DISCARD

Platt and Labate's
HEROIN ADDICTION

SECOND EDITION

HEROIN ADDICTION
Theory, Research, and Treatment

SECOND EDITION

JEROME J. PLATT

Hahnemann University School of Medicine
Philadelphia, Pennsylvania

ROBERT E. KRIEGER PUBLISHING COMPANY
MALABAR, FLORIDA
1986

Second Edition 1986
Original Edition 1976 by Platt and Labate

Printed and Published by
ROBERT E. KRIEGER PUBLISHING COMPANY, INC.
KRIEGER DRIVE
MALABAR FL 32950

Printed in the United States of America

Library of Congress Cataloging in Publication Data

Platt, Jerome J.
  Heroin addiction.

  Bibliography: p.
  Includes indexes.
  1. Heroin habit. 2. Heroin habit—Treatment.
  3. Narcotic laws—United States. I. Title.

RC568.H4P55   1986   362.2'93   83-19584
ISBN 0-89874-694-9

10 9 8 7 6 5 4 3 2

To Greg

Preface to the Second Edition

The need for a revised, updated second edition of *Heroin Addiction: Theory, Research and Treatment* arises from two sectors. First, the drug abuse research community is both a large and a very active one. It is prolific in its production of new literature reporting on the latest developments in the field. Secondly, new areas of investigation have been emerging with regularity, even as new findings appear in older, more established areas. Thus, a work completed less than a decade ago with the aim of providing a relatively comprehensive, yet reasonably concise overview of knowledge on the problem of heroin addiction — its etiology, manifestations, and treatment — is already dated in many areas. I have been aware, for several years now, of this need to bring the original edition up to date by the inclusion of the most recent material — in fact this awareness dated from the day the first edition appeared! It was clear, for instance, that certain areas needed greater exposition, and that studies of particular relevance could have been included to illustrate or illuminate a point.

In great part, the immediate stimulus for the revision of the book came from the readers themselves who contacted the author with their suggestions and comments. As this second edition is the result of an interaction between the author and the readers of the first edition, *they* deserve special thanks! Certainly, their comments and suggestions have been valued and an attempt has been made to revise the book with them in mind.

As was the case with the first edition, the mass of literature to be reviewed has been immense. At least 1,600 articles, books, monographs, and chapters have appeared since 1976. Also, as was true earlier, the final decision on incorporating a particular study, article, or book has been the responsibility of the author alone. Hopefully, no worker will feel slighted because his or her particular study has not been included.

Certain individuals have greatly contributed to the preparation of this work, and they deserve recognition. First, Dr. Christina Labate, co-author for the first edition, who has unfortunately not been able to participate in the preparation of the second edition. Her absence has been keenly felt, for the first edition was indeed a joint effort. Dr. Israel Zwerling, chairman of the Department of Mental Health Sciences, who has created an environment in which scientific inquiry and clinical application go hand in hand, and who on a more pragmatic level, arranged time for this work to be completed. Kay Platt, who somehow managed to critically read the work repeatedly in recent months, and who assisted in assembling the references, deserves special thanks, as does Vilma Rubero, who somehow managed to keep up with the typing, in addition to her usual duties, while maintaining her good humor!

Jerome J. Platt

Philadelphia, Pennsylvania
1985

Preface to the First Edition

Heroin addiction is a problem which has been in the national consciousness for many years and is currently undergoing a resurgence. Recently, substantial efforts have been made to determine the causes of heroin addiction and also to develop techniques for its treatment. These efforts have not been confined to any one particular professional field, for the literature contains contributions from psychiatry, social work, pharmacology, physiology, medicine, criminology, and psychology. The purpose of this book is to survey these contributions.

One may wonder why a work such as this is necessary, given the voluminous amount of literature available on the subject. The answer is threefold. First, the very volume of published material on the subject, in the form of journal articles, books, and chapters in reference works, is overwhelming. In the preparation of this work, we developed a working list of over 2000 published references relating exclusively to heroin addiction, and were well aware while doing so that we were far from exhausting the available material in the American and British literature alone. Such a plethora of material should not be considered surprising, however, given the broad spectrum of areas of knowledge, from neurophysiology to penology to law, in which contributions to the literature of heroin addiction may be found. It is the exceptional individual who has either the breadth of knowledge required or the time available to consult the literature in each of these areas to learn about the subject. Thus, one purpose of this book is to provide a survey of knowledge about the subject of heroin addiction, covering as many of the major areas of knowledge as is reasonably possible in a volume of this size. The material in this book is divided into four major parts. The first part discusses the historicolegal background to the development of heroin addiction in the United States; the second touches on the scientific basis of heroin addiction, primarily from the viewpoint of the medical and biological sciences; the third section deals with explanations of heroin abuse drawing upon formal and not-so-formal theories developed within physiologic, psychologic, psycho-analytic, and sociologic frameworks. This section also includes surveys of knowledge about the personality and personal and social characteristics of the addict. These are followed by a discussion of the various current treatment approaches to heroin addiction and an integrative summary.

It is our belief that each of the chapters in this book will provide the reader with an understanding of the recent and current approaches to a particular aspect of the problem of heroin addiction, relatively complete in and of themselves, and also provide a variety of points of entry into the original literature.

The second raison d'être for this book is also founded in the diversity of material available on the subject. Any single original source the reader consults will probably provide him or her with an explanation reflecting the unique vantage point of the writer. This lack of wider perspective is understandable in the journal article, in which the writer usually attempts either to rationally argue or empirically support a case within a limited space. This form of bias is compounded, however, because the majority of books on heroin addiction are compilations of collected contributions, each prepared by a prominent person in the area. Thus, books which could serve a broadly informative role all too often contain collections of narrowly defined reviews of a specific line of research or even reports of experimental work carried out within a specific theoretical context. It is of course understandable that with a large number of contributors even the best planned compilation of essays may leave large unfilled gaps in coverage. Several excellent broad summaries of knowledge on heroin addiction do exist, however, such as Jerome Jaffe's chapters in Goodman and Gilman's *The Pharmacological Basis of Therapeutics* or those in Oakley Ray's *Drugs, Society, and Human Behavior*. These, however, like journal articles, are confined to the space provided by one or a few chapters.

The third reason for preparing this book is closely related to the second. Authors of articles, monographs, or chapters who present their viewpoints rarely include any contradictory or inconsistent findings, except where they have been able to either explain or refute them. Where such contradictory viewpoints or inconsistencies exist in the areas covered by this book, we have referred to them.

This book is also not intended to fulfill certain roles. First, it is not meant to be comprehensive with respect to all the facts, viewpoints, and issues pertaining to the subject (even though this was the original, rather naive, intent of the authors). Rather, as mentioned earlier, it is designed to serve as a survey which not only represents the major viewpoints on heroin addiction as we see them, but also provides the citations so that the reader may consult the original sources.

The representations of specific theoretical viewpoints, the findings of studies, and even the inclusion or noninclusion of information are our interpretation of the facts, based upon the best available information. Accordingly, we apologize in advance to all those authors whose positions are not stated as they would have preferred. Here again, we urge the reader who is interested in learning more of a particular position or set of findings to consult the original source, to obtain the writer's own arguments for his position or interpretation of his findings.

The authors would like to acknowledge the contributions made by various individuals toward the preparation of this book. First, for the institutional environment which fostered the positive approach toward the remediation of mental health problems within which this book was conceptualized, Dr. Israel Zwerling, Chairman of the Department of Mental Health Sciences and Dr. Clifford J. Bodarky, Deputy Chairman and past Director of the Hahnemann Community Mental Health and Mental Retardation Center deserve recognition, as does Dr. Stephen Schwartz, Acting Director of the Center. Dr. George Spivack, Director of Research and Evaluation, also provided generous support in the preparation of this book.

Antonia Labate, who assembled much of the material for the chapter on the medical complications and side effects of heroin addiction, deserves our special thanks as do Robert Calvo, M.D., who generously contributed his comments on this chapter and on Chapter Four, Dr. Eugenie Flaherty who did the same for Part V, and Kay Platt who critically read parts of the manuscript. Janice Clarke, the librarian responsible for interlibrary loan, who secured much otherwise unobtainable material for us, also deserves acknowledgment. Patricia Erdenberger, Grace Verna, Zakia Amin, and Bertha Washington contributed to the typing of the manuscript, and their patient assistance is also acknowledged with thanks, as is that of Joan Bryson, who assisted in proofreading and indexing.

JEROME J. PLATT
CHRISTINA LABATE

Philadelphia, Pennsylvania
February, 1976

ABOUT THE AUTHOR

Jerome J. Platt, Ph.D. is Professor and Director of the Division of Research in the Department of Mental Health Sciences at Hahnemann University School of Medicine. He also holds appointments at other universities, including those as Adjunct Professor of Psychiatry and Human Behavior (Psychology) at Jefferson Medical College, and Consultant in Psychiatry at the School of Osteopathic Medicine, University of Medicine and Dentistry of New Jersey.

Dr. Platt is a member of numerous professional organizations and is a Fellow of the American Psychological Association, the Pennsylvania Psychological Association, the American College of Forensic Psychology, and a Clinical Fellow of the Behavior Therapy and Research Society. He is listed in Who's Who in the East, Who's Who in America, and Who's Who in the World.

Dr. Platt has served as a principal investigator and co-investigator on clinical research grants sponsored by the National Institute on Drug Abuse as well as by other public agencies and private foundations. He has also served on research grant review panels, on the editorial boards of professional journals, and as a consultant to treatment agencies, educational institutions, and hospitals.

In addition to Heroin Addiction: Theory, Research, and Treatment, Dr. Platt has authored or edited a number of other books with colleagues, including The Problem-Solving Approach to Adjustment, A Drug Abuse Primer for Criminal Justice Personnel, Evaluative Research in Correctional Drug Abuse Treatment, The Psychological Consultant, and Crisis Intervention. Two other works are currently in progress.

Contents

PART FOUR
TREATMENT OF THE HEROIN ADDICT

PART FIVE
CONCLUSIONS

APPENDIX
SCALES USED SPECIFICALLY IN THE ASSESSMENT
AND STUDY OF DRUG ADDICTION

PART ONE

The Historicolegal Context of Heroin Addiction in the United States

CHAPTER 1

The International Background to the Current Legal Status of Heroin in the United States

In order to fully understand the underlying issues in the development of antinarcotics legislation and policies in the United States during the last century it becomes necessary to view the American problem of heroin addiction from the perspective provided by the international situation in which this country found itself in the late nineteenth century. Primarily in response to the opium trade and its international complications, a quest gradually emerged for internationally based agreements for the regulation, manufacture, distribution, and use of narcotics. Some idea of the necessity for such regulation can be gained from the fact that control over a profitable worldwide opium trade had been the basis of two opium wars between England and China, the first resulting directly from an attempt by the Chinese to curtail the foreign opium trade.

When the United States emerged as a world power in the latter part of the nineteenth century, she also became increasingly concerned with the opium traffic because of self-interests. The desire to expand the American sphere of economic interest in China for instance, directly influenced the form of overtures designed to ease the strain in Sino-American relations. The impact upon China of U.S. policies regarding opium control in the

Philippines, which had recently been annexed, also played a role, as did the situation on the West Coast of the United States which was then experiencing an influx of Chinese laborers. These issues affected the decision to offer aid to China in developing opium control policies, and the United States remained at the forefront of the international movement to control narcotics partly out of a conviction that elimination of a domestic drug problem was contingent upon removal of foreign sources of supply. Furthermore, U.S. ratification of international opium conferences provided an impetus for the enactment of domestic antinarcotics legislation and also substantially influenced the final form of such legislation.

In an effort to understand the interaction between international, federal, and state narcotics legislation, and their ultimate effect upon heroin addiction in the United States, an overview of the development of antinarcotics policies at all three levels has been provided in this chapter and the two following ones.

INTERNATIONAL LEGISLATION

During the late nineteenth-century expansion of American influence in the Philippines and in China, the United States became aware of both the necessity for international opium trade agreements and the possible benefits to the U.S. which might acrue from them. Prior to this time, American interests in China had been restricted to scattered missionary outposts. However, the increasing westernization of China and her receptivity to foreign investment and development during this period attracted substantial international interest. The United States in particular faced difficulties from two sources when she attempted to expand her sphere of influence in China at this time. The European powers, already engaged in loan agreements with China during her push for modernization, were understandably reluctant to admit the competition arising from more diversified U.S. interests. There also existed a certain degree of tension between the United States and China that arose from American policies toward the Chinese: (1) the prejudicial treatment accorded Chinese laborers on the West Coast of the United States, and (2) antiopium legislation in the Philippines that was directed principally at the Chinese population. The latter condition originated with the U.S. acquisition of the Philippines following the Spanish-American War in 1898 and with it an established government monopoly on the opium market. The federal government had created a special commission responsible for investigating the unfamiliar "opium problem" in the Philippines. The recommendations of this commission resulted in antiopium legislation which provided a model for American narcotics policies during the early part of the twentieth century. The Philippines Opium Commission reported that drug use was an evil influence which must be prohibited, and recommended a gradual reduction in opium trade over a 3 year period. Legislation was enacted which would make opium use, other than for medicinal purposes, illegal at the end of that period. Addicts were required to obtain a license from authorities and were barred from government employment. Violations of these regulations were punishable by imprisonment. Inadvertently this legislation was directed at adult male Chinese opium addicts, since the preponderance of the opium-smoking population in the Philippines was Chinese. This lack of subtlety in approach and apparent prejudicial treatment of the Chinese population aggravated Sino-American relations.

However, in an effort to expand her interests in China, the United States offered to aid the Chinese in their attempted resolution of the opium problem in their own country. At the conclusion of the Boxer Rebellion of 1900, China began a concerted effort at modernization in which opium addiction was perceived as an obstacle to progress. In 1906 the convening of an international opium conference was suggested to President Theodore Roosevelt as a vehicle by which the United States and other foreign nations could ostensibly aid the Chinese in ameliorating the problem. The possible benefits to American interests in China through a strong offer of aid were immediately obvious. Since renegotiation of international treaties with China seemed imminent, American support for the antiopium movement might predispose the Chinese government to adopt a position more favorable to American interests. This overture might also reduce the strained Sino-American relations and place the United States in a more favored position than other European countries that already had an economic stronghold in China. Apparently the potential advantages were recognized by many other countries as the United States convened the first international opium conference with acceptances from nearly every nation with an interest in the Far East. Prior to the conference, a national survey of the existing body of knowledge about opium was undertaken so that American delegates might have substantial current information relevant to the problem. The lack of federal legislation restricting the importation, use, sale, and/or manufacture of opium as a result of the reluctance of the federal government to intervene in state affairs was an embarrassment to the committee delegates who felt that if the United States were to assume a position of leadership at the conference she should have exemplary opium laws. This concern generated several proposals for a federal law regulating opiates, specifically the smoking of opium. In 1909, prior to the conference, the legislation passed to control the opium problem in the Philippines was modified to prohibit the importation of opium for smoking into the United States.

The Shanghai Conference 1909

The first international opium conference was convened in Shanghai in 1909 with 13 nations in attendance. Problems beset the meeting from the beginning as there was an apparent lack of interest or sense of urgency on the part of some participants regarding the necessity for the international control of narcotic traffic. Since the United States entered the conference believing that a reduction in the severity of her own narcotics problem was contingent upon the enactment of laws by other nations to restrict the production and export of opiates, she adopted a strong position on the desirability of internationally based control measures. The committee itself, however, did not have the power to extract commitments from each nation to ratify articles of the convention and thus could only make recommendations. Governments were asked to reexamine their own laws in view of a gradual suppression of opium for other than medicinal purposes, and it was recommended that each nation become more sensitive to the potential international ramifications of proposed antinarcotics laws. Agreement was reached only on the issue of the desirability of legislation to severely curtail indiscriminate distribution of morphine and its derivatives. Although the necessity for adequate control of production and distribution of drugs was generally recognized, no action was outlined to implement these recommendations. The committee's recommendations did provide impetus and support for subsequent domestic American legislation. In essence, the Shanghai Conference was successful only insofar as it focused international attention on the extent of the narcotics problem.

The Hague Conferences 1912–1913

The inconclusiveness of the Shanghai Conference generated several suggestions for a second meeting. The United States had achieved one of her goals, and was encouraged by the resumption of friendly relations with China. It was hoped that a second display of American support would further incline China toward a favorable view of U.S. economic interests. The second international opium conference was convened at The Hague in 1912 and was attended by 12 nations. Once again the disparity between the stated goals of the conference and the actual preoccupation with individual concerns and mutual suspiciousness were apparent. Although the necessity for establishing internationally binding agreements was recognized by the majority of participants, it soon became clear that Germany in particular was concerned that other countries would take up the slack in the drug market if she restricted the production of her chemicals industry. Therefore Germany demanded unanimous agreement that this would not happen and voiced doubt about the actual enactment of Congressional support (which the United States guaranteed was pending) to enforce the convention. A number of other nations had already moved far ahead of the United States in passing stringent antinarcotics legislation and this weakened the American position. Ultimately, agreement was reached on several issues. The conference called for the control of all phases of the production and distribution of medicinal opium, morphine, heroin, cocaine, and any derivatives subsequently found to be dangerous. The distribution of raw opium would be controlled and the use of prepared opium would gradually be eliminated. The export of raw opium to countries prohibiting its importation was forbidden, and export to those countries restricting its distribution would be monitored. Use of the alkaloids of opium and, its derivatives were confined to legitimate medical purposes. A government license would be required of all persons engaged in the manufacture, sale, distribution, or import/export of the above-mentioned narcotics. All preparations containing more than .1% heroin would be controlled. The burden for the enactment of agreed upon measures of narcotics control was to be at the domestic level. However, the obvious major defect of the opium convention was that it failed to create administrative mechanisms for carrying out the recommendations. Neither were guidelines issued regarding the implementation of control over the production and distribution of narcotics. The convention delegates decided that all nations, not merely those present at the conference, must ratify the articles of the convention before they could be implemented. If the attempt to obtain a sufficient number of signatures were unsuccessful by the end of 1912, provision was made for a second conference to be convened in 1913. This conference was necessary and also proved unsuccessful in securing the 12 remaining signatures needed for ratification.

THE LEAGUE OF NATIONS

After World War I, the League of Nations undertook responsibility for supervising the international traffic in opium and other dangerous drugs and an advisory committee was established to centralize and coordinate the League's efforts. A certificate system was developed under which no government could allow the export of dangerous drugs unless the exporter produced a license from the importing country to the effect that the drugs were required for legitimate purposes. In an added effort to control the distribution of dangerous drugs, exports were limited to those nations which had ratified The Hague Conference. The 56 nations that had ratified the convention were to prepare annual estimates of the amount of narcotics they would require for all legitimate purposes so that production would eventually be limited to the amount specifically required. In 1922 in support of the League's efforts the United States enacted the Narcotic Drugs Import and Export Act specifically prohibiting the importation of heroin. A subsequent legislative amendment broadened the effectiveness of this Act by excluding the importation of opium to be used in the manufacture of heroin. From this point on, the manufacture of heroin in the United States ceased to be legal. In 1923, the national movement toward the abolition of heroin was mirrored at the international level when the Opium Advisory Committee recommended the total suppression of heroin internationally. At that time, although each of the member nations was asked for its opinion on the suppression of heroin a consensus was not reached. Since some nations were willing to consider the total abolition of heroin while others still considered it necessary for medical purposes, no action was taken.

In 1923 the U.S. Congress passed a resolution urging the President to consult with other nations to facilitate the international limitation of narcotics. The resolution called attention to the spread of the national drug problem and the continuing failure to suppress the illegal traffic in narcotics as strong reasons for calling another conference. Congress focused on the absence of effective controls on production in a number of countries as an urgent reason for calling an international meeting and proposed that the President issue a request to Turkey and several other nations to limit the production of raw opium. It soon became clear that another international conference could be the means toward this end.

The Geneva Conferences 1924–1925

At the first of the Geneva Conferences, convened in 1924, the United States took a strong position in the international antinarcotics movement. The American delegation hoped that other nations would adopt legislation to prohibit the importation of opium for the manufacture of heroin and thus suppress the legal manufacture of heroin. The purpose of the convention was to consolidate international agreements limiting the amounts of morphine, heroin, and cocaine that could be manufactured. However, the nations attending the conference were only able to agree on the substitution of government monopoly for all other narcotic control systems. No general agreement could be reached regarding (1) the registration or rationing of drugs to addicts, (2) uniform prices, (3) uniform penalties for violations, and (4) the limitation of imports.

A second Geneva Conference was called in 1925 with somewhat greater success. The American delegation felt that they were in a stronger position to influence the outcome of the conference because domestic legislation had banned the manufacture of heroin in the United States. The delegation was not authorized to sign any agreement that failed to include some way of limiting the production of raw opium. At the Conference the United States encountered reistance from the other nations who were somewhat reluctant to adopt the inflexible American position on narcotics. Thus, there was no agreement to the U.S. proposal to ban the manufacture of heroin or to lower the amount of current exemptions. Since no limitations were placed on the production of opium and no plans were incorporated into the original articles for limiting to medical requirements the quantities of drugs produced, the United States withdrew from the conference. China also withdrew, and the remaining delegates then drew up a protocol. In an attempt to avoid the defects of The Hague conventions, the ratifying states agreed that within a 5 year period they would do whatever was necessary to prevent the smuggling of raw opium from interfering with the effective suppression of prepared opium. To effect stricter controls of manufacture, an international commission was created to visit the opium-producing countries to determine methods by which production could be limited without causing "undue hardship" to the producing nation. All persons involved in the manufacture, sale, distribution, or export of heroin were required to obtain a license. An exporter would be required to obtain an export license from the government to be issued upon production of a copy of the import certificate from the importing country. A copy of the export authorization accompanying the shipment would state the number and date of this import certificate. A Permanent Central Opium Board was created to monitor the international opium trade and to investigate cases of excessive accumulation of narcotics. However, no proposals for the effective limitation of manufacture were accepted at that time. Although the American committeemen had urged the nationalization of factories manufacturing narcotics, the German delegates recommended their internationalization through the formation of international trusts holding controlling interests. Despite the fact that she had not participated in the conference, the United States agreed to cooperate with its principles. Arrangements were made with foreign law enforcement agencies to exchange information about the identity and operations of narcotics smugglers. However, despite substantial advances made in reaching an agreement, the convention obtained only 40% of the signatures needed to ratify the measures.

The Limitation Convention 1931

The continued illicit narcotics traffic necessitated a further agreement. To this end, the League of Nations convened the Conference on Limitation of Manufacture of Narcotic Drugs in Geneva in 1931. The Limitation Convention, so named because its purpose was to establish limitations on the manufacture and distribution of narcotic drugs to those amounts required for medical and scientific purposes, did much to overcome the defects of the 1925 Geneva Conference. Attended by 73 countries, this was the first general international convention purporting to create a complete system of narcotics regulations. The expressed goals were to adjust the manufacture of narcotics to legitimate world demand, to control all channels of distribution, and to entrust record keeping and supervision to international bodies. The contracting parties were required to furnish an annual estimate of the amount of drugs they would need for medical and scientific purposes, for the manufacture of preparations not requiring export authorization, for conversion to other drugs, and the amount required to maintain acceptable levels of government stocks. This estimate would then be reviewed by the International Drug Supervisory Body which could approve it or make substitute estimates of its own. A proposal was once again introduced to abolish the manufacture of heroin. It was rejected on the basis of objections that the drug possessed medical value, that almost none of it was escaping to illicit traffic, and that abolition would not prevent its manufacture from morphine. Restrictions were, however, placed on heroin so that exports were prohibited except at the specific request of a government which banned its domestic manufacture.

A number of steps were taken prior to World War II to reduce the illicit traffic in narcotics. In 1934 the League of Nations again polled foreign governments on the abolition or restriction of the use of heroin: 12 nations were opposed, 4 were in favor of restriction; 8 already had restrictions, 9 were in favor of abolition, and 7 had already abolished heroin use. Two years later, in June 1936, the Conference for Suppression of Illicit Traffic in Dangerous Drugs met to outline proposals to enhance enforcement potential, to improve detection techniques, and to provide international penalties for violations of narcotics laws. The final proposal provided for the extradition of narcotics traffic violators, so that an individual could be prosecuted in his own country for violations of foreign narcotics laws. Prior to that time the violator could have returned to his or her own country to escape prosecution. The Contraband Seizure Act of 1939 established a legal basis for seizure by the U.S. federal government of any vessel used in the transport, sale, or possession of illicit narcotics.

Although the rate of narcotics smuggling diminished during World War II, the Allied military authorities feared a sudden increase at the end of the war and issued several directives designed to control the illicit traffic. France and Belgium had already created effective controls, while Denmark, the Netherlands, and Norway informed the League of Nations that they believed their control mechanisms were satisfactory and did not warrant interference. Spain refused to provide any statistics to the League and continued to import narcotics in excess of her estimated requirements under the Limitation Convention of 1931. The primary problem remained in Germany. During the war Germany had produced morphine from poppies, the cultivation of which had become widespread. An attempt was made at uniform control throughout the zones by requiring a report to an inter-Allied Control Commission and by the licensing of poppy growth. Conditions in Iran and India remained the same as they had been before the war: Iran reported a high incidence of opiate addiction, and India continued to be a source of illicit narcotic traffic to the United States, England, and Canada.

In 1945 the San Francisco Conference of the U.N. organization suggested that the many specialized agencies operating under the existing treaties (e.g., the Permanent Central Opium Board) be subsumed under the functions of the United Nations. In 1946 all functions of the League of Nations were transferred to the U.N. Commission on Narcotic Drugs. The Commission, composed of members of those countries most heavily engaged in the production of opiates, was to carry out enforcement of the international conventions and to review continuously the problems of control. The Paris Protocol of 1948 transferred responsibility for the international control of narcotics to the World Health Organization. In 1952 the Commissioner of Narcotics in Washington, D.C., and the heads of 22 governments agreed to engage in a direct exchange of police information regarding the illicit traffic. Furthermore, the Opium Limitation Protocol of 1953 was enacted with the aim of reducing the annual world production of opium. Production was to be limited to seven countries in which a national opium monopoly was to be established; licensed cultivators of the poppy could sell only to the monopoly, and only the monopoly could engage in opium transactions. Opium production was to be restricted only to the amount needed for medical and scientific purposes. This protocol would have come into effect following ratification by 25 countries including three nations engaged in the production, and three in the manufacture, of drugs. As late as 1959, only India of the six producing or manufacturing nations had signed the protocol. Clearly, the need was felt for further agreement on the international control of opium, since there were nine treaties and a complicated mechanism for control of narcotics in effect by 1960. In 1961 the Single Convention on Narcotic Drugs was adopted to consolidate the efforts of the United Nations at control and to codify the existing body of international laws. This treaty replaced all preceding narcotic control treaties and was signed by more than 60 nations. It became internationally effective in 1964, was ratified by the United States in 1967, and is currently the international basis for the control of narcotics.

The major provisions of the convention are as follows: (*a*) four schedules of drugs were prepared for control measures, and decisions regarding categorization of drugs were the responsibility of the World Health Organization; (*b*) the availability and use of drugs was to be limited to medical and scientific purposes; (*c*) cultivation of raw materials from which narcotics and dangerous drugs were manufactured was to be controlled; (*d*) exportation of opium was limited in amount and authorization; (*e*) a licensing procedure for persons engaged in all aspects of drug trade was instituted; (*f*) treatment and rehabilitation of addicts was to be instituted. Further, provisions were made for two new divisions of the United Nations: the Commission on Narcotic Drugs composed of 24 nations to revise and evaluate current international agreements, and the International Control Board responsible for monitoring the legal production and distribution of world narcotics. Since it lacks enforcement powers, the Control Board can only negotiate with countries exceeding their annual narcotics quota. The Board's only recourse is to recommend an embargo on import and export of drugs from the offending nation. In essence, its purpose is to keep a record of the international flow of narcotics. The major flaw in the Single Convention on Narcotic Drugs of 1961 rests in its lack of enforcement machinery, since compliance with its articles is voluntary. The United States recommended several amendments to the convention in the 1972 Amending Protocol to the Single Convention: (*a*) they would permit the Control Board to challenge and to investigate the estimates of narcotics submitted by each nation; (*b*) they would authorize investigation into a nation's drug activities, and would allow modification of estimates determined to be in excess of a legitimate amount; and (*c*) they would authorize the Board to require an embargo in the event of continued violation. Extradition of illicit traffickers is also suggested. The obvious problems inherent in these amendments are that they would allow intervention in state sovereignty and would benefit the United States primarily. Although the United States ratified the Amending Protocol in 1972, other nations not possessing the same sense of urgency and perceiving heroin addiction as essentially an American problem, may be reluctant to authorize international intervention on such a scale (Simmons and Gold, 1973).

CONCLUDING COMMENTS

The problems of international control are immense and current enforcement procedures have not seriously decreased the illicit traffic in narcotics, since there has been no effective elimination of the raw materials from which narcotics are produced. The International Criminal Police Organization, Interpol, is perhaps best known for the important role it plays in the suppression of illegal narcotics traffic. Created in 1946, Interpol is the largest single, internationally cooperative organization of police. Quantities of information regarding suspected criminals are exchanged between member countries and arrested suspects are extradited to their own country. There are National Central Bureaus in each of the countries to coordinate police activities and to act as agents of Interpol. However, increased cooperation between police in countries either contributing to or suffering from drug problems continues to be necessary if disruption of the channels of supply is to be effected.

CHAPTER 2

The Development of Federal Antinarcotics Policies in the Twentieth Century

The need for narcotics control in the United States originated in the indiscriminate use of opium and morphine in patent medicines in the nineteenth century. Prior to 1800, opium was available primarily as an ingredient in multidrug preparations and in extracts such as laudanum. Advances in the chemical industry contributed to the eventual proliferation of drugstore and mail-order sales of hay fever remedies and other medicines containing morphine, cocaine, and heroin. The lack of federal requirements for labeling opiate content in patent medicines contributed to the widespread use of these drugs for their calming and soporific effects even after their addictive properties were discovered. In the absence of a domestically grown commercial supply of opium, overseas imports increased dramatically until

1900, partially as a consequence of the lack of federal restriction on crude opium imports other than a tariff prior to 1915.

Impetus for the creation of restrictive national opium laws was generated from two separate conditions in the United States around the turn of the century. First, about to enter into the First International Opium Convention in Shanghai, U.S. delegates found their envisioned role of aiding China in controlling her opium problem undermined by the embarrassment of having no nationally based restrictions on opium. Second, the public closely identified the nineteenth-century addict with foreigners and minorities, both groups being the object of social and legal restrictions. American prejudice against the Chinese was directed particularly at the custom of smoking opium. Cocaine usage also erroneously became associated with another repressed minority, the Negro. It was believed that drug usage by both groups would contribute to a desire on their part to undermine American society and to revolt against restrictive social sanctions.

Late in the nineteenth century, as recognition of drug addiction as a problem increased, several states enacted antinarcotics laws. Generally, these laws requiring the presentation of a physician's prescription for ordering a drug were overwhelmingly ineffective because of loopholes exempting patent medicines of a specified narcotic content. Problems continued even among those states with restrictive narcotics laws in the absence of mechanisms preventing purchase of prohibited narcotics in a neighboring state that had not passed controlling legislation. In 1900, the debate over the constitutionality of federal intervention in interstate commerce (and more specifically, narcotics traffic) postponed the enactment of federal laws controlling the sale and prescription of narcotics. It was not until the enactment of the Pure Food and Drug Act in 1906 that the pharmaceutical trade became a proponent of antinarcotics legislation.

Impetus for antinarcotics legislation also came from early reform movements directed at two conditions: individual immorality, and the disregard for public welfare on the part of growing corporations. The corporate reform movement was spearheaded by Samuel Adams in the "Great American Fraud" series published in *Collier's* (1905–1907). An advocate of regulatory laws aimed at the suppliers of medicines, Adams' position exemplified a concern with the dangers of patent medicines dispensed to an unsuspecting public (Musto, 1973). The other contingent of the reform movement, motivated by fear of the addict (particularly the Negro and the Chinese), felt that federal legislation against the drug user would reduce the perceived threat from the addict to society.

The health professions, increasing in status-consciousness, also had a vested interest in influencing the final form of narcotics legislation. The low status of physicians and pharmacists at that time was due primarily to weak licensing laws, minimal training requirements, and a surplus of practitioners. Doctors often relied heavily on symptomatic relief agents when cure was beyond their rudimentary medical technology. Both groups felt immediate pressure to take an active part in framing the drug laws for two reasons: (*a*) a belief that careful wording of the law would solidify and enhance the prestige of their institutions, and (*b*) fear that public interest would remove it beyond the sphere of their influence if they waited too long. Consequently, the American Pharmaceutical Association convened an Ad Hoc Committee on the Acquirement of the Drug Habit to study the drug problem. In 1903 the Committee recommended that the federal government ban the importation of opium and that prohibition of prescription and sale be enforced. It also recommended that heroin be dispensed only on the order of a physician and that the prescription not be refillable. The Committee's belief that the simplest method of controlling drugs lay in the state's (as opposed to federal) police powers was reflected in the structure of their proposed model state law. The trend toward harsh penalties for selling drugs as an effective deterrent and method of control originated in these early proposals. At that time, many competent physicians and pharmacists believed that denial of drugs to an addict might endanger his life. This explains the ambivalent attitude toward treatment of existing addicts in the Committee's recommendation that the sale of narcotic drugs be restricted but not prohibited.

DISTRICT OF COLUMBIA PHARMACY ACT OF 1906

Many of the Committee's recommendations in the model narcotics law were adopted by Congress in the District of Columbia Pharmacy Act of 1906. The law included generous compromises in the interest of physicians and druggists such as freedom of prescription for physicians and the exemption of minimal amounts of morphine, cocaine, opium and the derivatives of opium (specifically heroin) in patent medicines. However, prescriptions for narcotics could only be renewed by order of a physician. It is interesting to note the emergence of concern over addiction maintenance reflected in the legal requirement that a physician prove he acted "in good faith" in prescribing or renewing a prescription for narcotics. Acting in good faith would require a belief that such action was necessary to effect a cure. This legal definition of good faith later became the controversial focal point of several Supreme Court rulings on the issue of narcotics prescriptions and, by implication, of addiction maintenance. The Pure Food and Drug Act of 1906, closely following the District of Columbia Act, required the listing of narcotic content on all patent medicines traded in interstate commerce. In 1908, an amendment was rejected that would have eliminated from interstate commerce any medicines, except prescribed narcotics, containing addicting drugs.

ANTECEDENTS OF THE HARRISON ACT

Two factors strongly influenced the drive for national antinarcotics legislation following the First International Opium Convention in 1909. First, since the United States had urged the establishment of systems for international narcotics control at the conference, she felt that in order to honor her commitment to this position, she must have exemplary narcotics laws. Second, the recognition of the existence of a large number of addicts among the American population necessitated the establishment of control beyond the state and local levels. The Foster Antinarcotic Bill of 1911, a direct antecedent of the Harrison Act, proposed a plan for domestic legislation to control drug traffic through federal powers of taxation. The Foster Bill required revenue stamps on all drug containers of opiates, careful record keeping by retailers, and heavy penalties for violators. The bill proposed an essentially complicated and ponderous system which was opposed by the druggists, since the financial and time burdens would fall on them. Advocates of the bill attempted to encourage its passage by dramatizing the effects of addiction on Negroes, inciting them to revolt and to rape (Musto, 1973). The druggists, on the other hand, lobbied for exemptions, record-keeping simplifications, and softer penalties for infractions. After long controversy, the bill was ultimately defeated.

THE HARRISON ACT OF 1914

The Hague Convention of 1911 was followed by a change in the U.S. position on the seriousness of her national narcotics problem. Prior to this, the United States perceived her role in drug problems to be intervention on behalf of less developed countries. As a result of ratification of The Hague Convention in 1912 and assumption of responsibility for control of domestic production, distribution, and use of opium, a vehicle was created for increased public pressure for federal narcotics legislation. The shift in public belief that narcotics control was not exclusively a medical problem but one requiring the intervention of federal law offered a wide support for the antinarcotics movement. Public pressure from the antinarcotics movement supported by the necessity for fulfillment of an international commitment led to the proposal of the first Harrison Bill, which differed little from the earlier unsatisfactory Foster Bill. It retained such features as the issuance of revenue stamps, record-keeping, bond, license fees, and strict penalties for violations. No provision was made for the exemption of minimal amounts of narcotics in patent medicines. Since the new bill was still opposed by retail druggists, the American Pharmaceutical Association called a conference to discuss the complaints of the various components of the drug trade. Opposition to the current provisions of the Harrison Act was unanimous and several suggested revisions were later incorporated into the bill to facilitate its passage. The American Medical Association (AMA), however, favored federal assistance at that time, believing it would strengthen their national position. In order to write a bill that would be acceptable to the drug trades, the medical profession, and the Internal Revenue Bureau, a joint committee of the State and Treasury Departments was created. Several subsequent compromises were reached: record keeping was simplified; patent medicines containing no more than a permitted amount of morphine, heroin, cocaine, and opium were allowed to be sold in general stores and by mail order; and physicians were allowed to dispense drugs without keeping records while attending a patient. This revised bill quickly passed the House, but the presence of several amendments unacceptable to special interest groups prevented its immediate passage in the Senate. Again compromises were eventually reached which raised the level of exempted heroin content of medicines from 1/12 of a grain to 1/8 of a grain. The passage of the bill in its final form was ensured as enforcement powers were derived from its basis as a revenue measure. In bypassing a confrontation over the issue of the constitutionality of federal power to regulate interstate commerce in narcotics traffic, the simultaneous passage of penal controls was prohibited. It was hoped that by requiring government registration of all persons and firms handling drugs, the use of special forms in the transfer of drugs, the payment of fees, and a 1 cent tax per ounce, the process of drug distribution would become a matter of record. All persons who imported, manufactured, produced, compounded, sold or dispensed any derivative of opium were required to register with the Collector of Internal Revenue and to keep a record of all such transactions. Specific amounts of narcotics were to be provided for scientific use in analytic, educational, and research capacities by qualified persons. The Harrison Act of 1914 made dispensing of narcotic drugs unlawful except by physicians for legitimate medical purposes. Although there was no indication in the Act of any legislative intent to deny addicts legal access to drugs or to interfere with the physician's right to engage in legitimate medical practice, the statute lacked a definition of what constituted legitimate medical practice or prescription "in good faith." An addict was to obtain drugs from a registered physician and records of these transactions were to be kept. Although it did not classify addiction itself as illegal, the Act left the status of the drug addict undetermined.

The uncertainty surrounding the extent of legal control embodied in the Harrison Act extended to the question of enforcement by federal police in addition to federal revenue agents. Lacking legal sanction that allowed the intervention of federal police in each state the Act would be reduced to mere record keeping. Advocates of expansion of federal enforcement powers argued that the Act carried out Senate ratification of The Hague Convention and thereby took precedence over state law restricting federal intervention. The Public Health Service voiced the collective opinion that the Act was solely a method for information gathering, while the Bureau of Internal Revenue supported the broader interpretation that permitted it to bring action against violators. Physicians too had an interest, albeit primarily an economic one, in the resolution of this complicated and controversial issue. If the "nonmedical" use of narcotic drugs was not reduced, physicians, supposedly the sole legal suppliers of narcotics, would become a prime target for legal action.

Early in 1915 the Treasury Department was forced to establish guidelines for the enforcement of the Harrison Act designed to clarify the issue of whether the statute was primarily oriented toward record keeping. These guidelines stated that narcotics could only be obtained through a registered physician; record-keeping duties were maximal to monitor a physician's prescription philosophy; possession of narcotics obtained in any way other than by a doctor's prescription was considered a violation of the Act; and prescriptions for an addict would be considered valid only if they called for a "normal dose" of the drug. This was the legislative indication of a trend to eliminate nonmedical addiction maintenance. Again, in response to the druggists' complaint that the law was unclear on the question of proper dosage, the Treasury Department added a new regulation requiring that the quantity of drug prescribed be reduced over a period of time. In essence, by prohibiting addiction maintenance, this new interpretation made it almost impossible for the addict to obtain drugs from a legitimate source. The federal courts reacted to this interpretation of the Act by stating that intervention in private medical practice was unconstitutional. A flurry of court decisions followed the passage of the Harrison Act, as the intent of its powers was tested on legal grounds.

THE JIN FUEY MOY DECISION OF 1915

The early Supreme Court decisions did not uphold the broad interpretation of the Harrison Act. In *United States* v. *Jin Fuey Moy* (1915) the government brought a case against Dr. Jin Fuey Moy for prescribing $\frac{1}{16}$ ounce of narcotics for an addict. The government held that the physician conspired to prescribe for the maintenance of addiction. Since this prescription was a violation of the "good faith" clause in the Harrison Act, the possession of narcotics by the addict was thereby illegal. Implicit in this argument was the assumption that the maintenance of addiction violates the practice of medicine in good faith. The defense argued that since the addict was not required to register as a consumer of the drug, possession alone did not constitute a violation of the Act. The lower courts interpreted the Act strictly as a revenue measure and considered it unconstitutional for the government to intervene in the practice of medicine. The Supreme Court upheld the lower court decision and denied the government's attempt to expand its police powers. The majority opinion also refuted the argument that the Harrison Act was passed in fulfillment of treaty obligations and that its powers therefore took precedence over those of the state. This decision diminished the power of Congress to enforce its broad interpretation of the Act.

THE WEBB AND DOREMUS DECISIONS OF 1919

Following the Jin Fuey Moy decision, the Treasury Department attempted to secure an amendment to the Harrison Act that would make it easier to control illicit traffic in narcotics. Before such legislation was passed, however, two Supreme Court decisions strengthened the constitutionality of the Harrison Act. In *United States* v. *Doremus* (1919) the Supreme Court upheld an indictment against Dr. Charles Doremus for prescribing 500 ⅙-grain tablets of morphine for an addict. In the case of *Webb et al.* v. *United States* (1919), the Supreme Court ruled that prescribing drugs for an addict, not during the course of a cure but to maintain his habit, was a "perversion of [the] meaning" of the Harrison Act (*Webb et al.* v. *United States*, 249 U.S. 96, 1919). This decision constituted the first clear-cut court action against the practice of addiction maintenance. It must be remembered that the United States had emerged from World War I with a strong orientation toward nationalism. The "red scare" of 1919 had contributed heavily to the fear and repression of any actions that might conceivably aid the enemies of this country in their attempt to undermine American society. Addiction was perceived as a threat because it was believed to lead directly to antisocial acts (Musto, 1973).

In 1920 the Supreme Court ruled against Jin Fuey Moy when it directed that a physician could not legitimately prescribe drugs to "cater to the appetite" of a drug addict (*Jin Fuey Moy* v. *United States* 254 U.S. 189, 1920).

Shortly after the Supreme Court decision in the Jin Fuey Moy case, the government established a committee to recommend changes in the Harrison Act with a view toward eliminating any legal basis for addiction maintenance. In mid-1918 a bill was proposed that would make recording mandatory in the sale and manufacture of patent medicines, demand a tax of 1 cent per ounce of narcotics, and make possession of narcotics with a tax stamp (unless prescribed by a physician) *prima facie* evidence of illegal possession. The last measure was designed to close the loophole used by the defense in the Jin Fuey Moy case of 1915 and to permit prosecution of those persons holding large amounts of narcotics without a prescription. The committee also issued a report on the extent of the addiction problem to support its proposed amendments. The drastic overestimation of the number of addicts in the United States contributed to the hysteria surrounding the problem of addiction, and to the repressive nature of the court decisions prior to 1925. The committee's report described the drug addict as a weak person without moral sense, motivated to crime when denied drugs. However the committee did suggest that provision for emergency care be made for addicts, despite the fact that there was no known cure or consensus of opinion regarding the best treatment.

THE NEW YORK CITY CLINIC MOVEMENT

With the Webb and Doremus decisions of 1919 the government had set a legal precedent for the arrest of several physicians and druggists in New York City who were accused of supplying drugs to addicts. To stem the backlash of violence city officials had been led to expect by the Treasury Committee's report on the consequence of denying drugs to addicts, a temporary emergency clinic was established. The New York Clinic was structured to supply narcotics to addicts who were suffering as a result of having been severed from their legal medical sources. However, the city clinic did not permit maintenance for any substantial period, and the amount of narcotics given to an addict was reduced rapidly. Both inpatient and outpatient facilities were provided. The outcome of this experiment was extremely important because the success of this model treatment program would provide support for medical treatment of addiction. The model program was dealt a severe blow when the France Bill, a comprehensive federal plan calling for congressional appropriations and the cooperation of the Public Health Service in matching funds for the establishment of clinics, was defeated.

Late in 1919 the Narcotic Division was created within the Prohibition Unit and the Revenue Bureau was given the responsibility for the enforcement of narcotics laws. A report of the amended Harrison Act by the Treasury Department's special narcotics committee undermined the clinic movement by suggesting that the only known cure for addiction was elimination of available drugs to the addict. Once again the emphasis shifted to enforcement as the mechanism by which the drug problem could be eliminated. A survey distributed among physicians and scientists relating to treatment approaches revealed that the consensus of medical opinion opposed the antibody physiologic hypothesis, thereby casting doubt on the theory of heroin addiction as a disease (Musto, 1973). The Internal Revenue Bureau received a formal statement from the AMA opposing ambulatory maintenance programs. Consequently, as a result of an investigation of their effectiveness, the Narcotic Division decided to close the clinics and cited the lack of medical evidence supporting any method of treatment other than withdrawal, the high recidivism rates, and the minimal danger of death from withdrawal as rationale. The Bureau believed this action would reduce the supply of narcotics and establish potential legal grounds for the indictment of physicians who prescribed narcotics for addicts. Although it was comparatively easy to convict the street trader in narcotics, the sentences imposed were light and proved ineffective as deterrents. It was far more difficult to convict a physician, since juries often were sympathetic to the defense argument that a physician's professional responsibility included addiction maintenance until an effective cure was discovered. Probably at this point the medical profession began to regret its previous encouragement of government intervention, which was initially sought to enhance its national status.

By 1922, the Supreme Court seemed to be moving in the same direction as the Internal Revenue Bureau: doctors could not legally prescribe drugs to relieve withdrawal or to maintain a habit, but could only prescribe in reducing dosages under conditions of institutional confinement. In the case of *United States* v. *Behrman* (1922) the Supreme Court ruled that it was not legitimate medical practice to prescribe for an addict regardless of purpose. In effect this ruling eliminated the defense of acting in good faith and made it impossible for physicians to treat addicts privately in a manner that was satisfactory to law enforcement officials. By 1922 the ambulatory method of treatment had been condemned. Addicts were not readily treated in hospitals and doctors did not have access to institutional treatment facilities. The legal position of the addict was now clear: following the Behrman decision he was denied legal access to drugs and was thus forced to deal with the black market traffickers to support his habit. Lindesmith (1967) suggests that implicit in the decisions opposing maintenance is the assumption that addiction is not a disease but a "willful indulgence" requiring punishment as a deterrent. At this time, the only legitimate administration of drugs was limited to elderly or infirm addicts for whom withdrawal might constitute a threat to life and to persons afflicted with incurable diseases.

THE JONES-MILLER ACT OF 1922

The restrictive Jones-Miller Act or Narcotic Drugs Import and Export Act was passed in 1922, detailing heavy penalties for narcotics violations. Fines of not more than $5000 and imprisonment not to exceed 10 years were legislated for anyone convicted of illegally importing, buying or selling narcotic drugs. Under this Act possession alone was sufficient evidence for conviction and the burden of proving a legitimate reason for possession fell on the defendant. The Jones-Miller Act permitted the export of narcotics only upon receipt of assurance from the importing nation that it would strictly monitor the use and distribution of the drugs. To administer the Act, the federal Narcotics Control Board was established. Exports were limited to nations which had ratified The Hague Convention, had a satisfactory licensing system, and could provide proof that the use of drugs would be legitimate.

In 1924 legislation was proposed to ban the domestic manufacture of heroin. The testimony given during hearings on the bill was overwhelmingly critical: heroin was considered extremely addictive, its use was convincingly linked to crime, and the percentage of drug abusers using heroin was shown to be increasing (Brecher, 1972). The Deputy Police Commissioner of New York wrote that 94% of the criminal drug addicts arrested in New York City used heroin (Anonymous, 1953).

THE LINDER DECISION OF 1925

Despite urgent attempts of the Treasury and Justice Departments to strengthen the Harrison Act by amendment, the Supreme Court made a monumental decision in *Linder* v. *United States* regarding the physician's right to treat addiction. Dr. Charles Linder was indicted for having prescribed four tablets of a drug for a woman addict who entered his office complaining of symptoms associated with partial withdrawal. The woman, an informer, reported the transaction to the police. The lower court convicted Dr. Linder on the grounds that he had provided drugs for an addict to relieve withdrawal symptoms and to maintain the customary habit with no thought of cure. In a unanimous decision the Supreme Court overruled the conviction and espoused the view that addiction was a disease, and therefore a physician acting in good faith and according to fair medical standards could prescribe a moderate amount of narcotics to relieve withdrawal [*Linder* v. *United States* 268 U.S. 5 (1925).] Lindesmith (1967) suggests that the decision implies a belief on the part of the court that proper medical care of the addict should be the physician's responsibility.

Although it temporarily stemmed the tide of legislation against addiction, the Linder case had little effect on enforcement policies. Huberty (1972), in arguing the case against civil commitment of the narcotic addict, believes that the Linder decision introduced the issues of an addict's "right to treatment" by reversing earlier decisions in which medical treatment was denied. There appears to be a great deal of legal confusion in cases subsequent to the Linder decision. The Treasury Department, fearing another direct attack on the constitutionality of the Harrison Act, attempted to strengthen it by congressional amendment. In 1926 seven amendments were requested to the Harrison Act. These were intended to fulfill a number of purposes: to prevent addicted physicians from registering and to withhold for one year the registration of those convicted of Harrison Act violations, to prohibit ambulatory treatment of addicts and to require full records of drugs dispensed, to increase the responsibility of druggists in determining good faith prior to filling a prescription, to require record keeping of transactions involving previously exempted narcotics, and to make forging prescriptions illegal. None of the proposed amendments was enacted.

THE ESTABLISHMENT OF FEDERAL NARCOTICS FARMS AND THE FEDERAL BUREAU OF NARCOTICS

In 1929, partly in response to the Linder decision and to remedy the lack of community treatment facilities, legislation was enacted to provide for the establishment of two federal hospitals for the treatment of federal prisoners who were narcotic addicts. Actually, these federal narcotics farms were intended to serve as separate prison facilities for addicts. The institutions at Lexington, Kentucky and at Fort Worth, Texas were not opened until 1935 and 1938 respectively. They were operated by the Public Health Service under the auspices of the Justice Department and the Federal Bureau of Narcotics, a separate agency created in 1930 with national and international responsibilities to reduce smuggling and facilitate enforcement. Harry Anslinger, the first commissioner of the Bureau, was instrumental in establishing its policy until his retirement in 1962. The major thrust of the Bureau was to attack the supply of illicit narcotics traffic at its source, in the case of heroin in Europe and the Near East.

Originally, the Bureau concentrated its enforcement efforts on those drugs irrefutably considered dangerous (e.g., heroin) because of concern that arrests of persons abusing other drugs would be considered unwarranted interference in the lives of private citizens, and that such arrests would be overturned in the courts.

This concern stemmed partly from the Linder decision, which the Bureau suggested was due to a defect in the indictment (Lindesmith, 1967). Lindesmith, in a critical evaluation of the Bureau in *The Addict and the Law*, suggests that the Federal Bureau of Narcotics had fostered the punishment and nontreatment approach to addiction, had consistently failed to provide reliable statistics on the narcotics problem, and had been responsible for tightening the federal narcotics laws, thereby making arrests and convictions easier to obtain.

THE UNIFORM NARCOTIC DRUG ACT OF 1932

Upon its establishment in 1930, the Federal Bureau of Narcotics urged the cooperation of the states in the passage of the Uniform Narcotic Drug Act. Designed to facilitate enforcement, the law proposed cooperation between federal and nonfederal officers and uniform standards of record keeping. The Uniform Narcotic Drug Act, adopted by the National Conference of Commissioners on Uniform State Laws in 1932, makes no provision for the civil commitment of addicts nor does it contain specific federal recommendations of penalties for violations.

The strong prohibitive characteristics of legislation passed during this period and immediately after World War II encouraged the imposition of ultimate sanctions in criminal penalties. The problem of controlling the distribution and possession of narcotics was again increasingly delegated to the criminal justice system. While the Uniform Narcotic Drug Act allowed a physician to prescribe in "good faith," the problem continued to be one of interpretation of the term in light of increasingly repressive criminal law. The post-Linder cases are characterized by: (1) the lack of court definitions of good faith; (2) the failure of the defense that a physician's duty to relieve suffering extended to prescription of narcotics to addicts; (3) the increasing number of physicians arrested for narcotics violations; and (4) the lack of federal court restrictions consistent with a disease model of addiction.

THE BOGGS ACT (1951) AND THE NARCOTIC DRUG CONTROL ACT (1956)

The trend in narcotics legislation following World War II was toward stiffer penalties and mandatory minimum sentences as exemplified by the

Boggs Act (1951) and the Narcotic Drug Control Act of 1956. Hearings on both bills linked narcotics use to a Communist conspiracy to undermine Western society (Musto, 1973), and they were enacted in an atmosphere similar to that during the red scare in 1919.

The Hale-Boggs Bill of 1951 called for a mandatory minimum sentence of 2 years and a maximum of 5 years for a first narcotics offense, a mandatory 5 to 10 years with probation and suspension of sentence denied for the second offense, and a mandatory 10 to 20 years with probation and suspension of sentence denied for the third and subsequent offenses. The Narcotic Drug Control Act of 1956 called for even harsher and less flexible penalties: 2 to 10 years for first offense of possession, mandatory 5 to 20 years (probation and parole denied) for second possession or first selling offense, mandatory 10 to 40 years (probation and parole denied) for third possession or second selling offense, and 10 years to life (no parole or probation) and the possibility of a death sentence upon the recommendation of the jury for the sale of heroin by an adult (over 18) to a minor (under 18). Prior to 1951, federal judges could impose long sentences on large-scale narcotics dealers by a summation of consecutive sentences on multiple counts. However, employment of this technique was at the discretion of the judge. The 1951 and 1956 laws did not substantially alter the actual length of sentences for the major dealers, but served to force these sentences on addicts and small-scale pushers. Characterized by harsh and inflexible penalties, these two laws severely limited the judge's prerogative of taking into account mitigating circumstances in the consideration of sentences. Essentially the power to mitigate punishment was transferred to the enforcement officers who, by manipulating the charges against a violator, could effectively determine the length of sentence. The minimum mandatory sentences prescribed by the Boggs Act were perceived to interfere with the rehabilitative process. During the hearings before the Hale-Boggs subcommittee in 1955 and 1956, testimony from enforcement officers severely criticized federal judges for not issuing heavy penalties and for failure to secure convictions. Lindesmith (1967) suggests that perhaps this contention arose from the desire of federal judges to see justice done, from their abhorrence of the mandatory penalties which denied judicial discretion, and from the failure of both police and prosecutors to provide sufficient evidence to warrant a conviction under the harsher laws.

The Boggs Act and the Narcotic Drug Control Act gained enthusiastic support among enforcement officials who welcomed the increased leverage provided by mandatory minimum sentences. It has frequently been noted that a major problem in the control of illicit narcotics traffic is the victimless nature of the offense, since both buyer and seller willingly engage in the transaction and it is therefore unlikely that a complaint would be filed by either party. It then becomes necessary for the police to secure the cooperation of the participants to elicit any information regarding the "who" and "where," and "how much" of the transaction. The stiff penalties imposed by a conviction under violation of either Act and the ability to manipulate charges offer increased leverage to the enforcement officials in securing this cooperation. However, what is referred to as the "stool pigeon technique" proved to be ineffectual in providing a link with the major narcotics dealers who cautiously remain indirectly involved. Illicit drug traffic is relatively untouched by the numerous arrests of street addicts while the court system becomes clogged. Between 1950 and 1954, the total number of narcotic violations defendants remained constant, while the tendency for a defendant to plead guilty diminished (Lindesmith, 1967). By stiffening the penalties for conviction on a narcotics violation the Boggs Act has actually increased the caseload of the judicial system, with defendants demanding trial by jury in the hope of circumventing the long sentences.

THE JOINT COMMITTEE ON NARCOTIC DRUGS

Among the harshest critics of the strict penalties prescribed by the Boggs Act were members of the legal and medical professions. The American Bar Association (ABA) requested a subcommittee investigation in response to the preliminary statements of the Federal Bureau of Narcotics praising the efficacy of the mandatory sentences. Ironically, the outcome of the committee's report was the Narcotic Drug Control Act of 1956, which has already been cited for its even more severe penalty provisions. Dissatisfied, the ABA created its own Standing Committee on Narcotics and Alcohol, and in 1957 the AMA joined the ABA to establish the Joint Committee on Narcotic Drugs. The *Interim Report* of the Joint Committee issued in 1958 called for a softening of penalties and the establishment of an experimental outpatient clinic for the treatment of drug addicts. The response from the Federal Bureau of Narcotics to this report was both anxious and critical. Threatened by what it perceived as a potential reduction in surveillance efficiency as a result of numerous clinics, and the concomitant increase in required appropriations, the Bureau issued a report of its own. The controversy was settled in favor of the Joint Committee partly because of increasing interest in, and sophistication of, the mental health professions. Federal appropriations to the mental health professions had been steadily increasing since World War II. Members of the mental health professions argued that addiction was a psychological disease and should therefore be treated by physicians. Also, the failure of harsh penalties and mandatory sentences to prevent a rise in drug abuse provoked a search for an answer from the mental health professions. The New York State Medical Society submitted a proposal to the AMA that would legalize the distribution of narcotics to addicts and the Special Committee on Narcotic Addictions Report suggested outpatient rehabilitation programs and the institution of civil commitment as consequences of conviction for possession. In 1962, the White House Conference on Addiction called for a shift in national policy on the treatment of addiction. That same year witnessed the historic Supreme Court decision in the case of *Robinson* v. *California* that added judicial impetus to the civil commitment movement. California had enacted a statute making addiction a crime in and of itself. Any person convicted under this law would undergo a mandatory 90 day incarceration. The Supreme Court ruled this a violation of the Eighth Amendment as constituting "cruel and unusual punishment." The court proposed that addiction should not be punished as a crime but that states should compel addicts to undergo treatment and impose penal sanction only in the event of failure to comply with the civil commitment procedure (*Robinson* v. *United States* 370 U.S. 660, 1962). The Presidential Commission on Narcotic and Drug Abuse Report of 1963 provided further support in calling for (1) the relaxation of mandatory sentences; (2) an increase in appropriations for research; (3) dismantling of the Federal Bureau of ·Narcotics and transfer of its functions to the Department of Health, Education and Welfare and to the Justice Department; and (4) a reinstatement of the right of the medical profession to decide what constituted legitimate medical treatment of addiction. With the establishment of the Bureau of Drug Abuse Control in the Department of Health, Education and Welfare by the Drug Abuse Control Amendment of 1965, the constitutional basis of narcotic control shifted from taxation (where it had been since 1914) to interstate commerce.

Civil commitment became national policy in 1966, with the Narcotic Addict Rehabilitation Act providing for both inpatient and outpatient phases of treatment. The National Institute of Mental Health requested model treatment programs using multimodality mental health centers to treat large numbers of addicts. Civil commitment programs were predicated on the theory that addiction is a process requiring lengthy treatment that often incorporates legal controls. Since treatment and cure are not synonymous, the issue of volition becomes central. Huberty (1972) suggests that two criteria are used in resolving the issue of voluntary versus involuntary treatment: the right *not* to be treated is almost certainly denied when (1) it involves a risk to life, and (2) when the disease involves high societal costs. In the case of addiction, the societal cost outweighs the individual's right not to be treated. The courts, however, did not agree as to what constituted a civil as opposed to a criminal commitment. In 1967 the Presidential Commission on Law Enforcement and Administration of Justice criticized civil commitment as a violation of individual freedom. The Commission report suggested that the success rate for this procedure was too low to warrant continuation and recommended an increase in the enforcement staffs of the Federal Bureau of Narcotics and the Customs Bureau.

THE COMPREHENSIVE DRUG ABUSE PREVENTION AND CONTROL ACT OF 1970

A distillation of the various issues was made in the ultimate form of the Comprehensive Drug Abuse Prevention and Control Act of 1970. Originally a liberal administration proposal emphasizing research, education, and rehabilitation, the bill aroused considerable controversy in the Senate. An alternate bill favoring law enforcement had been proposed by Senator Thomas Dodd in 1969. After numerous revisions and compromises the final form of the Drug Abuse Act was enacted, replacing all preceding national laws relating to narcotics. For the first time, the bill explicitly states that federal law has jurisdiction over all drugs controlled by the Act. Provision has been made for the appropriation of funds for institutions engaged in prevention and treatment of drug abuse and in the rehabilitation of drug addicts. Power for enforcement of the Act is no longer derived from the federal powers of taxation but comes from the laws directly controlling narcotics. Responsibility for enforcement has been transferred from the Treasury Department to the Bureau of Narcotics and Dangerous Drugs in the Department of Justice. Decisions regarding the selection of specific drugs requiring federal control have been delegated to the Secretary of Health, Education and Welfare.

The law defines several "schedules" of drugs; division is on the basis of potential for abuse, and the recommended maximum penalties for each schedule are graded appropriately. For example, heroin is usually classified as a Schedule I drug together with other extremely addictive narcotics (other opiates and opiate derivatives) and carries the heaviest maximum penalties. Conviction on a first offense for heroin possession is punishable by a maximum prison sentence of one year and a fine of $5000. The second possession offense warrants two years imprisonment and a $10,000 fine. Conviction on a first offense for manufacturing or distributing carries a penalty of 15 years maximum imprisonment, $25,000 fine, and a 3 year mandatory probationary period following release. The second and subsequent offenses require 30 years maximum imprisonment, a $50,000 fine, and a 6 year probationary period. All persons engaged in the manufacture, distribution, and research of controlled drugs are required to register annually. Records of narcotics transactions must be kept for two years. The controversial mandatory sentences characteristic of legislation in the 1950s have been deleted from the 1970 act. There is, however, provision for dealing more harshly with the sale of dangerous drugs to a minor. An individual over 18 who distributes a controlled drug to a minor can receive twice the penalty for a first offense and three times the penalty for a second. Heavy increments of the penalty schedule are also specified in detail for those engaged in illicit drug enterprise, calling for life imprisonment and denial of probation in the hopes of deterring large-scale dealers. Leniency is recommended for the "onetime user," especially in cases of marijuana use, and there is a provision that deletes the conviction and arrest from the individual's record after a 1 year probation period.

Although it seems premature to attempt an evaluation of the 1970 Drug Abuse Act, the law does recognize, perhaps for the first time, a distinction between those constant or large-scale offenders who regularly profit from illicit narcotics traffic and the onetime experimental user. The scale of penalties graduated according to the severity of the offense and the provisions for leniency in the case of infrequent users have done much to reverse the trend of the 1951 Boggs Act and the 1956 Narcotic Drug Control Act.

FEDERAL STRATEGY FOR DRUG ABUSE AND DRUG TRAFFIC PREVENTION

The Drug Abuse Office and Treatment Act of 1972 called for the development of a federal strategy for drug abuse and drug traffic prevention. Prevention of drug abuse was to include activities in treatment, education, rehabilitation, and research, the policy for which would be established by the Special Action Office for Drug Abuse Prevention. Activities in drug traffic prevention were divided into two spheres of control: (1) international, coordinated by the Cabinet Committee on International Narcotics Control (1971) under the Secretary of State, and (2) domestic, controlled by the Special Consultant to the President for Drug Abuse Law Enforcement. The International Drug Control program would concentrate on seizure of illicit drug shipments, destruction of traffic patterns, and arrest and imprisonment of traffickers. A greater commitment to law enforcement by foreign governments against drug traffickers was considered necessary if the programs were to succeed. In 1973, the report of the Strategy

Council on Drug Abuse called for focus on the availability of heroin and other narcotics as the principal factor over which control could be exercised. The efforts at prevention were to be concentrated on reducing the availability of heroin, on heavy penalties to act as a deterrent, and on offering treatment to prevent the spread of abuse. Heroin was singled out as the most widely abused narcotic and priority in services was to be given to heroin abuse.

In an evaluation of treatment programs, the Council suggested that without a mechanism to retain those persons in civil commitment treatment, the high cost of the procedure relative to that of voluntary programs was such that its overall ineffectiveness did not warrant federal expansion. However, the Council did recommend continued federal support for those programs accepting state referral patients. In a search for efficacious treatment programs, the Council suggested three major voluntary treatment modalities for heroin addicts: (a) self-regulating therapeutic communities, (b) programs providing for withdrawal followed by aftercare and counseling in the community, and (c) methadone maintenance. It was felt that legalized distribution of heroin would not substantially alter the recruitment pattern of new addicts, therefore adoption of the British system of heroin maintenance was opposed by the Council. Regarding treatment, the Council took the following position: (a) the long-range goal of treatment should be abstinence; (b) maintenance should be employed only in the case of addicts with at least a 2 year history of abuse; (c) drugs in addition to methadone should be explored; and (d) the maximum dosage provided should not exceed 120 mg, and those persons receiving over 100 mg of the drug should be required to take it only in the clinic.

The federal government planned to expand all three of the treatment programs mentioned without replacing the individual states' responsibility for providing supporting resources. It was estimated by the Council that no more than one-half of the active narcotics users would seek treatment in any given year. The needed capacity for treatment was established at 200,000 to 250,000 (Strategy Council on Drug Abuse, 1973, p. 80). A change in the federal delivery of care was recommended to increase the responsibility at the state level to ensure efficiency of treatment. Each state would design a single agency to be responsible for coordination of various state programs and to recommend licensing procedures to assure minimum treatment standards. In this way programs could be tailored to meet the unique needs of individual states while concurrently fulfilling federal requirements. The Office for Drug Abuse Law Enforcement in the Department of Justice was requested to coordinate efforts at state, local, and federal levels to increase the efficiency of enforcement tools and procedures. As a result, the number of federally funded programs has risen from

36 in 1971 to 394 in 1973 (Strategy Council of Drug Abuse, 1973, p. 137).

NARCOTIC ADDICT TREATMENT ACT OF 1974

Responding to a need to establish clearer lines of federal authority and control over the treatment of narcotic addicts, Congress, in 1974, passed the Narcotic Addict Treatment Act (NATA). Under this act, the Department of Health and Human Services was delegated the authority to establish standards for the use by practitioners of narcotic drugs for maintenance or detoxification of narcotic-addicted persons. Actual regulation of narcotic treatment programs under NATA was delegated to the Food and Drug Administration (FDA).

The Food and Drug Administration's role in enforcing the Narcotic Addict Treatment Act includes (a) determination of the qualifications of proposed program sponsors to engage in maintenance or detoxification treatment; (b) determination of compliance by applicants for treatment programs with the standards established by FDA and the National Institute on Drug Abuse (NIDA) for the operation of narcotic treatment programs, and (c) the concurrent review of applications for narcotic treatment programs with the appropriate state, although the state must first grant initial approval before FDA grants final approval. Additionally, NATA requires that treatment programs must not only comply with HHS regulations but must also be registered with the Attorney General through the Drug Enforcement Agency (DEA).

In 1980, the FDA and NIDA significantly revised regulations governing the operation of treatment programs. This was done with the intent of (a) allowing programs greater flexibility in using methadone to treat narcotic addicts, (b) increasing the effectiveness of methadone treatment, (c) reducing the likelihood of methadone diversion by patients, and (d) establishing clearer treatment standards. Some specific changes in 1980 led to new requirements for the development of individualized treatment plans; for assessing an individual client's responsibility for handling take home medication; and for the delineation of specific requirements for the medical director and program physicians. Additionally, the regulations were changed to allow: (a) six-day take-home medication; (b) greater program discretion regarding staffing and patient admissions; (c) a reduction in required "history of addiction" for admission to maintenance treatment from two to one years; and (d) less frequently required urine testing.

By 1985, FDA had approved approximately 600 narcotic treatment programs in 41 states and three territories, as well as 200 hospital inpatient detoxification treatment programs nationwide. Approximately one-fourth of these programs receive routine on-site visits each year as part of a regular monitoring process.

In 1984, Congress passed legislation removing the 21-day cap on the allowed length of time for detoxification treatment and extending it to 180 days.

This law was to become effective on January 17, 1985, but has not yet been implemented.

CONCLUDING COMMENTS

The Board of Directors of the National Council on Crime and Delinquency (1974) noted that while there were many addicts in the 1920s, they were generally not criminals and lived much the same as did the nonaddict population. The Board believed that the illegal narcotics market produced by the introduction of legal restrictions on narcotic drugs originally forced the addict into his present lifestyle of criminal activity. One answer to this problem, they suggested, would be to undermine this illegal market by providing narcotics on a maintenance basis together with medical treatment. The issue of restrictive drug laws was also considered by Lindesmith and Gagnon (1964) who noted that society's reaction to the opiate user is an important factor in the use of such drugs. As proof for this theory they cited the high rate of use in the United States, a country with a restrictive drug policy, and the lesser extent of opiate use in England, a country without punitive legislation. In addition, the changing characteristics of the opiate addict population following the passage of the Harrison Act in 1914 were considered by Lindesmith and Gagnon to be directly related to the influence of a restrictive narcotics control policy. Prior to 1914 the addict was primarily white and upper middle class. The subsequent legislative trend toward criminalization of addiction led to its predominance in urban, poverty cultures. They concluded from the evidence that the characteristics of any country's addiction problem can be predicted from the type of control policy in force. One effect of restrictive legislation on drug use may be to drive the user to another drug. This resolution of the problem by substitution of another problem is illustrated by Hawks, Mitcheson, Ogborne, and Edwards' (1969) observation of a sharp increase in the intravenous use of methylamphetamine after legislation in England resulted in decreased availability of heroin and cocaine in 1968. When limits were then placed on the availability of methylamphetamine, the rate of intravenous use of barbiturates increased (Mitcheson, Davidson, Hawks, Hitchens, and Malone, 1970). Clearly, restriction of drug availability in itself is not the answer. This is particularly true in the United States where complete control of heroin traffic has never been and is unlikely to be achieved, and where heroin users tend toward multidrug abuse.

On the other hand, a relaxation of restrictions on narcotics traffic per se will probably increase the incidence of heroin addiction, since many marginal individuals who now have difficulty in successfully supporting the habit or in obtaining the drug will find it easier to do so. This is evident from the "Swedish experiment," in which relatively easy drug accessibility resulted in a substantial increase in the incidence of drug abuse.

CHAPTER 3

Antinarcotics Legislation
at the State Level

Prior to federal intervention in the narcotics problem, legislation at the state level constituted the only serious attempt to restrict the distribution and use of drugs. At this level, restrictions during the nineteenth century were embodied in antinarcotics laws that varied according to the salience of drug abuse problems in a particular community. The prevalence of any particular drug contributed to the degree of local concern. For instance, Pennsylvania, the site of a leading morphine manufacturer, enacted anti-morphine legislation as early as 1860 in response to local concern. By the beginning of the twentieth century, a possible contributing factor to this action and to general concern about the availability of drugs was the indiscriminate over-the-counter sale of patent medicines containing percentages of morphine, cocaine, and heroin.

STATE LEGISLATION PRIOR TO 1914

When state and local control finally developed, it was in the form of state legislation in three stages: (1) laws directed at the control of drug use, (2) laws to control and restrict the sale of drugs, and (3) laws directed at the treatment of the drug addict. The early state laws directed at the suppression of opium-smoking generally failed in their attempts to affect the drug trade because they lacked provisions for enforcement.

The antidrug movement was pioneered by California which passed legislation enacting the first antiopium statute in 1872. This law dealt with the administration of drugs with the intent to facilitate the commission of a felony (Levine, 1973). However, the failure of this law to restrict the legal use of opium led to further legislation in 1881, which declared it a misdemeanor to maintain a place where opium was sold or smoked. Much later, California was the first state to create an independent narcotics bureau and to offer treatment to addicts.

The first state to pass legislation directed at controlling the distribution of narcotics was Nevada, in 1877, making the sale of opium illegal except on the order of a physician's prescription. Most other Western states followed Nevada's example, but restricted the law's applicability exclusively to opium. The enactment of these laws may have reflected concerns generated by the influx of Oriental laborers and the introduction of the custom of smoking opium in the Western states at that time.

It soon became apparent that laws attempting to control drug use were insufficient, and in 1887 Oregon passed the first legislation directed at the restriction of sale. Licenses were issued for the sale of narcotics, and prescriptions were required for the possession and sale of narcotics. The antinarcotics laws of the 1890s requiring a physician's prescription were, however, beset by loopholes which provided for the continued legal procurement of patent medicines of unspecified narcotic content. At that time federal intervention in state antinarcotics legislation was believed to be unconstitutional. While there did exist some very specific conditions under which federal law took precedence, such as interstate commerce, these were too narrowly delineated and therefore ineffective in controlling the narcotics traffic. As a result, state laws varied widely in comprehensiveness and severity and lacked jurisdiction over the sale of drugs between states with differing antinarcotics laws. Typical state laws prior to the Harrison Act in 1914 provided for the unrestricted sale of patent medicines but required a physician's prescription for the purchase of pure drugs. This limitation was more theoretical than real, however, because inspection of prescriptions was extremely rare and was often overlooked by pharmacists. Additional problems with the early state laws in situations to which they applied were so restricted as to render them ineffective on other than a very small scale. For example, although Connecticut passed a law in 1905 directing that cocaine could be sold legally and possessed only with a prescription, it was not until 1913 that heroin and morphine were also covered by the law. The controversy that arose over the issue of refilling narcotics prescriptions eventually brought into focus the problem of legislative ambiguity with regard to addiction maintenance. The necessity for returning to a doctor to refill a prescription created both a financial burden on the poor and established a steady flow of patients to physicians. Even then, the vast majority of doctors were wary of maintaining addicts, despite the fact that the addict often had little trouble persuading a doctor of his need for narcotics. The prevalent concern over the possibility of death caused by the abrupt termination of an addict's supply of narcotics certainly had some effect on the individual physician's prescription philosophy. However, most of the legislatures were forced to rely on professional ethics among physicians to control narcotics use. Legal definitions lacked the power to discriminate between well-intentioned overuse and indiscriminate dispensing prior to enactment of the Harrison Act in 1914. The early legislative concern with establishing control over the sale of drugs clouded the more important issue of delineating criteria by which a legitimate need for certain drugs could be established.

Following The Hague Convention in 1912, an investigation was made by the Public Health Service into state laws relating to narcotic drugs. The Public Health Service report criticized state laws as ineffective and inconsistent and prompted legislative reform in a number of states. In 1913 Tennessee enacted the Tennessee Narcotic Act, requiring addicts to register ostensibly for the receipt of narcotics prescriptions and to insure the legitimacy of the drug traffic. Both physicians and druggists were blamed for local drug problems as responsibility for care of the addict population shifted to the state level. Interest in antinarcotic legislation also developed in New York State in 1913, where attempts were made to prohibit fraudulent professional credentials and to monitor the drug traffic. Early proposed legislation would have restricted to 3 weeks the length of time a physician could legitimately dispense drugs to an addict. It was hoped that such restriction would encourage addicts to seek treatment in a sanitarium. The law was opposed, however, by physicians who perceived it as a serious encroachment on their professional liberty and it was ultimately rejected.

THE BOYLAN AND WHITNEY ACTS (NEW YORK)

The second attempt at state antinarcotics legislation was the Boylan Act of 1914. This statute contained exemptions for medicines of less than a specified narcotic content, had no provision for refills, required verification of prescriptions ordering more than a predetermined maximum amount of narcotics, required record keeping of all narcotic transactions, and required commitment to a licensed institution for the treatment of addiction.[1] Although possession of narcotics without authorization was considered a misdemeanor, maintenance of addiction was permitted if the addict was under the care of a physician. In 1914 when the law went into effect, concern increased about the adequacy of available treatment facilities that would become increasingly necessary as addicts were legally required to enter treatment. Hospitals were encouraged to provide more beds for the number of addicts estimated to be seeking cures as their legitimate supply of narcotics was revoked.

With the passage of the Harrison and Boylan Acts, drug-related arrests and prosecution of drug violators increased, and heightened concern over the magnitude of the drug problem led to an amendment to the Boylan Act in 1915. By this amendment, the sale of drugs to a minor was upgraded to a felony and record-keeping requirements became stricter. The medical profession came under increasing attack because it was supposedly the only legitimate source of narcotics. Inevitably, several professional groups began a movement for the private physician to retain responsibility for treatment of the addict that was spearheaded by the Association of Physicians Economic League of New York. When compromise legislation could not be reached, the state legislature created the Whitney Committee to investigate the narcotics problem. In its preliminary report the Committee cited the medical profession as responsible for the confusion over what constituted effective treatment. Furthermore, addiction was defined by the Committee as a disease for which narcotics should be supplied until effective treatment was discovered. During the course of "treatment," addicts were to be committed to the care of a physician. The Committee's recommendations were included into the Whitney Act in 1917 with a rider that local boards of health could dispense drugs to an addict pending treatment.

An independent State Commission on Narcotic Drug Control was established by the Second Whitney Act of 1918. The report issued by this committee in 1918 recommended the establishment of a central state authority to organize narcotic control policies in cooperation with federal authorities and the provision for institutional treatment of addiction by the state. The Commission did not recommend the prohibition of heroin at that time. With the creation of the Department of Narcotic Drug Control in 1919, plans were initiated for the establishment of narcotics clinics.

[1] This trend toward compulsory treatment of addiction originated with a Connecticut statute in 1874 that declared an addict incompetent and remanded him to a state asylum for treatment. When voluntary treatment programs failed to attract significant numbers of addicts many other states, including New York, attempted to make treatment compulsory.

Detailed records of narcotic flow would serve to identify physicians and druggists who dispensed drugs commercially. A substantial number of such transactions actually were uncovered and provided a rallying point for those opposed to maintenance programs. The major loophole in the law, which exempted a physician from filling a prescription when treating a disease other than addiction, was closed in 1920 with the aim of curtailing such abuse. Institutional treatment was also supported by the commissioner, who believed the success of the ambulatory treatment method was minimal because it created a greater potential for abuse as well as difficulties in controlling distribution.

Two subsequent developments led to the abolition of ambulatory treatment in New York. The Supreme Court decisions against maintenance in the Webb and Doremus cases (1919) resulted in large-scale arrests of physicians and druggists in New York City who were believed to be supplying narcotics to addicts. As previously noted, a city clinic was created to absorb the overflow of addicts expected to be seeking drugs. The Department of Narcotic Drug Control supervised the establishment of state clinics, and the State Commission came under criticism from groups who feared massive state interference in the practice of medicine. The Physicians' Protective Association specifically fought the mandate that doctors must decrease their prescription dosages over a given period of time and argued that care of the addict was properly the responsibility of the private physician. Nevertheless, the number of addicts registering for treatment increased almost threefold from July 1919 to January 1920, (Musto, 1973). Several methods of registration were attempted in an effort to assure the success of the clinics. At one point, staining the hands with silver nitrate was tried. According to Musto (1973), this method was eventually abandoned in favor of a registration card showing the addict's photograph, signature, dosage, and physician. The treatment procedure adopted was to gradually decrease the narcotic dosage by ½ grain every other day and to offer institutional treatment at the point of withdrawal. Evaluation of the clinic procedure revealed its success rate to be low and its profit margin to be high, with addicts often traveling from one clinic to another to prolong maintenance. By 1920 the public attitude was largely fearful of addicts and favored repression of addiction maintenance. Following the strict interpretation of the amendment to the Harrison Act, the state and city clinics faced imminent closure. Similar problems were faced by narcotics clinics in Atlanta and Louisiana. Although those in Louisiana remained in operation longer than those in New York, they were eventually closed by the Harrison Act Amendment. The Atlanta clinic was closed in 1925.

THE UNIFORM NARCOTIC DRUG ACT

State narcotic legislation was essentially nonexistent in New York following the clinic closings in 1921. Responsibility for narcotics control reverted to the local communities, since attempts at the state level to deal with the problems of narcotic addiction had been overruled by recent federal legislation. Prior to 1930 and the establishment of the Federal Bureau of Narcotics, most states had thoroughly inadequate laws which could not control the sale, manufacture, or possession of dangerous drugs. Up to that time the control of narcotics had been primarily a federal concern. Following its inception, the Bureau was to assist the states in drafting legislation directed at the suppression of drug abuse in an effort to secure cooperation with its policies at the state level. Legislation was badly needed to assure uniformity of state laws to eliminate the possibility of obtaining drugs in an adjoining state that had no restrictions on the sale of narcotics. In 1932 this cooperative effort resulted in the passage of the Uniform Narcotic Act, which was subsequently adopted by most states with minor revisions (see Chapter 2). This Act attempted to prescribe uniform methods of record keeping in both state and federal agencies and to enhance enforcement potential (heretofore constitutionally restricted federal intervention in state concerns). It was hoped that the federal agencies would direct their attention to the large-scale wholesalers and interstate traffickers and that the states would concentrate on the peddlers and addicts. Although most states passed the Uniform Narcotic Act, the penalties for narcotics violations varied from state to state because it was the state's prerogative to determine the severity of appropriate and effective penalties in controlling its drug problem. In some states addiction itself was defined as a crime, and most state legislation was designed to permit the arrest and incarceration on sight of known narcotic users on charges of vagrancy and loitering. A tendency gradually developed toward heavier punishment at the state level, often involving the upgrading of violations from a misdemeanor to a felony. Lindesmith (1967) suggests that the logic behind upgrading possession offenses stems from the difficulties encountered in proving actual sale of narcotics in court. By upgrading the offense it thereby becomes possible to punish the violator (seller) on more easily proven charges of possession by sentencing appropriate in severity to the crime of the sale.

The Uniform Narcotic Act remained the basis of state laws throughout World War II during which time the national drug problem decreased in severity. As discussed earlier, the national atmosphere following the war was conducive to the enactment of stricter legislative controls. The

Uniform Act had not provided for variation in penalties between state and federal levels. An attempt to modify the Uniform Narcotic Act through the addition of mandatory minimum sentences was initiated in the Boggs Act (1951). Reported increases in rates of addiction and drug-related crime contributed heavily to a belief in the necessity for mandatory minimum sentences as deterrents. Many states passed acts in accordance with the aim of the Boggs Act. In 1956 New Jersey, for example, prescribed a mandatory minimum sentence of 20 years for the sale of narcotics by an adult to a minor. A first selling offense would be punished by a 10 year minimum sentence, a second offense by 20 years, and a third by 30 years. Suspension of sentence and probation were denied. Lindesmith (1967) quotes the Governor of New Jersey justifying his veto of this bill on the grounds that it implied that "injustice to individual defendants is a fair price to pay for deterrent effect upon the addict as well as the non-addict sellers" (p. 32).

THE UNIFORM CONTROLLED SUBSTANCES ACT

In 1969 the President requested passage of a federal law with the aim of consolidating the various state laws into a uniform code in accordance with federal guidelines. The Federal Bureau of Narcotics and Dangerous Drugs suggested the Uniform Controlled Substances Act which was adopted in 1970. This law is essentially a state-oriented codified system of drug control derived from the Federal Controlled Substances Act of 1970. The Act is identical to the Federal law in the following respects: (a) all narcotics and dangerous drugs are classified into five schedules according to discrete criteria; (b) states may amend the law based on emerging scientific evidence; and (c) provisions are made to restrict the distribution of controlled substances to those persons legitimately requiring them. As in the Uniform Narcotics Act, specific sentences for violation are left to the discretion of the states so that they may deal effectively with specific drug abuse patterns in their various geographical areas so long as such sentencing practices are not in conflict with the general Federal provisions. By 1972, 18 states had passed the Act and most others were considering it (an additional 22 states had passed it by 1973). Ultimately, the Act is designed to classify drugs into five schedules based upon their potential for abuse and on their known harmful effects, thereby making it possible to delineate penalties more appropriate to the dangerousness of the drug. Levine (1974) concisely evaluates this trend:

In essence, adoption of the Uniform Controlled Substances Act, which is a legislative prototype of federal dangerous drug laws, is an effort to establish a comprehensive, coordinated and codified legislative effort to prevent and control drug abuse. [p. 171]

Regarding the current status of antinarcotic legislation at the state level, two major trends have recently developed. Many states have adopted the Uniform Narcotic Drug Act with minor revisions of the five basic schedules. The remaining states have, with modification, provided penalties for two (or more) distinct categories of drugs: narcotics and dangerous drugs (nonnarcotics). Originally, many states classified marijuana with the narcotic drugs for punitive purposes. The current trend, however, is away from this classification with less harsh penalties. A few states have adopted the federal provision for the dismissal of charges against a first offender at the discretion of the court. Since it would be unwieldy to discuss individual state laws in this context, legislation of certain states will be reviewed, either because the laws are representative of many states or because they are unusual. The largest proportion of states provide sentences of not more than 5 years for the first offense of possession (Oklahoma, North Dakota, North Carolina, New Jersey, New Hampshire, Montana, Delaware, Connecticut, and South Dakota), with the addition of a mandatory minimum of 2 years in Tennessee, Pennsylvania, Ohio, Nebraska, Iowa, Georgia, Florida, and Arkansas. A few have a maximum of 20 years (Alabama, Minnesota, Kentucky, and Washington). Texas has the harshest law—a mandatory minimum of 2 years and a maximum of life imprisonment. West Virginia has the lightest penalty for a first possession offense— 90 days to 6 months. For the second possession violation, many localities prescribe a maximum sentence of 10 years (New Hampshire and Washington, D.C.) and a mandatory minimum of 5 years (Wisconsin, Tennessee, Pennsylvania, Oklahoma, Ohio, North Carolina, Nebraska, Iowa, Georgia, Florida, and Arkansas). Missouri and Texas have a maximum of life imprisonment, while Wyoming requires not more than 6 months. The first sales offense is more severely punished; five states provide a maximum life sentence (Texas, Missouri, Michigan, Montana, and Illinois). There is no consensus within the remaining states regarding sentencing; the penalties range from not more than 5 years in Oklahoma to 1 to 40 years in Virginia. Eight states have provision for life imprisonment for the second narcotics sale offense (mandatory life sentence: Illinois, New Mexico, Nevada, Indiana, Michigan, Virginia, Missouri, Texas), and all require a mandatory minimum of 10 to 20 years with no opportunity for suspended sentence or parole. The harshest laws exist in those states having specific sentences covering the sale of narcotics (especially heroin) by an adult to a minor. In Missouri, this is legally punishable by death, while Oklahoma, Texas and Alabama suggest death at the recommendation of the jury. A significant number of states require a life sentence with no probation or parole.

Many states have adapted the Uniform Code to meet the needs of their particular types of drug problems. Arizona and Alaska have made special prohibitions to prevent the importation of narcotic drugs into their states (maximum of life sentence for second offense in Arizona). Some states have directed their legislation toward the prevention of drug abuse. To this end Delaware, New Jersey, and Montana have provided for court discretion in conditionally discharging first offenders. This entails a lengthy period of probation after which the charges are dismissed if all the conditions of probation have been met. Kentucky and Maryland offer a similar progressive approach in the case of possession. Upon conviction for a first offense, the individual must report to a treatment and rehabilitation facility pursuant to court orders. After satisfactory completion of the rehabilitation or treatment program, the conviction is set aside. In Oklahoma, Georgia, and Illinois addiction itself is considered a crime and carries penalties of three to six months in jail. The Kentucky statute requires that an individual using a narcotic for other than medical treatment be confined in a county jail for one year. The legality of enforcement of these statutes requiring commitment to treatment is questionable in view of the Supreme Court decision in *Robinson* v. *California* (1962) discussed earlier. This issue is often avoided, however, when the addict is given the choice of volunteering for treatment or facing prosecution for a drug violation. The U.S. district court can suspend a criminal charge if it believes the individual is an addict and can be treated. In this case, the addict is committed to the custody of the Surgeon General and the charge against him is dropped if he completes the treatment program satisfactorily. Iowa demands civil commitment for an addict, the penalty being treatment until cured. Indiana declares (1970) a narcotics addict is

. . . dangerous in public places and is subject to three months confinement and a fine of $300. He is also prohibited from entering public places, including streets and highways, unless he can present positive proof that he is under the care of a licensed physician for the treatment of addiction [Levine, 1974, p. 75]

In addition, Illinois law provides that multiple punctures on skin surfaces or scars resulting from hypodermic use are *prima facie* evidence of repeated narcotics use. Those states (specifically Oregon and Pennsylvania) that have only general penalty provisions on the basis of broadly defined classes of narcotic/nonnarcotic drugs minimize the discretion of the court in imposing sentence. Perhaps the most unique specific provision under state law is that of Ohio (1970), making illegal the carnal knowledge of an individual who is under the influence of a narcotic; a first offense carries a 2 to 5 year sentence.

CONCLUDING COMMENTS

Problems of enforcement of antinarcotic laws at the state level arise from their lack of uniformity. In New York both the State Police and the Bureau of Narcotics Control are responsible for control. In contrast, California has delegated responsibility for enforcement to one agency, the Bureau of Narcotic Enforcement. Problems of cooperation among police departments in metropolitan regions often result in inconsistent enforcement and fragmented information. In several areas, metropolitan enforcement groups are organized as teams whose members are drawn from the various enforcement agencies in the area. The Bureau of Narcotics and Dangerous Drugs has urged support for these programs with federal funds. The teams consist principally of undercover agents and informers who transmit information to various local police departments in an effort to avoid duplication of data. In 1970 the International Association of Chiefs of Police published a report to be used as a guideline in establishing local narcotics enforcement units whose goals would be elimination of the illegal sale and use of narcotics and dangerous drugs. To this end education, treatment, elimination of drug supply, and police support would all be utilized. The local police agencies with primary responsibility could count on the state law enforcement agencies for support in resources (both personnel and information). It is logical that only through cooperation between agencies and the widespread dissemination of information can the locus of drug traffic be pinpointed and eliminated.

LEGAL CASES CITED IN PART I.

Jin Fuey Moy v. *United States,* 254 U.S. 189 (1920).
Linder v. *United States,* 268 U.S. 5 (1925).
Robinson v. *United States,* 370 U.S. 660 (1962).
United States v. *Behrman,* 258 U.S. 280 (1922).
United States v. *Doremus,* 246 U.S. 86 (1919).
United States v. *Jin Fuey Moy,* 241 U.S. 394 (1915).
Webb et al v. *United States,* 249 U.S. 96 (1919).

PART TWO

The Physiology and Pharmacology of Heroin Addiction

CHAPTER 4

Heroin: Administration, Action, Antagonists, and Substitutes

Heroin addiction, like many other forms of substance addiction, involves various processes that operate at various functional levels. Thus partial explanations of heroin use and its effects can be found at the following levels: the physiological, the individual psychological, the social, and the societal. The physiological level, discussed in this chapter, is particularly relevant in understanding addiction to heroin because of the essential role played by tolerance and physiological dependence. The first part of this chapter introduces the administration, dose level, and mechanisms of action of heroin. The second half focuses on the narcotic antagonists and substitutes because of the additional insight they provide into the mechanisms underlying heroin action.

WHAT IS HEROIN?

Heroin is derived from the opium poppy, *Papaver somniferum*, indigenous to the Middle East and Southeast Asia. This plant produces annually, for 7 to 10 days, a white, milky substance which becomes reddish-brown and gummy when dried in contact with the air. When further dried and powdered, this substance is known as opium. Morphine is the major alkaloid of opium, comprising about 10%. Other alkaloids naturally found in opium are codeine, papaverine, and noscapine. Heroin (diacetylmorphine), a semisynthetic derivative of morphine, is produced by exposing morphine to acetic acid. This induces a change in the chemical structure of morphine involving acetylation of the phenolic and alcoholic OH groups.

   The first step in processing raw opium to produce heroin requires successive boiling and straining in water to separate out the impurities. When the water is evaporated from this solution, a residue in the form of a thick black paste is formed. Opium can be used for smoking in this form. This process results in a 25% reduction in weight of the original raw opium. By the time heroin reaches the street, however, it is far from its original form. Heroin is often cut with lactose, quinine, and mannitol, sometimes resulting in less than 2% or 3% pure heroin remaining in the street form. Street heroin also contains many adulterants, particularly quinine, which was originally introduced as an adulterant to provide protection against malaria. Sapira (1968) notes two reasons for the preferred use of quinine as an adulterant of heroin: its bitter taste, which disguises the heroin content of the substance used, and its vasodilatory effects when injected intravenously. The latter effects produce a flush which may be mistaken by the novice addict for that produced by heroin. The use of

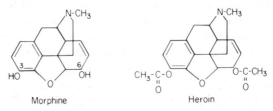

Figure 1. Structural formulas for morphine and heroin.

quinine may, however, be implicated in the development of tetanus in addicts because of its production of tissue abscesses when heroin is administered subcutaneously (Cherubin, 1967).

METHODS OF ADMINISTRATION

Heroin may be administered orally, inhaled, or injected subcutaneously or directly into the veins (Brown, 1961). The preferred mode of administration among addicts in the United States seems to be by direct injection into a vein or "mainlining"; other methods decrease the initial effect by the digestive and/or absorptive processes and also increase latency time before effects are felt. Ball (1966) noted that among a group of 107 Puerto Rican males he studied, 36% started using opiates by intravenous injection, while sniffing was the initial route for 39%, subcutaneous or intramuscular injection for 7%, and injection by an unspecified route for 8%. Among American soldiers in Southeast Asia, however, smoking was the most commonly used route of administration (Rosenbaum, 1971), sniffing occurred less frequently, and administration by injection was quite rare. According to one Congressional report, 5 to 10% of heroin-addicted U.S. servicemen in South Vietnam administered the drug by injection.[1]

Sinnett, Arata, and Bates (1974) surveyed a sample of drug users from three Kansas communities as to their knowledge and actual employment of methods of self-administration of heroin. Although 100% of the users were aware of "shooting up" as a method of heroin use, only 60% actually used this method. The most commonly used method was "snorting," used by 64%, and known of by 98% of the sample surveyed. "Dropping" (or eating) was known of by 70% of the users questioned, but used by only 8%. Smoking was least known (26%) and was used by 11%. As the authors point out, ". . . one cannot assume accuracy of stereotypes" (i.e., that heroin is taken only intravenously) "when one is assessing an individual user's practice." (p. 6).

Generally the street addict is very frugal with respect to achieving the maximum effect of the drug and, if possible, will always try to mainline it. The long-term addict however, eventually runs out of veins that have not been damaged by repeated injection. This leads him or her to seek other sites of entry, e.g., between the toes or fingers, or other parts of the body. Although the user of the 1920s and 1930s would inject relatively pure

[1] The World Heroin Problem, Report of a Special Study Mission by Morgan F. Murphy and Robert H. Steele, House Committee on Foreign Affairs, 92nd Congress, 1st Session 20 (May 27, 1971).

heroin into the flesh of his arm or leg, currently the primary route of injection is into the vein, reflecting in part the lower concentration of the product available on the street.

THE "MECHANICS" OF ADMINISTRATION

The procedure followed by street addicts in preparing and using heroin usually involves the following steps. The powdered heroin is first placed in a spoon ("cooker") or bottle cap. A small amount of water is then added to dissolve the powder, and the mixture is heated by applying a match flame under the spoon. Many addicts place a small ball of cotton in the spoon to act as a filter through which the liquid is drawn into an eye-dropper. This cotton filter is saved and can be used in an emergency (several of these are boiled in water and a heroin residue is extracted that can provide enough of the drug to stave off the symptoms of with-drawal). A hypodermic needle is tightly attached by a paper flange to the eyedropper, which Helpern and Rho (1967) suggest is much more easily manipulated than a plastic syringe. The area of the arm at which the in-jection is to occur is rubbed to facilitate injection. A tourniquet is usually applied to the arm to raise the vein into which the needle is inserted directly. Other modes of effecting entry into the veins include the use of safety pins, razor blades, needles, and other sharp objects. Not surpris-ingly, such practices can often lead to serious infections. Hepatitis is a common complication of chronic drug abuse since addicts occasionally use communal sets of "works" which rapidly become unsterile. The gen-eral issue of medical complications of heroin usage is discussed in detail in Chapter Six.

DOSE LEVEL AND COST

Winick (1965) noted that there had been a decline in purity and thus in the strength of heroin available to the addict since the 1920s. In earlier years it was possible to obtain 87% pure heroin which the addict cut him-self. He paid from $25 to $40 for an ounce of this relatively pure heroin. Between 1948 and 1953 heroin was available at 30 to 40% purity for $2 to $2.50 a packet. In the sixties, a 2% pure mixture cost $5. In their 1967 article Helpern and Rho reported contents of a "bag" to be 20 to 30 mg of heroin. According to Brecher (1972) the usual dose contained in a "bag" is 10 mg.

Commenting on the rising cost of heroin, DuPont and Greene (1973) reported the cost of a milligram of street heroin to be $1.53 in early 1972;

a year later it had increased to $5.80. The authors also noted that addicts entering treatment in November 1972 had noted an increase in the mean daily cost of their habit, from $39 to $52 over the previous three months. Bourne (1974) also noted a recent increase in price over an 18 month period, from 50 cents per mg to as much as $5 per mg. Citing government reports and other sources, Flaherty (1973) reported that heroin used by soldiers stationed at Ft. Belvoir, Virginia in 1971 was 5 to 7% pure and cost $10 per capsule. In Vietnam, 96% pure heroin used primarily for smoking or snorting cost about $2 for a 250 mg vial.

In an impressive study, Brown and Silverman (1974) determined the price of heroin in New York City, Detroit, and Los Angeles in relation to such variables as purity, quantity, and date of purchase. Using as their basic data the characteristics of heroin purchases by undercover federal, state, and local narcotics agents, the authors developed a carefully considered model which traced the market price of pure heroin on a monthly basis between July 1970 and June 1972. The apparent accuracy of their analysis is indicated by the correspondence of price fluctuations to external events affecting the supply of heroin. Thus, when dock strikes presumably reduced the amount of wholesale heroin imported, high retail prices resulted in the area of the country affected at the time. Other interesting data discussed in this study are the (inverse) relationship between quantity purchased and price; the relationship between price per gram and level of the distribution system at which the purchase took place (also inverse); the effects of time, reflecting such variables as inflation, stricter enforcement, and number of addicts upon price (direct, as might be expected); and the relationship between the price of heroin and crime (dependent upon the city studied). As Winick (1965) noted, one positive implication of the changing availability of pure heroin has been a diminution in the strength of the habit, reflected in the relative infrequency of severe reactions seen in addicts undergoing withdrawal today.

The English addict group of Blumberg et al (1974) reported a median daily dose level of about 50 mg, with 25% of the sample claiming daily use over 100 mg. Bewley and Ben-Aire (1968) reported that at the time of admission to treatment, most of their sample, also comprised of English addicts, had been taking 260 mg (4.3 grains) of heroin daily. The median level for their sample was 180 mg (3 grains).

The time of most frequent use of heroin on a habitual basis was found to be upon awakening. This was interpreted by Sinnett, Judd, Rissman, and Harvey (1980) as apparently being to ward off withdrawal symptoms. Heroin "chipping," or occasional use, was most frequent between 6 to 10 p.m., coinciding with the most common time of use for a number of illicit substances in various populations.

MECHANISM OF ACTION

While morphine is apparently responsible for the pharmacological effects of heroin (Jaffe, 1970c), heroin has an analgesia potency ratio, in contrast to morphine (which is generally used as the standard for this effect), of 2 or 3:1 (Martin and Fraser, 1961). In this regard Reichle et al (1962) examined the relative potencies of heroin and morphine with respect to the relief of postoperative pain during the first 150 minutes after administration. They found heroin to be two to four times as potent analgesically as morphine. As Janssen (1969) has noted, "the most potent analgesics known are pharmacologically and chemically related to morphine." Heroin, like all opiates, is a central nervous system depressant. In contrast to morphine it has been reported to be more euphorogenic, to produce greater respiratory depression, to be less constipating, and to have greater antitussive activity (Martin, 1963). The chief actions of heroin are a consequence of its rapid biotransformation by hydrolysis to 6-mono-acetylmorphine (MAM) and then more slowly to morphine. Because of their greater lipid solubility, heroin and MAM readily penetrate the brain where rapid deacetylation of these compounds to morphine occurs (Way, 1968; Way and Adler, 1960). Actually, heroin itself has minimal central nervous system effects and only when it is biotransformed to MAM does it become active, the MAM serving as a carrier to receptor sites. Way and Adler suggest, however, that heroin itself may have direct central nervous system effects when administered intravenously. The transformation of heroin to MAM is more rapid than the onset of pharmacologic effects when administration is subcutaneous. The authors therefore conclude that the route of administration is crucial in determining whether heroin has direct effects on the central nervous system. The pharmacologic effects on the brain are apparently due to morphine. Further evidence that the central nervous system effects of heroin are primarily due to the products of transformation comes from the finding that heroin disappears very rapidly from the brain (Way and Adler, 1960), as does MAM. The level of morphine in the brain, in contrast, is maintained for a longer period of time. Thus, any long-term effects of heroin must be due to the action of morphine. Heroin apparently acts as a carrier, is transported to the brain more readily than morphine, and is converted there to morphine (Martin, 1963). Although the blood-brain barrier generally impedes the entry of morphine into the brain, both heroin and MAM are more lipid-soluble and cross this barrier rapidly (Jaffe, 1970d). This rapid uptake of heroin by the brain itself was demonstrated in a study of rats by Oldendorf, Hyman, Braun, and Oldendorf (1972) who compared the brain uptake of morphine, codeine, heroin, and methadone 15 seconds after injection into the carotid artery. This procedure bypassed the blood-brain barrier. They found the uptake of heroin to be 68%, when it was taken as a percentage of a previously injected reference substance that served as a baseline. In contrast, the uptake of methadone was 42%; codeine, 24%; and morphine, too small to be measured. Oldendorf et al conclude that "the high uptake of heroin . . . indicates that an abrupt entrance of heroin into brain tissue probably occurs 10 to 20 seconds after the usual intravenous injection by addicts. This rapid entry relative to morphine may reinforce the addict's relating the act of drug administration to central nervous system response and thereby be a factor in the more intractable addiction to heroin" (p. 986).

SITE OF ACTION

Once it reaches the brain via the bloodstream, heroin, now metabolized to morphine, affects a number of sites. Jaffe (1970d) points out, however, that it is difficult to locate precisely those central nervous system sites where morphine produces its effects. In 1962, Guzman, Braun, and Lim demonstrated that the site of action of morphine and other opiates was definitely within the central nervous system, in contrast to the nonnarcotic analgesics. Narcotic analgesics such as morphine do not significantly affect peripheral reception or initial conduction of painful visceral stimuli. This is indicated in a study by Wagers and Smith (1960) which shows that large doses of morphine administered intravenously did not alter the responsiveness of dental nerves to mechanical and electrical stimuli. Another line of evidence suggesting a primary effect on the central nervous system rather than on peripheral conduction is the clinical observation that after morphine is administrated patients are still aware of pain, even though it has lost its aversive quality.

According to Seevers and Deneau (1963) and Seevers and Woods (1953), the pharmacologic effect of narcotics may occur through occupation of receptor sites on the surface of internuncial neurons and within neural cell bodies. Collier (1966) suggested that the site of action of opiates might be the 5-hydroxytryptamine (serotonin) receptors on appropriate brain cells, since the effects of opiate withdrawal in the dog and rat closely resemble those encountered in injecting 5-hydroxytryptamine. Abel (1974) concurred in suggesting serotonin as the transmitter substance involved in producing morphine's analgesic effects. He suggested, however, that the transmitter substance involved in the production of euphoria was norepinephrine. According to Paton (1969), the pattern of central nervous system effects of a synaptic transmitter depressant (such as morphine) depends not only upon the incidence of specific receptors for the drug, but also on the distribution of synaptic "safety factors," differing in sensitivity to transmitter output in different parts of the brain.

Attempts to locate the specific sites at which morphine acts in the brain have, until very recently, not been successful. As Way (1968) has noted, either the receptor sites did not show a preferential uptake of the drug, or the precision necessary to locate these sites was lacking. It was recognized for some time, however, that within the central nervous system several specific centers seem to be affected by morphine. These include certain complex pain-induced spinal cord reflexes which account for depression of the respiratory centers located in the brainstem. This effect upon respiration is caused primarily by decreased responsiveness of brainstem receptors to the increased percentage of carbon dioxide in the blood and by depression of centers responsibile for regulating respiratory rhythms. Often, this interference with the breathing mechanism can lead to death from respiratory failure. In addition, Wikler (1944) noted that morphine had an effect on the descending reticular system which modulates spinal cord mechanisms.

Way (1968) studied the responses of both cats and dogs to morphine and found no differential distribution of morphine in the brain, although, in both, grey matter had the highest concentration. Summarizing a number of studies, Way concluded that the hypothalamus and the immediately surrounding tissue seemed to be the areas most sensitive to morphine. Other sites particularly sensitive to the effects of morphine were the grey matter surrounding the third ventricle (Tsau and Jang, 1964), and the anterior hypothalamus. Functionally, in the former case, the presence of morphine led to elevations in the pain threshold to thermal stimuli, and in the latter case to decreased heat production and a fall in body temperature (Lotti, Lomax, and George, 1965). Ervin (1968) suggested that a number of the effects of the opioid drugs may be attributed to selective action upon the amygdaloid-hippocampal system. This system is involved in producing analgesia, mood-elevation, and "psychological goal-seeking" (p. 154) behavior.

Morphine and other narcotic analgesics may exert their effects by releasing endogenous opiates. Dewey, Fu, Ohlsson, Bowman, and Martin (1982) note the dose relationship between the distribution of endogenous opiates and stereospecific opiate-binding sites in the brain. They propose that morphine stimulates the release of endogenous opiates as a first step in producing its analgesic effects. These endogenous opiates then interact with stereospecific opiate-binding sites located on neurons in the brain and possibly the spinal cord, to produce analgesia.

OPIATE RECEPTORS

The search for a specific opiate receptor or macromolecule in the central nervous system to which opiates bind as a first step in producing their effects has been an active one since Beckett and Casy (1954) hypothesized a structure for one which would accommodate opioid compounds. As Simon (1973) pointed out:

The isolation of these receptors and elucidation of their interaction with drugs should provide a better understanding of the mode of action of narcotic analgesics and may aid in identifying the mechanism of addiction. [p.161]

A substantial advance in identifying an opiate receptor was made when Pert and Snyder (1973) were able to demonstrate direct stereospecific binding of the D (−) isomer of naloxone, and opiate antagonist (see below), to receptors in nervous tissues, including homologized rat brain and minced guinea pig intestine containing myenteric plexus. In 15 opiates they also found a direct and roughly approximate relationship between pharmacologic potency and affinity for receptor binding. Since Pert and Snyder (1973) found no opiate receptor binding in strips of guinea pig intestine that did not contain nervous innervation, nor in human red blood cells or bakers' yeast, they were able to conclude that ". . . the opiate receptor is confined to nervous tissue" (p. 1013).

In the study by Pert and Snyder (1973), the issue of localization of opiate receptors in the rat was also examined, and the greatest amount of binding was found to occur in the corpus striatum, which had a fourfold binding capability when compared with the cerebral cortex. At the other extreme, no binding took place in the cerebellum. This distribution of opiate receptors roughly paralleled regional variations in acetylcholine concentration.

In another study of regional localization of the opiate receptors, in monkey and human brain, Kuhar, Pert, and Snyder (1973) found the greatest concentration of binding in monkey brain to have taken place in the anterior amygdala, followed by the posterior amygdala and the periaqueductal area of the midbrain, and the hypothalamus and medial thalamus. Throughout all regions of the cortex and spinal cord, binding was much greater in grey than in white matter. In human brain the findings were similar, with the greatest amount of binding in the amygdala and the thalamus. Receptor binding was not affected by lesions of noradrenergic, serotoninergic and cholinergic pathways, suggesting, although not conclusively demonstrating, that receptor binding was not specifically associated with a particular neurotransmitter. Although results were not uniform throughout, they did suggest a rich opiate receptor distribution in structures comprising the limbic system.

Summarizing their distribution, Simon (1982) notes that most opiate receptors are found in the CNS and in nervous innervation of smooth muscle, although they are also found in endocrine tissue. Their function in the latter location, however, is not entirely clear. Within the central nervous system, almost all areas in which opiate binding sites have been demonstrated, if not associated with the limbic system, have been implicated in pain perception or modulation.

Martin et al (1976) suggested the possibility of multiple opiate receptors on the basis of the inability of certain opiates to suppress morphine abstinence symptoms in chronic spinal preparations. Martin et al's (1976) report was followed by a number of studies demonstrating the existence of a heterogeneity of opioid binding sites within the central nervous system. Herz, Schulz and Wuster (1982) further demonstrated the development of selective tolerance to different opiate receptor agonists. They note the relevance of this finding to understanding the development of tolerance and dependence in the light of the differentiation of types and subtypes of opiate receptors.

Opioid Peptides

The identification of opiate receptors in all vertebrate species soon led to a search for naturally occurring substances with opiate properties. This search successfully resulted in the isolation of naturally occurring opioid peptides or "endogenous morphines" by Hughes and Kosterlitz (Hughes, 1975) and Terenius and Wahlström (1975). Simon coined the widely used term "endorphins," a contraction of "endogenous" and "morphine," to describe these substances. As he notes, "the properties of the opioid peptides can best be summarized by stating that their pharmacologic effects are remarkably similar to those of the plant-derived and synthetic opiate alkaloids. Responses to these peptides include analgesia, respiratory depression, hypothermia, development of tolerance and physical dependence upon chronic administration, and a number of behavioral changes," among other properties (Simon, 1982, p. 331). Most recently, endorphins or, more accurately, their absence, have been suggested as playing a role in mental illness and its amelioration (Kleber, 1982; Berger et al, 1980), although this role is far from clear and contradictory evidence exists (Judd, et al, 1981).

DISPOSITION

Eventually morphine is absorbed relatively rapidly and concentrates in the internal organs such as the lungs, kidneys, liver, spleen, endocrine glands and, to a lesser extent, in skeletal muscle. This pattern reflects the affinity of these sites for morphine's properties as a base. Accumulation does not occur, however, and substantial excretion in the urine takes place within 24 hours of the last dose. At the time of excretion in the urine, some 50 to 57% of the original amount of morphine is recoverable, about 50% in the form of bound morphine and 7% as free morphine (Way and Adler, 1960). Some excretion also takes place through the alimentary tract, in the bile, and traces are even found in perspiration. In general, excretion is unimportant in limiting the effects of morphine, since the evidence (Way and Adler, 1960) presented suggests that "biotransformation is the chief factor limiting the intensity of response and duration of effect of morphine and its surrogates" (p. 402).

NARCOTIC ANTAGONISTS

The narcotic antagonists and methadone must occupy a prominent role in any discussion of the pharmacologic properties of heroin. Not only has the study of the narcotic antagonists and methadone led to a greater understanding of the mechanism of action of heroin, but their increasingly important role in the treatment of heroin addiction makes a discussion of their properties imperative.

Narcotic Antagonists

Substitution for the methyl group (Ch_3) on the nitrogen in the morphine, oxymorphone, morphinan and benzomorphan rings yields what currently are known as narcotic antagonists. The antagonists have four basic clinical uses: (1) they are useful in the treatment of narcotics addiction; (2) they produce analgesia; (3) they can be used to diagnose narcotics dependence; and (4) they are effective antidotes for narcotic analgesic intoxication. In addition, as a class of compounds they antagonize the depressant and other pharmacologic effects of narcotics. Szara and Bunney (1974) have listed the properties which the ideal narcotic antagonist should possess: (1) prevention of narcotic-induced euphoria; (2) minimal pharmacologic effects; (3) should not cause physical dependence or development of tolerance to its effects; (4) should have no serious side effects or toxicity under chronic administration; (5) should be easily administered at minimal cost; (6) should be long-acting; (7) should have sufficient potency to permit administration of small doses, and (8) should have little or no abuse potential. The authors noted that no antagonists available then met all of these criteria. Unfortunately, this is still the case in 1984.

Among the most widely used narcotic antagonists to be discussed here are nalorphine (N-allylnormorphine), naloxone (N-allyl-noroxymorphone), levallorphan (l-3-hydroxy-N-allylmorphinan), cyclazocine (2-cyclopropyl-methyl-2-hydroxy-5,9-dimethyl-6,7-benzomorphan), pentazocine [2-(3,3-di-methylallyl) hydroxy-5,9-dimethyl-6,7-benzomorphan], naltrexone (N-cyclo-propylnoroxymorphone)[2], and buprenorphine.

Antagonists have a close affinity for opiate receptor sites. When they occupy such sites, they block the access of agonists to them, resulting in a failure of the opiate agonists to produce a pharmacologic effect. (Renault, 1981). While they will not produce symptoms in opiate-free individuals, they will elicit the abstinence syndrome when administered to physically dependent opiate users.

Nalorphine, levallorphan, cyclazocine, and pentazocine are considered to be partial antagonists because each of these possesses analgesic, agonistic, and other morphinelike qualities in addition to inducing varying degrees of tolerance and dependence in the opiate-free individual. Naloxone and naltrexone are the only antagonists listed above that are considred to be "pure" antagonists because they have minimal or no agonistic effects. Both types of antagonists will precipitate the abstinence syndrome within minutes when administered to an individual who is dependent upon narcotics. Use of an antagonist by an ex-addict will prevent the experience of euphoria as well as protect against the development of opioid dependence.

The Partial Antagonists

Nalorphine. Nalorphine is rapidly taken up in the bloodstream when administered subcutaneously and reaches a peak concentration in the grey matter of the brain within 30 minutes. Its concentration in the brain is much greater than that of morphine although decay is more rapid (leaving only traces after 4 hours). However, the decay of nalorphine in the brain is more rapid than the decay of its agonistic effects, suggesting perhaps that it is more tightly bound to the active than to the inactive receptors (Martin, 1967). Although nalorphine antagonizes the effects of morphine on the brain, it does not consistently affect the brain concentration of morphine.

Nalorphine has been found to be roughly equianalgesic to morphine, although the data tend to be somewhat inconsistent and dependent upon the type of test used to measure analgesia. Like morphine, nalorphine also has respiratory depressant effects. However, these effects are maximal at 10 mg of nalorphine, whereas a ceiling is reached with as much as 70 mg of morphine. At low doses (5 to 10 mg) nalorphine has been known to produce euphoria, while at higher doses sedativelike effects such as sleepiness, fatigue, drunkenness, and dysphoric effects such as irritability, racing thoughts, and

---

[2] Despite popular misconception, methadone is not properly classified as a narcotic antagonist. It is a synthetic narcotic.

inability to concentrate have been noted. However, nalorphine has less of a disruptive effect on motor coordination than other antagonists such as cyclazocine for example.

Nalorphine has agonistic actions on circulation, the spinal cord, and on the gastrointestinal tract. In guinea pig ileum, it depresses peristaltic reflexes as does morphine. Some of its neurophysiologic actions are similar to those produced by barbiturates, interneuron depressants, and morphine An electroencephalogram (EEG) sleep pattern similar to that of morphine is induced by the administration of nalorphine which has been estimated to be roughly 10 times stronger than morphine in producing sedation (Martin, 1967). Tolerance is known to develop to all of the agonistic effects of nalorphine, and subjects exhibit cross-tolerance to cyclazocine.

The results of antagonizing the analgesic response to morphine with a narcotic antagonist such as nalorphine are complicated. Studies of nalorphine suggest that it is a "competitive antagonist" because the degree of antagonism increases as the dosage of the antagonist increases to a certain point and then declines with doses beyond that level (Martin, 1967). This biphasic response is characteristic of all the narcotic antagonists that possess analgesic effects (i.e., the partial antagonists). Nalorphine antagonizes a number of the effects morphine has on various bodily systems: the respiratory depressant effects, the miotic effects, the vasodepressor effects, the spasmatogenic effects on the intestine, the depressant effects on the spinal cord, the antidiuretic action, the hyperglycemic effects, and the hypothermic response. Tolerance to the antagonistic effects of nalorphine, in contrast to the agonistic effects, never develops.

Cyclazocine. Cyclazocine is similar to nalorphine in a number of respects. As a partial antagonist it also has agonistic effects, the most pronounced of which is the production of analgesia. In relation to morphine, it has been estimated to be roughly 40 times more potent as an analgesic: 2 mg administered parenterally produces analgesia equivalent to 10 mg of morphine (National Clearinghouse for Drug Abuse Information, 1973). It is excreted much more slowly than nalorphine and is still capable of blocking the effects of heroin administered subcutaneously up to 12 hours later. Cyclazocine also has respiratory depressant effects which reach a maximum at 0.25 mg. Among the side effects attributed to cyclazocine are dysphoria, "drunkenness," constipation, drowsiness, and feeling "high." Kleber et al (1974) note that of their heroin addict patients complaining about the "high" obtained on cyclazocine, most compared it to the high associated with psychotropic drugs rather than that with opiates and therefore found it uncomfortable and unfamiliar. However, cyclazocine apparently produces fewer subjective effects than nalorphine in heroin addicts. Additional agonistic effects include suppression of the flexor reflex, constriction of pupils, depression of nociceptive reflexes, respiratory depression, and depression of peristaltic reflexes in guinea pig ileum. As is the case with nalorphine, tolerance develops to the agonistic effects of cyclazocine.

Cyclazocine antagonizes the analgesic effects of morphine but apparently is significantly less effective in antagonizing morphine-induced respiratory depression than either nalorphine or levallorphan. It is also known to antagonize the emetic and nausea-producing effects of morphine, which may be offset by the fact that it causes constipation in man.

Levallorphan. Although levallorphan is classified as a partial antagonist, it shares many of the characteristics of the pure antagonist, naloxone. Its agonistic effects are less extensive or pronounced than those of nalorphine and cyclazocine, including minimal analgesic qualities at therapeutic doses (National Clearinghouse for Drug Abuse Information, 1973). However, Martin (1967) cites evidence that 8 mg per 70 kg of body weight of levallorphan is equianalgesic to 10 mg per 70 kg of morphine, which suggests that some of the findings are inconsistent. Like nalorphine, levallorphan is absorbed and excreted rapidly and has a much shorter duration of action than either its parent compound (morphinan) or cyclazocine. Other agonistic affects have been noted, including respiratory depression in man, subjective effects similar to those of cyclazocine and nalorphine, depression of peristaltic reflexes in guinea pig ileum, and constriction of pupils. Changes in EEG patterns, however, were the reverse of those produced by morphine.

The antagonistic effects of levallorphan are numerous. It has been described as five to eight times more effective than nalorphine in antagonizing narcotics-induced respiratory depression. Levallorphan is also an effective antagonist for the analgesic effects of morphine.

Pentazocine. Pentazocine is considered a very weak antagonist and has been clinically useful as an analgesic, despite its shorter duration and one-half to one-sixth the potency of morphine. However, it produces respiratory depression greater than that produced by an equianalgesic dose of morphine and only partially antagonizes the respiratory depression induced by morphine. Since only a mild dependence develops on pentazocine, it appears to have a low abuse potential.

Buprenorphine is a partial opiate antagonist which has the properties of (a) possessing a high affinity for opiate receptors, (b) exhibiting a strong and relatively long-lasting effect in both animals and man, approximately 30 times that of morphine, (c) having a longer period of effectiveness than equipotent doses of morphine, pethidine, or pentazocine, and (d) being a potent opiate antagonist, almost equal to nalaxone in effect. In a study by Yanagita, Katoh, Wakasa, and Oinuma (1982), the possibility of weak or practically negative addiction potential was noted, as was a lower reinforcing effect than pentazocine, and an absence during self-administration of marked depression, stimulation, or acute toxic effects. Yanagita et al conclude that, on the basis of these findings, the psychological dependence potential of buprenorphine may be lower than that of pentazocine.

Pure Antagonists

Naloxone. As a pure antagonist, naloxone has no agonistic effects when administered to individuals who are not using narcotics (Jasinski, Martin, and Haertzen, 1967). Although there are some conflicting findings with respect to analgesic qualities, the preponderance of results indicate that naloxone is devoid of analgesia. Furthermore, naloxone does not produce respiratory depression, has no subjective effects, does not induce EEG changes, and tolerance and dependence do not develop following chronic use. As an antagonist for narcotic-induced respiratory depression, naloxone is roughly 30 times more effective than nalorphine.

Although naloxone initially appears to be the ideal antagonist because it successfully reverses narcotic-induced changes in a number of functional systems and blocks euphoria while being devoid of agonistic effects, several problems mar its use as a therapeutic agent. Naloxone is a relatively short-acting compound, with a narcotic blockade of only four to six hours' duration at normal dosages. It is also relatively ineffective in oral administration, and the high cost of a single 100 mg oral dose required to block the effects of 40 mg of intravenous heroin is prohibitive. In a study by the National Clearinghouse for Drug Abuse Information in 1973, individuals receiving 2400 mg of naloxone daily were reported to experience only a partial blockage of heroin 24 hours later. On the other hand, Zaks, Jones, Fink, and Freedman (1971) achieved successful blockade of morphine effects with the use of large doses of naloxone.

Naltrexone. On the basis of pharmacologic and toxicologic studies of animals (Blumberg, Dayton, and Wolf, 1967; Blumberg and Dayton, 1972) this agent seemed to offer the advantages of almost twice the antagonistic potency of naloxone as well as a greater duration of action while having only slight agonistic properties. Studying its effects in man, Martin, Jasinski, and Mansky (1973) found that naltrexone has few agonistic effects and no evidence of subjective effects. At the same time, its potency was approximately 17 times greater than nalorphine, and its duration of action, while longer than that of naloxone was less than that of cyclazocine. With respect to the oral dose level of naltrexone required to produce blockade, only 30 to 50 mg a day were required to reach the level produced by up to 3000 mg of naloxone. At a dose level of 50 mg per day, the degree of morphine blockade is reported by Martin et al (1973) to be equivalent to 4 mg (orally) daily of cyclazocine. The authors concluded: "Because of its potency and longer duration of action and oral effectiveness, naltrexone has definite advantages over naloxone in the treatment of heroin dependence" (p. 791).

The Mechanism of Narcotic Antagonist Action

Various explanations have been offered for the mechanism whereby narcotic antagonists produce their effects. The most commonly held hypothesis is that the antagonist displaces morphine from the active receptors, thereby antagonizing the agonistic effects. Seevers and Deneau (1963) suggest that compounds such as nalorphine selectively antagonize the depressant effects of morphine while leaving the excitant effects unopposed. This action would account for the ability of the narcotic antagonists to precipitate the abstinence syndrome in dependent subjects. Martin (1967) notes, however, that a number of characteristic effects of the antagonists are inconsistent with the hypothesis of competition with the narcotic analgesics for receptors. The fact that nalorphine does not alter the brain concentration of morphine appears to contradict what one would expect if it were to displace morphine from the active receptors.

Martin (1967) carefully examined the phenomena of tolerance and dependence development in narcotic antagonists in light of this hypothesis. Following chronic use of cyclazocine and nalorphine, tolerance develops to their agonistic effects in addition to cross-tolerance between the two drugs. Upon abrupt discontinuation of either antagonist, an abstinence syndrome occurs that is qualitatively different from that of morphine. Lacrimation, yawning, chills, rhinorrhea, and diarrhea occur during abstinence from both cyclazocine and nalorphine but with less frequency than during abstinence from morphine. Concurrent loss of weight and appetite are also noted, as in morphine withdrawal. However, increase in blood pressure and respiration are much lower during nalorphine/cyclazocine withdrawal than during morphine withdrawal. In contrast to narcotic analgesic withdrawal, ". . . the narcotic antagonist abstinence syndrome is not associated with either an apparent drug need or drug seeking behavior" (Martin, 1967, p. 480). Martin suggests further that the phenomena of tolerance and dependence are related to the agonistic and not the antagonistic effects of nalorphine and cyclazocine. In support of this hypothesis he notes that tolerance is not developed to the antagonistic effects of these drugs and that there are no signs of abstinence upon abrupt discontinuation of naloxone (which has no subjective effects). Interestingly, Martin suggests that one implication of the above phenomena is that tolerance and dependence are related to the agonistic effects of any drug and not simply to receptor occupation.

Antagonists differ in their degree of activity on a number of functional systems such as those responsible for analgesia, respiratory depression, and the inhibition of release of acetylcholine. In this regard, Martin suggests:

> The ubiquitous distribution of the sites of actions of opioids and opioid antagonists in the central nervous system indicates that these agents affect a fundamental function of nervous tissue and that this function is mediated or modulated by a relatively specific drug receptor interaction. [Martin, 1967, p. 502]

The nature of this drug-receptor interaction is delineated by Martin as it relates to the hypothesized mechanism of competition between antagonist and analgesic for the same receptor. As was previously mentioned, a biphasic response occurs during which antagonists have analgesic effects: antagonism increases as the dose of the antagonist is increased to a certain point, and then decreases. Martin comments that if both antagonist and agonist are competing for the same receptor, one would predict that as the concentration of the antagonist is increased for any given dose of agonist the effect should approach that produced by the antagonist alone. This is not the case. The biphasic action of partial antagonists could be explained if the "analgesic effect of the antagonist is produced by occupying another receptor that is stereochemically similar to the narcotic analgesic receptor but different" (Martin, 1967, p. 484). Furthermore,

> this type of dose response relationship cannot be obtained by assuming there is one analgesic receptor and that competitive antagonism or competitive dualism obtains. It can be explained by assuming that there are two analgesic receptors, one where morphine acts as an agonist and nalorphine as a competitive antagonist, and the other where morphine is inactive and nalorphine is an agonist. [p. 508]

A study by Veatch, Adler, and Way (1964) proposes that the site of action of the analgesics where nalorphine is antagonistic are the "supraspinal inhibitory centers" stimulated by analgesics. Nalorphine does not act antagonistically at sites in the spinal cord. The authors suggest that perhaps nalorphine has a lower affinity for the morphine receptors in the spinal cord. In light of this controversy, it seems clear that a full understanding of the mechanisms underlying the action of narcotic antagonists must await further investigation.

NARCOTIC SUBSTITUTES

Methadone (dl-4, 4-Diphenyl-6-dimethylamino-3-heptanone)

As a synthetic narcotic analgesic agent, methadone possesses many of the pharmacologic properties of morphine. It is rapidly absorbed in the bloodstream and concentrates in the liver, lungs, spleen, and kidney, with minimal amounts reaching the brain. Its action lasts from 24 to 36 hours —significantly longer than that of most narcotic antagonists. Methadone is roughly equianalgesic to morphine, with 7.5 to 10 mg methadone producing analgesia equivalent to that produced by 10 mg of morphine (National Clearinghouse for Drug Abuse Information, 1974). Additional agonistic effects include marked respiratory depression, sedation, relaxation of smooth muscle, hyperglycemia, hypothermia, constipation, constriction of pupils, and EEG changes resembling sleep. Subjective effects are also similar to those produced by morphine, with many addicts reporting sensations of euphoria and well-being.

Tolerance to the agonistic effects (e.g., analgesic, sedative, respiratory depressant, cardiovascular) of methadone develops more slowly than it does to morphine, and cross-tolerance to other narcotic analgesics is also present in an individual tolerant to methadone. The abstinence syndrome indicative of physical dependence is slower in onset and milder but of longer duration than that for morphine. Symptoms appear roughly 8 to 24 hours after the last dose and the peak is reached after 6 days (vs. 4 to 6 hours and 2 days, respectively, for heroin). Withdrawal is usually complete after 2 weeks.

Numerous adverse side effects that have occurred with use of methadone include constipation, weight gain, numbness, and hallucinations. Methadone overdosing or poisoning can result in death from diminished pulmonary ventilation, and depressed respiration (National Clearinghouse for Drug Abuse Information, 1974, p. 6). Such symptoms may be reversed by administration of a partial narcotic antagonist, although naloxone is usually used because of its greater potency, longer action, and lack of agonistic effects. Administration of the antagonist must be repeated at several intervals to avoid relapse of respiratory depression due to the longer duration of methadone's action relative to that of the antagonist.

Methadone is clinically useful in narcotic maintenance and detoxification programs in addition to being effective as an analgesic. It appears to have the following advantages: (*a*) it can be taken orally; (*b*) it is long acting; (*c*) side effects diminish at maintenance doses; (*d*) it blocks the effects of heroin (rather than preventing heroin from occupying neuronal binding sites as a result of the development of cross-tolerance); and (*e*) it has no euphoric effects after tolerance has developed. The role of methadone in treatment of heroin addiction is further discussed in Chapter 12.

LAAM   (l-α-Acetylmethadol hydrochloride)

LAAM or acetylmethadol is a synthetic analgesic possessing many characteristics similar to those of methadone in composition and action. Its ability to prevent withdrawal symptoms for periods up to 72 hours, as first identified by Fraser and Isbell (1952) and later confirmed by Jaffe, Schuster, Smith, and Blachley (1970), makes it an attractive substitute for methadone. Clinically, when LAAM was administered three times weekly, generally at approximately equal or slightly higher doses than 'methadone, patients who were making satisfactory adjustments on methadone continued to do so on LAAM (Jaffe et al, 1970; Senay, Dorus, Renault, and Morell, 1975).

Propoxyphene Napsylate (PN)

PN is a weak morphine-like agonist which has been used both as a detoxification agent and maintenance medication. Jasinski, Pernick, Clark, and Griffith (1977) report its potency ratio, when compared with morphine, to be 50 to 60 mg of PN to one mg of morphine, administered subcutaneously. The toxic effects of PN are more potent than those of morphine—perhaps equivalent to 10 mg of morphine. Senay (1983) notes that PN in daily doses of above 1000 mg can produce the following side effects: hallucinations, seizure-like or frank seizure activity, and dysphoria. These limit its usefulness to mildly opioid-dependent individuals, but unambiguous data concerning the efficacy of PN are not yet available.

CHAPTER 5

Tolerance and Dependence

Two important factors in the process of addiction to heroin are the ability of the drug to produce both physiologic tolerance and dependence which, as Seevers and Deneau (1963) pointed out, "are the only elements of addiction which have been subjected to carefully controlled and objective physiologic experimentation" (p. 566). In addition to the development of physiologic tolerance and dependence, psychologic dependence frequently develops as use continues.[1]

TOLERANCE

Tolerance occurs when repeated administration of a certain amount of a drug fails to provide the same effects as the initial dose. Other definitions of tolerance include those by Seevers and Woods (1953) and Seevers and

---

[1] Theories of tolerance and dependence development focus on the effects of morphine, since (as indicated in Chapter 4) heroin's actions occur primarily through its metabolic product, morphine.

Deneau (1963). In both cases, tolerance was defined as a diminishing biological response occurring as a result of cellular adaptation to an alien chemical. To this definition Seevers and Deneau have added the qualification of repeated exposure to the alien chemical. Thus, in the case of heroin use, the addict must constantly be increasing the size of each successive dose in order to produce the same psychopharmacologic effect. There are several theories as to how tolerance develops and these will be more fully reviewed later in this chapter. One theory suggests that tolerance occurs as a result of diminished responsivity of central nervous system cells to the drug. An alternate theory suggests that tolerance is developed as the organism becomes adapted to new chemical substances and therefore metabolizes them more quickly. This accelerated breakdown of the drug is responsible for the increment in dosage required to produce the same effects. There remains a great deal of controversy regarding the mechanisms underlying tolerance, and Remmer (1969) feels that the reason for the development of tolerance to morphine is still not known and will not be known until the biochemical mechanism of the receptor site is understood. However, it is known in the case of analgesia and physical dependence that some very specific structural qualities such as a tertiary nitrogen, a central carbon atom not bonded to hydrogen, and a phenyl or structurally similar group bonded to a central carbon must be characteristic of the drug (Eddy, Halbach, and Braenden, 1956).

Tolerance can appear to any of the following effects of morphine: the euphoric, the analgesic, or the visceral. In terms of rate of acquisition, tolerance appears most quickly to the euphoric effects of morphine, secondly to its analgesic effects, and never to its effects upon smooth muscle (Jaffe, 1970d). Continued and increased use of opiates in the face of decrements in the level of euphoria obtained is due to the concurrent onset of withdrawal symptoms as tolerance develops.

DEPENDENCE AND THE ABSTINENCE SYNDROME

Dependence is not so easily defined since it can be both psychological and physiological in nature. Physical dependence refers to a predictable pattern of physiological responses which appear when regular administration of a drug is discontinued. Physical dependence is defined by Seevers and Deneau (1963) as "the state of latent hyperexcitability which develops in the cells of the central nervous system of higher mammals following frequent and prolonged administration of the morphine-like analgesics . . . [It] becomes manifest subjectively and objectively as specific symptoms and signs, the *abstinence syndrome,* or the *withdrawal illness,* upon abrupt termination of drug administration . . ." (p. 567). *Psychological dependence* refers to the need to avoid the aversive subjective effects associated with discontinuance of the drug. According to Levine (1973), psychological dependence (i.e., psychic dependence, psychic craving, compulsive abuse) refers to a condition "characterized by an emotional or mental drive to continue taking a drug whose effects the user feels are necessary to maintain his sense of optimal well-being" (p. 330).

The presence of physical dependence is clear from the appearance of the *abstinence syndrome*, which is characterized by such symptoms as anxiety, restlessness, irritability, lacrimation, general body aches, insomnia, perspiration, dilated pupils, "goose flesh," hot flashes, nausea, gagging, vomiting, diarrhea, fever, increased heart rate, increased blood pressure, abdominal and other muscle cramps, with dehydration and loss of weight accompanying the above. Additional symptoms during withdrawal may include nervousness, hyperactivity, leg cramps, generalized muscle twitches, and alternating profuse sweating and chills (Eiseman, Lam, and Rush, 1964). Intestinal symptoms may also include hyperperistalsis and gastric hypersecretion. Sapira (1968) reports the occasional occurrence of spontaneous erection and/or spontaneous ejaculation in male addicts undergoing withdrawal. Obviously, the severity of the abstinence syndrome is a function of the degree of dependence. According to the report of the Mayor's Committee on Drug Addiction (Lambert et al, 1930) the abstinence syndrome runs its course in 96 hours. However, Seevers and Deneau (1963) note that with long-acting compounds such as morphine symptoms of withdrawal will peak in from 24 to 48 hours and will require 7 to 10 days to subside completely. Himmelsbach (1942) reported that physical signs of morphine abstinence lasted for up to 6 months. Martin, Winkler, Eades, and Pescor (1963) confirmed this in their report that physiological signs of abstinence persisted in the rat for as long as 6 months.

Lewis et al (1970) found withdrawal from heroin produced abnormalities in REM sleep that persisted for several months. Withdrawal after one week of heroin administration results in a generally increasing percentage of REM sleep each successive night and this effect persists for about five weeks.

The appearance of the abstinence syndrome can be avoided or forestalled by the administration of heroin. Any other opiate may also be substituted and produce the same effects (Madinaveitia, 1969). Although they vary in potency and dependency liability, use of any of the opioids can lead to the development and maintenance of tolerance and dependence.

An interesting note is provided by Levine (1973) with respect to the fact that nalorphine, a morphine antagonist, produces physical dependence which is manifested as a withdrawal syndrome upon its discontinuation. However, since it is not accompanied by the development of psychological dependence, nalorphine has not become a drug of abuse. Levine argues that physical dependence alone does not lead to drug abuse, as evidenced by the fact that the vast majority of patients receiving therapeutic doses of narcotics, including morphine, demonstrate no desire for continued use after relief of the condition for which it was prescribed. However, physical dependence combined with psychological dependence becomes a powerful reinforcer for continued drug use.

In discussing the amount of the drug necessary to induce dependence and tolerance, Wikler and Carter (1953) have suggested that some degree of physical dependence may be induced by as little as a single large dose of morphine. This is, however, a debatable point. Seevers and Deneau (1963) believe that "continual neuronal exposure to the drug. . . without interruption" (p. 591) is necessary for physical dependence to develop. Using mice, Goldstein and Sheehan (1969) confirmed that tolerance could be initiated by a single injection of a synthetic opioid (levorphanol). They also found that this tolerance disappeared if another administration of the drug did not occur within approximately 48 hours, each successive administration having the same effect. Tolerance develops rapidly, however, with shorter intervals, and each successive administration produces less of an effect (i.e., the development of tolerance).

An excellent picture of the central nervous system effects accompanying the development of tolerance and withdrawal in man is provided by Martin and Jasinski (1969) who followed seven addicts through a cycle of morphine dependence for 74 weeks. Morphine was administered four times daily for the first 31 weeks of the cycle in increasing doses until (during the fifth week) a stabilization dose of 240 mg per day was reached. Prior to this 31 week period Ss were observed 7 weeks, during which time they were free of addiction. Using measures of physiologic parameters observed during the control period, the following changes due to chronic administration of morphine were observed: respiratory rate decreased; pupils were constricted; elevations occurred in systolic and diastolic blood pressure, pulse rate, and body temperature. Initial decreases in caloric intake and weight loss recovered to above normal levels until withdrawal. All changes, with the exception of body weight and caloric intake were statistically significant. Withdrawal, which took place gradually over a 2 week period, soon elicited the abstinence syndrome characterized by increases in systolic and diastolic blood pressure, pulse rate, pupil size, temperature, respiratory rate, and decreases in body weight and caloric intake, all of which (with the exception of respiratory rate) persisted for 4 to 10 weeks following withdrawal. Interestingly, from 6 to 9 weeks following initiation of withdrawal, blood pressure, body temperature, and pulse rate fell below preaddiction levels, as did pupillary diameter. These protracted or secondary abstinence effects can persist for from 4 to 6 months (Martin, 1971). The only permanent effect seemed to be decreased caloric intake, which did not return to preaddiction levels.

There are two slightly different schools of thought with respect to the issue of whether the processes of tolerance and dependence share the same underlying mechanism. Way and his associates (1974) suggest that tolerance and physical dependence do not seem to be readily separable, perhaps because they have closely related underlying central nervous system mechanisms. On the other hand, Seevers and Deneau (1963) maintain that tolerance and dependence develop concurrently and are interrelated but not interdependent. In support of the former view, interference with protein synthesis seems to prevent the development of morphine tolerance. Loh, Shen, and Way (1969) were able to block the development of physical dependence on and tolerance to morphine without altering the analgesic response to the drug by administering cycloheximide. Way (1974) notes that acetylcholine, norepinephrine, and dopamine seem to be related to the acute pharmacologic response to morphine as well as to certain aspects of the dependent state. To a lesser extent they are involved in the development of tolerance to and physical dependence on morphine. Morphine reduces the resting output of acetylcholine, a synaptic transmitter substance in guinea pig intestine, without depressing choline synthesis (Schaumann, 1956; 1957). Morphine also depresses the response of guinea pig ileum to the effects of brief shocks. Normally this response consists of twitches which result from the excitation of the cholinergic postganglionic nerves of Auerbach's plexus, which activates smooth muscle. At the same time, if acetylcholine is directly applied to smooth muscle, no response occurs (Paton, 1956; 1957). This finding leads to the implication that morphine interferes with the output of transmitter substance. Direct confirmation of this finding was obtained by Paton (1969). In a further study (Paton and Zar, 1968) it was shown that in the above studies morphine acted directly on nervous tissue and not on muscle.

The general conclusion to be drawn from these and related studies, according to Paton (1969), is that there is good reason to believe that the opiates, as well other drugs producing dependence, specifically depress transmitter release at the synapse. Norepinephrine, acetylcholine, and dopamine appear to be involved in actual signs of withdrawal. On the other hand, serotonin appears to be involved in the development of tolerance and physical dependence. Reduction of serotonin synthesis interferes with the development of tolerance and dependence (Way, 1974), whereas stimulation of serotonin synthesis by its precursor, 5-hydroxy-tryptophane, enhances the development of tolerance and physical dependence (Collier, 1965).

Way (1974), summarizing the biochemical literature on the development of morphine tolerance and physical dependence, lists several compounds that have the capacity to inhibit or to reduce the development of tolerance and dependence. These are: (a) narcotic antagonists (e.g., naloxone), (b) protein synthesis inhibitors, (c) serotonin synthesis inhibitors, (d) β-adrenergic blockers, and (e) γ-aminobutyric acid antagonists (e.g., bicuculline). On the other hand, a group of agents, including tryptophane, have been identified that can accelerate the development of tolerance and dependence. These agents are antagonistic to several of the morphine tolerance inhibitors cited above. At the same time, they antagonize the analgesic actions of morphine.

According to Way (1974), the ability to separate the pharmacologic actions of morphine from the development of tolerance to and physical dependence on it has important implications for the development of therapeutic programs. The possibility of developing a chemical agent which would block the development of physical dependence and tolerance without actually altering the analgesic qualities of morphine is highly desirable. Use of such an agent might reduce the physical reinforcement for drug abuse.

THEORIES OF TOLERANCE AND DEPENDENCE DEVELOPMENT

Research on the pharmacologic effects and neurologic mechanisms of morphine has led to a number of theories of the development of dependence and tolerance. None of these theories attempts to account for the initial use of heroin but simply suggests mechanisms whereby tolerance and dependence develop.

The Dual Action Theory

Tatum, Seevers, and Collins (1929) originally formulated a dual action theory of morphine addiction. This theory is based upon experimental evidence indicating that morphine has both stimulant and depressant effects on various parts of the central nervous system. The depressant effects first observed immediately after an injection of morphine are a result of decreased alertness and awareness and depression of the respiratory center, and are followed by longer acting stimulation related to increased activity of the spinal cord and certain (unspecified) regions of the brain.

Tolerance, which develops only to the depressant effects, occurs in local cells in several types of tissue. Recovery from these depressant effects is relatively rapid, resulting in increased excitability of certain parts of the central nervous system following repeated administration of morphine. During the course of addiction the initial central nervous system depression becomes increasingly less profound, since it must overcome longer lasting excitability resulting from the preceeding dose. Increasingly larger doses of morphine are required to produce the original level of depression as the long-lasting excitability continually accumulates with subsequent doses. Shortened duration and, eventually, disappearance of the pharmacologic effect at a given dosage appears in the course of tolerance development. Addiction is thus conceived of as a state of physiologic balance between stimulation and depression. Increasingly larger doses of morphine are required to maintain this state of equilibrium. When additional doses of morphine are withheld this balance is disrupted. Withdrawal symptoms (the abstinence syndrome) are a direct result of hyperexcitability due to the unopposed direct stimulant effects of residual morphine. This latent hyperexcitability, previously disguised by the simultaneous depressant effect of morphine, is now unmasked because tolerance has developed to the shorter acting effect.

Seevers and Woods (1953) modified the dual action hypothesis by suggesting there were two different sites on the neuron that acted as drug receptors. One of these sites is axonal, where the drug combines rapidly with the receptor, and the pharmacological effects occur only when the receptor is occupied by the drug. Occupation at the second receptor site is within the cell body, is much slower, and cellular excitation originates here. This state of excitability continues after morphine has been depleted.

Evidence accumulated by Seevers and Deneau (1963) since the original proposal of the dual action mechanism in 1929 fails to support the hypothesis that the hyperexcitability expressed in abstinence symptoms is due to unopposed direct stimulant effects of morphine and is qualitatively identical to the abstinence syndrome. Seevers and Deneau (1969) suggest a modification of the dual action theory in which the development of physical dependence is due to the continuous occupation of the receptor sites that induce depression. This continuous occupation leads to a semipermanent biochemical adaptive change (i.e., dependence) which results in the hyperexcitability of certain cell groups. Thus the signs of withdrawal are manifestations of the state of physical dependence but are not qualitatively identical to this hyperexcitability. As tolerance develops, increasing doses result in a summation of the direct stimulatory effects of morphine that contributes to (but is not the sole cause of) an overall hyperexcitability of the central nervous system and the acute symptoms experienced during the early phases of withdrawal. As morphine is excreted from the body, the adaptive responses to its depressant effect slowly decay.

Experimental evidence also suggests that the modification of Seevers and Woods (1953) may be accurate if one conceives of the stimulant and depressant actions of morphine occurring on two separate receptors. Tolerance and narcosis (two of four possible reactions a neuron may have to the presence of morphine) should occur on the receptor involved in the depressant effects. Dependence (the third response) may develop in the same receptor depending on its location in the neuron. The fourth response, excitation, should therefore occur in the receptor responsible for stimulant effects.

The Seevers and Deneau modification of the dual action theory necessitates a redefinition of tolerance and of dependence. Tolerance is now defined as a cellular adaptation to a foreign chemical that results in a decreased biological response (Seevers and Deneau, 1963). Physical dependence is now defined as a "state of latent hyperexcitability which develops in the cells of the central nervous system of higher mammals following frequent and prolonged administration of the morphine-like analgesics . . ." (p. 567). This is a highly specific phenomenon which can be induced only in the neuron by certain depressant drugs. Since hyperexcitability is unmasked only upon withdrawal of the chemical that causes it, the condition is considered to be latent.

Disuse Sensitivity Theory

Jaffe and Sharpless (1968) hypothesize that there are central nervous system mechanisms of physical dependence analogous to those involved in the development of peripheral denervation supersensitivity. They suggest that withdrawal phenomena involve a rebound reaction in which the functions (e.g., synaptic transmission) previously depressed by narcotic drugs become exaggerated during withdrawal. Although Seevers and Deneau (1963) defined dependence as a latent hyperexcitability of the nervous pathways during withdrawal that has been masked by the depressant effect of narcotics, Jaffe and Sharpless propose that this latent hyperexcitability is not caused by the presence of the drug but by a disuse of pathways induced by the drug. "In identifying the drug-induced depression rather than the drug itself as the primary causative agent, we are suggesting that drugs that act on different sites or occupy different receptors might still produce the same abstinence phenomena by causing, directly or indirectly, a diminution in the flow of impulses along the same nervous pathways" (p. 227). Jaffe and Sharpless' theory is similar to the homeostatic theories insofar as both suggest that physical dependence is a compensatory reaction to a change in nervous activity that is caused by narcotics. In contrast to the dual action theory, the mechanism of disuse supersensitivity requires only a single drug-receptor interaction to explain both the action of morphine and the development of dependence. The similarities to peripheral denervation sensitivity do not go beyond the phenomenon of increased sensitivity that results from disuse of pathways observed by Jaffe and Sharpless in narcotic dependence. Disuse sensitivity has three characteristics: (1) it develops slowly, (2) it is unspecific insofar as sensitivity is increased to both adrenergic and cholinergic influences as a result of blockage of either fiber, and (3) it is caused by any procedure that blocks the flow of impulses across a neuroeffector junction.

The specific mechanism involved in the alteration of sensitivity is unclear. It could be a change in the number of receptors or a change in the number of steps linking the transmitter-receptor combination to the cell reaction (Jaffe and Sharpless, 1968). However, the phenomenon of tolerance may also be related to an offsetting of the partial blockade of transmitter by an increased postsynaptic sensitivity.

Pharmacological Denervation Sensitivity Theory

According to Paton (1969), the physical mechanism underlying tolerance and the withdrawal syndrome is due mainly to the reduction of output of synaptic transmitters such as acetylcholine. This leads to an overabundant supply of the transmitter substance within the nerve terminals that accounts for the earlier stages of tolerance. Since there is a resulting rise in concentration of the transmitter substance within the terminal, the release of a small amount would still have the effect previously produced by release of a larger amount. At the same time, development of supersensitivity of the postganglionic structures to the transmitter substance would occur as a result of this pharmacologic denervation, which explains the later stages of tolerance. Each factor accounts for withdrawal symptoms. Thus, when the blockade of release of the transmitter substance occurs upon withdrawal of the drug, two events take place: a normal amount of transmitter would be released that would, in turn, elicit more than normal excitation from the supersensitive postganglionic cell.

Substantial evidence supporting the proposed mechanism is based upon research with other than nervous tissue, and one must assume with Paton (1969) that the same action is mirrored in the central nervous systems of humans. Paton also points out that the rapid rise of tolerance to opiates may occur in part because of their capacity to reverse their action as their concentration rises. Thus, tolerance should develop rapidly as higher doses are reached.

According to Paton (1969), one implication of the "surfeit" hypothesis is that both tolerance and the intensity of withdrawal symptoms can be attenuated by the identification of a substance or procedure that will prevent the accumulation of transmitter during the period when its release is inhibited.

Homeostatic Theory

Himmelsbach (1943) attempted to explain the phenomenon of physical dependence in terms of classic mechanisms of central autonomic homeostasis or the tendency of the organism to maintain a constant internal environment. It has been suggested that morphine acts directly on the hypothalamus (see Chapter 5), which also functions to maintain homeostasis by initiating compensatory reactions in response to changes in internal or external environments. Morphine affects the hypothalamus by initiating a reaction to its presence that increases in efficiency through repeated administration of the drug. This chronic adjustment results in a condition which requires the presence of morphine and generates an internal need to adjust to the presence of morphine in order to maintain homeostatic equilibrium. Himmelsbach has not, however, provided an explanation of how the original homeostatic mechanism is disrupted or what specific quality of morphine produces this effect.

Enzyme Expansion Theory

Goldstein and Goldstein (1968) proposed an enzyme expansion theory of drug dependence and tolerance based on the homeostatic adjustment of the regulatory mechanism in the brain that controls enzyme levels. The theory is predicated upon four interrelated physiologic processes: (a) synthesis of a neurohumoral substance, mediated by an enzyme or a protein, is regulated by both the rate at which it is produced and the rate at which it is degraded; (b) the protein mediator is regulated in a similar fashion; (c) a given drug operates to inhibit the protein; (d) repression of the protein end-product, that is, the neurohumoral substance, results in an alteration of the level of the protein. Essentially this is a classic homeostatic mechanism. The ultimate effect of narcotics administration is to inhibit the protein and thus produce a decreased level of neurohumoral substance that will consequently result in increased protein synthesis, so that the protein level returns to its original point. As this reciprocal process of inhibition and increased synthesis continues, more narcotic substance is needed to inhibit the increasing amounts of protein, resulting in tolerance. Although the level of protein is abnormally high in the tolerant state, its action is inhibited by the presence of narcotic substance. At this point the level of the neurohumoral substance is nearly normal because of the compensating increase in enzyme/protein synthesis. If the narcotic substance is suddenly withdrawn, the accumulated excess protein will be disinhibited, the neurohumoral substance will be overproduced, and withdrawal symptoms will result.

Homeostatic and Redundancy Theory

Martin (1968b) attempts to incorporate both elements of homeostasis and redundance (i.e., duplication of pathways) in his theory of dependence and tolerance. In this concept dependence is defined primarily as "a disease of adaptation to a toxin" (p. 206). Martin delineates two types of tolerance for which separate mechanisms are necessary to explain all of the phenomena. Redundancy theory postulates parallel pathways mediating a single physiologic response. Such a postulate is necessary to explain the following facts: (a) the rate of tolerance development varies in different functional systems; (b) the effects of abstinence appear at different points in time in each system; and (c) the effects of morphine in a tolerant individual can be of either long or short duration. Martin proposes that the administration of morphine interrupts one of these redundant pathways and not the other, so that the uninterrupted one will undergo hypertrophy with increased usage. Sharpless and Jaffe (1968), however, noted little evidence to support the assumption that increased stimulation of a pathway causes hypertrophy. Nonetheless, Martin suggests that this hypertrophied pathway will assume the functioning of the interrupted pathway. Tolerance is thus a consequence of the hypertrophy of a redundant pathway.

During withdrawal, the previously interrupted pathway returns to a normal level of excitability. However, the overall functioning of the total system is increased as the activity of the now normally functioning pathway combines with the increased activity of the redundant pathway. This result generates the hyperexcitability observed during abstinence. The actual effects of morphine and the development of tolerance depend upon two factors: the importance of the pathways in mediating a physiologic response and the capacity of either pathway to hypertrophy. Martin believes such a mechanism, can account for partial tolerance, acute and chronic tolerance, and the long- and short-term effects of morphine. Other investigators also provide evidence that redundant pathways exist in the central nervous system.

Martin suggests a mechanism for the hypertrophy of the redundant pathway. If there is a negative feedback mechanism which exerts an inhibitory influence on both redundant pathways, Martin proposes that this influence will itself be inhibited when one pathway is depressed by morphine. The two inhibiting actions would cancel each other out and result in increased stimulation of the uninterrupted pathway. This negative feedback is necessary if stimulation of the uninterrupted pathway, resulting in hypertrophy, occurs when there is a decrease in output from the whole system.

The second half of this theory relies heavily on a homeostatic mechanism resembling that of Himmelsbach (1943). Martin also proposes that acute physical dependence on morphine lowers a homeostat and creates a condition in which the internal state of the organism is too high for the new homeostatic equilibrium. This departure from homeostasis results in a "force" on the system to lower the existing state. For example, Martin suggests that such a mechanism would account for the lowered equilibrium temperature observed in morphine-tolerant dogs. Conversely, the homeostat returns to the pretolerant level during abstinence. The internal state of the individual is then too low for this new equilibrium level. This difference then results in a force on the system to raise the internal state to the homeostatic level. This process of readjustment would explain the shivering observed in dogs undergoing withdrawal.

Theories Based on a Change in the Number of Drug Receptors

Axelrod (1968) suggests that tolerance occurs as a result of cellular adaptation to the presence of a narcotic drug which leads to a decrease in responsiveness to successive doses. The basis for this development of tolerance is a reduction in the number of drug-receptor sites available. Axelrod observed that all narcotic substances are metabolized by N-demethylation by microsomal enzymes. He also noted that in morphine-tolerant animals there is a decrease in this enzyme activity that results in a loss of analgesic response. During withdrawal, recovery of both enzyme activity and analgesic responses are observed. In a series of studies on the response to morphine of the N-demethylating enzyme, Axelrod found support for his theory of tolerance in an analogous reaction. He noted a similarity between the properties of the enzyme with N-demethylated narcotics and the cellular adaptation of the narcotic drug receptors of the central nervous system to repeated administration of morphine. He observed an adaptive increase in responsiveness of certain cells that continue to respond in the presence of the drug. Examining the number of active metabolizing sites of the enzyme on continuous interaction with morphine, he concluded that the number of receptor sites is reduced by occupation by narcotics. Therefore the number of drug-receptor combinations is reduced, and the effect of repeated administrations of narcotics is ultimately a reduction in overall response. During withdrawal, however, when drugs are no longer present, sudden cellular overresponse results in the symptoms associated with withdrawal. Unfortunately, Axelrod's theory does not explain dependence.

Collier (1972) proposed a variation of Axelrod's theory that explains tolerance and dependence in terms of an adaptive change in the drug receptors. Collier (1965; 1966; 1969) has cast the supersensitivity theory into receptor terms by making three assumptions: (a) the magnitude of response to a transmitter agent is dependent upon the number of receptors; (b) depriving a cell of humoral transmitter substance increases the number of receptors for that transmitter on the cell; (c) subsequent exposure of the cell to transmitter reduces the number of receptors. Thus, deprivation of the humoral transmitter agent through blockade would increase the number of receptors and permit a stronger response to the available transmitter passing the blockade (development of tolerance). Upon withdrawal of the blockading drug, a greater amount of transmitter substance would become available, resulting in abstinence effects. Subsequent aftereffects would be due to the failure of all additional receptors to disappear (Cochin and Kornetsky, 1964).

Collier draws upon several facts implicating catecholamines in the development of tolerance and dependence. He observes that catecholamines are the humoral substances which control the cerebral reward-punishment mechanism. The administration of 6-hydroxydopamine depresses catecholamine synthesis and functionally terminates the self-stimulation of rats engaged in lever-pressing. The administration of disulfiram blocks the conversion of dopamine to noradrenaline and also results in the termination of self-stimulation by rats with an electrode implanted in the medial forebrain. A further observation that morphine increases the rate of biosynthesis of catecholamines in the brain leads to Collier's final conclusion that tolerance and dependence are different aspects of the same process and are generated by a drug-induced adaptive change in the number of receptors or binding sites available for narcotics.

Way (1974), on the other hand, suggests that catecholamines are involved not in the development of tolerance and dependence but in the acute pharmacologic response to morphine. He notes that 6-hydroxydopamine reduces catecholamines in the peripheral nervous system by causing a degeneration of the adrenergic nerve endings. Way postulates the synthesis of a macromolecule, different in form from the receptor protein, which is altered during the development of tolerance and dependence. As evidence for this hypothesis, he presents a series of studies which suggest the following: (a) the possibility of altering the acute pharmacologic response to morphine without interfering with the development of dependence or tolerance; (b) blockade of dependence and tolerance development can be accomplished without modifying the acute pharmacologic response of morphine; and (c) the possibility of the acceleration of the development of tolerance and dependence. Way was able to block the development of tolerance and dependence by administering cycloheximide, an inhibitor of protein synthesis, while concurrently observing no change in the analgesic response to morphine. This evidence is cited in support of the hypothesis that the macromolecule involved in the development of tolerance and dependence cannot possibly be the same one that is a receptor involved in the acute effects of morphine. On further investigation, Way concluded that the neurotransmitters acetylcholine, norepinephrine, and dopamine are responsible for the acute pharmacologic responses to morphine.

Immune Reaction Theory

Cochin and Kornetsky (1968) and Cochin (1974) attempted to explain the development of tolerance as an immunological reaction to morphine. A cornerstone of this hypothesis was derived from their original demonstration of (a) the development of long-term (up to one year) tolerance to the effects of a single injection of morphine (Cochin and Kornetsky, 1964); (b) the presence of a definite time sequence in its development; and (c) the inhibiting effects of cycloheximide and other agents upon tolerance development. However, as Cochin himself noted (Cochin, 1974) there are alternative explanations for these events as well as inconclusiveness in demonstrating related immunological phenomena such as transference of tolerance from donors to non-tolerant recipients.

CONCLUDING COMMENTS

Recently, Martin, Eades, Thompson, Huppler and Gilbert reported on the inability of certain opiates to suppress the appearance of the abstinence syndrome in chronic spinal dog preparations when morphine was withheld. This has led to consideration of the existence of multiple opiate receptors. The possibility thus exists that selective tolerance may develop to different receptor agonists. The potential importance of this is clearly noted by Herz, Schulz, and Wuster (1982), who observe that the opportunity now exists to study the mechanisms underlying tolerance and dependence, their separability, and mediation by different receptor types.

CHAPTER 6

Mortality and Medical Complications Among Heroin Addicts

A widely cited consequence of heroin addiction is the high death rate among addicts as a result of overdosing. Less widely known is the fact that heroin addicts are much more at risk than the general population with respect to increased mortality risk from a wide variety of diseases associated with heroin addiction but not directly attributable to heroin per se. One purpose of this chapter is to review evidence concerning the greater risk of mortality among heroin addicts as well as some of the factors that have been suggested to explain it, including overdosing, suicide, and death due to the medical complications of heroin addiction. This chapter will also examine the latest evidence regarding the mechanism by which acute heroin overdosing leads to death. Finally, the rates of occurrence, origins, and nature of certain specific medical complications often found in association with heroin addiction, including those involving the heart, circulatory, nervous, lymphatic and other systems will be surveyed, as will other specific complications related to pregnancy and childbirth, osteomyelitis, malaria, and tetanus.

MORTALITY RATES AMONG ADDICTS

Addicts die more frequently and at younger ages than the general population. Bewley et al (1968) observe that the data from published studies such as those by Vaillant (1965), Helpern and Rho (1966), Louria, Hensle, and Rose (1967), and Kavaler-Menachem (1967) all suggest an annual mortality rate of about 10 per 1000. Bewley et al (1968) point out that the mortality rate in England among heroin addicts up to 1966 was 27 per 1000 per year while the expected number of deaths in the same population was 2.45 per 1000 per year. Pescor (1943) observed a 7% death rate among 4700 male narcotics addicts released from Lexington. Duvall, Locke, and Brill (1963) reported an 11.5% rate, also among Lexington addicts, with slightly less than half of the deaths directly attributable to drug use.

Several investigators have attempted to identify factors that contribute to this higher death rate among addicts. O'Donnell (1969) found that of 266 white narcotics patients from Kentucky treated at Lexington, the mortality rate was 2.5 times as great as that expected for males, and 2.86 times greater for females. O'Donnell estimated that the males in his sample had lost one-third or more of their life expectancies and the females one-fifth at the time of their first admission to Lexington, and added that these figures were probably an underestimate. He attributed this high death rate to two factors: preadmission illnesses, such as tuberculosis and heart disease, and unnatural causes, such as accidents, suicide, and so on.

Sapira, Ball, and Penn (1970) examined the question of whether addicts died of ordinary causes in contrast to specific diseases that resulted in early death. They examined the causes of all deaths that occurred while addicts were in treatment at Lexington since 1935. The results of the study suggested that death was caused by a greater variety of diseases than would be expected in patients at a purely medical facility. Approximately one-third of the deaths were due to infectious diseases such as tuberculosis and bacterial endocarditis, and the authors point out that these illnesses could be directly attributable to addiction. Surprisingly, however, other diseases normally attributed to addiction such as septicemia, malaria, tetanus, and viral hepatitis were absent. The second major cause of death was from diseases of the circulatory system, especially cardiac failure. The authors attribute a significant decrease in the number of deaths in recent years partly to the younger mean age of addicts upon admission. Comparing causes of death for addicts at Lexington with those for the general U.S. population, tuberculosis and nephritis occurred more often in the Lexington population than would otherwise have been expected.

Baden (1975) reported the following breakdown of causes of death among the 1400 addicts who died in New York City in the previous year: adverse reaction to heroin or methadone with/without other drugs of abuse, slightly over 50%; violence (usually homicide), 40%; infection, 5%. Of particular interest is his comment that violent deaths among addicts have increased markedly in recent years. He attributes this partly to a possible shift toward a younger, more aggressive, and more antisocial addict population.

Glaser and Ball (1970) examined another aspect of mortality among addicts—death occurring in the course of treatment. They reviewed 55 cases reported in the literature in which death occurred during the process of withdrawal from opiates. Of the 33 cases with sufficient available information, death could be attributed to the following causes: suicide, 2 cases; overdose, 4 cases; illness, 3 cases; exacerbation of chronic illness or a pre-existing condition, 11 cases; and "over-zealous treatment," 10 cases. When the authors examined the causes of death in 25 patients who died during opiate withdrawal at Lexington (of the 29,581 patients going through the process between 1935 and 1966), none were due to the actual withdrawal of opiates, although 4 were due to concomitant barbiturate withdrawal.

Gardner (1970a) noted that 72% of 112 opioid users she had studied who died during the period 1965 through 1968 in England had died of drug misuse, including accidental or deliberate overdose, infection, or treatment. The most frequent cause of death, occurring in 46% of cases, was accidental overdose. Louria, Hensle and Rose (1967) estimated that overdose killed an estimated 1% of addicts in New York City annually. Of the 47 deaths that occurred from accidental overdose in Gardner's study, 32 had involved intravenous administration of heroin; 26 individuals died shortly after a period of abstinence. This frequent finding again suggests that the loss of tolerance to opioids, usually as a result of institutional commitment, is a contributing factor in addict deaths.

Bewley et al (1968) noted: "Heroin addiction in Britain at present carries a high mortality risk" (p. 725). They found an increase in the number of deaths during the period covered by their study as well as a decrease in the mean age at death: 30.3 years among nontherapeutic addicts prior to 1965, and 24.8 years in the period 1965-1966. Fifty percent of all deaths occurred before 28 years of age. Of 89 deaths, 9 were due to suicide, 7 more to an overdose from a drug other than the one to which they were addicted, 16 from accidental overdoses, 6 as the result of violence, and 15 were due to infection (sepsis). According to Bewley et al, the 12 natural deaths were "almost all directly or indirectly due to the consequences of drug addiction" (p. 726).

D'Orban (1974) found that 10 out of 66 female heroin addicts he studied in a 4 year follow-up to incarceration had died—a mortality rate of 15%—9 of the 10 had died of complications related to drug abuse (seven of overdoses of various drugs), and 1 was a suicide. Their mean age at death was 22.5 years. Interestingly, the 10 addicts who died were reported to have had the highest number of previous convictions as well as a history of delinquency before the onset of addiction. This suggests a possible relationship between greater deviancy and increased mortality among the female addicts in this sample.

At the peak of the heroin epidemic in Washington, D.C., in 1971, Dupont and Greene (1973) reported that 29 heroin overdose deaths occurred in a 3 month period. This decreased to a low of 1 during the first quarter of 1973. Coincidentally, during this time the variability of heroin content of packages purchased decreased, and this may have contributed to a decrease in the number of deaths due to overdoses. With respect to personal characteristics, in Washington, D.C., 80% of deaths classified as due to acute opiate overdoses occurred primarily in "young, black, inner-city males with a history of narcotics addiction" (p. 717). In 98% of these cases evidence of morphine was found in their systems, and no other causes of death were discernible. Overall, some 287 deaths directly attributable to narcotics use were found to have occurred in the District of Columbia between July, 1971 and December, 1979. Contributing factors in some cases were found to be lack of opiate tolerance, as well as conjoint abuse of ethanol (Zimney and Luke, 1981).

A detailed summary of a variety of factors related to deaths among narcotic addicts in New York City has been provided by Helpern and

Rho (1967) who found an increase in the percentage as well as the number of deaths attributable to narcotics in New York City for the period from 1950 to 1961. These deaths occurred most often in May for males and in August for females. The greatest incidence was among blacks (612.9 narcotic-related deaths per 10,000 deaths from all causes) —12 times as many as for whites (14.4 per 10,000 deaths). The ratio of black male to white male deaths was 10:1, the female black to female white ratio, 15:1. When examined by sex, irrespective of race, Helpern and Rho (1967) found the ratio of male to female deaths among narcotic addicts to be roughly 3.5:1. Ten percent of all narcotic deaths occurred in teen-agers, 25% in individuals under the age of 30, 75% before 35, and 90% before 50. The average age at death was 29 for males and 30 for females, and decreased slightly between 1950 and 1961. An average of 58.8% of the addicts were single (males 62%, and females 43%) which the authors note, is probably "indicative of a similarly high incidence among the entire addict population and thus a measure of social maladjustment" (p. 65).

Helpern and Rho (1967) also found an inverse relationship between mortality rate and occupational category, with the highest death rate among unskilled workers or laborers, and the lowest among skilled or semiskilled groups. Geographically, the greatest number of deaths occurred in poverty areas with high crime rates. The percentage of addicts who died there was greater than the number who resided there and suggested that they sought out these areas because of the opportunity provided for obtaining and using drugs. Furthermore, addicts who died from overdoses tended to be found in places where there was a high degree of privacy for drug use.

Finally, it should be noted that treatment does not necessarily reduce increased risk of mortality for addicts. Over a 79 month period, patients enrolled in methadone maintenance were found to have an overall mortality rate of 20 per 1,000. Even after discharge methadone maintenance clients have a mortality rate one and a half times the average for the community in which they resided (Concool, Smith, and Stimmel, 1979).

Suicide

In an examination of the possibility of death due to suicide, Chambers and Ball (1970) found a suicide rate of 3 per 10,000 hospitalized opiate addicts. This rate was three times as high as that for the general population but approximately slightly more than one-half of that for prison inmates, and less than one-third of that for mental hospital patients. Suicides were more frequent among males, older addicts, and whites, but were not related to religion, social class (including father's occupation and patient's education and occupation) parents' or patient's marital status, geographic place of residence, or physical condition. Of those patients committing suicide who had been evaluated psychiatrically, all had been diagnosed as having a "psychiatric deviancy" and almost 80% had been diagnosed as having more than one. The patients who committed suicide were experienced addicts (average length of addiction, 14.1 years), but inexperienced with respect to treatment. They tended to have begun drug abuse later in life, more frequently as a result of medical treatment for illness. In investigating the reasons for suicide among this addict group, such diverse causes appeared as difficulties of withdrawal, institutional adjustment, and acceptance of incarceration, as well as inability to cope with personal problems associated with addiction.

A reported 21 percent rate of past suicidal attempts by 98 "hard-core" heroin addicts, as reported by Frederick, Resnick, and Wittlin (1973), was the subject of further investigation by Emery, Steer, and Beck (1979). In the latter study, 191 daily heroin users entering a methadone maintenance program were questioned about past and current suicidal attempts and ideation. Rates of 9.9 percent past suicide attempts and 8.3 percent current suicidal ideation were obtained. Emery et al (1979) interpret their finding of low rates for past suicidal attempts as possibly reflecting differences in racial composition. Their sample was 66.5 percent black compared to 95 percent for Frederick et al's sample. The low rates for present suicidal ideation are suggested to reflect optimism upon entry into treatment, the point at which the survey was taken. When the role of hopelessness as a mediating variable between depression and suicidal behaviors was examined in a sample of 191 heroin addicts, suicidal intent was found to be significantly related to hopelessness, but not to depression (Emery, Steer, and Beck, 1981).

OVERDOSING AS A CAUSE OF DEATH AMONG ADDICTS

As indicated above, high rates of sudden death among addicts have been ascribed directly to self-administered overdoses of heroin (Helpern and Rho, 1966; Louria, Hensle, and Rose, 1967). Louria et al (1967) have suggested five ways in which such overdoses occur: (a) With heavy adulteration of heroin, the addict may have almost no idea of just how much of the drug he is injecting. Louria et al (1967) cite Helpern who reported that of 122 packages supposedly containing heroin (110 actually did), the concentration of heroin ranged from 1 to 77%. Noting that a heroin content of greater than 20% may be lethal, the authors concluded: ". . . a lack of awareness of the potency of the heroin packet is the most frequent cause of overdose" (p. 2); (b) injecting after not having abused heroin for a period of time (and subsequent loss of tolerance) of the previously used dosage; (c) the use by recently addicted addicts of the higher dose levels used by addicts who have developed a greater tolerance for the drug; (d) the street availability of virtually pure heroin by dealers who are evading the police; and (e) the deliberate attempt by a pusher to induce a lethal overdose by providing purer heroin than usual.

The physical signs of overdosing may include (a) pupillary constriction, (b) a lowered rate of respiration, perhaps as low as two to four respirations per minute, (c) cyanosis, (d) cold and clammy skin, (e) a progressive drop in blood pressure, (f) a decrease in body temperature, (g) flaccid skeletal musculature, and (h) a comatose state. Death, if it occurs, is often due to respiratory failure but can also be caused by complications developing during coma that include pneumonia, shock, and pulmonary edema (Jaffe, 1970d). Adding another possible complication, Lipski, Stimmel, and Donoso (1973) suggested that the high rate of electrocardiogram abnormalities seen in heroin addicts who had recently used the drug, including abnormalities of conduction, depolarization, and repolarization, and bradyarrhythmias, may "play a role in the production and facilitation of lethal arrhythmias and may be the mechanism of the acute fatal reaction" (p. 668).

According to Sapira (1968) four explanations have been proposed to account for sudden death due to overdosing, and for the pulmonary edema which is often seen on autopsy (Helpern and Rho, 1966; Silber and Clerkin, 1959): (a) pulmonary edema and subsequent death due to acute cardiac failure resulting from the large amount of quinine used as an adulterant in street heroin (Isbell, personal communication, cited by Sapira); (b) anoxia secondary to acute heart disease due to pulmonary hypertension resulting from disease of pulmonary blood vessels, with pulmonary edema also present (Burton, Zawadzki, Wetherbell, and Moy, 1965); (c) anoxia which occurs as a result of opiate-induced apnea, with the pulmonary edema a secondary finding (Louria, Hensle, and Rose, 1967; Siegel, Helpern, and Ehrenreich, 1966); and (d) an acute hypersensitivity reaction in the lung, leading to death from anoxia that results from impairment of normal pulmonary functioning (Helpern and Rho, 1966; Siegel et al, 1966; Cherubin, 1967). With regard to this last explanation, Cherubin (1967) notes that the injection of colloidal or particulate matter found in heroin, such as quinine, lactose or sucrose, procaine, magnesium silicate, and mannitol may result in a fall in blood pressure, tachypnea, cyanosis, and ultimately death. Cherubin suggests that the low concentration of actual heroin found in samples obtained on the street and the rapid onset of collapse and death in overdose cases seem to support an explanation of sudden death due to a hypersensitivity reaction, with pulmonary edema and vascular congestion as the immediate cause of death.

In an important paper on the contribution of drug-associated environmental cues in heroin addicts, Siegel, Hinson, Krank, and McCully (1982) address the question of why ". . . many experienced drug users die after a dose that should not be fatal in view of their tolerance" (p. 436). Noting that death may occur after administration of a heroin dose that was well tolerated on the previous day, Siegel et al propose that the "overdose" may occur from a "failure of tolerance." In their view, tolerance involves classical conditioning of environmental cues which elicit anticipatory conditioned pharmacological responses. These, in turn, attenuate the effects of the drug and thus increase tolerance. Using an animal analogue study to test this model, Siegel et al found that ". . . groups of rats with the same pharmacological history of heroin administration can differ in mortality following administration of a high dose of the drug: rats that received the potentially lethal dose in the context of cues previously associated with sublethal doses were more likely to survive than animals that received the dose in the context of cues not previously associated with the drug" (p. 437).

The wide spectrum of physical complications occurring as a result of use of street heroin is evident in the results of a study by Pearson, Challenor, Baden, and Richter (1972). In a group of New York City addicts, after administration of adulterated narcotics, the authors found the following complications: delirium, convulsions, coma, parkinsonianlike states, acute transverse myelitis, amblyopia, and other complications such as plexitis, peripheral neuropathy and muscular dysfunction at sites other than and remote from the sites of injection. Intellectual impairment and personality change were also noted. The results of postmortem examinations indicated the presence of occasional central nervous system changes including frequent astrocytic clasmatodendrosis, occasional diffuse brain swelling and also degenerative and reactive changes in the globus pallidus, and necrosis of spinal gray matter. Pathologic change in muscles and chronic inflammation in and degeneration of peripheral nerves also occurred.

SPECIFIC SYSTEMIC COMPLICATIONS

Pulmonary Complications

These are quite common among addicts and may arise from emboli resulting from endocarditis, the injection of inert substances, or bacterial infection. Respiratory impairment as a direct result of the effect of heroin upon respiratory reflexes also plays an important role in facilitating the development of these complications, as does the generally poor state of health of the addict.

The injection of substances prepared for oral use often leads to the presence of inert substances such as starch and talc which can embolize to the lungs (Sapira, 1968). These thrombi may in turn lead to such conditions as angiothrombotic pulmonary hypertension and right ventricular failure. Tumorlike granulomas may also develop in the lung after injection of adulterants or even from the fiber from the cotton ball through which the heroin is filtered while being prepared for injection (Von Glahn and Hall, 1949). This disease process may eventually result in decreased lung volume and diffusing capacity (Lerner and Oerther, 1966).

Pulmonary infections such as staphylococcal pneumonitis and tuberculosis may also result from the formation of pulmonary emboli, the latter especially when the emboli are the result of septicemia, or right-sided endocarditis. Louria, Hensle, and Rose (1967) have commented on the frequent presence of nonstaphylococcal pneumonia in addicts. Sapira (1968) suggests that one explanation for the occurrence of this type of pneumonia might be the direct effect of morphine in reducing lung expansion due to depression of the sighing and coughing reflexes, together with a decrease in tidal volume and alveolar hypoventilation. Other related factors might also include the entry of pneumococci from the throat by aspiration, the added decrease in lung volume due to cigarette smoking, and the effects of prolonged periods of maintaining a supine position with resultant accumulation of secretions in the lungs. With regard to this latter point, Curtis, Richman, and Feinstein (1974) found one-third of the addicts with endocarditis in their sample had been hospitalized for pneumonia immediately preceding the study. They attributed this high rate as "due in part to the problem of aspiration while the addict is obtunded" (p. 7), and noted that pneumonia is seen more often now than in the past.

Asthma may be induced as a result of (a) the constrictive effects of heroin upon the air passages, mediated by release of histamine, by direct effects upon the bronchial musculature, and by vagal effects, or (b) a direct hypersensitivity reaction of the lung (asthmatic diathesis). According to Sapira (1968) the latter explanation has many implications for the understanding of the sudden death mechanism in addicts that occurs as a result of a heroin overdose.

Helpern and Rho (1966), Cherubin (1967), and Felton (1975) all report a high rate of occurrence of tuberculosis among addicts. Felton reports a 3.74% rate of active tuberculosis among addicted patients. Cherubin, observing that addicts tend to live in those areas of the city that have higher than average rates of this disease, raised the question of whether this rate of occurrence was any higher than expected for non-addicted individuals living in the same environment. The evidence presented by Felton (1975) suggests that addicts do have a higher rate of tuberculosis, since he projected an incidence among addicts of 3740 cases per 100,000 population, versus 123 per 100,000 for nonaddicts in the same community and 15.9 per 100,000 nationally.

Heart and Circulatory System

Endocarditis

According to Sapira (1968), "the most important lesion affecting the heart is endocarditis" (p. 567). Helpern and Rho (1966) have suggested that endocarditis and sepsis accounted for almost 9% of deaths among addicts in New York City. Two basic types of this lesion are found—right-sided endocarditis which affects the tricuspid valve, usually due to *staphylococcus aureus*, and left-sided endocarditis with involvement of the aortic or mitral valves, often caused by a type of streptococcus. According to Cherubin (1967), left-sided endocarditis is the one usually found in heroin addicts. Louria et al (1967) found infecting agents "extraordinary." They compared their finding of 42% of cases of narcotic-induced endocarditis due to *staphylococcus aureus* to a maximum 25% of subacute cases in nonaddicts attributable to this cause. Minda and Gorbach (1973) found an even higher percentage; they attributed 70% of cases of bacterial endocarditis in their sample to *staphylococcus aureus*. In contrast, among nonaddicts, endocarditis is more likely to be caused by a species of streptococcus and to occur in individuals with a preexisting history of rheumatic or other heart disease.

Minda and Gorbach (1973) commented on the high mortality rate (69%) attributable to endocarditis in addicts as well as on the high rate of endocardial infection by a fungus, *Candida*, in cases with a previous history of heart disease. Stimmel, Donoso, and Dach (1973), however, reported a comparable rate of response to medical therapy among addicts (58%) and nonaddicts (62%), although more frequent and more serious complications occurred in addicts.

Stroke

Stroke has been identified as a significant consequence of drug abuse, especially in young adults and adolescents (Caplan, Hier, and Banks, 1982). This seems to be particularly relevant to heroin use where the drug is adulterated with such substances as "talcum, starch, curry powder, Vim, Ajax, Caffeine ('Chinese heroin'), strychnine, mannitol, quinine, or lactose" and injection is used as a means of delivery. Noting nine reports in the literature where stroke was directly attributable to heroin use, each was due to cerebral infarction following intravenous injection. Other cerebrovascular consequences noted by Caplan et al included infective endocarditis with cerebrovascular complications of embolization and subarachnoid hemorrhage following rupture of a mycotic aneurysm.

Other Infections

Septicemia arising at the sites of injection on the arms and legs has been suggested by Helpern and Rho (1966) as a possible explanation for as many as one in twelve deaths among addicts in New York City.

Electrocardiogram

Lipski, Stimmel, and Donoso (1973) compared the electrocardiograms (ECGs) of heroin addicts with those of nonaddicts and found a 55% rate of electrical abnormalities among addicts who had taken heroin in the preceding 24 hours in contrast to none in the control group. A third group of addicts who used methadone, alcohol, barbiturates, or cocaine showed a 60% rate of abnormal ECG patterns.

Spleen

Although heroin has no direct effect on the spleen, two disorders often seen in addicts, bacterial endocarditis and acute viral hepatitis, may be associated with splenic enlargement. Apparently, malaria as a cause of splenomegaly in addicts is a relatively remote possibility due possibly to the generally low incidence of this disorder in the United States and also to the presence of quinine in street heroin.

Lymphatic System

Sapira (1968) cited Siegel, Helpern, and Ehrenreich's (1966) observation that lymphadenopathy is present in over 75% of addicts, with lymph nodes sometimes increased to five times their normal size. "Addict's lymphadenopathy" may be due to the presence of particles of contaminants in narcotics or to a generalized hyperplasia of the entire lymphatic system. The occurrence of "puffy hand" syndrome in addicts is attributed by Ritland and Butterfield (1973) to lymphatic obstruction, possibly caused by quinine, and to the sclerosing action of the injected drug on the soft tissues and veins and the resultant collapse of hand and forearm veins. Often, addicts also have a high lymphocyte count and atypical lymphocytes (Sapira, 1968).

Hepatic System

Viral hepatitis was "the foremost cause of addict admissions to the medical service at Metropolitan Hospital in New York," according to Cherubin (1967). For Louria, Hensle, and Rose (1967), hepatitis was "the most frequently observed infectious complication requiring hospitalization" (p. 14), occurring in 42 of the 100 cases with complications studied. First recognized as a complication of heroin addiction by Steigmann, Hyman, and Goldbloom (1950), the prevalence of this disease among addicts has led Eiseman, Lam, and Rush (1964) to comment that "it is safe to assume that any confirmed addict has had hepatitis" (p. 753).

The high rate of viral hepatitis in addicts was also evident in the study by Potter, Cohen, and Norris (1960), who performed liver function tests on 69 heroin addicts incarcerated for six months at the time of the study and found that 52 out of 69 had at least one or more abnormal test results. This incidence was even more striking by comparison with a control group of 43 nonaddicts in which only 7 had one or more abnormal tests. Only 5% of the addicts had a history of jaundice. Kaplan (1963) also reported a high level of abnormal liver function tests (up to 75% in one sample) in addicts.

The etiology of liver dysfunction in addicts is unclear. Kaplan, in contrast to Potter et al, did not attribute the high level of liver dysfunction found in addicts to viral hepatitis. He based this interpretation on two points: first, there was no relationship between a history of jaundice and liver disease in his sample, and second, the rate of chronic liver dysfunction in addicts was much higher than usually found after acute hepatitis. Litt, Cohen, and Schonberg (1972), after reporting a 37% incidence of liver disease in a sample of 7272 adolescent drug users, were unable to rule out "a chronic, direct toxic effect of heroin on the liver . . ." (p. 241). On the other hand, Sapira's (1968) findings suggested a "mild, chronic, intermittently active anicteric serum hepatitis . . ." (p. 572), and that hepatitis was ". . . probably not due to a toxic or allergic effect of the opiate *per se* . . ." (p. 572). Likewise, Cherubin (1975) also favored a viral basis for hepatitis in addicts. He reported that 80% of initial episodes of viral hepatitis in addicts occurred within two years of initial injection of the drug. Obviously, the issue of etiology has yet to be settled. Finally, Eiseman, Lam, and Rush (1964), commenting on the relatively low incidence of alcoholic cirrhosis among addicts, suggested that this finding indicates a relative absence of chronic alcoholism in this group.

Nervous System

Heroin itself seems to produce few direct neurologic dysfunctions. Overdose, hypersensitivity reactions, and infection may, however, result in neurologic complications. Sapira (1968) stated that "...there are no clinical neurologic signs of chronic opiate addiction *per se*, and the presence of neurologic abnormalities should prompt a search for another disease [in addition to the addiction]" (p. 578). Neurologic complications may include purulent meningitis, brain abscesses due to septicemia, and cerebral emboli due to bacterial endocarditis. Heroin overdoses may result in neurologic complications as the result of anoxia or a direct toxic effect (Richter and Pearson, 1975).

Four cases of acute transverse myelitis involving thoracic spinal cord segments were reported as a possible complication of heroin addiction by Richter and Rosenberg (1968). In these cases the condition developed when heroin use was reinitiated after a period of abstinence. The authors suggested as the mechanism a "temporary vascular insufficiency" resulting from an allergic or hypersensitivity reaction to either quinine, some other adulterant, or to the heroin itself. Richter and Rosenberg (1968) further noted that (*a*) MacGregor and Lowenstein (1944) had reported that quinine could trigger a severe hypotensive reaction by depression of myocardium and peripheral vasodilation; and (*b*) heroin itself could have depressed central vasomotor control that resulted in decreased blood pressure. In addition to acute transverse myelitis, Ritland and Butterfield (1973) indicated several other possible peripheral neurologic complications of heroin use, including direct injury to nerves, polyneuritis, and ischemic neuritis. They listed among the possible causes, direct arterial ischemia, puncturing nerves during injection or other administration of the narcotic, scarring, and hypersensitivity reactions.

Other neurologic complications suggested to be related to heroin addiction include toxic amblyopia (Brust and Richter, 1971), and brachial and lumbrosacral plexitis (Challenor, Richter, Bruun, and Pearson, 1973).

In a postmortem comparison of the brains of a group of 20 heroin addicts who died immediately following injection and a control group, Pearson and Richter (1975) found evidence of cerebral edema, a marked reduction in the number of astrocytes present, and a reduction in the neuronal population of the *globus pallidus*, among other changes. In another study, Richter, Baden, and Pearson (1970) found cerebral edema in 60% of patients who died from acute heroin overdose. These findings may be attributable to increased intracranial pressure associated with pulmonary edema.

Eyes

The frequent presence of nystagmus in heroin addicts may suggest a concurrent addiction to barbiturates. Jaundiced sclera may result from the quinine with which heroin is adulterated and also from hepatitis, which is common among addicts. Miosis, or contracted pupils, persists during chronic opiate addiction (Sapira, 1968).

Sleep

The effects of heroin upon human sleep were evaluated by Kay, Pickworth, and Neider (1981), using seven non-dependent opiate addicts in a randomized double-blind crossover design. Drugs and dose levels employed were heroin (3,6,12 mg/70 kg), morphine (10,20 mg/70 kg), and placebo. The results indicated that (a) heroin produces a dose-related increase in wakefulness, drowsiness episodes, muscle tension, and shifts in sleep-waking states, (b) heroin produces a dose-related decrease in total sleep, sleep efficiency, delta sleep, and REM sleep, (c) heroin has twice the potency of morphine in producing insomnia of this type, and (d) morphine insomnia appears to be a characteristic initial effect of opioids, at least in the non-dependent opiate addicts studied.

Digestive System

Stomach

The relative incidence of peptic and duodenal ulcers may differ in heroin addicts. Sapira (1968) found a lower than expected incidence of peptic ulcer among narcotics addicts admitted to Lexington between 1961 and 1966. Complications, when present, were also no greater than anticipated. On the other hand, Cherubin (1967) reported a greater than expected incidence of duodenal ulcers among addicts in treatment at Daytop Village in New York City.

Intestinal Tract

Obstruction of the intestinal tract may occur in addicts as a consequence of chronic decreased gastrointestinal motility and resultant constipation. Another type of obstruction, reported by Sapira (1968), is the result of having swallowed drugs (often placed in a condom) in an attempt to smuggle them into a jail or hospital.

Rectum

Hemorrhoids are a frequently reported problem in addicts because of the chronic constipation induced by the effects of heroin on the large intestine.

Endocrine System

Decreases in the production of adrenocorticotrophic hormone and gonadotrophin after the administration of morphine have been demonstrated experimentally (Eisenman, Fraser, Sloan, and Isbell, 1958; Eisenman, Fraser, and Brooks, 1961).

Diabetes

Sapira (1968) noted that diabetes mellitus may be less common among addicts than nonaddicts. Although initial use of morphine raises blood sugar levels, tolerance to this effect soon occurs, followed perhaps by a slight hypoglycemic condition after administration.

Integument

Skin Lesions

Continued injection of heroin into the veins eventually leads to the characteristic "railroad tracks" seen on the bodies of heroin addicts that result from repeated punctures of the skin over the accessible veins and subsequent scar formation. These tracks, most often found on the forearm, hands, and feet, may be found almost anywhere on the body where veins are accessible. When all readily accessible veins have been sclerosed, the addict may turn to the external jugular and sublingual veins and the dorsal vein of the penis (Hofmann, 1975). Usually, however, tracks are found only in habitual users. The external evidence of injections in occasional users may range from single needle marks to hyperpigmentation over the points of injection. Unusually dark pigmentation may also be found when the tip of the needle has first been "sterilized" by being heated with a match flame. The resultant carbon accumulation is deposited under the skin during injection (Baden, 1975).

"Skin-popping," or subcutaneous injection, often leads to the formation of bacterial or chemical abscesses. Sapira (1968) noted that these are usually multiple lesions which can leave a characteristic pair of scars: one, hyperpigmented with vague margins ranging in size from 1 to 3 cm or more; the second, a round or oval-shaped punched-out lesion with sharply defined borders, ranging from 1 to 5 cm in diameter, in which the skin is atrophic, shiny and/or depigmented. The subcutaneous abscesses produced by skin-popping are usually found on the thighs and back (Baden, 1975).

Two other types of skin lesions are also reported by Sapira (1968) as common among heroin addicts. One is a "rosette" of cigarette burns on the chest resulting from nodding while having a lighted cigarette in the mouth; at the same time, the analgesic effect of the drug has prevented an immediate reflex withdrawal. The other kind of lesion is tattoos, either over the sites of scars resulting from repeated injections in an attempt to obscure them, or intended as a form of identification within the addict subculture. Baden (1975) reported that tattoos are found in more than 20% of addicts. Other skin problems found in heroin addicts are secondary infections due to scratching to relieve itching, lack of concern with personal hygiene, and the effects of adulterants.

Genitourinary System

Kidney

Renal disease in conjunction with bacterial endocarditis was found in 25.5% of a sample of addicts studied by Lessin and Siegel (1973). Sapira (1968) indicated that renal failure may occur in addicts as a result of bacterial endocarditis. He also reported an unusually high incidence of chronic glomerulonephritis in addicts at Lexington over a 30 year period, although he did not see renal disease in general as unusually common among addicts. Recently, Kilcoyne (1975) suggested a relationship between heroin use and the development of a nephrotic syndrome distinguishable from that occurring in nonaddicts.

Gynecological

Finnegan (1979) reports that 60 to 90 percent of female addicts have menstrual abnormalities, with amenorrhea the most frequently reported. Factors reported as contributing to this high rate include polydrug abuse, malnutrition, hepatitis, pelvic infection, other physical illness, and the stress of involvement in the unstable social, economic, and emotional environment of the heroin addict's world. Dysmenorrhea is also increased during addiction and withdrawal, although the cause may be secondary to pelvic infection. Significantly, Finnegan (1979) notes that women using medically prescribed narcotics and those in methadone maintenance usually do not have menstrual problems. Likewise, abstinence usually results in a return to menstrual regularity in 57 to 88 percent of women. Chronic female heroin users are reported by Smith et al (1982) to demonstrate a reduction of sexual desire and performance, as well as irregular menstrual cycles and occasional amenorrhea, as a result of the depressive effects of opiates upon pituitary hormones.

Venereal Disease

According to Sapira (1968) 25 to 35% of incarcerated addicts may have positive serologic tests for syphilis, although a high proportion of these may be false positives, due perhaps to the production of abnormal amounts of unusual serum proteins. Sapira (1968) cites a recent study by Harris and Andrei (1967) in which they found a 58% incidence of false positives among women arrested for prostitution. After examining the evidence, Sapira concludes that "there is both a high syphilis rate and a high rate of biologic false-positive reactors among addicts, although the exact incidence of each is yet to be determined" (p. 578).

A commonly reported side effect in heroin addicts is decreased sexual drive or libido (Isbell and White, 1953), although this finding seems contradictory to the high rate of venereal disease reported for this group.

NEONATAL ADDICTION

Children born to heroin-addicted mothers present a specific set of medical problems. Not only are these infants frequently more at risk with respect to mortality and morbidity because of poor prenatal care, but they also demonstrate the symptoms of the abstinence syndrome, because they have acquired the mother's need for periodic administration of the narcotic.

There has been increasing awareness of the magnitude of the problem of heroin-induced complications occurring in newborn infants. In New York City in 1960 only 1 in 164 deliveries was to a drug-addicted female. In 1972 this figure was 1 in 27 deliveries (Zelson, 1973). Infants born to addicted mothers have a high probability of showing withdrawal symptoms. Zelson, Lee, and Casalino (1973) reported that more than three-quarters of newborn infants born to heroin-addicted mothers in their sample showed signs of withdrawal within 48 hours following birth. Sometimes symptoms will not be obvious at first, but may take from two to four weeks to appear (Kendall and Gantner, 1974); more frequently, they will be evident within the first 24 hours after birth. In 1975, Glass, Evans, and Rajegowda reported that during the previous two years 1 in 20 infants born at Harlem Hospital Center developed withdrawal symptoms. These symptoms include marked tremors, hyperirritability, hypertonicity, vomiting, respiratory distress, fever, and a high-pitched cry (Zelson, 1973); Hofmann (1975) added the following: poor food intake, twitching, yawning, sneezing, nasal congestion, lacrimation, and sweating. There may also be abnormalities of sleep patterns, especially in REM sleep (Schulman, 1969). Low birth weight is frequently seen in infants born to addicted mothers (Zelson et al, 1973; Priestly, 1973). A system for the classification of severity of the major withdrawal symptoms in newborns has been developed by Kahn, Newmann, and Polk (1969).

With respect to the greater likelihood of mortality in these infants, Zelson (1973) notes a 3.5% mortality rate versus a 3.0% rate for the general nursery population. Reasons for this increased mortality rate may be the failure of pregnant addicts to seek prenatal care, poor maternal diet, and the relatively high incidence of venereal disease in addicted mothers (Glass et al, 1975). Finnegan (1979) observes that many pregnant addicts self-deliver or deliver at home without a physician in attendance. Furthermore, the majority do not obtain adequate prenatal care.

Hutchings (1982) reviewed the literature on the behavioral effects upon the neonate of methadone and heroin use by the mother during pregnancy. Hutchings concluded that clinical and animal studies were in agreement that prenatal exposure to opiates produces effects in two stages: (a) an acute stage consisting of a neonatal abstinence syndrome lasting from 3 to 6 months in humans and characterized by an increase in CNS arousal, and involving hyperactivity, disturbed sleep, and increased state lability; and (b) a less well-understood pattern of impaired organizational and perceptual skills, poor adjustment, and decreased motor inhibition. Reviewing the available literature, preschool children with a history of prenatal exposure to methadone showed no effects upon intellectual or cognitive abilities, but demonstrated increased activity or energy levels, impulsivity, and decreased attention span and persistence. Impaired motor inhibition ability was cited as an area of particular vulnerability.

In a comprehensive review of the literature on the medical impact upon infants of maternal narcotics addiction, Householder, Hatcher, Burns, and Chasnoff (1982) review the findings of some 78 studies. They find clear evidence for the following sequelae of intrauterine stress upon the developing fetus: low birth weight, meconium staining and perinatal asphyxia, and violent intrauterine kicking, possibly suggestive of in utero seizures or withdrawal during unavailability of narcotics to the mother. Perinatal complications seen include shorter than average labor times and increased incidence of malpresentations.

Postnatal complications outlined by Householder et al (1982) include some degree of narcotic withdrawal for 70 to 90 percent of infants born to narcotic-addicted mothers, with a variety of patterns of symptoms reflecting CNS disturbance. These patterns usually appear within 24 to 72 hours after delivery, resulting in an average hospital stay of from six to 20 days. Some ten percent of births display delayed onset of symptomatology possibly reflecting fetal accumulation and delayed excretion of drugs. Long-term greater risk during the perinatal period seems to be not only the continuation of these problems, but also the result of other non-withdrawal-related problems. These include greater incidence of venereal disease in addicted mothers, possible chromosomal aberrations, and increased incidence of sudden infant death syndrome (SIDS), the last possibly reflecting a depressed ventilatory response.

Problems in behavior and attachment during infancy seem to be unusually prevalent in infants of narcotic-addicted mothers. Householder et al (1982) note that "in general, narcotic-addicted neonates have an impaired ability to organize their responses to the environment, with a lessened capacity to attend and react to noxious stimuli and to habituate to disturbing events" (p. 460). Furthermore, irritability, hyperactivity and feeding and sleep disturbances are present, leading to disturbance of the development of mother-infant affectional bonding. Thus, the conclusion is drawn by Householder et al (1982) that the addicted neonate is at double risk—not only as a result of the direct physiological sequelae of addiction, but also as a result of the reactions evoked by their behavior on the part of caretakers.

In a study of the effects of heroin addiction upon fetal and postnatal growth, Lifschitz, Wilson, Smith, and Desmond (1983) compared the children of untreated heroin addicts, methadone patients, and a drug-free comparison group. Controlling for biologic, demographic, and health variables, it was found that mean birth rates for both drug-exposure groups was less than those for the drug-free comparison group. Another comparison, after adjustment for sex, race, prenatal care, pregnancy weight gain, maternal education, and smoking resulted in a loss of these differences. Adjustment for birth, length, parental height, and smoking did result in the methadone group being shorter than the children exposed to heroin in utero, with the comparison group intermediate between the other two. Lifschitz et al conclude that the effect of heroin and methadone on intrauterine growth cannot be differentiated from other associated factors, and there was no demonstrable impact upon postnatal growth, in comparison to other high-risk groups.

OTHER COMPLICATIONS OF HEROIN ADDICTION

Malaria

Biggam's (1929) report of malaria being transmitted among needle-sharing addicts in Cairo was followed by a number of reports of outbreaks among addicts in the United States during the 1930s (Helpern, 1934; Most, 1940a, 1940b). From 1942 to 1971 there had been no reports of malaria due to needle-sharing. Cherubin (1967) attributed the absence of malaria among addicts to the eradication of the disease in the United States. It has also been suggested that the widespread use of quinine as an adulterant was a factor (Louria, Hensle, and Rose, 1967).

In 1971, Bick and Anhalt reported observing 10 cases of malaria among heroin addicts in Bakersfield, California. The authors' suspicion that the outbreak may have been caused by a returning Vietnam veteran was confirmed in a final report on the outbreak, which eventually involved 47 persons (Friedmann, Dover, Roberto, and Kearns, 1973). All 47 individuals had shared needles, each with an average of 13 others. The veteran had returned from Vietnam in August 1970, after a clinical case of malaria, but had not completed treatment for it. A total of 330 needle-sharing contacts with separate individuals had been made by the 47 persons who contracted the disease!

Tetanus

This contemporary complication of heroin addiction was first reported a hundred years ago by Norman (1876) and, as noted by Helpern and Rho (1966) and Siegel, Helpern, and Ehrenreich (1966), may have accounted for 5 to 10% of addict deaths in New York City during the period from 1950 to 1965. In 1968, Sapira reported the increase of tetanus among addicts. Baden (1975) notes that almost all current cases of tetanus in New York City are attributable to heroin addiction and usually result from skin-popping. Sapira (1968) had also attributed tetanus in addicts to subcutaneous injection of narcotics. In addition, the use of quinine as an adulterant provides a hospitable environment for the development of tetanus organisms since it produces abscesses at the site of injection (Cherubin, 1967). Sapira reported that tetanus was much more frequent than expected in female addicts and cited Cherubin's (1967) explanation for the greater frequency of this complication in female addicts as being due to the relative paucity of veins suitable for injection in females and, therefore, greater use of subcutaneous injections.

Self-induced or Feigned Disorders

Addicts may present symptoms of various physical disorders to obtain medication from physicians. These feigned disorders may include cholecystitis, intestinal obstruction, renal colic, back pain, cardiac pain, acute porphyria, and arthritis. In the process of obtaining narcotics, addicts become well acquainted with hospital schedules and procedures, and frequent emergency rooms during the middle of the night with complaints of severe pain which is usually relieved rapidly by narcotic administration prior to a detailed medical evaluation (i.e., a complaint of renal colic or cardiac chest pain).[1] Eiseman, Lam, and Rush (1964) point out that many addicts will even convince surgeons that they require an operation to obtain a dose of narcotics.

[1] Robert Calvo, M.D., personal communication.

Osteomyelitis and Arthritis

Occasionally, involvement of the skeletal system is found in heroin addicts that can be ascribed to bacterial or fungal infections acquired as the result of using contaminated needles (Holzman and Bishko, 1971).

Sexual Functioning

Numerous clinical observations have been made regarding the relationship between sexual functioning and heroin addiction. The general consensus has been that sexual behavior is disrupted during addiction to heroin. (Some writers, particularly the psychoanalysts, have focused on the role of disturbances in sexual functioning in the development of addiction [see Chapters 7 and 8].)

In a study of the effects of heroin addiction on sexual functioning, Chein, Gerard, Lee and Rosenfeld (1964) reported a high rate of disturbance in the male addict group they studied, with nearly half of the sample reporting impotency. In one of the few published empirical studies directly focused on this issue DeLeon and Wexler (1973) surveyed addicts residing in a therapeutic community about their sexual behavior prior to, during, and after addiction. They found:

. . . during periods of heroin addiction, there is a relative 'loss' of sexuality. For most subjects, frequency of intercourse, masturbation, and nocturnal emissions all decrease as does the proportion of orgasms. [p. 37]

Other adverse effects reported were increased time to ejaculation, decreased quality of orgasm, and a low level of sexual desire. All aspects of sexuality recovered, however, in the postaddiction phase, actually reaching higher levels in some cases when compared to the preaddiction phase. This latter finding may be related residually to the sexual rebound effects which have been observed during withdrawal from opiates (Gebhard, 1965). Sexual dysfunction appears to persist, however, in some patients on methadone maintenance. Kreek (1975) reported libido and orgasmic abnormalities in 22% and 14% respectively of such patients.

The effects of *chronic* heroin use upon the sexual development of young men was studied by Mendelson and Mello (1982). They compared equivalent groups of former addicts who began heroin use during early puberty, current heroin users, and drug-free controls with respect to psychosexual development and pituitary gonadal hormone levels. Both the plasma testosterone and luteinizing hormone levels did not differ between the former addicts and formal controls. They were, however, significantly suppressed in the current heroin user group. No differences were found to exist with respect to sexual behavior or physical development, leading to the conclusion that recurrent heroin use in early puberty did not significantly disrupt pubertal development in males. Similar findings were obtained with respect to the impact of heroin use upon hormonal functioning. Mirin, Meyer, Mendelson, and Ellingboe (1980) found heroin use to acutely suppress luteinizing hormone released from the pituitary. This suppression of LH was then followed by a secondary drop in plasma testosterone levels.

Acquired Immunodeficiency Disease

Heroin addicts have been identified as being at risk for contracting acquired immunodeficiency disease or AIDS (Small, Klein, Friedland, Moll, Emeson and Spigland, 1983), and it appears that perinatal or in utero transmission of this disease can occur (Rubinstein et al, 1983). In 1985, the death rate from AIDS among addicts in New York City may have reached a high of up to 40 per week, then dropping to a median of 15 per week.

Chromosomal Damage

Heroin addicts may be at greater risk for chromosomal damage, according to the results of a series of studies by Falek and his associates. Summarizing their findings to date, Falek and Hollingsworth (1980) concluded that (a) heroin use results in a significantly greater increase in frequency of cells displaying chromosomal damage than would be expected in the general population, (b) chromosomal damage is found to be distributed randomly among addicts studied, and is thus not confined to only a few persons, (c) chromosomal damage is less evident after three months in a methadone maintenance program, but still present at reduced levels up to one year after admission, and (d) after one year in methadone treatment, damage declines to control group levels. Falek and Hollingsworth (1980) conclude that ". . . heroin addicts may be at an increased risk for mutation and carcinogenesis that declines over time after these persons cease the use of street heroin" (p. 228).

General Physical Condition

Christie (1972) noted that heroin-addicted U.S. servicemen in Thailand were in poor physical condition. He also reported a recent history of considerable weight loss, sometimes 9 to 14 kg over a period of two to three months. Ball and Urbaitis (1970) studied the long-term physical complications arising from chronic opiate use. In a sample of 37 chronic addicts, each of whom had been admitted to Lexington 20 or more times, and none of whom had started using opiates for medical reasons, 14 were categorized as being in good health and another 14 in fair health. This group was therefore in surprisingly good health. The authors pointed out, however, that these results may reflect the fact that only two of these addicts had used heroin as their principal drug; the majority had used morphine. Thus, these individuals were not as exposed to the many risks the heroin addict incurs in purchasing street heroin of unknown adulteration. These results are relevant in the study of heroin addiction because they suggest that use of morphine, the active ingredient in heroin, itself produces minimal physical complications.

PART THREE

Explaining Heroin Addiction

CHAPTER 7

Theories of Addiction

Theories seeking to explain the mechanisms underlying the development of tolerance to and physical dependence on heroin have been discussed in Chapter 5. By way of contrast, this chapter presents an overview of a number of current theoretical formulations which have sought to explain the mechanisms underlying the initial use of and the process of development of psychologic dependence on heroin. The range of theories covered in this chapter is very broad in terms of the kinds of explanatory mechanisms utilized and the particular scientific disciplines from which they are derived. Dole and Nyswander, for example, propose a theory of heroin addiction based on a metabolic deficiency in the addict. The social learning theories presented by Wikler and others differ greatly from the metabolic theory. Wikler proposes a conditioning theory which seeks to explain heroin addiction in terms of learning theory derived from the experimental psychology laboratory. Wikler also attempts to delineate possible underlying neural mechanisms for his conditioning theory. At another point on the theoretical spectrum are the explanations of addiction derived from sociology and related disciplines that seek to explain addiction in terms of social learning, utilizing constructs such as anomie and social deviance. The psychoanalytic theories occupy an extreme position in terms of minimal grounding in empirical referents.

Thus it is apparent that theories of heroin addiction have been invoked at many different levels of scientific explanation—from the molecular to the molar. In addition, there are often several different theoretical formulations at any one level.

CONDITIONING THEORIES

Several attempts have been made to formulate models of addiction based upon the principles of both classical and operant conditioning, the most notable being by Wikler. Some of these conditioning theories have accounted for a substantial number of phenomena observed in the process of addiction.

Two-Factor Theory

Expressing doubt that narcotic-induced euphoria and fear of aversive withdrawal states were sufficient to account for addiction, Wikler (1965) attempted to explain the self-maintenance of addiction to morphine in terms of learning theory. Two definitions, *pharmacological reinforcement* and *direct reinforcement*, are central to Wikler's (1973) detailed conditioning theory of drug addiction. Pharmacologic reinforcement occurs as ". . . the result of interaction between certain pharmacological effects of the drug and sources of reinforcement, i.e., organismic variables upon which the reinforcing properties of the drug are contingent" (p. 611). Such reinforcement is considered to be direct if its source is not engendered by the drug itself and indirect if it is. Direct reinforcement may be related to properties of the central nervous system (CNS) or to characteristics acquired during the development of personality. However, Wikler (1973) states that the only sources of indirect reinforcement are the CNS changes produced as a consequence of actual drug dependence.

In drug dependence the initial reinforcement for drug-taking is social in nature and diminishes in importance as dependence and tolerance develop. Wikler (1953) suggested that a personality structure which will enhance the attractiveness of morphine must precede the onset of addiction. Such a personality need not be neurotic or psychopathic, as many authors have suggested, but must predispose toward enhancing the attractiveness of the narcotic. The desirability of morphine is thus related to its pharmacologic properties, especially its ability to reduce anxiety relative to a primary need such as pain. Failure of the individual to gratify these needs in socially acceptable ways will increase the possibility that morphine use will appear to be an attractive substitute. Although secondary needs of social and interpersonal functioning may also be related to morphine use, they become tangential to the purposive aspects of morphine addiction (Wikler, 1953). Wikler (1965) proposed that in addicts physical dependence may become classically conditioned to the environmental situations temporarily contiguous to narcotic availability. Concurrently, the repeated experience of rapid attenuation of abstinence symptoms by administration of narcotics reinforces the instrumental behavior of seeking out the drug. Each administration of a narcotic induces "central counteradaptive changes" which are unconditioned responses to the drug action at the receptor site. If drug-taking continues, successive central changes eventually generate a homeostatic need for the drug that is reduced by further administration. Wikler suggests a process (modeled after Stein, 1964) in which conditioning occurs in the limbic system. The response-related stimuli (CS) and the reward (US) are paired. An hypothetical, medial forebrain "go" mechanism ultimately conditioned to the response-related stimuli activates this mechanism to engage in the rewarded behavior. What occurs in the case of drug addiction is a result of the conditioning of "central processing events" resulting from the action of a narcotic at a neuronal receptor site along the afferent pathways. Thus, some drug effects are reflexive adaptive responses to the action of the drug at the receptor sites, while others are compensatory responses to the drug effects at peripheral sites. The repeated pairing of neutral (e.g., environmental) stimuli with drug administration results in a conditioned response almost qualitatively identical to the above-mentioned drug effects. Drugs acting at the effector sites result in the conditioning of an unconditioned, acquired adaptive response. According to Wikler (1973):

. . . as drug administrations are continued in frequent temporal contiguity with certain exteroceptive or interoceptive stimuli, or both, these CSs come to elicit, as CRs, successive unconditioned adaptations and counter adaptations to the initial (agonistic) actions of the drug at receptor sites in afferent arms of neural reflex . . . circuits. [p. 614]

The possibility of "interoceptive conditioning" is raised by Wikler to explain continued use of the drug. In interoceptive conditioning the pattern of neural activity evoked by the drug (and responsible for its effects) tends, after repeated pairing with other physiologic stimuli resulting from administration of the drug, to be evoked by the physiologic stimuli alone. Wikler (1971) proposes that this phenomenon serves to maintain drug-taking behavior.

Psychic dependence is defined by Wikler (1973) as the ". . . reinforce-ment of drug-using behavior as a consequence of interactions between certain pharmacological . . . actions of a drug with certain organismic vari-ables that had *not* been engendered by previous doses of that drug" (p. 611). Physical dependence, on the other hand, is based on the interaction of the drug with organismic variables which have been engendered by previous administrations of the drug. However, Wikler notes that the hypothetical conditioning of intero- and exteroceptive stimuli eliciting adaptations to the drug at the receptor site blurs the distinction between psychic and physical dependence.

Relapse following withdrawal may be due to a reactivation of craving for narcotics by the conditioned extero- and interoceptive stimuli that are the conditioned central counteradaptations to the agonistic effects of mor-phine. Relapse is further facilitated by a reactivation of the underlying neural processes associated with this conditioning. The abstinence syn-drome itself can be conditioned by two procedures: (*a*) pairing of specific environmental stimuli with slow withdrawal, and (*b*) pairing discrete stimuli with antagonist-precipitated withdrawal, so that presentation of either CS will evoke conditioned abstinence symptoms. The existence of this phenomenon, that is, conditioned abstinence, has implications regard-ing the causes of relapse. It becomes impossible to state conclusively whether relapse is due to conditioning, protracted abstinence, or both.

Wikler (1973) suggest that the most efficacious treatment for drug addiction must take into account the principles of conditioning. The re-peated elicitation of the CR by the CS must be actively extinguished by blocking the reinforcing effects of the drug with antagonists. Additionally, the substitution of socially approved reinforcers should be accomplished if the patient is to remain drugfree.

According to Wikler (1965), this two-factor theory of addiction draws support from several sources. First, the quest for euphoria as an explan-ation for maintenance of the drug habit is unlikely because of the rapid development of tolerance to this effect; for example after the initial effect subsequent "highs" never achieve the same effect, even with increased dosage. Second, the fear of abstinence is not totally realistic, since addicts sometimes withdraw themselves relatively painlessly either by a gradual reduction of drug dosage or substitution of and subsequent withdrawal from methadone (Wikler, 1952; 1953). Third, being "hooked" provides the addict with reinforcement from his peers and prevents boredom because of the sustained activity necessary to obtain drugs (Wikler, 1952; 1965). Addiction provides clearly attainable goals insofar as daily activities re-quired for a continuous supply of narcotics are defined.

Important support for the conditioning approach proposed by Wikler comes from the work of O'Brien and his associates, in their demonstration of conditioned narcotic withdrawal responses in humans (O'Brien, O'Brien, Mintz, and Brady, 1975; O'Brien, Testa, O'Brien, Brady, and Wells, 1977). Essentially, evidence now exists to support Wikler's (1973) assertion that conditioned withdrawal response components include pairing of (a) pharmacological withdrawal with environmental cues, and (b) environmental stimuli with homeostatic mechanisms adapting to the onset of drug effects. Eventually, the environmental cues themselves come to elicit the withdrawal symptoms. Thus, a return by addicts to environments where they had previously used narcotics could result in the onset of withdrawal symptoms. Further support for conditioned abstinence was provided in a study by Sideroff and Jarvik (1980) who demonstrated that heroin addicts on methadone and completing a 14-day detoxification program, when shown a videotape of heroin-related stimuli, responded with increased levels of anxiety, depression, subjective craving, as well as increased heart rates and GSR responses. A control group showed no such changes.

Simple Learning Theory

Crowley (1972) also formulated a theory of drug addiction in terms of conditioning principles without atempting to delineate the underlying neural mechanisms to the extent that Wikler (1953, 1965, 1973) has done. The high degree of abuse potential of a narcotic such as heroin is derived from its properties as a "primary reinforcer." Heroin provides reinforcement in terms of a pleasurable subjective sensation almost immediately following injection. When reinforcement and operant behavior (in this case drug-taking) are in such close temporal proximity, the frequency of the behavior is likely to increase more rapidly than if the reinforcement were either reduced qualitatively or delayed in presentation. Crowley suggests that there are certain individuals who are more susceptible to heroin reinforcement than others, and who have come to believe, as a result of their past experiences that they cannot expect reinforcement from their environment. They seek forms of reinforcement more completely under the individual's control, such as that provided by the injection of heroin. On this basis narcotics have a high likelihood for abuse.

The principle of negative reinforcement, in which the termination itself of an aversive stimuli is reinforcing, also operates to increase the probability of continued drug abuse. The abstinence syndrome is clearly aversive and the successful and immediate termination of this condition by taking additional drugs reinforces the drug-taking behavior. Crowley (1972) notes that narcotics also probably act to reduce sensitivity to aversive environmental stimuli, thus providing an additional source of reinforcement.

A third phenomenon, that of secondary reinforcement, also operates to increase the likelihood of drug-taking behavior. The changes in an individual's behavior as a result of taking a drug may prove to be desirable to the user. These behavioral changes are both drug specific and dose dependent. For example, narcotics may reduce aggressive impulses or facilitate social interaction, while a drug such as alcohol may lower inhibitions. The more desirable these drug-induced behavioral changes appear to the user, the greater the likelihood that they will act as secondary reinforcers. Previously neutral objects, such as the syringe used to inject heroin, may also acquire reinforcing properties as a result of association with the primary reinforcing qualities of heroin.

Crowley (1972) supports Wikler's hypothesis that withdrawal can become conditioned so that withdrawal-like symptoms are evoked by previously neutral stimuli associated with actual withdrawal. ". . . [O]bjects or events regularly associated with an unconditioned aversive state would develop conditioned aversive properties" (p. 55). Such a process would constitute secondary negative reinforcement to the extent that the termination of this conditioned aversive state by further injection of narcotics would be reinforcing. Crowley notes that all four types of reinforcement mentioned earlier (primary, secondary, negative, and secondary negative) are operative in narcotics addiction. No other drug has as many reinforcing properties as heroin and this explains its extremely high abuse/addiction potential.

Drive Theory

Bejerot (1972) also attempted to explain addiction in terms of learning theory as an artificially induced drive. This hypothesis is based on the work of Olds (1962), which indicated that rats would stimulate themselves (operant behavior) to the point of exhaustion when an electrode had been implanted in the hypothetical pleasure center of the hypothalamus. Bejerot believed this corresponded to addiction phenomena in that "addiction may be considered as an artificially induced drive developed through chemical stimulation of the pleasure center" (p. 842). In principle, a certain amount of narcotics (as yet undetermined) administered over a given period would be sufficient for the development of drug dependence in any individual. The stronger and more pleasurable the drug effects, the more rapidly actual addiction develops. This process is based on the pleasure-pain principle which Bejerot feels is the "primary biological steering mechanism." Addiction "short circuits" the pleasure-pain principle by allowing the individual unlimited access to gratification ·through direct hypothalamic stimulation. Antecedent personality disturbance, a necessary predisposing factor in several other theories, is unnecessary for the development of addiction as a chemically induced drive (Bejerot, 1972). Addiction itself is not a symptom of an underlying psychological condition, but is a "deeply rooted morbid condition that [is] characterized by [its] own dynamics of development" (p. 842). As such, it is a purely biological phenomenon.

During the process of addiction the individual passes through an initial stage in which drug-taking behavior is still within his control. Once the individual has lost this voluntary control, he has entered the stage of dependence wherein drug craving has become an expression of an acquired drive. Bejerot feels the addict wants to rid himself of the legal, financial, and social complications of his addiction without ever actually relinquishing the source of his pleasure (i.e., heroin).

Peer-group Learning Theory

Paschke, (1970) attempted to integrate sociological observations of the importance of peergroup influence on individual behavior in his "learning theory-peer-group model" of the addiction cycle. His approach is derived from Hullian theory in that drug-using behavior is learned and is subject to habit strengths which increase through repetition and reward.

The initial decision to experiment with drugs can be schematized on an "approach-avoidance gradient." The individual perceives certain advantages of taking drugs at any given point in time that increase the approach tendency. However, the response of taking a drug is of minimal habit strength because such behavior has not been engaged in previously. This low position in the response hierarchy operates in the direction of avoidance. Further factors that would reduce the likelihood of engaging in drug-taking behavior might be fear of the consequences, and moral reservations. The incentive of curiosity and the desire for peer-group approval will interact with these factors to produce approach, so that the potential user resolves the approach-avoidance conflict in favor of taking the drug.

If the first experience with narcotics is rewarded by social and physical pleasure, the act of taking drugs is reinforced. Such behavior is therefore more likely to recur, with habit strength increasing each time drug-taking is repeated and rewarded.

In addition, the development of tolerance and the experience of withdrawal as unpleasant provide additional motivation for maintenance of the drug habit. The addict begins to use drugs in order to avoid withdrawal as well as for production of pleasurable physical sensations. The act of taking drugs has come to be reinforced because it allows the addict to avoid the unpleasant symptoms of withdrawal.

> By virtue of fractionated anticipatory responses . . . the individual learns to be sensitive to internal body cues of oncoming withdrawal effects well in advance of the actual illness effects. [Paschke, 1970, p. 75]

Continued administration of narcotics at more closely spaced intervals ensures that the addict will not experience withdrawal effects.

When an individual actively undergoes withdrawal and remains drug-free for some time, the habit strength of drug-taking behavior decays over the period of abstinence. However, upon reintroduction of the stimuli previously associated with drug-taking, habit strength tends to increase thereby increasing drive. The cycle of addiction is reinitiated in this manner and accounts for the phenomenon of relapse following a drugfree period.

The principal assumption underlying this model is that peer-group norms are transmitted to an individual through the consistent reward of conforming behavior. Both initial and continued drug use are based on membership in a peer group that approves of and is involved in drugtaking. Given these conditions, the social incentives for taking drugs are obvious and will vary with the individual's perceived value of group membership. The theory of cognitive dissonance further suggests that if group membership is highly valued, the pressure on the individual to conform to the group's behavioral norms will be strong. The group for which drug-taking behavior is normative reinforces conformity by alternatively providing support to and approval of the individual who takes drugs. Such intragroup processes have clearly defined implications for relapse. Following a period of abstinence, the former addict is often unable to join peer groups that are normatively different with respect to drug use. Habit strength of drug-taking is once again increased as the former addict rejoins his old peer group and pressures to conform reactivate the addiction cycle. In a learning theory-peer group model of drug addiction, individual pathology is not a prerequisite for the development of addiction.

METABOLIC DEFICIENCY THEORY

Dole and Nyswander (1967) also have proposed a tentative model of heroin addiction, the impetus for which was derived from the unexpected degree of success with a methadone maintenance program in New York. The majority of their patients received stabilization doses of methadone exclusively. Although ancillary services such as psychotherapy were available on demand for each patient, these were not utilized and few patients exhibited any problems that the authors felt might have been treated by these services. Nearly 70% of their patients were either back in school or legally employed 6 months following implementation of the maintenance program. This is a particularly noteworthy achievement, since almost all these patients had previous criminal records associated with their addiction problems. Dole and Nyswander raised the question of how these patients on methadone were apparently able to cope with reality in the absence of the euphorogenic effects of heroin which, according to traditional psychological theories of addiction, facilitate a desired escape from reality. The authors suggested that perhaps prior research on the addictive personality has propagated confusion regarding the distinction between a causal factor in addiction and a consequence of addiction. Furthermore personality traits such as sociopathy, previously attributed to addicts, may actually be consequences of addiction and the high cost of maintaining a habit in a society where heroin can only be obtained illegally. The conclusions on which traditional psychological theories of addiction are based may themselves be spurious because they are derived from studies of confirmed addicts. It is therefore confusing to attempt retrospective separation of those traits that may be causally related to addiction liability and those that are an outgrowth of addiction. Dole and Nyswander found that when the craving for heroin was eliminated by methadone, all the antisocial acts previously exhibited by their patients disappeared.

Strongly implied in Dole and Nyswander's (1967) observation that traditional psychotherapeutic techniques are often unsuccessful in the treatment of addiction is the conviction that psychogenic theories do not adequately explain addiction phenomena. If such theories were based on accurate assessment of the causal factors relative to addiction and the addict was actually motivated by a need to escape the stress of coping with reality, Dole and Nyswander suggest that such predisposing tendencies would be exacerbated during prolonged drug abuse. However, they found the reverse to be true of their methadone patients. On the basis of psychiatric evaluations, they concluded that the majority of these patients exhibited modes of coping with reality that fell within the normal behavior range (Dole and Nyswander, 1967).

Dole and Nyswander (1967) offer an alternative explanation. They propose that the real basis of narcotics addiction is an unspecified metabolic deficiency. This neurologic susceptibility mediates addiction in a manner analogous to that of the addictive personality construct. Initial experimentation with drugs arises from normal curiosity and is not based on individual psychopathology. However, in the individual suffering from this neurologic susceptibility, there is an altered response to the initial effects of narcotics so that euphoria is produced instead of nausea and other aversive side effects often reported in first experiences with heroin. Methadone, in alternatively correcting this metabolic deficiency, allows the addict to lead a normally productive life by eliminating his other drug-seeking behavior. Dole and Nyswander support their hypothesis by noting the apparent ease with which their patients were able to return to school or work once they were stabilized on methadone. Furthermore, they propose a redefinition of successful outcome in drug treatment programs to focus on a return to productive life rather than remaining drug-free.

SOCIOLOGIC THEORIES

On the basis of personal interview data obtained from 60 to 70 opiate addicts, Lindesmith (1947) attempted to construct a theory of opiate addiction that would explain the greater likelihood of certain individuals to become addicts. Lindesmith suggests that theories focusing on the presence of personality defects which predispose to addiction, such as the desire to escape from life, and the predominantly psychopathic classification of addicts are inadequate. Particularly in the case of predisposing personality defects, Lindesmith (1947) states that he can find no evidence in support of such a theory. Addiction is not a symptom of maladjustment.

> . . . [T]he question of the addict's normality or abnormality is considered irrelevant . . . addiction appears . . . as the unavoidable product of a sequence of events and processes which could be evoked in any individual provided only that certain specific conditions are met. [p. 174]

Lindesmith (1938) also criticizes theories similar to Ausubel's (1961, 1964) in which the euphorogenic properties of opiates are causally related to the development of addiction. He observes that although the initial effects in the nonaddicted person are euphoric, this condition is reversed as tolerance develops. Once this stage is reached, the addict begins to need drugs simply to feel "normal," as opposed to "subnormal" or "supernormal." Once opiates cease to produce pleasure, their use must be continued to avoid pain. Lindesmith (1938) believes this reversal of effect explains the "seductiveness" of opiates. Opiates are useful because of their ability to facilitate a normal or more desirable state in individuals suffering from depression, anxiety, and fatigue.

The initial effects consist largely of a general dulling of sensibilities accompanied by a pleasant though not sensational . . . state of mind which is characterized by freedom from pain and worry. . . . [p. 24]

Lindesmith's theory (1938, 1947) is composed of a three-stage process of addiction including (a) recognition of dependence on drugs, (b) a concomitant restructuring of the self-concept to include this recognition, and (c) a preoccupation with drugs and assimilation into the addict culture. An essential requirement for this redefinition is the experience of withdrawal followed by the recognition that the abstinence symptoms are due to the absence of opiates. The further use of opiates to relieve this withdrawal distress cements the drug-taking behavior pattern as the addict becomes increasingly sensitive to impending withdrawal symptoms.

Initial drug use is related to both the availability of opiates and to peer-group normative behavior. The individual often begins taking a drug for a variety of reasons: alleviation of pain, production of pleasure, or enhancement of sociability—reasons which, Lindesmith (1947) points out, are different and distinct in motivation from those for which he continues taking drugs once he has recognized that he is dependent upon them.

The casual way in which the drug was first used may be compared to the manner in which a child sometimes eats candy simply because he enjoys its taste, without any thought of ultimate consequences. [p. 78]

The element of compulsion in opiate use is absent in the early stages of the addictive process, as evidenced by the user's lack of concern regarding an uninterrupted future supply of drugs. The development of subsequent preoccupation with a continuous supply arises from the experience and true understanding of withdrawal. The initial user cannot conceive of himself as an addict, nor does he really believe that withdrawal exists or that it will happen to him. This belief in his own omnipotence allows him to become careless. Lacking deterrents such as an expensive habit or the discomfort associated with the development of tolerance, the initiate has little motivation for abandoning drug use. By the time he recognizes the imminence of both complications, it is too late to avoid withdrawal. The process of becoming an addict commences with the discovery that the discomfort he feels during abstinence is due to the absence of opiates in his system. Once withdrawal is experienced and opiates are used to relieve it, the addict realizes he is "hooked." "The knowledge or ignorance of the meaning of withdrawal distress and the use of opiates thereafter determines whether or not the individual will become addicted" (p. 69). The availability of opiates during the experience of withdrawal strongly influences the likelihood of use to alleviate this discomfort.

The experience of avoiding withdrawal by further narcotic injections results in the addict's recognition that he is "supported" by the drug. He realizes that his "normalcy" is related to and dependent upon the presence of opiates. Lindesmith feels addicts have a fantastic belief in the potency of opiates that contributes to the escalation of drug abuse. Once the drug has become indispensable to the addict, he learns to react to all stressful situations with the drug-seeking behavior originally elicited only by withdrawal. Drugs are taken to alleviate any and all forms of distress when the addict discovers he can endure everything that goes wrong in his life more easily if he is on drugs.

The addict's tendency to increase each successive dose of narcotics arises from his increased awareness of and sensitivity to withdrawal symptoms. Once withdrawal itself has been experienced, the earliest signs of abstinence, magnified as expectations of future discomfort, become motivators of drug use. The addict now takes the drug at shorter and shorter intervals to avoid symptoms he imagines to be imminent, and the effect (assessed by comparing before-and-after injections states) is less than he anticipated (Lindesmith, 1947). This progression, combined with the ability of the body to adapt physiologically to a given amount of drug, leads to rapid dose increments. The size of a given opiate dose is therefore a function of both the amount necessary to stave off withdrawal and the additional amount the addict believes necessary to remain normal once he realizes that he is hooked.

Having learned to value the physical impact of the drug for its symbolic significance [security against withdrawal], he may strive to enhance this symbol quantitatively. As a result, he creates the illusion that he feels well. [Lindesmith, 1947, p. 85]

Lindesmith (1947) believes that the phenomenon of addiction can only occur in an organized society because such a phenomenon depends heavily on the traditional symbols and attitudes of a culture that are transmitted through language. As an individual assimilates his experiences by conceptualizing them in terms of societal categories, the process of becoming an addict involves an essentially linquistic transformation.

It is through the use of the social symbols of language in conversation with himself and with others that the personality changes involved in becoming an addict are initiated and carried out. The individual, when he uses the symbols which society provides him, also assumes the attitudes appropriate to those symbols when he applies them to himself. [Lindesmith, 1947, p. 166].

In this context the issues of causality in drug addiction become very complex. Lindesmith (1947) believes the ability to perceive how one feels and to relate this effect to having taken a drug requires a complex learning process, as does the equally essential recognition of an association between the physical discomfort experienced during withdrawal and the removal of drugs from the body.

Lindesmith (1938, 1947) explains the high incidence of relapse among opiate addicts in terms of his three-stage theory of addiction. He believes the addict sincerely wants to be cured and is not motivated by a desire simply to reduce the size of his habit or to restore the original euphorogenic experience, as other authors have stated (e.g., Rado, 1933). Once the addict has come to recognize his dependence on the drug and to perceive himself as an addict, there is a concurrent recognition that his drug-related behaviors are widely condemned. To the extent that he has internalized negative cultural attitudes toward addicts, societal pressure will motivate him to seek a cure. However, once withdrawal sets in and serves to separate him from the social order, he is motivated only by the physical craving to alleviate his distress. The struggle to quit in which the addict repeatedly fails further strengthens his self-identification as an addict.

Lindesmith (1938, 1947) suggests that the process of relapse is subtle and the factors contributing to it are insidious. Few former addicts intentionally plan to use enough of the drug to become readdicted. Both the smallness of the dose required to reexperience pleasurable feelings and the fact that withdrawal is not immediately experienced with intermittent use tend to confirm the former addict's rationalization that he won't be hooked. Other factors that tend to produce relapse include external circumstances, such as having friends who are addicts, the availability of drugs, having been labeled an addict and experiencing the associated loss of status, and being unable to obtain a job as a result of this stigmatization. The daily routine involved in obtaining drugs is very hard to abandon, as there is often no immediate substitute motivation for living. Attitudes formed during the process of addiction, such as a fantastic belief in the drug's potency, persist after "cure" and tend to incline toward relapse.

A wide range of criticisms have been leveled at Lindesmith's (1938, 1947) theory of opiate addiction, some of which center around methodologic flaws. Many of Lindesmith's conclusions are based on the personal interview data collected from 60 to 70 addicts and are clearly subject to reservations regarding the validity of self-report techniques in this population. This reflects the widespread assumption about the unreliability of information obtained from addicts. In addition, the fact that addiction is based on cognitive processes unique to man has been cited by Miller (1969) as eliminating the possibility of studying the addiction process with infrahuman subjects.

Deviance Theory and Anomie

Several authors have outlined general theories of deviance and anomie that have been applied to the phenomenon of drug addiction. The principal support for and interest in the formulation of these theories derives from the field of sociologic investigation where group processes and social learning provide the primary foci.

Deviance Theory

Deviance refers to a socially defined standard of behavior such that a given act of behavior is labeled deviant only in reference to societal norms. In this definition, norms ". . .refer to those shared expectations or standards of appropriateness upon which members of social groups can rely for the orderly regulation of social behavior." (Jessor, Graves, Hanson, and Jessor, 1968, p. 25).

Rotter (1954) suggested a social learning theory in which behavior occurs as a result of a selection/decision-making process in which alternative behaviors are evaluated as to their likelihood of leading to a valued goal in any given situation. Two factors influence this selection: (a) the expectation that the chosen behavior will lead to a given outcome and (b) the value placed on that outcome. ". . .[D]eviant behavior occurs when the expectation of its maximizing valued goal attainment or preferred outcomes is higher than that for conforming behavior" (Jessor et al, 1968, p. 42). The presence of antecedent psychopathology is irrelevant.

Deviance is goal-directed learned behavior for seeking success or for coping with failure. When conforming behavior has failed to achieve the desired goals, alternative behaviors will be explored, some of which will probably be deviant. Specifically with reference to drug use, valued goals exist that are both direct consequences and symbolic implications of its use. The direct outcomes are related to the pharmacologic effects of narcotics such as reduction of anxiety or fear, and euphoria. The symbolic outcomes refer to peer-group status, a sense of belonging engendered by the shared experience of drug use, and feelings of power.

Merton (1957) introduced the concept of "opportunity structure," which is particularly relevant to the choice of deviant behavior, and refers to the socially structured, institutionalized, legitimate means of access to desired goals. In the United States, however, the institutionalized channels of access to these goals are unevenly distributed among the various strata of society, with the lower socioeconomic components having fewer opportunities to utilize socially prescribed routes. This limited access to legitimate means to cultural goals exerts a force toward deviant alternative means of achieving these goals. "It is the *disjunction* between culturally induced high aspirations and socially structured obstacles to realization of these aspirations which is held to exert distinct pressure for deviant behavior" (Merton, 1957, p. 174).

Cloward and Ohlin (1960) propose a modification of this concept, the "differential opportunity structure," in which the individual is in both the legitimate and the illegitimate opportunity structures simultaneously. The delinquent response will vary to the extent that illegitimate means are available and legitimate means are limited.

Anomie

The normative structure of a society constitutes the culturally defined acceptable means to strive for these goals. Social norms serve to regulate individual behavior and are necessary to insure the stability of a society. Norms determine both which goals are valued and the means by which these goals are to be achieved. Durkheim (1951) referred to the breakdown of these regulations as "anomie." From a slightly different perspective, Merton (Jessor et al, 1968) suggested that the "value-access disjunction" contributes to the tendency toward deviance and to the state of anomie by putting stress on the normative structure as it fails to provide legitimate means for large segments of society. In this way norms necessarily become less authoritative, thereby contributing to anomie. Furthermore, the degree of anomie will be related to the degree of disadvantage within the opportunity structure (Merton, 1957). This idea has been modified slightly by Jessor et al (1968) who suggest that conforming behavior is unsuccessful in achieving desired goals in some situations for a certain group of individuals, particularly those occupying socially disadvantaged positions. It is this condition in which the failure of conformity creates a situation in which deviant behaviors are selected despite the likelihood of societal censure or punishment.

Jessor et al (1968) propose that the social control structure relative to (a) the opportunity to learn deviance, (b) the opportunity to understand the nature and probability of sanctions, and (c) the opportunity to perform deviant acts will affect the incidence of deviant behavior. An additional contributory factor to anomie is membership in a group that has an alternative normative structure, for example, a drug-taking subculture. To the extent that the individual observes norms being broken successfully and without negative sanctions, the validity of those norms will be questioned. For the drug experimenter, observation of peer-group members engaging in drug use unaccompanied by either arrest or rapid physical and psychologic deterioration which the experimenter has been led to believe are imminent, results in doubt regarding the validity of norms proscribing drug use. The opportunity to learn deviance and to observe its consequences is related to Sutherland's proposal (Bloch and Geis, 1965) that deviance occurs as a result of excessive criminal association in comparison with noncriminal association. To the extent that the individual perceives similarities between himself and criminal role models, assumption of deviant behavior in other areas will occur. Concurrently, the effectiveness of social sanctions regarding deviant behavior depends on the degree to which an individual's behavior will be regulated by the group, and is determined both by the value placed on group membership and the extent to which the individual is a group member. The opportunity to engage in deviant acts, particularly drug use, is salient to the extent of occurrence of such behavior. Greater access to drugs, less supervision by authority, and greater anonymity in urban areas all contribute to the opportunity for deviant, drug-related behavior and to the ineffectiveness of social controls among this group.

The adequacy of anomie theory as an explanation of drug addiction has been criticized by Lindesmith and Gagnon (1964). The authors pointed out that there is a major problem with definitions of deviance insofar as the concept of deviance is relative and depends upon the context of group membership. Specifically, drug-taking behavior is not considered deviant by some groups, in different cultures, and under certain circumstances (e.g., medically prescribed use).

Lindesmith and Gagnon (1964) question the premise that anomie is a contributing factor to drug addiction. In order for this to be the case, a condition of anomie must precede drug use. Historically, however, the drug addict has not always come from the lower socioeconomic class, minority group, or urban background considered to be conducive to anomie. In the nineteenth century, the addict was often female, older, from the middle or upper classes, and nondelinquent. It was not until the introduction of legal sanctions in the Harrison Act of 1914 that narcotics use became prevalent in delinquent and criminal populations. The authors feel that anomie theory cannot explain this difference in the population.

An alternative explanation is offered by Lindesmith and Gagnon (1964) for this shift in demographic characteristics of the addict. They suggest that making addiction illegal and cutting off legal access to drugs created an illicit traffic in narcotics. In order to obtain opiates one had to have connections with individuals engaged in illegal activities. This factor of differential access to drugs ensures that the highest concentration of addicts will occur among the lower/criminal classes who have the easiest access to supply. The authors noted that in countries where there is legal access to drugs, the distribution patterns of addiction more closely resemble those of the United States in the nineteenth century—addicts are older, more likely to be female, and there is little association between addiction and crime. However, if a relationship exists between the national control policy and the distribution patterns of addiction, a change in this policy should alter the addict population but should have no effect on conditions of anomie. Lindesmith and Gagnon (1964) proposed that availability is the relevant factor affecting incidence, and that changes in the opportunity to use drugs and not changes in anomie account for the shift in the addict population. The high rate of addiction among physicians and the improbability that this group as a whole is more subject to anomie are cited in support of their interpretation. The authors suggest that anomie theory may have relevance for the addict population in the urban ghetto, where limited access to legitimate means of making money may have motivated some individuals to assume the high risks involved in selling drugs for the high profits possible. However, both anomie and the increased availability of drugs in the urban ghetto must be taken into account in attempting to explain the shift in the distribution of addiction.

As mentioned previously, Cloward and Ohlin have modified Merton's suggestion that the addict finds legitimate means to success blocked, has inhibitions against illegitimate means, and therefore retreats into drug use. Cloward and Ohlin (1960) suggest the "double failure" hypothesis, wherein the addict has failed at both legitimate and illegitimate means and has removed himself from competition through the abuse of drugs. Lindesmith and Gagnon (1964) believe these theories are very limited in applicability. Neither theory is an adequate explanation of the high incidence of addiction among physicians or of the characteristics of the pre-1914 addict. There appears to be no empirical evidence to support the pre-addiction double failure hypothesis. On the contrary, the authors agree that in order to support an expensive daily habit, the addict must be at least moderately successful at stealing.

. . . [I]t is still necessary to distinguish sharply between those who are failures because they are addicts and those who are addicts because they are failures. [Lindesmith and Gagnon, 1964, p. 177]

According to Merton, and Cloward and Ohlin, addiction is a form of retreat precipitated by inner conflict.

. . . resulting from the discrepancy between aspirations and goals which eliminates the inner problem or conflict by a renunciation of both the culturally prescribed goals and the means of achieving them. [Lindesmith and Gagnon, 1964, p. 178]

A direct contradiction to this interpretation would seem to be the necessity of dealing intensely and continuously with the world in order to support an expensive habit (Lindesmith and Gagnon, 1964). The pharmacologic effects of opiates and the onset of tolerance ensure that a retreat will be short-lived.

Finally, Lindesmith and Gagnon (1964) suggest that while anomie is sometimes a cause of addiction, addiction itself generates anomie. As addiction progresses, the gap between goals and the means of achieving them widens, disjunction increases and engenders feelings of alienation and despair.

Social Deviance

Hill (1962) attempted to delineate empirically the concepts of deviance and, to a lesser degree, of anomie on the basis of Minnesota Multiphasic Personality Inventory (MMPI) profiles. In a study of the development of narcotics addiction from a review of the literature and his own experience with the MMPI, Hill concluded that the only characteristic addicts had in common was social deviance—or preferably "conduct disorder"—which antedates the onset of addiction and acts as a causal factor.

Four main factor profiles of social deviance were delineated by the MMPI: (*a*) *undifferentiated psychopath* exhibiting an elevated psychopathic deviate (*Pd*) scale, no neurotic or schizoid tendencies, and a marked absence of self-criticism; (*b*) *primary psychopath* exhibiting, in addition to an elevated *Pd* scale, an elevated hypomania scale, strong aggressive and antisocial behaviors, and a complete absence of guilt feelings; (*c*) *neurotic psychopath*, characterized as an "inadequate" social deviant; and (*d*) *schizoid*, exhibiting classical retreatist modes of adaptation, strong depression, and paranoid features. All these profiles were characterized by an elevated *Pd* scale which Hill (1962) believes has the potential for distinguishing between pathology which is personal or idiosyncratic, and social pathology. This distinction is central to the formulation of an hypothesis of narcotics addiction based on the socially deviant personality.

Social behavior involves those responses to a given situation that are shared by members of society, which is itself structured by and composed of these shared responses. Social deviance, on the other hand, is defined and evaluated with respect to these shared responses, or norms, of the dominant middle class in the United States. The social deviant does not possess these shared responses which have been labeled appropriate and acceptable by the dominant proportion of society.

Four factors characteristic either of the social deviant or of the narcotic addict interact to initiate addiction. First, those characteristics of the social deviant that make him vulnerable to addiction are often produced in a deprived urban slum environment which provides easy access to drugs and wider exposure to drug-using models. The second major factor in narcotics addiction is the lack of social controls or shared responses in the social deviant that determine the acceptability of drug experimentation. The drug user comes from a family in which there has been a marked absence of internalization of social controls. Often, parents have made inconsistent and unrealistic demands which have precluded the development of mature and independent behavior patterns during adolescence. The social deviant lacks "counteranxiety" or guilt which might restrain him from further experimentation with drugs. Counteranxiety is evoked by either the performance or anticipated performance of an act that would probably result in societal sanctions, and thus acts as a social control. The low level of counteranxiety in the social deviant makes it doubtful that he will view continued drug use as unacceptable behavior. Hill (1962) considers the social deviant's acceptability of deviant behavior the most essential factor in addiction.

> . . . [T]he degree of social deviance exhibited by an individual is a measure of the effectiveness of his social controls, and the degree of such effectiveness is determined by the development of preference and inhibitions which are held in common by the larger society. [p. 571]

The third causal factor in addiction is the susceptibility of the social deviant to desiring immediate rewards. Lacking the ability to delay gratification, the deviant is unable to find satisfaction in or reinforcement from his daily life to prevent him from seeking alternatives to acceptable behavior. The interaction of few social controls and lack of daily satisfactions result in a predisposition toward drug-produced euphoria, which is more acceptable to and more easily induced in the social deviant (Hill, 1962). This euphoria may take the form of relief from boredom or anxiety, frustration, and pain. As support for this interpretation, Hill (1962) cited the self-reported, initially pleasurable experiences of addicts with narcotics.

The final factor contributing to narcotics addiction derives from the pharmacologic effects of any given drug. The use of drugs, and particularly of opiates, allows the social deviant to alter his personal state to a more desirable one. His preestablished individual response hierarchies can be rearranged through the use of opiates, so that a weak desired behavior may be produced more often when under the influence of drugs. These response hierarchy rearrangements are drug specific, notably the opiate-induced decrease in emotional lability, aggression, and conflict. Certainly this drug effect provides further reinforcement for continued drug use.

It should be obvious that many of the criticisms which have been made of deviance theory and anomie can also be made of Hill's (1962) integration. There is ample evidence with which to question the essential role that Hill attributes to euphoria as a factor in addiction. As was noted in Chapter 5 and commented upon by many investigators, initial use of narcotics often results in aversive effects rather than in the uniform production of euphoria, even in those individuals who have subsequently become addicted. Also, this theory seems unable to adequately explain addiction in physicians and the characteristics of narcotic addicts of the nineteenth century (Lindesmith and Gagnon, 1964). Difficulties in measuring counter-anxiety as a social control are encountered, although Hill (1962) suggested this area deserves further investigation. It must be noted that Hill considers his hypothesis but "one formulation of the development of addiction [at times based on] unsystematically collected clinical data and on speculation" (p. 562). Such an hypothesis was intended to generate research possibilities rather than to serve as a definitive explanation.

FAMILY THEORY

Stanton and his colleagues have attempted to explain heroin addiction, and drug abuse in general within a context reflecting familial and interpersonal issues. As presented by Stanton (1978; 1979; 1980), addiction is seen as a *symptom* arising within an interpersonal context and bearing *meaning* for both the symptomatic individual and those within his *system*. Thus, homeostatic and feedback mechanisms are involved, accounting for the relative failure that results from attempts to change the individual without regard to the context within which he functions.

According to Stanton (1980), there are a number of contributing factors to drug abuse, when it is viewed as a family phenomenon: (a) *Traumatic Loss.* Noting the often observed relationship between immigration and parent-child cultural disparity on the one hand and addiction on the other, Stanton suggests that the immigrant family is under stress. In part this stress reflects the difficulties of coping with the new environment, and in part, the "loss" of the family left behind. As a result, immigrant parents may tend to depend significantly upon their children for support, emotional or otherwise, and become terrified by the individuation process in adolescence. Similarly, non-immigrant families of drug abusers show more early deaths or tragic losses than expected, leading to the possibility that ". . . the high rate of death, suicide, and self-destruction among addicts is actually a family phenomenon in which the addict's role is to die, or to come close to death, as part of the family's attempt to work through the trauma of the loss . . . " (p. 149); (b) *Fear of Separation.* Stanton notes the strong fear of separation on the part of addict families, and the resultant dependency and lack of readiness to assume responsibility on the part of addicts. Further, when addicts show success at work, in treatment, or elsewhere, crises invariably occur in their families that lead to failure on the part of the addict and the resultant resolution of the family crisis. Thus, both the family and the addict are *interdependent* in maintaining family closeness. (c) *Addict-Family Context.* A number of studies by himself and others are cited by Stanton to support a "close family tie" hypothesis for addicts, in comparison to non-addict peers. (d) *Family Structure.* The "typical" addict family structure of intense involvement on the part of one parent, usually of the opposite sex, and distant, punitive, or absent presence on the part of the other parent, is seen by Stanton as resulting in the (future) addict becoming "stuck" at adolescence and becoming involved in a repetitive failure to successfully individuate. The reason underlying this failure is based on the parental panic on the possible loss of a child who has served a pathological, but necessary, role for the communication by his parents with each other.

Stanton (1978, 1980) lists a number of factors which tend to differentiate the drug abuser's family from other families in which a pattern of overinvolvement by one parent and distance/absence by the other occurs. These include: (a) high frequencies of chemical dependency across generations, particularly for males, and other addictive-like behaviors, such as gambling, (b) primitive and direct expression of conflict, (c) the quality of parental behavior being "conspicuously unschizophrenic," (d) the presence of a peer group to retreat to following family conflict, thus reinforcing an illusion of independence, (e) greater presence of "symbiotic" maternal behaviors, (f) a greater frequency of untimely deaths and/or death themes, (g) a "pseudo-individuation" from the family, and (h) the greater incidence among offspring of immigrants, suggesting the importance of parent-child cultural disparity.

The model Stanton presents is clearly stated as homeostatic in nature, in which addiction is conceived of as a cyclical process usually involving the addict and two other persons, usually parents. Any threat to the equilibrium of this balanced, intimate, and interdependent interpersonal system results in the addict member focusing attention on himself by engagement in deviant acts. These acts serve a *protective* function in maintaining the *homeostatic* balance of the family. Stanton's theory is perhaps one of the most clearly articulated theories, and one which takes into account, in an explanatory fashion, more of the often disparate facts about the addict which have been reported in the literature. It also provides for more readily derivable elements of the intervention process than is the case with most other theories. Overall, in its scope and integral soundness, it is an impressive accomplishment.

Finally, the involvement of the family in the treatment of the heroin addict, while relatively recent (Stanton, 1979), seems to be firmly established as a recognized treatment modality. Coleman and Davis (1978) reported that a survey of over two thousand drug programs revealed that some 93 percent were providing at least some family services or family therapy to their clients.

PSYCHOANALYTIC THEORIES

In general, early psychoanalytic literature focused on the perceived relationship between drug abuse and the libido. One of Freud's few references to drug addiction was in a letter to Fliess in 1897 stating that addictions to morphine and to alcohol were simply substitutes for masturbation, which he considered to be the "primal addiction" (Freud, cited in Yorke, 1970). In 1898 Freud wrote that narcotics such as morphine serve as substitutes for sexual satisfaction, and that until it is possible to reestablish normal sexual functioning relapse following abstinence from narcotics is inevitable. It is interesting to note, particularly in light of his relative silence on the subject, that Freud was a heavy user of cocaine for 3 years, although there has been speculation about whether he actually was addicted to the drug.

Rado (1933), a well-known psychoanalyst, formulated a prototypical explanation of drug addiction utilizing principles of psychoanalytic theory. He perceived all drug addiction to be a single disease based on the ability of certain drugs to affect an individual's emotions in distressing situations. According to Rado, a drug with abuse potential can have two effects: the reduction of pain and the production of euphoria. Thus the addict takes drugs because they are pleasurable and provide relief from characteristic tension. The potential addict is therefore characterized by a high degree of tension, an intolerance to pain, and is in a state of what Rado terms "tense depression." The individual experiencing this tense depression is especially susceptible to the effects of narcotics as a result of his overwhelming need to relieve his tension. "The role of the initial depression is to sensitize the patient for the pharmacogenic pleasure-effect" (p. 5), during which the individual experiences increased self-esteem and mood elevation when using narcotics. Rado (1933) believed that this subjective experience of elation was an ego reaction to the pleasure effect which develops in early childhood.

According to the analytic theory, as the child develops from a stage of narcissism in which his wishes have been immediately gratified to a stage where he must assume responsibility for coping with the environment, the ego begins to take over the function of sustaining the individual. Disturbance of this development results in impairment of the ego's ability to cope with reality at a later stage in life, and the original narcissistic state remains an ideal for the ego. Through the pharmacogenic elation provided by narcotics the ego is allowed to return to this narcissistic state, although there is concurrent disruption of ego functioning and destruction of the saliency of reality. ". . . this illness is a narcissistic disorder, a destruction through artificial means, of the natural ego organization" (Rado, 1933,

p. 9). As the drug effects wear off depression returns, made all the more acute by comparison with the preceding elation, and the addict then experiences a renewed craving for the drug. At this point the ego is under what Rado terms a "pharmacothymic regime," in which there is exclusive focus on the problem of depression, and the only certain means of combating this depression appears to be continued use of the narcotic.

Rado notes that the phenomenon of tolerance is an important factor in repeated drug-seeking behavior. As drug-taking continues, accompanied by the development of tolerance, the experience of elation becomes increasingly elusive. In addition, Rado suggests that a growing fear on the part of the addict that the drug will lose its powers of inducing elation gradually reduces the probability that the drug will actually be effective. A vicious cycle is established in which a reduction in subjective effect is experienced, the depression component becomes stronger, and anxiety results to further exacerbate the state of tension. Finally, pursuit of the drug becomes of paramount importance to the addict.

At this point in the cycle of addiction, the pharmacogenic pleasure effect supplants experience of and desire for sexual pleasure. In effect it becomes the sexual goal. In the sense that this pleasure is autoerotic (being both self-induced and sexual in nature) objects become unnecessary and irrelevant to this primary goal. Fort (1954) noted:

> Rado has pointed out that since the injection of a narcotic substance can be accomplished in a few seconds, this gives the pharmacological orgasm remarkable advantages over the complicated interpersonal orgasm. [p. 256]

The ego responds to this transformation with fears of castration (analogous to castration anxiety following the prototype of masturbation), but it is unable to relinquish drug use because it has become completely dependent on drug effects. This concomitant fear of castration further enhances the fear that the pleasure effect will diminish because the addict's investment in this effect has been doubled.

By this time, Rado (1933, 1963) believes the ego is under the control of masochism and the death instinct. Drug-related behaviors become increasingly self-destructive as social, familial, financial, and academic responsibilities are ignored. However, since the addict characteristically believes himself to be invulnerable, the ego remains under this pharmacothymic regime. At some point the drug fails to produce the essential pleasure effect and the "pharmacothymic crisis" of withdrawal occurs. Once the ego is denied elation, it is overcome by masochism and the individual focuses on the physical tortures of withdrawal. Rado (1933) believes only three outcomes following withdrawal are possible: (*a*) the individual goes through a drug free period for the sole purpose of resurrecting the effectiveness of the drug; (b) the individual succumbs to masochism and commits suicide, or (c) he descends into psychosis.

Savitt (1963) also focuses on the role of the ego in his formulation of an analytic theory of narcotic addiction. On the basis of clinical observations, Savitt believes all addicts are characteristically in a state of intolerable tension due originally to maternal neglect and lack of love, and to passive, ineffectual father figures. Federn (1972) confirms, on the basis of his clinical experience, that all individuals who resort to drug abuse have experienced a severe disappointment in a love object very early in their lives. The decisive factor in this failure of early object relations is a specific disappointment in the same-sex parent that occurs during the oedipal phase. Furthermore, Fort (1954) suggests that the predominance of over-protective, controlling, and indulgent mothers in conjunction with the lack of strong, masculine father figures among his heroin-addicted patients is causally related to the development of addiction. Mothers of these addicts fostered dependency and further prevented adequate masculine identity in their sons by severely criticizing the absent father. Strong underlying feelings of aggression against the mother, from which narcotics offered an escape, were also characteristic of these addicts. Savitt suggests that drugs provide a release from this tension in a fashion analogous to sleep in infancy, which follows the immediate gratification of the infant's needs. Addicts are extremely tense as a result of ambivalent feelings toward and dependency on their mothers and, therefore, experience insomnia. To the addict, sleep represents a cessation of anxiety and drugs serve to induce a sleeplike stupor. In contrast to Rado, who believes that the euphoria-producing characteristics of narcotics are of paramount importance, Savitt (1963) believes the drug-induced stupor analogous to sleep is the crucial factor in addiction.

Several additional features are usually present in the individual specifically susceptible to drug abuse. Savitt notes that the ego organization necessary for delay of gratification is absent in the addict. Lacking past experience in which needs are gratified despite delay, the ego becomes disorganized and the addict regresses to "primary processes" such as the search for immediate gratification. The immediacy of the subjective effect following the injection of narcotics contributes significantly to their appeal for individuals who are unable to delay gratification. Savitt (1963) further notes that addicts often have an archaic type of object relationship so that incorporation results in the total destruction of the object. The addict cannot experience love through the more "normal" channels of incorporation or introjection, and this increases the likelihood that the love object will be completely destroyed by the injection of narcotics. The development of tolerance is important in exacerbating this tendency toward immediate consumption, but it is not the salient factor. "It is only a complication, a secondary elaboration of the addiction" (p. 48). What is crucial to Savitt's theory is the addict's psychic need to fuse with the mother in an attempt to relieve his tension. The injection of heroin is analogous to "mother-breast-food" (Savitt, 1963). In the use of a hypodermic, Savitt (1963) sees a regressive wish to bypass oral gratification and to return to an even more primitive means of satisfaction. He speculates that this action represents a symbolic return to the fetal/umbilical stage involving primacy of vascular routes of sustenance. The addict thus imitates the fetal relationship with the mother through this form of instantaneous gratification. The injection of heroin releases tension and ego integrity is restored, but at an infantile stage where fusion with the mother is essential.

One additional feature of heroin addiction, the loss of sexual desire, functions as a motivationally desirable effect. Savitt notes that in his clinical experience intolerable incestuous desires were characteristic of all of his addict patients. Heroin, in eliminating sexual desire, further allows the addict to regress to a pregenital stage where the breast and food are of primary importance.

The role of the ego in the development of addictions is viewed in a less exclusively psychoanalytic fashion by Khantzian, Mack, and Schatzberg (1974). Although ego impairment is also a causal factor in heroin addiction in their model, the use of opiates is seen as a unique way of dealing with ordinary human problems. Addicts use drugs because they have failed to develop the usual adaptive defense mechanisms for dealing with stress and have substituted heroin use as a method of coping with a wide range of problems and of resolving conflicts. The pharmacologic effects of the opiates abet this substitution by influencing the emotional state of the addict in such a way that it is perceived as adaptive. Emotional distress is relieved and becomes manageable. The action of the drug serves to mask emotions and to "solve" problems in interpersonal relationships ". . . opiates provide a chemical buffer for dealing with various human interactions" (Khantzian et al, 1974, p. 163).

The rituals associated with heroin addiction and the addict subculture are significant insofar as the addict experiences a sense of belonging, often for the first time. Heroin addiction fills an emotional and personal vacuum, provides a daily goal where previously there was none, and eliminates the need for personal involvement.

Both societal and intrafamilial influences interact to produce ego impairment, so that the individual fails to develop the usual coping mechanisms and must later resort to drug use. Deprivation can lead to such ego impairment. Conversely, maternal overindulgence can have the same effect insofar as it reinforces dependency needs and denies opportunities to experience the world and to develop methods of coping independently with problems. In the addict, ego impairment is specifically related to functions of self-care, and it is the experience of deprivation/overindulgence which results in this failure to establish self-preservative functions in the ego. Khantzian et al (1974) believe the developmental crises faced by the addict are not unusual in themselves, but the fact that, as a result of ego impairment, the addict hasn't learned adaptive solutions with which to respond in a crisis sets him apart. Resorting to drugs in an effort to resolve problems further precludes the development of adaptive responses. Use of drugs eventually becomes the addict's characteristic way of dealing with the world and with his own emotions.

Khantzian (1982), more recently, presented a hypothesis concerning the specific appeal of opiates and how this appeal interacts with those vulnerabilities possessed by addicts. Noting that a major appeal of opiates is their anti-aggressive action, he suggested that addicts have had both life-long exposure to physical abuse, violence, sadism, and brutality on the one hand, and possess strong feelings of aggression and sadism on the other. The use of narcotics by these individuals presented for addicts an opportunity to escape from the dysphoria associated with anger, rage, and related feelings, thus allowing them to feel normal, calm, and relaxed. According to Khantzian, "Opiates reversed regressed ego-states by counteracting the disorganizing influences of aggression on the ego, helping addicts to feel and become more organized, and thus, better able to cope with life's demands and challenges" (p. 29).

PSYCHOSOCIAL THEORIES

Ausubel (1961) attempted to integrate both the psychologic and the sociologic theories of narcotic addiction in the belief that neither was sufficient in itself to explain the observed phenomena. Ausubel's psychosocial theory is based on the precept that both internal and external factors are inherent in addiction, and that each factor has precipitating or predisposing causes. The predisposing internal factors originate within the individual, while the precipitating external factors are essentially environmental. These interact in varying degrees so that the predominance of one factor will obviate the degree of effectiveness of the other factors necessary to result in addiction. The likelihood of relapse following a period of abstinence is also a function of the intensity of each of the causal factors.

The primary external precipitant factor is the availability of drugs. Ausubel believes the proliferation of narcotics in slum areas strongly influences the high incidence of narcotics addiction observed in these areas.

Community tolerance of drug use is another predisposing factor that might explain the differences in addiction incidence observed in populations with relatively equal exposure to drugs. Furthermore, the relationship of the individual to his primary social group will strongly influence his initial attitude toward drug use and also affect the probability of his continuing to use drugs once the experimental stage has passed. The relative status of his peers, the strength of the individual's need to belong, and therefore to conform to group norms, will affect the degree to which the individual adopts his peer-group values. Additionally, the peer-group reaction to the initial experimentation with drugs will affect the likelihood of further experimentation to the extent that the peer group is valued by the individual. Ausubel (1961) believes that all these external factors interact either to increase or decrease the likelihood of individual drug use if certain predisposing internal factors are present.

Internal factors resulting in a "differential susceptibility" to drug abuse interact with the above-mentioned external factors. Ausubel (1961, 1964) outlines three types of addiction which arise both from interrelated internal factors and from the pharmacologic properties of narcotics. First, the euphoria-producing properties of narcotics are responsible for addiction to the degree that they have adjustive value for the individual. In the process of addiction certain personality changes occur that are relatively permanent and exacerbate the tendencies responsible for initial drug-taking. A permanent change in personality occurs when the drive for euphoria replaces all other more socially adjustive drives and becomes the primary adjustive mechanism for the individual. Clearly, Ausubel perceives the occurrence of this change to depend upon both the euphoria-producing properties of the drug and on certain predisposing personality factors that he has classified as leading to three types of opiate addiction. In each of the three classes of addiction (primary, symptomatic, and reactive) adjustive value provided by the opiates serves as the basis for the classification. *Primary* addiction occurs as a function of the specific adjustive value of an opiate. *Symptomatic* addiction occurs only as a symptom of a behavior disorder. *Reactive* addiction results from the temporary adjustive value provided by opiates in stressful developmental situations.

Primary addiction comprises two subcategories of personality: the inadequate personality, and anxiety and reactive depression. The first is by far the more common and is characterized by a motivational deficiency which Ausubel calls "motivational immaturity." The individual who has failed to develop the motivational characteristics of normal adults seeks immediate gratification in the form of narcotics. Such a person, Ausubel (1961, 1964) observes, is characteristically irresponsible, passive, lacking in self-discipline and in the ability to delay gratification. These personality traits or internal predisposing factors originate in the nature of the parent-child relationship in one of three possible ways: (*a*) the overprotecting parent consistently denies the child the opportunity to act independently; (*b*) the underdominating parent never makes demands on the child for responsible actions, thus fostering the child's belief that he is privileged and not subject to the usual social sanctions; (*c*) the overdominating parent imposes unrealistic goals and standards of behavior on the child and invites rebellion when the child realizes he cannot meet these standards. Any one of these patterns of parent-child relationships may provide the basis for the development of an inadequate personality and, subsequently, for the development of primary addiction. Opiate use provides a specific adjustive function for the inadequate personality seeking an undemanding and pleasant environment. Narcotics tend to dull the individual's sensitivity to self-criticism while offering an immature adjustment to problems through immediate gratification, an increase in self-confidence, and a sense of omnipotence. The relief from immediate distress provided by opiates generalizes in such a way that use of narcotics becomes the predominant mode of dealing with any and all forms of stress. This pattern is further reinforced as the concurrent development of physical dependence ensures that opiate use must be continued to avoid withdrawal.

Anxiety and reactive depression are somewhat rarer than inadequate personality as a subcategory of primary addiction. Ausubel observes that such individuals have high aspirations coupled with low self-esteem, so that continued striving for unrealistic goals engenders feelings of inadequacy and anxiety. Opiate use offers specific adjustive value to the individual suffering from anxiety or reactive depression because it reduces responsiveness to stressful situations, thus reducing anxiety.

The second type of addiction, symptomatic addiction, ". . . occurs primarily as a nonspecific symptom in aggressive antisocial psychopaths" (Ausubel, 1964, p. 49). Such individuals have a history of delinquent behavior, lack adequate superego development, and use opiates primarily as an outlet for overwhelming antisocial tendencies.

In contrast, Ausubel suggests reactive addiction is a transitory developmental phenomenon occurring in essentially normally adjusted individuals as a temporary outlet for rebellious, defiant, and aggressive urges. Characteristically, this is a phase of adolescence in response to developmental pressures that often predominate in slum environments. Adolescents growing up in slums often have fewer socially acceptable outlets for their needs, and membership in drug-using peer groups is facilitated by both the greater availability of drugs in such areas and by greater community tolerance of drug use. Drug use provides entrance into and is supported by this peer group. The predisposing internal factor of adolescent defiance of traditional behavioral norms is enhanced and is reinforced by the peer group for which drug use becomes the vehicle for expression of these feelings. Such needs diminish as the adolescent matures and begins to focus on family and vocational responsibilities. Eventually drug-taking is no longer adjustive and is terminated.

Perhaps most importantly, Ausubel (1961, 1964) strongly emphasizes that in all cases of drug use the less specific adjustive value a narcotic has for an individual the less susceptible he will be to developing chronic patterns of addiction.

Buckman (1971) also focused on the role of adolescent conflicts in providing a basis for drug addiction in his psychosocial theory. He cites Berger and Porterfield (1969) as enumerating three reasons for drug use: (a) to be freed from personal problems and to achieve a sense of well-being; (b) to identify with a subculture: (c) to rebel against society and "establishment" restrictions. Buckman feels the personal motivations for drug use arise from intrapsychic conflicts which are especially acute during adolescence. These conflicts may focus on identity problems, dependency needs, sexuality, and hostility. Various components of society contribute significantly to the selection of drugs as the means chosen by the adolescent to cope with these conflicts. Buckman blames television and the pharmaceutical industry for exacerbating a feeling of pessimism about the state of the world, for enhancing the value of escape (TV, amusement, vacations, sleeping pills, etc.), for engendering a belief that one must use drugs to alleviate tension, to sleep, to be beautiful, and so on. Buckman says that ". . . the best way to persuade people to buy is to have the product promise to alleviate some of the sources of suffering and the feelings of inadequacy" (p. 99) .

He believes that during the period of adolescence, contemporary problems that are suddenly brought into focus appear insoluble. Concurrently, the disruption of family life and the prolonged period of dependence necessitated by the extended educational process combine to produce a high level of anxiety and a strong need for escape from these tensions. Buckman (1971) feels that adolescents are particularly susceptible to the lures of drug abuse because adolescent defense mechanisms are "brittle," and the continued use of drugs tends to dissolve ego defenses and to increase feelings of depersonalization in a self-perpetuating motivational cycle. Drugs further reduce the sense of personal isolation commonly experienced in adolescence by providing a clearly delineated subgroup of users to which one belongs only by virtue of using drugs. An additional motivation for drug use is based on the ability of drugs to allay anxiety and to provide an outlet for rebellious feelings in a manner similar to that described by Ausubel (1961, 1964) . Buckman also suggests that drug use tends to heighten the perpetual conflict between adolescents and the older generation, and becomes a further source of conflict, sense of isolation, and lack of direction. Feelings of aggression, hostility, and sexuality are suppressed by chronic heroin use, and thus an entire realm of typical adolescent conflicts is eliminated by ingestion of a single drug. "Prone to use heroin will be those already in physical and psychic pain and those who tend to cope with problems by withdrawal and oblivion" (Buckman, 1971, p. 101).

A METATHEORETICAL ANALYSIS: EXPOSURE VS. ADAPTIVE ORIENTATIONS

Alexander and Hadaway (1982) attempt to resolve the problems posed by the dilemma of "chaotic and bewildering" theory and research findings on heroin addiction by identifying two basically inconsistent orientations that pervade the literature. They identify the *exposure orientation*, reflective of the view that "opiate addiction is a condition that occurs when opiate drug use engenders a powerful tendency towards subsequent, compulsive use," and the *adaptive orientation,* in which "opiate addiction is an attempt to adapt to chronic distress of any sort through habitual use of opiate drugs" (p. 367). Certainly Alexander and Hadaway (1982) are able to muster a solid case for their adaptive orientation viewpoint. First, they demonstrate that exposure to opiates does not necessarily result in addiction by reviewing the relevant literature related to this issue. To support their position, Alexander and Hadaway cite work such as Zinberg's (1974) on nonaddictive opiate use. They also cite Robins' (1973) reports of low relapse rates to addiction among returned Vietnam veterans as being inconsistent with an exposure view. They do admit to the primacy of theory and data emphasizing metabolic changes (*e.g.*, Lindesmith, 1968; Goldstein, 1972) and conditioning (*e.g.*, Wikler, 1971; Wikler and Prescor, 1967), particularly the animal pharmacological studies, as supporting the exposure orientation. To support the adaptive orientation, Alexander and Hadaway (1982) call upon studies of familial distress (Coleman and Stanton, 1978), endorphin deficiency (Goldstein, 1976), and protective functions served by addiction, such as calming and reducing unpleasant affect and fear (Khantzian, Mack, and Schatzberg, 1974).

Admitting to the existence of problems which may impede acceptance of the adaptive orientation viewpoint, they consider each of the following four problems, suggesting answers for each. They are (a) failure of adaptive theories to explain the progressive, self-destructive nature of severe addiction; (b) the support for the adaptive viewpoint lying primarily in clinical, and thus anecdotal and retrospective data, rather than in quantifiable data; (c) the reluctance of psychologists to reject outmoded theoretical viewpoints; and (d) the failure to have demonstrated successful psychotherapy for the addictions.

The ideas and literature marshalled to support the adaptive view are impressive and this paper may prove to be one of the more important metatheoretical contributions to the understanding of heroin addiction. Whether one agrees with the arguments presented, this paper certainly deserves reading.

CHAPTER.8

Personality and Psychopathology in Heroin Addicts

Much of the search for the "type" of person who becomes an addict has been based upon tacit acceptance of the premise that particular types of persons become addicts. That is, persons who posses certain specific personality characteristics are often considered more likely to become addicts than persons not possessing these traits. This line of reasoning has raised a number of specific questions with regard to the addict. Is he, for instance, basically an inadequate person seeking escape from an environment with which he cannot cope, or is he an incorrigible sensation-seeker always searching for higher levels of stimulation? Or is he perhaps a disturbed individual who engages in drug abuse as an attempt to escape from, avoid, or resolve intrapsychic conflicts? All these characteristics have been ascribed to addicts at one time or another. This chapter aims to review the available evidence concerning personality traits and adjustment characteristics that have been postulated as characteristic of or empirically linked to heroin addiction, and will attempt to reach some conclusions about the current status of "the addictive personality hypothesis."

PSYCHOPATHOLOGY

Extent of Psychopathology Among Heroin Addicts

Research on the personality characteristics of narcotic addicts has generally revealed the presence of a significant degree of pathology. However, the types of disorders observed cover a wide range of psychopathologic diagnostic categories. Heroin addicts have been classified by various authors as neurotic, psychotic, having inadequate personalities, or being sociopaths, based on psychological tests and clinical observations.

One point on which there appears to be little disagreement among investigators, however, is that psychopathology is a frequently observed characteristic of heroin addicts. Sheppard, Fracchia, Ricca, and Merlis (1972) found only 6% of their male heroin-user sample exhibited profiles without pathology when they administered the MMPI. Sutker (1971) reported only 12% of her heroin addict sample had normal MMPI profiles. Again, in a comparison of street addicts, heroin addict prisoners, and nonaddict prisoners, Sutker and Moan (1972) found only 21% of the female street addicts and 18% of female prison addicts had normal MMPI profiles, in contrast to 48% of nonaddict prisoners. Hill, Haertzen, and Glaser (1960) reported that although only 5.5% of their narcotic addict sample had normal MMPI profiles, 30.5% had psychopathic profiles. English and Tori (1973) found a sample of heroin addicts—most of whom were in treatment voluntarily in a methadone program—possessed a greater degree of psychopathology and fewer ego defenses than users of other hard drugs. Staff and soft-drug users were not distinguishable in this respect, being equally at a higher level of ego strength.

Monroe, Ross, and Berzins (1967) examined MMPI indices of psychopathology among four groups of narcotic addicts admitted to the National Institute of Mental Health (NIMH) Clinical Research Center at Lexington. The following four groups were studied: (a) civil commitment admissions under the Narcotic Addict Rehabilitation Act (NARA) of 1966, (b) prisoners sentenced by federal courts, (c) volunteers for treatment, and (d) persons required to seek treatment as a condition of state or municipal probation. In a sample of 845 patients, the NARA admissions exhibited the broadest spectrum of psychiatric disturbance of all four groups, almost evenly divided among character disorders (31%), emotional disturbances (31%), and thinking disturbances (29%). Volunteers tended to have a relatively greater incidence of character disorders (39%) and emotional disturbances (36%), but a smaller frequency of thinking disturbances (18%). Character disturbances were most prevalent among the probationer (45%) and prisoner (52%) groups. The incidence of emotional disturbances was 26% and 23% respectively among probationers and prisoners; thinking disturbance rates were 22% and 19% respectively in these two groups. While admitting the possible contamination of their results by methodologic factors such as the high selectivity of each sample, the authors conclude that in contrast to the other groups the NARA patients were more heterogeneous (and also the most psychiatrically disturbed group).

With respect to the relationship between psychopathology and race, Sutker, Archer, and Allain (1978) found black addicts to demonstrate less psychopathology than whites, as demonstrated by less elevated MMPI scores. In a factor analytic study of the MMPI with heroin addicts, Shaffer, Kinlock, and Nurco (1982) found essentially similar factor structures for black and white addicts. The white addict group, however, displayed significantly more psychopathology than did the black addicts. Similarly, Penk, Robinowitz, Woodward, and Hess (1980) found white addicts to demonstrate more anxiety and repression than blacks.

That maladjustment is a relatively common characteristic of heroin addicts is also suggested by the finding of Gardner (1967) that a cut-off score, reported as useful in identifying maladjusted subjects on the Rotter Incomplete Sentences Blank (RISB), correctly identified 80% of male and 100% of female heroin users. In the following sections, evidence will be reviewed which relates to the existence of specific psychopathologic traits in heroin addicts.

Neurosis

There is substantial empirical evidence linking neurotic personality patterns with narcotic addiction, primarily on the basis of MMPI data. However, the incidence of neurosis among heroin addicts appears to be lower than character disorders, psychopathy, and psychosis. Hill, Haertzen, and Glaser (1960) classified 19% of their sample of 270 adult and adolescent black and white narcotic addicts as neurotic on the basis of MMPI profiles. A similar incidence in which 16% of their sample demonstrated neurotic disturbances was reported by Sheppard, Fracchia, Ricca, and Merlis (1972) who administered the MMPI to 336 male narcotic addicts undergoing treatment. Their sample of neurotics showed symptoms of anxiety and depression, which the authors attributed to feelings of inferiority and inadequacy.

Beckett and Lodge (1971) reported that 20 of 34 male heroin addicts in treatment had overt childhood neurotic manifestations and another 5 had disturbances during puberty. The authors are surprised at the few instances of such problems, given the family pathology in the patient backgrounds.

Anxiety and reactive depression appear to predominate in the neurotic narcotic addict. Ausubel (1958) stated that psychoneurotic individuals who become addicts are motivated by high aspirations toward success but lack self-esteem. In the face of constant failure to achieve unrealistically high goals, these individuals feel inadequate and depressed. Anxiety increases greatly as repetitive failure and lack of self-confidence characterize encounters with the world. The chronic abuse of narcotics serves to reduce this anxiety.

Eveson (1963), on the basis of clinical observations, also believed anxiety plays a crucial role in narcotic addiction. He suggested a causal interrelationship between anxiety and hostility in drug addiction and believed that these are the only two dimensions required for an individual to become an addict. Characterizing the addict as an inadequate, passive individual with a low threshold of anxiety and a high level of hostility as a result of early environmental rejection, Eveson believed the use of narcotics reduced the pressures of hostility and the fear of expressing this hostility. Wikler (1952, 1953) suggested that the source of this characteristic anxiety in the narcotic addict is sexuality and the expression of hostility. Conflicts with aggression, pain, and sexuality are the sources of anxiety (Wikler and Rasor, 1953) and narcotics tend to suppress these drives. Jaffe (1970c) referred to this use of narcotics as a notably passive adaptation to inner conflict. In contrast, Korin (1974) found no marked differences between heroin and nonopiate user psychotic and nonpsychotic groups on the Multiple Affect Adjective Checklist (MAAC) scales of anxiety, hostility, and depression.

Savitt (1963) observed strong incestuous desires in his addict patients. The intolerability of these desires motivated the patients to use heroin as this addiction reduces sexual drives. (That this actually occurs was recently confirmed in research by DeLeon and Wexler [1973].)

A combination of sexual disturbance and a high level of anxiety was also a frequent factor noted by Kraft (1970) in his clinical observations of narcotic addict patients. In three case histories representative of narcotic addicts there was severe personality disturbance prior to taking drugs. All three individuals demonstrated neurotic symptoms such as sexual problems, high social anxiety, and strong sadomasochistic trends. Kraft suggests that the drug-taking began as an alternative satisfaction of neurotic needs and provided relief from these symptoms. Similar themes were also seen by Chein, Gerard, Lee, and Rosenfeld (1964), who reported that the Thematic Apperception Test (TAT) stories of adolescent opiate addicts had central characters involved in "murder, rape, strangulation, fatal cancer, rotting away, failure and impotence," reflecting depression and pessimism.

Zuckerman, Sola, Masterson, and Angelone (1975) found that while 39 percent of new admissions to a therapeutic community displayed depressive and neurotic symptomatology, virtually all such patterns of behavior disappeared during treatment. Haertzen and Hooks (1969), Martin, Jasinski and Haertzen (1973), and Mirin, Meyer, and McNamee (1976) all reported the presence of depression in individuals maintained on narcotics, either morphine or methadone.

Henriques, Arsenian, Cutter, and Samaraweera (1972) attempted to clarify the role of anxiety and depression as motivation for heroin use. They investigated the question of whether clinical syndromes of anxiety and depression as identified by the MMPI differentiated heroin addicts, barbiturate users, and amphetamine users. On the basis of previous clinical observations, they expected heroin and barbiturate users to be anxious, preferring drugs that act as physiologic depressants. Amphetamine users, on the other hand, would already be depressed and might therefore prefer stimulating drugs. Mean differences between heroin users and other groups on these scales were not significant, although the authors did find a greater number of barbiturate users (45%) than heroin addicts (27%) or amphetamine users (11%) had scores on the depression scale which ranked highest or second highest among the various clinical scales.

Woody and Blaine (1979) estimated that about 30 percent of lower class addicts in methadone treatment are depressed, although they note that this figure is higher if depression is assessed prior to stabilization on methadone. When Weissman, Slobetz, Prusoff, Mesritz, and Howard (1976) studied the incidence of clinical depression among young lower socioeconomic status male clients in a methadone maintenance program, they found approximately one-third were depressed. Furthermore, the depressive symptomatology was associated with impaired social functioning, increased stress, and a history of alcohol abuse.

Negative findings emerge from two additional studies. Gritz, Shiffman, Jarvik, Haber, Dymond, Coger, Charuvastra and Schlesinger (1975) found a relative absence of mood deviations in both methadone patients and abstinent addicts, while Ling, Holmes, Post, and Litaker (1973) found that 53 percent of male methadone clients they studied were otherwise free of psychiatric syndromes. Another 30 percent were classified as having antisocial personality disorders, and 22 percent had significant drinking problem. While ten subjects had some affective symptomatology, none had diagnosable psychiatric syndromes.

Significant interest has been addressed to the extent psychosocial stressors in the form of recent life events (RLE), such as arguments, conflicts, deaths, marital separations, etc. may precede the onset of depression. In the first prospective study specifically addressing RLE and depression in heroin addicts, Kosten, Rounsaville, and Kleber (1983) evaluated change in depressive symptomatology over a six month interval during which the occurrences of RLE were recorded. Their findings were that among addicts with low numbers of RLE, 23 percent either remained or became depressed, while among addicts with high numbers of RLE, 50 percent either remained or became depressed. Furthermore, when RLE were classified into "argument" vs. "exit" (loss or separation) events, argument RLE were most strongly related to depression, and exit RLE to resumption of illicit drug use during treatment. The relationship between stressful life events and return to heroin use in methadone maintenance patients was evaluated in a study by Krueger (1981). His results indicated the influence of such events as recent loss, depression, and the exacerbation of intense affect as coinciding with renewed heroin use. Furthermore, the number and magnitude of such events was significantly related to failure to adhere to methadone maintenance and return to heroin use.

Psychosis

While several empirical studies have suggested that many narcotic addicts fall within the neurotic classification, a greater number of addicts have been considered psychotic. However, this number is generally smaller than those addicts in the personality and character disorder category. Hill, Haertzen, and Glaser (1960), in their MMPI study of adult and adolescent black and white narcotic addicts at Lexington, found 17% were schizoid. Sutker and Moan (1972) obtained similar MMPI results in a comparison of female street addicts, heroin addict prisoners, and nonaddict prisoners: 26% of street addicts and 29% of prison addicts had psychotic profiles in contrast to 4% of nonaddict prisoners. Most of these addicts were labeled "antisocial psychotics," reflecting "pronounced antisocial tendencies in concert with idiosyncratic and irrational thought processes" (p. 112). An earlier MMPI-based study by Sutker (1971) resulted in 23% of the addict sample being characterized as psychotic. In yet another MMPI study, Sheppard, Fracchia, Ricca, and Merlis (1972) found a slightly larger percentage (36%) of psychotic male heroin addicts; 32% of this sample was schizoid, and the remaining 4% had affective disturbances. The authors suggest that heroin use in this sample was a means of coping with basic withdrawal defenses, and acted as a protection against sadistic feelings. Of their cases, 24% also showed signs of paranoia. An unusually high percentage (71%) of male NARA (1966) narcotic patients at Lexington were judged psychotic by Berzins, Ross, and Monroe (1971). They suggested that this group appeared to be more egocentric, defensive, sexually confused, and socially maladjusted than earlier groups of patients observed at Lexington.

Gerard and Kornetsky (1954) also studied male heroin addict hospital admissions at Lexington. On the basis of responses to the Rorschach and Human Figure Drawings (HFD) tests, the authors classified their subjects into four diagnostic categories that included overt and incipient schizophrenia. Drug-taking was adaptive because it facilitated denial and avoidance, reduced anxiety, and increased withdrawal, thereby treating the psychiatric symptomatology. Bender (1963) reviewed a Columbia University followup study of adolescent drug (primarily narcotics) users treated at Riverside Hospital in New York City, in which 21% of the sample exhibited psychotic reactions.

Uhde, Redmond, and Kleber (1982) made the point that while psychosis is not generally associated with opioid withdrawal, acute withdrawal may precipitate the emergence of pre-existing psychiatric illness, including symptoms of schizophrenic, phobic, and panic disorders. Furthermore, such patients may require special treatment not usually available at methadone or other drug treatment clinics, possibly including the prescription of psychotropic medication in addition to a maintenance narcotic, and supportive psychotherapy.

Personality Disorders

There appears to be substantial evidence linking various personality and character disorders to narcotic addiction. Ausubel (1958) specifically delineates two personality types for whom drug abuse has adjustive value: the first corresponds to what was described earlier in this chapter as the neurotic type, and the second is the inadequate personality. Ausubel cites clinical evidence obtained from psychiatric histories and the results of psychological tests given to adolescent heroin addicts at Bellevue Hospital as well as Lambert's classification of 58% of 318 adult addicts at Bellevue as inadequate personalities to support his conclusion. According to Ausubel, such an individual is passive and dependent and unable to delay gratification. Drug abuse allows him to avoid environmental demands and provides immediate pleasure in illusory feelings of self-confidence and omnipotence.

Weak ego development was found to be characteristic of the "heroin addict type" in a study of 65 adolescent addicts by Zimmering, Toolan,

Safrin, and Wortis (1952). On the basis of the HFD and Rorschach tests, Zimmering et al characterized the heroin addict as a nonaggressive, nonimpulsive individual in whom self-esteem plays an important role. His interpersonal relations are tenuous and he fears new situations calling for active mastery or initiation of activity on his part. Low frustration tolerance and weak ego development force him to deal inadequately with inner conflicts. He relies on primitive drives as a result of immature emotional development. His emotional impulses cause conflicts to which he reacts with defense mechanisms of repression, inhibition, restriction, denial, reaction formation, projection, and rationalization. As a result, anxiety is easily evoked while aggression is markedly absent. Under conditions of threat or frustration, the addict tends to withdraw into a narcissistic level of adjustment and fantasies of omnipotence. Zimmering et al conclude that the self-concept of the addict is one of inadequacy, confusion, and impotence. This is often reflected in a morbid preoccupation with body image. The self-reported subjective experience of heroin addicts reveals that they feel a reduction in anxiety, an increase in self-esteem and competence, and omnipotence. Chein et al (1964) note the description of the heroin addict (given by an addiction clinic staff) as an individual having low frustration tolerance and readiness to collapse and retreat into passivity.

Inability of narcotic addicts to delay gratification and threatened ego disintegration have been observed by Savitt (1963). He saw the impulse to use drugs originating in the addict's great need to fuse with his mother to relieve his tension and depression. The addict is unable to experience love. Gratification cannot be delayed because he has no reason to believe it might be forthcoming at some later time. In regression to a primitive level of functioning, the immediate gratification of narcotics is sought and the ego is subsequently threatened by disintegration.

Low tolerance for discomfort, frustration, and feelings of inferiority were cited by Felix (1944) as factors leading to narcotic addiction. He suggested that addiction is not a disease but a symptom of underlying personality difficulties. The addict is an inadequately adjusted individual who uses drugs to reduce discomfort and to give himself a feeling of control. In essence, Felix proposed that life proves too complicated for the addict, who possesses only limited emotional resources.

Chein et al (1964) noted that the adolescent addict initially avoids situations that lead to the acquisition of competence for the normal adolescent and may passively go along with others until he reaches the point where he engages in drug use as an evasion of responsibility. In their study of adolescent narcotic addicts at Lexington, Gerard and Kornetsky (1954) found evidence suggesting that both inadequate personality and character disorder dominate the addict's personality. In a comparison of addicts and control Ss on the Rorschach and HFD tests, the addicts responded with meager, constricted drawings and an inability to produce fantasy or emotionally determined material. Since the addicts made little use of determinants other than form, the authors concluded that they "lack the richness and variety of resources necessary to function in novel, unstructured, or stressful situations" (p. 466). A second Rorschach test given immediately following the first revealed that the addicts provided few responses, used color regressively and showed decreased form levels.

Chein et al (1964) also reported that addicts were much more constricted than nonaddicts in their performance on the Rorschach. The authors saw the addicts as leading "much more impoverished lives, inwardly and outwardly, than their immediate situations required of them" (p. 200). Chein et al (1964) further confirmed the findings of Gerard and Kornetsky (1954) when they observed adolescent users were less aware of supportive or enriching experiences around them, engaged in a narrower ranger of leisure activities, and had little interest in extracurricular programs and politics. The authors suggest two explanations for these findings: the life space of the addict is restricted directly as a result of living in a chronically impoverished environment, and this constriction represents a defense against disappointment and frustration. Chein et al believe the latter is the more probable explanation. When asked to make human figure drawings, the addicts produced childlike body images more often than did the control Ss. They also produced rigid, in contrast to animated, drawings. On the basis of these data, the authors attempted to identify personality malfunction with constricted emotional responsivity, inability to sustain close peer relations, and with a tendency to withdraw under stress. Chein, Gerard, Lee, and Rosenfeld (1964) noted that adolescent heroin addicts are unable to enter into almost any kind of close relationship. Typically, therefore, they have marginal friendships.

Despite the essentially consistent picture given above of the addict as suffering from personality disorders, Sarg (1972) provides a counterpoint. He suggested that the majority of cases of heroin addiction seen in Vietnam were "basically physically and mentally healthy, with a striking absence of character disturbances and personality impoverishment peculiar to heroin dependents in the United States" (p. 111). He believed heroin use was due to environmental conditions associated with military service in Vietnam, and that most addicted servicemen would not return to the use of heroin when the "emotional support of home, family and friends" was present. Christie (1972), however, strongly disagreed with Sarg's observation. Citing his own experience in Thailand, he noted, ". . . almost without exception, the presence of striking character and personality disorders of the passive-aggressive, passive-dependent, antisocial types. Furthermore, the cases were characterized," he observed, by a "lack of basic trust and trustworthiness and [a] long history of chronic complaining and troublemaking." He concluded that heroin users he observed were "... rather sorry, hostile, distrustful and insecure" young men (p. 609).

Psychopathy and Sociopathy

A once popularly held view of the addict was that psychopathic and sociopathic traits were predominant in his psychologic make-up. Kolb (1925), for example, argued that addiction liability was restricted to psychopaths since the "sensual pleasures" of opiates could only be experienced if one were a psychopath. The sole experience of a normal person receiving an opiate would be reduction of pain. More recent data relevant to this issue is primarily empirical in nature, being based upon studies using the MMPI.

Hill, Haertzen, and Glaser (1960), and Hill, Haertzen, and Davis (1962) examined the MMPI profiles of male narcotic addicts at the U.S. Public Health Service Hospital in Lexington. A factor analysis revealed that of five subgroups among the addicts, three exhibited sociopathic characteristics in varying degrees. The first group, accounting for 30.5% of the variance, were labeled undifferentiated sociopaths, while the second factor identified primary and secondary sociopaths (an additional 24% of the variance). Elevations on the Psychopathic Deviate (*Pd*) scale were characteristic of these addict subjects. A total of 54% of the addict sample presented predominantly sociopathic profiles, and the authors concluded that psychopathy was the characteristic personality type of the narcotic addict. Gilbert and Lombardi (1967) attempted to replicate the finding of Hill's studies while controlling for socioeconomic background in samples of male narcotic addicts and nonaddict controls. The MMPI was administered to both groups and significant differences were obtained on the Depression, Psychopathic Deviate, Psychasthenia, Social Introversion, and Hysteria scales. The authors concluded that psychopathic traits were the outstanding characteristic of the narcotic addict sample, and group differences in willingness to admit to socially undesirable characteristics were not responsible for the findings.

Similar findings were obtained by Sutker (1971) and Sutker and Moan (1972). Sutker (1971) compared heroin addicts and nonaddict inmates on the MMPI, using a carefully controlled procedure. While the nonaddict prisoners fell within the normal range, elevations on the Psychopathic Deviate and Depression scales dominated the addict profiles. Sutker found addicts were more depressed, anxious, and concerned with bodily ailments than nonaddict inmates. Of the addict sample, 50% were classified as socially deviant. A further study by Sutker and Moan (1972) examined the MMPI profiles of street addicts, heroin addict inmates, and non-addict prisoners. Again, both addict samples contained a sizable proportion of antisocial psychopaths (street addicts 26%, prison addicts 24%).

MMPI profiles for narcotic addicts consistent with the above findings were obtained by Overall (1973). The profile pattern of his addict group was a "4-9" code type (i.e., a profile type characterized by high elevations on scales 4 and 9, the Psychopathic Deviate and Mania scales, respectively), suggesting (according to Marks and Seeman, 1963) a sociopathic, emotionally unstable personality often characterized by sexual problems. Gilberstadt and Duker (1965) have described the 4-9 profile type as immature, hostile, poorly socialized, impulsive, and of low frustration tolerance.

Sheppard, Fracchia, Ricca, and Merlis (1972) attempted to provide more detailed data relating to the variety of MMPI profile types obtained with narcotic addicts. They administered the MMPI to 336 male narcotics users undergoing treatment. Of this sample, 33% demonstrated sociopathy with subgrouping along the primary and secondary dimensions suggested by Hill et al (1960, 1962). In another study with similar findings, Hampton and Vogel (1973) classified into diagnostic categories on the basis of the MMPI, 101 returning Vietnam veterans who were found to be heroin users. Using Meehl's system of differential diagnosis, they found a total of 55% of the sample were "psychiatrically abnormal." Slightly less than half of this number were classified as conduct disorders. (The actual incidence of pathology would have been higher in this study if the authors had first removed invalid profiles, which accounted for 10% of the sample, from their total before calculating their percentages.) Finally, Hekimian and Gershon (1968), not using the MMPI, diagnosed sociopathic personality in 15 out of 20 heroin addicts studied at Bellevue Hospital's psychiatric division. In all the above-mentioned studies, empirical evidence from the MMPI suggests that a large proportion of narcotic addicts possess sociopathic or psychopathic characteristics.

Monroe, Ross, and Berzins (1971) expressed concern that the resulting stereotype of the addict as a sociopath would interfere with potential rehabilitation programs because psychopathy is believed to be resistant to treatment. They therefore studied narcotic addicts admitted to treatment under the NARA of 1966, that is, civil commitments. Eight clinical scales of the MMPI, including the *Pd* and *Ma* scales, were administered to three samples of approximately consecutive admissions: voluntary admissions, probationers, and prisoners. The results indicated that drug addiction is not confined to the sociopathic personality, since it occurs with almost equal frequency among a variety of character disorders, neuroses, and psychoses. (In all three samples sociopathy was characteristic of less than 20% of the Ss.) This point is worth emphasizing. Studies reviewed in this chapter relative to the existence of distinct personality types among narcotic addicts repeatedly suggest that heroin addiction is not confined to any one personality disorder, but seems to occur in association with, and with varying incidence rates in, neurotics, psychotics, and persons with personality disorders.

Similarly, after studying the incidence of various forms of pathology in a heroin addict population, Sheppard et al (1972) concluded: "addicts are a heterogeneous psychopathological patient group" (p. 358). One implication of this finding is that the various diagnostic groups require different treatment modalities, since, as Sheppard et al note with respect to the schizoid group, representing 36% of the sample:

Obviously, focusing on the drug addiction in this patient group will not be sufficient, especially if the choice of heroin abuse was developed as a means of coping with a basic withdrawal, defensive operation, or protection from sadistic urges or feelings. [p. 359]

Onset of Psychiatric Illness

The relationship between drug use and the onset of psychiatric illness was evaluated in a sample of drug abusers admitted for inpatient treatment to an urban Philadelphia V.A. hospital at least yearly over a six year period (McLellan, Woody, and O'Brien, 1979). Relating psychiatric symptomatology to pattern of illicit drug use, they concluded that the abuse of specific drugs played a major role in the development of certain psychiatric syndromes. Essentially similar in status at time of first admission, six years later 6 of 11 stimulant users had been diagnosed as schizophrenic, and psychodepressant users similarly demonstrated profound changes in psychological status, with 8 of 14 demonstrating significant depression. By contrast, the opiate group, despite heavy use, initial sociopathic and psychopathic character disorders, and pervasive related problems of an interpersonal and criminal nature, showed surprisingly little change. McLellan et al (1975) suggest two possible explanations for these findings. Either (a) the symptoms seen were initially present below threshold levels and resulted in differential drug use with the aim of symptom relief, or (b) the prolonged use of the specific drugs had a direct effect upon the development and expression of the disorders. The lack of change in the opiate group is seen as reflecting the antidepressant, antipsychotic, and other psychopharmacologic qualities of opiates.

OTHER PERSONALITY CHARACTERISTICS

There have been many attempts to delineate the personality characteristics of narcotic addicts along more narrowly defined dimensions than the global personality types revealed by MMPI studies. Such dimensions as self-esteem, sensation-seeking, future time perspective, anomie, and need patterns have been studied. Two early studies were carried out by Brown (1935, 1940). In one study (1935) he attempted to verify empirically McDougall's (1929) suggestion of a relationship between introversion and opioid drug use. Brown sought to determine the proportions of introverts, ambiverts, and extroverts among morphine addicts, using Kretschmer's body type classification. Brown justified this method by "the close affinity between Kretschmer's cyclothymic and schizothymic temperament with the generally recognized aspects of extraversion and introversion" (p. 555). Not surprisingly, the results of this study failed to confirm Brown's expectation of a relationship between temperament (via body type classification) and morphine addiction, the "average addict" being pyknoid. Brown also administered the Bernreuter Personality Schedule and the Neymann-Kohlstedt Introversion-Extroversion Schedule, but came to the conclusion that both tests were "of limited scope in connection with studies on drug addiction" (p. 563).

In a second study, in 1940, Brown examined the relationship between body build and addiction to alkaloid drugs in a sample of 400 native-born white, male federal prison admissions. Based upon McDougall's (1929) theory of temperament, Brown expected to find the alkaloid addict group was predominately introverts. His discovered, however, that the addict group he studied were average or slightly above in height and weight, had body builds within normal limits, and a tendency toward the pyknic end of the distribution. In addition, the lower than normal weight of this sample upon admission, which increased rapidly to the normal range after admission, suggested that the lower initial admission weight was the result of inadequate nutrition. Brown concluded that the etiology of drug addiction could not be ascribed (in his sample at least) to "gross constitutional weakness" (p. 1962).

Self-esteem

Perhaps the most widely noted characteristic of the narcotic addict is his lack of self-esteem. Hoffman (1964), on the basis of clinical observations of narcotic addicts, cited low self-esteem as the most striking feature of the addict. He believed this to be at the basis of the "addiction-prone personality," for whom the chronic use of narcotics serves to provide a sense of self-esteem. Other characteristics of narcotic addicts were perceived by Hoffman to derive directly from this lowered self-esteem. Thus depression is the result of low self-esteem, while hostility emerges as a defense; anxiety stems from fear of this hostility.

Kaplan and Meyerowitz (1970), in their review of the literature relating to narcotic drug addiction, proposed a model in which the need to enhance self-esteem or to avoid self-derogatory attitudes becomes the motivating force for the addict. All other observed characteristics such as feelings of hopelessness, weak superego development, problems of sexual identity, weak interpersonal relationships, and low tolerance to anxiety and frustration are interpreted by the authors as reflections of reactions to a negative self-attitude and of mechanisms for dealing with lowered self-esteem.

Laskowitz (1961) also believed that self-esteem plays an immportant role in the addicts motivation for using drugs. According to Laskowitz, the adolescent addict characteristically seeks paths to his goals that involve the least threat to his self-esteem. He has an incorrect view of his own importance and simultaneously lacks the confidence to reach a goal "without loading the dice in his favor" (p. 69).

Schiff (1959) compared the self-esteem of addict and nonaddict prisoners under and over 21 years of age as measured by a Q-sort procedure. His over-21-year-old addict group was further divided into two groups: one had become habituated before age 21, and the other had become addicted after this time. All groups were required to carry out five Q-sorts of the 80 items on the scale: one sort was for a description of the individual's present self, one for the kind of person he would like to be, the third for the kind of person his parents would like him to be, the fourth for the kind of person his friends would like him to be, and the fifth was based on what he thought a person whose opinion was important to him would like him to be. Schiff found that the under-21 and nonaddict groups did not differ in level of self-esteem, and also did not differ from adult users who had become addicted before the age of 21. All three of these groups, however, had a higher level of self-esteem than the nonaddict adults and adults who had become habituated over 21. These two later groups did not differ from one another. It is difficult to interpret these findings since, as Chein et al (1964) pointed out, in this case all adolescents and adult users who had become addicted under 21 had higher self-esteem. Both Chein and Schiff note that one would expect the opposite to be true. Chein (1964) cited Fenichel as noting that an important element in drug use is the resulting great increase in the typically low level of self-esteem of drug addicts.

A valuable contribution to understanding the role of self-esteem in heroin addiction was made in a study by Ogborne (1974) of a group of British heroin addicts who responded to a list of 80 items dealing with psychological and emotional reactions to heroin and its effect upon inter-personal functioning. Factor analyzing their responses, he identified two major subgroups of addicts: one group, which endorsed items relating to increased self-esteem and general awareness, he labeled "enhancers," and the other, which chose items relating to a decreased awareness of the world and of individual emotions and needs, he labeled "avoiders." Al-though the two addict groups did not differ from each other in their stated daily use of the drug, their recent pattern of use, or in terms of demographic and attitude variables, Enhancers were significantly older and had used heroin for a longer period of time. Enhancers tended to say they used heroin to "help concentrate," whereas avoiders gave "avoid responsibilities" and "escape from problems" as their reasons. Ogborne suggests that the two groups he identified are analogous to the psycho-pathic and neurotic addict types identified by Ausubel (1964) and Wikler and Rasor (1953), but that the kinds of reactions reported "reflect self-esteem and other aspects of the self-image" (p. 240).

Self-concept

In one study, addicts entering Lexington from metropolitan areas were more likely to view themselves as "essentially healthy persons who use drugs for kicks" in contrast to addicts from the South who perceived themselves as "being ill, and as using narcotics—rarely heroin—as medi-cine" (O'Donnell, 1969, p. 5).

English and Tori (1973) found in their sample of heroin addicts in methadone treatment that hard- and soft-drug users showed poor self-conception integration and perceived social status. As drug users, they saw themselves as unacceptable people. The opiate users tended to be at a level of social competence between the hard- and soft-drug users on the one hand and the staff on the other. English and Tori interpreted this last finding to reflect ". . . a certain amount of social competence . . . necessary for survival on the street" as well as due to the fact that "drug use is less deviant behavior in their cultural reference group" (p. 406).

Needs

Several studies have focused on the need structures of addicts, using Murray's need system and employing a variety of measurement instru-ments. When the Edwards Personal Preference Schedule (EPPS) was administered by Sheppard, Ricca, Fracchia, and Merlis (1974) to a sub-urban heroin addict sample and to a control group of nonaddicts, signifi-cant differences were obtained, with higher scores for the addict sample, on the heterosexuality, autonomy, and change need scales, and lower scores for the addict group on the endurance, deference, order, affiliation, and dominance need scales. The authors concluded that the need to be free of restraints and responsibilities as well as the desire for new and exciting experiences reinforced drug-taking.

Chambers (1972), using the Picture Identification Test (PIT), obtained the following differences between the need associations of addicts and normal control groups: (a) the inability of addicts to react appropriately to frustration as a result of being unable to choose between persistence and self-justification when things go wrong, for which the instant gratification provided by drugs offers a possible solution; (b) peer relationships, as viewed by addicts, provide protection and security, in contrast to controls' concept that these relationships provide pleasure and recognition; (c) tendency of addicts to confuse affiliation and succorance leads to unsatisfying peer interaction; (d) addicts find it more difficult to maintain peer relationships in the face of frustration; (e) addicts, in contrast to normals, do not associate desire to succeed with fear of failure, a combination that usually produces high levels of motivation for long-range goals; and (f) in interpersonal situations, the benevolent feelings of addicts are compromised by aggressive and destructive impulses.

Another study (Chambers and Lieberman, 1965) found male addicts, when compared to controls, possessed (a) positive attitudes toward needs for deference; (b) negative attitudes toward needs for nurturance; and (c) lower scores for abasement need. These results support the above-mentioned study in that Chambers (1972) suggests, "addicts tend to quickly express aggression and resentment, [and] are unwilling to assume responsibility for others" (p. 469). Interestingly Scherer, Ettinger, and Mudrick (1972), in a study of hard-drug users among college students, found (in contrast to soft-drug and nonusers) they scored highest on the need for social approval as measured by the Crowne-Marlow Social Desirability scale. The authors suggest that the need for approval makes these individuals more susceptible to peer pressure in drug-taking.

Values and Attitudes

A subject of current interest to researchers is that of the values and attitudes held by heroin addicts and other drug users. Studies on these issues fall into three major categories: investigations of the value structure of the addict, examination of attitudes held by addicts toward heroin and other drugs as well as toward addiction, and those studies that have focused on staff attitudes toward the addict himself. Each of these will be examined.

Miller, Sensenig, and Reed (1972) compared the relative importance given to common values by narcotic addicts in treatment at Lexington, and a sample of college students. They concluded that "the addict subculture sampled in this study is not greatly different from the general population . . ." (p. 6) with respect to their rankings of common values. It is interesting, however, that addicts ranked as more important (*a*) "avoiding loss in games," (*b*) "your own life" (in contrast to "physical safety of husband/wife"), (*c*) "making a meaningful contribution to society," and (*d*) "your leisure time pursuits." The authors interpreted these findings as suggesting that while addicts share many common values with other populations, they possess "an overconcern with self in contrast with important social others," and "a high concern with vocational goals and aspirations" (p. 7).

When Miller, Sensenig, and Reed (1972) examined the value given by addicts to risky situations, they found the addict consistently undervalued the risk involved. They suggested the addict may avoid taking chances because he devalues his ability to control his own fate, or he may just be "playing it cool" and not taking risks for anything or anybody.

English and Tori (1973) found no overall differences on the Rokeach Value Survey between heroin addicts in methadone treatment, users of other hard and soft drugs, and staff members. There was a tendency (perhaps due to chance) for heroin addicts to rank relatively high values such as family security, ambition, cleanliness, and self-respect (the last in conjunction with the high ranking given this concept by staff). The authors attributed the values assigned by opiate addicts to their relatively deprived backgrounds.

In a follow-up study, Miller, Sensenig, Stocker, and Campbell (1973) examined the value systems of 284 consecutive male and female, black and white admissions to Lexington without comparison to a nonaddict group. They found the black addicts projected a greater concern with conventionally defined social values, including equal opportunity and affluence. White addicts, on the other hand, were much more concerned with interpersonal and self-concept issues. The authors saw the blacks as far less alienated and more middle class in their value system. Female addicts tended to be less concerned than males with achievement and competence-related values and more concerned with interpersonal and intrapersonal issues.

The perception of risks involved in using opiates as well as other drugs was examined by Kolb, Gunderson, and Nail (1974) in a group of Navy enlisted men entering treatment for drug problems. Social risks tended to be most salient for both light and heavy users of opiates, although medical risks were also perceived as quite high. In contrast, psychiatric risks, with the exception of "isolation from others" and "loss of interest in surroundings," were perceived as less applicable. Overall, the perception of risks by opiate users was quite high and tended to increase with the amount of use. Seventy-four percent of heavy users and 64% of light users reported risks associated with using the drug, in contrast to 47% of nonusers. These results seem entirely reasonable, given the predominant concern in this population of the necessity for conformity to clearly delineated standards of social behavior.

In an attempt to learn what drugs mean to the user, Robbins (1972) had heroin addicts in methadone treatment rate a number of drugs on the Semantic Differential (SD). With respect to the evaluative factor, he found that heroin was ranked lowest and marijuana highest, followed by methadone, which was ranked significantly higher than heroin. Heroin did not differ from methadone or other drugs in its ranking for potency; but otherwise, there was little similarity in the ways heroin and methadone were perceived. However, there was similarity in the ways heroin and marijuana were viewed. Interestingly, length of marijuana use was positively related to the perceived potency of heroin.

Robbins suggested that the more favorable view of methadone versus heroin may offer encouragement for methadone treatment. However, he ended with a word of warning in regard to the generally more positive perception of heroin and other drugs on each scale. He noted, "if drug addicts can go through all the personal and social problems that follow addiction to heroin and still think it relates more closely to 'wise' rather than 'foolish,' it does not bode well for the treatment of the addict" (p. 369).

In a study of college students' attitudes toward drugs, Brehm and Back (1968) found that males were more willing than females to use opiates. Furthermore, when attitudes about hard drugs (e.g., opiates, hallucinogens, and energizers), social stimulants, and sedatives were related to use, the use of all drugs by males and females was found to be related to insecurity, wish for self-change, and a general confidence in the effectiveness of drugs. Both males and females also associated hard-drug use with curiosity about their potentialities, and males related use to lack of denial of effects and lack of fear of loss of control. The general conclusion reached by Brehm and Bach was that factors related to willingness to use drugs were dissatisfaction with one's self and lack of restraints for drug use; the latter condition including both lack of fear of control and of bodily damage.

Soverow, Rosenberg, and Ferneau (1972) examined attitudes toward drugs and alcohol in a group of heroin addicts in methadone treatment. They found the addicts viewed addiction to alcohol and drugs as similar in ". . . the amount of the addictive substance needed to qualify for dependence; the nature of the addiction as a character defect, an illness or a harmless indulgence; and the addicting potential of the substance itself" (p. 196). The addicts did perceive the following differences between alcoholism and drug addiction: (a) emotional difficulties played a greater role in the etiology of alcoholism; (b) the alcoholic had less control over his use of the addicting substance; (c) a better prognosis for the alcoholic's recovery; and (d) the alcoholic possessed a higher social status than the addict.

When attitudes toward drugs of addicts and staff were compared, there was close similarity on the following points: (a) addict's loss of control over the amount of drug needed, (b) the nature of addiction as a character defect, (c) the addict's social status, and (d) the addictive potential of the drugs. The staff, however, saw a greater involvement of emotional factors in the etiology of heroin addiction, a better prognosis for recovery, the possibility of developing addiction with small doses of drugs; they also expressed a greater acceptance of addiction as a disease, and were less willing to view it as a harmless indulgence.

A comparison has also been made of attitudes toward drug users[1] on the part of drug treatment staff members, addicts in treatment, and social work students, the last chosen because they were closer to the addicts in age than the staff (Lincoln, Berryman, and Linn, 1973). Lincoln et al had her subjects rate a series of concepts on the SD. The concepts rated included "police," "amphetamine user," "marijuana user," "heroin user," "LSD user," and "pusher." The only significant finding relative to the heroin user concept was that for drug users; ratings for this concept and pusher were equally and most negatively viewed. Both staff and students viewed pusher most negatively, but the difference in attitudes toward heroin user between the groups was not significant.

Finally, attitudes toward heroin users were not related to staff, student, or user characteristics, including age, sex, marital status, parenthood, education, years worked, and having friends who were either users or nonusers of drugs.

Trust

Blumberg et al (1974) found their English addicts seeking treatment ranked low in trust and authoritarianism, but were in the normal range for anxiety and extraversion as measured by the Eysenck Personality Inventory (EPI), although they suggested this latter finding might be

---

[1] Drug users were not limited to heroin users, although 75% of the group had used heroin. This study is included, however, because of the data obtained about staff attitudes toward heroin users.

partly due to drug use.

Habitual drug users (including users of heroin) among high school students were found by Adler and Lotecka (1973) to trust their parents least of all drug-using or nonusing groups surveyed. On the other hand, habitual drug users trusted friends more than all other groups. This is not surprising, if the peer-group orientation of many drug users of this age and the poor family relationships evident among drug users are considered.

Future Time Perspective

Future time perspective (FTP), defined as a "general concern for future events" (Kastenbaum, 1961), has been observed to be deficient in several groups that appear to overlap the heroin addict population. These groups include delinquents and individuals with problems of impulse control. Likewise, the addict's approach to living has been described by Laskowitz (1961) as being one of "live today—there may be no tomorrow," in which the addict is seen as being concerned only with the here and now and the immediate future (e.g., the next "fix"). According to Laskowitz, anticipating the future has meager appeal for the addict who has had little experience in formulating long-term goals.

An empirical study of FTP in heroin addicts was reported by Einstein (1965), who examined personal future extension, defined as "the length of the personal future time span conceptualized." This measure, introduced by Wallace (1956), requires the respondent to list 10 events that could happen to him during his lifetime and indicate his age at each event. The median difference between the subject's present age and his projected age for each event was used as his FTP score. Einstein compared the FTP scores of a group of adolescent nondelinquent addicts in a treatment program with two groups each of delinquent and nondelinquent nonaddicts. The results indicated that in one set of comparisons the adolescent heroin addict group had a significantly less extended FTP in contrast to the nonaddict nondelinquent group but did not differ significantly from the nonaddict delinquent group. This finding tends to support Laskowitz's description of the addict as possessing a limited future orientation. In the other set of comparisons, the addicts had significantly more extended FTPs than either the delinquent or nondelinquent control groups. The latter pair of comparisons should probably not have been reported, however, because of the incomparability of the two groups. Finally, Einstein's conclusions regarding data on the relationship between ethnicity and sex and the heroin addict's FTP were as follows: (a) adolescent male and female addicts did not differ in FTP; (b) black, Puerto Rican, and white addicts did not differ in FTP; and (c) there was no significant interaction between sex and ethnic background.

Sensation-seeking

Three studies reported on the relationship between sensation-seeking, or the optimal level of stimulation or arousal sought by an individual, and heroin use. The issue of sensation-seeking was discussed in Willis' (1969) study of British and American heroin addicts. When asked about reasons for heroin use, curiosity about the effects of heroin was the most common response given by majorities of both the British and American male samples and by the American female sample. This could be interpreted as reflecting desire for exciting experiences in these groups and as further evidence implicating sensation-seeking as a characteristic of heroin addicts.

In the second of these studies, Zuckerman, Neary, and Brustman (1970) found that only male college students rated high on sensation-seeking, as measured by the Sensation-seeking scale (Zuckerman, Kolin, Price, and Zoob, 1964), and exhibited greater use of opium derivatives. In the third study, Platt (1975) compared groups of heroin addict and nonaddict incarcerated youthful offenders and found the addicted adolescents showed significantly greater levels of general sensation-seeking. This study also compared the two youthful offender groups on a number of subscales, each dealing with a specific aspect of the sensation-seeking dimension. The addicts and nonaddicts differed on the Experience-seeking scale, which contains items reflecting the need for a broad variety of inner experiences achieved through travel, drugs, music, art, and an unconventional lifestyle. Items on this scale also reflected resistance to irrational authority and conformity. The two groups did not differ, however, on the Disinhibition, Boredom Susceptibility, or Thrill and Adventure-seeking scales. Thus their greater level of sensation-seeking was of a very specific type.

Locus of Control

The locus of control variable (Rotter, 1966) can be conceived of as a bipolar dimension with poles labeled internal locus of control and external locus of control, respectively. At the internal extreme is the generalized expectancy that important reinforcements in one's life are controlled by the actions of an individual. At the external extreme is the belief that these same reinforcements are controlled by luck, chance, fate, or powerful other individuals. In a large body of literature on the subject, the general finding in reviews (Lefcourt, 1966; Joe, 1971) has been that internal control is associated with membership in the more successful, stable, and higher status segments of society, whereas external control is more characteristic of the unsuccessful, the maladjusted and, in general, the lower status groups in society. In a fascinating study of the locus of control variable in opiate addicts, Berzins and Ross (1973) tested the hypothesis that addicts would be more internal than appropriate control subjects. They based their expectation on the fact that addicts, like other "self-indulgent, egocentric, antisocial, or sociopathic" groups display a "behavioral independence that seems to bespeak an underlying belief in a variant of internal control" (p. 84). Berzins and Ross (1973) further state that the strength of this dimension "can be inferred from [the addicts'] refractoriness to traditional treatment approaches, their surreptitious but zealous pursuit of drug related goals even when institutionalized for treatment, their high recidivism rate, and their apparent willingness to try almost any drug" (p. 84). The study's results confirm this hypothesis. Addicts were differentiated from nonaddicts on items related to feelings of personal control. Berzins and Ross relate this internal control orientation to the intrinsic rewards to the addict of drug-engendered mastery of his feelings and conflicts, which he obtains as a result of his addiction. Further, they see this belief in internal control as separate from and having no basis in the addict's social reinforcement history.

Calicchia (1974) undertook to replicate the Berzins and Ross study and also to test some specific hypotheses derived from the narcotic-induced internality position they espoused. First, Calicchia suggested that if the internal locus of control is related to the reinforcing, self-controlling effects of the narcotic, those addicts in treatment receiving a substitute drug such as methadone should be more internal than those undergoing abstinence treatment. Second, if addiction involves a set of reinforcing, self-controlling experiences, then a lengthy addiction should result in a stronger set of internal locus of control beliefs than a short habit. Not only did Calicchia confirm the original finding of an internal locus of control associated with heroin addiction, but he also verified his other two hypotheses. Heroin addicts in methadone treatment were more internally oriented in their locus of control than addicts in abstinence treatment, but the degree of internal control was directly related to the length of addiction. Of course these results are correlational and, as Calicchia himself notes, cannot be used to establish the validity of the underlying model suggested by Berzins and Ross (1973), but they do provide support for the earlier findings.

Contradictory results were obtained by Obitz, Oziel, and Unmacht (1973) in an examination of 80 incarcerated juvenile drug users, 50% of whom had used heroin at least twice during the previous year. Using Rotter's (1966) norms for comparison, Obitz et al found their sample was more external than the following four groups examined by Rotter: general normal group, black college students, prisoners from 18 to 26, and 18-year-olds from the Boston area. Obitz et al then administered a scale designed specifically to measure the perceived locus of control as related to drug-taking behavior. On this scale Ss did not endorse externally keyed items any more frequently than those internally keyed. In a second study that focused on a group of heroin addicts in a detoxification program similar results were obtained for both locus of control and nonendorsement of externally keyed items on a perceived locus of drug-taking control scale (Obitz, Cooper, and Madeiros, 1974). While it is admirable to see a replication such as Obitz et al carried out with a more clearly heroin addict sample, both studies would have been more valuable if there had been comparable nonuser control groups for the two addict groups. It is possible that Rotter's norms, which were used as baselines in both studies, were not appropriate for the populations studied.

A fifth study of the locus of control dimension in addicts provides some support for the Berzins and Ross study, or at least does not provide inconsistent findings. Platt (1975), in a carefully controlled comparison of heroin addict and nonaddict offenders, found no difference between these two groups on the locus of control variable when group differences on important demographic variables were controlled by means of a covariance procedure. Addict and nonaddict group means, *before* application of the covariance procedure, showed the addict group to be more internal in locus of control than the nonaddict group.

THE "ADDICTIVE PERSONALITY"

Almost without exception, the thrust of the literature cited earlier has been directed toward identification of specific predisposing characteristics in heroin addicts or demonstration of what has been called the "addictive personality." This idea of predisposing personality factors that lead to the development or maintenance of heroin addiction came under major criticism in a series of papers by Gendreau and Gendreau (1970; 1971; 1973). These writers believe that many of the positive findings of personality differences between addicts and nonaddicts in the previously cited studies by Gerard and Kornetsky (1955), Hill et al (1962), Gilbert and Lombardi (1967), Zimmerling, Toolan, Safrin, and Wortis (1952) and by Sutker (1971), among others, may actually be artifacts partly because of the failure of the investigators to match addict groups appropriately with equivalent controls. For example, Gendreau and Gendreau (1970) point out that Gerard and Kornetsky (1955) paid their controls but not their experimental subjects to participate, and that blind scoring of the projective tests was usually not done, and when it was done, resulted in the loss of group differences. Likewise, Zimmerling et al (1952) failed to use statistical tests in comparing his addict and nonaddict groups; Gilbert and Lombardi (1967) failed to match their addicts and nonaddicts in level of criminal activity; the groups studied by Hill, Haertzen, and Davis (1962) differed with respect to IQ, and in addition, the controls were drawn from a maximum security prison.

Other examples of poor and inadequate, or even absent, control procedures can be cited from the literature. One of the most disturbing is the failure of writers to define their experimental groups adequately. For example, Lombardi, O'Brien, and Isele (1968) compared matched pairs of addicts and nonaddicts on individual MMPI items but failed to define the nature of the addiction in their experimental Ss. One does not know if they were users of heroin or other narcotics, nor whether addiction was defined in terms of length, frequency of use of a drug or drugs, or the presence of the abstinence syndrome (i.e., withdrawal symptoms when the drug was withdrawn), or some other criterion. Thus one is tempted to believe there is clear substantiation of the point made by Gendreau and Gendreau (1970), even to the extent of suggesting that poor control and design flaws have been the major characteristics of personality studies of the addict in general and heroin addict studies in particular prior to the appearance of Gendreau and Gendreau's article.

In fairness to the authors of the studies criticized for their design faults, however, the other side of the coin is worth considering. Heroin addicts are rarely accessible as research subjects, since they are usually found in groups in correctional or treatment settings, where they are preselected by virtue of their incarceration, voluntary commitment to treatment, or other factors. Also, they present an extremely difficult group for which to find appropriate controls. For instance, where does one fiind a group comparable to those men in treatment at the Public Health Service Hospital at Lexington, Kentucky? Assuming, however, that the issue of obtaining appropriate controls for addicts is a problem, it is still necessary to conduct well-designed research on the subject. Gendreau and Gendreau (1970) attempted to do this by comparing jailed addicts and nonaddicts on the MMPI after determining equivalence with respect to socioeconomic level, after both groups had had the opportunity to obtain narcotics but had not become addicted, where both groups had criminal histories, and where they differed minimally with respect to age and IQ. The authors found no significant differences between the heroin addict and nonaddict groups on any of the scales, and therefore concluded that ". . . significant differences between addicts and non-addicts reported in previous studies may have been in part due to failure in sampling techniques" (p. 21).

In a second paper, Gendreau and Gendreau (1973) focused their attention specifically on Sutker's (1971) MMPI comparison of heroin-addicted and nonaddicted prisoners. Their argument was that her addict subjects were predominantly volunteers, in contrast to her nonaddict subjects, and that this factor may have confounded Sutker's (1971) results for a number of reasons.

Evidence from their earlier study (Gendreau and Gendreau, 1970), in addition to the finding of Berzins, Ross, and Monroe (1971), indicated that elevations for volunteer addicts exceeded those for nonvolunteer prisoner addicts on a number of MMPI scales. Gendreau and Gendreau (1973) also presented data that showed prisoner volunteers for treatment demonstrated elevated MMPI profiles regardless of addiction status. Finally, they reported, contrary to the results of Sutker's study, that volunteer nonaddicts had elevated MMPI profiles in contrast to nonvolunteer addicts.

These two studies by Gendreau and Gendreau prompted a reply from Sutker (1974), who reported that MMPI profiles of volunteer and compulsory applicants for treatment were very similar, with the exception of *Pd* scale elevation, in which volunteers significantly exceeded nonvolunteers. However, Sutker agreed with Gendreau and Gendreau that addict-nonaddict differences may not necessarily reflect addiction-proneness. She saw them mirroring the influences of long-standing personality characteristics and also "a heightened response to transitory pressures, environmental stimuli, and the physiological demands of an addiction typically supported by illegal means" (p. 464). In support, she cited a study by herself and Allain (1973).

Sutker and Allain (1973) examined the MMPI characteristics of three groups: the first was a group of unincarcerated street addicts; the second, a group of prison inmates with a history of heroin addiction; and the third, nonaddict inmates. Street addicts, in contrast to the other two groups, scored significantly higher on the Hypochondriasis, Hysteria, Depression, Psychopathic Deviate, and Psychasthenia scales. This group's mean profile, in contrast to either incarcerated group, suggested greater levels of depression, anxiety, bodily concern, and social deviance. The authors interpreted their results as an indication that unincarcerated addicts, as a function of the pressure placed on them by their addictions, were "psychologically more uncomfortable and socially more deviant" (p. 246) than either of the two groups with which they were compared.

Commenting on the study by Sutker and Allain (1973), Sheppard, Ricca, Fracchia, and Merlis (1973b) raised the question of whether the MMPI scores reported by Sutker and Allain reflected a lifestyle or a certain personality type before drug use. Their expectation was (based upon the Sutker and Allain findings) that the MMPI profiles would be very similar among various samples of street drug abusers. Sheppard et al (1973b) collected MMPIs from two groups of addicts, one admitted for treatment to a state hospital as part of a court procedure, and the second volunteering to participate. Data collected on a third group in a methadone maintenance program represented a sample of suburban addicts seeking supportive maintenance. Congruent with the expectation derived from Sutker and Allain's hypothesis, both actively addicted samples obtained significantly higher elevations on the Hysteria and Hypochondriasis scales of the MMPI. Both these studies suggest that MMPI scale elevations are a transient rather than a permanent characteristic of heroin addicts.

Sutker, Allain, and Cohen (1974) found significant personality changes occurring in addicts whose patterns of drug-related activities were interrupted by incarceration or hospitalization. Sutker (1974) interpreted this finding within a state-trait framework. In doing so, she provided a succinct statement of her position:

Thus, it would seem that there are certain possibly predisposing personality features which contribute to the addictive process, while at the same time there are a number of transitory states or fluctuations in psychological symptoms which vary depending upon the environmental circumstances and pressures present at the time of evaluation. [p. 464]

Empirical research, including studies by Gendreau and Gendreau (1970, 1973) and Sutker (1971, 1974), on the addictive personality can perhaps also be criticized for having permitted an extremely narrow focus in the number and kinds of personality dimensions studied. The MMPI, for instance, has been used as the source of personality traits to be studied in the majority of the most frequently cited empirical studies (e.g., Gilbert and Lombardi, 1967; Hill et al, 1960, 1962; Olson, 1964; Sutker, 1971; Gendreau and Gendreau, 1970, 1973). At the same time, only a limited number of studies have focused on other traits (e.g., Martin and Inglis, 1965). Thus it seems that the current research findings used to argue for or against validity of the addictive personality theory are open to additional criticism because they have been based upon a relatively narrow group of personality dimensions provided mainly by the MMPI and related measures of psychopathology.

To obtain evidence about the validity of the addictive personality in terms of variables other than MMPI scales, Platt (1975) compared addict and nonaddict youthful offenders on a series of 34 variables, many of which were previously uninvestigated, including self-evaluation, social self-esteem, anomie, locus of control, death concern, general sensation-seeking, thrill and adventure-seeking, experience-seeking, disinhibition, and boredom susceptibility, and also the self-concept and need scales of the Adjective Checklist.

In order to avoid some of the criticisms leveled at earlier studies because of design faults (cf. Gendreau and Gendreau, 1970, 1973), this investigation employed several control procedures. All subjects were drawn from a single population in which the incidence of heroin addiction at the time of the study made it possible to obtain a sufficient sample size of both addict and nonaddict subjects. All personality instruments were administered and scored without knowledge of an individual subject's drug history; heroin use history was determined from a number of different sources and then verified independently; and finally, addicts and nonaddicts were statistically equated with respect to the following demographic characteristics: (a) age at first arrest, (b) marital status, (c) religion, (d) IQ level, (e) educational achievement, as measured by the Stanford Achievement Test, Intermediate Battery, and (f) number of prior arrests.

In his discussion of these findings, Platt (1975) raised the question of whether the addict-nonaddict differences found in his study provided sufficient support for the addictive personality hypothesis. To do so, he suggested, these results needed to be definitive, consistent with, and meaningfully interpretable in terms of addiction-prone theory. He concluded that the results of this study, in which 7 out of 34 comparisons were significant, suggested some interesting personality differences between addicts and nonaddicts but failed to provide clear-cut evidence for the existence of an addictive personality. Also, some of the differences between the addict and nonaddict groups were in directions other than anticipated. For instance, it was difficult to reconcile higher addict scores on two of the Sensation-seeking scales with the suggestion of Khantzian, Mack, and Schatzberg (1974) that a major factor in the etiology of heroin addiction is an attempt by the addict to reduce the negative effect associated with the failure to cope. Similarly it was difficult to explain the higher scores obtained by the addict sample on the ACL Heterosexuality scale, since this finding was inconsistent with expectations based on addiction-prone theory. Further, when comparing groups in which one already exhibits pathology, there is no way to state unequivocally that the differences obtained are not the result of the disease process itself, that is, of having been a heroin addict at the time of admission in this instance. If these differences were the result of addiction, the findings obtained on both the Autonomy and Exhibitionism scales could be understood more readily.

Finally, differences clearly expected on the basis of addiction-prone theory did not emerge from the Self-control, Personal Adjustment, Achievement, Order, Nurturance, Affiliation, and Deference subscales of the Adjective Checklist. In its failure to find substantial and meaningful differences between the addict and nonaddict groups this study paralleled other similar studies (cf. Gendreau and Gendreau, 1973; Stuker and Allain, 1973).

Type I and Type II Addicts

A reasonable conclusion to draw from the studies reviewed above is that it is difficult to attempt to characterize the heroin addict in terms of a single personality type, since there are many more than one personality type among addicts. Berzins and his associates addressed themselves to this issue.

In a sample of over 800 admissions to Lexington between 1965 and 1970, Berzins, Ross, English, and Haley (1974) attempted to identify homogeneous groups among opiate addicts. They used a clustering technique that grouped highly similar MMPI profiles, and two distinct profile types emerged from 10 independent samples differing in sex and type of admission (e.g., civil commitments, voluntary, probationary, and prisoner). One group, labeled "Type I" addicts, tended to have the highest elevations on the Depression, Psychopathic Deviate, and Schizophrenic scales of the MMPI. According to Berzins et al this pattern reflected high levels of subjective stress, nonconformity, and confused thinking. In addition, Type I addicts "attributed a wide range of psychopathology to themselves and also depreciated themselves *as addicts*" (p. 72). "Type II" addicts, on the other hand, tended to have a single peak elevation on the *Pd* scale and were characterized by Berzins et al as "self-satisfied as persons and as addicts" (p. 72). In terms of overall incidence approximately one-third of the sample was identified as Type I and about 1 in 14 as Type II. The remaining 59.5% were not categorized in any homogeneous subgroup. After noting a strong similarity between these addict groups and groups of alcoholics identified in another study, Berzins et al suggested the existence of a substance abuser type characterized by these MMPI profile types. With respect to the opiate addicts, they further suggested: ". . . Type I subjects may employ drugs to control or attenuate feelings of anxiety, depression, distress, and so on, while Type II subjects may use them to enhance hedonistic pursuits or possibly, to reduce feelings of hostility or resentment" (p. 72).

CONCLUDING COMMENTS

What do the results of the numerous studies reported in this section mean? First, they demonstrate a long-standing interest by many writers attempting to explain addiction in terms of the identification of a specific personal trait or set of traits. Second, much of this research has generally employed inadequate research techniques, including poor control groups (if they have been used at all). When these facts are taken into consideration, however, some general findings are substantiated. The most important one is perhaps that heroin addicts demonstrate a significant amount of psychopathology, including high levels of anxiety, psychopathy and also neurotic and psychotic characteristics.

The following specific personality traits and disorders have also been associated with heroin addiction: personal inadequacy, inability to delay gratification, low frustration tolerance, poor self-image, and low self-esteem, to mention a few. The problem, however, has been that none of these traits has been documented consistently or employed satisfactorily to explain heroin use in all addicts. There is actually contradictory evidence on many points.

The most reasonable conclusion to draw based on available data, particularly the evidence presented in the studies reviewed in this chapter, would seem to be that although addicts generally exhibit pathologic traits, there is a low probability that a common pattern of personality traits is present in all addicts. Thus any attempt to specify an addictive type or addictive personality in terms other than a general level of disturbance will probably prove unproductive. One can only concur with Craig's (1982) conclusion, after reviewing the research on personality characteristics of addicts, that measurement of the presence or absence of a particular trait or characteristic is no longer sufficient. Rather, he suggests there is a need for typologies within an interactional framework systematically relating traits to such variables as recidivism, treatment retention, and etiology. The implications of these findings for a general concept of addiction will be discussed in the final chapter.

CHAPTER 9

Personal and Social Characteristics
of Heroin Addicts

The heroin addict is often pictured as an individual who possesses the most undesirable characteristics in our culture. He is perceived as a person coming from a background that involves substantial familial pathology, which includes poor parental relationships, absent parents, and broken homes; as a person emerging from the lowest socioeconomic levels of our society, often belonging to a minority group and having a poor employment record; and as a person with relatively few marketable skills and a poor education. Although many of these conceptions about the addict are supported by fact, others are more apparent than real, and may actually be contradictory to the available data. Currently, some of these conceptions are the center of controversy among individuals working in the drug field. This chapter will review recent and current findings relating to the personal and social characteristics of the heroin addict; in the process, some unexpected findings emerge.

THE FAMILIES OF ADDICTS

A number of authors have focused on the early family structure and related experiences of the addict as salient to the understanding of later addiction. Among the issues of particular concern are the role of parental influence and the high rates of parental social pathology.

Familial Characteristics and Influence

Familial Stability

Baer and Corrado (1974) studied the role of parental influence in the etiology of heroin addiction by comparing the responses of addicts and nonaddicts on a life-history questionnaire. Their specific interest was in the kinds of relationships addicts had had with parents in childhood and early adolescence. The findings were that, in contrast to a group of equivalent nonusers, although addicts more often reported an unhappy childhood, they were more likely to wish more often to relive part of it. The addicts reported more physical punishment and greater employment among mothers during childhood, more evening freedom as teenagers, less encouragement to bring friends home, and less parental interest in their school performance. They also reported less parental cohabitation, less career-planning assistance, and parents having less influence on their conduct. Finally, the addicts reported religion as a less important aspect of family life, a greater tendency toward parental condemnation of premarital sex, and less inclination to turn to their parents for sympathy or support. Baer and Corrado (1974) concluded that the majority of addicts in their study had led "an unhappy childhood which included harsh physical punishment and a general pattern of parental neglect and rejection" (p. 102).

A similar note was struck by Beckett and Lodge (1971) who reported that 85% of their heroin-addicted patient sample "had had a considerably diminished opportunity of establishing normal relationships during their formative years" (p. 31). This was often due to the presence of familial pathology such as alcoholism, physical or psychiatric illness, desertion and subsequent placement in foster homes, parental deaths, and so on. In relationships with fathers, a lower quality of such relationships was reported by heroin addicts than by groups using other drugs (Bucky, 1971). Chein et al (1964) also observed that the fathers of addicts were frequently emotionally distant or hostile, and that some form of familial pathology (e.g., divorce, hostility, poor interpersonal relationships) was present in almost all the families of addicts.

Crowther (1974) conducted an interview study in which she gathered information on a group of college opiate users in a "Midwest metropolitan area." Heroin users, in contrast to users of other opiates, reported greater prevalence of family disturbance (parental divorce, separation, death, etc.) during childhood and adolescence, and also less paternal education, lower socioeconomic status (within middle-class ranges), and a lower number stated a religious preference.

Broken homes were found more common in the backgrounds of addicts than controls by Kaplan and Meyerowitz (1970). The respective rates for parents living together, or both parents dead, or parents separated or divorced were 49%, 22%, and 28% for the addicts versus 79%, 12%, and 9% for the nonaddicts. Also, the data suggested that black addicts were more likely to come from a broken home than nonaddicts (Chambers and Moffett, 1970).

Johnson (1973) found heroin use in the year following high school related to parental divorce but not to parental death, in contrast to users of all other drugs in whom both parental death and divorce are related to drug use. When the quality of parents' personal relationships were examined, the heroin and amphetamine user groups had the highest percentages (30% and 28% respectively) in the fair to poor range, closely followed by the LSD user group (24%) (Bucky, 1971). A particularly striking finding was that only 19% of the parents of the heroin group were still living together in contrast to 65 to 77% of parents of all other drug-user groups (Bucky, 1971).

The above data suggest that the early family environment of addicts is of poor quality generally characterized by substantial pathology in child rearing patterns as well as poor parental adjustment and overall familial instability. Coleman (1980) has proposed that death, separation, and loss are significant etiological factors in heroin addict families. These variables are seen by Coleman as part of a homeostatic pattern that maintains the drug-abusing family member helpless and dependent and remaining at home with the family. She conceptualizes the drug-use process as reflecting an underlying sense of family hopelessness and lack of purpose in life.

Parental Absence

Another issue of importance and one on which several authors have commented specifically has been the factor of parental absence, often due to death. Beckett and Lodge (1971) reported that the mothers of seven addicts and the fathers of four (of his sample of 34) had died before the patients were 15 years of age. Fort (1954) noted the frequent absence of addicts' fathers, as did Chein et al (1964), who found the father or father figure to be frequently or totally absent in about half of their addict group. The father was present in only 40% of the homes of heroin addicts studied by Goldsmith, Capell, Waddell, and Stewart (1972), while the mother was present in 80%. Only 63% of the heroin group in Bucky's (1971) study of Navy enlisted men definitely knew that their fathers were still alive in contrast to 93 to 97% of other groups. A similar finding occurred with respect to mothers: only 70% of the heroin group definitely knew their mothers were living, while other groups ranged from 93 to 96%. A full 20% of the heroin addict sample did not know if their fathers were living, 17% were unaware whether their mothers were still alive; at the same time, only 0 to 3% of the other groups did not know this (Bucky, 1971). Other investigators (Eldred, Brown, and Mahabir, 1974; and Lieberman, 1974) have also observed the relative absence of parents, literally or figuratively, in the families of heroin addicts.

As often occurs in research reviewed here that deals with the personal characteristics of heroin addicts, the findings are far from unanimous. With respect to the issue of parental death, Blumberg et al (1974) did not find a higher incidence of such events in opiate users seeking treatment in London than in samples of psychiatric patients or normal controls.

Perception of Parents

Addicts tend to perceive their parents in a less than positive fashion. Adler and Lotecka (1973) found that a substantial proportion of habitual drug users (more than half) did not view their home in positive terms, and more than a quarter were clearly alienated from parents. Parents of habitual users of heroin and other drugs were often perceived as habitual drinkers and users of amphetamines and barbiturates. Interestingly, perceived habitual drinking was the only way in which habitual drinking and drug-taking on the part of children was related to the same parental characteristic. Likewise, the heroin-addict sample in the study of Baer and Corrado (1974) described their fathers as "pals" and their mothers as being well-intentioned less often than did nonaddicts.

Family Size and Birth Order

Heroin addicts come from the largest families of all drug-using groups, according to Bucky (1971). In his survey heroin users also represented the highest percentage of only children (11%) and the lowest percentage of youngest children (9%). Birth order tended to be more frequently in the middle than in other groups. Similarly, 18% of the addicts in the Kaplan and Meyerowitz (1970) sample were only children, versus 6% in the control group. The authors attributed this significant difference to the high divorce rate among parents of addicts in their sample. When the addict had a sibling, the addict was more likely to be last born (27% vs. 14% of control subjects). Again, the picture is less than unanimous, since O'Donnell (1969) found no relationship between sibling position and opiate addiction in his study of Kentucky-born admissions to Lexington.

The issue of sibling drug use was addressed by Blumberg et al (1974) who found that most of the English addicts in their study seeking treatment had between three and five siblings. Of those addicts with at least one sibling, 20% reported that the sibling had used an opiate, 39% that they had used marijuana, and 31% that at least one sibling had been arrested.

PERSONAL CHARACTERISTICS OF ADDICTS

Age Characteristics

The age characteristics of addicts have been touched upon in two ways. First, several authors have reported age characteristics of their samples in light of either national or local trends. Often these numbers reflect the age at which heroin addicts come in contact with a particular agency. Other authors have focused on the age of onset of drug use as it relates to severity and duration of later use.

Age Trends

According to Ball and Chambers (1970) the mean age of addicts admitted to the Lexington and Fort Worth Public Health Service hospitals in 1963 was 32.9 years for males and 33.5 years for females. The largest proportion of females (25.6%) were in the 25- to 29-year-old category. While 23.7% of males also fell into this category, the 20- to 24-year-old total was almost 23.3%. As Ball and Chambers (1970) note, most addicts are young; 80% are under 40. Their summary of admission statistics to Lexington and Fort Worth indicated that only 20% of admissions were 40 years of age or older.

In 1965, Winick noted that ". . . opiate users today are primarily young adults" (p. 7). With the mean age decreasing, this trend seems to be on the increase. Similar trends have been noted by Scher (1973), who reported that in 1973 the average age of addicts in Cook County Jail was 21 years, compared with 28 some 13 years earlier; by the Board of Directors of the National Council on Crime and Delinquency (1974), who noted that the average age of addicts in the United States had declined while their number had increased in the 10 year period from 1964 to 1974; and by Ball and Chambers (1970), who reported that the median age of addicts admitted to Lexington and Fort Worth in the period between 1937 and 1962 had decreased from 39.1 years to 33.5 years.

In England, Bewley and Ben-Arie (1968) found that the mean age of male heroin addicts upon first admission to London's Tooting Bec Hospital was 24.7 years for those born in England and Ireland and 33.5 for those born overseas, very similar to recent U.S. figures. English and Tori (1973) reported opiate users in their sample, most of whom were voluntarily undergoing methadone treatment, had a mean age of 22.8 years.

Compared with users of other drugs, Nurco and Lerner (1972) found male heroin users in Maryland corrections to be older. Of their sample, 48% of heroin abusers were under 25 years of age in contrast to 73% for users of other opiates and synthetics and 70% for all others. Similarly, the 15- to 19-year-old group accounted for 14%. Platt, Hoffman, and Ebert (1976) reported that within a representative sample of youthful offenders in New Jersey, heroin addicts were consistently older than nonaddicts each year during the period from 1968 to 1971. In 1972, the mean age of addicts declined slightly, while nonaddicts who had been increasing in mean age from 1968 increased substantially. The mean age of addicts in 1968 was 20.8 years, which increased to 21.2 years in 1972. This trend continued throughout 1974, with the average age increasing to 22. On the other hand, DuPont and Greene (1973) reported the average age of incarcerated addicts in the District of Columbia increased from 23.1 to 25.7 years from January 1971 through August 1972; during the same period, no similar changes occurred among nonuser offenders. The authors interpreted these findings as an indication that fewer new users were being created and many users were quitting.

Age of Onset of Addiction

Beckett and Lodge (1971) found that the average age of onset of heroin addiction was 20 years in their sample of addicts in treatment. This finding is congruent with the observation of Bourne (1974) that ". . . 19 is the age of greatest vulnerability to heroin use . . ." (p. 9). The largest grouping according to age in the Beckett and Lodge study was 56% in the 20- to 24-year-old category, followed by 23.5% in the under 20 group, and 14.5% in the 25- to 34-year-old bracket. The smallest percentage was in the 35- to 49-year-old group (6%). In contrast, the most common age category represented in the London sample of Hewetson and Ollendorf (1964) was the 25 to 34 year group (42%), followed by the 20 to 24 year group (36%) and the 35 to 49 year and under 20 year groups with 15% and 7% respectively. Beckett and Lodge (1971) also report the following figures representing the addict population known to the Home Office in 1966: under 20, 25%; 20 to 34, 41%; 35 to 49, 12%; and over 50, 21%. The authors suggest that the high rate of admission for treatment between the ages of 20 and 34, 70.5%, nearly double the reported percentage of this age group in the general population, indicates the point at which heroin produces progressively less pleasure for the addict and leads him to seek treatment.

Bewley and Ben-Arie (1968) found the following percentages of their English sample of admissions to treatment had begun taking heroin at each of the following successive age levels: 16 to 18, 16%; 19 to 21, 34%; 22 to 24, 27%; 25 to 27, 11%; over 27, 11%. Use of other drugs started earlier: 13 to 15, 16%; 16 to 18, 21%; 19 to 21, 38%; 22 to 24, 7%; 25 to 27, 5%; and over 27, 3%. With respect to users of different types of drugs, Nurco and Lerner (1972) found no differences among their heroin abusers, abusers of opiates and other synthetics and other drug abusers in age at first use. All began abusing their drug of choice in their teens.

Winick (1965) noted that the earlier in life opiate use begins, the longer it is likely to continue. He suggests that for every year that drug use is delayed in onset, the overall length of use is decreased by one-eighth to one-ninth of a year.

Cohen and Klein (1972) studied the relationship between age of onset and later drug use in white middle-class psychiatric patients 15 to 25 years of age. They found that while earlier age of initial use was strongly related to later involvement, this was not true for males who use heroin. In this group, later onset of drug use led to a lesser involvement with a variety of drugs but to a greater involvement with heroin. As Cohen and Klein note, their finding contradicts that of Robins and Murphy (1967) who found in a sample of normal black males that the earlier drugs were used, the greater the risk of heroin use. Females, on the other hand, were more likely to use heroin and other drugs if they started drug use at an early age; females starting later rarely became involved in heroin use. Cohen and Klein (1972) suggest two explanations for the disparity of these findings with those for males. First, they suggest that "heroin use starts within a certain age range which the younger male users have not yet reached" (p.

269). They cite as support for this viewpoint the observation of Chein et al (1964) that 16- to 17-year-old boys are most susceptible to becoming "hooked." Second, they suggest that earlier users tend to be motivated more by sensation-seeking, trying a variety of drugs. In contrast, later users are seen as attempting to reduce the level of sensation or, as Cohen and Klein suggest, to "narcotize themselves." There is some support for this idea in the data presented in Chapter 10. Comparing the more recent findings with those obtained at an earlier time, Ball and Chambers (1970) note the striking overrepresentation (53%) of male Lexington patients admitted in 1966 who began their opiate use before the age of 20 in contrast to a very small percentage who began using opiates before the age of 20 in 1936 (16%).

In their study of addicts at Lexington and Fort Worth Ball and Chambers (1970) noted that the greatest percentage of patients (47%) started to use opiates between the ages of 15 and 19, and the next greatest (25%) between 20 and 24 years of age. Only 7% had become users during their 30s and only 4% during their 40s. Overall, 61% of males had started to use opiates before the age of 21. Ball and Chambers note a striking resemblance of their data to New York City data in which 64% of male addicts had begun opiate use before age 21.

Onset of opiate addiction for southern whites admitted to Lexington and Fort Worth occurred at a later age than for any other racial or ethnic group, including northern whites. They also tended to have a high rate of legal employment, reflecting the higher overall social competence of this group. Heroin, in contrast to other opiates, was less frequently used and a smaller proportion of the opiate was obtained from illegal sources.

Race and Ethnicity

Winick (1965) summarized several studies which suggested that the last several decades had seen a greater proportion of addicts in large cities with large minority group populations. He felt there was little question about the high prevalence of opiate users in slum areas of large cities, where racial minorities also reside in great concentrations.

According to Ball and Chambers (1970) the racial and ethnic composition among admissions to Lexington in 1963 was as follows: black, 29.8%; white, 44.1%; Mexican, 12.2%; and Puerto Rican, 13.9%, approximately half of whom were residents of Puerto Rico. In a comparison of the racial composition of their admissions with the U.S. population, minority groups showed an incidence of addiction three to nine times greater than those groups represented in the general population. Ball and Chambers (1970) reported that Pescor found nonwhites constituted only 11.6% of addicts at Lexington in 1936. By 1966, this percentage had risen to 56% of the addict population. The racial pattern of admissions to Lexington is largely a function of state of origin. In 1963, while two-thirds of patients from New York, the District of Columbia, and Illinois were black or Puerto Rican, these racial groups constituted only 10% of admissions from Alabama, Georgia, and Kentucky (Ball, 1965).

Kaplan and Meyerowitz (1970) found an overrepresentation of minority group members among their addict sample in Houston. The racial distribution was white, 42%; black, 23%; and Hispanic, 35%; compared to Houston's adult population distribution of 81%, 13%, and 5% respectively. Ball and Chambers (1970) comment that the major demographic change that has occurred in the addict population in the last 40 years has been mainly from white males to members of minority groups. They note this figure reflects the high incidence of heroin addiction among poverty groups in large urban areas comprised primarily of minority members. Seeking to explain racial differences such as those described here, Vaillant (1966e) also noted the greater than expected prevalence of post-war urban narcotic addiction among ethnic minority groups and suggested three possible reasons for the problem. First, minority group status has associated with it uncertain and devalued identity. Second, "socio-economic deprivation and the contagious delinquency (are) associated with urban slums" (p. 534). Third, there is also the social stress associated with recent emigration to the city. Thus all these conditions create the kinds of stresses that foster an environment in which drug use is more likely to occur. It has also been suggested by Nurco (1979) that black addicts come from families which have not been as able as their white peers to prepare their children for the demands of an urban society.

Yet these racial-ethnic differences are not necessarily a consistent finding. Among black males, addicts were found to be more likely than experimenters or nonusers to come from broken homes, to have friends who were involved in serious types of drug use and other illegal activities, and to drop out of high school (Crawford, Washington, and Senay, 1980). Examining a younger population group, Johnson (1973) found much higher rates of use of heroin and other drugs among blacks than among whites during high school. In the year following high school, however, this difference narrowed and whites approached rates similar to those for blacks. Finally, racial-ethnic differences were found *not* to be clearly related to treatment outcome in the DARP studies by Sells and his associates (Simpson and Sells, 1982).

Sex

According to Winick (1962), and Lindesmith and Gagnon (1964), prior to the Harrison Act there were more women than men using opiates, primarily for relief of pain, but the relative number of men using opiates has increased since then. In 1970, Ball and Chambers noted that females constituted 16 to 21% of addicts in the United States. Winick (1957) estimated a male-to-female ratio of 3:1 among narcotics users. The Treasury Department reported a 4.4:1 ratio in 1962 (U.S. Treasury Department, 1962b).

Marital Status

The general finding seems to be that married individuals are in the minority among heroin addicts. For instance, Blumberg et al (1974) found 20% of their sample of English addicts seeking treatment were married and living with their spouses, and 19% with steady friends of the opposite sex. Twenty-five percent had boy- or girlfriends who were not living with them, and 34% reported no steady boy- or girlfriends. Bucky (1973) found that 17% of his Navy enlisted man heroin-user group were married, the highest percentage of all groups of drug abusers he studied. If the younger age of Bucky's subjects is taken into account, this percentage is probably not very different from that reported by Blumberg.

Of 536 heroin addicts Goldsmith et al (1972) studied in New Orleans, 29% were married at the time (including common-law marriages), a figure the authors believe to be an underrepresentation of marital status in this group as compared with the general population. In contrast, Bewley and Ben-Arie (1968) did not find any significant difference between the marital status of male heroin addicts discharged from Tooting Bec Hospital in England and the general population.

When addicts are married, the quality of their marriage is often poor, with a high incidence of separation and marital maladjustment. Bucky (1973) found his heroin-user group had the highest percentage of divorces (17%) and poor marriages (18%). In the Beckett and Lodge (1971) sample of male addicts in treatment, 71% were single, and 7 of the 10 married addicts were separated. In three cases, the wives were also using heroin. In all marriages there were pressures of tension and sexual frustration.

Kaplan and Meyerwitz (1970) noted that 41% of their addict sample versus 17% of a normal control group had been previously, but was not married at the time of their study. Of the married addicts 24% had previously been married compared with 9% of nonaddicts. Nurco and Lerner (1972) found a smaller percentage of single men among heroin abusers (64%) than among abusers of opiates and synthetics or all other drugs that were similar to each other, 73% and 74% respectively. The proportion of separated heroin addicts was only slightly higher than for other drug groups. Chambers and Moffett (1970) reported black addicts were no more often married than expected, but, if married, were more likely to have an unsuccessful marital relationship.

The destructive nature of the heroin world upon interpersonal relations, particularly love relationships, is described by Rosenbaum (1981). Initially providing an addicted couple with communality of interest, heroin soon undermines other important aspects of the love relationship, leading to embitterment of the woman with men in general, and the male addict in particular.

Socioeconomic Status

A general assumption of many studies has been that addicts usually come from the most deprived levels of our society. In support of this point, Winick (1965) summarized a number of studies and noted they suggest that "socioeconomic status is a crucial contributor to opiate use in America" (p. 14). One reason for this, he suggested, was the high level of mistrust, negativism, and defiance found in the lower socioeconomic areas in which heroin addiction is most common. Likewise, Kaplan and Meyerowitz (1970) found that their addict group came from families of lower social status than the nonaddict controls. However, the picture remains unclear. For example, although Chein et al (1964) found black users were more deprived socioeconomically than nonusers, they also found that white and Puerto Rican users were more often of a higher socioeconomic status than nonusers. The investigators were unable to offer an explanation for this pattern.

Kleinman (1978) makes the thought-provoking observation that while socioeconomic status factors have a significant effect on age of onset for addiction for inner-city natives, no such effect appears upon migrants to the city. Thus, socioeconomic factors would seem to be operative only where the individual has already been acculturated to the environment.

Currently, addicts can be found in all segments of our society. In a study by Beckett and Lodge (1971) the addicts in treatment represented the entire range of social classes from professional to unskilled laborer. Most of their addicts "came from homes headed by a successful father as, for example, a government executive officer, two bank managers, a buyer, a grocer who had built up a small chain of shops, a company director, and a housemaster" (p. 30). Lukoff et al (1972) found reported heroin use by self or kin occurred most frequently in families with white collar occupations and higher incomes, in contrast to families not reporting heroin use. With respect to social origins, more reported use occurred where the father was a white collar worker and had at least some high school education.

Johnson (1973) found that the lowest and second highest socioeconomic groups reported greater heroin use than any others. Finally, Bewley and

Ben-Arie (1968) found the fathers of a sample of 100 male heroin addicts studied did not differ in social class from the general population. The addicts themselves seemed to be downwardly mobile, since those addicts whose fathers were at the upper end of the social distribution scale tended to be in the lower status groups. A similar finding is reported by Chambers and Ball (1970) who noted that among opiate addicts who committed suicide while in treatment at Lexington, 38.5% were downwardly mobile with respect to occupational status when compared with their fathers. In a survey of 2707 students in New Orleans parochial and private schools, Clack (1972) found admitted use of narcotic drugs to be unrelated to social class (and also to race and sex).

With respect to occupational status, Kaplan and Meyerowitz (1970) found 56% of their addicts (in contrast to 21% of normal controls) fell into semiskilled or unskilled categories. Addicts also tended to have lower occupational aspirations even when age and social class were taken into account. Further, the addicts anticipated a lower rate of peak earnings and aspired to membership in a lower social status group. These results persisted after age and social status origins were considered. Generally, the prevalence of blue-collar or unskilled workers has been observed in various studies of addict populations. In 1930, the Mayor's report (Lambert et al, 1930) noted unskilled laborer was the most frequent occupation among narcotics users. Winick observed that the typical user for the 15 year period preceding his (1965) summary probably had no established occupation.

Nurco and Lerner (1972) found no differences in occupational distributions among abusers of heroin, opiates, other synthetics, and other drugs, with the major representation being in the structural and building contracting trades and the service occupations. Fewer craftsmen and professionals and more farmers were found among a heroin-user group than among other drug-user groups by Bucky (1971). Family income tended to be lower, with heroin users having the highest percentage (13%) of all groups reporting under $5000 annually.

Education

There is some disagreement in the literature regarding the educational characteristics of heroin addicts compared with their nonaddict peers. Several investigators have reported that addicts either had poorer educational backgrounds than comparable groups, or that they were not appreciably different from them. For instance, heroin addicts in the Kaplan and Meyerowitz (1970) study had completed an average of 9.4 years of education compared with 11.4 years for their nonaddict control. Nurco and

Lerner (1972) found addicts in the Maryland correctional system had a substantially lower percentage of high school graduates among them (12%) than other opiate and synthetic drug abusers (24%) and about the same as abusers of other drugs (14%). Only 2% of heroin abusers in contrast to 6.5% of the abusers of all other drugs had any college education. Several writers have also reported a greater frequency of behavioral problems for addict groups in school. Beckett and Lodge (1971) found that 6 of the 39 male addicts they studied had been expelled from school, and Bucky (1971) reported that the greatest frequency of school problems among all addict groups was found among heroin addicts; 82% reported truancy and 69% had been expelled.

No differences in educational level between addicts and nonaddicts have been reported in several studies. For instance, Bewley and Ben-Arie (1968) found no differences in educational level between addicts in treatment in their English sample and the general population. Similarly, Blumberg et al (1974a) did not observe any differences between their London sample seeking treatment and the general population.

College attendance and performance, and type of school attended by heroin addicts were also examined in two studies. Bucky (1971) found that heroin addicts did not differ from other addict or nonaddict groups with respect to the percentage who had a college education, and Johnson (1973) found no relationship between use of any drug and college grades. Also, no differences were present with respect to type of college attended— community college, liberal arts college, or university. The incidence of reported heroin use was equally present in public and private colleges (2% each) in contrast to denominational colleges (1%) (American Institute of Public Opinion, 1971). In terms of area of study, the greatest incidence of heroin use was among students in the humanities (3%), followed by those in the social sciences (2%), business and education (1% each) and math, science, and engineering (0%).

In contrast to the above findings, a grouping of recent studies in the literature provides evidence that the heroin addict is at a higher educational level than his nonaddict peers. Although Ball and Chambers (1970) found a normal distribution of addicts at Lexington with respect to educational level, with fewer at either extreme than the general population, this group was above average in years of education for their respective neighborhoods of origin. Heroin addicts had graduated from high school more frequently than other groups of drug users in Bucky's (1971) survey of Navy enlisted men. He found the heroin users had completed high school at an earlier age than users of other drugs or nonusers.

In a study that received substantial attention in the news media, Lukoff, Quatrone and Sardell (1972) reported that families in the Bedford-

Stuyvesant section of New York City who reported heroin use by self or kin were more often better educated. Platt, Hoffman, and Ebert (1976) found that heroin users among incarcerated youthful offenders in New Jersey had attained more formal education than nondrug users. In addition, over the 5 year period from 1968 to 1972, the heroin user groups in each successive year had attained a greater number of years of formal education.

Intelligence and Intellectual Functioning

There is little agreement in the literature as to the intellectual level of the heroin addict. Among those writers reporting data on the subject, Zimmering et al (1952) found their sample of adolescent addicts covered the intellectual range from borderline to high-average on the Wechsler-Bellevue Scales, with a mean in the dull-average range.

Brown and Partington (1942a) found that a sample of 371 narcotics addicts tested in 1939 and 1940 possessed an average IQ of 101 as measured by the Wechsler-Bellevue. The scores ranged from defective to very superior, and were very similar to those of the general population in that a bell-shaped curve was obtained with most scores in the middle (or average) range. The percentages of addicts at the extremes of the distribution were smaller, however, than expected. This finding is in agreement with the findings of Panton and Behre (1973), and Platt, Hoffman, and Ebert (1976), who found their groups of addicts had IQs within the average range. Panton and Behre's sample of adult felons had a mean IQ of 105.3 on the Revised Beta while Platt, Hoffman, and Ebert (1976) reported a mean IQ of 94 on the Revised Beta for a sample of 390 addicts with a mean age of 21 years. There was, however, a racial difference in the latter study, in which white users tended to have a higher mean IQ level than black users.

Bewley and Ben-Arie (1968) found an average IQ of 103.5 for a subsample of their English group of consecutive admissions to treatment. Disparate findings presenting a case for both a higher and lower than average addict IQ include the observation of Ball and Chambers (1970) that opiate users are of average or above average intelligence, with an underrepresentation of below average intelligence. This is congruent with the finding of Beckett and Lodge (1971) that 56% of their heroin addicts in treatment had an IQ of 110 or higher. On the other hand, Johnson (1973) found heroin use occurred most often in the lowest intellectual group before and after high school graduation.

With respect to patterns of intellectual functioning and related skills, additional findings in Brown and Partington's (1942a) study were as follows: (*a*) no decline of IQ with age; (*b*) no discrepancy between performance and verbal abilities; and (*c*) no differences in IQ between prisoners and probationers. A slight superiority of volunteers over prisoners in verbal and total IQs was found. The authors attributed this to the overrepresentation of professionals in the volunteer group as compared with the prisoners. Volunteers had the highest mean educational level (tenth grade) compared with prisoners (seventh grade) and probationers (eighth grade).

In a further study of the intellectual functioning of narcotic addicts, Brown and Partington (1942b) compared addicts and attendants on the following measures and skills: (*a*) Ferguson Form Boards; (*b*) analogies; (*c*) Number Series Completion, a task modified from the Army alpha examination, (*d*) mazes; (*e*) Knox cubes; (*f*) Healy Picture Completion Test; (*g*) perseveration; (*h*) memory for names and faces, taken from the Social Intelligence Test; .(*i*) paper form; (*j*) Cancellation of Forms Test; (*k*) block-counting; and (*l*) distributed attention, as measured by a modification of the Taylor Number Series. The findings were that no differences existed between the narcotic addict and nonaddict groups on untimed procedures. Where speed was involved, however, there was a tendency for addicts to do better. The addict group tended to surpass the attendants on the following tests: cancellation of forms, distributed attention, and speed in adding, subtracting, and multiplying simple numbers. When different kinds of tasks were mixed, the addicts' scores tended to be lower than their performance levels for similar tasks (e.g., all addition, all multiplication, etc.) than those of the controls.

Korin (1974) found no differences in performance on the Kent Series of Emergency Scales between psychotic and nonpsychotic heroin users and psychotic and nonpsychotic nonopiate-user controls. He did, however, find certain deficiencies evident in both his psychotic and nonpsychotic heroin-user groups on the Bender Gestalt. Both heroin-user groups displayed marked degrees of errors in reproduction of Bender figures, reflecting the presence of perceptual motor disturbance. In fact, the nonpsychotic heroin users did more poorly on this task than psychotic nonheroin users. Korin concluded that the responses of the heroin patients probably reflected personality traits. This seems a reasonable conclusion, since scores for detoxified and nondetoxified heroin addicts did not differ.

Neuropsychological Functioning

A number of recent studies have evaluated the degree to which heroin users demonstrate neuropsychological deficits. One of the problems of this research has been the general lack of specificity of the nature of drug abuse in the samples utilized, thus limiting any interpretations. Thus, Grant, Adams, Carlin, Rennick, Judd, Schooff and Reed (1978) report results in a sample of "poly-drug users, many of whom used opiates." The results of Grant et al's (1976a, 1976b, 1978) studies variously found 37 to 64 percent of "poly-drug abusers" to demonstrate neuropsychological deficits. On the other hand, studies by Bruhn and Maage (1975) and Fields and Fullerton (1975) failed to find such deficits in opiate addicts when the Halstead-Reitan Battery was employed under well-controlled conditions.

Employing an abbreviated, economical battery of tests, Rounsaville, Novelly, Kleber and Jones (1981) evaluated the neuropsychological functioning of 72 opiate addicts. They found moderate to severe impairment in some 53 percent of subjects, and mild impairment in 26 percent. Only some 21 percent demonstrated no evidence of impairment. This distribution was found to be generally comparable to a group of diagnosed epileptics with respect to presence of evidence reflecting general cerebral dysfunction. Antecedents of greater impairment appeared to be childhood hyperactivity, early school dropout, poor educational achievement, and greater severity of use of alcohol and cocaine. Impairment was found not to be related to histories of head injuries, duration or severity of illicit use with the exception of cocaine, criminal history, psychiatric symptoms, social functioning, or personality pathology. The study contains many possible sources of confounding variables, which are discussed by the authors, and thus great caution needs to be exercised in interpreting these findings. This is particularly true in the light of the inconsistency in reported findings on this issue by other investigators.

SOCIAL CHARACTERISTICS OF ADDICTS

Social Pathology

The relationship between the incidence of narcotic addiction and social pathology in Baltimore was examined by Nurco and Lerner (1972) on a geographic basis. They compared incidence rates for narcotic addiction with indices of financial dependence, adult arrests, and juvenile delinquency on a census tract by census tract basis and found that narcotic addiction is found in the same areas where one finds extreme deprivation, crime, and juvenile delinquency. However, the extent to which each of these indices of social pathology was present was much more closely related to the other two being present than to the extent of narcotic addiction. Thus the presence or absence of narcotic addiction did not follow the extent of deprivation as closely as these other indices.

Residential Factors

Generally there has been little doubt that large urban centers usually have high rates of heroin addiction. In cities the high population concentration of high-risk groups with multiple problems as well as overall greater levels of environmental frustration, social stress, and deviant peer culture, tends to provide the medium from which epidemics of heroin use can originate. In 1970, Ball and Chambers reported that there had been a significant increase since 1937 in the number of addicts admitted to Lexington and Fort Worth from northern metropolitan areas. In part this reflects the shift, since the thirties, away from the type of addict characterized by several writers as the white, southern opiate user, and toward the northern ghetto dweller, mainly from minority groups. As observed by O'Donnell (1969), these two groups of addicts differed in several ways upon admission to Lexington. First, they differed in self-concept, with the urban addicts seeing themselves as healthy persons using drugs "for kicks." The rural addicts were often medical addicts who viewed themselves as ill. Second, the narcotic used was usually heroin only in the urban group. Third, the source of drugs for the urban addict was more likely to be the illicit market, whereas the rural addict usually secured narcotics from legal sources. Finally, a substantial drug culture existed for the urban addict that was almost nonexistent for the rural addict. By the 1970's, however, the situation had changed to its present state. Johnson (1973) found little difference between communities of different sizes in regard to heroin use among young people. He suggested that "there is little evidence . . . that being in a large city makes a person of this age substantially more susceptible to involvement with heroin" (p. 100). Further, Dr. Robert DuPont, director of the National Institute on Drug Abuse, testified on October 7, 1974, before a House subcommittee that the incidence of drug use was increasing in smaller cities and rural areas. Noting that there had been an "unexpected increase in heroin addiction in smaller cities like Macon, Georgia, Des Moines, Iowa, or Jackson, Mississippi," he went on to attribute this increase to a radiation of such use out from the major population areas, following a "reasonably predictable time lag."[1]

Residential Mobility

In general, addicts seem to be a stable group geographically. Ball and Chambers (1970) reported that addicts seeking treatment at Lexington tended to be "reasonably stable in their place of residence" (p. 10). Similarly, Ball and Bates (1970) did not find opiate addicts in treatment to be any more geographically mobile from birth to first admission to treatment than

---

[1] *Philadelphia Evening Bulletin,* October 8, 1974.

the general U.S. population. In fact they suggested that addicts "would be less mobile than the general population if unemployment, socio-economic status, race, and city were controlled" (p. 105). With respect to specific ethnic groups, Ball and Bates (1970) found both northern blacks and New York City Puerto Ricans are no more mobile than their respective base populations. The authors concluded that there was no evidence to support a relationship between mobility and addiction patterns.

The issue of the influence of parental mobility on the development of addiction in offspring is not quite as clear. The research of Ball and Chambers (1970) indicates that "most addicts are native born of native parentage . . . [and that] the foreign-born are under-represented when compared to the general population" (p. 10). Ball and Bates (1970) examined the relationship between parental mobility and opiate addiction, and found a strong correlation between parental migration and opiate addiction among offspring, especially among black patients.

Two studies (Ellinwood, Smith, and Vaillant, 1966; Vaillant, 1966e) indicated that first-generation residents of the ghetto are most susceptible to drug addiction. To explain this finding, Ellinwood et al (1966) suggested that the children of black migrants from the South and Puerto Rican children did not usually internalize parental values, but sought values from their peer groups instead, particularly when the value systems of the parents were at odds with the general ghetto culture. In the same way, Ellinwood et al noted, the increased incidence of drug use among middle-class American youth may reflect this generation gap.

Vaillant (1966e) found that narcotic addicts admitted to Lexington from New York City consisted of three times as many first-generation New Yorkers as immigrants, and that minority group membership was another important variable in admissions. Strong support for this hypothesis came from Vaillant's finding that the ethnic composition of the Lexington population tended to follow the immigration patterns of the parents of these ethnic groups. Vaillant notes that the oldest ethnic group at Lexington in 1961 was the Chinese, followed by non-Hispanic whites (usually Mexicans). The reason for this, suggests Vaillant, is that the first-generation child experiences a greater alienation, being torn between the values of his parents and those of his culture. At the same time, his parents spend a disproportionate amount of time coping with their new environment, and the mother, deprived of her own family ties, may be less able to meet the needs of her dependents.

Employment Patterns and Occupations

Scher (1973a) reported the results of a survey of 34,000 employed heroin addicts conducted by the Center of Urban Studies of the National Institute of Mental Health as follows: 9.8% were professionals, technical workers, managers, and owners; 22.0% were clerical and other white collar workers; 19.5% were skilled and semiskilled workers; and 29.3% were salespeople. Goldsmith et al (1972) found female addicts had a poorer record of job experience than male addicts. Their interpretation of this finding was that the types of employment open to many male addicts (e.g., longshoreman, construction worker) were intermittent in nature and thus permitted of a greater amount of flexibility in contrast to the kinds of jobs open to women. Chambers, Hinesley, and Moldestad (1970) found that 47% of their sample of female drug addicts admitted having engaged in prostitution.

With respect to patterns of employment and unemployment, Ball and Chambers (1970) reported that 31% of their admissions to Lexington and Fort Worth were unemployed, 31.7% were engaged in criminal activities, and 33.1% were employed. Ungerleider (1973) reported that of 1000 opiate addicts seen in a recent year only 25% were employed.

Blumberg et al (1974a) found 39% of their sample who sought treatment were working full time, 4% were employed part time, 7% were housewives, and 50% were unemployed. They reported that 36% of their sample had lost a job because of drug use, due to poor work performance, among other reasons, rather than to discovery. When questioned about their sources of income during the preceding month, 66% reported own or spouse's earnings, 49% borrowing or sharing with friends, 38% relatives, 37% selling things other than drugs, 34% social security, 32% selling drugs, and 22% stealing.

Beckett and Lodge (1971) found that of 11 addicts in their English sample who had left school at 15, 6 had been out of work upon admission. The educational level of those who left school at 17 or 18 was not as high as would normally have been expected, when their intellectual capacity and education were considered. Crowther (1974) found that only 50% of her sample of college opiate users had ever held a full-time job, although 42% reported having held a job for 2 years or more. As Crowther points out, however, this greater rate of steady employment is probably related to the fact that her sample had attended college, "itself a responsible action in our culture" (p. 251).

Yet, being a heroin addict does not seem to necessarily disqualify one from being employed, according to Nelson (1981). He cites a number of studies which reveal long-term employment of heroin addicts in a broad range of jobs, ranging from blue collar to professional. Chapter 11 contains a section focusing specifically upon the relationship between employment and treatment outcome.

Criminality

A history of criminal deviance seems to be a common characteristic of many heroin addicts. Of admissions to Lexington and Fort Worth, 86.6% had a record of arrests prior to admission (Ball and Chambers, 1970). Only 13.4% had never been arrested. Ball and Chambers comment that this latter percentage is high, considering the average of 9.9 years of opiate use in this group. Fifty percent of addicts in treatment both at Phoenix House and among New York City welfare applicant and recipient samples were found to have records of prior arrests (Biase, 1972). In Nash's (1973) examination of 19 narcotics treatment programs in New Jersey, he found that 83% of the clients in methadone treatment and 57% of those in drugfree programs had been arrested before entry into treatment. The average number of arrests for these two groups were 5.7 for those in methadone programs and 2.3 for those in drugfree programs. This difference was artifactual, however, since persons entering methadone programs tend to be older. For both groups, the average number of arrests was two for every 3 years between age 18 and entry into treatment.

Among Navy enlisted men, heroin users comprised the greatest percentage going to Captain's Mast (57%), and having been court-martialed (25%) (Bucky, 1971). Both of these percentages far exceeded those of other drug-user groups. Heroin users in this sample also had the largest percentages of arrests (70%) of all user groups. Bewley and Ben-Arie (1968) found that among their sample a history of convictions prior to first admission to the hospital for treatment was common. Only 17 of the 92 admissions they studied had no prior convictions, and 57% had two or more. Their conclusion was that "generally there was a history of deviant behavior even before drug-taking in this group" (p. 728). Brown, Gauvey, Meyers, and Stark (1971) found that 74% of adult male addicts, 78% of juvenile male addicts, and 40% of adult female addicts had committed illegal acts prior to their initial use of heroin. Furthermore, arrest rates for these three groups prior to using heroin were 53% for adult males, 55% for juvenile males, and 20% for adult females. Brown et al concluded that "this study lends support to the findings reported elsewhere suggesting that the addict—and particularly the male addict—is drawn from a culture or subculture already invested in illegal activity" (p. 642). Nurco and Lerner (1972) found that of drug abusers known to the police before their present arrest, heroin abusers represented a larger proportion (91%) than those unknown (60%). Data are also available on the extent of drug-related arrests as well as the time sequence relative to the onset of addiction. Beckett and Lodge (1971) noted that of the male addicts they saw in treatment only a small number had not had legal difficulties; 32% had been to court before the onset of addiction, and 44% afterward for the first time. According to Kaplan and Meyerowitz (1970), the mean age for the first arrest of their addict sample was 16.1 years; drugs were first used at 18.3 years, and the individual was hooked at 20.8 years.

Blumberg et al (1974a) found 80% of the 208 persons of their English addict sample had at least one court conviction, 46% had been convicted in the 12 months prior to seeking treatment, and 69% before that; 52% had been convicted of at least one drug offense, and 59% of at least one nondrug offense; 47% had at least one conviction prior to their first fix. The female addicts in Blumberg's sample had fewer convictions than the males during the preceding 12 months. Crowther (1974) reported that 70% of her college addict sample had never been arrested; 85% of those who had, however, were charged with a drug offense. In contrast, Crowther (1972) found that 69% of Mexican-American addicts in a Fort Worth hospital had been arrested prior to their first use of narcotics, and 55% were under 16 years of age. Blumberg et al (1974a) reported that admitted illegal activity in the three months prior to interview included the following: illegal possession of drugs (95%), selling drugs (50%), knowingly receiving stolen goods (41%), stealing goods (33%), and obtaining by false pretenses (22%). Nurco and Lerner (1972) reported that heroin addicts in the Maryland correctional system were more likely to have been convicted of a nonviolent offense (78%) than either abusers of other opiates and synthetics (58%) or other drug abusers (36%). However, Kozel, Dupont, and Brown (1972), in their examination of offenses attributed to heroin addict and nonaddict inmates in the District of Columbia jail, found no difference between them in the commission of crimes against property as opposed to crimes against persons. In their study of female opiate addicts, Chambers, Hinesley, and Moldestad (1970) found a high incidence of narcotics sales (25%), prostitution (50%), adolescent arrests (75%), and arrests prior to drug use (21%). Among addicts in treatment in New Jersey between 1972 and 1973 there were twice as many arrests for crimes such as breaking and entering and robbery as there were for narcotics-related crimes such as sales and abuse (Nash, 1973).

Goldsmith, et al (1972) reported white rather than black, addicts had been arrested at consistently earlier ages, and averaged less time between arrests. Chambers and Moffett (1970) found black addicts were illegally employed more often than black nonaddicts. Black female addicts were more often involved in selling and/or prostitution than comparable white female addicts and had also been arrested more frequently for these activities (Chambers, Hinesley, and Moldestad, 1970). In Nash's sample (Nash, 1973), whites had a greater proportion of arrests for narcotics-related offenses than did nonwhites.

CONCLUDING COMMENTS

The conclusion that may be drawn from the data in this chapter is the realization that the portrait of the addict in terms of his personal and social characteristics is not entirely clear. Even when a preponderance of evidence exists to support a particular characteristic, such as socioeconomic status, there are still sufficient findings available to the contrary to preclude presuming that this is a universal characteristic of all addicts. However, several characteristics may be attributed to addicts in general. First, addicts tend to have had relatively poor familial environments in the formative periods of their lives. For instance, their parents tended to have a high incidence of serious problems of a psychiatric, physical, or interpersonal nature. Home life was usually unstable because of parental absence for any of a number of reasons. Heroin addiction is more common among ethnic and social minorities in our country and, although it tends to be most prevalent among the economically underprivileged elements of our society, also occurs elsewhere. Further, those persons who become addicted are usually an unlikely subgroup within a poverty culture. There is evidence to suggest, for instance, that this subgroup is often (although not exclusively) comprised of persons within the culture who have the highest levels of social competence. The fact that several recent and extensive studies have indicated that the addict is an individual who possesses higher levels of intelligence and educational experience relative to his peers and/or cultural background carries important implications with respect to developing an increased understanding of the dynamics of heroin addiction. An integration of the material presented in this chapter as well as in the other chapters comprising Part Three will be provided in Part Five.

CHAPTER 10

Issues Related to the
Course of Addiction

This chapter discusses the addict's behavior at certain points in his career as a heroin user. Thus, for example, relevant issues early in this career, such as reports of why the addict uses heroin, the role played by his peers in initiating use, and the prior use of other illicit drugs are reviewed. Temporal considerations in addiction, such as the length of time between initial drug use and addiction, and the relationship of early drug use to later addiction are dealt with, followed by an examination of the relationship between heroin use and criminal activity. Finally, issues related to the outcome of the addictive process, such as entry into treatment and rates of relapse after treatment, are considered. The aim of this chapter is to fill out the picture of the addict as developed from preceding chapters, which have focused on his personality and personal characteristics.

INITIAL USE OF HEROIN

Reasons for Initial Use of Heroin

A decade ago, Bowden (1971) summarized a number of factors related to initial use of heroin. He listed seven factors which he believed influence the first use of opioids, given that more than one of these is usually operative at any one time: (a) diminished self-esteem, due to ". . . early family disruption, lack of role models for successful function through legitimate pursuits, poor educational and vocational skills, unsatisfactory work habits, and lack of general social skills. . . . These often combine to give a sense of purposelessness in life" (p. 136); (b) interpersonal strivings in which the addict fantasizes that ". . . opioids will solve problems of social isolation or sexual inadequacy, either magically per se or through diminishing anxiety or other unpleasant emotions . . ." (p. 136). Also included in this category is the instrumental use of the drug to achieve intimacy and/or acceptance by others; (c) proselytism, to convince others to join him in drug use to enable him to "cope with his own sense of shame and his need to protect his self-image" (p. 137); (d) ignorance of opioid effects, particularly of one's ability to resist becoming addicted; (e) pleasure of a fantasized nature being expected from drug use or, similarly, the quest for mystical or transcendental experiences, usually by young persons, often those with serious emotional difficulties; (f) tranquilization, to reduce anxiety, and to help one cope with unpleasant affect states; and (g) pain, for which opiates are administered in order to provide analgesia.

Life Disturbance

The general theme of "life disturbance" as a causal factor in heroin addiction has been touched upon by many writers and was discussed in detail in the previous chapter. Several of the factors suggested by Bowden (1971) could result from such disruption, specifically diminished self-esteem and the attempt on the part of the addict to deal with unpleasant affect states. Certainly, the lives of many addicts both prior to and after becoming addicted are less than stable. In this respect it has been suggested that addicts lead lives that involve a substantial and sustained degree of change. Dudley, Rozell, Mules, and Hague (1974) studied this issue and found that the recent level of life change in both heroin addicts and alcoholics had been unusually high. A related finding was that heroin addicts had normal to augmented perception of the impact of life change and physical disease severity, but did not relate these conditions to their addiction. In contrast, alcoholics underperceived such events.

Focusing more specifically on the failure of the addict to cope with the many life changes with which he is faced, Flaherty (1973) quoted a military commander as noting that "drug abusers [in the service] are those who . . . are generally unable to cope with the stresses of a disciplined military society" (p. 7). He cites another officer as saying: "Many of the participants [in a drug program] are losers. I have yet to meet a participant who has not had some kind of family background problem such as alcoholism, divorce, bigamy, or incest" (p. 8). On the other hand, Bourne (1974) noted that some individuals functioning at a borderline level prior to becoming addicted have found the structuring of their daily lives around heroin to help them to maintain some degree of equilibrium. He comments further that these individuals are the ones most likely to succeed in a heroin maintenance program and the least likely to succeed in a drug-free program.

The Addict's Own View

Brown, Gauvey, Meyers, and Stark (1971) solicited heroin addicts' descriptions of why they began using heroin. While 44.9% of adult male addicts and 40.0% of adult females cited curiosity as a major reason, only 28.8% of juvenile males did. However, 65.8% of the juveniles cited the influence of friends, making this the major reason given by this group and also by adult females (51.4%). Adult males were as likely to attribute their first use of heroin to the influence of friends (43.9%) as they were to curiosity (44.9%). Initial use of heroin for the relief of personal problems was cited by 20.0% of adult females but only 7.1% of adult males and 12.3% of juvenile males gave this reason. Seeking a high was described by 16.3% of adult males and 15.1% of juvenile males, but only by 5.7% of adult females. Females' first use of heroin was more influenced by relatives (14.3%) than that of either adult males (3.1%) or juvenile males (2.7%). Thus, this study identified four reasons given by addicts for starting on heroin: curiosity, the influence of others, relief of personal problems, and mood change.

Some Specific Factors in Heroin Use

Escapism

One reason for using heroin may be to enable the individual to avoid, escape, or change an otherwise unpleasant existence. Oswald, Evans, and

Lewis (1969) note that "drugs of addiction are taken because, initially at least, they make possible an escape from reality. Those most vulnerable are people whose personalities bring them conflicts and anxieties, but little solace, from contacts with the real world. Given access to the drugs, they are enabled to escape to a less harsh world, a world more removed from reality and nearer to dreams" (p. 243).

Mood

Willis (1969) reported that of 108 English and American addicts studied, 32% reported mood disturbance (e.g., depression) as the chief reason for taking heroin. The nationality and sex breakdown was as follows: 43% British males versus 9% American males, and 56% British females versus 33% American females gave mood disturbance as their main reason. Thus taking heroin to influence mood seems to be a more commonly given reason for British addicts as opposed to their American counterparts, and this difference is especially significant between British and American males. Interestingly, however, Willis (1969) reported that only in three of his British patients was there actually "any substantial evidence of manifest mood disturbance of any severity" (p. 306). The desire to elevate mood above normal did not emerge as the chief reason for drug use, however, since this was reserved for curiosity about the effects of heroin (54%). Only 18.5% of respondents gave the desire to elevate mood above normal as their reason for using the drug. In this study then, the euphoria associated with drug use was not the desired effect for which heroin was used. Most respondents said that this effect could be achieved by the use of amphetamines or cannabis. In this regard, Crowther (1974) suggested that college heroin users tended to use drugs for their own sake rather than for their effects.

In contrast, however, Hekimian and Gershon (1968) found a desire for euphoria to be a common characteristic of heroin addicts, and saw these findings as supporting the hypothesis of Eddy et al (1965) "that narcotic addiction has a strong psychic dependence factor based on the desire for euphoria or avoidance of psychic pain" (p. 78). Hekimian and Gershon further suggested that "a depressive component is temporarily relieved by the drug" (p. 78). The desire to change mood as a reason for heroin use was also implicated in several other studies. For instance, Bucky (1971) reported that of his group of heroin users among U.S. Navy enlisted men, 33% started because it "feels good," and 15% because they were unhappy. Boredom was cited as a reason for drug use by Crowther (1974), Flaherty (1973), and Adler and Lotecka (1973). In the first study, boredom or a simple need to experiment were seen as motivating forces in addition to maturational difficulties. Adler and Lotecka found that habitual users of heroin and other drugs more often saw their world as boring, in contrast to users, tasters, or habitual alcohol users.

A study of mood states of pregnant (N=52) and non-pregnant (N=276) heroin addicts found no differences between the two groups. Both groups were similar to psychiatric outpatients in the mean levels of their moods. Although there was a slight trend for greater tenseness and anxiety among the pregnant addicts, the conclusion was drawn that the moods of pregnant and non-pregnant addicts were comparable (Steer and Schut, 1980).

Peer Influence

Several writers have referred to the important role played by peers in initial heroin use. For instance, Golosow and Childs (1973) studied a sample of military heroin addicts and also found most of their sample had been "introduced to heroin by their friends, who frequently exerted considerable influence through enticement and ridicule" (p. 10). He cites the means by which this pressure was exerted: "One reward for using heroin was a sense of acceptance. Discontinuation of its use was punished by mistrust, ridicule, and rejection by the peer group" (p. 10). Similarly, Blumberg et al (1974) suggested that the need for anxiety reduction and affiliation were important elements in the initial use of opiates. Also with respect to the influence of peers, Hunt (1974) notes: ". . . it is now generally believed that drug use spreads naturally . . . by interpersonal contact among associated individuals in peer groups" (p. 3). Specifically Blumberg et al (1972) reported that in 80% of their opiate addict sample at least one of three close friends had used opiates. Before starting opiate use, some 98% of the sample had known someone who had "fixed," the median number known being nine. Furthermore, friends of addicts were more likely to have used drugs than those of nonaddicts in a study of addicts and nonaddict controls by Kaplan and Meyerowitz (1970). Bucky (1971) noted that 15% of his Navy enlisted men studied indicated that they had used heroin because of friends.

Ball (1966) found that over 85% of his male subjects reported being initiated into heroin use by addict friends. This occurred usually in response to a request by the subjects for drugs from older addict friends. Ball saw the adolescent heroin-user peer group as exerting a dominant influence upon the younger subjects in his study. Typically, the younger subject requested of this group that he be included in the group's primary activity of heroin use. This assumption of the norms of the addict subculture was the predominant mode of first heroin use among males. Ball saw no evidence ". . . that the onset of drug use was a consequence of proselytizing, coercion, or seduction" (p. 126).

Nurco (1979) observed that ". . . there appears to be no doubt that peer pressure in beginning narcotic use is overwhelmingly important." (p. 318). He observed that first use of heroin tended to occur in small groups of from two to six persons, 90 percent of whom were male, with whites being present in smaller groups than blacks until recent times, when this pattern reversed itself. When circumstance surrounding initiation into the heroin user community in Washington, D.C., was examined, it was found to both be mediated through close friends, and to occur in a secure atmosphere in which anxiety and guilt are minimized (Gibbons, Brown, Greene, and DuPont, 1981). Initiators of drug use in novitiates tended to be older, male, intimate friends who were held in high regard by the novitiate.

According to Brown et al (1971) the role played by the encouragement of friends in initiating heroin use is more relevant for adolescents than for adults. This factor is extremely important, and its preeminence is probably most clearly seen in the adolescent's progression from marijuana to heroin use. The importance of this element has been recognized by a number of writers whose observations are summarized in the following section.

USE OF OTHER DRUGS BY HEROIN ADDICTS

Prior Use of Marijuana and Other Drugs by Heroin Addicts

The need to experiment with other drugs before starting on an "addictive career" has been observed to be the case by Nurco (1979). He noted that there has been relative stability in the age of first opiate use by addicts except during "heroin epidemics." Such periods result in a decline in age of first use, later reverting to "preepidemic" levels as the epidemic passes.

Kandal, Treiman, Faust, and Single (1976) proposed a three stage model of adolescent drug abuse. The first involves the use of legal drugs, such as alcohol, and is primarily influenced by societal mores. The second stage involves marijuana use and is one in which the primary influence is that of peers. The third, the frequent use of other illegal drugs, appears contingent on the parent-adolescent relationship.

Examining the patterns of primary drug abuse for a sample of 102,062 subjects, Tyler and Sheridan (1980) found that when first drug use occurred at age 15, marijuana was used first, followed by heroin, amphetamines, and cocaine. When age of first use was 16, a pattern of heroin followed by marijuana, amphetamines and cocaine emerged. In this study, heroin was found to be abused more by blacks than whites or Hispanics. With respect to females entering treatment, Tyler and Thompson (1980) found heroin to be most abused in the 19 to 20 year age at first use category, with marijuana the second most abused. For women whose age at first use was older (26), sedatives were the second most frequently abused drug. Heroin was found to be more frequently used by women with high school educations than by those with ninth grade educations.

Marijuana

Ball (1966), in his study of marijuana-smoking and later heroin use in Puerto Rican addicts, found a clear association between use of the two drugs. In 91% of the subjects he studied who smoked marijuana, heroin use was preceded by such smoking. Since 87.6% of his addict sample had smoked marijuana, this pattern of drug use was characteristic of a large portion of the population under study. Typically, marijuana-smoking began at age 18. Blumberg et al (1974) also found that over 90% of their sample of opiate addicts had at least tried marijuana and also amphetamines, methadone, and tranquilizers. Contrasting drug-using and nonusing female delinquents, Noble, Hart, and Nation (1972) found that 40 out of 194 girls who were using nonnarcotic drugs between 1966 and 1968 subsequently used narcotics, while only 1 out of 100 nonusers from the same population became users. A history of marijuana use was often found to be associated with heroin dependence among admissions to the Fort Worth and Lexington U.S. Public Health Service hospitals by Ball, Chambers, and Ball (1968). Although all these studies suggest that prior exposure to marijuana is related to later heroin use, there is no evidence of a causal relationship.

A suggestion as to the nature of the relationship between use of the two drugs is provided in a study by Fracchia, Sheppard, and Merlis (1973b) of cigarette smoking and later heroin use. The authors noted that prior cigarette smoking, like marijuana smoking, was related to later heroin use. Specifically, Fracchia, Sheppard, and Merlis (1973b) noted that median ages for first smoking cigarettes, first using an illicit drug, and first using heroin were 14.6 years, 15.5 years, and 17.3 years respectively. Cigarette smoking preceded heroin use in 98% of applicants to a methadone treatment program studied by Fracchia et al (1973b). It was suggested that cigarette smoking at an early age may reflect personality problems and that these problems may also lead to later drug use, "facilitated by the reinforcement achieved through early smoking behaviors" (p. 373). Martino and Truss (1973) also suggested a correlation between marijuana smoking and drug use. They saw use of both drugs as a reflection of similar underlying characteristics of the user. Later or concurrent marijuana use may also reflect the same motivations. The data of Fracchia et al concerning smoking is very similar to that obtained in England about the incidence of smoking in heroin addicts. Only 7% of the addict sample of Bewley and Ben-Arie (1968) were nontobacco smokers, compared with 40.2% and 33.5% in the 16- to 24-year-old and 25- to 34-year-old groups of all English men, respectively.

Ball, Chambers, and Ball (1968) suggested that marijuana use and delinquency were predisposing factors to opiate use among adolescents in U.S. metropolitan areas. They suggested a number of similarities between use of marijuana and heroin that might contribute to a relationship between prior marijuana use and later heroin use. These include the use of marijuana to produce a high, obtaining both drugs from illegal sources, drug use in a peer-group setting, and the use of heroin with the same friends who initiated marijuana use. This pattern, typical of metropolitan areas in the East and Far West, did not however occur in the southern states where the opiates used are usually nonheroin drugs.

Robins and Wish (1977) reported that, among urban black males, the following factors tended to precede opiate use: early sex experience, marijuana use, and dropping out of high school. Overall, however, opiate use seemed to be most related, as a deviant behavior, to the *total* number of other deviant behaviors observed in subjects. Thus, rather than being the outcome of these other acts, it was more a part of the overall *pattern* of such acts.

Black females were found by Chambers, Hinesley and Moldestad (1970) to have used marijuana as their first illegal drug and to have advanced to opiates in a peer-group setting. This pattern may be contrasted with the one for white female addicts who had not used marijuana but had become addicted to opiates through medically related routes, and who tended not to use heroin as their opiate of choice.

In a study by Ball (1966), the factors underlying the onset of female Puerto Rican opiate use were quite different from those for males. Typically, opiate use began as the result of medical treatment rather than as a result of same-sex peer influence. In addition, there was little prior marijuana use for female opiate addicts, heroin was less often the drug of choice, and fewer females tended to be arrested.

Lipscomb (1971) rejected the notion that marijuana use leads to other drug use. He noted that the data he obtained from a survey of drug use in ghetto youths cast doubt on the hypothesis that regular or experimental use of marijuana led to use of more devastating drugs. While 54% of his sample admitted to marijuana use, only 3% admitted to heroin use. This issue is explained more fully by Johnson (1973) who found the correlation of heroin use in a high school sample the year after high school to be +.32 with marijuana use while in high school. In addition, the relationship of later heroin use to use of other drugs in high school also is higher than for marijuana. The correlation between barbiturate use and later heroin use, for example, is +.48. This suggests that heroin use after high school is more strongly related to the use of drugs other than marijuana while in high school.

The general implication of the above findings seems to be that marijuana use does not in itself lead to later heroin use. Rather, the heroin user has generally tried marijuana first and then moved on to heroin, this pattern reflecting either the influence of the peer culture or other unspecified underlying factors. As usual, however, there is a discordant finding. Kozel, DuPont, and Brown (1972) found almost no difference between heroin addicts and nonaddicts in terms of the number who had used marijuana. Thus, although 75% of the addicts and 68% of the nonaddicts had used this drug in the past, this difference was not significant.

Prior Use of Drugs Other than Marijuana

With respect to drugs other than marijuana, it is the minority of heroin users who start with heroin itself as the first drug of abuse. Crowther (1974) found that 39% of her college heroin-user group had used the drug as their first narcotic. Some 16% reported having first used cough syrups containing narcotics, and 32% of her total sample of opiate users had used opium first; the use of this latter drug usually reflected initial use while in the armed forces. Interestingly, only 1 of 24 heroin users and 4 of the nonheroin opiate users reported having started use of opiates for a medical reason. Use of another illicit drug prior to using heroin seems to be the pattern for later heroin users, as reported by 74% of heroin users in the study. Similarly, heroin was the drug first used by 26% of the correctional drug-abuser population studied by Nurco and Lerner (1972). Of those who had started with another opiate, 81% had changed to heroin. Many initial users of barbiturates, marijuana, or other psychotropic drugs also switched to heroin. Exact percentages were 70% for the barbiturates, and 72% for marijuana and the psychotropics. Smaller numbers of those who had begun drug abuse with amphetamines or other drugs had progressed to heroin. When heroin was the first drug abused, a massive 96% continued to use it. Johnson (1973) also noted that use of one or more amphetamines, barbiturates, and hallucinogens tends to precede heroin use.

The possibility also exists, as suggested by Ball, Chambers, and Ball (1968), that there may be drug-specific addictions. This interpretation was based on their finding that few meperidine and methadone users among admissions to Lexington and Fort Worth had ever used heroin.

Concerning the broader issue of the relative preference of addicts for heroin versus other drugs of abuse, Blumberg et al (1974) reported the most commonly used drugs for his addict sample (in descending order of preference) were heroin, methadone, alcohol and marijuana, the last being used less than once weekly prior to attending the clinic. In a correctional setting, Nurco and Lerner (1972) found 73% of their abusers preferred heroin as their drug of abuse, 5% chose another opiate or a synthetic, 6% abused barbiturates, 5% used psychotropics including marijuana, 4% cocaine, 2% each amphetamines or LSD and other hallucinogens, and 1% preferred glue. Nurco (1979) notes that despite the fact that the age at which *both* addicts and nonaddicts begin drinking alcohol has been dropping, those teenagers who become narcotic addicts tend to begin using alcohol earlier than their age and social class peers. He attributes this to greater overall deviance on the addict's part during the teenage years.

ALCOHOL AND HEROIN

Alcoholism in treated opiate addicts was found by Rounsaville, Weissman, and Kleber (1982) to be a very significant problem, occurring at rates far above those in comparable community groups. Furthermore, when the sequence of alcoholism vs. drug use or seeking of treatment for opiate addiction was examined, alcohol problems were found to have been the first to occur. Entry into treatment did not appear to significantly impact alcohol abuse, one way or the other, and alcohol abuse, when present, continued through treatment. Finally, alcoholic addicts, when compared with nonalcoholic addicts, had fewer assets and greater liabilities, including histories of more disruptive childhoods, more legal problems, more polydrug abuse, more severe problems of social functioning, and higher rates of psychiatric problems. Overall, however, follow-up findings six months later found that alcoholism was of *little* prognostic significance in relationship to treatment outcome. Kaufman (1982) found alcohol abuse by heroin addicts to increase when heroin purity decreased and the addict cycled through a methadone program. In clear agreement with Rounsaville et al, Kaufman found much of the alcohol abuse of his sample to predate the onset of heroin use and dependence.

After reviewing the relevant literature, Stimmel (1979) concludes that "with respect to concomitant use of alcohol and heroin, anywhere from 25 percent to 80 percent of heroin addicts are found to consume a considerable quantity of alcohol on a regular basis, with up to 25 percent noted to be overtly alcoholic" (p. 175). He also notes that "excessive use of alcohol in methadone programs has also been shown to be considerable, with prevalence rates of problem drinking ranging from 12 percent to 40 percent and alcoholism noted in four to seven percent" (p. 175).

Kreek (1981) makes the interesting point that co-existence of narcotic and alcohol abuse and addiction, whereas thought a decade ago to be relatively infrequent, is today quite common. As yet, however, she observes, while there is no evidence of a definite relationship between alcoholism and narcotic addiction, there are several possible mechanisms of narcotic-ethanol interaction and/or commonality in effects. In this regard, she cites (a) the findings by Ross and his associates that both chronic morphine and ethanol treatment results in the selective depletion of brain calcium in animals (Ross, Medina, and Cardenas, 1974), (b) the possible reaction of ethanol with endogenous transmitter amines to form alkaloids which share some properties with narcotics (Cohen, 1976; Myers and Melchior, 1977; and Blum, Hamilton, Hirst, and Wallace, 1978), (c) the possible release of endorphins by ethanol, resulting in effects similar to those produced by opiates (Ho and Ho, 1979; Verebey and Blum, 1979), (d) possible interactions between narcotics, usually morphine and naloxone, on ethanol consumption in rats (Myers and Melchior, 1977; Ho, Chen, and Morrison, 1977), and (e) the suppression by' ethanol of naloxone precipitated abstinence syndrome in animals (Bass, Friedman, and Lester, 1978; Ho, Chen, and Kreek, 1979). Kreek (1981) summarized a number of studies which showed that chronic ethanol administration alters methadone disposition in the rat. Chronic methadone also accelerates ethanol metabolism, while chronic administration of both ethanol and methadone results in an even greater rate of ethanol elimination than either substance alone.

Substitution of alcohol for opiates, or at least the existence of such a relationship between alcohol use and methadone or heroin use, has been suggested by both Waldorf (1973) and McGothlin, Anglin, and Wilson (1977). These authors reported a significant increase in alcohol consumption while addicts are in methadone treatment or abstinence compared to such use while actively addicted. On the other hand, Green and Jaffe (1977) concluded that Vietnam Veterans demonstrated no subsequent increase in the rate of alcohol problems subsequent to termination of addiction. Gordis and Senay (1980) found former narcotic addicts to do poorly in alcoholism treatment. This was the case irrespective of whether they had had a methadone maintenance experience. Alcohol use preceded heroin use in more than half the cases, and was often heavy. The authors conclude that a history of narcotics use reduces markedly the likelihood of successful outcome in conventional alcoholism treatment, and that alcoholism and narcotic addiction are independent in their development.

Stimmel, Korts, Cohen, Jackson, Sturiano, and Hanbury (1981) suggest that while alcoholics and narcotics addicts represent an extremely heterogeneous population, serious consideration should be given to the formulation of a feasible common treatment approach for the two kinds of addiction. Gordis (1981) notes that while he is not certain as to whether alcoholism is more frequent among methadone clients than among matched non-narcotics users from the same area, alcoholism is "the leading cause of failure in drug treatment programs" (p. 57). He also reports on two clinical observations which he believes merit research attention: (a) the failure of both alcohol and opiates to relieve each other's withdrawal symptoms, and (b) the relative intractability of alcoholism in persons with a heroin use history.

A cautionary note is, however, raised by Kreek (1981). Noting the lack of clear evidence that the high rates of alcohol abuse in heroin addicts, both during and after treatment, is greater than for appropriately matched control groups, she concludes that there is no definite evidence of a link between alcohol and narcotics addictions, although clinical observation and some preliminary studies suggest the existence of such.

Noting the increasing awareness of the need to consider both drug and alcohol abuse as part of one overall picture requiring a combined therapeutic approach, Stimmel (1977) listed five relevant issues requiring attention: (a) the need for carefully designed studies to determine actual prevalence of dependency to two or more mood-altering substances, (b) funding of more basic studies of alcohol-drug interactions on the biological level, (c) development of effective designs for the evaluation of existing therapies for drug and/or alcohol abuse, (d) encouraging innovative treatment approaches with adequate experimental designs including follow-ups, and (e) supporting feasibility studies for combined treatment of alcohol and drug dependency.

Concurrent Use of Other Drugs

A characteristic of heroin users seems to be their sustained use of a wide variety of other drugs while using heroin. This finding is almost universal, and is amply illustrated by a study by Bewley and Ben-Arie (1968) who reported that at the time of admission to treatment nearly all of their heroin addict sample had used drugs other than heroin: 79% had used marijuana before becoming heroin dependent, 4% cocaine, 59% amphetamines, 18% barbiturates, 10% other opiates, and 6% or less had used intravenously administered amphetamines, or LSD, or opium. The following percentages of addicts had first used other drugs after heroin dependence had developed: marijuana, 4%; cocaine, 63%; oral amphetamines, 1%; barbiturates, 22%; other opiates, 23%; intravenous amphetamines, 17%; LSD, 9%, and opium, 1%. Thus 97% of the sample had used other drugs either before or after addiction to heroin, 34% had used two or less other drugs, and 66% tried three or more. Beckett and Lodge (1971) also noted that all but one of their male addict sample in treatment had been using other drugs before admission. The most commonly used drugs were cocaine (32%), marijuana (31%), and amphetamines (21%). Barbiturates, Methedrine, and LSD were used only by 10% or fewer of the subjects. According to Abeles, Plew, Laudeutscher, and Rosenthal (1966), at least 40% of heroin users in New York City were using barbiturates concurrently.

Simpson and Sells (1974) examined patterns of pre-treatment drug abuse in a sample of over 11,000 drug users entering treatment. The most prevalent pattern of abuse, found in 28% of the sample, was the daily or weekly use of heroin alone. The combination of heroin and cocaine, heroin and marijuana, or heroin and both cocaine and marijuana on a daily or weekly basis also occurred frequently. These four patterns accounted for over 52% of the patient population. Also, a group (18%) of polydrug abusers who used at least three nonopiates was identified. Over two-thirds of this group also used opiates either daily or weekly.

Noble, Hart, and Nation (1972) found that narcotics users among a sample of English delinquent adolescent girls had used a greater variety of drugs than either nonnarcotics users or girls who had not used narcotics but would do so within the following 3 years. The mean number of different drugs used by the three groups were 5.1, 2.2, and 2.4, respectively. When Bucky (1971) examined this issue in his sample of Navy enlisted men using heroin, he found that 72% had used amphetamines, slightly less than 50% had used barbiturates, and only 8.5% had used LSD. In another study, narcotics abuse was found to be relatively common among young users of psychedelic drugs. Heavier users of these drugs and alcohol tended most frequently to have tried narcotics (Crowley, Chesluk, Dilts, and Hart, 1974).

Crowther (1974) found her sample of college heroin users had tried a greater variety of drugs than users of other opiates. Her entire sample of 24 heroin users reported having used at least three different opiates, and 7 reported using 10 or more different opiates. In contrast, her nonheroin users had used only one or two other opiates. Heroin users also admitted greater use of barbiturates and stimulants as well as many different hallucinogens. With respect to marijuana use, the majority of heroin users reported first having used it in high school, whereas the majority of users of other opiates reported initial use of marijuana in college. Interestingly 67% of users of other opiates reported less marijuana use after starting use of opiates, in contrast to heroin users of whom only 29% reported less current use of marijuana. As Crowther points out, college addicts differ from street addicts in the college addicts' use of hallucinogens, and their use of a wide variety of drugs. This author concludes from her findings that ". . . the picture that emerges is one of a multiple drug user who has tried a wide variety of different drugs. The heroin user appears to be more deeply submerged in this drug culture and reports more experimentation with different types of drugs than does the non-heroin user" (p. 245).

Examining drug preferences among a sample of 190 experienced polydrug abusers, Kliner and Pickens (1982) found a highly consistent ranking of preference, with heroin ranked as most preferred, followed by (in descending order of preference) amphetamines, alcohol, pentobarbital, secobarbital, marijuana, cocaine, codeine, diazepam, LSD, and hashish. Furthermore, Kliner and Pickens found this preference ranking to be unrelated to incidence of use or drug accessibility. Tyler and Frith (1981), in a study of primary patterns of abuse among women admitted to treatment, found heroin to be the most abused drug. The fact that this sample was based upon admission to treatment strongly biases it, however, toward more "serious" drug use, such as heroin. Sutker, Archer and Allain (1978) found that women drug abusers tended to use fewer categories of drugs, and did not differ from males in age at first drug use, frequency of drug use, or drug preference. They also found black addicts to report use of fewer categories of drugs, and to prefer depressants, such as opiates, over stimulants.

In regard to trends, Chambers, Hinesley, and Moldestad (1970) indicated that there had been an increased incidence of simultaneous use of opiates and sedatives in addicts at Lexington between 1944 and 1966, and that this concurrent use was the typical pattern at the time the article was written. Also, over one-third of all opiate addicts admitted for treatment required concurrent treatment for a sedative addiction.

An interesting and potentially quite important finding is reported by Lahmeyer and Steingold (1980), who note that pentazocine and tripelennamine are supplanting heroin use as a primary drug of abuse among Chicago drug addicts. They suggest that initial use of these two drugs is generally related to (a) an attempt either to withdraw from heroin or to "slow down" their level of heroin use, or (b) the poor quality of heroin available to them.

NON-ADDICTIVE OPIATE USE

Zinberg (1979) makes a convincing case for nonaddictive opiate use. He obtained a sample of 90 controlled opiate users—subjects who had used opiates at least 10 times per year for more than two years, but at least twice during a six month period preceding an interview in depth. Furthermore he required that his subjects (a) had not had more than one "spree" or episode of opiate use for from 4 to 15 days in any one year; (b) were not using any other drugs in a controlled manner, and (c) had not been in a drug free or methadone maintenance program or other confining institution during their years of controlled use. Demographically diverse, but obviously more socially competent than most samples of heroin users, he found that over 80 percent of his sample had used heroin, some for up to five years in their current period of use. Infrequent use seemed to be the rule: about 20 percent used opiates less than monthly, 40 percent monthly, 20 percent weekly, and the remainder in various patterns. Twenty-five percent had either a history of addiction to opiates or a history of compulsive use of another drug, or both. Such periods were significantly shorter than the current period of controlled use, a fact suggesting the existence of controlled use as a stable style.

Perhaps the most interesting finding reported by Zinberg was the manner in which his subjects had come to be controlled users. *All* of his subjects had first tried heroin as part of a pattern of experimentation and had found the experience "particularly pleasing." Recognizing that they had no preparation for opiate use, they attempted to learn all they could about the drug from peers, suggesting that they had not gone through the social drug education process typical of alcohol users. The primary problem reported by those non-addicted users seemed to have been how to integrate the drug high into a pattern of work and social relationships.

Zinberg eventually identified six levels of controlled use: (a) the several times daily user who was stereotypically addicted and who used as much heroin as was available, (b) the physiologically addicted individual who nonetheless placed limits on his use, (c) the individual whose physiological addiction did not disrupt his functioning, (d) those persons who were not addicted, but who had a recent history of addiction such that they could not be considered controlled users, (e) occasional users who were more or less compulsive users of other drugs, and (f) individuals neither clearly controlled *nor* addicted, labeled "marginal users."

The concept of the nonaddictive heroin user has been challenged by Robins (1979) who notes that two problems exist in accepting such a model of heroin use: (a) one cannot say with certainty that the user *will never*, during some future time period, become addicted, since he may be just slower on the route to addiction, and (b) failure to know the actual amount of drug consumed because of dilution may mean consumption of minute amounts. Robins presents a brief but interesting review of the published findings relating to this issue, examining some of the relevant literature and pointing out its shortcomings in providing conclusive evidence on nonaddictive opiate use.

TEMPORAL CONSIDERATIONS IN THE COURSE OF ADDICTION

The length of time involved in going from initial exposure to narcotics to addiction has also been explored. Cushman (1974a) reported that the sample of New York City addicts he studied in methadone treatment averaged 5 to 7 months between their first exposure to narcotics and the onset of daily use. He considered this time before the onset of daily use to be a period of experimentation. Cohen and Klein (1972) presented evidence suggesting that for male psychiatric patients, later age of initial drug use was associated with a rapid progression from early experimentation with a variety of drugs to heroin use. Early onset of drug use in males was associated with use of a greater variety of drugs. For females, on the other hand, later use of heroin was associated with early onset of drug use. There was no heroin use in the group of females who had a late onset of drug use. Cohen and Klein note that these results, for males at least, are inconsistent with those obtained by Robins and Murphy (1967) who found that among normal black males, earlier use of drugs was associated with a greater risk of later heroin use.

In reviewing several studies, Robins (1979) noted a wide range of typical intervals between first use and addiction, concluding that this period ranged from 5 to 18 months, with considerable intersubject variation. This wide variability is reflected in Waldorf's (1973) findings of a range of three weeks to six years, with a median of 11 months. Other intervals presented by Robins are those of a mean of 18 months for inner-city blacks (Halikas, Darvish, and Rimmer, 1976), about one year for English addicts (Blumberg et al, 1974), and an average of "less than a year" for New York City addicts in treatment (Hendler and Stephens, 1977). In this last study, some users were reported to have become addicted from their first use.

There is apparent agreement that the first year of heroin use is a crucial one in the development of addiction, during which the addict is most likely to influence the addiction liability of others. Bourne (1974) for example, noted it is during this first year of heroin use, while the addict is still outside the addict subculture, that he is most "contagious"—that is, likely to influence others to use the drug. As his addiction continues, he tends to enter the addict subculture and thus become isolated from his former friends. Hunt (1974) concurs, stating that "the beginning year of epidemic use is a crucial period during which there is little time to act, since large numbers of susceptible individuals will, within a brief period, become users of the drug" (p. 17).

CRIMINAL ACTIVITY AS A CONSEQUENCE OF HEROIN ADDICTION

One widely accepted consequence of addiction to heroin is involvement in criminal activities to obtain funds for the purchase of the drug; often this is followed by subsequent arrest and incarceration. Although involvement with the criminal justice system is not necessarily the outcome of criminal behavior in every instance, the high rates of such behavior by addicts make it an eventual probability in the careers of most addicts.

Evidence presented in Chapter 9 about the criminal histories of heroin addicts strongly suggests that the majority of heroin addicts have been arrested at some point in their lives, many of them before having become addicted. Although addiction to heroin is certainly not limited to those with a criminal background, heroin use and criminal behavior seem to arise most frequently in similar sociocultural and socioeconomic circumstances. The high, relatively sustained rates of heroin use among New Jersey reformatory inmates studied by Platt, Scura, and Hoffman (1973) from 1968 to 1972 seem to support this view. In this study and in subsequent data collected from 1973 to 1974 (Platt et al, 1976), documented heroin use was found in substantial percentages of successive groups of reformatory admissions. These figures ranged from a low of 29% for 1968 to a high of 71.5% in 1971, to 50.5% in 1974. These rates were statistically independent of arrest rates for drug offenses, which were never higher than 30% in any one year (1971). These figures do not, of course, answer any questions about the existence of a causal relationship between heroin use and criminal behavior. That such a relationship exists may be inferred from estimates such as that of Scher (1973a) that each addict stole $50,000 to $150,000 of merchandise, equipment, or funds each year from business and industry. Further, Scher suggested that 50% of all property damage and 60% of all violent crimes are secondary to drug addiction or alcohol abuse. Since a heroin addict requires between $50 and $100 a day, 63,000 known addicts are estimated to be stealing $3.5 million in cash or $35 million a day in merchandise in the United States. This is a substantial increase from Winick's (1965) estimate that heroin addiction costs the community over $250 million annually.

This issue of the relationship between the incidence of crime and heroin addiction was discussed by DuPont and Greene (1973) who noted both an increase and a decline in crime in Washington, D.C., which paralleled the rapid increase and decline of heroin addiction in the city during the same period. While carefully noting that it was not possible to postulate a causal relationship between the two trends, they listed three observations which suggested a correlation. First, the decline in the crime rate started when drug treatment became available in the District of Columbia. Second, the rates of crimes against property accounted for much of both the rise and decline in crime rate. Finally, the authors observed a strong inverse relationship between the number of patients in treatment and the property crime rate.

The chronic nature of criminal behavior among heroin addicts is underscored by D'Orban's (1974) finding that 33 out of 53 female heroin addicts were convicted of further offenses in the 4 years he followed them after initial identification. Furthermore, this continued criminal behavior seemed to be closely related to continued narcotic dependence.

The relationship between the cost of heroin and criminal activity was studied by Brown and Silverman (1974). They reviewed the literature and found that Ausubel (1961), Maurer and Vogel (1962), Cohen and Short (1958), and Duvall, Locke, and Brill (1963) supported the view that as the retail price of heroin rises so will the crime rate, as addicts increase their level of criminal activity to obtain sufficient money to support their habits. Brown and Silverman (1974) test the alternate viewpoint in which criminal activity is unrelated to the price of heroin. It may be that an increase in price causes addicts to consume less heroin. After studying the available data on fluctuations in the retail price of heroin and crime rates in several major cities, the authors found their results indicated different relationships between these variables in different cities. Thus, for New York City, which harbors the greatest concentration of addicts in the country, there was a positive correlation between crime rate and the price of heroin. Most significantly, this relationship applied to revenue-raising crimes (e.g., robbery, larceny, auto theft) rather than nonrevenue-producing crimes (e.g., manslaughter, forcible rape). That these relationships were not replicated for other cities was interpreted by Brown and Silverman as a possible reflection of the fact that addict-related crime in cities other than New York is small relative to the total, and of less available price data for cities other than New York.

Taylor and Albright (1981) found little association between the age at which heroin use starts and the ages at which various non-drug-related crimes were first committed, thus suggesting that non-drug criminality predates heroin use. Secondly, they found that heroin users commit income generating crimes regardless of whether or not they are violent, and third, the success of treatment directed toward reducing non-drug criminality is related to the extent of prior criminality. With respect to the issue of drug vs. alcohol use and crime, Green (1981) reported that person crimes and victimless crimes were less likely to be committed under the influence of drugs, when compared with alcohol. Property crimes were more likely to be used to support a drug or alcohol addiction than were person or victimless crimes. While agreeing with Taylor and Albright (1981) that criminal behavior predated regular drug use, the fact that a large proportion of addicts in their survey started substance abuse in the same year or in year previous to having launched their criminal careers cannot be ignored.

The general implication of these results is that Brown, Gauvey, Meyers, and Stark (1971) were probably correct in their assessment that the inner-city heroin addict is one ". . . whose addiction is superimposed on his criminal adjustment . . ." (p. 642). This finding led them to conclude that ". . . any treatment program intended to serve effectively the inner-city addict population must address itself to providing an alternative not only to the addict life style, but to the criminal life style as well. The treatment program organized must therefore provide the client a range of new adjustive skills and behaviors that make it unnecessary, if not undesirable, for him to remain a part of the criminal subculture. Thus, the client will require the vocational and academic training and the counselling needed to permit him to change his role and functioning in the community." (p. 642)

THE CYCLE OF ADDICTION

A number of investigators have proposed conceptual models of the cycle of addiction that seem particularly relevant to the discussion of treatment in the next chapter. Alksne, Lieberman, and Brill (1967) conceptualized four phases through which the addict moved in a life cycle of addiction: (a) tolerance for potential addiction, (b) tolerance of the addiction system, (c) tolerance for potential abstinence, and (d) tolerance of abstinence. Several preconditions must also exist for an individual to be amenable to the "addiction set," since the availability of drugs is not in itself sufficient to account for drug abuse. Both a psychiatric precondition such as an inadequate personality or weak ego and a sociologic precondition such as anomie could interact to create such amenability in a social setting involving a change in status through drug use.

Phase I, tolerance for potential addiction, begins with the experimentation stage which is facilitated by the availability of drugs. Initiates rarely resort immediately to intravenous injection of heroin, since this act represents a symbolic commitment to a practice closely identified with "junkies." However, as the need develops for large doses, the experimenter must learn the skills and attitudes necessary to maintain a fairly regular supply of heroin. Those individuals who cease drug-taking after the experimentation stage do not have what Alksne et al (1967) term a tolerance for potential addiction, either because of initial adverse reactions to heroin, disinclination to alter their self-image, or greater influence of conventional norms. However, the authors note that ". . . it is during this *experimentation stage* that the immediate effects of the drug have a bearing upon the emotional component of the predisposing addiction set" (p. 227) involving reduction in anxiety most often. Intermittent use soon leads to regular use, at which point the user is not necessarily addicted but characteristically uses heroin regularly. This activity prepares the addict for the later stages in the cycle of addiction by reinforcing and creating relationships to the addiction system. The user discovers how helpful drugs are when he reaches the addiction stage and experiences symptoms of abstinence for the first time. His self-image has begun to alter and increasingly to tolerate the label of "junkie" by the time the transitional stage to the addiction system is reached. Being a junkie implies involvement in a hustling syndrome which the addict recognizes following the first experience of withdrawal. To continue as a user he must expand his drug-seeking behavior which requires that his self-image must conform to this expansion. "In effect, he will develop a self-image which incorporates expectations of the others in the addiction system which will help provide the basis for knowledge of how to act appropriately" (Alksne et al, 1967, p. 230). This is essentially a socialization process in which the addict becomes willing to accept increased involvement in criminal behavior and alienation from conventional roles to avoid withdrawal and reentry into the nonusing culture. In this final transitional phase the addict still vacillates and is not completely ready to identify himself as an addict, using avoidance detoxification in an attempt to eliminate further drug involvement. Avoidance detoxification in the transitional phase only serves to reduce the amount of drugs used and to increase tolerance to the addiction system unless other salient factions in the addict's life have changed.

When he progresses to Phase II, tolerance of the addiction system involves the ". . . addict's full incorporation of the individual and sociocultural values as well as the knowledge of the mechanisms that have come to be associated with narcotics use in our society" (Alksne et al, 1967, p. 233). Narcotics use and membership in the drug-using subculture function to provide alternative status within a deviant population and to give positive value to a way of life generally condemned by society. The addict generates rationalizations for this way of life because there are many components of this lifestyle (e.g., rejection, constant surveillance) that he must tolerate. His drug-acquiring skills must be sophisticated and his activities must be restricted to those only involving the addiction system.

Phase II also involves a transitional stage on the way to abstinence during which withdrawal is attempted once again. The meaning of this withdrawal attempt is different, however, from that undergone in the transitional stage between phases I and II, when the user was attempting to avoid identification as an addict. This second withdrawal attempt involves an effort to abandon the addict identification. Ray (1961) conceives of this stage as the "inception of cure," which begins with thoughts arising from circumstances in the addict's life that cause him to be dissatisfied with his situation. The major problem in attempting withdrawal in the transitional phase is that the addict's primary self-image is involved in the addiction system (Alksne et al, 1967). The addict further questions his identification with all the secondary status characteristics of being an addict and begins to reject this identity (Ray, 1961). If he undergoes what Alksne et al term "rehabilitative detoxification," which is controlled by an outside agent, it will not result in the achievement of a drugfree state until the emotional component is modified so that the addict no longer identifies with the addiction system.

Phase III, tolerance for potential abstinence, involves a stage of experimentation with relapse that is not considered a failure because any experience with abstinence will reinforce a movement toward it. During this phase the addict tries to break away from the addiction system and fails because the unfamiliar nonusing system is uncomfortable. He must not only develop new skills, but must also seek new associations more appropriate to abstinence before he can succeed at being drugfree. It is during the adaptational stage, in which tolerance for abstinence is generated, that supportive chemotherapy is most useful. Ray (1961) suggests that the period immediately following withdrawal is most difficult for the addict, and involves wrestling with social identity and developing expectations regarding a drugfree future. In these early stages of abstinence there is a great deal of ambivalence about the relative status in addict or nonaddict groups. Addiction is no longer a personally meaningful experience, but the abstinent identity has not yet been formulated (Ray, 1961).

Phase IV, tolerance of abstinence, is reached when the former addict is emotionally and socially ready for membership in the conventional system (Alksne et al, 1967). He has begun to act as a nonaddict and attempts to take his place in the nonusing culture. It is at this point, however, that Ray (1961) believes the process of relapse is initiated. When the social expectations the former addict has developed are not met, and he perceives that he is still different from the nonaddict, social stresses begin to have a strong effect. The former addict begins to reexamine the meaning of abstinent life, and any further experiences he has with other addicts tend to facilitate relapse. Unfortunately, experiences with nonaddicts also tend to facilitate relapse when the former addict finds he is granted only marginal status and that the nonaddict culture does not believe he is cured. An encounter with relapse at this point raises questions about the meaningfulness of his abstinent experience. The former addict is called upon to recommit himself to the norms of addiction, to redefine the ways in which he can relate to nonaddicts. This experience with relapse results in feelings of isolation from the nonaddict group, as he readopts the secondary status characteristics of being an addict, and encourages self-identity as a chronic addict.

REASONS FOR SEEKING TREATMENT

Although it is the rare addict who does not seek treatment at some time, the reasons for doing so vary. The main reasons London addicts gave for seeking treatment were the cost of their habit, or that they wanted to reduce or stop drug use. The principal reasons given by their addict friends who did not seek treatment were infrequent use, or desire not to become involved with the clinic or other official agencies (Blumberg et al, 1974). On the other hand, Brown, Gauvey, Meyers, and Stark (1971) found the most common reason given by both adolescent (34.8%) and adult male addicts (38.7%) for initiating first withdrawal from heroin was an attempt to change the overall pattern of their lives. Female addicts gave this response 27.3% of the time, but cited drug-related physical problems as their main reason for first withdrawal (45.9%); 19.4% of adult males and 21.7% of juveniles responded in a similar fashion.

Surprisingly, concern about punishment for illegal acts was never given by adult males or females, although 13% of male juveniles cited this reason. The influence of friends was a relatively minor reason for all three groups to undergo first withdrawal, although it was slightly more salient for juveniles (13.0%) than for adult males (3.2%) or females (4.5%). When the three groups in this study were asked to give their major reason for currently attempting withdrawal, the males still were primarily concerned with changing their overall functioning and life patterns; for females, family problems and physical problems became important.

When Stephens and Cottrell (1972) asked abstaining narcotic addicts their reasons for doing so, the most frequent response given was the "desire to stay clean" (68%). Effectiveness of therapy was given by 36%, and support of family and nonaddict friends by 27% and 14% respectively. Counselors saw the same reasons for abstinence as their clients: 62% reported "the patient's desire to stay clean" as important; effectiveness of therapy, 19%; and support of the family, 15%. Fear of the consequences of continuing drug use was cited by 15% of the counselors and 14% of the addicts.

TREATMENT OUTCOMES AND RELATED ISSUES

Rates of Relapse after Treatment

Typically, rates of relapse after treatment for heroin addiction are discouragingly high. In the first follow-up study of narcotics addicts treated at Lexington, Pescor (1943) found that of 4766 males released between 1936 and 1940, only 14% were known to be abstinent. Of the remaining 46% on whom data were available, all but a total of 7% who had died had returned to narcotics use. In another study fifteen years later, Hunt and Odoroff (1962) found that 90.1% of detoxified patients released from Lexington between 1952 and

1955 were readdicted, and only 6.6% were abstinent! In studies by Duvall, Locke, and Brill (1963) and Vaillant (1966a), the general finding was that this extremely high relapse rate decreased with the passage of time—in 5 years, Duvall et al's 6 months abstinence rate of 9% became 25%, and the almost total relapse rate in Vaillant's study was only 46% at 12 years following treatment. O'Donnell (1969) found a 29% abstinence rate in his sample of Kentucky opiate addicts who had gone through Lexington. Of his sample, 2% had no addiction problems after their first admission. At any one time, however, only about one-third of all persons leaving the hospital were addicted to narcotics. The general pattern found in 60% of cases was a constant shift between addiction to narcotics, addiction to other drugs, and abstinence.

Hunt and Bespalic (1974) compared relapse rates for heroin addicts after treatment in a number of programs with similar rates for graduates of programs for tobacco and alcohol addiction. They found similar curves for the three addictions, with a rapid relapse rate during the first 3 months which decreased rapidly between the third and sixth months and then reached an asymptote at about 25%. Hunt and Bespalec suggest their data indicates a common factor in the various addictive processes (as well as difficulty in dealing with them). The authors presented the following interpretation of their findings:

We are more inclined to consider the possibility of two kinds of learning, one representing the usual reinforcement paradigm with the gradual extinction of the learned behavior as shown in the early part of the curve, the other representing some kind of decision making process or encoding, which isolates the response in question from the usual mechanisms of reinforcement and establishes the permanence of the behavior outside the influence of reinforcement. [Hunt and General, 1971, p. 68]

Maturing Out

Frequently, addicts stop using heroin spontaneously after a number of years. Winick (1965) reported that the typical opiate addict uses the drug for 8.6 years; only 7.25% use opiates for 15 years or more. Furthermore, older addicts, that is, those over 30, have a lower relapse rate after treatment, especially after an addiction of about 10 years' duration. To explain the relative lack of older addicts, as shown by the decline in incidence over age 30, Winick suggested the "maturing out" hypothesis, which states essentially that the addict in his thirties no longer needs opiates to avoid coping with the demands imposed on him to make decisions regarding vocation, marriage, and other issues of living. At an earlier age, opiate use replaced the need to make these decisions with an absorbing avocation, such as obtaining drugs, by providing membership and acceptance in a peer group and also by decreasing drives related to sex and aggression. In the fourth decade of life, the original environmental demands have lost their urgency, the pressure of police harassment is felt, and the addict gradually tends to drift away from drug use. Beckett and Lodge (1971) are in substantial agreement with Winick's analysis, noting that at some point in the course of addiction the addict reaches a point at which he has a general sense of well-being—usually after heroin use has produced an initial "marked sensation of pleasure and gratification" (p. 34). After this point has been reached, however, "heroin merely changes the state of the user from abnormal to comparatively normal" with an accompanying decrease in euphoria. Similar findings were obtained by Nurco and Farrell (1975). In a study of male addicts in Baltimore, only 7% were found to be users when evaluated in a long-term follow-up.

Stephens and Cottrell (1972) present evidence that suggests there is far less regular narcotics use and readdiction in the over-30 segment of the addicts they studied than in those under 30. They believe this finding may be directly related to Winick's notion of the older addict "burning-out." Stephens and Cottrell's data did not, however, support Winick's hypothesized relationship between length of addiction and relapse since they found that "slightly more persons addicted for ten years or less were abstinent and slightly less were addicted." (p. 48)

On the other hand, Harrington and Cox (1979) carried out a twenty year follow-up of heroin addicts arrested in Tucson, Arizona, in 1955 through 1957 in order to test the maturation hypothesis. They concluded, based upon the fact that they could only positively identify one individual as drug-free or abstinent, that the maturation hypothesis did not hold for their sample.

Some rather unusual findings were reported by Oppenheimer and Stimson (1982) concerning heroin use and clinic involvement. Their seven year follow-up of heroin addicts showed a marked decrease in overall drug use in each year, with the most marked decrease in use of heroin. It was found, however, that hard-core heroin users were still using heroin after several years of clinic involvement. In this study the use of illegal opiates *without* clinical attendance was relatively rare. Thus, this study underlines the danger inherent in assuming absolute homogeneity of heroin user samples.

Heroin Use in Vietnam Veterans

Great concern was expressed about the rates of heroin use among soldiers in Vietnam. Concern was particularly expressed that exposure to relatively pure and inexpensive heroin in Vietnam would result in high rates of addiction upon discharge and subsequent return to the U.S. Yet, Robins, Helzer, Hesselbrook, and Wish (1977) found only 12% of returning veterans who had been addicted in Vietnam to have been addicted in the first three years after return. The follow-up data for those who had been re-addicted in the three years after return indicated that 70 percent of this group were *not* re-addicted during the next two years. Examining the characteristics related to initial addiction in Vietnam and continued use of heroin upon return to the U.S., Robins (1976) reported that being young and black predicted initial addiction, with dependency upon return being related to being white, older, and having parents who were alcoholic or who had been arrested. Overall, the data on addicted Vietnam veterans suggest that exposure to, and even brief periods of addiction to, a higher quality supply of the available drug does not necessarily result in longterm addiction.

Factors Related to Abstinence and Relapse

Snarr and Ball (1974) studied the extent to which involvement in a drug subculture was related to opiate use in a sample of Puerto Rican narcotic addicts who had been treated at Lexington. Based on the fact that degree of involvement in a specific subculture reflects a greater commitment to the modes of behavior associated with it, the authors hypothesized a negative relationship between degree of involvement in a drug subculture and abstinence following treatment. This hypothesis was supported in that 38% of individuals with little involvement remained abstinent in contrast to 10% of those with extensive involvement. This relationship held for various social-class subgroupings, with little change from class to class except for a higher abstinence rate after treatment among middle and upper-class subjects. When age was introduced as a variable, strong support for the original hypothesis was seen among those who began using opiates at age 21 or over, although the extent of involvement in the drug subculture was not related to abstinence in individuals who had started using opiates under 21. The authors interpret this finding as suggesting that the adolescent's involvement in the drug culture is probably part of his search for new experiences, which lose their appeal as he begins to assume legitimate adult roles. On the other hand, the late-starting addict may have failed to establish himself in these legitimate roles.

Stephens and Cottrell (1972) found that addicts employed after release from treatment at Lexington had a lower relapse rate (81%) than those unable to obtain a job (94%). An interesting finding was that 48% of the sample reported they encountered no problems while looking for a job. Some 29% of the sample relapsed before obtaining employment, or were not motivated to seek a job. Only 6% encountered difficulties because of lack of occupational skills and/or past criminal and addiction histories. Platt and Labate (1976a), in a study focused on factors related to recidivism in youthful heroin offenders, also found a significant inverse relationship between employment and drug use on parole. Only 29.4% of parolees who obtained steady employment used drugs, whereas 60.7% who were unemployed were users. As might be expected, both employment status and drug use on parole were significantly related to parole success. Of those individuals with postrelease unemployment or intermittent employment, 75% failed versus 4.8% of those steadily employed. Likewise, 51.9% of drug users during parole failed versus 4.2% of the abstainers. When the variable of preincarceration work experience was examined in another study of factors related to parole success in heroin addicts, length of preincarceration work experience was found to be significantly related to parole outcome. Parole successes had an average of 37.6 months of work experience versus 28.7 months for parole failures (Platt and Labate, 1976b).

McLellan, Woody, Evans, and O'Brien (1982) found the "opiate only" patient in contrast to "opiate plus other drugs" patients to have the best general prognosis due to their having (a) developed skills readily applicable to employment, and (b) fewer psychiatric symptoms which could interfere with interpersonal relations.

Other findings in the Stephens and Cottrell (1972) study included the following: (a) little difference in relapse rates between racial groups (while whites were more frequently abstinent, their rate was 84.3% compared with 88.2% of Hispanic addicts and 91.4% of blacks), and (b) a lower relapse rate among addicts with 4 years or more of college (60%) than among those with some college education or a high school diploma (81.8%), some high school (90.0%), or less than 9 years of education (88.2%).

Of the group of 19 preincarceration demographic variables (including those related to personal characteristics, employment history, military experience, criminal history, and educational, psychological, and medical status) that Platt and Labate (1976b) examined in relation to parole outcome in a group of 48 youthful heroin offenders, only three were related to positive outcome—being older, having fewer arrests, and being white. In a replication of this study with a larger sample ($N = 175$), the variables related to positive outcome were age, greater likelihood of being married, and the greater work experience mentioned earlier.

When Stephens and Cottrell (1972) asked the addicts in their study why they had relapsed, 49% cited the "enjoyment of narcotics," and 25% cited either "use of drugs to alleviate stress" or "to combat his own faults or depression." Interestingly, when the addicts' aftercare counselors were asked the same question, the most often cited reason was "to alleviate stresses which the patient encounters in interactions with others" (p. 51). Secondary reasons given by counselors were enjoyment of drug states or peer pressure. The third reason cited was depression after failure to cope with problems, and subsequent relapse.

When heroin addicts in the Brown et al (1971) study were asked why they had failed in early attempts to withdraw from heroin use, the most common reason given by both male and female adult addicts and male juvenile addicts was that "they had given up drugs only physically, and that a psychological need remained" (p. 639). Relief of personal problems, a less frequent reason, seemed to be a greater factor for females than males, while easy availability of heroin was more salient for both adolescent and adult males in contrast to females. In addition, the influence of friends was more frequently cited by juveniles than adults.

On the other hand, several investigators have examined the factors involved in successfully maintaining abstinence. Bess, Janus, and Rifkin (1972) randomly selected 17 former addicts from a variety of rehabilitation programs who had been drugfree for a minimum of 2 years. Of these, 14 came from intact families (despite general reports of relatively poor relationships with their fathers), and 15 reported that their friends had pressured them into experimentation with drugs for the following reasons: 7 "acceptance," 4 "kicks," 4 "curiosity." However, 10 of the 17 subjects had experienced an overt trauma coincidental with the onset of drug experimentation. The authors concluded that the "burn out" theory of narcotics renunciation did not play a significant role in the abstinence of these former addicts, and that their fathers provided suitable models for work roles. Bowden and Langenauer (1972) also examined variables differentiating those who were successful (no opioid use 6 months after release from Lexington) and those who failed (opioid use in each of 6 months after treatment). These subjects were all patients in treatment under the NARA of 1966, in which Title I allows the federal courts to remand an addict to treatment if a physician feels the addict can be rehabilitated. Title I commitments usually involve 36 months of inpatient and outpatient care. Title IV provides for the civil commitment of addicts and involves 6 months hospitalization followed by 36 months of compulsory supervised aftercare.

. . . [T]he typical successful patient lived with both parents at least until the age of 6. He was more likely to be white and to have completed high school. He began using opioids later in life and had greater external pressure to comply with the treatment program . . . his work performance was good. He did not get into trouble with the law and did not use other drugs. [Bowden and Langenauer, 1972, p. 855]

Similarly, Zahn and Ball (1972) found successful former addicts among Puerto Ricans were usually married and living with spouse, steadily employed, older, and had fewer or no arrests. They studied a group of 108 male Puerto Rican addicts admitted to Lexington between 1935 and 1962 in whom the "cures" were determined as those individuals for whom all sources indicated abstinence for 3 consecutive years prior to the study. Individuals were considered to have relapsed if they used opiates at any time within the 3 year period. Evidence was obtained from interviews, urinalysis, and medical records, with two or more sources of information required for each subject. Although no differences between groups were found relative to education or occupational status, the cure group generally had not used heroin as the primary drug of abuse at the time of their first admission. The cure rate was highest among those who had started opiate abuse after the age of 32, although the probability of cure was usually greater for later initiates to drug abuse. Zahn and Ball (1972) feel ". . . the most crucial age for the beginning of addiction is at the transition period between childhood and adulthood. . . . Addicts who begin drug use at this time develop fewer alternative statuses to that of 'junkie' than do those who begin later in life" (p. 242). They found addicts who started drug use at 16 or 17 were most likely to relapse. Bowden and Langenauer (1972) echo this sentiment:

Narcotic addiction is generally such a time-consuming behavior, so overwhelming in restructuring the individual's priorities, and such a ready escape from any discomfort that it does not allow for much in the way of maturation —psychologically, educationally, or vocationally. Because of the early beginning of addiction, many of the patient failures may not have completed the normal developmental tasks of adolescence, thus making their rehabilitation much more difficult. [p. 855]

Concurrently, they learned that the earlier treatment interrupts the addiction process, the greater the probability of cure—those treated within the first year of abuse had a 100% cure rate, whereas only 13% of those treated after 4 years or more of addiction were cured. Furthermore, treatment modalities with an element of compulsory supervision were more likely to effect cure (62%), a finding confirmed by the extensive follow-up efforts of Vaillant.

Vaillant (1966d) noted that little was known about the determinants of abstinence because the former addict does not often attract the attention of medical or legal authorities. In a 12-year follow-up to investigate the determinants of abstinence, Vaillant (1966d) studied 30 male addicts who had achieved abstinence for 3 years or more. In general the results indicated abstinence was related more to the presence of alternatives satisfactory to the addict than it was to the type of treatment experienced. Interviews were conducted with the former addicts to determine (a) with whom they lived, (b) the stability of address, (c) the important people in their lives, (d) whether they maintained cordial relationships with their families, (e) the type of employment and salary, (f) the degree of dependence on others (g) the occurrence of medical or psychological problems, (h) their reasons for remaining abstinent, and (i) substitutes for drugs in their lives. The former addicts generally resided in one community for 3 years or more without using narcotics, maintained abstinence up to the time of study, and had no convictions for narcotics or property offenses for at least 4 years. These results were compared with those obtained for a group of 30 chronic addicts who spent less than 20% of their time abstinent, who had been actively addicted for at least 5 years excluding time spent in prison, and who were still alive 10 years after their admission to Lexington. Vaillant's (1966d) major finding was that the important variables in determining abstinence were severity of addiction, length of abstinence, and the circumstances surrounding abstinence. Addicts did not tend to "burn out" or to "mature out" in their midthirties, because 5 had achieved abstinence between the ages of 20 and 25, 11 between 26 and 30, 9 between 31 and 35, and 5 between 36 and 40. Former addicts were more likely than chronic addicts to be independent and to have their own families and jobs. Relative to criminal behavior, 77% of the former addicts had at least one conviction since their release from Lexington, although the type of crime committed did not differentiate them from chronic addicts.

Relocation of residence was found to have a positive impact in a study by Maddux and Desmond (1982). In a 20 year study, 248 addicts were found to have been voluntarily abstinent 54% of the time during relocation and 12% of the time during residence in their hometown, San Antonio, Texas. Treatment preceding relocation resulted in a 31% frequency of abstinence compared to relocation alone (17%), or treatment and/or correctional interactions (6%) alone. When abstinent addicts returned to San Antonio, some 81% resumed opioid use within one month. Drug availability, conditioned abstinence, and peer modeling all appear to have played a role, leading the authors to suggest the encouragement of relocation.

In agreement with Zahn and Ball (1972), Vaillant (1966d) found that addiction for longer than 3 years was unfavorable for subsequent abstinence. Interestingly, "within limits . . . future chronicity of addiction was not significantly correlated with the quantity of narcotic injected in the past" (Vaillant, 1966d, p. 576), a finding over which there is some disagreement. Slightly more former addicts were diagnosed as passive, dependent, or neurotic, and more chronic addicts were considered inadequate personalities or sociopathic. In regard to employment, the findings of numerous other investigators were confirmed: chronic addicts were singularly unable to remain stably employed prior to admission. The absence of stable employment both prior to and following treatment was the best single predictor of subsequent chronicity. Roughly 70% of the former addicts were employed. Several differences between groups emerged that were not statistically significant: favorable outcome was more likely for those who had become addicted after the age of 25, and less probable for those whose homes were broken before they reached the age of 6, and also for those whose parents came from a foreign culture. Reasons for abstinence ranged from the discovery of a substitution for narcotics, the largest principal one being alcohol, to the establishment of meaningful relationships and moving to an area where there was little drug abuse. Interestingly, having significant others depend on them was a reason for remaining abstinent to many ex-addicts. The issue of compulsory supervision was found to be extremely important, having a high correlation with abstinence. However, Vaillant (1966) notes that ". . . addicts capable of finding on their own an alternative source of gratification to addiction . . . seemed less dependent upon external control for their abstinence" (p. 579). Again in agreement with other researchers, Vaillant found the presence of good premorbid adjustment to be a good predictor of later abstinence, particularly when drug abuse appeared to be reactive or as a response to stress.

However, despite their drug-free state, Vaillant (1966) found few of the ex-addicts to know where they were going and many to have a feeling that something was missing from their lives. They often exhibited problems in channeling aggression and a need to be cared for by others. "Relapse to drugs seemed to result more from a poverty of familiar alternatives than because drugs powerfully answered the addict's needs" (Vaillant, 1966, p. 582). Furthermore, Vaillant (1966) states

. . . if addiction is conceptualized as a form of immaturity, then it is not surprising to find that: a) the disorder, like adolescence, gets better with time; b) when symptoms are removed, they need not be replaced with others; and c) ex-addicts can manifest new defenses. [p. 583]

Regarding reports of successful outcome, Bowden and Langenauer (1972) cautiously note that ". . . several [studies] have done so only by defining the sample as those who complete treatment and by making the conditions for staying in treatment similar to the criteria for successful outcome" (p. 853). Despite this concern, Zahn and Ball (1972) reported only 20% of their sample of 108 male Puerto Rican addicts admitted to Lexington over a period of almost 30 years had successfully achieved abstinence for a 3 year period prior to the study. Similarly, Levy (1972) followed 50 narcotic addicts only 20 of whom were considered "good outcomes." A closer look at these good outcomes, however, revealed only 9 were abstinent while 11 occasionally used drugs. Apparently, what differentiated the good outcomes, most of whom were employed, full-time homemakers, or students, was the degree of support they received from and were called upon to give to abstinent friends and relatives. They had succeeded in moving away from their old environment, in contrast to the "poor outcomes" who mentioned problems in breaking away from the drug subculture.

A study employing 282 drug abuse clients in treatment at three V.A. Medical Centers (two inpatient and one outpatient) and conducted by McLellan, O'Brien, Woody, Luborsky, and Druley (1982) resulted in the following conclusions concerning the effectiveness of drug abuse treatment: (a) highly significant improvements were found in both composite and individual criteria; (b) while most significant improvements were found in the area of drug abuse, highly significant improvements also occurred in the areas of employment, legal, family, and psychological status – – no change occurred in medical status or physical health; (c) the magnitude of change resulted in up to a 67 percent reduction in opiate use, a 50 percent reduction in stimulant use, a 67 percent reduction in crime days, and a 386 percent increase in earned pay; (d) drug abuse treatment effects were equal to those seen in studies of professional psychotherapy in criterion areas of drug use, employment, and legal status, while overall treatment effects were greater in the psychotherapy treatments; and (e) when short-term versus long-term favorable discharge patients were compared, the long-term stay patients showed a significantly greater degree of change. McLellan et al conclude that these findings "provide a clear and valid demonstration of substance abuse treatment effectiveness" (p. 229).

When one examines the results of the follow-up component of the DARP research conducted by Sells and his associates (Simpson and Sells, 1982), the following major results related to prediction of post-treatment outcome emerge: (a) treatment effects appeared to be unrelated to sex, based upon no findings emerging in post-treatment with respect to sex differences in illicit drug use; (b) males, in comparison to females, had higher rates of post-DARP criminal involvement; (c) ethnic differences in outcome were unclear, as they are confounded by geographic and sociocultural factors; (d) the strongest predictive relationships existed between similar behaviors pre- and post-treatment, e.g., pre-treatment alcohol use best predicted post-treatment alcohol use, pre-treatment criminal involvement best predicted post-treatment criminal involvement, etc.; (e) the strongest background predictor of unfavorable outcome on drug abuse, employment, and criminal involvement indicators was the presence of extensive criminal involvement; (f) favorable post-treatment outcome was most clearly related to favorable treatment performance on drug use, criminality, and employment; (g) outcome of treatment of less than 90 days' duration, regardless of modality, was relatively poor, and not different from detoxification and intake-only conditions; (h) a direct, linear relationship existed between time spent in methadone maintenance, therapeutic community, and drug-free treatment and positive outcomes; and (i) no optimal match of client types and treatment types was found.

Thus, Simpson and Sells (1982) conclude that "the major predictions of post treatment outcomes were pre-DARP criminal history and performance and length of time spent in treatment. The relationships of these variables with outcome measures tended to remain stable across the treatment groups and cohort samples studied." Of importance also is ". . . the lack of evidence found for an optimal match of client type and treatment type" (p. 12).

CONCLUDING COMMENTS

Once introduced to heroin, the addict rapidly progresses to regular use and usually begins or continues involvement in a pattern of criminal behavior. Abandoning this lifestyle is quite difficult as the constant cycle of addiction, abstinence, and withdrawal demonstrates. Perhaps, as Bourne (1974) has suggested, this life serves a purpose, providing for some a point around which to structure their lives. For others the escape from unpleasant affects or reality may be highly reinforcing, and still others may find peer acceptance in the addict culture, or excitement in the life. Again, the social context in which heroin use begins and is maintained seems to assume great importance. Thus it seems that treatment which does not in some way take into account this social context will probably fail. This issue will be elaborated upon further in Chapters 11 and 12.

PART FOUR

Treatment of the Heroin Addict

CHAPTER 11

Major Treatment Modalities for Heroin Addiction

Evidence presented in the preceding chapter clearly suggests that it is possible to interrupt the cycle of addiction with some degree of success when the addict has resolved to abandon the "addiction system" which no longer has meaning for him. However, it is equally clear that meaningful alternatives must be provided to avoid relapse. The subjects in Levy's (1972) study suggested treatment efforts would be more effective under the following conditions: (a) if confirmed addicts were separated from novices (Alksne et al, 1967 also noted that one should avoid placing a confirmed addict with one who has not yet identified with the addiction system); (b) if drug laws were able to discriminate between different types of users to provide greater latitude in treatment; (c) if more former addicts were used in the treatment process; and (d) if more emphasis were placed on the development of ability, ways of dealing with stress, and new ways to achieve satisfaction. Vaillant (1966d) suggested that treatment efforts should focus on ways of helping the addict to find ". . . the best possible dependency object, to sustain employment via external support, and to discover a more mature way to deal with his instinctual needs than solitary gratification" (p. 583). The treatment modalities reviewed in this chapter have incorporated elements of these suggestions to varying degrees. The approaches to treatment range from the self-help therapeutic communities, founded on the belief that until an individual is drugfree he will not face the irresponsible and immature behavior that led him to become an addict, to the use of narcotic antagonists that represent an empirical attempt to test conditioning theories of addiction.

PSYCHOTHERAPY

Perhaps one of the oldest forms of treatment, and certainly one which has generally proven unsuccessful, is the traditional psychotherapeutic approach. Switzer (1974) noted that the individual approach in psychotherapy with its ". . . emphasis . . . on overcoming emotional repression and achieving the . . . catharsis of feelings as the basis for achieving true psychic health" (p. 20) was derived from Freud's original concept of catharsis and abreaction in reexperiencing early trauma. Consistent with the psychoanalytic approach of focusing on past experiences is Janov's primal therapy which proposed that ". . . drug use constitutes self-medication as a defense against the catastrophic and unbearable emotional pain suffered through early childhood rejection and other emotional deprivations" (Switzer, 1974, p. 22). One must break through these defenses by generating a therapeutic milieu in which the individual can come to express these basic feelings. Feeling therapy (Switzer,

1974) incorporates components of reality, primal, and gestalt therapies into three processes of abreaction, proaction, and counteraction. In the process of abreaction the patient reexperiences painful childhood traumas which may provide insights into present behavior patterns; counteraction, on the other hand, refers to abandoning the acting out of old behavior patterns; and proaction refers to an opening up of the individual to new ways of dealing with life situations (Switzer, 1974).

However, individual psychotherapy with heroin addicts suffers from the same limitations as with any population. Harms (1972) has pointed out that psychotherapy is often based on an intellectual approach whereas the "drug experience" is diametrically opposed to this path. The rational approach of talking through one's problems is not meaningful to the heroin addict. Therefore Harms (1972) suggested that psychotherapy with the addict should focus more heavily on ego therapy. He also criticized group encounter therapy, believing that ". . . these group techniques function by little more than allowing blindfolded human beings to communicate with one another" (p. 2). Harms observed that such groups are too often composed of individuals who may or may not be compatible. In an examination of the validity of this criticism Einstein and Jones (1965) attempted therapy for a heterogeneous group composed of addicts and nonaddicts, with some degree of success. In using the group approach, Einstein and Jones felt they could draw upon a prior history of group affiliation among addicts, deemphasize verbalization, and avoid the pitfalls of individual psychotherapy with addicts. Further, the investigators felt the use of a heterogeneous group would be less artificial, provide an opportunity for identification with nonaddicts, and would also meet an expressed desire of the addict members to be part of a group that was not homogeneous. The attempt was successful insofar as the isolated status of the addict members was altered, long-term relationships were established, and the perceptions of the addict by nonaddicts were also modified.

In general, Harms (1972) also questioned the value of using former addicts as group leaders, despite the claims of many addict respondents cited in Levy's (1972) study who wanted more former addicts involved in the treatment process. Harms took a staunchly "medical model" approach to treatment in his belief that former addicts were not qualified to lead a group simply on the basis of their past addiction experience. Lacking objectivity, he felt the former addict is often single-minded and proselytic regarding the "right" way to approach a given problem. Finally, Harms believed that the addict group member requires very careful professional handling to achieve rehabilitation, which the former addict is unable to provide.

Wesson and Smith (1979) have outlined the different orientations and foci of psychotherapy most relevant at different points in treatment: They see directive and/or instructive problem-resolution psychotherapy as being useful during crisis intervention. Individual psychotherapy can serve a supportive role during the detoxification process, as a means of dealing with emotional issues which emerge as drug use decreases. At this point "regular psychotherapeutic sessions" may assist in retaining the client in treatment. From this point on, the therapist-client relationship can serve a number of purposes including (a) identifying new problem areas, (b) defining goals, and (c) assessing the need for, and impact of, other treatment interventions. For patients whose drug use was motivated by a need to self-medicate neurotic conflict or affective disorder, or emergent psychotic process, Wesson and Smith see the need for a more psychodynamic or "insight-oriented," non-directive form of treatment at this stage, although the transition to it may prove difficult for the patient. Finally, these authors note the usefulness of separating the medical management and psychotherapeutic roles between two persons so as to avoid an over-focus on medication-related issues in therapy sessions.

Reality Therapy

One modification of traditional psychotherapy that has achieved a degree of success with narcotic addicts is based on Glaser's reality therapy. Instead of expending a great deal of energy focusing on the past, which is unchangeable, reality therapy attempts to deal with present behavior and the responsibility for fulfilling one's needs without depriving others of the right to fulfill theirs. Basically, psychiatric symptomatology is considered a reflection of the degree to which the individual is unable to fulfill his needs in the context of his current lifestyle because of his inability to recognize how to deal with reality in relation to need fulfillment (Switzer, 1974). Bratter (1973) notes:

> When drug experimentation and exploration becomes a preoccupation or an adaptive mechanism to compensate for a personal, social, or intellectual deficiency, then it becomes abuse and must be viewed as symptomatic of a problem. [p. 586]

Bratter's extensive experience with adolescent drug abusers led him to believe that repeated adolescent failure is a result of retreat from responsibility; thus the drug abuser can rationalize his failures as a consequence of not having tried (Bratter, 1973). The adolescent drug abuser views his failure as temporary because he believes he still possesses the same resources he had prior to the onset of his addiction.

Bratter (1973) suggested a combination of reality therapy, confrontation, and the psychotherapeutic approach with the following major components of treatment: (a) establishment of therapeutic alliance, (b) forced behavioral change, (c) reorientation and reconstruction of behavior, and (d) growth and development. The problems of establishing a therapeutic relationship with a suspicious drug-abusing adolescent are compounded by his fears of detection and incarceration. Bratter placed the responsibility for establishing rapport on the therapist, advocating that the therapist honestly express his personal views on the destructiveness of taking drugs. The therapist can use his role as a parental surrogate to establish limits with regard to crisis intervention and to convince the patient that the therapist cares about him. This commitment to the patient is demonstrated (*a*) by maintaining consistently high expectations for the patient to fulfill, which reflect a belief in the patient's potential; (*b*) by setting increasingly higher goals; and (*c*) by acting aggressively in the patient's behalf (Bratter, 1972, 1973). Although it is important to attempt to deescalate drug dependence, it is unrealistic to expect immediate abstinence. In the event of imminent danger to the patient, however, Bratter (1973) advocates immediate intervention: "Any intervention by the therapist is justified when it enables the individual to survive long enough to make a rational decision" (p. 590). Often, Bratter (1973) advocates using confrontation in the form of a nonnegotiable contract if the patient wishes to remain at home, or the choice between entering a treatment facility or a therapeutic community. The goal of therapy is to make the patient aware of both his behavior and its consequences. Bratter's (1973) "confrontation-teaching-interpretive-reasoning" approach focuses on the self-defeating quality and irresponsibility of the addict's behavior. He stresses the patient's capacity to control his own behavior, forcing him to decide whether he wishes to change when confronted with the humiliation and discomfort of facing his previous actions. Psychotherapy is used in a process of joint continual assessment of the patient's growth by writing up successive contracts with specifically outlined goals. A vital factor in this therapy is the therapist's commitment to act as an advocate of the addict in an attempt to manipulate the environment so that the patient can achieve his goals. The extra effort of obtaining a special service on behalf of the patient often adds impetus for meeting the outlined expectations because the patient's failure reflects unfavorably on the therapist's credibility (Bratter, 1972). In also serving as a role model, the therapist attempts to help the addict contain his self-destructive behavior and to maintain continually high expectations of improvement.

Bratter (1972, 1973) claimed to have had significant success with this approach, particularly with alienated, affluent adolescent addicts. Outcome reports on 75 patients indicated 10 were in college, 45 continued their education or went to work, 35 were abstinent, and 19 were failures. He has adapted the confrontation-teaching-interpretive-reasoning approach to group process with a flexible 1 to 7 hour program (Bratter, 1972). When the addict is shown his irresponsible and self-defeating behavior, he becomes aware of the impact of this behavior on others. As the consequences of this behavior become clear, responsibility is taken for these actions. Bratter (1972) found that issues of irresponsibility are more difficult to avoid in a group than in individual therapy. He stated: "The ritual requires that the individual risk being ostracized by self exposure which involves putting aside his defenses" (Bratter, 1972, p. 309). He must learn to rely on his own resources and make the commitment to change his behavior. Eventually, the individual discards his identification with failure and experiences some success in learning to control his response to external conditions.

Raubolt and Bratter (1974) have further modified Bratter's (1972, 1973) approach into a confrontation-reality therapy incorporating five similar treatment goals: (a) the elimination of overt self-destructive behavior, (b) the encouragement of expression of feelings, (c) the use of these feelings in productive behavior, (d) the development of responsible concern, and (e) the encouragement of independent thinking and action. The focus of their treatment is the addict's current behavior. "Addiction consists of a pattern of manipulation to avoid loneliness, failure, isolation and despair. While this behavior is self-destructive it is also stable, safe." (Raubolt and Bratter, 1974, p.3). Again, Raubolt and Bratter perceived that the addict's previous failures are used as rationalizations and excuses for continuing irresponsible behavior. Confrontation forces the individual to change his behavior, to accept responsibility for this behavior, and helps him to understand and accept the consequences of his behavior, as well as helping the addict to rely on his personal resources (Raubolt and Bratter,1974). To these ends, three stages were considered part of confrontation-reality group therapy: (a) establishing relationships, (b) inducing a therapeutic crisis, and (c) restructuring behavior. In the first stage the therapist must prove that he is competent and that he cares by challenging irresponsible behavior, exposing manipulation, being firm and willing to help, and clearly defining and upholding limits. The effective therapist is characterized by "responsible concern" in which he adopts the attitude that "they (drug addicts) do not have drug problems, they have people problems such as loneliness, fear, anger, and failure" (Raubolt and Bratter, 1974, p. 5). The antisocial attitudes and behavior of the addict must be channeled into constructive agents of social change. Eventually, the group members begin to depend on each other rather than on the therapist. This is particularly difficult when the old behavior patterns have been destroyed and have been replaced by feelings of fear and inadequacy, which must be further replaced by new ways of coping within the group through the use of confrontation to produce introjection and to establish peer dependence. In the third stage when there is a general acceptance of the need for behavioral change, the therapist adopts the role of teacher and suggests viable options. Group members write up individual contracts outlining sequential goals beginning with simple, easily achieved ends and progressing to long-range goals. Failure to meet these contract goals is never excused by the therapist. As peer interaction becomes increasingly important, the therapist assumes a less directive role and the group members become role models and, eventually, group leaders.

Rational Authority

Vaillant (1966d) presented evidence that compulsory supervision was a salient factor in effecting abstinence, and this suggestion has been incorporated into treatment approaches based on rational authority. Brill and Jaffe (1967) suggested that the use of authority to structure and hold addicts in treatment was particularly effective with addicts displaying character disorders, personality disorders, or sociopathy; all of which symptoms are egosyntonic. Rational authority involves cooperation between the community and court agencies and is derived from the courts and the Department of Probation. There must be complete sharing of all information among agencies to use authority effectively to set limits and establish controls over antisocial behavior. In this effort coercive measures such as hospitalization, close supervision by parole officers and, ultimately, the power to remand an addict to jail are utilized in an attempt to make authority real and visible. The use of such authority to keep an addict in treatment and to curb destructive behavior has been found by Brill and Jaffe (1967) to be most effective with adolescents.

McGlothin (1979), in reviewing the status of heroin treatment programs in criminal justice settings, saw a growing trend towards lessening criminal justice sanctions for drug use and possession. He concluded that the trend was "movement away from the concept of compulsory treatment justified as being in the client's best interest" (p. 207), as exemplified in the rational authority approach.

Behavior Therapy

Behavior therapy employs a learning model to explain the acquisition and maintenance of addiction. Essentially it sees modeling and the reinforcing qualities of drug use, such as the "rush" of heroin, the emphasis on relaxation associated with drug effects, or the socially reinforcing attributes of acceptance by the drug-using culture, including acceptance into a peer group, friendships, and feelings of self-esteem, as strengthening the drug use habit. Physiologically, the development of tolerance and dependence results in repetitive reinforcement, in terms of the cessation of aversive withdrawal symptoms, upon administration of the next dose of heroin. As noted elsewhere in this volume, such reinforcing effects of heroin may be maintained over a long period of time and craving may be triggered by environmental stimuli associated with past use.

A detailed behavioral analysis of drug abuse may be found in Callahan, Price, and Dahlkoetter (1980). Their view of the role of behavioral interventions in the treatment of substance abuse has been one of a gradual evolution from overly simplistic models to the realization that the drug abuser is a unique individual with a variety of behavioral assets and deficits. With respect to treatment, they organize the current approaches based upon behavioral intervention models into the following categories: (a) *Chemical aversion therapies*, mostly earlier studies, in which punishment or classical conditioning of drug taking is employed through means of aversive conditioning, or covert conditioning; (b) *Electrical aversion therapy*, which while less distasteful and more controllable than chemical aversion treatments, and in fact, apparently more successful, is rapidly losing popularity with behavior therapists as aversion treatment is used less frequently; (c) *Covert sensitization*, employing verbal aversion pairing with the unwanted behavior, but a method for which clear evaluation of effectiveness with heroin addicts is still unavailable; (d) *Extinction*, employing narcotic antagonistics to block the effects of heroin; (e) *Contingency management*, with careful employment of principles of reinforcement via the use of reinforcers such as access to recreation by means of a contingency contract. Synanon is cited by Callahan et al as one environment in which contingency management is clearly employed, while noting that supportive behavioral treatment approaches are more likely to have effective outcomes than confrontative ones; and (f) *Community-based behavioral* treatment programs, in which the contingency contract is used to shape behaviors leading towards appropriate goals.

From their review of behavioral interventions for drug abusers, Callahan, Price, and Dahlkoetter (1980) derive five critical treatment target behaviors: (a) substance abuse, (b) therapy attendance, (c) drug urges, (d) work behavior, and (e) a non-abuser life style. They see the most effective treatments, in terms of modifying these respective behaviors, as (a) inpatient detoxification and urine testing for drug abuse, (b) contingency contracting for therapy attendance; (c) use of a blocking agent such as naltrexone and covert sensitization for extinction of drug urges, (d) contingency contracting for appropriate work behavior, and (e) life management training and contingency contracting for developing a nonabusive life style. Callahan et al describe several excellent studies, including one in which they found that the impact upon heroin addicts of behavior therapy alone and in conjunction with naltrexone antagonist therapy resulted in an initial superiority of the combined treatment, but a loss of differences between treatments over time (Callahan, Rawson, McCleve, Arias, Glazer, and Liberman, 1980).

In two other recent behavioral intervention studies, more positive outcomes were obtained. Hirt and Greenfield (1979) evaluated the effectiveness of short-duration (12 sessions) implosive therapy as compared with eclectic counseling or no treatment for heroin addicts during detoxification from methadone. They found the implosive therapy group to be the only one to show a significant reduction of methadone level during treatment and follow-up periods. While the results are impressive in terms of the short duration of the treatments, Hirt and Greenfield appropriately warn of possible methodological limitations of their study, something done all too infrequently by treatment researchers in the drug abuse field. Hollonds, Oei, and Turecek (1980) compared a behavior therapy program with a methadone withdrawal program to evaluate relative efficacy in preventing relapse after methadone treatment. The behavior therapy program included elements of systematic desensitization and assertiveness training directed at increasing coping and social skills. In addition, there was a combined treatment group and a no-treatment control group. As expected, there was a significant acquisition of social skills and decrease in fear levels in the group receiving behavior therapy. This group showed a prevention of relapse; the combined behavior therapy and methadone withdrawal group, a decrease in rate of relapse; and the methadone alone and control groups, no change. Rate of relapse was found to be related to fear of withdrawal, fear of negative evaluation, social avoidance and distress, and lack of interpersonal assertiveness.

In summary, the literature on psychotherapy with heroin addicts is both sparse and unencouraging. Apparently the recent modifications of reality therapy and confrontation-reality therapy are more successful than the traditional forms of individual psychotherapy. The psychoanalytic literature reveals a similar lack of effectiveness probably for the same reasons: psychoanalysis requires a great deal of motivation, which is uncharacteristic of addicts in general, to remain in analysis for several years; it places strong emphasis on intellectual and verbal skills; and it also appears to have little impact on interrupting the cycle of addiction and on providing viable alternatives to drug-taking. Psychoanalytic case histories of drug addicts were generally so specific and idiosyncratic as to offer little in the way of generalization, insight, and evaluation, and have been omitted from review for this reason. If there is a bright spot in the psychotherapy literature, it is with respect to the application of behavior therapy to the problem of heroin addiction. It is clear from the presentation made by Callahan, Price, and Dahlkoetter (1980) that behavior therapy has a great deal to offer in the treatment of heroin addiction. The careful analysis of the behavior involved in addiction as well as the systematic approach to treatment programming is at the basis of good scientific research. It is unfortunate that relatively few studies on substance abuse have appeared so far, particularly since some of the findings appear to be promising.

THERAPEUTIC COMMUNITIES

Synanon

The model for all residential, self-help, drugfree therapeutic communities is Synanon, founded in 1958 by Charles Dederich, whose early success was attributed to his charismatic and exhibitionistic nature (Cherkas, 1965). The first house opened in Santa Monica with 50 residents entering into what was at that time a new approach to drug addiction, modeled after the self-help efforts of Alcoholics Anonymous. The Synanon Foundation grew rapidly into a series of multiple facilities; today it covers several states and is managed almost entirely by former addicts. Efforts were successfully made in this expansion to use the press to disseminate information to the public about Synanon, and to use Synanon graduates as public speakers to attract community financial support.

Synanon prohibits drug use of any sort among its members, offering them in return a program designed to foster self-esteem and a sense of involvement and responsibility. Cherkas (1965) states:

> There is no expectation to 'cure' the addict any more than a realistic psychotherapist *expects* to cure schizophrenia . . . the goals of Synanon are rather to understand the addict, provide him with adequate biological supplies . . . , and to help him find need-satisfying roles in a drug-free unique community. [p. 1065]

The primary requisite for admission to Synanon is motivation, which is strongly tested in the initial interview conducted with a completely non-permissive atmosphere. "At the time of the initial interview the applicant is further smashed by a calculated effort to demolish his self-image by confronting him with his obvious lack of success and futile incompetency in living" (Markoff, 1966, pp. 298–299). A total investment of the self in the program is required, through which it is hoped the addict will be able to identify with the former addicts at Synanon and desire to emulate them. Each applicant is required to sever all former associations and contacts with relatives and friends for the first few months. This period of isolation is believed necessary to break the patterns of irresponsible behavior, avoid temptations and rationalizations, and to provide time to instill the Synanon philosophy. Once admitted, the addict immediately undergoes withdrawal "cold turkey," reinforced only by the emotional support the other members offer to mitigate the experience.

Once withdrawal is complete the individual is assigned work projects to occupy his daily life that are structured in a status hierarchy, in which the individual receives greater freedom, material benefits, and higher status as he becomes more mature. The small, highly structured community is authoritarian, demanding a high degree of conformity to its rules which is reinforced by group pressure. Transgressions are severely punished by public humiliation, reprimands and, in extreme cases, head-shaving as a public statement of how weak and irresponsible the transgressor has been. Shame and guilt are constantly used to force the individual to accept the group's clearly defined approved behavior codes. Rewards for conformity are offered through movement up this hierarchy of positions. The novitiate begins at the bottom post with the most menial jobs, such as washing toilets, and as he demonstrates his conformity and allegiance to the group's principles he is allowed to move up to positions of greater responsibility. Sabath (1967) observes that this strict regulation of daily life promotes a feeling of security and stability so markedly absent from the addict's prior life-style.

Markoff (1966) observed that there are four stages in the Synanon program. The first involves the decision to enter and to comply with group roles. The second phase involves a 3 to 6 month period during which the newcomer undergoes severe depression arising from contemplation of himself and his former behavior patterns. At this time many persons choose to leave. The third phase is reached around the anniversary of the first year, when the member makes the commitment to understanding himself. Between 18 months and 2 years the member reaches the fourth stage: the former addict is stabilized, controls have become internalized, and he is more or less self-sufficient. Readiness to graduate from Synanon is assessed by the former addict's ability to be in touch with his feelings and to communicate them, to deal with job responsibilities, and to deal with other people.

Daily activities include an hour-long meeting following lunch at which members are encouraged to discuss philosophy, listen to lectures, and give speeches. Discussion of tapes of administration meetings and debates are often part of the daily meetings. "This system of daily group meetings is a deliberate effort to inculcate habits of thinking and communication, and thereby subtly to enhance self-esteem, self-confidence and a sense of personal significance" (Markoff, 1966, p. 304). On Saturday evenings there is an Open House to which the public is invited, to secure financial support from the community and to keep the Synanon members exposed to the outside world. Group solidarity is certainly promoted by these constant meetings, as the individual's stake in the program increases when he is encouraged (almost forced) to regard the group as his "family." Switzer (1974) notes perceptively that "as the individual's dependency is shifted from drugs to the group, a powerful leverage on his behavior is created" (p. 29). Individual loyalties are supplanted by an overwhelming commitment to the group, since responsibility to the community forbids covering up for another's transgression. The entire street-addict mode of operation, of manipulation, and conning must be demolished. Further efforts to solidly replace individual values with those predominantly middle-class values of the group include Saturday night celebrations of the 12 month anniversary of each member. At this time the member is called upon to make a statement to the group about what Synanon has meant to him.

Prototypically, Synanon emphasizes confrontation as a vehicle to break down an addict's defenses and thus facilitate emergence of the "real person." In essence, the Synanon approach is founded on the belief that defenses are masks which allow the addict to manipulate others. Self-appraisal is constant and required. Addicts are believed to be "emotional infants" for whom drug use was a substitute for mother's love (Markoff, 1966, p. 301). The group member must recognize that his former behavior was not only absurd and useless but also self-destructive and disgusting. Any feelings of security that might have grown out of the addict's former lifestyle are systematically destroyed by a group process designed to take everything away from the individual and then replace feelings of inadequacy with superiority and strength derived from group membership. The addict will discover subsequently that the system against which he directed his hostility and passive-aggressive behavior is absent from Synanon, and thus there is nothing against which he needs to fight.

To the end of achieving insights and more responsible behavior both "games" and "trips" are utilized as psychotherapeutic devices. "The game" involves 12 members who meet three or more times a week to examine each others' attitudes and to engage in critical self-evaluation. These sessions often involve verbally abusive confrontations overseen by a group leader who has structured the group's membership around the interpersonal difficulties of group members. Several purposes are served by the game: an increased awareness of one's responsibility to the community may be achieved; and often, the exchanges encountered during the game constitute the first experience of peer-group concern for many addicts. Further, the game serves as a force in promoting adoption of the group values, leading Weppner (1973) to comment: "Actually, the game appears to be more of a control device than a therapeutic method . . ." (p. 74). Similarly, "the trip" involves a marathon of group therapy to renew the original concepts of Synanon and to reaffirm each member's commitment to them.

Synanon has been a controversial approach. Its proponents argue that it fosters resocialization, emphasizing honesty, trust, and responsibility. Most importantly, the measure of a group member's progress is his ability to perform in the group and to express his feelings honestly. However, the problem of assessing a therapeutic community such as Synanon is to determine what constitutes success. The attrition rate is extremely high: of 844 persons entering Synanon between September 1958 and April 1964, 459 left prematurely (Scott and Goldberg, 1973). Although the Synanon approach involves only a small number of highly motivated addicts, even some of this group drop out. Of those who complete the program and leave the sheltered community, at least 75% relapse to drug use within 2 years (Switzer, 1974).

Systematic efforts to evaluate the Synanon program have not been encouraged in the past by Synanon. In fact, it has been stated that "research criteria or statistical studies are secondary and may even be harmful to the milieu of this admission phase" (Markoff, 1966, p. 299). Actually, Synanon perceives itself as a social movement and an educational process rather than as a treatment center (Markoff, 1966). "Synanon seeks to preserve itself in pure culture uncorrupted by what it regards as the dilutions and compromises of the professionally affiliated treatment efforts" (Markoff, 1966, p. 308). In its release solely of data informally collected by Synanon itself, Synanon claimed that as of January 1, 1964, a total of 140,227 "clean-man days" had been achieved by its members (Cherkas, 1965). Further, Synanon claims a 25% success rate of abstinence after 2 years of follow-up, and of those remaining 3 months or longer in the program over 65% are abstinent at 2 years (Markoff, 1966). However, the high success rates claimed are undocumented. Of 844 admissions from September 1, 1958 to April 1, 1964, 359 were still in residence, and an additional 26 members had graduated to living on the outside (Cherkas, 1965). Scott and Goldberg (1973) comment that retention rate may be used as a valid measure of success because the group members are drugfree while remaining in the House. Switzer (1974) has observed:

It would seem that for some, the relative success of this approach to drug abuse results from an exchange of a chemical dependency for a group dependency. As long as the group dependency is maintained, the drug dependency can be avoided." [p. 32]

Only 26 of the 94 persons who completed 2 years of the Synanon program by April 1964 had left (Scott and Goldberg, 1973). Therefore, Scott and Goldberg (1973) remark that the criterion of returning graduates to the community is not a valid index of success for the Synanon type of program. Synanon graduates are doubly handicapped in their search for stable jobs on the outside by a lack of education and a criminal record. Scott and Goldberg suggest that one of the major reasons for a former addict to remain in the residential community may be that it provides him with status and an income that he is unlikely to obtain on the outside because of prejudice, lack of education, and a criminal record. Despite the criticism, however, Markoff (1966) notes favorably:

Whether the former addict elects to take his place individually in the general population or to continue as a worker for Synanon . . . his social and personal significance have been considerably enhanced. [p. 308]

Phoenix House

The Phoenix House program is similar to that of Synanon in many respects but has been evaluated more systematically. As part of the Addiction Services Agency in New York City, addicts are admitted to Phoenix House through 12 units located throughout the community. Unlike Synanon, addicts spend from 1 to 3 months in the center program breaking their habit, or they may be detoxified at the Morris J. Bernstein Institute. When they are ready for the residential rehabilitation program, they move to Phoenix House for a period of 12 to 18 months. Finally, when they are ready to reenter the community, residents move to Addiction Services Agency Phoenix Reentry Houses for a period of 6 to 12 months.

Each of the Phoenix houses contains 70 to 80 residents 20 to 30% of whom are women. Demographically, mean length of drug abuse is 10 years, mean age of residents is 27, 85% of the men have arrest records with an average of four convictions, and 53% of the men have no regular occupation. Phoenix houses are located in neighborhoods having a high drug abuse rate, thus making help clearly visible and available to those who need it most. Residents refurbish these houses themselves and are thus constantly in a position to compare their new life styles with their old patterns. However, to avoid risk of association with old addict friends, residents are not assigned to houses located in their home neighborhoods. New members are not allowed to have visitors or to leave the house unescorted for the first 2 months of their stay, as in Synanon. They also must submit to random weekly urinalysis to determine the extent, if any, of continuing drug abuse. Each house contains three paid staff members, a director and two assistants (one male, one female), all of whom have overcome some serious problem like drug addiction in the past. Additionally, each house has two coordinators and seven department heads responsible for the daily organization.

George DeLeon and Mitchell Rosenthal of Phoenix House (1979) stated the broad philosophical basis of the therapeutic community in the following manner:

"No single theory—social, psychological, or medical—guides or explains the activities, therapeutic techniques, or daily routine in the TC. Drug abuse and criminal behavior are viewed as signs of social disorder, family disturbance, and individual maladaptation. To effect change requires ongoing multidimensional influence and training, which for most can occur only in a residential setting." (p. 40)

Similar to the Synanon philosophy, Phoenix House operates on the principle that the addict's lack of identity other than that of an addict can best be overcome by offering suitable role models of former addicts who demonstrate effective alternative methods of coping with stress. Honesty and openness are strongly encouraged. Each member is given the responsibility of making certain that house rules are obeyed. Transgression is punished by penalties determined by the director that are similar to those employed at Synanon, such as head-shaving and wearing signs. The entire Phoenix House community meets once a day in a structured session dealing with some specific issue or activity of importance. Again, as at Synanon, individual problems are handled in encounters which a resident attends at least three times a week. The house coordinator arranges the encounters to bring together persons having similar problems. All encounters focus on present behavior and may be of two types: a floor encounter having no leader in which the emphasis is on emotional catharsis; a tutorial encounter directed by a senior staff person with both educational and cathartic functions. However, in both types of encounter, members are encouraged to attack irresponsible behavior, to strip the "target" person of his defenses in order to promote understanding and recognition of responsible behavior. Encounters serve the same purpose for Phoenix House residents as does·"the game" for Synanon, and they can become equally abusive verbally. To safeguard the continued, smooth operation of the program, members are not allowed to take their explosive behavior outside of the encounter. They must respond with civility and politeness to an individual who perhaps 20 minutes earlier has been extremely critical and hostile.

As in all self-supporting therapeutic communities, members are given daily jobs around the house that have been organized into a hierarchy. Rapid changes in job allocations occur to reflect promotions or demotions based on the maturity of the individual's behavior. Jobs are organized under seven departments: service, kitchen-commissary, supply, building, administration, archives, and education. All residents pool their funds and receive in return 50 cents to $3 weekly, depending on their progress. Such measures serve simultaneously to enhance a feeling of community and to reduce operating expenses. There is also an educational program of seminars with lectures given by residents who have researched a given topic, followed by a discussion or debate.

Phoenix House has been far more systematically evaluated than Synanon, and it is possible to give some overall impressions of its effectiveness. Rosenthal and Biase (1969) note that since the time Phoenix House opened in May 1967, of the 600 admissions, 17% dropped out and 72 were in the reentry phase. However, Scott and Goldberg (1973) note that a dropout rate of roughly 60% was maintained by Phoenix House in the first 3 years of its operation.

DeLeon, Skodol, and Rosenthal (1973) investigated the changes in psychopathologic signs of Phoenix House residents, since the program operates on ". . . the assumption that addiction is associated with, or a manifestation of, personality and behavioral disturbance" (p. 131). Five Psychopathologic variables—depression, anxiety, hostility, locus of control and psychoticism—were examined in 208 residents. Scores on these variables were recorded at several stages in the program and within a subgroup of subjects over a 7 month period. Pretest scores resembled the profiles obtained from a psychiatric population with high externality, high Sc, moderate depression, and high anxiety, leading DeLeon et al (1973) to remark that on the whole they were "distinctly psychopathological" (p. 133). Scores obtained at the beginning of the induction period were also significantly more pathologic than those obtained after a period of residence. Those subjects who had dropped out of the program by 6 months had significantly higher pathologic scores than those who remained in the program. The authors suggested that, with the emphasis on addiction as a sign of emotional immaturity, it was possible that the new inductee was responding to pressure in reporting himself as "sick," while those who had been in residence longer perceived themselves as getting better. However, DeLeon et al (1973) did not believe this was an adequate explanation of the observed decrease in psychopathologic signs, and suggested that the Phoenix House program really did have a therapeutic effect in addition to removing the symptoms of addiction.

A long-term measurement of emotional change in Phoenix House residents was undertaken by DeLeon, Rosenthal, and Brodney (1971). Measures of emotionality were taken from the Narcotic Addiction Evaluation Program Questionnaire relative to four moods: depression, anxiety, anger, and suspicion. Ratings were obtained monthly on a 4 point scale from residential staff members. All four moods were averaged to obtain a monthly composite emotionality score on 50 active residents and 45 dropouts. Results indicated that the starting scores for the active group were significantly higher than scores obtained at any other point during 3 month intervals (over 19 months). Similarly, the dropout group also showed a significant overall decrease in emotionality. However, for the dropouts ". . . a reciprocal relationship is suggested between length of stay in the program and the magnitude of the initial emotional ratings" (DeLeon et al, 1971, p. 598). Overall the authors found the data inconclusive, but suggested that initial emotionality may have an effect upon how long an addict will remain in treatment.

In one of the few objective studies of therapeutic community residents relative to criminal activity (a major index of success for methadone maintenance programs), DeLeon, Holland, and Rosenthal (1972) compared 254 dropouts to 104 individuals remaining in residence for 22 months. The percentage of the dropout sample arrested during the year prior to admission was compared to the percentage arrested 1 year following program termination. The percentage of the dropout sample arrested during the period of treatment was also determined. However, for those individuals remaining in the Phoenix House program 22 months, percentages could be obtained only for those arrested in the 22 months prior to admission and those arrested during their 22 months in the program. Results indicate that for dropouts the preadmission arrest rate was 49.2%, the during residence rate was 2.8%, and the 1 year following termination arrest rate was 31.1%; for those still active, the preadmission rate was 45.2% and the during treatment arrest rate was 4.8%. The largest decrease in arrest rate from preadmission levels for dropouts was in the group who remained in the program 12 months. The greatest decrease in arrest rate was among those nonvolunteers who had been referred to the program by the state, indicating that motivation prior to treatment may not be a significant factor in altering criminal behavior. When examining the percentage of change in arrest by time period, the arrest rate decreased by 6.7% for those in treatment less than 3 months, by 40 to 50% for those in treatment 3 to 11 months, and by 70% for those in treatment more than 12 months. The fact that even those individuals who failed to complete treatment exhibited reduced arrest rates was attributed to the influence of the strong socialization process, which increased the longer one stayed in the program (DeLeon et al, 1972). The authors concluded, on the basis of their evidence, that the Phoenix House program was successful in reducing criminal behavior, not only in those who completed treatment, but also in individuals in residence for as little as 3 months.

When DeLeon and Andrews (1977) conducted a long-term follow-up of 60 male Phoenix House graduates randomly selected during 1970-71, they found a significant impact of treatment upon arrest rates. While 72 percent of graduates had been arrested in the five years prior to entering the program, only approximately 27 percent were arrested in the five years following graduation from the program.

DeLeon and Andrews (1977) reported that for participants in the Phoenix House program who did not complete the program, magnitude of outcome in a positive direction on a wide variety of outcomes was directly related to the amount of time spent in the program. The greatest amount of change was observed six months after "dropping out," with the maximum reached at 36 months in a 60-month follow-up. Likewise, Simpson, Savage, Lloyd, and Sells (1977) found favorable outcome after treatment to be related to time in treatment, with the best results occurring where residents had been in treatment for at least one year. This was also true, however, of methadone maintenance and drug-free programs.

Odyssey House

Odyssey House[2] represents the third major category of drugfree therapeutic communities, and is at the opposite end of the spectrum from Synanon in its emphasis on returning the graduate to the mainstream of community life. In fact, this emphasis is so strong that less than 40% of those completing the Odyssey House program remain in the addiction field. Odyssey House was founded in 1966 to meet the need for a therapeutic community which prepared its graduates for a vocation. The employment of rehabilitated former addicts was not a focal concern for the Synanon-type programs, since most of their few graduates remained in the Synanon community as staff members. In addition, prejudicial treatment of former addicts that often excluded them from business contributed strongly to recidivism. Like Synanon and Phoenix House, Odyssey House is a drug-free residential therapeutic community employing encounters, marathons, and ". . . a hierarchical normative system of social control" (Densen-Gerber and Drassner, 1974, p. 3). However, it differs in providing a variety of special programs for different addict subgroups, in using professionals, in doing a complete medical and psychological work-up on each admission, in emphasizing education and training for outside jobs, in offering workshops for business training, in having a residential vocational counseling and testing program, and in providing for a system of aftercare.

Based essentially on a belief that drug addicts are not a homogenous group and therefore should not all receive the same treatment, Odyssey House has developed a variety of programs designed to meet the needs of the adolescent addict, the gifted addict, addict parents, the schizophrenic addict, the retarded addict, and the Vietnam veteran who is also an addict. Professionals are used in this endeavor because of their greater expertise and because they can provide a wider range of role models with which the former addict can identify. The sentiment of Harms (1972) is echoed in the belief that paraprofessional former addicts cannot recognize certain behavior patterns as easily as professionals, and this expertise is a necessity in the rehabilitation effort.

In providing residents with the skills to obtain jobs outside the addiction field, the directors of Odyssey House feel:

---

[2] The description of Odyssey House was obtained mainly from Densen-Gerber and Drassner (1974). Page numbers refer to the reprint.

. . . [the] employment of paraprofessionals in the drug abuse treatment area must be a positive choice rather than one based on personal limitations arising from ineffective treatment, dependency needs, debilitating anxieties, and fear of an inability to 'cut it' on the outside. [Densen-Gerber and Drassner, 1974, p. 4]

Furthermore,

Primary amongst the dangers inherent in assuming the role of an ex-addict paraprofessional is the constriction of lateral and vertical mobility outside of the therapeutic community. [Densen-Gerber and Drassner, 1974, p. 13]

Each resident is required to develop skills which will make him mobile in the external society before he is allowed to remain in the therapeutic community as a staff member. Requisite to being hired by Odyssey House, the resident must present evidence of having a high school or equivalency diploma, a driver's license, and the offer of an alternative job. In this way Odyssey House hopes to ensure that residents will not remain in the addiction field because they lack the necessary skills to move to the out-side employment field, or are dependent, anxious, and afraid of trying to make it on their own.

Odyssey House has an on-site educational facility consisting of a public school. The necessity for providing an opportunity to develop new skills is based on the following principle:

It is only through the acquisition of enhanced abilities and ego satisfactions that many drug abusers will be able to relinquish their involvement in deviant cultures which in the past has permitted them to experience a sense of achievement while circumventing the middle class value system. [Densen-Gerber and Drassner, 1974, p. 14]

Such efforts at providing skills are in accord with the expressed belief of many researchers that in order to avoid relapse meaningful alternatives must be provided for the former addict (Snarr and Ball, 1974; Bowden and Langenauer, 1972; Vaillant, 1966d; Levy, 1972). Furthermore, these meaningful alternatives most consistently include stable employment (Bowden and Langenauer, 1972; Zahn and Ball, 1972; Vaillant, 1966d), which is often achieved via education. Odyssey House ensures that both adolescents and adults have an opportunity to obtain a regular high school diploma. In fact, 75 of their residents obtained a diploma while participating in the program (Densen-Gerber and Drassner, 1974). For those who wish to further their education beyond the high school level, there is also a college-bound program at Odyssey House.

The development of skills appropriate to working outside the therapeutic community is fostered through an extensive workshop program in which residents participate. Work pressures are gradually increased as the resident progresses to approximate those encountered in external work situations. Special projects are created for residents either possessing or wishing to acquire special skills. The directors of Odyssey House believe the work program facilitates the former addict's reentry particularly when Odyssey House's own business shops provide work experience. In addition, there is an in-residence vocational counselor who can facilitate service provision and who has available a wide range of information about a given resident to accurately assess his/her potential. Odyssey House is unique among treatment programs because the vocational counselor focuses on the skills the addict may have acquired on the street and determines how to best utilize these assets vocationally. Vocational inventories are used in assessing the employability of a resident as well as his performance in structured work situations, his punctuality, and his initiative. Often, unrealistic goal aspirations contribute to relapse, and the Odyssey House counselors foster a positive self-image while helping residents adjust to more realistic goals. Representatives from various professions and trades are frequently invited to speak, and Odyssey House residents subsequently are given opportunities to observe a variety of employment situations. The terminal phase of the program involves job placement. Odyssey House counselors work closely with potential employers to obtain equal opportunities for former addicts and to inform them of the specific assets of an employable resident.

Appeals to the 'corporate social conscience' are strictly anathema for it is recognized that businesses cannot be social welfare agencies, and that jobs preferred through pity rather than corporate need are valueless, demean the employee and lessen his/her self-esteem which are the opposites to the values of the treatment process. Often where ex-addicts are hired feeling they haven't earned the job, their sociopathic, conniving, 'beat the system' attitudes are reinforced. [Densen-Gerber and Drassner, 1974, p. 27]

Residents are required to obtain jobs on their own merit. In the case that a resident fails to be hired, the counselor attempts to determine the reasons and to program remedial steps to increase the likelihood of later employment. Once employed and outside the therapeutic community, graduates return for aftercare therapy groups. In many ways this phase is the most crucial because the social expectations of others are often not met, and resulting disillusionment leads to relapse (Alksne et al, 1967; Ray, 1961).

Conclusions

In 1966, Jaffe noted that ideally treatment should focus on drug use, social functioning, and character to make a person responsible, mature, productive, and drugfree. However, he also observed that all of these goals were not achieved in any then current treatment program. The therapeutic communities have utilized rehabilitated former addicts as staff members, thereby giving status to those who behave maturely and who identify with common goals. For the former addict such a role decreases his sense of alienation and provides him with a stake in the future. Cohen (1974) noted, however, that the number of persons reached via the self-help drugfree therapeutic communities was roughly a pitiful 2%, and it is doubtful that this figure has changed a decade later.

Katz, Long, and Churchman (1975) carefully evaluated a halfway house program patterned after a therapeutic community in Los Angeles, following 118 clients from four to 18 months upon leaving the program. Using multiple sources of information which allowed for verification of findings, Katz et al found that approximately two-thirds of their Ss had been employed for 17 to 19 weeks, 20 percent had been arrested, and that some up to 60 percent had used drugs up to the time of the follow-up interview, although only eight to 16 percent were actually using drugs *at the time* of the interview. As in many other studies reviewed in this chapter, length of time spent in the program was predictive of post-treatment rates of employment, arrest, and drug use. Again, the age of first drug use and number of arrests prior to program entry also predicted post-treatment drug use.

Coombs (1981) evaluated the impact, for 208 addicts, of participation in two California therapeutic communities, one 3 months and the other 10-12 months in length. Follow-up interviews 11 to 18 months after leaving the program found only 4.3 percent of the participants to be totally abstinent from drugs. A marked decrease was noted, however, from pre-treatment rates of drug use, crime, and unemployment. The greatest changes occurred in participants in the long-term versus short-term program, and among program graduates versus dropouts.

After critically reviewing some 25 therapeutic community treatment outcome studies, Bale (1979) notes a wide range of methodological limitations, including (a) retrospective designs, (b) unclearly defined outcome variables, (c) low follow-up completion rates, (d) lack of descriptive data on the treatment processes in the patients, (e) inadequate sampling, (f) lack of comparison control groups and (g) lack of validating data for self reports. Obviously Jaffe's (1966) concern is still valid. At that time, he observed that accurate evaluation of therapeutic communities as well as comparison with other modalities in terms of outcome was extremely difficult. Problems are confounded by high screening levels and high rates of attrition, making it impossible to determine how much of the program's success is actually due to the program and how much of it is a function of the high motivation levels displayed by its members.

MULTIMODALITY PROGRAMS

The inauguration of large-scale multimodality treatment programs in New York City and Washington, D.C. represent two major attempts to deal with the problem of narcotics addiction by mobilizing all potential treatment resources under one administrative program. The Narcotic Addiction Control Commission (NACC) (later known as the Drug Abuse Control Commission) of New York approached the problem of addiction on two levels, as a physical ailment and as a mental disorder (Wright, 1974). The treatment approach involves involuntary incarceration for therapy "... because the illness is recognized as a personality disorder and a disorder of the willpower" (Wright, 1974, p. 374). Wright (1974) states that most addicts do not recognize that they need treatment, and to "... protect society from their unlawful activities.." (p. 438) the government must assume powers of involuntary incarceration. For this purpose, an annual budget of $75.2 million was allocated in 1974 (of which $40 million was allocated to local addiction programs) to treat 15,000 addicts (Wright, 1974). The money was distributed among treatment and rehabilitation centers, centralized support services, and prevention and community agencies for research and testing and administration.

The Washington, D.C. program was similar to that of New York City in many respects. Following the sudden escalation of the heroin epidemic to crisis proportions in the late 1960s, with concomitant increases in crime, the Narcotic Treatment Administration (NTA) initiated a large-scale multimodality program in 1970. In the absence of screening procedures, facilities for treating inpatients, outpatients, adults, juveniles, voluntary and criminal justice referrals reached an estimated 2300 addicts in the first year of operation (DuPont and Katon, 1971). Nearly 70% of those addicts were receiving methadone (DuPont and Katon, 1971). Modeled after the Narcotics Addiction Rehabilitation Center (NARC) which first treated heroin addicts from Washington, D.C. prisons, the NTA delineated three objectives: (a) to stop illegal drug use, (b) to stop crime, and (c) to promote employment or education for heroin addicts (DuPont and Katon, 1971). Initially former heroin addicts were used as counselors, and a preliminary report by DuPont and Katon in 1971 revealed 14% of the patients were voluntary referrals, 41% were from prisons, and 45% were referred by other criminal justice agencies. In 1970, of a total of 150 patients (99 in methadone maintenance), 14.7% were arrested (DuPont and Katon, 1971). By 1972, 734 adults were in long-term methadone maintenance or abstinence programs (Brown, DuPont, Bass, Glendinning, Kozel, and Meyers, 1972), and the majority of the NTA patients were young, black males. Treatment objectives included: *(a)* retention, *(b)* abstinence from illicit drugs, *(c)* lack of arrests, and *(d)* employment, job training, or school. Adult addicts were given the option of abstinence, high-dose (greater than 60 mg) or low-dose (less than 60 mg) methadone maintenance, or methadone detoxification. Both professional and former addict counselors were used in individual or group therapy, and vocational and academic counseling.

Brown, DuPont, Bass, Brewster, Glendinning, Kozel, and Meyers (1973) examined a sample of 150 adult voluntary outpatients, 150 voluntary adult outpatients and residents, 150 involuntary adults, and 150 juvenile patients in the NTA program. Their results indicated the high-dose methadone maintenance patients were most likely to remain in treatment at 6 months (74%), and the abstinent patients were the least likely to remain (14%). An overall retention rate of 55% at the end of 6 months (Brown et al, 1973) and of 52% at 1 year was recorded; 14% had dropped out and then returned, and 38% were in treatment continuously (Brown et al, 1972). Relative to arrest rates, 11% of the high-dose methadone maintenance patients and 39% of the abstinent patients had been arrested at 6 months (Brown et al, 1973), and an overall arrest rate (including dropouts) of 23% that included 18% of the maintenance patients and 43% of the abstinent patients was obtained at 1 year (Brown et al, 1972).

While in treatment, the methadone maintenance patients were arrested once every 71 months (Brown et al, 1972). This rate is significant when compared to one arrest every 28 months for the same population following termination of maintenance (Brown et al, 1972), and is consistent with data presented in Chapter 12. Interestingly, Brown et al (1972) found the converse to be true of abstinent patients with one arrest every 21 months while in treatment and one every 34 months after having dropped out. No explanation was given for this unexpected finding. Overall, the NTA patients were arrested once every 52 months while in treatment programs, and once every 33 months after they had dropped out (Brown et al, 1972).

In examining criteria of employment or education, Brown et al (1973) found 52% of those patients remaining in treatment at 6 months were in jobs, job training, or school, with no differences between treatment groups. At the end of 1 year, 65% of the adults still in treatment were working full time or were students (Brown et al, 1972). Brown et al, (1972) note that employment is a major problem in the assessment of treatment program effectiveness. Although it is often selected as a criterion of success, it is a factor over which the treatment staffs have little control. Employability depends partly on individual skills, the availability of jobs, and the attitude of employers, and less on the abstinence of the patient. For these reasons, Brown et al (1972) suggest that employment not be considered a measure of program effectiveness.

Relative to criteria of retention and continued use of illicit drugs, Brown et al, (1972) found no evidence of illicit drug use in 55% of the NTA patients. At 6 months Brown et al (1973) found no differences between treatment groups; 7% of the NTA patients used drugs regularly and 38% were occasional drug users. Examination of retention rates revealed that methadone maintenance patients were much more likely to remain in treatment than methadone detoxification or abstinent patients (Brown et al, 1972). Further, clients on high doses of methadone usually remained, rather than those on low doses (Brown et al, 1972). Overall, 24% of the adults retained in treatment for 1 year met all the criteria for treatment effectiveness (Brown et al, 1972); an additional 28% were retained for 1 year but failed to meet one or more of these criteria (Brown et al, 1972). In addition, the high-dose methadone clients were most likely to meet all the criteria for success while the abstinent clients were the least likely to do so (Brown et al, 1972). Both studies concluded that high-dose methadone maintenance was superior in terms of the four outlined criteria for success. High-dose methadone maintenance may satisfy drug-craving and, since it is addicting, Brown et al (1973) note this dependence will obviously increase the probability that methadone clients will remain in treatment. However, they indicate it is possible that whatever factors led a particular client to choose methadone maintenance might also affect the greater likelihood of a successful outcome.

. . . [I]t may be argued that those persons who elect to be placed on methadone differ in important ways from those who elect abstinence and that consequently that choice is itself an important measure of who will remain in treatment. [Brown et al, 1973, p. 55]

Brown et al (1973) point out that once in treatment the high-dose methadone maintenance client is no more likely to achieve a prosocial lifestyle than those engaged in other treatment modalities. Methadone is useful in allowing the client to explore alternative lifestyles, but other problems arising from the rehabilitation process will require additional services. Brown et al (1972) suggest that ancillary services can focus on either developing individual skills or on modifying the community to which the former addict will return. In attempting to modify the community so that it becomes more supportive of a prosocial adjustment, community agencies should be called upon for assistance in finding jobs, housing, and social activities for the former addict (Brown et al, 1972, 1973).

Burt and Associates (1977) conducted two follow-up studies of multimodality programs in New York City and Washington, D.C. respectively. Each involved multiple sites. The New York programs consisted of 782 clients in 14 methadone maintenance, drug-free ambulatory therapeutic community and residential therapeutic community programs. In Washington, D.C. a sample of 360 clients admitted to methadone maintenance and detoxification-abstinence treatment were studied. Control groups of early dropouts, who were defined as having left the program in less than five days, were used. The results indicated that, when compared with two-month periods preceding admission, a high degree of positive change had occurred. Such change was, however, *independent of the type of treatment*. Surprisingly, however, "no treatment" controls for both groups did as well as those in treatment. Sample specific positive outcomes were present, however, in that ASA clients in treatment over one year had better post-discharge employment records than ASA clients with less time in treatment, and ASA therapeutic community clients had better post-treatment employment records. Contrary to studies by others (see in particular the review by Simpson and Sells, 1982), no relationships were found between demographic or background variables on the one hand and post-treatment outcome on the other.

Lexington and Forth Worth Public Health Service Hospitals

Civil commitment under the NARA to either Lexington or Fort Worth has been discontinued, with both institutions now administered by the Federal Bureau of Prisons. Yet, their place in the historical development of heroin addicts treatment in this country requires that studies pertaining to their effectiveness be briefly reviewed.

Prior to the NARA of 1966, an early 5-year follow-up of Lexington releases was conducted by Duvall, Locke, and Brill (1963). Results indicated that only 9% of the population was voluntarily abstinent 6 months after discharge, while 67% were readdicted, and increased to 17% voluntarily abstinent 2 years after discharge with 53% readaddiction, and to 25% voluntarily abstinent at 5 years (46% readdicted). The highest abstinence rate (55%) was found among white male volunteers whose first admission to Lexington occurred after the age of 30. However, only 42% of those who were voluntarily abstinent at 2 years remained abstinent at 5 years, while 51% who had become readdicted in the 2 years following their release were still readdicted 3 years later. Duvall et al (1963) estimated that only 40.1% of the population released from Lexington were voluntarily abstinent at some time during the 5-year follow-up. Even more striking, 52 of the 453 released former addicts had died during the follow-up period with an annual death rate of 16 per 1000 for those under 30 and 30.7 for those over 30. A significant 78.9% of the deaths occurring in the under 30 group were directly attributable to drug use.

Baganz and Maddux (1965) noted in a study of Fort Worth patients that of 63% who were later employed, significant correlations were obtained between employment and years of education, completion of high school, and the use of psychological help while at Fort Worth. Furthermore, 75% of those who were employed had taken advantage of the psychotherapy available at Fort Worth. The authors observed that the motivation which led these subjects to seek psychological help may have also motivated them to hold jobs.

Perhaps the most extensive study of readmission rates to the U.S. Public Health Service Hospital at Lexington was conducted by Ball, Thompson, and Allen (1970). During the 32 years between the opening of the Lexington Hospital in 1935 and the initiation of civil commitment in 1966 there were 77,076 admissions involving 43,215 patients. Of those, ·70% were voluntary and 30% were federal prisoners, with 66.7% having only a single admission, 17.3% had two admissions, and 16% had three or more. Almost 25% of those subsequently returning to the hospital did so within the first year following discharge, 50% by 2 years, and 90% by the end of 6 years. When rates of readmission were calculated to account for differential years at risk male volunteers had a rate of 40.0% and male prisoners a rate of 36.1%. The voluntary readmission rates for nonwhite addicts was significantly lower than that for white addicts (36.7% vs. 42.1%), and for nonwhite prisoners (29.8%) versus white prisoners (40.7%). The younger patients had higher rates of admission even when years at risk were controlled. Apparently the age at first admission is a crucial factor in readmission: the younger the addict at first admission, the more likely he is to return. This finding is completely contrary to that expected from hypotheses suggesting that the earlier treatment is begun in the addiction cycle, the more likely it is to be effective.

Ball et al (1970) found that of the voluntary admissions more than half were unwilling to stay in treatment a month, and only one-fifth continued treatment for the recommended time to be considered cured. Actually, the rate of readmission for those considered cured was not very different from those who had terminated treatment very early (37.4% vs. 39.9%). Despite considerably more exposure to medical and psychological treatment, these patients did not show any significant decrease in rates of readmission. For voluntary patients between 21 and 30, then, the length of hospital stay was unrelated to the probability of readmission. Ball et al (1970) conclude that 40 to 50% of the addicts admitted in the 32 year period since the opening of the Lexington PHSH relapsed, and the rates of readmission were higher for younger patients, voluntary patients, and voluntary AMA discharges. Ball et al (1970) state:

We concluded that a positive association exists between relapse to drug abuse and both the youthfulness of addicts and the inadequacy of brief periods of voluntary hospital treatment. [p. 616]

Unfortunately, the advent of civil commitment in 1966 did not change these statistics significantly. Langenauer and Bowden (1971) followed the first 252 NARA civilly committed male patients released from Lexington. At Lexington, these patients led a fairly flexible life with therapeutic opportunities available, job assignments, education opportunities, and group therapy. However, in the first month of aftercare, 45% of the patients used opioids and an additional 5% used other drugs. This percentage remained fairly constant, so that only 14.4% of the patients in aftercare had not used opioids by the end of the sixth month. While opioid use increased the probability that patients would subsequently undergo detoxification, this effort was of little use. The relapse rate was extremely high, despite the fact that 71% of those in aftercare were self-supporting by the fifth month.

The California Civil Commitment Program

A review of the early California Civil Commitment Program reveals that participants were primarily addicts who would otherwise have been imprisoned (Kramer et al, 1968). Stated objectives included the altering of personality patterns believed to underlie chronic drug abuse:

> . . . drug use is merely a symptom of aberrant personality patterns and inadequate socialization and that it is useless to hope to change the symptom without effecting changes in patterns of thinking and reacting [Kramer et al, 1968, p. 817]

The California program began in 1961, as part of the Department of Corrections, to treat, rehabilitate, and control drug abuse and abusers. At that time it was possible to commit a person to treatment on the basis either of his being an addict or being in danger of becoming an addict (Kramer et al, 1968). Once committed to treatment, the addict underwent a statutory minimum period of 6 months' institutionalization followed by lengthy parole. Institutional treatment consisted of a therapeutic community ". . . modified to meet the special restrictions of the law, the terms of commitment, the rules of the director of the Department of Corrections, the superintendent of the institution, and the paroling authority" (Kramer et al, 1968, p. 817). Once released to outpatient status the patient had to report regularly to a parole officer, undergo routine nalline testing or urinalysis, and might be required to attend group counseling. Obviously the use of narcotics and dangerous drugs was prohibited as an outpatient, and only moderate amounts of alcohol were tolerated. A total of 13 conditions had to be met in order to remain in outpatient status. Violation of any condition was sufficient to bring about reinstitutionalization, the most common violations being drug use, arrests, and absconding from supervision. Less justifiable and clearly oppressive restrictions were embodied in violations constituting "examples of poor adjustment" such as frequent changes of job or residence without permission from the authorities, failure to attend scheduled counseling sessions, and continued association with known addicts (Kramer et al, 1968). The demands for conformity were clearly rigid, and termination of commitment was made by recommendation of the Narcotic Addict Evaluation Authority (NAEA) after completion of a minimum of three years satisfactory outpatient status. However, suspension of parole required both documentation and the approval of the parole board of the NAEA.

Although the minimum inpatient treatment period was statutorily set at 6 months, Kramer et al (1968) noted the median length was 13.7 months. At one point an unsuccessful attempt was made to reduce this amount of time, resulting in an increased return rate. After 1 year of outpatient status (OPS), 35% of 1209 patients were in good standing and 64% were not (Kramer et al, 1968). Results of 3 years OPS following first release indicated that only 16% were in good standing (i.e., representing only those who were continuously in good standing from the time of their first release) and 81% were not (Kramer et al, 1968). One year following the second release from inpatient status revealed that 26% were in good standing. Further, Kramer et al (1968) noted that not only were 56% of the outpatients detected using drugs in their first year of OPS, but 20% of those following their first release were convicted for a misdemeanor in the first year.

The authors cautioned, however, that problems in comparative evaluation of treatment programs often arise from differences in criteria for improvement, length of follow-up, and the nature of the population. They further point out that a "failure" in many programs may not be restricted to relapse to drug abuse.

O'Donnell suggests that many follow up studies are being misinterpreted as indicating that opiate addiction is a more intractable phenomenon than it actually is since provision is seldom made for evaluating subsequent remission or determining diminution in degree of addiction. [Kramer et al, 1968, p. 821]

Since their evaluation of the California Civil Commitment Program suggested that one out of three patients were in good standing after 1 year OPS and one out of six after 3 years, Kramer et al (1968) could only conclude that the program was effective for some people. Further, a period of civil commitment might have delayed a return to drug use for many people as well as possibly changing their self-perception. However, Kramer et al (1968) acknowledge that a negative reaction to both the correctional setting and the element of compulsion may have interfered with the degree of positive benefits derived. They comment that the duration of commitment was too long in light of the fact that although those addicts convicted of a felony (70% of the commitments) would spend more time in prison, a substantial percentage of the addicts had been convicted of a misdemeanor or no crime at all and would have spent far less time in prison. In their examination of the results of Vaillant's (1966a, d) studies indicating programs with compulsory supervision have the highest degree of successful outcome, Kramer et al (1968) do not feel that the California program's effectiveness was increased because of its rigidity.

Among the self-imposed restrictions may be included a treatment program which operates with little variation and which excludes psychiatrists and psychologists from direct participation. The few mental health professionals associated with the program are used only peripherally. [p. 822]

Compulsory parole supervision will induce periods of abstinence in some addicts, but Kramer et al (1968) believe this number is substantially lower than Vaillant's studies have projected. The authors suggest that the consequences of failure in the California program are particularly salient because the majority of patients fail every year. The fact that the ". . . periods of intermittent incarceration are about equal to the time spent on parole . . ." (p. 823) implies the existence of consequences different from those following failure in a voluntary program.

The ultimate effect has been to produce a system into which a large number of addicts are locked, most of the addicts shifting between approximately equal periods of incarceration and parole. [Kramer et al, 1968, p. 823]

McGothlin, Anglin, and Wilson (1977b), in an evaluation of the California program, interviewed some 756 of a sample of 949 male admissions some five to 12 years after admission. Their interest in the incarceration, criminal, and drug involvement of this sample revealed that continuation in the program resulted in better performance during commitment, compared to a matched control group released shortly after admission. Similar results, although of lesser magnitude, were obtained following discharge. In general, success and program compliance at time of discharge were related to success at followup, and the availability of methadone maintenance was significantly related to a reduction of heroin use. In 1979, Sells concluded that the California Civil Commitment Program appeared to have "demonstrated worth" (p. 115) for narcotics addicts.

TREATMENT OF THE ADDICT OFFENDER

In many ways the treatment of narcotic addicts in correctional settings seems a very logical approach. Because of the high rate of involvement of almost all addicts in criminal activities, sooner or later most will find themselves incarcerated. Thus, access to the client exists. Secondly, the correctional setting provides relative isolation of the addict from sources of narcotics, although it is clear that there is some availability of drugs, including opiates, in most correctional facilities. Relative isolation from the drug abuse culture exists, although here incarceration, together with a population consisting of a high proportion of drug abusers (Platt, Scura, and Hoffman, 1973), maintains many elements of the interpersonal context of drug abuse. Yet, relatively few correctional drug abuse treatment programs have been established, most likely reflecting both the relative lack of treatment rehabilitation programs in corrections as well as the realistic financial constraints and need to address the more basic problems of correctional settings, such as housing and maintaining an ever-expanding correctional population. One such correctionally based treatment program is described by Platt, Metzger, and Perry in Ross and Gendreau's (1980) *Effective Correctional Treatment*.

Literature that relates to treatment of the incarcerated addict is sparse despite an obvious need for such programs in the prison setting. The very fact that possession or consumption of heroin constitutes an illegal act ensures the involvement of many heroin users with the criminal justice system. Platt, Hoffman, and Ebert (1976) found documented heroin use in admissions to the New Jersey Reformatory Complex over a 5 year period (1968-1972) increased from a minimum of 25% in January 1968, to a maximum of 73% by July 1971. This rate had leveled off to a still substantial 68% by July 1972. Thus, based upon data collected in New Jersey, the proportion of the offender population who require some form of treatment for narcotics involvement is not inconsequential.

Helms, Scura, and Fisher (1975) have noted that opportunities for obtaining adequate treatment in a correctional institution are limited. Rehabilitation programs within prisons focus on psychotherapy, vocational, group and educational counseling, and only recently have incorporated chemotherapeutic techniques (e.g., antagonists and methadone detoxification), which have generally proven ineffective in meeting the needs of the incarcerated addict. As Helms et al (1975) point out:

. . . psychotherapeutic and counseling programs depend on an individual's desire to explore himself and change. [p. 361]

Neither of these desires may apply to the offender who is forced into treatment he does not want as a prerequisite for parole. Furthermore,

Helms et al (1975) suggest that the freedom to determine both the nature and duration of the therapeutic process, which is absent in the correctional institution, may be a crucial factor in successful treatment.

The Guided Group Interaction Approach

One of the few group treatment approaches which has been slightly more effective, particularly with youthful offenders who are also drug addicts, is Guided Group Interaction (GGI). The GGI technique was originally developed in the Highfields Project (McCorkle, Elias, and Bixby, 1958), and requires youthful offenders to examine their behavior within the context of intensive group discussion. As Wicks (1974) observed:

> The object of GGI sessions is to provide members with enough information, understanding, and motivation to adapt to society. [p. 50]

The following five stages are usually involved in the process of adaptation: (a) the offender begins to recognize and to abandon the defenses he has previously used in dealing with the world; (b) the offender examines his interpersonal problems in the context of group evaluation; (c) the inmate begins to evaluate the problems he has faced and will face upon reentry into the community; (d) the process of reeducation becomes firmly established as the inmate begins to accept his problems responsibly; and (e) an "outline of a plan to change" is created to which the inmate commits himself in future behavior (Wicks, 1974). Generally this treatment model involves a degree of responsible employment and community involvement for the group participants.

Reports of success utilizing the GGI approach are inconclusive, however. Platt et al (1977) provided an evaluation of a GGI-oriented narcotics treatment program for youthful addict offenders with respect to both immediate impact and long-range postrelease behavioral effects. Four groups of subjects comprising two treatment and two control groups were examined relative to performance on scales measuring five personality variables (self-evaluation, anomie, locus of control, death concern, and sensation-seeking), and to parole behavior. The treatment subjects progressed through four consecutive phases in the program. Phase I involved evaluation for and orientation to the program, initiation of group therapy or individual counseling, and assumption of responsibility for routine jobs. The second phase focused on the acquisition and development of good work habits and personal responsibility during a minimum of 2 months. Continued participation in therapy, in a work program, and the opportunity for participation in a voluntary school program characterize phase II. The third phase is entered upon satisfactory completition of phase II. Since phase III is essentially a transitional phase, inmates are offered weekend trips to the community and jobs of increasing responsibility. The fourth and final phase comprises a work-release promotion.

In addition to the activities outlined in the above-mentioned four phases, therapeutic components to the program included guided group interaction designed to facilitate resolution of interpersonal conflicts, communication, the acquisition of problem-solving skills, couple therapy, work-release therapy focusing on problems related to employment, and family or individual counseling.

Results obtained at 6 months following release indicated that program graduates were significantly more successful on parole than controls, suggesting the existence of a relationship between program completion and parole success (Platt, 1977). Furthermore, the finding that program graduates were significantly more successful on parole than nongraduates strengthens this conclusion. Data on the pre-post administration of the personality instruments indicated movement in a positive direction on several dimensions, suggesting decreased susceptibility to drug use. (Platt et al, 1977) concluded that a treatment program emphasizing the development of cognitive skills related to the successful attainment of personal goals was effective in providing certain skills necessary to cope with problems encountered on parole. However, he cautions that differential motivation for treatment might have been a salient factor in the success of the treatment groups because random assignment of inmates to treatment and to control conditions was not effected. Such control procedures are of course necessary to ensure unambiguous findings. This study reflects a problem unfortunately encountered all too often in conducting evaluative research—the need to modify research design so as to accommodate the very real day-to-day requirements of a treatment facility.

Platt, Labate, and Wicks (1977) provide an overview of the issues facing the evaluator of narcotics treatment programs in correctional settings. Noting the increased need for, and acceptance of, treatment programs in correctional settings, they provide an introduction to the methodology (and problems) involved in organizing and implementing such research. Among the issues of primary importance to be considered in evaluation research in correctional settings, according to Platt et al, are the following: (a) selection of appropriate outcome indicators (b) treatment designs to be employed, (c) nature of the reporting of results, and (d) the forum within which results are to be reported. Each of these seemingly simple questions carries with it potentially significant implications which must be considered in the light of the unique setting corrections provides with respect to the conduct of evaluative research.

An Aftercare Rehabilitation Program for Offenders

The crucial role played by aftercare treatment in the rehabilitation of the paroled former addict offender was highlighted by Peck and Klugman (1973) in their study of a Los Angeles program, which still provides a model for a high standard of care. Aftercare treatment services were provided over a 3 year period following release of 145 federal parolees who had been committed to correctional institutions under Title II of the NARA of 1966. The program components were designed to offer an extensive range of services. The Active Prerelease Program involved inmate consultation with counselors and paraprofessionals prior to release regarding problems anticipated on parole. Planning for job training and placement or education was also undertaken at this time. Treatment consisted primarily of individual counseling conducted partly by former addict paraprofessionals. Roughly 45% of the staff parolees also had access to group therapy and crisis intervention facilities as needed. Psychiatric consultation involved dispensing medication, evaluation of behavior problems, and recommendation for treatment. An outreach program, considered by Peck and Klugman (1973) to be one of the most successful components of aftercare, made a staff member available to visit the homes of parolees experiencing difficulties.Peck and Klugman (1973) believed that this immediate intervention, in addition to increasing rapport between staff and patients, resulted in containment of certain problems before they reached crisis proportions. In the job placement program the aftercare staff coordinated efforts with federal community programs to obtain employment for patients, and a program vocational counselor was available. Eventually, a residential treatment center was included for patients who became readdicted, or who were in imminent danger of becoming readdicted, or who were temporarily unable to take care of themselves. This center offered a highly structured drugfree program that included many of the characteristics of the therapeutic communities such as work responsibilities, job counseling, and individual and group therapy. In addition, provision was made for continual urinalysis and ancillary health care services. Methadone maintenance was incorporated into the program for those patients demonstrating an inability to remain drugfree. Detoxification was provided on an inpatient basis for patients who had become readdicted.

Results reported by Peck and Klugman (1973) indicated that this multimodality approach to aftercare was significantly effective relative to the stated goals of abstinence, abandonment of criminal activities, and development of a productive lifestyle. More than 80% of the urine tests each month were drugfree. Positive urines accounted for 17% of all samples, with roughly 8% positive for morphine. Arrest data indicated that of the 25% of program participants who had been arrested only half were convicted, principally for drug-related offenses. Relative to involvement in productive activities, 50%

of the participants were employed for over 3 months, 5% were in school, and 3% were both working and attending school, for an overall total of 58% in work and/or school. However, counselor ratings indicated 62% were "doing well," 24% were experiencing "moderate difficulties" and 14% were experiencing "severe difficulties" (Peck and Klugman, 1973, p. 21). The authors concluded that 62 to 86% of the program participants were "functioning at a satisfactory to adequate level" (p. 22).

Peck and Klugman (1973) felt that a factor contributing to the failure of some of the program participants was an inability to tolerate success and stability.

It is our hypothesis that these individuals become frightened by their stable life style and the ensuing sense of boredom, which is akin to a depressive state, and they feel the need to do something to relieve this growing tension. This may reflect an inability to tolerate the negative feelings the person has about himself, which his previous manipulative, hustling life style enabled him to avoid. [Peck and Klugman, 1973, p. 22]

In combating this sense of inadequacy, the authors indicated that outreach, job placement, and residential treatment opportunities were likely to be most effective. Admitting that their results were only preliminary, they suggested:

Our results, thus far, indicate that the combination of a multimodality approach and dedicated staff can tip the balance in favor of success in working with drug dependent offenders. [Peck and Klugman, 1973, p. 23]

Issues and Criticisms

Helms, Scura, and Fisher (1975) have been cited previously as pointing out some of the major problems arising from and inherent in designation of the criminal justice system as the principal control mechanism for drug abuse problems.

In most of our legal jurisdictions, a considerable proportion of the available law enforcement resources is expended to arrest drug users. . . . The prisons become more and more crowded with the drug offenders sentenced to these facilities. [Helms, Scura, and Fisher, 1975, p. 360]

Such overcrowding ensures tension within the prison arising from a necessity to focus on security measures to the disadvantage of rehabilitation efforts. Helms et al (1975) further observe that overcrowding both restricts access to limited numbers of treatment personnel and limits the amount of space available for allocation to treatment programs. In fact, the authors state, ". . . only 10 percent of those persons requiring drug treatment services are currently receiving them in the New Jersey prison system" (p. 361).

In regard to the issue of the potential to conduct effective treatment within a coercive and restrictive environment, Helms et al (1975) comment:

Treatment efforts . . . are seriously compromised in a prison system, where the client is additionally an 'offender', and as an offender, is told to accept treatment, and change behavior by criteria defined and imposed by an authority responsible for determining the length of punishment by confinement. [p. 362]

Helms et al (1975) suggested an alternative approach for treating the drug-addicted offender that would utilize community treatment programs and avoid many of the problems outlined earlier. Addicts would be paroled to those licensed community treatment programs most appropriate for meeting the individual's needs as a requirement of parole. The linkage between the community drug programs and the prison system would be monitored by a central intake and referral system, which would increase efficiency and accuracy in appropriate allocation of resources. Helms et al (1975) believed that such a cooperative effort would not only facilitate reentry to the community, but would also reduce pressures of overcrowding to allow for more effective rehabilitation of those remaining in the correctional institution.

AFTERCARE AS A TREATMENT MODALITY

Aftercare has become an integral part of treatment in several major human service fields, including mental health, alcoholism, and criminal justice. Essentially, aftercare refers to a transitional stage between formal treatment and full adjustment during re-entry into the community. Brown and Asherly (1979) briefly outline the considerable literature which has developed in the mental health and alcoholism fields. With respect to drug abuse, however, they note that ". . . with the possible exception of vocational rehabilitation, considerably less has been written regarding aftercare initiatives in the field of drug abuse. This situation exists in spite of expressed concerns that addict clients in particular are often ill equipped to cope with societal demands . . ." (p. 166). Among the reasons they cite as being causes of ill preparation are inadequate education, limited vocational skills, and inappropriate patterns of socialization. Brown and Asherly attribute this relative absence of aftercare strategies in the drug abuse field to a number of possible causes, including (a) a relative absence of deinstitutionalization problems, as compared to mental health and criminal justice problems, (b) a high rate of utilization of community resources, at least in terms of service providers, with some 33 percent of them being volunteers, (c) the emphasis upon vocational rehabilitation in the drug abuse field to the de-emphasis upon other modalities, (d) the orientation of methadone programs to heroin addiction as a recurring illness, resulting in an emphasis upon ability to return to treatment, rather than upon aftercare, (e) a relative absence of skills relating to the extra-treatment community among counseling staff, and (f) a tradition within clinics of development of coping skills based upon the counseling/psychiatric model, rather than upon one encouraging re-entry into the community.

Brown and Asherly (1979) divide aftercare intervention models into three groups: (a) self-help efforts, (b) service delivery community efforts, and (c) nonprofessional and university efforts. While the reader is referred specifically to their detailed review for specific references and details of specific programs, a brief summary of each approach will be provided here.

Self-help Groups. These typically involve group support with the aim of maintenance changed behavior, with a lesser focus upon individual growth and change. Essentially based upon a helper-therapy model in which individuals are maintained in a new identity by helping other persons, strong emphasis is placed upon modeling and a supportive network, with ideology transmitted through group membership, regular meetings, and group solidarity. Narcotics Anonymous is the major formal organization in this area, with over 700 chapters in 1977 (Brown and Asherly, 1979).

Service Delivery Community. This approach involves follow-up of clients by staff members of the treatment program from which the client is "graduating." It may involve counseling staff entering the community to monitor client progress and to provide support, placement in group living situations in which the clients assume primary responsibility for themselves, but meet weekly with staff and fellow residents in support groups, or referral of the discharged client to stable work groups composed of fellow clients.

The Non-professional Community. In this approach, carefully screened non-addict volunteers are assigned to clients similar in demographic characteristics and they meet frequently to participate jointly in appropriate community activities with the goal of the client learning from an appropriate role model.

Certainly, the aftercare model, with demonstrated success in other areas of human service delivery, holds significant potential for having the same impact on narcotics addiction rehabilitation. As Brown and Asherly (1979) point out, there are many questions still to be answered concerning the most efficacious approach for such an effort to take. This is clearly an area in which further research, and particularly the evaluation of seemingly successful programs to identify effective program elements, would be most profitable.

DETOXIFICATION

Detoxification treatment of addicts has as its aim the symptomatic relief of symptoms associated with the opioid abstinence syndrome while physical dependence is being eliminated (Resnick, 1983). Detoxification has, however, occupied a rather controversial status among addiction treatments, particularly when it has been employed as the sole form of treatment. Typical of the views taken by many clinicians is that of Ramer and Flohr (1974) who noted that "Detoxification as a sole treatment modality served only to facilitate a 'revolving door.' Addicts would enter the hospital, spend five to seven days receiving doses of methadone, and then be discharged as 'drug-free.' Within a few days, they were back on the streets using narcotics to an even greater extent" (p. 72). Zinberg (1974) concurs, noting that such relapse can be understood by applying a simple behavioral model. "The detoxified addicts leave the protected atmosphere to return to a less structured life filled with potential dangers. The sight of a friend or a familiar atmosphere revives powerful old memories and sets in motion the series of conditional acts that ends in shooting up" (p. 165). Implicit in both of these statements is adherence to Wikler's (1974) conditioning model of opioid dependence, which leads to the conclusion that ". . . mere detoxification, with or without conventional psychotherapy and prolonged retention in a drug-free environment does not result in extinction of the conditional responses . . ." (p. 16).

While not necessarily accepting or rejecting the conditioning model, there have been a large number of critics of detoxification as treatment. Kahn et al (1976) and Campo et al (1977), for instance, are critical of the 20 day detoxification programs because of their lack of effectiveness in altering the pattern of addiction and relative failure to hold the patient in treatment.

In a clear dissent from these writers, Newman (1979) makes the following statement about his pro-detoxification position.

Detoxification of narcotic addicts is highly successful, relatively cheap, applicable on a very large scale, associated with virtually no morbidity or mortality, and is acceptable to a very large proportion of the population, including those who are otherwise "unreachable." (p. 21)

Newman readily admits that the effectiveness of narcotic addiction treatment "regardless of modality and irrespective of the criteria used to measure success" is a direct function of length of time in treatment. On the other hand, he is in agreement with Lindesmith (1947) that detoxification of acute physiological dependence associated with chronic narcotics use is a major goal inasmuch as narcotics use is as often directed towards avoidance of "cold-turkey" withdrawal at all costs as from an attempt to gain euphoria, especially when a high degree of tolerance is present (Newman, 1979, p. 22). Newman's position is that providing symptomatic relief from the withdrawal syndrome is the primary objective of detoxification treatment. At the same time, crisis intervention, referral for long-term treatment, job training and placement, medical evaluation, and other services can be instituted as needed by the client, with referrals made by the detoxification staff. In summary, Newman sees detoxification as complementing and supplementing long-term treatment modalities while having clearly defined objectives of its own—the elimination of acute physical dependence on narcotics.

Recently, there has been a clear resurgence of interest in the opioid detoxification process, with a number of studies having been initiated with the aim of experimentally evaluating a number of variables in the treatment process. These variables include use of different detoxification agents, the effects of pretreatment, length of time over which the dose of the agent has been reduced, and degree of patient involvement in, or control over, the treatment process, including self-vs. program regulation of detoxification agents.

The basic reason for these studies has not only been the search for improved efficacy of treatment, but more basically, the existence of serious questions concerning the effectiveness of rapid detoxification from opiates. Senay, Dorus, and Showalter (1981) summarize the criticisms made of short-term detoxification with methadone as follows: (a) dropout rates are high, (b) success in achieving abstinence is low, and (c) success in maintaining abstinence is almost zero. They cite a number of studies to support their position. Typical is one by Tennant, Russell, Casas, and Bleich (1975) who reported that of 25 of 36 patients who participated to completion in a three week detoxification program, only 25% exhibited urines free of morphine during their third week of detoxification. At follow-up one month later, 47% were using heroin, 42% had entered program maintenance, and none were drug-free outside of a program.

Treatment Program Elements

To a great extent, outpatient detoxification treatment has been a highly homogeneous procedure as practiced by different programs at least in terms of length of time the addict may spend in a detoxification program. This is due to the fact that outpatient detoxification programs were instituted primarily for addicts who, because of a history of opioid dependence of less than two years, were ineligible for methadone maintenance. Federal standards require that such treatment may not extend beyond three weeks for patients with less than a two year history of opiate addiction. Furthermore, the time interval between treatment episodes was to be not less than 28 days (U.S. Department of Health, Education, and Welfare, 1972). The major criterion for admission to treatment programs has only been current physiological dependence upon narcotics, and this has usually been based upon the presence of visual evidence of heroin use, such as "track marks," verbal self-report, or where question exists as to the presence of physical dependence, the elicitation of abstinence by administration of a narcotic antagonist such as naloxone. Senay et al (1981) note that these regulations lead recently addicted persons to either avoid treatment altogether or to misrepresent the length of their addiction, since they know that 21 day detoxification is all that is available to them.

Methadone Detoxification

Methadone is commonly employed as the detoxification agent in opioid dependence, although as Resnick (1983) notes, any opioid drug could be used for this purpose because of the cross-tolerance and cross-dependence among them. The detoxification process essentially involves stabilization on a sufficiently large dose of methadone to prevent withdrawal symptoms, followed by stepwise reductions in the daily dose of the drug.

Rate and Length of Detoxification

According to the available literature, both rate of dose reduction and the period of time over which it is carried out appear to be related to successful outcome in detoxification. Although there is a lack of agreement concerning the nature of the relationship with respect to dose level, both Asher (1973) and Resnick et al (1975) report, in what are essentially case studies, that rapid reduction in dose level resulted in minimal symptomatology. Asher (1973) found this to be true for three jailed addicts in which rapid withdrawal was used. In all three cases, slow withdrawal prior to incarceration had resulted in severe symptomatology. Resnick et al (1975) found no overt signs of withdrawal, with the exception of insomnia and irritability, when he used daily dose decrements of up to 50 percent each in treating four hospitalized patients. Senay et al (1977) found that for patients in methadone maintenance treatment, a 10 percent, in contrast to a three percent, weekly reduction in dose rate resulted in greater symptomatology, higher dropout, and greater use of illicit narcotics. When patients were allowed to regulate the dose of methadone received during the first 14 of the 21 day period of detoxification, Fulwiler et al (1979) found a preference for higher dose levels and fewer "dirty" urines.

In what appears to have been one of the most carefully controlled studies in this area, Senay et al (1981) evaluated the relative effectiveness of a rapid detoxification on a 21 day schedule as compared with an 84 day schedule. Using a double blind procedure with random assignments to the two programs, the following outcome variables were examined: length of treatment, heroin use, discomfort experienced during withdrawal, and ability to reach and maintain abstinence from opiates. Their results indicated that those Ss in the 21 day program, in comparison with those Ss in the 84 day program, (a) dropped out of treatment earlier, (b) had a higher percentage of "dirty" urines, in terms of morphine being identified, (c) reported more symptomatology, (d) had a lower likelihood of remaining drug-free, and (e) expressed more negative feelings about the program. Neither group, however, had a large percentage of patients who reached abstinence and remained drug-free. Stimmel et al (1982), on the other hand, found no relationship between duration of detoxification and the patient's ability to complete the full course of detoxification.

When an attempt is made to detoxify clients who have been in methadone maintenance, symptoms frequently emerge during or immediately following withdrawal. Resnick (1983) notes that extending the period of withdrawal to a minimum of four to six months is recommended for methadone maintenance patients. Yet, he notes that even with individualized and very gradual dose reductions, "considerable withdrawal discomfort at methadone doses below 20 mg." (p. 160) may be experienced.

Using a case study presentation of four patients, Sorensen, Hargreaves, and Weinberg (1982a) illustrated the difficulties of brief-stay outpatient detoxification from heroin with the use of LAAM. They note that prior studies employing either grouped or single-case study presentations have not adequately communicated the difficulties of brief-stay outpatient detoxification from heroin. Sorensen et al conclude that while clinicians may only expect to see "small steps" towards rehabilitation during a patient's attempts to taper off heroin use, even such minimal progress may justify detoxification as a link between "street life" and the decision to enter long-term treatment.

Clearly, the results are not yet in with respect to the issues related to the most effective dose level reduction rate, and length of time in methadone detoxification, although the Senay et al (1981) study does seem to provide some very convincing data with respect to the latter issue.

Clonidine

Clonidine, an alpha-adrenergic agonist, has attracted a great deal of attention as a detoxification agent. Originally introduced as an antihypertensive drug, it has been suggested to have been introduced into clinical use in its role as a detoxification agent without a full appreciation by some researchers that it had investigational-drug-only status (Ginzburg, 1983). While it is not known just exactly how clonidine acts pharmacologically, or at what sites it acts, there is significant evidence available that it is effective in alleviating the signs and symptoms of opiate withdrawal (Gold, Redmond, and Kleber, 1978; Washton, Resnick, and LaPlaca, 1980).

First identified as relieving opiate withdrawal signs in rats by Tseung et al (1975), clonidine was then demonstrated to possess dose-dependent analgesic and anti-withdrawal qualities by Fielding et al (1978). Gold et al (1978) reported that a single dose of clonidine could relieve the abstinence syndrome in humans, demonstrating successful detoxification of addicts in an outpatient treatment facility. The fact that clonidine is neither an opiate drug, nor does it have addictive or euphoric qualities itself only underlined its potential usefulness in the treatment of opiate dependence. This suggested applicability in preventing the appearance of the abstinence syndrome during methadone detoxification. Thus, clonidine could prove useful in assisting addicted patients to bridge the gap between discontinuation of opiate use and commencement of naltrexone therapy.

Some controversy still exists regarding the demonstrated usefulness of clonidine as a totally safe and effective agent for the detoxification of patients who have been stabilized on relatively low (generally less than 40 mg) doses of oral methadone (Ginzburg, 1983). On the other hand, Gold et al (1980) have listed a number of advantages of clonidine as a non-opiate treatment for rapid detoxification. These qualities are 1) rapidity of action, 2) nonopiate, 3) non-euphoria-producing, 4) high success of inpatient detoxification, 5) high success of naltrexone induction, 6) provision of a drug-free or naltrexone alternative to methadone maintenance for: (a) iatrogenic actions, (b) pill, cough medicine, "non-street" opiate addiction, (c) suburban addicts with no previous exposure to clinic-related drug abuse and crime, 7) ideally suited for the working addict, 8) enhance the role of M.O. and M.D.-patient relationship, and 9) define and limit the role of maintenance methadone (p. 99). Although all the foregoing appears to be true, some adverse effects of clonidine have been noted. These include overdose and hypotensive effects, sedative effects, acute psychotic and other psychiatric problems after clonidine detoxification, toxic effects of abrupt cessation following prolonged administration, and risk in misuse by opioid addicts (Ginzburg, 1983).

A series of crossover studies evaluating the efficacy of clonidine in morphine withdrawal was reported by Jasinski, Haertzen, Henningfield, Johnson, Makhzoumi, and Miyasato (1982). They concluded that clonidine (a) more completely suppressed autonomic signs of withdrawal when compared with morphine, (b) was less effective than morphine in suppressing subjective withdrawal discomfort, with only slight alleviation of illness late in the withdrawal period and (c) in contrast to morphine, produced marked sedation and orthostatic hypotension, although this effect was probably unrelated to the alleviation of subjective discomfort.

Lofexidine

Lofexidine is an analogue of clonidine that appears to suppress opiate withdrawal signs with less potent hypotensive and sedative effects (Wilkins et al, 1981). At the same time, Washton and Resnick (1983) note that lofexidine is comparable to clonidine in terms of anti-withdrawal efficacy, thus suggesting ". . . a more clinically useful and viable treatment than clonidine in opiate detoxification, especially with ambulatory outpatients . . ." (p. 48). In addition, the authors note that the lower level of side effects may permit detoxification from higher doses of opiates than is the case with clonidine.

Washton and Resnick (1983) note some possible situations where non-opiate treatment with clonidine or lofexidine may be preferable to the use of methadone. These include: (a) the treatment of addicts with low levels of opiate dependence where methadone may cause an increase, (b) the treatment of iatrogenic addiction to prescription opiates where exposure to methadone and/or methadone treatment facilities may be undesirable, and (c) where detoxification with methadone is inappropriate, unsuccessful or unavailable.

Detoxification Plus Psychotherapy

Considering the many suggestions that pharmacotherapy may be most efficacious when teamed with psychotherapy, it is surprising that so few studies have tested this hypothesis. This is particularly true in the area of detoxification, especially since the relatively short duration of treatment makes this such a feasible research project. In one of the few studies available in this area, Chappel et al (1973) found that during detoxification from methadone, group therapy was most clearly related to positive treatment outcome than was individual milieu or non-specific group therapy. More recently, Resnick, Washton, Stone-Washton and Rawson (1981) studied the impact upon outcome of naltrexone detoxification of high intervention (psychotherapy) vs. low intervention (no attempt at psychotherapeutic contact) conditions. The results indicated a greater rate of retention in treatment and a greater likelihood of opiate-free status at three and six month follow-up for the psychotherapy plus other treatments vs. the medical and social service treatment group only. Stone-Washton, Resnick, and Washton (1982) then conducted a follow-up study (a) employing detoxified heroin addicts and excluding patients detoxified from long-term methadone treatment, (b) employing more stringent control of therapist intervention, and (c) extending the follow-up period to 18 months with more effort to obtain follow-up data. The results obtained in this study were consistent with those of the earlier one, with the naltrexone plus psychotherapy condition showing better treatment retention and a higher level of opiate abstinence than naltrexone alone. The efficacy of combining psychotherapeutic counseling with 21 day heroin detoxification was evaluated by Rawson, Mann, Tennant and Clabough (1983) who randomly assigned patients to detoxification alone or detoxification plus mandatory counseling conditions. The results indicated (a) no significant difference in number of patients successfully detoxified, but (b) improved attendance during detoxification for the counseled group, and (c) a higher rate of entry into long-term treatment following detoxification for the counseled group.

Stimmel, Goldberg, Rotkopf, and Cohen (1977) found that as many as 35 percent of clients who had completed methadone detoxification were narcotic-free and doing generally well up to six years afterwards. These investigators found the following variables associated with continued abstinence after detox-ification: length of duration in methadone maintenance treatment, negative urines, development of insight concerning personal needs, concern over long-term goals, increased frustration tolerance, stable home life, improved interper-sonal relations, meaningful use of home, and vocational stability. On the other hand, higher recidivism was related to premature detoxification from methadone maintenance.

Variables associated with successful completion of an opiate detoxifica-tion program were found by Craig, Rogalski, and Veltri (1982) to include (a) greater absence of staff and primary therapist, (b) patient census increases during hospitalization, and (c) prescription of methadone. After cross-validating these results, the authors concluded that treatment dropout was more dependent upon situational interactionism than on individual determinism.

Dole and Joseph (1977) found the best outcomes after detoxification for a subset of addicts with histories of a relatively brief period of addiction prior to treatment and with many indicators of social competency, including relatively young age, employed, responsible in behavior, and not alcoholic.

Noting initial responses to outpatient methadone detoxification to differ markedly in individual clients, with some showing almost continuous positive tests for opiates and others being opiate-free, McCane, Stitzer, Bigelow and Liebson (1983) examined correlates of these two patterns, in particular out-come status. Their results failed to demonstrate differences either in pre-treatment demographic variables, pre-treatment behaviors, including use of sedative drugs, or most importantly, in ultimate treatment outcome, in terms of continued illicit opiate use. The only significant differences which did emerge in their study reflected greater adherence to the treatment regimen among patients who curtailed street use of opiates early in treatment.

A review of 20 studies published during the 1970s was conducted by Mad-dux, Desmond, and Esquivel (1980). They concluded that (a) none to 62 per-cent of the patients completed withdrawal, (b) none to 35 percent became abstinent at termination of withdrawal, and none to 38 percent were absti-nent at follow-up. Admitting to the ambiguity of these results, Maddux et al concluded that outpatient withdrawal did not lead to prolonged abstinence in most heroin users. Sells (1977) clearly states his belief that "detoxification as an entry procedure for drug free treatment or as a means of recruitment to treatment may be well justified, but the evidence reviewed does not justify consideration of detoxification as an effective independent treatment" (p. 115).

THE OPIATE ANTAGONISTS

The clinical use of narcotic antagonists in the treatment of heroin abusers represents the second significant chemical approach to such treatment (the major chemical approach being methadone). Since the pharmacology of the antagonists has been reviewed previously in Chapter 4, it will only be discussed here as it relates to the treatment of heroin addiction.

Jaffe (1970b) notes that there is no single reason why a person begins using drugs, nor is there a single pattern of drug abuse. Contributory factors may include: characterologic problems, pain, anxiety and depression, or interpersonal relationships for which drug use may serve as reinforcement. Ideal treatment should produce a stable, productive, law-abiding citizen who is drugfree (Jaffe, 1970b). Since this is not always possible, a hierarchy of goals should be established for the treatment of the individual patient. The foundation for use of the narcotic antagonists in this treatment effort is the belief that

. . . if addicts could be protected against the effects of narcotics and the development of tolerance and physical dependence could be prevented, the pharmacological factors contributing to relapse could be controlled and the prognosis for continued abstinence could be improved. [Martin, Gorodetzky, and McClane, 1966, p. 456]

Although antagonist therapy, involving almost exclusively the chronic administration of a chemical substance, does not by its nature have the capacity to modify any of the psychological, characterologic, or situational factors operative in heroin addiction, Martin et al (1966) clearly indicated that it does have the potential to prevent reactivation of the physiologic factors. To the extent that tolerance and physical dependence are salient factors in drug abuse, their elimination might substantially affect the probability of relapse. In decreasing the risk of dependence development and therefore the likelihood of continued abuse following a temporary "spree" for sporadic users of heroin, chronic administration of an antagonist will reduce the probability that such use will result in an escalating involvement with drugs. Kurland, Krantz, Henderson, and Kerman (1973) express the hope that lengthening periods of abstinence will result from these efforts. Further, Kurland et al (1973) point out that antagonists used as therapeutic agents to block heroin-induced euphoria have the potential to extinguish drug-seeking behavior which has been conditioned by the reinforcing properties of the drug. The conditioning theories of narcotic addiction (as outlined in Chapter 7) propose that drug-taking is a conditioned response, both classical and instrumental in nature. Drug-using behavior is perpetuated by the reinforcement of reduction in such aversive states as anxiety and pain. It is further reinforced by the onset of physical dependence, at which point drug-taking acquires the additional reinforcing properties of avoiding an aversive withdrawal state. According to conditioning theories, the use of antagonists should extinguish drug-taking behavior because such behavior will repeatedly fail to be reinforced. Jaffe (1970b) suggested that the occupation of the receptor sites by the antagonist would prevent both the subjective effects of heroin (as it will be unable to reach these receptor sites) and the development of physical dependence. The conditioned withdrawal syndrome will also be extinguished, as the conditioned stimuli (e.g., places where withdrawal was previously experienced) are repeatedly presented without the unconditioned stimulus (actual withdrawal). Without physical dependence, conditioned stimuli will lose their capacity to elicit drug-taking behavior. In the absence of physical dependence there will be no withdrawal symptoms; therefore there will be no relief from withdrawal upon taking heroin. The reward has been eliminated. However, Jaffe (1970b) noted that "in any case, the use of narcotic antagonists will prevent physical dependence, and the value of preventing physical dependence is quite independent of the validity of the conditioning hypothesis" (p. 556).

Irrespective of which antagonist is to be used, the procedures for detoxification from heroin are essentially the same in most cases. The withdrawal phase is often managed by methadone detoxification because methadone taken orally does not produce euphoria, although it is long-acting. Oral methadone dosages can sometimes be reduced by 5 mg per week over a period of 4 to 6 weeks to avoid hospitalization. However, Jaffe (1970b) notes that ambulatory withdrawal has the disadvantage of failing to isolate the addict from contact with other active users. Relapse is a possibility in ambulatory procedures, despite attempts to control illicit diversion of methadone by requiring its ingestion under direct staff supervision. Jaffe (1970b) recommended isolation of the addict in an environment where he could be denied access to any drug for a period extending 7 to 14 days beyond withdrawal.

Methadone detoxification is a standardized technique based on the phenomenon of cross-tolerance and the existence of an inverse relationship between the duration of action of a drug and the intensity of withdrawal symptoms. Suppression of the abstinence syndrome is achieved by stabilization of the patient on oral methadone for 24 hours (maximum of 20 mg twice daily for the first 24 hours) before initiating reduction of the methadone dosage (Jaffe, 1970b). A gradual reduction of 5 mg per day usually ensures that the patient will experience only mild discomfort. Once withdrawal is complete, a test dose of 3 mg of nalorphine is administered subcutaneously from 48 to 72 hours after the last dose of methadone (Jaffe, 1970b). If no discomfort is experienced, an additional 4 mg is administered

10 minutes later (Jaffe, 1970b). If the nalorphine still fails to produce any discomfort, the test is considered negative and antagonist therapy is commenced the following day.

Cyclazocine

The most extensive clinical experience with antagonists has involved cyclazocine, an N-substituted benzomorphan derivative possessing both antagonistic and analgesic qualities. As a potent analgesic and respiratory depressant, small doses produce subjective effects resembling those produced by moderate doses of morphine (Martin, Gorodetzky, and McClane, 1966), while oral administration avoids the subjective effects resulting from subcutaneous use (Fraser and Rosenberg, 1966). These effects are lost at larger doses, and tolerance to the subjective effects is developed following chronic administration.

Cyclazocine induction may begin 24 hours after the completion of methadone detoxification in the method reported by Jaffe (1970b). Initial doses range from 0.10 mg to 0.25 mg, and there may be some residual distress experienced by patients involving restlessness and insomnia (7 to 10 days) in this method because withdrawal from methadone may not be complete (Jaffe, 1970b). The cyclazocine dose may be increased an average of 0.25 mg daily with a range from 0.10 mg every 3 days to 0.50 mg daily (Jaffe, 1970b). A gradual increase will minimize the experience of side effects until, over a period of several weeks, a stabilization dose of 6 to 8 mg daily is achieved (Jaffe, 1970b).

This procedure has undergone variation by a number of investigators. Freedman, Fink, Sharoff, and Zaks (1963) experimented with cyclazocine in liquid form (0.1 mg per cc), in capsules (0.25 mg), in tablets (0.1 mg and 1.0 mg) and by intravenous administration (0.5 mg per ml). Of 60 subjects beginning the experimental treatment, 58 completed induction and achieved methadone detoxification in 4 to 7 days. Cyclazocine induction to a stabilization level of 4.0 mg per day was achieved under a variety of conditions: four groups of four patients each were placed on 10, 15, 20, or 30 days schedules. Freedman el al (1963) noted many complaints from those patients receiving increments of 0.4 mg on the 10 day schedule, and no complaints of secondary symptoms from those patients on either the 20 or 30 day schedules. This experience confirms that of other investigators, notably Jaffe (1970b), who find gradual induction reduces the incidence of side effects. Freedman et al (1963) ultimately settled on a 0.2 mg increment in liquid form over a 10 day period, then switched to 0.4 mg per day for 5 days. Cyclazocine was given twice daily (each dose was one-half the daily amount) until the 4.0 mg stabilization level was reached at 15 days.

After 20 days patients were switched to a single daily 4.0 mg dose. Fink, Zaks, Resnick, and Freedman (1966) attempted gradual induction to a 4.0 mg daily dose of cyclazocine over a 40 day period. Following a drugfree period of 7 to 10 days, patients began liquid cyclazocine at 0.2 mg per day with an increment of 0.2 mg per day for 10 days. In the absence of adverse effects patients switched to a 0.4 mg per day increment for the next 5 days, receiving cyclazocine in two half-doses daily. Side effects included constipation, elation, anxiety, dizziness, headaches, restlessness, and insomnia during the first 4 to 6 days, which diminished during the second week. No side effects were reported in patients after a 2 year period of cyclazocine maintenance. Results of a heroin challenge indicated that 4 mg of cyclazocine blockaded 25 mg heroin over a 6 hour period. Tolerance did not develop to this antagonistic quality, and the duration of cyclazocine effectiveness was determined to be 20 hours. The experience of Freedman et al (1968) with a 15 mg heroin challenge given 1 week after stabilization on 4.0 mg of cyclazocine had been achieved revealed the following: (a) of 8 patients given heroin 6 hours after cyclazocine, only 1 experienced euphoria, which was nòt repeated at a second challenge on 5.0 cyclazocine; (b) of 19 patients given heroin 1 to 3 hours after cyclazacine, 3 experienced euphoria; and (c) of 18 patients given heroin 24 hours after cyclazocine, 6 experienced euphoria. The authors concluded that the effective duration of cyclazocine is 20 hours, peaking at 6 to 8 hours, and then rapidly declining after 28 hours. These observations were confirmed by urinalysis. In patients who received 4.0 mg cyclazocine at 8 A.M., there was a maximum concentration of cyclazocine in the urine late in the afternoon and no detectable amounts present the following morning. Tòlerance did not develop to the antinarcotic effects, and after 1 to 4 weeks on cyclazocine the level of blockade was maintained.

Freedman, Fink, Sharoff, and Zaks (1967) reported similar results. Patients underwent cyclazocine induction after a drugfree period of 1 week, starting with 0.2 mg per day and increasing 0.2 mg per day for 10 days. An increase to 0.4 mg per day for 5 days was then given, reaching a total of 4.0 mg per day after 15 days. The shift to a single 4.0 mg dose was made at 20 days. Patients volunteering for a challenge with intravenous heroin were given 8, 15, or 30 mg of heroin, 0.5 or 1.5 mg cyclazocine, and saline. Of seven preliminary challenges, five subjects correctly identified 15 mg of heroin and two subjects identified 30 mg of heroin. Of an additional 42 patients receiving a challenge after 1 week of stabilization, 40 received 15 mg of heroin. The results were identical to the preceding study with 1 of 8 subjects reporting euphoria at 6 hours, 6 of 18 at 24 hours, and 8 of 19 at 1 to 3 hours. Freedman et al (1967) noted that relief from side effects was accomplished by dividing the regular daily dose into two equal parts.

Martin et al (1966) attempted to determine the time course of action of single doses of cyclazocine (1.0 mg per 70 kg), nalorphine (8.0 mg per 70 kg), and morphine (8.0 mg per 70 kg) at 1, 2, 3, 4, 5, and 12 hours in patients at the Public Health Service Hospital at Lexington. Drug effects were determined by examination of pupillary diameter and the use of questionnaires. The time course of morphine (25 mg per 70 kg subcutaneously) antagonism after a single dose of cyclazocine (0.6 mg per 70 kg subcutaneously) was observed at 4, 12, and 24 hours; similar studies were made of nalorphine. The antagonistic action of chronically administered cyclazocine on single doses of morphine and on chronically administered morphine were investigated. The latter study involved administration of 60 mg of morphine sulfate four times a day for 9 days, abrupt withdrawal of morphine, and continued maintenance on 4.0 mg cyclazocine. Results indicated that cyclazocine was much longer acting than either morphine or nalorphine, with a maximal effect with regard to opiate signs at 2 to 3 hours. Martin et al (1966) also determined that the blocking action of cyclazocine was comparable to the time course of its analgesic qualities, with the effects of 30 and 60 mg morphine on 2 mg of cyclazocine being less than those produced by 10 and 30 mg on controls. The effects of 60 mg per 70 kg of heroin administered intravenously were blocked. Nalorphine was also found to be an effective antagonist, but Martin et al (1966) concluded that the effects of morphine observed after 4 to 6 hours resulted from the nalorphine abstinence syndrome and were therefore not directly attributable to the morphine. The abstinence syndrome experienced by subjects chronically receiving morphine and cyclazocine was very mild upon withdrawal of morphine and significantly milder than that experienced by patients not receiving cyclazocine. A mild abstinence syndrome was observed upon withdrawal of cyclazocine, the greatest intensity occurring after 48 hours. Martin et al (1966) concluded that premedication with cyclazocine antagonized both euphoria production by narcotics and the development of physical dependence. In addition, the use of cyclazocine would prevent an individual who was not tolerant to heroin from dying of a heroin overdose.

Fraser and Rosenberg (1966) also examined the comparative effects of chronic administration of cyclazocine and morphine, and the effects of substitution of nalorphine for cyclazocine. They found cyclazocine withdrawal was mild after chronic administration of 9.2 mg subcutaneously for 55 days. Substitution of nalorphine for cyclazocine did not precipitate an abstinence syndrome suggesting cross-tolerance, but the substitution was considered unpleasant by patients.

Clinical experience indicates that cyclazocine is accepted as a valid treatment modality by heroin addicts. Jaffe and Brill (1966) found that moderate doses of 0.4 to 0.8 mg are almost as agreeable to patients as 10 to 20 mg morphine administered parenterally. Unlike the use of Antabuse (disulfiram) in the treatment of alcoholism, an individual receiving cyclazocine regularly will not experience any serious toxic effects upon administration of heroin.

Retention rates for addicts in cyclazocine programs vary. Freedman et al (1967) found 30 out of 52 patients returned to a clinic for cyclazocine three times a week for a period of 2 months. Freedman et al (1963) found 27 out of 58 patients returned for 2 months or more despite the absence of specific rehabilitation measures offered at the clinic. Both Freedman et al (1968) and Fink et al (1966) reported an increase in social activity, a reduction of anxiety, reduced interest in narcotics, increased interest in vocations, and a reduction in crime among cyclazocine-maintained patients. Fink et al (1966) found 15 out of 74 patients undergoing cyclazocine induction were retained in antagonist treatment, 11 switched to methadone maintenance, and 48 relapsed. Jaffe and Brill (1966) found 82% of patients started on cyclazocine had remained in treatment despite increases in concurrent use of other drugs.

Resnick, Fink, and Freedman (1970) attempted to determine criteria for selecting patients most likely to succeed in cyclazocine treatment in a study of 31 male heroin addicts who underwent standard cyclazocine induction procedures. During the drugfree period prior to induction, subjects were interviewed as to what function heroin use had served for them. Two groups were delineated on the basis of differential functioning of heroin: the "normalizer" group for whom heroin improved the capacity to function, and a second group for whom drug-seeking was related to external environmental factors. The authors suggested these two groups would respond differentially to cyclazocine treatment and that those who did not need heroin to be "normal" would respond to cyclazocine more favorably. Those for whom heroin use functioned as a "normalizer" would more closely resemble the type of patient described by Dole and Nyswander and would respond best to methadone. An 11-item questionnaire relating to heroin use was administered and scores on each item ranged from "always true" to "always false" (1–5). Fifty percent of the patients remained in cyclazocine treatment with a mean length of outpatient treatment of 20 months. Those patients remaining in treatment had significantly higher questionnaire scores than those who dropped out (39.7 vs. 28.4, $p < .05$). Furthermore, Resnick et al (1970) found addicts with stable heterosexual relationships, which exert an influence on the addict to avoid relapse, to be more successful on cyclazocine. The authors suggested that wives might be utilized as "auxiliary therapists" to administer the daily dose of cyclazocine, in an attempt to prevent manipulation of dosage and to decrease chances of "experimenting" with heroin. The authors concluded that those patients who perceive the role of heroin in their lives as effective in "reducing anger, tension, and disappointment and increasing their ability to work or study, to relate to others and to express themselves" (p. 1259) conform to the Dole and Nyswander hypothesis of opiate dependence as a self-induced metabolic deficiency. For the group of patients for whom heroin facilitates social interaction and not functioning, Wikler's conditioning theory might provide a more appropriate model. These patients would be more readily treated by cyclazocine.

Additional insight into the factors related to the successful use of cyclazocine is found in a study by Fink, Simeon, Itil, and Freedman (1970) reporting on the antidepressant activity of cyclazocine. Since both the clinical and EEG patterns of cyclazocine were similar to those of the tricyclic antidepressants, Fink et al (1970) were prompted to investigate its effectiveness in the treatment of depressive disorders. In 80% of the severely depressed chronic mental patients who were given 1 to 3 mg of cyclazocine daily for a period of 4 weeks, marked improvement was noted in depressive symptoms and clinical evaluations. This antidepressant activity was correlated with EEG patterns, and was unrelated to the antinarcotic activity of cyclazocine. Overall, in chronic patients with symptoms of depression, apathy, withdrawal, and disinterest, improvement responses on cyclazocine ranged from mild to significant. In acutely ill patients, over half showed moderate to marked improvement. In general, Fink et al (1970) found the degree of sustained improvement was inversely related to the daily dosage of cyclazocine. Although they concluded that the severity of side effects precluded the general clinical usefulness of cyclazocine as an antidepressant, the authors suggested that the range of usefulness might be expanded by concurrently administering naloxone to antagonize the agonistic actions of cyclazocine. In regard to the treatment of heroin addiction, Fink et al (1970) state:

> The prevailing view is that clinical benefits are related to narcotic blockade and a deconditioning which is said to take place as reinforcement is denied when injected opiates no longer elicit a 'high.' [p. 46]

However, as addicts are also often withdrawn and apathetic, the use of cyclazocine results in increased interpersonal activity. Additional results indicate that cyclazocine does not depress activity to the extent that chronic morphine use does (Fraser and Rosenberg, 1966). Fink et al (1970) comment:

> Perhaps the behavioral improvement of opiate addicts with cyclazocine may be related in part to direct antidepressant effects as well as to its antinarcotic activity. [p. 46]

There are a number of advantages to using cyclazocine. It is possible to give fairly large, single daily doses (as with methadone) to reduce the number of times a patient must return to a clinic for treatment. Furthermore, since cyclazocine has a much lower abuse potential than methadone it has no market value, and therefore patients may be given greater latitude in frequency of required contact with the clinic (Jaffe and Brill, 1966). Cyclazocine is unlikely to be subject to illicit diversion to the black market, so patients may be given several days' supply at one time. The fact that it is orally effective further increases the ease of treatment. Jaffe and Brill (1966) point out one advantage of using cyclazocine is that it reduces the amount of time required for inpatient detoxification, thereby reducing the overall cost of care. The usual 3 week minimum inpatient treatment required to avoid immediate relapse can be reduced to 2 weeks by daily outpatient treatment with cyclazocine 14 to 16 days following withdrawal.

There are, however, limitations to the widespread use of cyclazocine in the treatment of heroin addiction. Jaffe and Brill (1966) note that while patients receiving 6 to 8 mg of cyclazocine are unable to feel the effects of 20 mg heroin within the first 14 to 18 hours, a larger dose administered later will produce some effect. It is possible to evade the antinarcotic action of cyclazocine by taking larger doses of heroin nearer the end of the time period of effective duration (e.g., 18 to 20 hours) and before the next dose of cyclazocine has been administered. Furthermore, Jaffe (1970) observes that cyclazocine maintenance does not reduce the addict's craving for narcotics as does methadone. Abuse of other drugs is common. Thus for these reasons much of the initial interest in cyclazocine has now shifted to the longer acting antagonists such as naltrexone.

Brill and Jaffe (1967) suggest that cyclazocine is most useful with highly motivated ambulatory patients; the majority of patients volunteering for such programs are middle-class, educated, and have avoided the constant shifting from prison to hospital that is characteristic of the methadone patient. Consensus of opinion indicates that cyclazocine is a useful but limited treatment approach requiring (a) the additional support services of group and individual therapy, and vocational counseling to be effective, and (b) great degrees of individualization in treatment regimen to minimize side effects. Fink et al (1966) comment:

> In our experience we have found cyclazocine to be less effective in reducing the conditioned drug-seeking response than in providing engagement to a therapy program and preventing the development of tolerance and withdrawal. [p. 288]

According to Resnick, Schuyten-Resnick, and Washton (1979), early clinical trials with cyclazocine usually resulted in relapse to opiate use within a few months. Treatment success, defined as opiate free status at follow-up, rose substantially, however, when cyclazocine was administered as part of a comprehensive treatment program offering a variety of rehabilitative services.

Naloxone

Naloxone (N-allyl-noroxymorphone) is the second antagonist that has been used on a major scale in treating heroin dependence. Naloxone, as are all the N-allyl derivatives of the narcotic analgesics, is capable of antagonizing narcotic-induced respiratory depression in relatively small doses (65 mg per kg). As noted in Chapter 4, however, naloxone has no respiratory or circulatory effects of its own when given to patients not pretreated with narcotics (Foldes, Lunn, Moore, and Brown, 1963), in contrast to nalorphine or cyclazocine. On a milligram per kilogram basis, naloxone is at least six times more potent than levallorphan, and 30 times more effective than nalorphine in antagonizing respiratory depression (Foldes et al, 1963). Sadove, Balagot, Hatano, and Jobgen (1963) suggest that the basis for effectiveness in antagonizing respiratory depression is a group specificity of the antagonists derived from similarity in chemical structure.

Jasinski, Martin and Haertzen (1967) compared nalorphine, naloxone, levallorphan, cyclazocine, and a placebo with respect to pharmacology and abuse potential. The opiatelike effects of the four drugs were studied at 30 minutes, 1, 2, 3, 4, 5, and 12 hours after administration by the completion of opiate questionnaires (including a 20-item questionnaire of the LSD Pattern scale to assess psychotomimetic changes) and examination of pupillary diameter. The ability to precipitate the abstinence syndrome in morphine-dependent subjects, with the intensity of withdrawal assessed by the Himmelsbach scale, was also comparatively examined. Results indicated that naloxone was indistinguishable from the placebo in terms of pupillary response and subjective drug effects. Potency in precipitating abstinence in relation to nalorphine was 0.52 levallorphan, 0.14 naloxone, and 0.18 cyclazocine. Duration of action of naloxone was relatively short (up to 9 hours) and the blocking activity decreased as the interval between naloxone and morphine administration increased. No physiologic changes were observed following chronic administration of naloxone, and no significant withdrawal symptoms occurred upon abrupt termination. Jasinski et al (1967) observed that a high level of blockade was maintained during chronic administration, the effect of which decayed over a 3 hour period. The conclusion that naloxone was without side effects, subjective morphinelike effects, and agonistic effects, and therefore had no abuse potential of the morphine type, made naloxone an attractive candidate for use in narcotic antagonist therapy.

Fink, Zaks, Sharoff, Mora, Bruner, Levit, and Freedman (1968) extended these studies to examine the role of naloxone in heroin dependence. Patients underwent methadone detoxification. In a series of "acute" studies, 19 patients were given 10 to 20 mg heroin in 2.0 cc saline followed in 8 to 32 minutes by intravenous administration of 0.7 to 10.0 mg naloxone in 2 to 5 cc saline, and 10 patients were given the naloxone before receiving the heroin. EEG readings were taken before, during, and after each injection. The "chronic" studies consisted of naloxone-maintained patients responding to heroin challenges (20 mg in 2 cc saline). Results of the short-term studies indicated that naloxone at even the lowest dosages terminated the heroin "high" within 30 seconds to 2 minutes. However, duration of its antagonistic effects was shorter than the duration of heroin effects, so that patients reported a recurrence in sensation of the heroin effects within 3 to 5 hours. When patients were pretreated with naloxone, 8 of the 10 reported feeling no effects of the heroin injection. Again, after 3 hours the antagonist's effects seemed to wear off and patients were able to report experiencing the heroin effects. The long-term naloxone studies were based on dosages of naloxone dependent on individual reaction to heroin challenges. At 100 to 120 mg given in two daily doses with 20 mg heroin given 4 to 6 hours after naloxone, 71% of patients reported some reaction to the heroin; at 200 mg the blockade was complete. When 100 mg doses were given twice daily, a challenge with 40 mg heroin 5 hours after the first 100 mg dose of naloxone elicited effects in only one out of three patients. There were no abstinence signs upon withdrawal of naloxone, little or no side effects, and no long-term changes in EEG or other systems. Fink et al (1968) concluded that naloxone seemed the ideal antagonist and had no systemic or gross central effects, particularly in comparsion with the short duration and hallucinogenic potential of nalorphine and the widespread secondary effects of cyclazocine. They suggested that 1 mg of naloxone administered intravenously would block 40 mg of heroin. However there were major problems in clinical application because of the short duration of action, the high dosages required to maintain blockade, and the cost incurred in making naloxone from the expensive compound thebaine in amounts large enough to be clinically useful.

Other investigators have commented on the prohibitively high doses of naloxone required to establish an effective blockade. Fink et al (1966) noted that dosages as high as 2400 mg may be required in some cases to block the effects of 50 mg heroin. Use of naloxone in treatment has met with only limited success. Zaks, Jones, Fink, and Freedman (1971) attempted naloxone maintenance in nine voluntary, hospitalized addicts with a mean length of addiction of 12 years. Preliminary results suggested that as low as 0.7 mg naloxone administered parenterally was effective, but

200 mg per day orally was only effective in antagonizing 20 mg intravenous heroin. Patients were withdrawn from heroin by methadone detoxification over a period of 7 to 10 days. They were then given naloxone orally in single daily doses: three patients were given daily increments of 50 mg, four were given increments of 100 mg, and two of 300 mg. At 400 mg, patients were unaffected by 25 mg or 50 mg of heroin 6 hours after naloxone administration. By 18 hours, however, they were able to experience the full effects of the heroin. At 800 mg, there was no response to either 25 or 50 mg heroin after 18 hours. An attempted replication of these results required as high a dose level as 1200 mg to blockade 50 mg heroin for 18 hours, and at 24 hours the effects of heroin were still noticeable. In an attempt to extend the duration of blockade by increasing the daily dose, 1500 mg failed at 24 hours, and at 2400 mg a partial blockade to 25 mg heroin (full reaction to 50 mg) was achieved at 24 hours. One subject required 3000 mg of naloxone to effect a complete blockade to both 25 and 50 mg heroin challenges at 24 hours. Even at these extreme levels, however, there were no side effects on bodily functioning. Zaks et al (1971) suggested parenteral administration was far more effective, as might be the development of a slow-release implantable pellet.

In an attempt to avoid the problems involved in massive doses of naloxone, Kurland, Hanlon, and McCabe (1974) examined the effectiveness of a partial blockade. Subjects were parolees who volunteered for participation and were divided into three groups: controls ($N=41$) receiving only weekly group therapy, naloxone group ($N=39$) receiving both naloxone and group therapy, and a placebo group ($N=39$) who received a placebo and group therapy. Naloxone was dispensed daily in doses ranging from 200 to 800 mg. Criteria of treatment effectiveness were retention and abstinence. Of those who completed the 9 month program, individuals were categorized according to those who were abstinent, those who exhibited only a minimum of narcotics use in urinalysis testing, and those who were hospitalized or arrested. Only the first two categories were considered to be successful outcomes. Results indicated that naloxone was no more effective than the placebo at the end of 9 months. Abuse tended to occur within the first 3 months of participation in the program. Kurland et al (1974) concluded that there was ". . . little differential effect between the placebo and naloxone, at least as far as retention rates and the maintenance of complete abstinence . . ." (p. 669). The initial deterrent effect resulted from the expectation of a blockade and was the same for both the placebo and naloxone groups. Kurland et al (1974) note that since naloxone does not reduce the urge to take drugs, complete abstinence was unlikely. However, while there was no significant difference between the placebo and naloxone groups with respect to retention and complete abstinence, there was less overall narcotics use by the naloxone group (30.2% vs. 10.9%).

Kurland, Krantz, Henderson, and Kerman (1973) also attempted a low-dose maintenance program with naloxone in another population of male parolee volunteers. Partial blockade was attempted and subjects received 4 tablets of naloxone nightly at the clinic to enable them to endure evening hours without resorting to drug use. Urinalysis was conducted and parolees were required to attend a weekly therapy group. Two groups of subjects were selected: those admitted directly following their release from prison, and those admitted as transfers from an abstinence program. Dosage ranged from 200 to 800 mg (via a 200 mg tablet) depending on the results of heroin challenges. Relative to retention rates, 34.7% of the transfers remained at 6 months and 4.7% at 1 year, whereas 59.6% of the direct admissions remained at 6 months and 13.4% at 1 year. A total of 34.7% had either completed the program by the expiration of their parole or were still participating. Another 21.3% were removed, and 40.8% absconded. Over 50% of the population still in treatment at the completion of the study had clean urine. Kurland et al (1973) suggested that administration of high doses of naloxone to establish a 24 hour blockade at times when an individual is relapsing, and discontinuation when he is abstinent, might result in more effective management and avoid the prohibitive expense of maintaining a high-dose blockade. Further, in addition to adequate supervision, the authors suggested use of a 500 mg tablet might allow greater latitude in the manipulation of dosage and an extension of blockade. They also felt the likelihood of success was greater with subjects undergoing naloxone induction immediately following a drugfree period than with those who had failed at abstinence.

Kleber (1973) examined the effectiveness of using narcotic antagonists in conjunction with other therapies in a multimodality treatment program. Subjects initially receiving naloxone were 14 to 24 years of age, with a minimum of 3 months' heroin use. Individuals with major medical complications, acute psychosis, or severe mixed addictions were excluded. Methadone detoxification was accomplished by both inpatient and outpatient methods with subjects beginning naloxone 5 to 7 days after the last dose of methadone. The first day subjects received 100 mg of naloxone in the morning and, in the absence of withdrawal signs, received a second 100 mg dose in the afternoon. Increments of 100 mg per day were instituted until an 800 mg dose level was achieved, which blocked 50 mg heroin for 18 hours. When initially attempted in a day treatment program incorporating group and reality therapies, a 70% dropout rate resulted. When the program's emphasis was shifted to education and vocational training with confrontation group therapy and work assignments, the retention rate increased to 70% at the end of 1 year. It was felt that the day hospital approach allowed exposure to outside problems while continuing to provide a supportive environment in which such problems could be discussed. Naloxone was given for 4 months, then subjects continued in the day program for 2 to 3 months, finally going to work or to school during the day and returning for evening groups. Of the 70% who were still in treatment at the end of 1 year, less than half were still receiving naloxone; 11% had successfully completed both phases of the program, and 18% had left. Less than 2% of the urines tested revealed heroin use over 1 year, and less than 4% indicated other drug use. Kleber (1973) observed that the minimal testing of the blockade might have been a result of misconceptions that heroin would make one "sick," in a fashion similar to Antabuse. This would indicate that a true test of Wikler's conditioning hypothesis was not adequately conducted. However, Kleber did suggest that the use of antagonists alone was not sufficient to keep addicts in treatment, as evidenced by the high dropout rate when patients did not feel the original program had anything to offer them. On the other hand, outpatient abstinence therapy without the use of antagonists also has a high relapse rate. Both therapeutic structure and the use of antagonists were believed to be important in retention.

Although the retention rate has traditionally been one of the parameters considered in evaluating program success with narcotic addicts, it clearly is not one of the crucial outcome variables more closely related to success in the 'real' world. [Kleber, 1973, p. 218]

Naloxone has also been used to facilitate transition from an opiate dependent state to antagonist maintenance on an agent such as naltrexone. Judson and Goldstein (1983) cite Blachly, Casey, Marcel, and Denny (1975) as having used naloxone, in repeated administrations, to reach fast detoxification both in heroin addicts and methadone patients. In the study by Blachly et al, clients were admitted to an inpatient unit about one day following last use of an opiate and generally discharged 24 hours later. Naloxone was first administered at a dose level of 0.08 mg, with increments determined by the patient's response to the prior dose. Both Resnick, Kestenbaum, Washton, and Poole (1977) and Kurland and McCabe (1976) are cited by Judson and Goldstein as using short-term (either 24 or 48 hr.) procedures for rapid detoxification via naloxone between opiates and naltrexone. Addicts in the Resnick et al (1977) study are said to have preferred the rapid detoxification procedure with considerable discomfort to a prolonged one with less discomfort. Naloxone was combined with clonidine by Riordan and Kleber (1980) in a three day outpatient treatment which required the client to remain in the clinic during all three days. Clonidine only was given on the first day, after a pre-treatment dose to assess reaction to the drug. On days two and three, both clonidine and naloxone were administered. On day three clonidine was discontinued, with one dose of naloxone 1.2 mg, i.m. given at 8 p.m. If no withdrawal signs were elicited, naltrexone was then started. This procedure was used to minimize withdrawal symptoms of naloxone. Judson and Goldstein note, however, that more recent evidence suggests that lofexidine may prove superior to clonidine for this purpose.

Buprenorphine

Summarizing research conducted at the NIDA Addiction Research Center on the usefulness of buprenorphine as a treatment drug in narcotic addiction, Jasinski, Henningfield, Hickey, and Johnson (1983) compared its effects to those of naloxone in methadone dependent subjects. Naloxone, compared to a placebo, produced signs of withdrawal including pupil dilation, increased blood pressure, lacrimation, rhinorrhea, perspiration, and subjective reports of withdrawal sickness. Buprenorphine produced mydriasis and hypertension, but no subjective reports of withdrawal sickness. Two doses of buprenorphine produced feelings of relaxation, coasting, and typical opiate-like subjective effects. Naloxone, in contrast, produced nervousness and upset stomach. Jasinski et al interpreted these findings as suggesting a lack of cross-tolerance in methadone dependent patients to some of the effects of buprenorphine. They also found no evidence to suggest that, in maintenance patients on up to 45 mg of methadone, buprenorphine precipitated clinically significant withdrawal. When the severity of withdrawal from buprenorphine and methadone was compared, the syndrome was found to be similar in degree and severity, suggesting that discontinuation of buprenorphine led to a reemergence of the methadone withdrawal syndrome. Jasinski et al concluded that buprenorphine would partially substitute for methadone, alternating the methadone withdrawal syndrome. Thus it can be used in the detoxification of methadone dependent patients with minimal discomfort or behavioral disruption.

Naltrexone

Naltrexone is a potent narcotic analgesic with many positive qualities, including a long duration of action (up to 3 days) and absence of agonist activity, thus producing a nearly asymptomatic induction phase. Naltrexone is administered either in liquid or capsule form, although the use of the latter carries with it the risk of diversion. It is administered either daily as a dose level of 50 mg or on a thrice weekly basis of 100 mg each on Mondays and Wednesdays and 150 mg on Fridays. Nonphysically dependent post-addicts are generally inducted onto naltrexone by 10 mg increments until the 50 mg level is reached. They are then converted to a 100-100-150 mg schedule. It may not be necessary, however, to follow such a course of induction in nonaddicted ex-addicts.

With regard to effectiveness, Resnick and Washton (1978) reported a clear relationship between time on naltrexone and opiate-free status in a sample of 267 patients who had been off naltrexone for at least six months. They reported that 31% of patients who had taken naltrexone for three months or longer were opiate-free at follow-up, in comparison with only two percent who had taken naltrexone for less than three months. Similar findings are reported by Greenstein et al (1976) and Lewis et al (1976).

Judson, Carney and Goldstein (1981), using a double-blind design, evaluated the safety and efficacy of 60 mg vs. 120 mg of naltrexone administered thrice weekly. They found neither clinically significant nor treatment retention differences between the two dosages. Approximately half their patients used heroin during the course of the study, with, however, only 9% of urine tests positive for opiates. Heroin craving usually disappeared by the end of the first week, and no side effects or toxicity were found.

When Greenstein, Evans, McLellan and O'Brien (1983) attempted to identify predictors of successful outcome following naltrexone treatment using a multivariate approach, they found two such variables significantly related to one month outcome status: (a) pre-treatment employment earnings, and (b) days of naltrexone treatment, with at least 30 days of naltrexone therapy necessary for significant improvement. Further analysis, however, showed outcomes not to differ following treatments longer than one month. Length of stay in treatment was, in turn, predicted by marital status and employment during the month preceding naltrexone treatment. In their article, Greenstein et al note that in another study, a composite estimate of the seriousness of a patient's psychiatric symptomatology which they labeled "psychiatric severity" was the best general predictor of outcome in therapeutic community and methadone maintenance treatment. Summarizing a series of studies on the interaction of narcotic antagonist therapy and psychosocial and drug history variables in relation to treatment outcome, Resnick, Schuyten-Resnick and Washton (1979) concluded that success in naltrexone treatment is associated with (a) presence of a meaningful relationship with a nonaddict mate, (b) full-time employment or school attendance, (c) living with family rather than friends or alone, (d) longer histories of addiction, (e) longer drug-free periods between addiction cycles, and (f) less dependence on opiates immediately preceding detoxification; the latter three factors being associated with freedom from opiates one year from the start of naltrexone treatment (Resnick and Washton, 1978). While one is always pleased to see significant relationships between history and treatment variables identified, none of these specific findings should come as a surprise to any researcher or clinician in the drug abuse field. Renault (1981) observed that many narcotic addicts find the idea of methadone maintenance unacceptable, preferring instead total abstinence. He includes in this group (a) recently detoxified addicts, (b) those to be released from prison, (c) individuals who are at risk of renewed heroin use due to emotional pressures or ready availability of heroin, or (d) new heroin users at risk of becoming dependent, particularly adolescents. Noting the immense pressures confronting "abstinent addicts"—patients who have at one and the same time a strong craving for narcotics and a strong motivation to seek treatment—he sees narcotic antagonist treatment as meeting the needs of these patients. Taking into account the clinic setting in which naltrexone is administered is critical to its successful use, according to Renault, since it is not a treatment in itself, rather a pharmacologic adjunct to treatment.

According to Renault (1981), the concept of narcotic antagonist therapy has been criticized on the basis of its failure to do anything "positive" for the user. It produces an "absence of effect" when opiates are used. It also has no pharmacological consequences, such as withdrawal symptoms, when not used. Thus, say its detractors, compliance in antagonist treatment is a problem. Renault lists three solutions which have been suggested to meet this objection: (a) long-acting antagonists could be used, with action lasting up to a month, (b) coercion could be employed, with criminal justice or civil commitment consequences for non-use, and (c) an antagonist could be developed with agonistic euphoriant properties, thus acting as a reinforcer and encouraging compliance. The general problem of compliance has led to two basic philosophies in the use of naltrexone. These are use (a) as a maintenance drug for a period of one or two years or even indefinitely, and (b) as a crisis medication when the patient feels at risk of resuming heroin use.

Kleber (1973) had suggested that in light of more important variables such as employment, education, reduction in illegal activities, and overall social adjustment, the multimodality treatment program employing narcotic antagonists offers encouraging preliminary results. As Kurland et al (1974) had also noted, motivation appears to be a salient factor in the effectiveness of the antagonist treatment method. The use of antagonists will reduce the likelihood of readdiction for the motivated subject who occasionally experiences relapse. It appears that the narcotic antagonists are effective in managing heroin addiction within fairly restricted guidelines. Naloxone is short-acting and expensive and requires massive oral doses to effect a blockade to 50 mg heroin for 24 hours. Cyclazocine is longer acting, less expensive, but limited in clinical usefulness by disruptive side effects. Naltrexone has a long duration of action and no agonist activity. Yet, use of none of the antagonists alone seems to increase significantly the probability of sustained abstinence, although their use in conjunction with other therapies appears to be encouraging initially.

HEROIN MAINTENANCE

Occasionally, the issue is raised that perhaps heroin should be provided in some controlled legitimate fashion to addicts until an effective cure is discovered. There is little disagreement that the current treatment effort is inadequate and ineffective. Rector (1972) stated that rehabilitation programs in the United States reach only roughly 10% of the addict population, and further, that less than 10% of those treated result in a successful outcome. In addition, the monopoly on the heroin supply held by underworld organizations ensures unwarranted expense and an escalating involvement in criminal activities for many addicts (Rector, 1972). Rector (1972) cited former New York City Police Commissioner, Patrick V. Murphy, as having attributed half of that city's crime to addicts at a cost of over $150 million. It is no wonder, Rectgor suggested, that the addict must commit crimes to support his habit when he pays over $1000 for 100 tablets of heroin in the United States costing him $2 in England. Rector (1972) felt, as do many others, that until we can both understand and cure heroin addiction, heroin should be made available to addicts in some controlled manner. Although the success of the British experience with heroin maintenance is often cited in support of such an approach, a closer examination of the differences between the British heroin problem and that in the United States may indicate that heroin maintenance is by no means the obvious solution.

At the beginning of the twentieth century both the United States and England had fairly substantial narcotics problems. However, after U.S. enactment of the Harrison Act in 1914 the two countries pursued divergent addiction control policies. England chose to allow private physicians complete discretion in maintaining addicts on heroin, partly because the policymakers believed addicts had become addicted in the course of medical treatment (Lidz, Lewis, Crane, and Gould, 1975). The "typical addict" in England was believed to be an individual who became hooked on morphine or heroin after having taken it to relieve severe pain (Lidz et al, 1975). Those prone to addiction were perceived as being somewhat weak but essentially blameless, in complete contrast to the predominant stereotype in the United States (Lidz et al, 1975). This perception is grounded in fact insofar as, through the continuing process of obtaining a supply of heroin from a physician, many English addicts actually did come to view their addiction as essentially a medical problem. This policy of private maintenance worked fairly smoothly until the 1960s, prior to which time the British government knew of less than 500 addicts in the whole country while estimates of the number of addicts in the United States ran into the hundreds of thousands. However, by 1968 the British addict population had suddenly doubled, and a flurry of investigations were authorized to determine the cause of this epidemic. The major conclusion, perhaps an overly simple one, was that the sudden growth in the number of addicts resulted from profligate prescription practices on the part of a small group of physicians. Lidz et al (1975) propose an alternative explanation based on what they perceived to be a change in the demand for heroin. This change in demand was reflected in an increased interest in drugs as "agents of pleasure," generated by counterculture figures of the early 1960s. A new type of addict, more closely resembling his American counterpart, began to emerge—young, rebellious, and pleasure-seeking. Nonetheless, in response to this escalation of the heroin problem the British government established centralized clinics for dispensing heroin in the hope of eliminating irresponsible prescription practices. While this effort was largely successful in halting the increase in the number of new addicts, an increase in the demand for black market heroin arose when clinic dosages were kept at a minimum. Despite this relative epidemic the heroin problem in England has not approached the proportions it has in the United States where, despite intensified law enforcement efforts and widespread access to methadone maintenance clinics, the population of heroin addicts continues to grow.

While many observers have commented on the impossibility of comparing the U.S. experience with that of England because of massive cultural differences, Lidz et al (1975) believe the real difference lies in the type of policy each country has pursued in attempting to control heroin addiction. They point out that the demand for heroin is qualitatively different under such different approaches. The British "therapeutic addict" had little desire for more heroin than was necessary to avoid withdrawal because he was not primarily seeking a "high." On the other hand, the American addict was constantly forced to escalate his dosage as tolerance developed in order to reexperience the euphoria associated with early heroin use. Furthermore, Lidz et al (1975) suggest that while cost is an irrelevant factor to the therapeutic addict, a prohibitively high price will force the unaddicted pleasure-seekers out of the market. But "cost" really reflects more than simply a financial drain, as many observers have commented. It includes the cost of a particular lifestyle: in the United States, one of hustling, maintaining a low profile, and avoiding the police in England, one of daily contact with a clinic. In essence, ". . . the 'cost' of heroin reflects the social conditions under which heroin is available . . ." (Lidz et al, 1975, p. 10). However, the British policy makers decided early that the demand for heroin would remain the same irrespective of the "cost" to the individual. For this reason they believed a humane approach would be to provide easy access at a low financial cost to the addict. Although the recent inauguration of the clinic system does restrict completely free access, the monopoly on the heroin market maintained by the British government has resulted in a reduction of complications associated with black market heroin. In contrast, the American government has no such monopoly and all attempts to reduce the supply of heroin available to the addict have only succeeded in raising the overall "cost" of addiction. There is no medically based heroin control system as there is for methadone, and hence Lidz et al (1975) feel there can be no "medical addicts" in the United States. Furthermore, while escalation of law enforcement activity has assured that the street heroin will be expensive, it has, in so doing, indirectly provided impetus for a clinic system. However, Lidz et al (1975) point out that in order for clinics to attract large numbers of addicts their "cost" should be competitively low, and this is unfortunately not the case with methadone maintenance.

Many advocates of heroin maintenance have argued, on the basis of the British experience, that provision of legitimate access to heroin has actually reduced the rate of addiction rather than resulting in an increase anticipated from increased availability. Even if a sudden increase in heroin availability in the United States resulted in a rise in the addiction rate, Lidz et al (1975) observe that the meaning of being an addict would be changed. "What seems like a good deal to an already addicted user may not look like such a good deal to the young person considering whether or not to become an addict" (Lidz et al, 1975, p. 16). To "medicalize" the demand for heroin, Lidz et al suggest, would decrease the attractions of the heroin lifestyle and would change the characteristics of the addict population over a long period of time.

Proponents of heroin maintenance have also argued that legal access to heroin would reduce crime, based on the common assumption that money for heroin is obtained through acquisitive crime. However, Lidz et al (1975) suggest that evidence indicates most addicts support their habits through crimes of vice and sales, which, they feel, a heroin clinic would not affect. They further suggest that the underlying assumption that the total amount of crime committed depends upon the total number of criminals is erroneous; rather it is based on the demand for illicit services and the market for stolen goods. Thus, removing addicts from such a system would not eliminate the demand for stolen goods. On the other hand, Lidz et al (1975) point out that the American addict perceives himself as having a "special need" for money, and an elimination of this need might reduce the incidence of high-risk crimes. All concerned agree that a heroin clinic system would result in a substantial reduction in the profits accrued by organized crime from control of the black market in heroin.

Despite what Lidz et al (1975) perceive to be flaws in the proposals of heroin maintenance proponents, they believe that the legal-punitive control policy adopted by the United States has done very little to reduce the scale of the problem. The demand for heroin must decrease; otherwise arrests of big suppliers will simply result in a price increase and someone else will move in to take up the slack. Lidz et al (1975) state: "There is no reason to believe that there is a 'threshold' of pressure beyond which suppliers will no longer find it worthwhile to supply heroin" (p. 22). Furthermore, the extent to which the repressive legal policy was expanded to incorporate civil commitment not only of addicts, but also of those in danger of becoming addicted (particularly in the state of California) involves important issues of civil liberties that cannot be ignored. "The use of heroin is itself a mild problem compared to the problems that develop when the society tries to prohibit its use" (Lidz et al, 1975, p. 25). Therein lies the principal difference between the success of the British heroin maintenance system and the failure of the legal control policy of the United States.

The Drug Abuse Council has systematically analyzed the relevant issues in heroin maintenance as an alternative solution to the problem of heroin addiction in the United States. Their report (1973) will be drawn upon heavily in the following discussion. There are several alternative modifications of the maintenance proposal: heroin could be legalized, or it could be distributed by individual physicians under a system of medical control, or heroin induction could be instituted to secure an addict in treatment later to be transferred to another modality. Many of the physiological problems involved in heroin maintenance arise from the pharmacologic properties of the drug. Since prolonged use results in tolerance and dependence, it is not known if it is possible to find a stabilization dose high enough to avoid withdrawal but low enough to avoid producing euphoria. Other problems arise from heroin's short duration of action which requires the addict to secure repeated doses at short intervals, roughly 3 to 5 times a day, in order not to alternate between being high and being sick. Constantly returning to a clinic for injections or, alternatively, fluctuating between states interferes with normalization of the addict's life. However, there is little empirical work on the subject, and there may actually be a wider range between doses producing euphoria and doses staving off withdrawal than is currently anticipated. There are also problems of determining the correct dosage and individual variations in the processing speed of heroin. Further, to date there is no answer to the question of whether addicts will accept a stabilization dose or will constantly try to raise or supplement it. Although this would not necessarily be a problem for the motivated addict, the Drug Abuse Council (1973) points out there is no evidence that such addicts comprise the majority of the addict population. It is certainly reasonable to wonder whether the motivated addict might have done equally well in some other treatment modality. However, inherent in this concern is a presupposition that the underlying motivation for heroin abuse is euphoria production—a controversial issue at the very least (see Chapter 7). In the establishment of heroin maintenance clinics there is the risk that the heroin clinic will be used as a source of cheap heroin by the unmotivated addict. As the opponents of heroin maintenance point out, it is possible that the casual user may become an addict if admitted to a maintenance program which lacks stringent screening procedures. If heroin detoxification is attempted, problems will be encountered in tapering off an injectable drug with some evidence to suggest an attachment to the needle. Furthermore, statistics relative to recidivism after enforced detoxification indicate a relapse rate of 80 to 90% (Drug Abuse Council, 1973). Finally, chronic heroin use appears to interfere with the user's functioning by reducing motivation and interfering with sustained effort on a given task.

There are also a series of problems that arise in the determination of a target population. Evaluation of eligibility and setting age limits create potential problems of establishing addiction in a casual youthful user. On the other hand, the Council argues, there may be a greater chance of stabilizing life if one interrupts the cycle of addiction at an earlier age. In attempting to reach the hard-core addict who is untreatable by other means, issues that must be resolved include how many prior failures over how long a period of time should be required for admission. Problems are compounded by attempts to define how large a habit should be necessary, particularly since there is no evidence that a small daily habit is any easier to eliminate than a large one (Drug Abuse Council, 1973).

It has been argued by many that the very existence of the option of heroin maintenance would tend to undermine the efforts of other treatment programs because addicts might merely put in the required amount of time, moving from one program to the next until they acquired enough failures to be eligible for maintenance. However, it is equally possible that the necessary restrictiveness of returning to the clinic several times a day for heroin may prove too inconvenient for those who have any desire to stabilize their lives. In any event, heroin clinics would ensure the quality and purity of the heroin that addicts injected and would eliminate the preponderance of unsterile conditions that lead to major medical complications of heroin addiction.

Regarding the assumed outcome of reduction in crime subsequent to the establishment of heroin clinics, the Drug Abuse Council (1973) cautions that this is by no means guaranteed. While there is evidence that heroin itself does not incite an individual to commit crimes, the hypothesis that addicts steal to obtain funds to support their habits may be an oversimplification of the relationship between addiction and crime. It is estimated that roughly 50% of the heroin used is financed through "dealing," and an additional 10 to 20% through victimless crimes such as prostitution (Drug Abuse Council, 1973), leaving only an estimated 30 to 40% of the drug funded through crime. Furthermore, the Drug Abuse Council (1973) cautions that projections of the cost to society of addict crimes, based upon estimates of the number of addicts multiplied by estimates of the size of the average habit, are extremely unreliable. There is also evidence to indicate that many addicts were already engaged in criminal activities prior to the onset of addiction (see Chapter 9) and, to the extent that this condition represents a significant proportion of the population, it would remain unaffected by heroin maintenance. There seems to be little disagreement that heroin maintenance would undermine the black market. However, the Drug Abuse Council (1973) proposes an alternative in which supply and quality of heroin provided on the black market might increase and price might decrease in order to be competitive with clinic heroin. Almost certainly the imposition of a lower age limit of 18 or 21 on admissions to heroin clinics would ensure that these users would be forced to obtain heroin elsewhere, that is, from the black market. The data relative to age at first use of heroin (Chapter 9) strongly suggest that this subgroup is a significant proportion of the addict population.

The effects of heroin maintenance on the spread of addiction are equally hard to project. Although it is possible that control of the supply of heroin might reduce the spread of addiction, it is also possible that it might legitimize heroin use (Drug Abuse Council, 1973). In the event that a black market response were to increase the quality and decrease the price of its heroin, more individuals might be willing to try it because the deterrent effect of an undesirable lifestyle to support a habit would then be removed. If availability is a salient factor in experimenting with heroin, an increased supply might encourage use.

There are even problems in deciding locations for maintenance clinics. Many neighborhoods are averse to having them because they believe problems would arise from loitering outside the clinic and patients crowding public transportation facilities several times a day. Adequate facilities are expensive and administration costs would be high, particularly if each addict had to be supervised and injected at the clinic three to five times daily.

Finally, the Drug Abuse Council (1973) recommended a limited pilot study of heroin maintenance which would be valuable in terms of research. Such a pilot is contained in the Vera Institute proposal of heroin induction for 30 hard-core addicts over a 1 year period. Heroin would be offered as a lure, with eventual transfer to another treatment modality. Ideally the use of heroin would facilitate establishment of a therapeutic relationship, making a later shift to a nonheroin modality more likely. While such a proposal is valuable, the Drug Abuse Council (1973) raises questions about the validity of results obtained from such a small-scale program when they are applied to managing the maintenance of 500,000 addicts. Certainly it seems that the success of a heroin maintenance program, based as it must be on medical treatment approach, is doubtful in a concomitant atmosphere of repressive legal sanctions and control characteristic of the United States. The two appear almost mutually exclusive. Some questions, such as the possibility of determining a stabilization dose, could be answered by attempting maintenance on a small scale; most of the other issues remain unresolved. Thus from almost any vantage point, heroin maintenance is not the ideal solution. The pharmacologic properties of the drug make rigid structuring of the maintenance patient's life a necessity, and the degree to which this structuring and restriction would eventually interfere with attempts to lead a productive life is unknown. Furthermore, the necessity to inject heroin continually, because it loses much of its potency in oral administration, does not decrease the probability of long-term damage to the circulatory system. In many respects—if a maintenance regimen is to be initiated—perhaps methadone with its longer duration of action and oral effectiveness might avoid many of pharmacologic drawbacks of heroin. However, since either maintenance system relies on a chemical solution to a complex behavioral problem and —in the absence of massive efforts at supportive therapies, educational and vocational counseling, and the improvement of interpersonal skills— it seems unlikely that the roots of the problem will be touched so as to provide a long-term solution.

Many of the concerns raised by opponents of heroin maintenance seem to have been confirmed in a recently reported study. In a controlled trial of heroin maintenance, a group of 96 confirmed heroin addicts requesting heroin maintenance were randomly allocated to treatment with injectable heroin or oral methadone. The results of a 12 month follow-up indicated that heroin maintenance had little impact, with most individuals under this regimen continuing to self-inject illegal heroin and maintaining an intermediate level of involvement in the drug culture and criminal activity. Those patients offered oral methadone tended to be either in the high or low categories of involvement in drug use. While there were no differences between groups in employment, health, or use of non-opiate drugs, clients in the methadone condition who were refused heroin dropped out, had higher abstinence or higher illegal heroin use rates (Hartnoll, Mitcheson, Battersey, Brown, Ellis, Fleming, and Hedley, 1980).

EMPLOYMENT AND TREATMENT OUTCOME[3]

Employment has been viewed as an essential element in the successful rehabilitation of the methadone client. On this point, based on a number of small studies he conducted, Smart (1977) stated: "the major factor may be getting a job and not whether a drug is given or not" (p. 181). Other researchers agree that, for the ex-heroin addict to reach a successful outcome, employment is crucial in making the expected life adjustments (NIDA, 1979; Waldorf, 1970; Preble and Casey, 1976).

Generally, the employed methadone client is more likely to be successful than the unemployed methadone client not only with respect to securing employment, but also in terms of other outcome criteria. Vaillant (1966) and others (Waldorf, 1970; Dole and Joseph, 1977) have reported that employment appears to be related to abstinence form opioid and non-opioid drugs. Other investigators have found a strong association between employment status and criminality among methadone clients. The employed methadone client is more likely to have shorter periods and/or fewer instances of incarceration (Bass and Woodward, 1978; Nash, 1973). Retention in treatment has also been related to employment. In an effort to stabilize their lives, clients are maintained on methadone for what are often lengthy periods of time. Although retention rates in methadone maintenance programs were reported to be around 50% overall (NIDA, 1976), cumulative evidence (Babst et al, 1971; Berle and Lowinson, 1970; Chambers et al, 1970; Sells, Chatham, and Joe, 1972) consistently indicated that employment status was directly related to retention in treatment. Those clients who are employed have a higher retention rate. The conclusion drawn from these studies is that the employed client is, from all indications, likely to meet many criteria used to define a successful treatment experience. The pattern of these results appears to indicate that to understand the issues involved in employment, and to understand the factors involved in overall successful rehabilitation, one must examine the individual client and his personal qualities and/or resources.

Characteristics of the Employed Client

The abilities and resources of the employed methadone client which enable him to secure and maintain employment are of a multidimensional nature. A host of internal forces (i.e., values, confidence, motivation, personal decisions, etc.) and external forces (i.e., employment opportunities, social matrix, etc.) come together to render the client employable as well as employed. In addressing these abilities within the context of employment and training of ex-drug users, Presnall (1975) stated:

[3] The author acknowledges David Metzger's significant contribution to the preparation of this section.

One . . . can improvise a fairly effective rehabilitation process, provided an ex-drug user has well developed survival skills and is not too distant from the language and cultural value system of the middle class business world. (p. 1212)

Richman (1966) agreed and further delineated the factors involved in the success of rehabilitation: "degree of identification with and conformity to conventional modes of behavior and the degree of criminality" (p. 260). There is, in fact, increasing evidence that it is the "type" of client involved which best clarifies the relationship found between employment status and overall success at rehabilitation:

Most of the outcome status variance from which we could account was related to characteristics of the patients before they entered the sample treatment program . . . the type of patient served may outweigh program impact. (Mandell et al, 1973, p. 122)

Other researchers have arrived at the same conclusion. Katzker et al (1974) and Joe (1973) found that the success experienced on the various outcome measures, such as retention and employment, appears to be dependent not on treatment, but on the personal qualities and social resources that the individual client has prior to entering treatment.

The ability to secure employment is, of course, more than simply going out and getting a job. For example, one can make some reasonable assumptions which are, even in their simplicity, worthy of mention. First, the client who successfully goes out and gets a job placed some value on being employed. Second, he believed that job opportunities do exist. Third, he had realistic goals in view of his skills and abilities, and he had confidence in applying these resources and seeking and securing employment. Fourth, the employed methadone client was motivated and made the decision to do so. Finally, he was successful in overcoming or dealing with the fears and anxieties associated with locating, applying for, and being accepted (or rejected) for employment. It is thus clear that the ability to maintain employment is more than merely applying the skills required in performing the given work task. In this regard, Richman (1966) stated:

Work requires at least two attributes, namely the skill and ability to perform the task required and the social ability to be part of the social matrix which is the job environment. (p. 254)

The implication of the above findings is that the typical ex-heroin addict in making a successful rehabilitation must engage in what could be called a "cultural transition." The extent to which the addict internalizes and identifies with the drug subculture where he feels accepted has been explored and documented through the literature (Chein et al, 1964; Waldorf, 1970; Senay,

1975; Coombs et al, 1976). The addict, through involvement in the drug sub-culture and a drug-seeking career, becomes enmeshed in a way of life which is far removed from that of the dominant culture.

The employed methadone client, given his success at rehabilitation, appears to have the abilities and resources required to make this cultural transition. There is, in fact, some evidence that the employed methadone client is not as far removed from the dominant culture as are addicts in general. Caplovitz (1976), in a study of working addicts, concluded that the social characteristics of the working addict are more similar to the nonaddict population than to addicts in general. This finding was substantiated by Hughes et al (1971), who found that the working client is a good treatment prospect, given his abilities with respect to psychosocial functioning. Further, the employed methadone client, according to Dole and Joseph (1977), has a relatively shorter history of addiction; that is, he has had less involvement in the drug sub-culture than the unemployed methadone client. Finally, there is considerable evidence that a stable work history prior to admission is indicative of subsequent success at employment (Koenigsburg and Royster, 1975; Vaillant, 1966); the employed methadone client had experience in applying his personal and social abilities within a job environment prior to treatment.

Overall, there appears to be a pattern which emerges from the literature with respect to the employed methadone client. First, he is successful not only in securing employment, but also on other outcome measures; the employed client is considered successful in terms of overall rehabilitation. The success experienced in each of these areas appears to be dependent on personal qualities and resources which typify the employed methadone client. Finally, the employed client has the abilities required to seek and gain employment and the social skills that enable him to interact with the nonaddict population found in the job environment.

Recent Findings: A Controlled Study of the Methadone Rehabilitation Process
Platt, Flaherty, Morell, and Metzger (1982) evaluated the rehabilitative potential of providing interpersonal cognitive problem-solving training to methadone clients. An important aspect of the research was focused upon investigating the demographic, psychosocial, treatment involvement, and interpersonal problem-solving characteristics associated with the employment status of these clients. Of the 191 methadone clients included in the final analysis, 25% were employed.

Perhaps the most striking finding was that the employed group and the unemployed group were very similar in terms of the demographic and what Platt et al termed "personal characteristics." There was no clear evidence that the employed group was more similar to the nonaddict population than the unemployed group. However, the trends noted did lend support to past research findings. From the overall study sample, it was noted that white male clients from non-urban, higher socioeconomic areas were more likely to be included in the employed group. Also, these clients tended to have a shorter length of involvement in drug abuse and, therefore a shorter period in which the drug culture, with its attendant beliefs, attitudes, language and behavior, could be internalized.

Regardless of the extent to which the drug culture is internalized, it appears that there remain essential differences which the methadone client must deal with when involved in a working environment. The employed methadone client, interacting within a different social matrix, that of the employed non-addict population, had a significantly lower sense of self-confidence in his ability to deal with social situations. It is perhaps for this reason in part that the employed client is more likely than the unemployed client to maintain a relatively extensive support system. It was also found that the employed client was not only more likely to be married, but was also more likely to indicate that, when needed, he had someone to whom he could turn for help. Most frequently, when faced with a problem, the employed client—unlike his unemployed counterpart—felt that he could turn to clinic staff for support.

In addition to having a support system available to him, the employed methadone client was able to view problems from various perspectives. He displayed a stronger ability to make causal connections between actions and consequences and, perhaps for that reason, was also able to cite more solutions to a particular problem. This finding is particularly noteworthy. Although two groups were similar in their ability to cite the various types of problems that people routinely encounter, the employed methadone client was able to conceive of significantly more alternative solutions. Although cognitive abilities are usually viewed as stable constructs, there is ample evidence that these abilities can change with time, training, and/or experience.

The analysis of employment status and related variables was conducted in order to examine client characteristics associated with employment, a common goal of treatment. Results showed the employed clients to be demographically very similar to their unemployed counterparts. They were also essentially equivalent in terms of their past and current treatment involvement. Employed clients, however, were receiving significantly higher doses of methadone ($\bar{X} = 50$ mgs vs. $\bar{X} = 38$ mgs). The employed clients also had significantly lower self-evaluations and a greater willingness to take risks. With regard to problem-solving skills, employed clients were able to generate significantly more alternatives to problem situations and evidenced significantly greater causal thinking ability. Together, these similarities and differences suggest that employment is related to interpersonal cognitive processes and of course job availability. There were few demographic and treatment-related differences other than clinic and dose between those who had jobs and those who did not. While employment may be an almost universal goal of treatment programs and clients alike, the data suggest that gaining employment brings with it an increased need for supportive counseling services.

OTHER INTERVENTIONS

Wesson and Smith (1979) note the usefulness of a number of psychopharmacological agents in the treatment of polydrug addicts. They suggest tricyclic antidepressants for the treatment of depression frequently seen in addicts, although they recommend careful monitoring of dispensing of antidepressants where suicidal depression is present. Lithium carbonate is also suggested for use with affective disorders and the somatic symptoms associated with them, particularly manic-depressive illness, unipolar mania, and some unipolar endogenous depressions. Phenothiazines, including chlorpromazine (Thorazine), trifluoperazine hydrochloride (Stelazine), fluphenazine hydrochloride (Prolixin) as well as another antipsychotic, haloperidol (Haldol) are suggested as indicated where a thought disorder is precipitated by drug use or masked by heavy drug use. Based on the hypothesis that complex biochemical processes which accompany addiction may play a casual role in the development of the depression found by many investigators to accompany opiate addiction, Woody, O'Brien and Rickels (1975) administered the antidepressant doxepin to addicts receiving methadone. Using a double blind design, the control group received methadone plus a placebo. The findings indicated a clear decrease in depressive symptomatology in the methadone plus doxepin group, when compared with the control group. Furthermore, the experimental group demonstrated significantly less amphetamine use, and a trend towards lowered rates of treatment dropout and street drug use. Similar findings were obtained by Spensley (1974) in an open study, also with methadone patients. Both of the above studies reflect a concern with attempts not only to "discover" a solution to the heroin addiction problem through pharmacologic means, but also the increasing awareness that treating the psychopathology that is often found concomitantly with heroin addiction can lower the risk of continued addiction and contribute to more successful treatment outcomes. Kleber (1983) presents an excellent review of the usefulness of a variety of pharmacologic substances in the treatment of opiate addicts with other psychiatric diagnoses, and the reader should consult this source for further information.

Two other treatment approaches appearing in the literature are acupuncture and biofeedback.

The first reported use of acupuncture in the treatment of heroin addiction was by Wen and Cheung (1973), who reported that acupuncture when paired with electrical stimulation effectively relieved narcotic withdrawal symptoms. Using treatments of up to 30 minutes, they found that withdrawal symptoms disappeared after ten to 15 minutes, as did craving for narcotics. This report was soon followed by similar positive reports by other investigators (Sainsbury, 1974; Sacks, 1975; Patterson, 1976; Tennant, 1976). The impact of these favorable reports is, however, tempered by a critical review by O'Brien and Ng (1979), who note the failure of these and similar studies to control for expectational and ritualistic effects. They conclude that the effectiveness of acupuncture must remain in question until properly controlled studies are conducted. Further studies by Ng, Dauthitt, Thoa, and Herbert (1975) and Pomeranz, Cheng, and Law (1977) suggest that the mechanism underlying acupuncture effects may reflect stimulation of sensory nerves which activate the pituitary or brain stem to release endorphins. These in turn may mediate some acupuncture effects. Electromyographic (EMG) biofeedback involves the use of physiologically based indicators of degree of muscle relaxation to assist the patient in learning how to induce a state of significant relaxation. A number of studies appeared in the literature which initially suggested the usefulness of this procedure in conjunction with either methadone maintenance (Goldberg, Greenwood, and Taintor, 1976) or opiate detoxification (Cohen, Graham, Fotopaulos, and Cook, 1977). In both studies, positive results were obtained, with Ss reporting decreased drug use (Goldberg et al) and decreased withdrawal discomfort (Cohen et al). In the latter study, however, introduction of a double blind procedure resulted in loss of differences between experimental and control groups.

ISSUES RELATED TO TREATMENT

Classification of Programs

Beigel and Bower (1972) suggested that the treatment of heroin addiction could best proceed if one had a clear idea of the types of treatment programs available. They developed a simple, straightforward classification system that offers a clear picture of the range of treatment facilities currently in operation. *Intake facilities* generally involve small organizations or offices established primarily to make the first contact between the addict and the treatment system. While many intake facilities also provide assessment, counseling, crisis intervention, or referral services, the most important factor is their easy accessibility and 24 hour-a-day availability. *Short-term 24 hour facilities* can either be hospital based for patients still on drugs with medical or psychological complications, or they can be non-hospital based either as a detoxification facility or for populations not having medical or psychological complications. *Medium-term 24 hour facilities* are also hospital-nonhospital based. The hospital-based facilities are usually specialized inpatient treatment programs designed to separate the patient from his pattern of drug-taking behavior. Psychotherapy is usually offered in conjunction with a stay in the psychiatric unit of a hospital. Generally, however, these programs provide access to a variety of treatment modalities. The nonhospital-based programs usually attempt to meet the needs of those patients not wanting or needing hospitalized psychiatric treatment. *Long-term 24 hour inpatient facilities* can be hospital based for those who have developed severe psychological disturbances, or can be nonhospital-based residential programs such as Synanon or Phoenix House. *Part-time facilities* are available to patients not requiring full-time care and are often structured during specified hours of the day or evening. They offer less restrictive programs and are used also as a transitional stage for patients in the process of returning to the community. In controlling against further drug use, they function to separate the patient from an unhealthy home situation while providing access to rehabilitation. Such efforts include halfway houses, day programs, and weekend programs. *Community facilities* are established for addicts who report at intervals for some rehabilitation-oriented activity. They function to aid the former addict in reestablishing himself in society. The community mental health centers aid in the achievement of self-understanding through individual or group therapy and counseling. Rehabilitation programs offer a variety of services to facilitate education, job training, and vocational counseling. Court clinics offer diagnosis, referral, evaluation, and brief treatment services for those patients coming through the criminal justice system. Also included in the community facilities are methadone maintenance clinics and recreation programs. The authors suggest that a structured consultation service should be established in the communities to provide access to expert advice and to act as a liaison between agencies that deal specifically with drug abuse and those that do not. Coordination of services must be achieved either under the auspices of a single authoritative agency overseeing programs or through a formal agreement between the separate agencies. Dembo and Hendler (1982) describe the problems associated with the rational assignment of drug abusers within a large treatment program. Problems such as custodial/management considerations were found to significantly influence treatment assignments. They suggest the need to develop means to meet client needs, in contrast to staff and organizational needs. In an effort to increase the effectiveness of dealing with the problem of drug abuse, Beigel and Bower (1972) recommended prevention through education, evaluation, research, the establishment of community organizations to arouse citizen interest in various programs, and the utilization of advisory and control groups to manage the delivery of services.

The Problem of Who Comes for Treatment

It should seem obvious that different types of treatment programs attract different types of addicts. For example, addicts entering methadone programs tend to be older and to have spent a longer time involved in the drug subculture. On the other hand, the drugfree programs tend to attract short-term, fairly young addicts (Johns Hopkins School of Hygiene and Public Health, 1974). McKee (1972) analyzed the successes of three different treatment programs in an attempt to identify which types of addicts were best served by each: a residential therapeutic community, a religious therapeutic community, and a methadone clinic. Essentially the individual with problems should be treated by a group approach, although programs emphasizing confrontation and group encounters are unsuited for addicts who have language problems. These addicts are better served by the methadone approach, in which requirements for interaction are kept at a minimum. Furthermore, McKee (1972) suggested that the residential communities were best suited to younger addicts whose lives and responsibilities are flexible, since the extended period of separation required is less likely to retain the older married addict. Residential programs that are strongly authoritarian seemed best able to provide treatment for addicts without a strong authority figure and who have undemanding parents. The deeply religious programs seemed unsuited for the addict who is better educated.

The Problem of Treatment

Dealing with broader issues of treatment, Einstein and Garitano (1972) noted that treatment programs often fail because they have homogenous goals for a heterogenous population. Personnel are often inadequately trained and are unaware of the complexities of the drug scene. However, the authors point out that many issues are involved in delineation of treatment, not the least of which is the definition of drugs. The socioreligious orientation defines drug use along dimensions irrespective of the medical consequences of drug use. Medical definitions focus on legitimate purposes for drug use, whereas legal definitions involve delineation of which drug substances can be used freely and which require application of external controls. The scientific orientation focuses almost exclusively on drug effects on functioning. Einstein and Garitano (1972) point out that in defining drug abuse as a symptom of psychopathology

The trap . . . is that many kinds of people are involved in all types of bizarre, irrational, illogical behavior, and may not necessarily be psychologically or socially sick, given the agreed upon mores and rituals of the time. [pp. 324–325)

Once the view that drug abusers are sick is adopted, treatment becomes imperative. The authors suggest that effective treatment must involve an assessment of the strengths and weaknesses of the individual and the establishment of goals based on that evaluation. Abstinence is by no means the only valid goal, unless medical evidence has indicated that the chronic use of a certain substance is harmful. In order to change drug behavior, Einstein and Garitano (1972) indicate it will probably be necessary to change a number of other behaviors and, before this is undertaken, a critical examination of which behaviors can and cannot be changed is essential if realistic goals are to be set. Goals should be meaningful, achievable, acceptable, and flexible. The authors point out that it is not yet possible to say which goals are achievable with different types of therapies. However, follow-up criteria for successful outcome usually involve the following: (a) nonuse of specific drugs, (b) employment or being in school, (c) no legal involvement. Relative to these three criteria, Einstein and Garitano (1972) critically suggest:

This triad is in part a piece of drug use stereotype. Obviously a real bona fide drug abuser uses illicit or licit drugs for the wrong reasons, doesn't work, and therefore has a criminal status. If he's cured—through our efforts—he may drink and smoke, be unemployed or employed in a job he may be ill suited for, or which is only minimally productive for his community, and hopefully his criminal acts will fit into blue or white collar categories. . . . [p. 329]

Although this assessment seems slightly harsh, it may be related to the overall ineffectiveness of treatment programs in modifying significantly the pattern of heroin addiction. Dole, Robinson, Orraca, Towns, Searcy, and Caine (1969) commented:

Most addicts are miserable much of the time. Almost every addict has made several serious attempts to escape the slavery of heroin dependence. If he lacks enthusiasm for another term in jail, or more group therapy, it is not because he enjoys addiction but because experience has destroyed his faith in these kinds of treatment. [p. 1372]

O'Malley, Anderson, and Lazare (1972) found it extremely difficult even to engage addicts in treatment, as indicated by their failure to return for a second appointment. Of 206 addicts requesting help from a walk-in psychiatric clinic at Massachusetts General Hospital (MGH), 96 were offered treatment at MGH, and 87 were referred to other outpatient facilities. Of the 96 offered treatment at MGH, 58 were offered outpatient methadone detoxification and none returned for a second visit; and of 22 offered psychotherapy, 19 did not keep their second appointment. This failure to engage addicts in treatment was compared to a control group drawn from all diagnostic categories, of which 97% returned for the second visit.

O'Malley et al (1972) suggest this failure ". . . may be conceptualized as divergence of expectational models between therapist and patient" (p. 867). While there is support for this position, O'Malley et al (1972) disagree strongly with the impression of Dole et al (1969). They note: "The patients . . . appear to request administrative sanction for the pursuit of an experience that is uniquely pleasure for them" (p. 867). It is not surprising that inconsistency of treatment goals, generally poor outcome, and lack of understanding of the problem's complexities arise when there is so little agreement in perspective among those engaged in treating heroin addiction.

A study by Glaser, Adler, Moffett, and Ball (1974) surveying the quality of drug abuse treatment programs offers a possible empirical basis for what Dole et al (1969) consider the addict's lack of faith in the treatment process. A detailed questionnaire covering the number of staff, patients, allocation of funds, and so on, and also a team on-site investigation, was the basis for assessing the quality of 76 narcotic addict treatment programs treating 10 or more patients in Pennsylvania. A global (A–F) rating of the quality of the program not based on specifically delineated criteria, but showing a high interrater reliability was used. Although the authors caution that their results can only be considered preliminary, a shockingly small 29% of the programs received a rating above C+. Further, that 29% served only a discouraging 22.8% of the population receiving treatment. Interestingly, the predominant modalities that received a rating above C+ were the therapeutic communities or modifications of them. ". . . [A] therapeutic community program was defined as one in which the social structure of the program itself was deliberately used as the primary therapeutic tool . . ." (Glaser et al, 1974, p. 599). The frequency of the ratings above C+ for the therapeutic communities in comparison with other modalities was significant beyond the .001 level. Unfortunately, however, the quality of treatment provided must be considered along with the fact that the therapeutic communities reach only a very small proportion of the addict population and are beset by their own outcome problems, as was noted earlier. The authors suggest that the relatively poor overall quality of treatment casts doubt upon the validity of outcome studies and indicates that a lack of resources and an underutilization or misuse of those that exist makes it extremely difficult to come to any valid conclusions about effectiveness of treatment. Who knows what might prove effective if overall quality improved so that maximum utilization of resources were the norm? Certainly one cannot blame the addict for avoiding a treatment program of poor quality whose effectiveness he apparently has a right to doubt. Glaser et al (1974) suggested several factors which might be correlated with high quality treatment: ideological intensity, quantity of therapeutic effort, staff-patient ratio, management efficiency, staffing patterns and size. The authors further suggested the establishment of minimum standards for each treatment modality in an effort to raise the overall quality.

The Problem of Evaluating Treatment

Lack of adequate program evaluation has also been a serious block to improving treatment for heroin addicts. According to an analysis by Morell (1975) this lack is based on the co-occurrence of two factors. First, few studies are methodologically sound: treatment variables are not well defined, control groups are not used, and clients are not allocated randomly to experimental conditions. Evaluation usually involves testing a large ill-defined program. Thus even if "success" is detected, there is no way to know which aspects of treatment caused the observed effect. Controls and randomization are difficult to implement in an evaluation setting. As a result the prevailing attitude seems to be that many poorly controlled studies using large numbers of subjects will make up for a lack of methodolgic rigor. Morell concludes that this is not true. He also proposes methods by which difficulties in implementing controlled evaluation can be surmounted. These include teaching program staff the advantages of evaluation, methods to minimize the disruption that research can cause in a clinic setting, and the use of controlled intraprogram comparisons to determine the validity of treatment.

Second, current evaluations attempt to measure variables that are highly resistant to change, including drug use, employment/school behavior, illegal activity, program attendance, and dropout rate. Rarely is an attempt made to study the intermediate variables that lead to these changes. Such intermediates might include attitudes toward work, amount of effort put into trying to change, perceptions of the value of rehabilitation, and so on. This type of information would tell a clinic if their attempts were oriented correctly and also where they failed. Without such information there is only all or none information, with no feedback on how to improve rehabilitation efforts.

Dole and Warner (1967) offered some specific suggestions relative to evaluation of treatment program effectiveness that might prove useful in reaching some valid conclusions. First, an independent committee with the ability to verify critical data while maintaining confidentiality should be empowered with the evaluation. The use of standardized forms would allow for comparison of effectiveness between programs. In an effort to classify patients residing in hospitals, jails, or sheltered environments, Phase II should include those patients who have been living in the community less than a year, and Phase III should include those living outside for more than a year who are employed or in school, and who are not abusing drugs. Such a classification would simplify comparisons between different treatment techniques. Since cost is crucial in the formulation of public policy, those programs that require long periods of hospitalization which are very expensive should be closely examined for their relative effectiveness. The evaluation committee could also prove useful in clarifying treatment goals such as abstinence or productivity.

As Dole and Warner (1967) observed, the literature relating to treatment is chaotic and therefore precludes drawing conclusions about effectiveness. They strongly urge the adoption of basic standards to ensure routine collection of data regarding the persistence of abuse, progress in social rehabilitation and health, and cost. Certainly, until uniform standards for treatment and for the evaluation of treatment are instituted, it will remain impossible to draw valid conclusions about the relative effectiveness of different treatment modalities.

Yet, the past 15 years have seen an increasing degree of concern with the effectiveness of treatment programs designed for heroin addicts. This trend reflects a number of underlying questions, basically centered on the issues of determinating whether or not programs reach the goals set for them. and whether they do this in a cost-effective manner. In addition, the question of *relative* effectiveness of different treatment approaches has become an increasingly important one. Perhaps the most widely known effort in this area is the massive effort put forth by Sells and his associates (Sells, 1974, 1976, 1979, Simpson and Sells, 1982). Essentially, Sells has applied a model involving quasi-experimental research designs to drug abuse treatment programs, and has carried out a long-term prospective study of drug abuse patients from admission through treatment to follow-up in the community. It is important to note that Sells has included in his analyses several sets of covariants, based upon the client's demographic characteristics, background factors, and prior substance abuse experience, thus allowing for a more accurate and comprehensive evaluation of treatment outcome than would otherwise be the case. Sells (1979) notes a number of methodological issues which emerged in the DARP evaluation. While developed specifically in the course of his project, they have broad relevance to the issue of evaluation of all drug abuse treatment programs. Among the issues he identified are (a) *Problems of comparison among treatments*, reflective of the often inherently different characteristics of clients entering different treatment modalities. He notes, for instance, that most clients entering the methadone treatment tend to be "male, older, black, and including 94 percent daily opioid users at admission, while the (drug free) sample includes significantly more females, is considerably younger, and predominantly white, and has only 35 percent daily opioid users" (p. 109), (b) *Evaluation during post-treatment.* Sells notes the need to consider each phase separately because of their close relationship to each other. Thus, not only is compliance while in treatment important as a predictor of eventual treatment outcome in the post-treatment period, but it is an important social goal of treatment itself, (c) *Base periods for measurement of change.* Comparisons of drug use behavior during followup requires, according to Sells, the need to derive base-line comparison data from both the acute and chronic stages of the problem, since neither is necessarily a sufficiently adequate base against which to measure posttreatment behavior. (d) *Validity of interview data.* Recognizing that most data is obtained from interviews, Sells notes that this data is remarkably consistent with that obtained from other, more official sources, and (e) *Random assignment of patients to treatment.* The problems inherent in arranging and implementing rigorous design procedures, such as random assignment of *Ss* to treatment conditions in the real world, is noted by Sells as presenting the researcher with almost impossible problems to overcome, including ethical issues relating to treatment enrollment. He favors the use of an analytic model including robust multivariate methods to compensate for the lack of such traditional experimental conditions as random assignment.

The Problems of Methadology and Recruitment in Treatment Research

It is obvious now that serious problems exist in terms of (a) the quality of research in the heroin addiction field, as well as (b) the often unrepresentative sampling of heroin addicts in treatment research. These issues have been addressed by Nathan and Lansky (1978) and Platt, Morell, Flaherty, and Metzger (1982) respectively.

An extremely important article, one which is a *must* for all potential researchers, as well as consumers, of research into opiate addiction, deals with the issues of common methodological problems in addiction research. Nathan and Lansky (1978) identify these problems as follows: (a) overly selective reviews of the literature in order to support a particular theory or interpretation of the facts, (b) problems of subject selection, including the use of appropriate diagnostic and selection criteria, (c) inadequate matching criteria for comparison groups to assure equivalent motivational, experimental, and related facts, (d) the problem of using analogue groups, such as substance-abusing college students, because of the unavailability of the actual target group, (e) not taking fully into account the impact upon design of dropouts when evaluating the impact of treatment programs, (f) the focus of studies upon readily accessible, highly visible groups such as "street addicts" who are not truly representative of the majority of substance abusers, and from whom data may have only limited generalizability, (g) inherent limitations in both single-subject and group designs in comparative treatment studies, (h) lack of comparability of therapists' experience and commitment when comparing different treatments, (i) non-equivalent length of treatment sessions and inter-treatment intervals between treatment conditions, (j) non-equivalent levels of quality of treatment, in terms of planning, comprehensiveness, and related factors across treatments, (k) failure to extend length of follow-up sufficiently to fully assess long-term effects of treatment, (l) lack of reliability and validity data on outcome measures, (m) the problem of lack of knowledge of the correspondence of analogue paradigms to actual behaviors of interest, (n) experimenter bias effects, (o) failure to take into account demographic correlates of substance abuse which can be incorrectly identified as explanatory variables, (p) over-enthusiastic reporting of findings, (q) over-interpretation of statistically significant findings as being clinically significant in magnitude, (r) lack of statements by investigators concerning limitations of generalizability of findings, (s) failure to consider alternative explanations for findings, or (t) failure to consider data representing both sides of a position. The problems inherent in collecting uniform data on drug abuse treatment, particularly on an international basis have been noted by Ball (1979): "...most studies refer to a single nation, province, or city; report on a single treatment program or type of drug abuse; and employ an improvised research methodology. Consequently, it is often difficult and sometimes impossible to obtain an accurate and comprehensive view of the treatment which is available in a given nation" (p. 367). Unfortunately, to some extent, the same must be said, although perhaps to a lesser degree, about treatment programs within this country as well.

If there is one over riding point to be made concerning design, interpretation, and related issues in drug abuse research, it is that the field is *at least as* prone as any other field, if not more so, to the kinds of problems which are inherent in all research in the mental health sciences. Caution, reflection, and consultation are very much needed in the design, conduct, and implementation of quality "high-yield" studies on addiction.

With respect to client recruitment, Platt, Morell, Flaherty, and Metzger (1982) outlined a 5 step model in their multi-clinic study of the methadone rehabilitation process. *Phase 1* involved gaining access to the program environment. Noting the critical importance of access as not being just acquiring administrative approval, but the involvement as well of program staff, extensive discussion with supervisory staff was aimed at clarification of roles and responsibilities, time commitments, protection of client confidentiality, and nature of research procedures. Program staff concerns centered on the potential for negative impact of the study upon the program and exceeded concern about potential project findings. *Phase 2* centered on client involvement. A major effort was made here to involve line staff by providing them with an understanding of the project goals and activities. A major focus here was upon regular meetings, both of a formal and informal nature, with the aim of informing staff about the nature of the research, the experimental procedures, confidentiality protections, and the investigator's perceived importance of their support in providing project visibility. *Phase 3* focused on promoting project visibility among program clients through posters and handouts. Project and program staff were also available to discuss the project with clients, and brief descriptions of the the project and expectations concerning client involvement were widely distributed. These emphasized only those aspects of the research which could be delivered with certainty (i.e., confidentiality, participation incentives, testing sessions, research conditions, etc.). Care was taken to avoid giving promises of positive impact or help. *Phase 4* involved the actual sign up of volunteers with project staff being available to answer questions. This was the first phase in which research staff interacted directly with clients. The likelihood of suspicion among clients was anticipated and confirmed. Concerns included the confidentiality of information, the "government's" use of the data, the affiliation of the research staff, and the nature of the research procedure. Positive aspects and benefits of involvement, as well as time commitments and requirements, were presented clearly. An attempt was made to convey the message that clients were being hired by the project to provide an honest evaluation of the experimental program. *Phase 5.* The final step was the scheduled administration of informed consent statements and pre-test questionnaires. Each client who had signed up was contacted individually. The final responsibility for participation then rested with the individual.

This recruitment procedure resulted in both a high proportion of volunteers (30% of the clinic's registered clients) and a high average "show" rate for both testing and treatment sessions, with 73% attendance for those who entered the ten session sequence.

Bale (1979) has suggested incorporating a number of elements in planning for an outcome evaluation of a treatment program. While his concern was with primarily therapeutic communities, his points have broader applicability within the drug abuse treatment field. His points include: (a) utilization of a prospective design, with use of parallel testing instruments at intake and follow-up; (b) preparation of subjects for follow-up contact at specific dates; (c) assessment to be done by personnel other than directly involved clinical staff; (d) variables should be clearly defined, selected with the input of project staff, gathered in a standardized manner, and designed to sample a wide variety of aspects of social functioning; (e) both graduates and dropouts among former clients should be sampled, with sampling done on a random basis within a stratification for degree of contact with the program; (f) treatment structure and process should be described, using standardized procedures where possible; (g) independent verification of self-reported data should be carried out, either on the whole sample or on a subsample; (h) program cost-effectiveness per successful outcome should be assessed; and (i) in the event different modalities are to be compared, a random assignment design should be used, where possible.

Given what has been set out in this section about methodology in the evaluation of drug abuse treatment, it is apparent that increasing concern now exists about the lack of well-designed evaluation studies which could yield data upon which to assess the effectiveness of such treatment. Considering the serious need for evaluation of various narcotics treatment modalities as a first step in making knowledgeable treatment planning and funding decisions in an era of shrinking resources, the collection of evaluation data should be considered an essential element of every program.

CHAPTER 12

Narcotic Substitution Therapy: Methadone

A tremendous volume of literature has been written about the pharmacology and abuse potential of methadone as well as its implementation in a variety of therapeutic programs. Actually the volume of this literature nearly equals that recently written on all other therapeutic modalities combined.

For this reason, an entire chapter is being devoted to an examination of the validity of claims to widespread success with methadone in "curing" and rehabilitating heroin addicts and also of the equally adamant claims that methadone exacts a more tenacious hold over the addict than does heroin. Few other therapeutic modalities have elicited the controversy that methadone maintenance has aroused, and certainly none has been available to as great a number of addicts since the 1960's. The early astonishing claims by Dole and Nyswander of an 85 to 100% rehabilitation rate of hard-core heroin addicts have given way to a more cautious optimism, as methadone maintenance has for the most part become the treatment of choice in major municipal and federally funded programs.

PHARMACOLOGY

Although the psychopharmacology of methadone has been discussed in some detail in Chapter 4, a review of the early research on its addiction liability and its use in the treatment of heroin withdrawal is both useful and interesting. Isbell and Vogel (1948) found that subcutaneous administration of doses of 20 mg or more of methadone produced euphoria which was slower in onset and of longer duration (48 hours) than that produced by heroin, and was also qualitatively indistinguishable from heroin-induced euphoria. Further investigation with four daily subcutaneous doses ranging from 5 to 10 mg per dose to 100 mg per dose revealed that at the lower dose levels no euphoria was produced. However there was a cumulative effect at 10 to 15 mg four times daily, accompanied by behavioral changes that were similar to those exhibited by morphine addicts (e.g., cessation of activity, nodding). Chen (1948) suggested that the sedative effects of methadone were due to depression of the sensory areas of the cortex because he noted that the amount of methadone required for sedation was substantially greater than that required to produce analgesia. Performance on tests of visual-motor coordination contained a greater number of errors following administration of methadone (Isbell and Vogel, 1948). Furthermore, when the Rorschach test was given to subjects before and after receiving methadone, changes in test protocols were always found:

Those subjects whose primary difficulty appeared to involve inhibition conflicts in relation to the expression of their instinctual drives showed, during addiction, a decrease in the guilt and anxiety associated with these conflicts, accompanied either by increased sensuality, immaturity, and egocentricity or by decreased accessibility to affective stimulation. [Isbell and Vogel, 1948, p. 910]

The local anesthetic action of methadone was observed in Germany during World War II. Chen (1948) proposed that the mechanism for methadone anesthesia involved raising the pain threshold by depression of the somesthetic area of the brain. Respiratory depression, as measured by a decrease in respiratory rate, amplitude, and volume of expired air was also thought to be effected by a depressive action of methadone on the respiratory center of the medulla (Chen, 1948). In addition the vomiting center of the medulla was thought to be stimulated by methadone, giving rise to the emetic properties methadone has in humans. Although Chen (1948) observed hyperglycemia, hypothermia, and emesis following methadone administration in human subjects, he concluded that it was more toxic than morphine only in subhuman species. Finally, Chen (1948) noted that the *l* isomer was more potent than the *d*, but a racemic mixture was more toxic than either optical isomer alone. Elimination of the amino-*N* resulted in loss of activity of the compound.

Since methadone had so many effects similar to those produced by morphine and was chemically a synthetic narcotic analgesic, Isbell, Wikler, Eisenman, Daingerfield, and Frank (1948) systematically investigated its potential addiction liability in a series of three experiments. Methadone was first administered to individuals undergoing morphine withdrawal to assess its effects relative to Himmelsbach's hypothesis that a drug which will alleviate withdrawal will itself produce physical dependence. Second, methadone was substituted for morphine and then withdrawn, to determine cross-tolerance and addiction liability. Third, an attempt was made to produce addiction to methadone itself via prolonged administration. Results indicated that in 10 individuals exhibiting moderate to severe abstinence signs 32 hours after the last dose of morphine, methadone administration was found to relieve withdrawal symptoms in every instance. The larger the amount of methadone administered, the greater the degree of relief with a dose ratio of methadone to morphine of 1:4 providing greater relief than a ratio of 1:5. The authors concluded that methadone could relieve the morphine abstinence syndrome. When 1 mg of methadone was substituted for every 4 mg of morphine, 12 morphine addicts were unable to report experiencing effects indicative of a change in compound. Considerable cross-tolerance was further noted in that doses which produced marked sedation in nontolerant subjects had no sedative effects on the morphine addicts. Following abrupt withdrawal of methadone an abstinence syndrome occurred, slower in onset and milder in intensity than that following the termination of morphine. The methadone abstinence syndrome began 3 days after the last dose of methadone, reached a peak intensity at about 6 days, and was complete in roughly 10 days.

It is also possible to create physical dependence on methadone directly, with subjects exhibiting behavior exactly like the behavior of morphine addicts. Tolerance to a given dosage was developed within about 2 weeks, at which time subjects became more alert, active, and requested increases in their doses. Following each increase, and prior to the development of tolerance to the new dose level, subjects showed a marked decrease in efficiency of intellectual functioning on the Otis arithmetic, coordination, and perseverance tests. During the course of addiction to methadone, a slight increase in temperature was observed, and also a slower pulse rate, depressed respiratory rate, constipation, development of tolerance to pupil constriction effects, lethargy, and twitching while asleep. The only change noted in the ECG was the development of sinus bradycardia; the EEGs exhibited slower frequency, slower alpha frequency, a delta increase, and the disappearance of beta entirely. Tolerance developed to the analgesic, sedative, EEG, and miotic effects of methadone. As noted earlier, withdrawal from methadone was marked only by the absence of cramps associated with morphine withdrawal. Overall, the major feature of methadone withdrawal seemed to be an absence of the autonomic signs which characterize morphine withdrawal. As mentioned previously, methadone withdrawal was milder than that of morphine. On the Himmelsbach rating scale of the intensity of the objective physical signs of withdrawal an average of 25 points were scored at the peak on the sixth day, in contrast to the 50 to 60 points scored for the third day peak of morphine withdrawal. However, there appeared to be some long-term physiologic changes following withdrawal from methadone: temperature, pulse rate, and respiratory rate did not return to normal even after 14 days. Interestingly, when the subjects were offered a choice between morphine, heroin, Dilaudid, or methadone at the conclusion of the experiments, the majority unhesitatingly chose methadone. Clearly, on the basis of experimental evidence, Isbell et al (1948) concluded that methadone was a drug of high abuse potential and great addiction liability.

More recently the addictive properties of methadone and the phenomenon of cross-tolerance have been utilized as the foundation of methadone maintenance programs. The large number of addicts in methadone maintenance programs over the past decade have provided evidence unavailable to early researchers about the long-term physical effects of methadone addiction. Nyswander (1971) observed no damage to the liver, kidneys, bone marrow, respiratory tract, central nervous system (CNS) or neuromuscular system in addicts who had been maintained on methadone for 5 years. This was further supported by a report from Kreek (1973) on the medical safety and side effects of methadone because no significant change was found in liver function or serum protein test values in subjects addicted to methadone for 3 years. This 3 year follow-up of 214 methadone maintenance patients showed no instances of hospitalization for side effects or toxicity related to methadone administration (Kreek, 1973). Nyswander (1971) observed no impairment of reaction time, affect, or IQ in her subjects after 5 years on methadone. Finally, methadone appears to be compatible with virtually all other medications making it of potential wide-ranging clinical usefulness. Excellent recent reviews by Kreek (1979, 1983) are available on the health consequences of methadone use.

ORIGINAL DOLE AND NYSWANDER METHADONE MAINTENANCE PROGRAM

Background

As noted in Chapter 7, Dole and Nyswander were singularly unimpressed with the effectiveness of psychotherapeutic approaches in rehabilitating the narcotic drug addict. They state:

A careful search of the literature has failed to disclose a single report in which withdrawal of drug and psychotherapy has enabled a significant fraction of the patients to return to the community and live as normal individuals. [Dole, Nyswander, and Kreek, 1966, p. 304]

Believing that heroin addiction is a medical problem whose solution should be the responsibility of medical research efforts, Dole and Nyswander have observed that incarceration fails to alter drug craving and, further, that the confinement of addicts under stringent legal sanctions fails to constitute therapy. The failure of the legal approach for over 40 years led to their early investigations of the potential therapeutic benefit to be derived from treating drug addiction with drugs.

As the heroin addict vacillates between being high and being "sick" with the early symptoms of abstinence, he finds himself without time to devote to a normally structured life. The relatively short duration of heroin action assures that he will continue in this constant state of vacillation. Therefore any drug that is substituted for heroin with any degree of success in freeing the addict from this constant preoccupation must be relatively long-acting. Further, in seeking to break the pattern of heroin addiction, such a drug must have the pharmacologic potential to avoid producing either extremes of high or "sickness" (Nyswander, 1967). The experience of Dole and Nyswander indicated an absence of consistent psychopathology among heroin addicts, suggesting that once freed of constant drug craving, the addict might restructure his resources to cope with daily community life in a fairly competent fashion. Clearly, the long duration of action of methadone (48 hours) made it an attractive alternative drug. Originally Dole and Nyswander (1966) claimed that methadone functioned as an "antinarcotic agent" by blocking the euphorogenic action of heroin. It has become obvious in light of additional research, however, that the basis for this effect is actually cross-tolerance among the narcotic analgesics. Nonetheless, Dole and Nyswander were able to obtain a grant from the New York City Health Research Council in 1963 to pilot their first methadone maintenance project at Rockefeller University. Their program was eventually expanded to the Morris J. Bernstein Institute at Beth Israel Hospital on the strength of very positive results from the pilot and, by 1967, was being funded by the New York State Narcotic Addiction Control Commission. Originally Dole and Nyswander explored morphine maintenance, which proved unsatisfactory because patients remained sedated and drug-oriented. The investigators then tried methadone in both intramuscular injection and oral form, and the oral doses proved more satisfactory. The patients receiving oral methadone were not sedated, exhibited no distortion in affect or perception, experienced a relief of drug craving, and developed tolerance to the euphorogenic effects of methadone. Stabilization of dosage, previously believed impossible with narcotic drugs, was achieved with patients not requesting an escalation of dose over a 2 year period (Dole, Nyswander, and Kreek, 1966).

An independent evaluation committee at the Columbia University School of Public Health and Administrative Medicine, directed by Frances Gearing, examined Dole and Nyswander's reports of success, supported the methadone maintenance program, and strongly recommended expansion of its facilities. The evaluation indicated a higher proportion of white addicts were participating in the program than were represented in the New York City Narcotics Register in 1967, and these white addicts were more likely to be discharged from the program for continued drug abuse while blacks were more frequently discharged for alcohol abuse. However, Gearing (1970) stated that the committee was unable to differentiate addicts who were most likely to succeed in the program. On the whole, the committee (Gearing, 1970) concluded that methadone maintenance was an effective form of treatment for large numbers of "selected" heroin addicts: none of the patients remaining in the program became readdicted to heroin, the majority returned to school or employment, and evidenced a significant reduction in arrests in comparison to both preadmission rates and arrest rates of addicts in other treatment programs matched for age, sex, and ethnicity. In February 1970, the New York State Medical Society passed a resolution recognizing the Dole-Nyswander methadone maintenance program as a valid treatment approach and funding was increased to $15 million for year 1970–71 (Langrod, Brill, Lowinson, and Joseph, 1972).

Admissions Criteria

Initially, the Dole and Nyswander target population was the hard-core heroin addict who had been repeatedly unsuccessful in other treatment modalities. A 4 year history of mainlining heroin was required, with repeated experience of failure in treatment and no legal compulsion to enter into further treatment. Originally, those patients exhibiting mixed addictions or a history of alcohol abuse were denied admission to the program because these factors might have obscured interpretation of the data. Furthermore, patients with medical conditions such as epilepsy and diabetes, which required medication, were screened out because it was not yet known what effect mixing drugs might have. Admissions were required to be between the ages of 21 and 40 to avoid inadvertent addiction of an adolescent who was only in the experimental stages of drug abuse and was seeking a new, free, and legitimate high, and to explore the validity of Winick's maturing-out hypothesis (Langrod et al, 1972). Eventually these criteria were relaxed to allow admission of 18-year-olds, individuals having only a 2 year history of heroin use or mixed drug abuse, and persons having additional medical complications, when it became clear that methadone did not adversely interact with other medication.

Procedure

A three-phase process of treatment was initiated, beginning with a 6 week induction period of hospitalization on open wards to establish a "blockade" level of methadone (Dole, Nyswander, and Warner, 1968). In reaching the blockade level, Dole et al believed a small dose of methadone relative to the level of tolerance was required in order to avoid producing narcotic effects (Dole, Nyswander, and Kreek, 1966). The process of induction was begun with small doses of methadone, half of which were given twice daily in a liquid vehicle until a stabilization level was reached (80 to 120 mg per day), at which time patients were shifted to a single daily dose. It was noted that as tolerance to methadone developed, the side effects observed earlier began to diminish.

During Phase I the addict begins to be freed of drug craving and is increasingly more able to explore educational and vocational opportunities. The second phase begins when the patient is discharged to the community and returns daily to the clinic to receive his medication. Methadone is given in sufficient quantity to cover the weekend period when the clinic is closed and, as individuals prove their reliability, they may be given several days' supply at once to decrease the amount of time spent in daily clinic visits. Urinalysis is done daily for the first 3 months and then once or twice weekly to make certain that patients are taking their methadone and not diverting it or hoarding it to produce a high, and to control for other drug abuse as shown by the presence of illegal drugs in the urine. The earlier part of Phase II constitutes an interim period in which the addict seeks employment and establishes a home routine. The emphasis is on getting a job or going back to school and increasing his meager skills. Dole and Nyswander (1967) carefully note that treatment programs for the street addict cannot ignore the social deficits which have been engendered by both a poverty culture background and a preoccupation with securing a continuous supply of narcotics, and which have resulted in arrest of social maturation. The second half of Phase II consists of the establishment of an acceptable daily routine with infrequent or no experimentation with drugs. The addict continues to need the support of the clinic staff as he becomes increasingly concerned with his performance and acceptance of responsibility. Phase III, the final phase of treatment, occurs when the addict is a responsible member of the community, no longer needs the support of the clinic staff, is well established in his new routine, and feels himself cured. However, Dole and Nyswander (1967) caution against weaning the addict from methadone at that point because he may be vulnerable to readdiction to heroin as complacency develops from his early success.

Treatment Goals

Prior to the establishment of methadone maintenance, the criteria by which the success of a given treatment program was measured invariably included abstinence or a drugfree state. The goals of methadone maintenance programs represent a radical departure from those of other treatment modalities because the emphasis is on social functioning and a wide range of activities rather than on abstinence. Obviously, as methadone is an addicting drug and patients are required to take daily doses of methadone, maintenance of abstinence is impossible. Instead, successful outcome is assessed by voluntary retention in treatment, increased productivity (as evidenced by employment or education), cessation of criminal behavior, and termination of drug abuse.

Success of Early Program

In a preliminary report on 22 patients in their pilot project, Dole and Nyswander (1965) noted an astonishing degree of success relative to the goals just mentioned. Addicts often requested admission to the program while in the initial stages of withdrawal, were between 19 and 37 years old, and had failed repeatedly at abstinence. They were given methadone on individual schedules to accommodate variations in tolerance to narcotics.

With methadone maintenance . . . patients found that they could meet addict friends, and even watch them inject diacetylmorphine, without great difficulty. They have tolerated frustrating episodes without feeling a need for diacetylmorphine. They have stopped dreaming about drugs, and seldom talk about drugs when together. [Dole and Nyswander, 1965, p. 649]

Relative to criminal behavior, in a later study Dole and Nyswander report that prior to treatment 91% of their patients had been in jail for a total of 52 convictions per 100 man-years of addiction (Dole, Nyswander, and Warner, 1968). Since entering treatment 88% of these patients were arrest-free (at 3 months or more), with 51 convictions per 880 man-years of treatment or 5.81 convictions per 100 man-years (Dole, Nyswander, and Warner, 1968). All of those who were convicted were removed from the program, as were those patients constantly exhibiting uncooperative behavior or other drug abuse. When the Dole-Nyswander patients were compared to a control group at a detoxification unit, it was found that at 3 to 5 months 6% of 473 methadone patients had been arrested versus 25% of 100 detoxification patients; at 6 to 11 months, 11% of 353 methadone patients had been arrested versus 37% of 100 detoxification patients; at 12 to 18 months, 8% of 326 methadone patients had been arrested versus 36% of 100 detoxification patients; at 19 to 24 months, only 3% of 185 remaining methadone patients had been arrested versus 18% of the detoxification patients (N = 100); and at 2 years or more, less than 1% of 101 methadone patients remaining in treatment had been arrested versus 22% of 100 detoxification patients (Methadone Maintenance Evaluation Committee, 1968). Of the 871 persons admitted to the methadone maintenance program as of March 31, 1968, only 14% were no longer participating for the following reasons: 10% discharged, 3% dropped out, and 1% died (Methadone Maintenance Evaluation Committee, 1968). At the time of admission only 28% were employed and 40% were receiving welfare; after 5 months in the program 45% were employed; after 11 months, 61% were employed or in school, and after 24 months, 85% were employed or in school (Methadone Maintenance Evaluation Committee, 1968). The number of patients receiving welfare also declined: at 5 months it was 50%, 22% at 1 year, and 15% at 2 years (Methadone Maintenance Evaluation Committee, 1968). None of the remaining patients were readdicted to heroin. Furthermore, over 80% of the patients admitted to the methadone maintenance program over a 6 year period remained in treatment

(Langrod et al, 1972). Among reasons for discharge, 50% were due to continued drug abuse and alcoholism and usually occurred during the first year of treatment (Langrod et al, 1972).

While these results certainly appeared to be encouraging, the degree of success claimed soon came under increasing scrutiny by other investigators.

MODIFICATIONS OF THE ORIGINAL DOLE AND NYSWANDER METHADONE MAINTENANCE PROGRAM

Outpatient versus Inpatient Treatment

The original group of Dole and Nyswander patients underwent a 6 week period of hospitalized detoxification and methadone induction, based on the belief that maximum supervision was necessary to ensure continued treatment. However, the existence of long admission waiting lists characteristic of many methadone programs prompted Nichols, Salwent, and Torrens (1971) to attempt to bypass the hospitalization phase outlined by Dole and Nyswander (1965) and to begin induction with ambulatory patients. Patients were stabilized over a 3 to 4 week period beginning with 20 to 30 mg of methadone given twice daily until the usual stabilization dose range of 80 to 120 mg was reached. A comparison was made between 19 patients who had undergone ambulatory induction and 37 patients who had experienced the usual hospitalized induction. It became clear that the selection criteria for ambulatory patients favored those who were employed or were full-time students, with preadmission differences of 53% ambulatory induction patients (AI) employed versus 27% of the hospitalized induction patients (HI). In addition, only 21% of the AI patients were black versus 54% of the HI patients. The HI patients also had a record of more unsuccessful withdrawal attempts than the AI patients. When both groups were compared after achieving full maintenance on methadone Nichols et al (1971) found that there were no real differences in concurrent drug abuse, although alcohol abuse was discovered more often among the AI patients. Outcome in terms of productive social behavior reflected an increase for both groups with 94% of the AI group and 88% of the HI group engaged full time in work, school, or homemaking activities. However, follow-up reports indicated that the percentage of individuals receiving "negative productivity" reports was greater among the HI group than among the AI group. There were no significant differences with respect to arrests or antisocial behavior. On the basis of their data the authors concluded that outpatient induction to methadone maintenance treatment was not only a viable alternative to hospitalization, but one which represented both greater efficiency in treating large numbers of addicts and a substantial reduction in the overall cost of methadone maintenance.

Similar results were reported by Wilson, Elms, and Thomson (1975) regarding outpatient versus hospitalized methadone detoxification. Random assignment of 40 addicts to either inpatient or outpatient detoxification conditions for a period no longer than 10 days revealed a lack of significant differences between groups on outcome criteria. Overall, few patients were drugfree at the end of the 10 day detoxification period. Further, at a 3 month follow-up of seven hospitalized patients none had remained abstinent. Of the outpatient group consisting of 19 patients followed for 2 months only two were still drugfree. Although outpatient detoxification entails roughly one-tenth the cost, it was noted that ambulatory patients rarely returned to the clinic for their methadone. Similarly, the hospitalized group often requested discharge before stabilization had been achieved. Both resulted in similarly poor outcomes. Wilson, Elms, and Thomson concluded: (a) there were no significant differences in the effectiveness of outpatient and inpatient detoxification procedures, and (b) short-term methadone detoxification has no lasting effect on drug abuse and should not be considered a valid rehabilitation method.

Knowledge of Dosage and Methadone Self-Prescription

The original methadone maintenance procedure as outlined by Dole and Nyswander (Nyswander, 1967; Langrod et al, 1972; Dole and Nyswander, 1965, 1967; Dole, Nyswander, and Warner, 1968; Dole, Nyswander, and Kreek, 1966) called for physician-controlled dosage schedules probably as a result of previous experience with addicts who attempted to obtain as large a quantity of narcotics as often as possible. However, Renault (1973) experimented with allowing patients attending a methadone maintenance clinic to know their daily dosage of methadone to investigate whether knowledge of dose would promote competition among patients to obtain as high a dose as permitted, with all of the attendant conning and manipulative behaviors. The results indicated the exact opposite to be true. Patients became more responsible and adult in their behavior, especially with respect to their treatment regimens.

Similar results were obtained by Angle and Parwatikar (1973) when nine subjects who volunteered for a detoxification study were stabilized on methadone, and then allowed to control their own dose levels, limited only to the extent that they could not exceed the stabilization dose. Each person knew his own dosage and all dosages of the entire group were publicly posted for 28 days. The results were surprising, particularly in light of preexperiment expectations that patients would increase physical complaints as a rationalization for raising their doses, that competition would develop among subjects to see who could get the most methadone, and that general deterioration of morale and motivation for treatment would occur. Actually, the opposite was true: strong competition emerged between subjects to reduce their methadone intake to very low levels, suggesting that addiction is a controllable process "influenced by environmental contingencies" (Angle and Parwatikar, 1973, p. 212). Complaints of physical symptoms were markedly less than when the staff controlled dosage and patients were unaware of how much methadone they were receiving. The authors note:

. . . [I]t may be suspected that an aspect of the withdrawal symptom complex is the subject's anxiety of not knowing his current drug level and anticipating symptoms that are controlled indirectly by the clinical staff. From this anxiety the subject may develop a greater awareness or sensitivity to physical symptoms, even though these symptoms may very likely be unrelated in origin to drug withdrawal. [p. 213]

Once again more responsible behavior with respect to treatment was shown by the subjects, and it is interesting to speculate on the role played by the individual having control over at least one segment of his life in the production of responsible behavior. Angle and Parwatikar (1973) cautiously noted that the factor of group pressure to reduce dosage would be impossible to maintain outside of the confines of the methadone clinic, but encouraged future research to identify the self-versus-group-control variables which might prove valuable in treatment.

Another addict-controlled detoxification program was initiated on the inpatient psychiatric unit at an urban hospital by Stern, Edwards, and Lerro (1974). Previous experience with standard detoxification procedures had proven them to be disruptive and unpleasant for both the staff and the addict patients. Characteristically, the physician-controlled regimen elicited constant attempts on the part of the addict to con the staff into giving out greater amounts of methadone. The authors felt that this behavior represented an attempt to "beat" the authoritarian system of physician-controlled detoxification in an extension of street behavior oriented toward beating the societal system. This factor of an adversary relationship alone might have been sufficient to produce the preponderance of sociopathic behaviors observed on the ward (Stern, Edwards, and Lerro, 1974). As a result of a rigidly defined treatment program precluding natural responses and fostering a preoccupation with conning behavior, the staff had minimal opportunities to perceive the addicts as individuals possessing their own particular strengths. In deciding to place the responsibility for detoxification on the addict, it was hoped that the need for manipulation would be eliminated. There was no selection procedure for the 11 addicts who were informed they would receive 5 mg doses of methadone on demand with no limit placed on the amount they could take. The only restriction was that each dose had to be taken under a nurse's observation; and nurses were instructed not to discourage the addict in any way from taking more methadone. If it became obvious after a 10 day period that an addict was making no attempt at withdrawal, consideration would be given to discharging him. Results indicated that addicts spent an average of 7.9 days in the hospital, which falls roughly in the middle range of time spent in other detoxification programs. However, the total amount of methadone taken by these addicts was less than that given in other programs. An average of 2.4 fewer days were spent in the hospital and 3.7 mg less methadone was taken than during the physician-controlled program. In eliminating the adversary relationship, the constant complaints of physical distress during withdrawal also disappeared. Actually, since none of the patients exhibited any objective signs of withdrawal it became easier to recognize and deal with individual problems. While acknowledging the possibility that some addicts were merely trying to reduce the size of their habits, the authors concluded: (a) it is possible to make the addict responsible for his own withdrawal schedule without his abusing that responsibility, and (b) such a shift in responsibility fosters a positive change in staff-patient interaction.

Since the methadone-on-demand technique seemed to avoid pathological confrontations by placing the major onus of treatment on the addict himself, and since this inclusion of the addict in the treatment planning has the effect of appealing to his maturity rather than to the regressive and childish aspects of his personality, we believe there is reasonable justification for this approach to detoxification. [Stern, Edwards, and Lerro, 1974, p. 871]

Resnick, Butler, and Washton (1982) evaluated the effect upon the methadone treatment process of client self-regulation of dosage without having to see a counselor or the clinic physician. Their design allowed clients stabilized on at least 20 mg of methadone to adjust their dosages up or down by 5 mg steps at the time of their next clinic visit, with a limit of two such changes per week. Consistent with earlier findings by Goldstein, Hanstein, and Horns (1975), they found (a) little change in methadone dose under patient control, and (b) overwhelming preference for this procedure by both staff and patients.

Maintaining comparable dose reduction periods (90 days) but manipulating the degree of information available to patients as well as the degree of control patients could extend over the dose reduction schedule, Stitzer, Bigelow, and Liebson (1982) compared blind, informed, and self-regulated detoxification procedures. They then studied five outcome variables for their 60 male opioid addict subjects, including (a) success at dose reduction, (b) retention in treatment, (c) patient symptomatology, (d) illicit drug use, and (e) follow-up status. Their results were as follows: (a) while blind and informed dose reduction conditions were equally effective, both were substantially more effective than the self-regulated condition (65 and 71.4 percent reaching a methadone dose of 5 mg or less vs. 26.3 percent), (b) blind and informed conditions differed highly in days in treatment (69.8 vs. 61.5 days), while the 74.1 days in treatment for the self-regulated group was not comparable as patients in this group tended not to detoxify, (c) symptoms tended to increase in the blind group while decreasing in the informed group for patients who were retained for the entire 90 days, (d) while the high rate of illicit drug use reduced sample size to where meaningful comparisons could not be made, no change appeared in the self-regulated group, while both other groups increased in drug use to about 50 percent as methadone dose fell below 10 mg, and (e) some 20.0 percent of the entire sample were opioid-free at follow-up anywhere between two and three weeks to two and a half months. No differences appeared between the groups in drug-free status. Stitzer et al (1982) conclude that while no outcome differences were obtained, procedural differences during detoxification may influence process measures of outcomes while being unrelated to relapse after completion of detoxification.

Thus, it seems reasonable to conclude that allowing the addict greater control over and responsibility for his own treatment, far from resulting in wild abuse, manipulative behavior, and complete failure, appears to encourage responsibility and maturity in a population notably characterized by the absence of both. These preliminary findings may ultimately constitute a significant contribution to the understanding of addiction and the addict and to the direction to be taken in increasing the effectiveness of treatment procedures.

Use of Other Treatment Services During Methadone Maintenance

One of the major concerns about methadone maintenance is that it will be utilized simply as a maintenance procedure to the neglect of long-term attempts at rehabilitation (Perkins, 1972). A wide variety of other services have increasingly been offered in conjunction with methadone in an effort to substantially affect the rehabilitation of the addict by decreasing or eliminating criminal behavior, increasing social interaction in appropriate ways, and increasing self-esteem (Senay and Renault, 1971). Jaffe, Zaks, and Washington (1969) investigated the effects of methadone in a multimodality narcotics treatment program on the basis of an expressed belief that narcotics users are an heterogenous group for whose needs one type of treatment would prove inadequate. The goal of treatment was not so much immediate abstinence as enhancing productive and acceptable behavior. Methadone was used in both maintenance and detoxification procedures. Patients received ambulatory treatment of low-dose methadone (45 mg per day), were unaware of dose levels, and underwent no preliminary screening. With regard to retention, 75% of admissions were still in active treatment 1 month later. Heroin was not being used on a regular basis since only 10 to 20% of the patients were experimenting with illicit narcotics. Upon admission 58.4% of the patients were employed, increasing to 75% at the end of 1 month of treatment. The incarceration rate had dropped from 28.9% at the time of admission to 4.4% at 1 month. The authors suggest that their results indicate low-dose short-term methadone use can be effective in an outpatient program. However, Senay and Renault (1971) underline the need for supportive services by noting that in a maintenance program the addict suddenly finds his energies released from the daily hustle of obtaining heroin and begins to seek satisfying personal relationships. Programs which include a group experience will help the addict to establish a feeling of relatedness. The authors believe that neither methadone nor rehabilitative efforts alone will prove effective over a long period of time.

Ramer, Zaslove, and Langan (1971) comment that as a result of the proliferation of methadone programs, problems related to competition for funding are being experienced. The addition of ancillary support services to the basic methadone maintenance program substantially raises the cost of treatment from the $2000 annual per addict estimate of Nyswander and Dole (1967). To investigate which ancillary services proved most beneficial to addicts and were utilized most frequently, in the hope of determining the most efficient allocation of funds and resources, Ramer et al (1971) evaluated a methadone program that provided a variety of basic services to each addict. Twenty-seven adult male addicts with at least a 2 year history of heroin use, repeated relapses, multiple felony convictions, and no history of psychosis or alcoholism were maintained on 80 to 120 mg methadone on an outpatient basis. Patients were gradually allowed take-home doses of methadone, after they had proven themselves responsible in receiving medication under direct supervision 6 days a week at the clinic with one take-home dose for Sundays. All addicts had free access to group and individual psychotherapy, crisis intervention, and vocational guidance, and the use of each service was carefully recorded. The basic services provided to all addicts included a physician who undertook the initial screening, induction, crisis intervention and group therapy, and a nurse who administered the methadone, was available for counseling, and acted as group cotherapist. Ancillary treatment included crisis intervention, individual, group, and family psychotherapy, marriage counseling, vocational and educational counseling and placement, medical diagnosis and treatment, dental care, and legal aid. The breakdown by service of the utilization of ancillary treatment revealed 79% of the patients used crisis intervention; 48% used vocational guidance; 34% medical diagnosis and treatment; 23% individual psychotherapy; and 30% group therapy. Overall roughly 80% of the patients used some form of psychotherapeutic aid during the course of their treatment. However, 41% of the patient population was diagnosed as having gross psychopathology and this was usually associated with a higher rate of use of ancillary treatment.

Ramer et al (1971) concluded that methadone is an extremely powerful tool and that ". . . receiving methadone brings about major disruptions in [the addict's] life, and these disruptions require swift, supportive, and wise treatment" (p. 1043). For this reason the availability of crisis intervention facilities was deemed imperative for methadone maintenance programs. However, the authors felt it was unnecessary for all treatment personnel to be highly skilled psychotherapists. Vocational guidance was also very important on the basis of frequency of use, suggesting methadone programs should employ highly experienced professionals with skill in placing the marginally employable (Ramer et al, 1971). The authors suggest further that the remainder of services be made available to addicts on an individual referral basis because it is unnecessary for them to be incorported in each treatment program. Outcome results indicated that while 70% of those admitted remained on methadone, of whom approximately half had not shown a single narcotics abuse in regular urine testing, those addicts who required individual psychotherapy had the poorest success rate overall. Drawing heavily on a variety of ancillary services, this program was successful in eliminating much of the socially unacceptable behavior of its addicts, in effecting employment or schooling for most of the patients, and in reducing known crime to insignificant levels.

Willett (1973) closely examined the effects of group psychotherapy on interpersonal behavior in a methadone outpatient program by placing addicts in three treatment groups: an analytic therapy group, a *T* group, and a control group receiving only methadone. The Interpersonal Check List (IPCL) (Leary, 1957) evaluating traits along eight dimensions of interpersonal behavior was administered to all addicts in a pre-post treatment design. The only significant pre-post change to emerge was an increase on the rebellious-distrustful dimension among those patients participating in the analytic group. As there was no change in the control group, Willett concluded that administration of methadone alone does not affect interpersonal behavior. Changes approaching significance for both therapy groups were interpreted as indicating that mode of therapy was salient, with the analytic group showing a greater number of changes than the

T group (Willett, 1973). However, the limited examination of interpersonal behavior in only analytically oriented therapy and *T* groups, as well as the lack of significant findings, necessitates caution in the interpretation and generalization of these results.

LAAM (Methadyl Acetate)

A series of studies on the usefulness of LAAM as a temporary chemotherapeutic support was reported by Lehmann (1976) who administered it to young addicts aged 16 to 21 years every 72 hours. While some discomfort appeared after 60 hours, symptomatology was in most cases mild and no dosage adjustment was required. The results of this and related studies indicated few differences between LAAM and methadone with respect to treatment retention and outcome.

Large-scale evaluation of LAAM in comparison to methadone in order to collect data regarding safety and treatment efficacy was conducted by the Special Action Office for Drug Abuse Prevention (SAODAP) and the Veterans Administration Alcohol and Drug Abuse Service. This study took place in 16 non-VA and 12 VA hospitals and clinics respectively between 1973 and 1976. The VA study, involving 430 patients, under the overall direction of Dr. Samuel Kaim, utilized a double blind design comparing 80 mg of LAAM given three times a week versus methadone at 50 mg and 100 mg daily dose levels respectively for male clients not yet on methadone treatment. A placebo was used for LAAM clients on days when LAAM was not administered.

The SAODAP study, under Dr. C. James Klett, using 636 male clients already in methadone treatment, employed flexible dose levels with random assignment to either methadone or LAAM. Length of treatment was 40 weeks in both cases (Ling and Blaine 1979). The results indicated that 61 percent of patients in the LAAM group terminated early versus 40 percent in the methadone group. In addition, termination in the LAAM group occurred earlier. The authors emphasize, however, that almost all LAAM early terminators returned to methadone treatment while almost all methadone early terminators are lost to the treatment system. Elsewhere, Blaine, Levine, Whysner, and Renault (1977) note that the high rate of early termination from LAAM may have been a function of the relative inexperience of the investigators with LAAM, particularly during induction and crossover from methadone.

Ling and Blaine (1979) make a persuasive case for use of LAAM in preference to methadone in treatment programs. They suggest the following advantages of LAAM: (a) the elimination of the risks of take-home methadone, including accidental ingestion of the drug by family members and the possible diversion of methadone into street trafficking (thus rendering unnecessary both the need to take more drugs than necessary and the bargaining for higher doses of the drug), (b) the reduction in number of visits to clinics which do not give take-home methadone, (c) the smoother and longer acting drug effect, resulting in more emotional stability, (d) breaking of the addiction routine of daily ingestion, and the reinforcement effect of immediate gratification, and (e) freeing of staff time from routine dispensing of drugs to more therapeutic activities.

Most addicts in the study found LAAM acceptable as a maintenance drug, and some even preferred it to methadone. However, Ling and Blaine note that LAAM poses the risk of acute overdose, as all opiates do, particularly since its delayed onset of action may lead to the ingestion of other psychoactive drugs, especially CNS depressants.

When clients were given a choice of LAAM under a three times a week clinic visit schedule versus daily methadone on a six times a week clinic visit schedule, equal patient acceptability was found. Acceptance of LAAM was found to be maximized by making supplemental methadone available to prevent abstinence symptoms during the initial induction period to LAAM (Resnick, Washton, Garwood, and Perzel, 1982). The only complicating factor in this study was the fact that a choice in favor of LAAM was acceptable only if the patient did not meet FDA eligibility rules for take-home methadone. To further evaluate the acceptability of LAAM, Hough, Washton, and Resnick (1983) performed a follow-up study in which LAAM maintenance was offered as the *sole* treatment. Their results suggested that LAAM was a "clinically viable treatment" even where take-home methadone was readily available in other closely located clinics.

Freedman and Czertko (1981) provided some powerful evidence of the efficacy of LAAM. Forty-eight employed addicts in methadone maintenance were randomly assigned either to continue in the same treatment or switch to thrice weekly LAAM. The outcome of this study indicated less illicit drug use and longer treatment retention for the LAAM group than for the methadone group. There was also a preference for LAAM on nine of 15 criteria, including dosage schedule, feeling "normal," and reduced craving for heroin. On the other hand, Sorensen, Hargreaves, and Weinberg (1982) evaluated the usefulness of LAAM versus methadone and the standard three week vs. an extended six week treatment period in a randomized clinical trial, employing a double blind procedure. The results indicated that LAAM performed similarly to methadone in most respects when compared on such outcome measures as retention in treatment (to the end of the dosing schedule), use of illicit drugs during treatment, subjective discomfort, satisfaction, staff ratings of global progress, and durability of change at a three month follow-up. The six week withdrawal period showed some temporary benefits over standard treatment, but not necessarily of sufficient magnitude to outweigh the greater cost of the six week treatment and similarity of outcome.

Judson and Goldstein (1982a) examined the relative presence of side effects in patients maintained on methadone, LAAM, and naltrexone and non-drug-using controls. Their results indicated that (a) methadone patients had more complaints than non-drug-using controls, (b) methadone patients felt worse when using heroin than when not using heroin, (c) methadone, LAAM, and naltrexone patients felt worse while in treatment than when not in treatment *and* drug-free, and (d) abstinent heroin users did not differ in level of complaints from non-drug-using controls. These results should be interpreted, however, in the light of the difficulties inherent in ascribing symptom complaints to drugs without placebo-treated control groups.

Abuse of Drugs While in Methadone Programs

The abuse of other drugs while on methadone maintenance is a significant problem. These drugs include heroin, cocaine, benzodiazepines and tricyclic antidepressives, amphetamines, and PCP (Kaul and Davidow, 1981). In one survey of methadone maintenance patients in Philadelphia, Stitzer, Griffiths, McClellan, Grabowski, and Hawthorne (1981) found diazepam to be the most commonly abused drug, with some 93 percent of patients surveyed indicating use. Some 65 to 70 percent of clients had positive urine tests for diazepam, with the usual daily dose from 40 to 50 mg, although 31 percent reported daily doses between 70 to 300 mg, and 62 percent had experience with doses of 100 mg and higher. In most cases, the diazepam was taken in a single daily dose within one hour of daily methadone, with some 72 percent of the sample indicating that diazepam "boosted" the methadone effects. Barbiturates apparently did not influence the effects of methadone.

The use of illicit drugs by clients in methadone treatment is commonly dealt with by either (a) verbal encouragement to eliminate use, or (b) threats of sanctions if use continues (Stitzer, Bigelow, and Liebson, 1982). In an innovative approach to this problem, Stitzer et al (1982) provided alternative reinforcers contingent upon reduced use of illicit drugs as documented by urinalysis. Using benzodiazepine drugs as the target of drug abuse, Stitzer et al offered a choice of three reinforcers for benzodiazepine-free urines: (a) two methadone take-home doses, (b) $15 cash, or (c) two opportunities to regulate the methadone dose by up to ± 20 mg. Over a 9 to 12 week period, the results showed a clear increase in benzodiazepine-free urines during the intervention period, when compared to the pre- and post-intervention periods. However, data is not presented on the relative effectiveness of the three reinforcers. The problem of illicit drug use by maintenance clients was approached by temporarily increasing maintenance doses of prescribed opiates in a study by Gossop, Strarg, and Connell (1982). They found such an increase to lead to a reduction in illicit drug use as well as an improvement in social functioning. While recommending that clinics be alert to the need for such temporary increases, Gossop et al urge them to take precautions in patient monitoring.

Urine Monitoring

Urinalysis as a determinant of drug use while in treatment has been a consistent element of methadone programs. It also has been a source of continuing controversy, with its basic usefulness and validity as the issues. Atkinson and Crowley (1982), for example, recently described it as the source of "the most valid indicators of patients' actual drug use" (p. 460), while Havassy and Hall (1982) come to exactly the opposite conclusion. Originally collected on a daily basis when first introduced, random collection schedules are the rule today both because of the staff time and laboratory costs involved, as well as the unpredictability of such schedules to the client who wishes to avoid detection of drug use. Random collection schedules are also less aversive to the client.

When fixed versus random collection schedules were evaluated in a retrospective study, Harford and Kleber (1978) found a dramatic decrease in opiate use. They attributed this to an increase in the likelihood of detection as well as to the application of clinical sanctions for detection. In an attempt to rule out alternative explanations for this study which resulted from the lack of a control group, Atkinson and Crowley (1982) implemented a study comparing the performance of clients who were maintained on a semi-random urine collection schedule with known "safe periods," with clients on a fully randomized collection schedule. Using a partial clinic sample, Atkinson and Crowley (1982) first found a consistent but insignificant difference between groups, with slightly more opiate use in the random schedule group. In a second study, involving all new clients admitted to the clinic, more opiate use was detected on the regular schedule group in seven of the ten months. They concluded that failure to obtain a decrease in opiate use on the random schedule reflected the inadequacies of the sanctions for detection in altering the client's drug-taking behavior. Thus, the patient did not attempt to avoid detection. Atkinson and Crowley (1982) conclude that urinalysis is a "vitally important tool," but that it "must be used therapeutically with immediate rewards and sanctions contigent upon the results of the analyses" (p. 465).

The usefulness of urine monitoring procedures in preventing illicit drug use by methadone clients has been questioned, however, particularly in light of (a) the difficulties of effective collection and the resistance on the part of clients (Lewis, Peterson, Geis, and Pollack, 1972), and (b) the low level of accuracy in identification of drug use (Gottheil, Caddy, and Austin, 1976). At least two studies have been directed towards the central question of effectiveness of urine monitoring procedures in preventing drug use. Goldstein and Judson (1974b) found no differences in illicit drug use between monitored and unmonitored methadone clients. In a carefully evaluated study on this issue which employed 431 clients at five different clinics, Havassy and Hall (1982) found no consistent differences between the monitored and unmonitored groups in terms of illicit drug use. They did, however, find (a) a higher rate of treatment termination in the monitored condition, and (b) no observed differences between treatment groups in terms of overall level of treatment satisfaction, although unmonitored subjects tended to *perceive* improved avoidance of illicit drug use. Harvassy and Hall (1982) concluded that their results did not suggest that urine monitoring had any strong uniform deterrent effects upon illicit drug use.

PROPOXYPHENE NAPSYLATE

Propoxyphene napsylate (PN) has been used over the last decade both as a detoxification agent and as a maintenance medication. In a series of reports in 1973, Tennant (1973a, 1973b, 1973c) initially demonstrated the utility of PN both in detoxification and maintenance of heroin addicts. In an initial clinical study (Tennant, 1973a) 64 of 102 inpatients were successfully detoxified, using a five day regimen. Minimal side effects were observed, and these consisted of mild sedation and slurring of speech. Fifty percent of 38 heroin addict outpatients were also successfully detoxified. Doses of PN used daily in the two programs ranged from an initial 1600 mg in the inpatient program to an initial dose range of 1000 to 1400 mg with the outpatients. Maintenance doses for 16 outpatients ranged from 600 to 1400 mg. Even higher detoxification rates were reported in Tennant's two other 1973 papers (Tennant, 1973b, 1973c). These were an 83 percent success rate with 280 inpatients, and a 62 percent success rate with 50 outpatient heroin addicts. These papers, and another one following in 1974, provided clinical evidence of the apparent utility, safety, and patient acceptability of PN. In 1975 Tennant, Russell, Shannon, and Casas reported on the usefulness of PN in withdrawal from methadone maintenance. One group of methadone maintenance patients was reduced in dose level to 40 mg of methadone daily with PN initiated in divided daily doses of 600 to 1400 mg. Methadone was then discontinued, and PN withdrawn in from "two to four weeks." Another group was directly transferred from 30 mg or less daily of methadone to PN with no reported adverse effects. A total of 17, or 60 percent, of 30 patients, in the two studies achieved abstinence. Significantly, withdrawal from PN was not possible because of the severity of the withdrawal syndrome. In a review of this literature, Senay (1983) notes that these clinical reports suggest "a low toxic therapeutic ratio which while limiting its abuse potential also appears to limit its usefulness in withdrawing or maintaining high dose heroin addicts or high dose methadone maintenance patients." (p. 230).

Senay also notes the possible unacceptability of reported side effects such as hallucinations and dysphoria.

A double blind comparison of the effectiveness of propoxyphene napsylate (PN) and methadone was carried out by Wang, Kochar, Hasegawa, and Roh (1982). They compared PN in two divided doses of 400 mg each to methadone at 10 mg, 20 mg, or placebo. Their findings were that (a) PN did not alleviate withdrawal symptoms in patients who had been maintained at 20 mg, (b) PN produced an "overmedicated" effect in detoxified ex-methadone clients, and (c) PN was equivalent to methadone in suppressing the abstinence syndrome in methadone patients previously stabilized at 10 mg doses. Wang et al (1982) conclude that it is only with mildly addicted patients on 10 mg or less of methadone daily that PN can be of value.

Suggestions concerning the appropriate place of PN in treatment exist. A 21 month study of the efficacy of propoxyphene napsylate (PN) therapy in a group of 178 heroin addicts suggested similar outcome in terms of employment and heroin use to that of a group of methadone maintenance patients. The authors suggest the usefulness of PN when the ability to discontinue and reenter treatment on a discretionary basis is one criterion for entry into treatment of some addicts (Tennant and Rawson, 1981). In concluding his review of the literature on the efficacy of PN in detoxification or maintenance of opiate addicts, Senay (1983) suggests its usefulness for minimally dependent patients or for patients from communities with a strong anti-methadone bias. Considering the low toxic therapeutic ratio and need for twice daily administration, he suggests its usefulness to be limited, with the exception of concurrent use with methadone as an adjunct to detoxification.

DETERMINING THE EFFECTIVENESS OF METHADONE MAINTENANCE

Program Retention

Perkins and Richman (1972) consider program retention to be the most important evaluation criterion, particularly in light of the fact that specific goals of treatment often vary from program to program. Retention also seems to be a particularly relevant criterion for the multimodality programs. There is some theoretical justification for the weight given to program retention because it is impossible to provide continuity of treatment and to have an impact upon patients who do not stay in treatment, and also because addicts are a population noted for their resistance to treatment and their intermittent and sporadic participation in such treatment. By defining "prevalence of participation" as the number of patients continuously in treatment in any unit and not only in the original treatment unit, Perkins and Richman (1972) hoped to obtain a more accurate reflection of the retention power of any given treatment modality. Using this definition, the authors found a 73% retention rate overall for the methadone programs they examined, which was surprising in light of their expectation that since admissions criteria had been relaxed to allow the more difficult patients to be admitted a reduction in favorable outcome would occur. This is a particularly high rate, considering the retention power of the other therapeutic modalities discussed in Chapter 11.

Bass and Brown (1973) also compared methadone maintenance and methadone detoxification programs in terms of retention and client characteristics. Their review suggested that methadone maintenance programs are more successful than detoxification programs, partly as a result of the satisfaction of drug-craving provided in the treatment process itself. Actually, the authors suggest, client variables may be the more salient factor in the greater success of the maintenance programs because those addicts who choose maintenance may be very different from those choosing detoxification. It becomes difficult, however, to accurately assess this interpretation since the authors did not define what constituted "success." All clients were selected from the Washington, D.C., Narcotic Treatment Administration programs, and were allowed to choose detoxification or maintenance in an agreement to remain in treatment for a minimum of 6 weeks. The results were assessed in terms of the respective retention rates for maintenance and detoxification procedures. At the end of 6 months a 72% retention rate was obtained for maintenance, versus a 49% retention rate for detoxification. On closer examination, however, maintenance clients had tended to be living with relatives, to be older, and to have used heroin longer. There was no difference in retention rate between the younger (21 or younger) and older (26 and older) clients within each modality, but the older maintenance sample was more likely to stay in treatment than the older detoxification sample. Bass and Brown (1973) suggested that those addicts selecting maintenance were more motivated than those choosing detoxification, with greater age and family involvement indicating (a) greater perception of community responsibility, (b) greater maturity and therefore dissatisfaction with the addict lifestyle, and (c) greater difficulties encountered in continued hustling on the street. Support for this interpretation was derived from the fact that the relationship between retention rate and living arrangement or age was lost when the authors controlled for modality.

Consequently, the maintenance client, having faced limitations in his functioning not yet faced by the detoxification client, would be more willing to undertake the lengthy and demanding regimen involved in the selection of methadone maintenance as his treatment modality. [Bass and Brown, 1975, p. 8]

However, the data also indicated that the older addict was more likely to remain in maintenance than he was in detoxification, suggesting that the older addict has a greater investment in the street-addict lifestyle and requires long-term involvement with supportive services to change. "...[F]or the older client with his more prolonged history of addictive adjustment, the discipline provided through a maintenance regimen may be importantly related to his efforts at rehabilitation" (Bass and Brown, 1975, p. 10).

Simpson, Sells, and Demaree (1976) reported that for clients entering methadone treatment between 1969 and 1973, average treatment duration was about fifteen months. They noted, however, a drop in duration of treatment in subsequent years. While 59 percent of DARP clients admitted to methadone treatment in 1969-71 were still in treatment one year later, the percentage dropped to 40 percent for the 1972-73 cohort, and to 24 percent for those admitted in 1976.

The psychosocial correlates of retention in methadone maintenance were examined by Steer (1980) in a sample of 207 heroin addicts. He found living with other addicts to be related to length of stay in treatment but not to dropping out. Variables inversely related to dropping out included being black, admitting to past suicide attempts, and describing oneself upon admission as vigorous and active. Steer notes that these findings may be program-specific and not generalizable across common treatment modalities, a conclusion that may be only *too* applicable to research in this area!

A large-scale study of the relationship between methadone dosage policy and retention in treatment was conducted by Brown, Watters, and Iglehart (1983). In their survey of 113 methadone maintenance programs in 11 states, Brown et al found that flexible dosage policies, where no single dosage policy predominated, were associated with higher levels of treatment retention. Such programs retained clients some nine months longer than other programs. Furthermore, retention in treatment was found not to differ among high, middle, and, low dose programs when client characteristics were controlled for. Craig (1980) found that addicts in low dose methadone maintenance (i.e., 30 mg daily) performed at similar success rates as did Ss in other studies with high dose levels, but that fewer clients on low doses remained in treatment at the end of one year. Ling, Charuvastra, Kaim, and Klett (1976) reported a double blind, randomized comparison of LAAM at 80 mg thrice weekly and methadone at maintenance dose levels of either 50 mg or 100 mg daily for a period of 33 weeks at the full dose levels. When the groups were compared on a variety of outcome measures, clear evidence was found for the superiority of the 100 mg fixed dose over the 50 mg dose in suppressing opiate abuse during the course of the study. Opiate abuse was lower in the high dose group, as were staff ratings of improvement. No differences were found in retention rates or symptom complaints. When the group of addicts who had been in the double blind study of 50 or 100 mg daily of methadone or 80 mg LAAM three times weekly were switched to an open dose of 60 mg daily of methadone, several results occurred. Those decreased from 100 mg of methadone or 80 mg of LAAM were quicker to ask for dose increases than were those who had been at 50 mg of methadone. The eventual percentage of each group who asked for an increase over a six week period did not differ. Very surprisingly, however, the low dose patients showed a significant decrease in opiate abuse during the restabilization period. The 100 mg group increased their opiate abuse during the same period, but not significantly. This study provided evidence that dose level made a difference in opiate abuse in patients stabilized in methadone treatment (Ling, Blakis, Holmes, Klett, and Carter 1980). Hargreaves (1983) reviews the evidence for the most efficacious methadone dosage level and concludes that the evidence presented by Ling, Charuvastra, Kaim, and Klett (1976) is persuasive for the greater effectiveness of suppressing opiate abuse during the first five to ten months of maintenance. Hargreaves is careful to point out that not all patients need a dose this high, but that "at least ten percent of patients, and probably more, will do better if maintained on some dose higher than 50 mg during their first five to ten months in treatment." (p. 53)

Sells (1979) reported that methadone maintenance clients remained longest in treatment of clients in any modality. In the DARP study, median time in treatment for methadone maintenance patients was over 12 months, less than four months for therapeutic communities and drug-free programs, less than one-half month for inpatient detoxification, and between one and two months for outpatient detoxification. More patients "graduated" from therapeutic communities and detoxification than from methadone maintenance. While the most frequent manner of termination irrespective of type of program was "quit," this was highest in outpatient detoxification. In all treatment modalities, Sells (1977) found length of stay and favorable outcome in treatment to be significantly related to final outcome. With respect to client characteristics, favorable posttreatment outcomes in Sells' studies (1977) were related to the following characteristics: age (older), ethnicity (white), and favorable background (low criminality). The only exception was for methadone maintenance, where most patients showed significantly lower drug use and criminality post-treatment. Sells (1977) suggested the existence of two factors related to outcome. There is a *compliance factor*, "reflecting response to coercive entry and program surveillance or during treatment outcomes" (p. 114). Continued improvement was also related to a *therapeutic change factor*, particularly in methadone maintenance.

Summarizing the results of Sells' study, he found the rates of successful outcome for the treatment modalities under study broke down as follows: methadone maintenance: 30 percent, therapeutic communities: 37 percent, drug free: 34 percent, detoxification: 21 percent, and control (intake only): 21 percent. Sells concludes by evaluating these differences in the following manner: Based upon predictors of outcome using a multiple discriminant analysis approach, outcomes for methadone maintenance and therapeutic communities exceeded expectation, the drug free programs did more poorly than expected and the detoxification and control groups fell far below expectations (Sells, 1979). This summary, however, cannot do full justice to the DARP results, and the reader is referred to the comprehensive report. Overall, however, Sells reports that the methadone maintenance as well as the therapeutic community approaches have demonstrated worth for narcotics treatment, while outpatient drug-free programs are seen as mainly useful for youthful non-opioid and polydrug users.

McGlothlin and Anglin (1981) compared follow-up results, over a six to seven year period, for first admissions to methadone maintenance programs which varied in their treatment policies. Two of the programs had a high dose, long-term retention, flexible conformance policy, while the third followed a low dose, high conformity policy with involuntary termination for violations of program rules. McGlothlin and Anglin provide convincing data for the significantly more effective performance of clients in the two high dose, long-term, flexible conformity programs than in the low dose, high conformity program. In terms of six of ten outcome measures, the two high dose programs outperformed the low dose program in terms of (a) mean time incarcerated, (b) daily opiate use, (c) no opiate use, (d) alcohol abuse, (e) dealing, (f) employment and crime days per year. When the "social cost" of each of the programs was calculated, the more costly high dose, long-duration programs resulted in a significantly lower social cost (based upon costs of arrest, trial, incarceration, legal supervision, property crime losses, and welfare costs *less* treatment costs) than the costly low dose program with less treatment.

Pointing out that no controlled study has yet been conducted to compare the efficacy of different durations of methadone maintenance, Hargreaves reviews those correlational studies which bear on this issue. He concludes that the time has come to examine current program practices. These include (a) the association of high methadone dose with long treatment duration, and (b) the extremely poor outcome results concerning complete abstinence following completion of methadone treatment and detoxification. He concludes that

(a) methadone clients terminated before achievement of stable social functioning are very unlikely to stay abstinent, and (b) termination under the best of circumstances still results in a less than 50 percent chance of remaining abstinent as long as three years. He thus concludes that forced termination may place even well-functioning methadone patients at serious risk of re-addiction.

Effects on Criminal Behavior

One of the most dramatic consequences of methadone maintenance and one most often cited in support of such programs is a drastic reduction in the number of crimes committed by methadone maintenance patients. It has been repeatedly suggested by investigators, including Dole and Nyswander, that the addict engages in criminal behavior to secure funds for narcotics, and once his drug-craving has been eliminated the necessity for criminal behavior will also disappear. In effect, methadone purportedly serves this purpose.

Dole and Nyswander (1968) showed that prior to treatment 91% of their addicts had been in jail at a rate of 52 convictions per 100 man-years of addiction. Since entering treatment, 88% of these addicts were arrest-free with 5.8 convictions per 100 man-years. Jaffe, Zaks, and Washington (1969) also found the incarceration rate of patients in a maintenance program dropped from 28.9% at the time of admission to 4.4% at 1 month. Dale and Dale (1973) examined a group of 814 maintenance patients who had been admitted without undergoing screening procedures. In the 12 month period preceding admission, 36% of these patients had been arrested, compared with 6% in the 3 month period following admission.

Many investigators have examined the effects of methadone maintenance on criminal behavior with similar results. Newman, Bashkow, and Cates (1973) compared the arrest histories of voluntary admissions to a methadone maintenance program, including those subjects who had dropped out of treatment, before and after admission. The arrest rate remained relatively steady until 6 months prior to application for treatment, at which point it increased by 38%. An additional 12% increase occurred subsequent to application but prior to admission, indicating to the authors that motivation for treatment alone was insufficient to account for the decrease in arrest rates following admission. Roughly 40% of the patients had been arrested at least once in the year prior to admission at a rate of 70.6 arrests per 100 person-years. The postadmission rate for the first 6 months of treatment declined 57% to 30.2 per 100 person-years. The total postadmission rate during the first year fell to 26.8 from 69.2 prior to admission. For those clients in treatment 13 months or more the arrest rate prior to admission was 92.6 per 100 person-years, dropping to 14.8 after the first 6 months and leveling off at 22.2 after the second 6 months for an overall decline of 82% in the first year. Women had a 48% lower arrest rate than men prior to admission. After admission, the arrest rate decreased by 55% for men during the first 6 months and 73% for women; after the second 6 months, 59% for men and 72% for women; and at 13 months or more, there was an 80% decrease for men and 100% for women. Blacks had the highest preadmission arrest rate of 79.3 per 100 person-years, and whites the lowest with 63.0 per 100 person-years. Both rates decreased steadily after admission. The highest arrest rates were found in those addicts under 30 years old, and declined in all age groups after admission.

Cushman (1972) examined the arrest records of heroin addicts admitted to a New York City methadone maintenance treatment program by submitting the names of 151 patients to the New York City police department. Pretreatment lifetime arrest rates were 42 per 100 patient-years, dropping drastically to 6.1 per 100 patient-years during treatment. During the 12 months immediately preceding treatment the arrest rate was 42 per 100 patient-years; during the first year of treatment, 8.3 per 100 patient-years; during the second year, 4.8 per 100 patient-years; during the third year of treatment, 5.4 per 100 patient-years; during the fourth year 4.8 per 100 patient-years; and during the fifth year of treatment 0 per 100 patient-years. Further investigation revealed that 47% of the arrests made prior to treatment were for crimes directly involving narcotics, an addtiional 32% were for crimes involving money, and a further 6% were for prostitution. Arrests for all of these categories decreased during the course of treatment. Cushman (1972) was careful to note that the police did not change their criteria for making arrests during this period, thus it was safe to assume that the substantial reduction in arrest rate he observed was real. Cushman (1972) draws a conclusion considered debatable by many investigators:

Since arrest frequency is a measure of criminal activities, and criminal activity in these patients is a measure of drug-seeking behavior, it can be inferred that drug abuse was sharply reduced after entry into methadone treatment. [p. 1754]

While this inference is open to criticism, it is difficult to argue with his further statement:

. . . [N]ot only did the patients studied exhibit less criminal behavior, but also the nature of their few offenses committed during treatment were less disturbing to society than those committed before treatment was started. [p. 1754]

Since the lifetime arrest rate and that of the year immediately preceding treatment were in such close agreement, Cushman (1972) felt it reasonable to assume that the pretreatment rate would not have changed in the absence of treatment.

Cushman (1974) carried out an additional longitudinal study of the criminal activity of 269 New York City narcotic addicts before and after methadone maintenance treatment. In this population, predominantly of lower socioeconomic status and nonwhite, Cushman found the arrest rate increased drastically during the period of addiction to heroin from preaddiction rates. Primarily, the increases represented drug law violations, prostitution, violence, property crime, and misbehavior. Arrests during preaddiction periods increased from 3.1 per 100 person-years to 35.1 per 100 person-years during the period of active addiction. During methadone treatment the arrest rate decreased to 5.9 per 100 person-years and the frequency of occurrence of dangerous drug law violations, prostitution, and property crimes declined; crimes related to misbehavior and violence declined at a somewhat lower rate. For a subsample of 46 addicts who had been discharged from methadone treatment, the arrest rate increased only slightly after discharge to 9.0 per 100 person-years, suggesting that the long-term benefits accrued during maintenance may transcend the simple elimination of drug-craving (Cushman, 1974).

Similarly, the Methadone Maintenance Evaluation Committee (1968) found the arrest rate of patients in a maintenance program decreased significantly over a 2 year period. Of 473 patients in the program for 3 to 5 months, 6% were arrested; at 6 to 11 months 11% of 353 patients were arrested; at 12 to 18 months, 8% of 326 patients were arrested, at 19 to 24 months only 3% of 185 patients had been arrested, and at 24 months and longer less than 1% of 101 patients had been arrested. The methadone patients were compared to a control group of 100 patients undergoing detoxification with the following results: at 3 to 5 months 25% had been arrested, at 6 to 11 months 37% had been arrested, at 12 to 18 months 36% had been arrested, at 19 to 24 months 18% had been arrested, and at 2 years or more the arrests leveled off at 22%. Clearly, the committee concluded that methadone maintenance was not only effective in reducing the arrest rate of patients, but it was more effective than detoxification procedures.

When the effect of being on civil addict parole status was compared with matched controls entering methadone treatment, Anglin, McGlothlin, and Speckart (1981) found the results of a seven year follow-up suggested a large decline in daily heroin use and related criminal behavior. Ss in the parole supervision plus urine testing condition did only marginally better than maintenance alone, although parole status did significantly reduce intervals of daily heroin use both preceding and following entry into methadone treatment.

Cushman (1971) effectively dramatized a point in regard to the effects of methadone maintenance on criminal addicts in terms of the financial cost of addiction to society. He calculated the cost in 1969 of the methadone maintenance clinic at St. Luke's Hospital in New York City to be $180,000. The mean daily census at St. Luke's was 69 patients, with an annual direct cost per patient of $1450. The mean total cost per patient was estimated at $2750. All 57 patients enrolled in the program as of January 1, 1969, and an additional 33 patients were asked to compare their drug and income-related activities during 1 year on methadone with the year preceding treatment. Estimates of the annual payments for narcotics were made by multiplying the average daily cost of heroin by the number of days heroin was actually used. The amount and type of illegal activity required to obtain some percentage of the daily habit cost was also estimated for the interview. Eighty-one patients had a mean daily habit of $34.85 with a range of $0 to $150, and only 37% were employed in the year prior to treatment. The total amount spent for heroin by the 81 addicts was obtained in the following manner: $455,000 from selling drugs; $258,000 from stealing, and $86,800 from prostitution. The total amount obtained by all methods was $887,800. It was also estimated that in order to obtain $258,000 from stealing, the fair market price of the stolen goods would have been $720,000.

Cushman (1971) further found the average income declared by these addicts prior to maintenance was $1500, and labeled them as very poor income tax payers. This income more than doubled during treatment. In addition, the number of welfare months decreased from 23,800 to 17,425 after treatment. These figures suggested to Cushman (1971) that the high incomes of these patients prior to treatment were needed to support a drug habit and not to maintain a given standard of living, since the addicts were able to live on substantially less money as soon as the need for heroin abated. Furthermore, the cost of heroin-related hospital care (with the exception of detoxification attempts) was calculated at $12,000 before treatment, which diminished to nothing during methadone maintenance. These 81 addicts spent a total of 1931 days in jail in the year immediately preceding treatment, at an estimated cost of $28,226. Again, treatment represented a substantial savings since during the first year of methadone maintenance no days were spent in jail. There were numerous indications that the decrease in illicit activities and in hospitalizations were a result of methadone maintenance and would not have occurred otherwise.

Clearly, addiction represents a staggering cost to society above and beyond the criminal activities of these addicts (although the preponderance of costs accrued in terms of stolen goods, police protection, and supportive services of criminal justice agencies). Compare the $180,000 cost of the maintenance clinic with the estimated $720,000 worth of stolen goods, $12,000 in heroin-related hospital care, $28,226 in jail costs, and uncalculated welfare payments incurred by these 81 addicts, all of which were either eliminated or substantially reduced (in the case of welfare payments) during maintenance. The effectiveness of detoxification was minimal, with almost immediate relapse in the case of most patients and at an inpatient detoxification cost of $67,260. Furthermore, Cushman (1971) confined his report to those costs which could be substantiated or very closely approximated. Cushman (1971) concludes, justifiably on the basis of the evidence he presents, that methadone maintenance represents an enormous saving to society and transforms former heroin addicts into assets instead of liabilities.

While inflation certainly has affected the figures cited above, the relative costs of treatment versus the costs to society of addicts remain in the same proportion. In 1981, McGothlin and Anglin estimated the annual pretreatment cost to society per addict to range between $16,900 to $19,300.

Effects on Employment and Education

Repeatedly, a striking finding by Dole and Nyswander was that heroin addicts who were unemployed at admission to the methadone maintenance program became productive members of the community while in treatment, either by obtaining employment, going back to school, or engaging in some other acceptable full-time activity. The authors concluded that when the addict was relieved of the necessity for securing a continuous supply of heroin, the energies previously concentrated on satisfying drug-craving were freed to be utilized in a more productive manner. These results have been confirmed directly by reports of increases in employment rates from a number of different maintenance programs, and indirectly by reports of addicts utilizing vocational and educational counseling (Ramer, Zaslove, and Langan, 1971).

Dole and Nyswander (1966) observed that 71% of their patients were employed or going to school after starting treatment. The Methadone Maintenance Evaluation Committee (1968) reported that at admission to a New York City methadone program only 28% of 544 heroin addicts were employed, and 40% were receiving welfare payments. After 5 months in the program 45% were employed, after 11 months 61% were employed or in school, and after 24 months 85% were employed or in school. A concurrent reduction in welfare support also occurred, with 50% receiving welfare at 5 months, 22% at 1 year and 15% at 2 years. A study of 521 admissions to the Morris J. Bernstein Institute conducted by Perkins and Bloch (1970) revealed 41% were employed during treatment compared to 27% at admission, 7% were in school compared to 0% at admission, and 36% were self-supporting. Significantly, Perkins and Bloch (1970) further found that continued drug use in this population was associated with unemployment and not being self-supporting. Cushman's (1971) sample taken from the methadone maintenance clinic at St. Luke's Hospital revealed only 37% were employed during the year prior to treatment, while 72% were not only employed but received higher salaries and assumed greater job responsibility during the course of methadone maintenance. Similarly, Jaffe, Zaks, and Washington (1969) found employment was up to 75% from 58.4% on admission at the end of 1 month of maintenance treatment. Of those patients active in a methadone maintenance program after 2 months, only 19% were employed on admission and 23% of those inactive at 2 months were employed on admission (Dale and Dale, 1973). At the end of 8 months, 38% were employed (Dale and Dale, 1973). Gearing (1970), in her evaluation of the New York City methadone maintenance program, also found substantial increases in employment and education. Only 29% of 990 addicts were employed on admission. At the end of 6 months, 45% of 816 patients in treatment were employed and 3% were in school; after 12 months, of 672 addicts still in treatment 61% were employed and 4% were in school; at 18 months 66% of 515 patients still in treatment were employed and 6% were in school; at 24 months 70% of 364 patients in treatment were employed and 4% were in school; at 30 months 77% of 223 patients were employed and 3% were in school; and at 36 months 88% of 88 patients remaining in treatment were employed and 4% were in school.

FACTORS ASSOCIATED WITH SUCCESS OR FAILURE IN METHADONE MAINTENANCE

While the evidence presented above indicates that methadone maintenance is more successful than most other treatment modalities when assessed by criteria of retention power, increase in productive behavior, and decrease in illegal and antisocial activities, a significant number of patients either drop out of programs or are discharged for a variety of reasons. Several investigators have recently begun to examine factors which might be associated with success or failure in a methadone maintenance program. Rosenberg, Davidson, and Patch (1972) investigated patterns of dropouts from a maintenance program and found that when such programs initiate more liberal admissions policies than the original Dole-Nyswander program, the success rate drops lower than the reported average of 80%. Their review indicated dropout rates ranging from 50% at 24 weeks (Jaffe, 1970) to

37% overall (DuPont, 1970). They reported on a Boston City Hospital program in which treatment was free to proven narcotic addicts in Boston. Demographic characteristics of the population studied were similar to those of other programs: mean age was 24 years, 80% male, 60% black; mean length of addiction was 2 to 4 years, and all patients were voluntary admissions. Initially all patients who applied were admitted. When a waiting list policy was instituted, however, the authors noted fewer than 56% of those who had initially applied returned for treatment. Most of the patients who eventually dropped out did so within the first 2 weeks of starting treatment, when patients originally underwent methadone detoxification before being admitted to the maintenance program. Once in the maintenance program the monthly dropout rate fell from 40% to 10%, with many dropouts occurring later in treatment. More patients who dropped out later in treatment were working at the time of admission (67%) than those who dropped out early (40%), more were living with their families (70% vs. 53%), and had a larger preadmission daily heroin habit. Concurrently, it was found that after 9 months roughly one-third of the urines analyzed revealed the presence of drugs other than methadone.

Dale and Dale (1973) observed that of 814 patients admitted to a methadone maintenance program, 190 had been discharged after 2 months, and 304 after 8 months, the majority of whom (75%) were discharged for failed appointments. Those patients who were still active after 2 months were older and less likely to be black. Those who had failed tended to receive outside support for their habits, and the authors suggested they were perhaps less motivated for treatment. Since nearly twice as many failures as those still active were compelled to enter the program by the courts, one must again question the role of motivation in successful outcome despite the claims made by some methadone maintenance proponents that methadone is effective with addicts who have repeatedly relapsed and who display little overt motivation. This is further supported by the fact that missing four appointments, the predominant reason for discharge, could hardly be interpreted as evidence of continued motivation.

Weiss and McFarland (1973) compared methadone clinic patients and dropouts on the Leary IPCL dominance-submission and love-hate dimensions. Their results indicated that the patients who dropped out were significantly more passive and less aware of their passivity. The authors suggested their findings confirmed the hypothesis derived from the description of Chein, Gerard, Lee, and Rosenfeld (1964) of the addict as passive, dependent, hostile, alienated, and unrealistic in self-perception.

Perkins and Bloch (1971) studied 53 patients who had failed in a methadone maintenance program, and found that 16 had been discharged for uncooperative behavior, nine for drug abuse, seven for psychological problems, six for alcohol abuse, and five for being arrested. The length of treatment varied from less than 1 month to 31 months with 53% discharged during the first 6 months and 75% during the first year. Overall, the risk of failure was greater for those who were unemployed or unmarried, confirming their earlier work (Perkins and Bloch, 1970), which suggested that unemployment was associated with continued drug abuse. This earlier study indicated that reasons for discharge were substance use, criminal involvement, and behavior problems, with a higher proportion of discharges of patients with more extensive arrest records. Discharge usually occurred in the first 6 weeks among those patients on low doses of methadone (Perkins and Bloch, 1970). The authors noted:

Specifically, we found that patients who are unemployed, do not reside with their families, are involved with the law, manifest behavioral problems, and continue substance use have a significantly higher proportion of discharge than patients who function more adequately in these areas [Perkins and Bloch, 1970, p. 1393]

Of those 53 patients who were discharged, only 15 were employed full or part-time or were in school at the time of follow-up, 10 were in jail, and 14 were engaged in criminal activities. Seventy-five percent had been arrested since discharge, with a total of more than 110 arrests and 63 convictions among them. Of the 38 patients who were not institutionalized at the time of follow-up, 36 reported using drugs or alcohol, 19 indicated they had not undergone a single period of voluntary abstinence since discharge, and 17 reported they had undergone only one such period. Additional rehabilitation attempts had been made one or more times by 31 subjects. Interestingly, 49% said their problems had gotten worse since their discharge, 73% indicated they were the same or worse, and 88% said they were the same, worse, or that they had developed new difficulties. Overwhelmingly, the subjects perceived a decline in their physical and mental health, and 60% reported their most serious problem was drug-related.

Similar results were obtained by Moffett, Soloway, and Glick (1972) in a comparison of 21 subjects who had been detoxified and were drugfree at the time of discharge from an ambulatory methadone detoxification program and 34 subjects who had left this program against medical advice (AMA). At the follow-up interview, urinalysis was done to confirm or to disconfirm drug use reports. At the time of termination of treatment 33.3% of the detoxified patients were legally employed, versus 44.1% of the AMA patients. However, 38.1% of the detoxified patients had subsequently been arrested compared with 52.9% of the AMA patients. At the time of follow-up, 9.5% of the detoxified patients were drugfree while 12.5% reported abusing heroin; 11.8% of the AMA patients were drugfree and

61.5% reported heroin abuse. The total relapse rate for both groups was 89.1%, and 47.6% of the detoxified group returned to opiate use within 1 month of discharge. Concurrently, an increase in frequency of abuse of methadone obtained on the street was reported with 34.7% abusing methadone at follow-up, 8.2% of whom said this was their only form of drug abuse. The reasons given for methadone abuse were not surprising: it was cheap and reliable. The greatest risks for the AMA dropout group were legal involvement, family disorganization, multidrug abuse, and unemployment, confirming the findings of other investigators relative to methadone maintenance program dropouts.

Based on their data, Moffett et al (1972) suggested revision of detoxification programs along a number of dimensions. First, greater structure within the treatment program might decrease the rate of premature termination. Second, since the detoxification patients who subsequently relapsed had spent an average of 6.1 months in treatment, while those who did not relapse averaged 2.8 months, the authors suggested a short-term highly structured detoxification program might be maximally effective. Furthermore, they stated:

If the detoxification process is not structured to include unlimited supportive counseling, and a rigidly enforced short-term detoxification schedule, the patient will probably fail and terminate from the program. [Moffett et al, 1972, p. 215]

In contrast, Levine, Levin, Sloan, and Chappel (1972) examined the personality correlates of success in a methadone maintenance program, and the results delineate a picture of the addict who is able to become a more conventionally productive member of society. In addition to the termination of illicit drug use, "the expectations of the clinic staff [were] that the patient [would] change life-style from the underground culture of the drug world . . . to the conventional ethic of the American middle class" (p. 456). The successful maintenance patient should obtain legitimate employment, terminate illegal activities and associations with drug users, and become family- and community-oriented. To this end, individual and group therapy were employed in a clinic managed by four former addict counselors, two nurses, and a part-time psychiatrist. Members were required to attend a weekly 2 hour group meeting and were maintained on low doses of methadone (40 mg per day). Patients were categorized on the basis of outcome into the "stepped-up group," those who were most successful, working, and drugfree at 6 months; the "re-entry group," those who had originally failed and later returned to the program; and the "dropout group," those who had failed. Data were obtained at follow-up from an individual psychiatric interview, unsupported by the administration of objective tests. This method of data collection forces a cautious interpretation, since interview data are notoriously unreliable. No differences emerged between the three groups relative to psychiatric diagnosis. However, the dropout group was most depressed, while the stepped-up group displayed the highest degrees of anxiety and compliance.

Levine et al (1972) suggested a number of possible interpretations of these results. First, degree of anxiety and depression might be true predictors of success. Second, they might also be artifacts of participation in the program, so that the stepped-up group might be most concerned about rules and least depressed because they had been successful, while the failures would be depressed as a result of continued heroin use. Thirdly, they might merely reflect the pharmacologic effects of heroin in that the stepped-up group was drugfree and therefore could be high anxious and not depressed, while the dropout group using heroin would be low anxious and very depressed. Certainly anxiety and compliance would tend to facilitate conformity to middle-class American values, and thus it seemed quite logical that addicts who were successful in the maintenance program would exhibit these traits.

Generally, it seems that the high anxious, compliant person who is able to remain in a fairly stable family situation, terminate illegal activities, and obtain steady employment tends to succeed in a methadone maintenance program that emphasizes productive behavior and varying degrees of conformity to middle-class mores. Yet, the relative inability to precisely predict long-term outcome for clients admitted to a methadone maintenance program was recently demonstrated by Judson and Goldstein (1982). They found that involvement with criminal justice agencies before treatment, heavy alcohol use before or during treatment, continued daily heroin use, living with an addict during treatment, or minority ethnicity were all associated with a poor outcome. For even the strongest predictions, however, the correlations with three different outcome criteria were weak, with the highest r only .26. Judson and Goldstein concluded that none of the 19 variables they studied could provide an *a priori* judgment at the time of admission about long-term outcome.

DETOXIFICATION OF THE METHADONE MAINTENANCE PATIENT

One of the major concerns with methadone maintenance as a rehabilitation measure is that in substituting one narcotic for another the individual remains addicted to drugs in spite of apparent increases in appropriate social functioning. Many critics, particularly members of therapeutic communities such as Synanon and Daytop, argue that an addict is not cured until he is completely drugfree. Until that time he has escaped dealing with problems of immaturity and irresponsibility. However, Dole and Nyswander did not originally recommend attempting to detoxify the methadone patient, fearing that such attempts, if premature, would result in relapse because the addict was complacent and overconfident of his invulnerability to drug craving.

Investigators have attempted to detoxify methadone patients with varying degrees of success. One early study was conducted by Berger and Schwegler (1973) who gradually reduced the dose level of 17 methadone patients voluntarily requesting detoxification by 10 mg per week. At the time the zero level was reached patients continued taking the liquid daily in which the methadone had been dissolved as a placebo, to avoid anxiety related to the knowledge that they were no longer receiving drugs. Any patient experiencing withdrawal effects was allowed to stabilize before continuing to reduce dosage. Of these 17 patients, nine were able to successfully detoxify, the remaining eight giving the primary reason for failure as anxiety about being drugfree. The authors delineated several factors apparently related to successful outcome: steady employment, self-support, middle-class background, high school graduation, lower arrest and conviction history, cooperation with program rules, younger age, shorter history of addiction, and better relationships with counselors.

Another early attempt at detoxification of rehabilitated methadone maintenance patients was conducted by Cushman and Dole (1973). Excluded from participation in the study were those patients who had been in treatment less than 8 months, those of known drug abuse occurring within 4 months prior to the study, and those who were considered "insufficiently stable" as demonstrated by acting out or problems in accepting dosage or schedule. Patients could terminate the process at any time and return to methadone maintenance. Dosage was reduced more slowly than in the Berger and Schwegler (1973) study, decreasing by 10 mg every 2 to 3 weeks until a 20 mg level was reached. At that time further decreases were 2 to 5 mg biweekly, with a placebo of orange juice and quinine given after the zero level had been reached. Patient response to detoxification was divided into four categories: (a) patients ($N = 3$) quitting early before reaching withdrawal, as a result of high anxiety about being without methadone; (b) patients failing to complete detoxification within 12 months because of withdrawal symptoms ($N = 4$); (c) patients completing detoxification and then resuming maintenance ($N = 10$), of whom five underwent a second detoxification attempt; and (d) patients who were successfully detoxified. Of 48 patients who had completed detoxification, 79% were still abstinent at follow-up for a mean of 9.4 ± 6 months and 16 patients were retreated with methadone. In an examination of reasons for detoxification, patients who expressed motivation and confidence were more successful than those who felt going to the clinic was a nuisance (75% vs. 16%). Furthermore, patients who had previously undergone periods of abstinence of some duration tended to be successfully detoxified more often than patients whose history of heroin abuse was uninterrupted. Interestingly, Cushman and Dole (1973) found no relationship between employment status and outcome. Relative to the actual process of detoxification, 34% of the patients did not experience any symptoms of withdrawal while 37% of the males experienced some sexual disturbance, notably premature ejaculation, which ultimately disappeared. Seventy-eight percent of the patients reported feeling no desire for heroin after detoxification.

Cushman and Dole (1973) cautiously note that the subjects who were successful were highly motivated, had stable families and jobs, and were far from representative of the population in treatment. Although a reduction in dose from 80 to 120 mg methadone per day to 40 mg per day should not produce major withdrawal symptoms, the authors warn that this reduction should not be attempted with relatively new patients because the heroin-taking habit has not yet been extinguished. They suggest that high levels of methadone (80 to 120 mg per day) should be maintained for at least a year to achieve stable rehabilitation. Finally, they note that a failure on the first attempt by no means indicates that subsequent detoxification efforts will fail. "The patients in the present study had major advantages in remaining abstinent in that they started from a point of considerable economic, social, and psychological strength" (Cushman and Dole, 1973, p. 752).

In general, little success has been achieved in finding effective procedures for detoxification from methadone. Procedures which have been tried include 21-day detoxification programs (Newman, 1979), 42-day detoxification supplemented by propoxyphene napsylate (PN) (Tennant, Janowski, Shannon, & Bleich, 1978), and the provision of counseling services during detoxification (Resnick, Washton, & Stone-Washton, 1981).

To date, the coupling of psychotherapy with detoxification seems to offer some increased power in increasing success rates (Resnick et al, 1981), but one is forced to join with Resnick (1983) in concluding that:

"There does not appear to be any optimum method of detoxification that is applicable to all patients, nor is it likely that one will be defined among the options now available." (p. 163).

CRITICISMS AND ISSUES IN METHADONE MAINTENANCE

Since its inception as a treatment modality reported to have an almost unequaled potential for success, with the pilot of Dole and Nyswander in 1964, the use of methadone has spread to an impressive number of treatment programs. It was estimated by Cushman (1974) that methadone would reach 80,000 heroin addicts in treatment by the summer of 1974. On the basis of the preceding studies providing evidence of the potential for successful treatment of previously unreachable hard-core addicts, methadone maintenance has become the treatment of choice for heroin addiction in the United States. The actual number of addicts in treatment in 1979 approached the 80,000 figure (Lowinson and Millman, 1979). However, an increasing number of investigators raised questions and voiced criticisms as the seeds of disenchantment with methadone maintenance as the simple, ideal solution it was once thought were sown.

Methadone was held out as the last chance at rehabilitation for the original group of heroin addicts treated by Dole and Nyswander, most of whom had been repeated failures in treatment programs with a long history of addiction. However, as early as 1971, Gould notes that in recent years the trend had been away from the concept of methadone as a "last hope," to the concept of methadone as the treatment of choice for heroin addiction. This situation has not changed in 1985. This policy continues to maintain a high risk situation because methadone has a very high abuse potential and, without the support services of rehabilitation programs for ghetto youths who need vocational and educational training to acquire necessary skills to function productively, the underlying determinants of drug abuse will not change.

Further, the sociopathic traits exhibited by some addicts will not simply disappear once they start taking methadone, and these individuals will still constitute the serious risk of illegal diversion of methadone suggested by Gould (1971). The problem of diversion of supply is a primary concern of the opponents to the expansion of methadone maintenance programs both then and now.

CONCLUDING COMMENTS

At the time the first edition of this book appeared, almost a decade ago, there was intensive debate about a number of issues related to methadone maintenance including the following: (a) the perception of methadone as a high risk drug in terms of its own abuse potential, thus providing the addict with a higher quality drug offering more dependable results; (b) the fear of methadone-related overdose and deaths from overdose; (c) the fear that many younger addicts, particularly adolescents who were not yet dependent upon heroin, might be "forced" into methadone programs, resulting in the creation of an addiction where previously there was none; (d) the precise definition of exactly what criteria constitute rehabilitation in methadone treatment;

(e) the high incidence of "cheating" or continued drug use among methadone clients, leading to additional questions concerning the effectiveness of methadone; (f) the problem of lack of appropriate evaluation of the effectiveness of methadone treatment by means of careful evaluative studies; (g) the problem of failure of methadone *by itself* to produce change in the "true" problems underlying heroin addiction; including familial and interpersonal disruption, the lack of marketable skills, the cycle of failure and unrealistic goals, and the inability to cope with often significant and realistic feelings of inadequacy, loneliness; and (h) the serious criticism the use of methadone often engenders, reinforcing "...the popular illusion that a drug can be a fast, cheap, and magical answer to complex human and social problems" (Lennard et al, 1972, p. 88).

The status of the above issues was reviewed in detail earlier (Platt and Labate, 1976, pp. 288-307). In 1985, it is clear that at least some of them are at or nearer resolution, such as the concern over methadone's safety (Kreek, 1983); the suggestion of stabilizing and therapeutic effects for some patients of methadone by itself, leading at times to successful treatment outcomes *without* psychotherapy (Cooper, 1983); the increasing use of rigorous designs for evaluating the effectiveness of methadone treatment (McLellan, Luborsky, Woody, and O'Brien, 1983b); and the positive impact of methadone upon illicit opiate use and criminal behavior (Hubbard et al, 1983). Other issues, particularly those more related to statements of values than existent scientific findings, are still focal points of intense discussion.

Perhaps the most concise statement of the current status of methadone treatment is the concluding statement by James R. Cooper in his introduction to the 1983 National Institute on Drug Abuse monograph *Research on the Treatment of Narcotic Addiction: State of the Art.*

Methadone maintenance has, thus far, proved to be the most effective biological tool available to the clinician for the modification of addictive behavior. It has offered many addicts an opportunity to begin their psychosocial rehabilitation. (Cooper, 1983, p. xvi).

Conclusions

Conclusions

Each of the preceding chapters has focused on a particular aspect of heroin addiction. Beginning with a survey of the historical roots of heroin addiction in the United States, our current knowledge of the problem at a number of levels—from the biochemical to the individual to the social—has been examined. While the data at each of these levels helps to explain, or at least provides a greater degree of understanding of some particular aspect of heroin addiction, it is evident that the task of integrating all this information within a single theoretical framework is exeedingly difficult, if not impossible. Integration is made even more complex because much of the information at any single level of explanation is not complete in itself. Thus, at the biochemical level we find an incomplete understanding of the mechanisms by which morphine, the agent through which heroin produces its primary effects, induces euphoria. Also, we do not know with certainty the specific central nervous system sites at which morphine acts although we know a good deal more than we did a decade ago. At the individual psychological level, we find a growing recognition that there is no single "addictive personality" associated with heroin addiction, although there may be a number of types of addicts, each with a different set of dynamics surrounding use of the drug. However, research directed at identifying common personality traits, usually psychopathologic in nature, persists. At the sociologic level, there is substantial inconsistency to be found among the results of studies by different investigators, for example, the conflicting findings in regard to the relative social competence of the addict. Thus, one reason an integration of what we do know about heroin addiction may not be possible is because the findings themselves are often either incomplete or inconsistent, and are certainly not definitive.

Two additional facts make the task of integrating our theoretical knowledge into a single theoretical framework difficult. First, much of the research on the social and psychological aspects of heroin addiction is just not good research, and does not provide clear statements of relationships among variables. As writers in all areas of addiction research have continued to point out, there are substantial methodological faults in many of the studies done in the heroin addiction field. Particularly in the areas of personality and evaluation of treatment, research efforts have been characterized by inadequate control groups, data collected on shrinking samples, and the absence of standardized outcome criteria which would allow for comparisons between modalities.

In addition to the lack of methodologically sound research on many aspects of heroin addiction, much of the literature on other than the biological and biochemical aspects of the problem is not empirical, and therefore contributes little except a statement of the writer's personal observations. This is not to say that there is not a place for such statements, but rather that they account for too great a proportion of the published work in the field. Perhaps it would be more profitable in developing an understanding of addiction if the energy devoted to preparing such statements were redirected to some extent toward attempting to replicate the results of other studies or to test the validity of hypotheses drawn from the plethora of existing theories. Any well-designed study, regardless of how modest or of whether its findings support or refute the hypothesis being tested, makes its contribution to the development of a mosaic of understanding. In this regard, editors of journals which publish reports in the addiction field could contribute substantially to general improvement in the quality of publication by encouraging authors to publish reports of research programs incorporating a series of studies around an issue rather than by publishing them in the piecemeal fashion so common today.

Let us now direct our attention toward the implications of the evidence reviewed for understanding and controlling heroin addiction.

THE HISTORICOLEGAL CONTEXT OF HEROIN ADDICTION

There is good reason to believe that drug use would exist in our society regardless of the level of control attempted by governmental agencies. Government efforts directed toward decreasing the drug problem focus primarily on control of the drug supply. This control approach will probably not succeed for several reasons. First, there is reason to believe that if heroin were not available some other drug would be used instead. This actually happened in England when supplies of heroin and cocaine were less available in the late 1960s and, given the multidrug abuse pattern of the American addict, is a highly probable event when supplies of heroin are tight in this country. Indeed, one explanation suggested for a decline in heroin use in this country has been a shift to illegal methadone use, which has a number of advantages to the user that include lower cost.

A second consequence of the major effort at control of heroin in this country is the underworld monopoly of supply and the high cost of the drug. This has necessitated the addict's involvement with black market operations and has probably led in turn to greater criminal activity on the part of addicts to raise funds to maintain their habits.

A third consequence, resulting from the second, is that the early decision to attempt a solution of the heroin addict problem via the criminal justice and law enforcement systems has resulted in a significant modification of what it actually means to be an addict. Because possession and use of heroin are illegal, the addict must maintain a low profile and must be constantly suspicious and "cool" in the process of procuring a drug, the need for which ensures that the addict is anything but cool. The necessity for clandestine drug-taking behavior also means that if an addict overdoses or develops complications (which as indicated in Chapter 6, are associated with chronic use of an illegal substance) he is less likely to obtain prompt, adequate, and knowledgeable care from the appropriate source. Furthermore, some investigators have even suggested that the illegality of heroin use establishes an adversarial relationship between the addict and the rest of society, the existence of which is partly responsible for the sociopathic behavior characteristic of many addicts.

It is also possible that the effort at control of heroin has indirectly resulted in making a deviant and criminal lifestyle more attractive to youth of poverty backgrounds. This may even have played a significant role in determining the nature of the addict population.

In conclusion, there are several reasons why the control approach has not been successful, as shown by the continued availability of heroin. This should not be surprising, given the huge profits involved in the heroin trade. The future will also witness a continuation of the problem as new suppliers enter the lucrative business of providing the world's addicts with opiates. On the other hand, any relaxation of controls would probably lead to an immediate resurgence in heroin use.

One must consider the implications of an all-out attempt at controlling the importation of heroin into this country. If it were stopped completely, there would be no heroin problem. However, given the extent of polydrug abuse there is a good chance a drug problem would still exist, with heroin being replaced by other drugs of abuse.

The logical conclusion implied by the control effort and the considerations discussed above is that to eliminate all drug problems, there must be complete and absolute control of all drugs of abuse. However, such a control effort would involve huge expenditures and would therefore result in fewer dollars being directed toward treatment and prevention.

THE PHARMACOLOGY OF HEROIN ADDICTION

The effects of heroin are relatively short-acting. Without constant access to the drug, the addict vacillates between states of intoxication, either actively searching for a "fix" to stave off the symptoms accompanying withdrawal, or attempting to secure the funds to obtain one. Thus, addiction precludes a normal daily life. The search for the drug and the necessary funds to purchase it, however, provide a highly structured and full daily regimen for the addict. For some time, the primary motivation for this behavior has been seen by many to be one of staving off the abstinence syndrome. Based upon the most recent estimates of actual heroin content of the "bag" purchased on the street, it seems unlikely, however, that the small amounts of the drug contained in a bag actually are capable of producing strong enough physiologic dependence to cause severe symptoms of withdrawal. That this is the case is borne out by the fact that a large proportion of admissions to treatment programs are not physiologically addicted upon admission. Clearly then, a treatment approach based principally on administration of chemical substances dealing only with the factor of physical dependence must prove ineffective.

THEORIES OF HEROIN ADDICTION

The strong appeal of the conditioning theories of drug addiction lies in their clarity and internal consistency. Heroin's alleged functions as a positive reinforcer in the production of euphoria and as a negative reinforcer in the termination of aversive states such as anxiety are straightforward and easily understood. Furthermore, the role played by the development of physical dependence, the experience of withdrawal, and the termination of withdrawal upon further administration of heroin, is clearly explained by the conditioning theories. What the conditioning theories have to offer is a paradigm, a model for understanding how drug-taking behavior is maintained once it is initiated—a model that is logically compelling and satisfying. What these theories cannot account for is the cause, the motivation underlying the initial experimentation. Thus, an explanation must be sought outside the framework of conditioning theory.

Conditioning theories have contributed greatly to our understanding of the factors salient to relapse. Because of their clarity they offer a unique opportunity to test their validity empirically in a way not possible with most other theories. For example, if the conditioning theories provide an adequate explanation of heroin addiction based on the principles of reinforcement and learning, it should be possible to extinguish this drug-taking behavior effectively via the same principles. According to these conditioning theories, behavior repeated in the absence of reinforcement will gradually be eliminated. Thus, if heroin administration is no longer reinforced it should cease. The narcotic antagonists make it possible to avoid producing physical dependence while blocking the subjective physical effects of heroin. Use of such antagonists ensures that reinforcement of drug-taking behavior will not occur. Conditioning theories would thus predict that antagonists would constitute an effective treatment modality. However, as was clear in the chapter dealing with antagonist therapy, the use of antagonists alone is ineffective in treating heroin addiction: retentive power is weak, drug-craving is unabated, and narcotic abuse continues. Patients fail to return daily to the clinics, they "forget" to take their medication, or they delay taking it in order to experience a "high." Clearly then, the compelling conclusion to be drawn is that the principles of conditioning offer only a partial explanation. There remains a strong motivational component in heroin addiction which the conditioning theories do not adequately explain.

In contrast to the conditioning theories, Lindesmith's (1968) theory of addiction emphasizes the cognitive behavior of the addict in the development of his addiction. The major role played by cognitive processes is evident in Lindesmith's (1947) three essential stages in the development of addiction: (a) the addict's own recognition of his dependence on the drug; (b) his reorganization of his self-concept to admit and incorporate this fact; (c) his total involvement with the heroin culture. Lindesmith's theory strongly emphasizes the role played by cognitions at the time of addiction, and minimizes the existence of predisposing factors in the development of addiction. There is strong evidence for a position supporting the lack of importance of predisposing factors in three areas. First, studies (Berzins et al, 1974; Platt, 1975) on the personality of the addict have failed to demonstrate the existence of a single, unique, universal personality type associated with heroin addiction. Second, some of these studies suggest (Berzins et al, 1974; Ogborne, 1974) there may be subgroups of addicts, each using heroin for a different purpose. For example, on subgroup may use heroin to increase their levels of stimulation, while another may use it to narcotize themselves against such stimulation. Third, many studies, including the above, have consistently failed to demonstrate a specific type of psychopathology to be associated with heroin addiction.

The role played by cognitive processes in the development of addiction is also evident in the deviance theories of heroin addiction. These theories suggest that the addict initially was pursuing unrealistically high culturally induced goals, but because the legitimized means of access to such goals were blocked (Merton, 1957) a cognitive disparity developed. The addict then seeks alternative goals which will provide him with a sense of belonging and positive self-esteem. As Merton notes:

. . . aberrant behavior may be regarded . . . as a symptom of dissociation between culturally prescribed aspirations and socially structured avenues for realizing these aspirations. [p. 134]

While there is support in some of the findings for a position relating low socioeconomic status to heroin addiction (Winick, 1965), more recently the picture has changed. In addition to heroin users deriving from the lowest socioeconomic strata, a substantial proportion of addicts come from middle-class backgrounds (Chein et al, 1964; Lukoff et al, 1972). Furthermore, there is some suggestion that addicts are often better educated than nonaddicts from similar backgrounds (Bucky, 1971; Lukoff, Quatrone, and Sardell, 1972; Platt, Hoffman, and Ebert, 1976). One wonders if the failure of middle-class addicts to achieve culturally prescribed goals is also ascribable to limited societal or personal means for reaching them. Perhaps it might prove more productive to propose the existence of an additional subgroup of addicts. Certainly there are those addicts who, because of limited societal means, respond to blocked opportunities by engaging in alternatively satisfying behavior, that is, heroin abuse, as Merton proposes. However, it seems apparent that a second group of addicts exist who simply do not have the individual means required to meet their expectations and goals. It may be that both blocked societal opportunity and inability of the individual himself to take advantage of such opportunity where it exists, because of his inability to conceptualize the means of achieving satisfying goals, result in heroin abuse. There is some empirical evidence to support this hypothesis.

The major problem of Lindesmith's theory and the theory of social deviance is that while they both suggest that cognitive elements are important in the addiction process, neither specifies the nature of the individual cognitive processes involved in operational terms. One suggestion as to the nature of these cognitive processes comes from a study of a specific aspect of social cognition, interpersonal problem-solving thinking. Platt, Scura, and Hannon (1973) found that in contrast to an equivalent group of nonaddicts, addicts were less capable of conceptualizing the step-by-step means of reaching goals in real-life interpersonal problem situations. Furthermore, means-ends scores were unrelated to age, education, or intellectual level. This suggests that one possible reason that addicts are unable to achieve the valued goals in their lives may be that they are deficient in the ability to think through the specific steps involved in reaching their goals. Thus, at all socioeconomic levels, there are individuals who do not possess the cognitive means of reaching their goals. The particular salience of this deficiency is underlined by the frequent tendency of the addict to set unrealistically high, and therefore difficult, goals for himself. This view is similar to that proposed by Ausubel, who suggested that the addict is basically an inadequate individual, and this fact, combined with his setting of unattainable goals, guarantees his subsequent failure.

We propose that goal-setting is related to the socioeconomic level from which one starts and, given the economic realities of the past few years, some failure to reach prescribed goals probably exists at all societal levels. The person particularly at risk would seem to be the individual who (a) has even greater achievement potential than his peers, based upon his higher level of intellectual functioning or achievement in the educational setting, thus setting higher goals for himself, and (b) is deficient in his ability to think through the specific steps toward goal achievement. When faced with failure, his level of subjective distress will be even greater than would otherwise be the case. From this point on, the route described by Lindesmith and the deviance theorists in the development and maintenance of addiction would seem to be operative.

Also, it should be noted that there appears to be evidence in treatment evaluation research that when addicts have vocational and educational counselors who are able to assess accurately potential abilites of each addict, and who are then able to work out a plan of realistic goal expectation with the addict, such a joint effort most often results in a satisfactory outcome.

PERSONALITY AND PSYCHOPATHOLOGY IN HEROIN ADDICTS

The major conclusions to be drawn from studies of personality variables in heroin addicts is that there is little basis for assuming commonality of such traits among addicts. This is as true for such commonly observed traits as psychopathy as it is for more specific traits such as temporal perspective or locus of control. In fact some of the most contradictory results are found with respect to the latter personality traits. For example, Einstein (1965) reported addicts had greater future time perspective on one measure and less on another. Likewise, several studies have reported addicts have an internal locus of control (Berzins and Ross, 1973; Calicchia, 1974), while another (Obitz, Oziel, and Unmacht, 1973) found them to be more external. Platt (1975) found that an apparent difference, with the addicts more internally oriented in their locus of control, was lost when a statistical procedure was used to control for group differences in demography.

Based upon findings such as these, it is difficult to reach any conclusion other than that there is little commonality among addicts. Even where subgroups of addicts are identified (Berzins et al, 1974; Ogborne, 1974) the number of individuals classifiable into homogeneous subgroups is never great. In the Berzins et al (1974) study, for example, over 59.5% of the subjects could not be classified into the two major categories identified.

Perhaps rather than theorizing in terms of different preexisting personality types among addicts, it might be more profitable with respect to understanding addiction to focus on the different purposes served by use of the drug. Such purposes include (a) removing the addict from an environment with which he cannot cope, (b) decreasing subjective discomfort through reduction of unpleasant affect states (e.g., anxiety, depression) resulting from actual or perceived failure to cope with reality, (c) establishing or enhancing self-esteem through membership and acceptance in an esteemed peer group, (d) maintaining equilibrium through engaging in a full-time avocation—drug-seeking behavior, and (e) attempting to cope through the use of heroin as a crutch. Certainly there appears to be a subgroup of addicts who report that heroin merely functioned to make them feel "normal." Although there is little empirical support for the Dole and Nyswander hypothesis that a self-induced metabolic deficiency is at the basis of heroin addiction, this does not by any means eliminate methadone maintenance as a valid treatment modality. For those addicts for whom heroin represents an attempt to cope, a removal from conflict, or membership in a meaningful peer group, perhaps other therapeutic foci would prove more effective.

PERSONAL AND SOCIAL CHARACTERISTICS OF HEROIN ADDICTS

The evidence regarding the family backgrounds of addicts seems to suggest that the largest grouping of addicts comes from familial environments containing substantial pathology. These backgrounds tend to be characterized by frequent parental absence, and by minimal attention on the parents' part. Winick (1965) further characterizes the addict's background as containing a high level of mistrust, negativism, and defiance. Other forms of pathology, such as alcoholism and physical and psychiatric illness, are also common. Generally, families such as these are unable to provide the developing child with appropriate role models as well as the cognitive means for achieving such roleś, and thus cannot contribute to the development of healthy children.

Furthermore, even where the addict does share the normally valued roles of society, he usually does not possess both the cultural and personal means of attaining them. Merton (1957) made this point years ago when he describes the lower socioeconomic strata as having fewer opportunities to utilize socially prescribed routes. On the personal level, this type of addict is also unlikely to possess the interpersonal skills needed for successful attainment of goals (Platt, Scura, and Hannon, 1973). Thus, given the adoption of a set of values different from those of the larger society, the limited routes of access available for advancement, and the poor personal resources he possesses, the addict seems predestined to failure in reaching conventionally defined goals in our society.

As noted above, a different type of addict has been described in the literature. He tends to have a higher personal social competence level than comparable nonaddict groups, as reflected in higher levels of education and intelligence (Lukoff, Quatrone, and Sardell, 1972; Platt, Hoffman, and Ebert, 1976). This type of addict may also come from a higher socioeconomic level (Johnson, 1973). Rather than being deficient in the intellectual or educational skills required to reach his goals, this type of addict may be deficient in the personal skills he needs for success, or may be frustrated by economic realities. With increased expectations of ready access to culturally defined goals, such as a job, and status—developed on the basis of his high attainment relative to comparable nonaddicts—the addict's failure to reach these goals has a detrimental effect upon his self-esteem and he turns to heroin use to escape from the unpleasant subjective consequences and negative affect that result. A study by Platt and Spivack (1973) provides some support for this hypothesis. Substantially greater levels of anxiety and lower levels of self-esteem were found in young adults in whom there was a greater discrepancy between personal goals and perceived achievement in attaining them. Although this study has not been replicated with heroin addicts, there is no reason to believe that this might not also be the case.

TREATMENT FOR HEROIN ADDICTION

If the heroin addict is an individual who lacks the personal skills necessary to reach his desired goals, particularly when these goals are unrealistically high, one would expect that certain types of therapies would be more effective than others. Specifically, approaches emphasizing the attainment of skills appropriate to achieving or redefining goals might have a higher rate of successful outcome when such outcome is defined in terms of adjustment, productive behavior, and the replacement of addiction with alternative means of satisfaction. There is some support in the literature for this suggestion, despite the fact that an assessment of the literature relating to treatment of the heroin addict is confounded by many problems. While it is very difficult to make comparisons of effectiveness between therapeutic modalities, there do seem to be several specific findings which relate to the proposed explanations.

Essentially, although methadone maintenance has substantial retentive power and offers the addict an opportunity to rechannel his energies in a more productive direction by satisfying drug-craving, it does not have the therapeutic power originally anticipated. However, the effectiveness of maintenance becomes highly significant when supportive therapies are offered in conjunction with methadone. Although maintenance alone frees the addict from his preoccupation with securing a constant supply of heroin, it fails to offer direction and guidance on how to spend this sudden wealth of time and energy. Those methadone programs that attempt to remedy this by providing educational and vocational counseling in addition to group and individual therapy seem to enhance the potential for successful outcome, particularly in light of the retentive power of such programs. Certainly the addict himself is more likely to be retained in a program he perceives to be worthwhile and relevant and which differentially utilizes ancillary services such as vocational counseling. Perhaps the function of such supportive services is to provide the means for achieving newly defined goals. Educational and vocational counseling are particularly valuable in delineating the means, which are now more readily available, to achieve an alternatively satisfying life situation.

Similar results are obtained with antagonist therapy. Once again, administration of an antagonist alone neither ensures that an addict will remain in treatment nor that he will abstain from the use of illicit substances. Actually, in the absence of supportive therapies, the retentive power of the antagonist modalities is even weaker than that of many other programs.

There are certain therapies besides chemotherapy that have a number of common elements which seem to be somewhat effective in treating heroin addiction. Therapeutic communities reach a very small number of addicts, but are able to provide meaningful alternatives to addiction for participants. Essentially the structure of such programs is rigid and clearly outlined. As Glaser, Adler, Moffett, and Ball (1974) pointed out, "a therapeutic community program [is] one in which the social structure of the program itself [is] deliberately used as the primary therapeutic tool. . ." (p. 599). The therapeutic communities provide a clearly delineated hierarchy of goals, and the means by which these goals can be achieved are identically structured for every member of the community. Each member knows exactly what he must do to achieve status and responsibility which are desirable goals in the context of the group. Furthermore, he is provided with an esteemed peer group membership and a rigidly structured itinerary of daily activities, all of which have been proposed as salient dimensions in heroin addiction. However, in replacing individual goals with those of the group in a situation in which the former addict is removed from the outside community, he is unable to transfer his achievement to life in the outside community. A dependency has thus been established so that the former addict lacks confidence in his ability to make it on the outside. On the other hand, a therapeutic community such as Phoenix House, which prepares its members for a return to the outside community by providing them with the opportunity to acquire marketable skills (in terms of education and vocation), is significantly more effective in rehabilitating former addicts. In this case there is a congruence of valued goals between the group and the external community so that adaptation and reentry are facilitated.

Essentially the rational authority, reality therapies, behavioral therapy, and Guided Group Interaction (GGI)-oriented programs focus on similar ways of working though specific inabilities to cope. They all have in common an emphasis on recognizing the consequences of one's behavior and on defining ways in which one needs to change. Goals are clearly stated and examined, and discussion of responsible behaviors for achieving these goals plays a crucial role in the effectiveness of these therapies.

Perhaps the most promising new development of the last several years, however, has been the attempt to explain heroin addiction within a family-relational context. Perhaps more than any theory with the exception of Wikler's conditioning model, Stanton's model ties together what have heretofore been highly disparate findings of individual research studies, providing a number of readily desirable, testable hypotheses regarding intervention. It comes as no surprise to see recently published studies (O'Brien et al, 1975; 1977; Sideroff and Jarvik, 1980) which have provided empirical support for Wikler's theoretical approach at both the human and animal analogue levels.

The use of role models as a therapeutic tool may prove flexible enough to meet individual variations in deficiencies and needs. A wide variety of therapeutic programs use role models who demonstrate alternatively effective ways of coping to the addict—from the use of former addicts who are successful within the Synanon community to the psychotherapist who guides and exhibits "responsible concern." The choice of a particular role model which will be effective depends a great deal upon the specific deficiencies and needs of the addict. For those addicts who require marketable skills and for whom the heroin lifestyle served as an alternate to blocked goals, professionals in a variety of relevant fields may serve as role models. For those addicts requiring strong guidance and support in learning to cope with and to reenter the experience of life, and for whom heroin served to decrease stimulation in an escape, perhaps mental health professionals such as therapists might prove effective models. For those addicts for whom heroin served as a link with an esteemed peer group, the therapeutic community and the former addict as role model might be appropriate.

Irrespective of the particular therapeutic tools to be used, a treatment approach that emphasizes the acquisition of problem-solving skills appears likely to facilitate the rehabilitation of the former addict. If the factors outlined here should prove salient to understanding heroin addiction, then focusing on delineation of realistic goals and increasing the ability to conceptualize the means for achieving a satisfying alternative lifestyle would be an important component of the therapeutic process for the heroin addict. A recent study by the author and his associates (Platt, Morell, Flaherty, and Metzger, 1982) demonstrated the feasibility of teaching interpersonal cognitive problem-solving (ICPS) skills to methadone maintenance clients. Significant acquisition of skills took place and retention was demonstrated for at least a one year follow-up period. Greatest skill acquisition was found to take place among those clients who had entered the program with the lowest levels of interpersonal problem-solving skills and who thus could be identified as those clients with the lowest likelihood of successful outcome. In this regard, the importance of both interpersonal issues and coping skills in the rehabilitation of heroin addicts was underscored in another recent study. When methadone clients were asked to what they would attribute their past and future successful rehabilitation, they listed the following variables: (a) a supportive relationship, particularly with a drug-free individual, (b) a satisfying job, and (c) personal coping skills (Abrahams, 1979).

THE IMPACT OF HEROIN ADDICTION TREATMENT[1]

The major issue in heroin addiction treatment today may be said to be the assessment of treatment impact: the relationship between program participation and client change. A careful appraisal of this literature reveals several consistent sets of findings relating to the assessment of treatment impact: (a) some, although an unimpressive portion of the client population, is judged to be improved following treatment; (b) abstinence rates generally increase over time, not over the short course, but over a period of years; (c) there has been an inability to attribute improvement at follow-up to participation in specific elements of treatment; and (d) there is an absence of procedures and

[1] The author is indebted to David Metzger for his significant contribution to the presentation of the ideas contained in this section.

instrumentation necessary for the codification of client service involvement while in treatment.

Early Studies of Treatment Outcome

An early study by Hunt and Odoroff (1962) identified a pattern of rapid relapse after discharge. In this one year follow-up study of 1,912 New York City addicts discharged from the Public Health Service Hospital in Lexington, Kentucky, between 1952 and 1955, 90% of the subjects were readdicted within the study period. These results helped to develop an understanding of the "careers" of addicts by documenting a rapid rate of relapse immediately following discharge from treatment. A full 90% of those who "relapsed" did so within the first six months of discharge. A stratified subsample of these discharged patients was then selected and followed for five years. In reporting the results of this five year follow-up, Duvall, Locke, and Brill (1963) state that "although 97% became readdicted" during the study period, "by the fifth year after discharge 49% were abstinent, either voluntarily (25%) or involuntarily (24%)."

In 1966, Vaillant reported the results of his 12 year follow-up study of 100 New York City narcotics addicts. These subjects had been first treated at the U.S. Public Health Service Hospital in Lexington, Kentucky, between August 1, 1952 and January 31, 1953. Aside from the methodological problem of a non-random sample and the lack of control groups (which Vaillant himself identifies), the study found that within 10 years of the first treatment, only some 30% of the subjects had been able to maintain abstinence for a minimum of three years. The results of the Vaillant study mirror the findings of a follow-up conducted by O'Donnell (1964). In this long-term follow-up study of 266 white residents of Kentucky who had been treated at Lexington between 1935 and 1955, a high relapse rate was identified and associated with a low rate of addiction at any one point in time. Of those who were living, 81% had become readdicted after treatment; yet 41% were abstinent at the time of follow-up contact.

Langenauer and Bowden (1971) conducted a six month follow-up of 252 individuals discharged from Lexington between July 1968 and June 1969. These clients were monitored monthly in the community by aftercare counselors. Using an expanded range of dependent variables the study found that of those who remained in aftercare, 14% had not used opiates during the entire study period.

Together, these follow-up studies of NARA clients define an addiction-abstinence pattern. This pattern is characterized by an early return to narcotic addiction after discharge, followed by a gradual increase in abstinence rates. These findings support the "maturing out" theory presented by Winick

(1962), in which it was proposed that a major portion of the addict population become abstinent in their thirties, reflecting a correlation between age and abstinence.

Several studies were also able to define a relationship between enforced community supervision and abstinence. These results led Vaillant and Rasor (1966) to argue for an enforced parole program for "virtually the entire addict population." With greater frequency, the drug treatment community began to focus its attention upon the non-institutional post-discharge involvements of clients.

The NARA-based studies provided a foundation for understanding the power (or lack of it) of treatment. None of these studies was able to directly link abstinence with program involvement. At best they demonstrated that "hospital treatment can initiate rehabilitation but it must be completed after the patient returns to the community" (Hunt and Odoroff, 1962). A more pessimistic view is that treatment merely provides an opportunity to study the natural course of addiction but does nothing to alter it.

The absence of a link between treatment and rehabilitation in these studies reflects obvious design issues (see Chapter 11). These include the absence of a) control groups, b) random assignment, and c) treatment specification. The utilization of random assignment to treatment and non-treatment experimental conditions has long been viewed as the ideal approach for assessing treatment impact (Morell, 1977). Such random assignment to experimental and control conditions, however, has been almost consistently not implemented for both practical and ethical reasons (Simpson, 1981). This is true not only for early studies, but of the more recent ones as well. It is the job of treatment programs to provide the best possible services to individuals in need. Random assignment to no-treatment conditions is thus an unacceptable option. This, however, does not explain the absence of data defining the service involvement of clients while in treatment. In fact, the need for such specifications is intensified when experimental controls are not present.

Studies of Treatment Outcome Related to Process

The results of the NARA studies coincided with the awareness of the growing increase in the use of narcotics in the middle and late 1960s. The "heroin epidemic," as it has come to be known, demanded a large-scale systematic response to the treatment of addicts. This resulted in a rapid increase in the number of community-based drug treatment programs, particularly methadone maintenance.

This change in the nature of treatment programming was propelled by a number of studies which demonstrated a sharp reduction in crime among clients in treatment (DuPont, 1972; Brown et al., 1972). This was especially true of clients involved in methadone maintenance. The original work of Dole and Nyswander (1965) provided a foundation for a shift in focus among researchers from status after treatment to performance during treatment. With this focus upon success while in treatment, retention became a frequent outcome variable. Szapocznik and Ladner (1977), in reviewing over 50 studies of retention conducted during the late 1960s and early 1970s, concluded that neither client nor treatment variables alone can predict outcome (retention). They concluded, in arguing for an interactional model of treatment and treatment research, that "...research must address the issue of goodness of fit among treatment, program variables, client characteristics and expected outcome..."

The past 17 years have produced a large volume of research related to drug abuse and its treatment. However, the primary emphasis in the majority of reported studies on drug abuse rehabilitation is on the treatment procedure used. Callner (1975) reports that most studies provide detailed treatment descriptions and little else. The descriptions often omit critical information on the duration, sequence, timing, and actual procedure of the treatment, making replication of the treatment by another investigator nearly impossible. Furthermore, the impossibility of exact replication prohibits attempts to reproduce results. The inadequacy of most treatment descriptions thus retards both the improvement of rehabilitation procedures used and the advancement of our knowledge about the rehabilitation process (Morell, 1977).

There have been several important follow-up studies conducted since the late 1960s. Of particular interest are those studies conducted by Burt Associates and Sells and colleagues at the Institute of Behavioral Research. Both represent large-scale multi-site and multi-modality studies. Both projects included follow-up of individuals who had completed an intake procedure but had not participated in treatment. Although not a randomly selected control group, this provides a comparison group of similar individuals. The studies of the Drug Abuse Reporting Program (DARP) represent an important effort in the assessment of treatment programming. Established in 1968, the DARP data base incorporated admission information from 52 agencies throughout the United States and Puerto Rico. Collection of admission information began in June 1969 and continued to March 1973. Information on over 40,000 admissions to these federally supported programs was incorporated into the data base. One year follow-up evaluations, based upon samples of admission cohorts drawn from this data base, were conducted.

The DARP data suggest that at one year after treatment, those clients who participated in methadone maintenance, therapeutic community, and outpatient drug-free programs had "highly favorable outcomes" in 27%, 28%, and 24% of the cases respectively. For those clients who were treated in outpatient detoxification programs, 15% achieved highly favorable treatment outcomes, and for clients who were involved only in an intake interview, 14%

achieved this positive status (NIDA, 1981). These data suggest that for black and white males, at best, involvement in an intensive treatment program improves one year post-treatment recovery rates by 14% above that achieved by the intake only group. The DARP data have been the basis for a large amount of additional research and analysis. Yet, as Sells (1979) states,

although the DARP data in particular link post-treatment measures with participation in treatment, . . . they do not link outcomes with treatment process. (p. 115)

Similarly, the follow-up study conducted by Burt, Brown and DuPont (1980) utilized an equivalent no-treatment comparison group who had completed the intake process yet left treatment within five days. Follow-up interviews were conducted with 81% of the original sample. The results identified "full recovery rates" of 15% for methadone maintenance clients, 26% for clients who had spent the majority of their treatment experiences abstinent, and 26% for the intake only clients. The lack of difference in the rates of recovery between the treatment and no-treatment groups suggest that "treatment, whatever its humanitarian virtues, had no impact on client outcome" (Burt et al, 1980).

These studies are important in that they, like the NARA studies cited earlier, define change among a substantial portion of the client population. As each of the authors recognizes, however, their results cannot—and should not—be viewed as tests of treatment impact. This is due in large part to the absence of control groups. In spite of this design issue, the overall consistency of the findings is impressive. Equally impressive is the fact that when comparison groups are studied, they too show substantial change.

The questions regarding impact raised early in the development of drug abuse treatment remain unanswered. Knowing that client change takes place refines the question related to treatment effectiveness. The question is no longer: "Do clients change?" but "Which clients change and why?" And ultimately: "Is client change related to treatment?" It cannot be assumed that those clients who show improvement at follow-up do so as a result of their treatment involvement. "What is still at issue is not that change occurs, but rather the degree of change which can be attributed to the treatment process, and also which programs affect which individuals" (Jaffe, 1979).

One can conclude at this point that the use of intake only comparison groups of clients cannot alone bridge the gap between treatment participation and outcome status. This has led to a general awareness of the need for outcome evaluation to focus attention upon the assessment of the treatment process: "Do successful clients receive different services than those who do not achieve success?" Given the variability of client service involvement within treatment programs (Sells, 1979), the identification of a client's modality of treatment alone cannot be used to define his treatment process. In the conclusion of their study, Burt, Brown, and DuPont (1980) state:

Special attention should be paid to the treatment and how it effects treatment outcomes. The treatment process should not be considered as a "Black Box." Follow-up studies will be more useful if they investigate the various types of counseling and counselors, staffing patterns, vocational rehabilitation, etc. (p. 407)

Such specification of treatment process requires assessments of the full range of services which clients receive in treatment. Also, given that service involvement is variable over time, such assessments must be conducted at more than one point in time. The technology for conducting such assessments of the treatment process has not yet been developed. One cannot help but agree with Simpson (1981) who states:

...The specific attributes of treatment that facilitate favorable patient responses (as well as the relevant patient characteristics) have not been systematically examined either in clinical trials or field-based research. (p. 880)

CONCLUDING COMMENT

The above discussion suggests that what is needed is a means of classifying or typologizing clients and the treatment process. This would remediate a significant weakness of much of the past research on drug treatment outcome, a weakness which has hampered efforts to identify those specific features of service delivery that are encountered or experienced by clients in the achievement of their treatment goals. Using service involvement profiles, one may find that the service involvements of clients while in treatment do not relate to outcome. Regardless of the services received, clients may change in much the same way. In this case, one would conclude that outcome is independent of specific ingredients of the treatment process. On the other hand, one may find that positive treatment outcomes are much more likely among clients who involve themselves in similar services while in treatment, in which case one would conclude that a certain pattern of service involvement while in treatment is related to functioning during and after treatment.

To date, significant effort has been devoted to identifying personality and demographic characteristics of "treatment successes." These efforts have not produced a consistent profile of the clients most amenable to treatment. The clients most likely to succeed thus represent a heterogenous group. This finding has led a number of treatment observers to conclude that success is an interactional process, a reflection of a certain match of clients and programs. The interaction of clients and programs is the definition of treatment process which is best defined through the assessment of service involvement. While the specification of service involvement cannot compensate for the absence of random assignment to control conditions, relating impact to service involvement can provide evidence concerning the relative efficacy of treatment in relation to specified differential outcome.

APPENDIX

Scales Used Specifically in the Assessment and Study of Drug Addiction

A great variety of clinical scales have been used in the study of heroin addiction. Some of these scales have been widely used personality inventories such as the Minnesota Multiphasic Personality Inventory. Others have been developed specifically to fill a need for instruments sensitive to drug effects. It seems useful to provide the reader with a description of three scales referred to in the text that have been designed to measure specific aspects of drug (or heroin) addiction: the Addiction Research Center Inventory (ARCI) Scales, the Heroin Scale (He) of the MMPI, and the Himmelsbach Withdrawal Intensity Scale. It is neither possible nor appropriate to review all scales which have been used in the attempt to understand heroin addiction, or all the literature on each of these scales included here. The reader is referred to the original literature for a description of general personality inventories mentioned in the text, such as the Minnesota Multiphasic Personality Inventory (MMPI), the California Psychological Inventory (CPI), and the Rorschach.

THE ADDICTION RESEARCH CENTER INVENTORY (ARCI) SCALES

The ARCI is perhaps the most extensively used and widely studied scale that has been developed to assess drug effects and addiction status. There are well over 100 citations of studies utilizing this inventory in a variety of forms since its development at the Addiction Research Center at Lexington, Kentucky. While the inventory is comprised of a number of individual scales designed to measure specific drug effects and general pathology, only a few of the major scales can be reviewed appropriately in this section. Representative references have been provided in this appendix for readers desiring further information.

Test Development

The Addiction Research Center Inventory (ARCI) scales were originally developed to meet a need for measurement of subjective drug effects. Haertzen, Hill, and Belleville (1963) felt standard psychological inventories were inadequate in the assessment of drug action. In this regard, they comment:

They seem fairly efficient when the actions being tested simulate serious behavioral abnormalities, e.g., the similarity of effects of LSD-25 to some aspects of schizophrenia, but they are inadequate in detecting effects which characterize many other drugs. [Haertzen et al, 1963, p. 156]

The range of drug effects which Haertzen el al wished to measure included physical, emotive, cognitive, and subjective effects. Originally, a list of 200 incomplete sentences were administered to subjects under a variety of drug conditions: no drug, morphine, LSD-25, amphetamine, pentobarbital, chlorpromazine, and SKF-5390. Subjects were asked to complete the sentences according to how they felt on the day they were answering the questionnaire. This method of testing was abandoned very early, as it became clear that many of the responses were unintelligible or were duplicated under a variety of different drug conditions. Haertzen et al (1963) then tried an "alternative stem method" in which effects were contrasted, a paired comparisons method, and a ranking of the intensity of sensation.

Eventually, a 550-item true-false questionnaire to measure the subjective effects of drugs with a diversity of pharmacologic actions was developed. Subjects were asked to answer all items on the basis of how they felt on the day they took the drug and answered the questionnaire. Both oral and intravenous administrations were used in the 11 drug and placebo conditions with the exception of alcohol.

In an attempt to construct a scale of items which discriminated the placebo from each separate drug condition, the following types of data were gathered over a period of years: (*a*) cross-validation studies (100 Ss), (*b*) validity generalization studies (30 Ss), (*c*) retest studies (30 Ss), (*d*) alcohol studies, and (*e*) dose-effect studies. Responses under all drug conditions were compared with those under placebo condition on two separate groups of 50 subjects. Those items which discriminated at the 5% level in a chi-square design were retained in the questionnaire and were referred to as the Significant Scale (S-scale). Those items which discriminated at the 5% level on the group of 100 men (two groups of 50 combined) were added to the original items and are referred to as the Marginally Significant Scale (M-scale).

Validity

The validity of the ARCI was assessed by (*a*) a 23-item scale measuring carelessness, confusion, or illiteracy, (*b*) cross-validation on two groups of 50 men each, (*c*) analyses of variance for replicated measures under control and each drug condition, (*d*) analyses of variance for independent measures on the differences between the initial group and the retest group, and (*e*) analyses of variance for independent measures on the dose-effect data (Hill, Haertzen, Wolback, and Miner, 1963).

Reliability

Reliability was determined from product moment correlation coefficients between scale scores for placebo and no-drug conditions in the initial group, between placebo and drug conditions, and between drug conditions (Hill et al, 1963).

All ARCI scales were standardized on a sample of opiate addicts of average intelligence and not significantly different from the general population of addicts admitted to Lexington in 1959 (Hill et al, 1963; Haertzen, 1974; Haertzen, Hill, and Belleville, 1963).

Preliminary results indicated that certain items were differentially associated with certain drugs. For example, alcohol was associated with aggression, emotional lability, excitement, and problems with the law. Amphetamines were associated with items reflecting good judgment, energy, active intellect, many sexual and similar problems. Cocaine was associated with hallucinations, racing thoughts, the urge to do harm, restlessness, and fear. Barbiturates were associated with items reflecting "can't," for example, problems of concentration, memory, and lack of energy. Marijuana was associated with fun, social grouping, and energy. Morphine was associated with distrust, secretiveness, irritation, worry, and disappointment (Haertzen, Hill, and Belleville, 1963).

Items were then classified under five headings: general information, interests and drives, sensation and perception, bodily symptoms and processes, feelings and mood. The greatest changes in drug effects were observed on items relating to sensation, perception, anxiety and mood, bodily symptoms, and activity level, and the fewest changes were observed on items relating to personality characteristics, occupational interests, general attitudes, or philosophies of life. Some items were selected for inclusion in the 550-item ARCI that indicated the major disorders of personality, even though response to these items would not be altered by any drug condition. The majority of these items were related to psychopathy, which appears to be characteristic of a significant proportion of the narcotic addict population in the United States (Haertzen and Panton, 1967).

The original 3300 items were reduced to 550, with a representative content for each of the five categories outlined above. The 550 items were selected with regard to sensitivity to drug effects. As Haertzen, Hill, and Belleville (1963) note ". . . each judge sorted all items with regard to representativeness of content . . . , probable sensitivity to drug effects (both specific and non-specific), and content which might simulate some of the more common behavioral abnormalities" (p. 163). In total, there are 30 items on the validity scale either repeated exactly or in their negative form, 40 items from the MMPI, and 510 original items. The average ARCI question is just above the third grade level of reading difficulty with the majority of items below that of the sixth grade. Furthermore, the test print is very large to ensure its usefulness for persons of moderate vision impairment.

The ARCI Scales

The ARCI may be administered in two forms: the subject either responds according to how he feels when actually answering the questionnaire or how he feels (or imagines himself to feel) when under some specified state. There are also a number of short forms which can be used to distinguish specific drug effects: for example, the LSD scale can be used to assess psychotomimetic effects, the PCAG scale to evaluate sedative effects, and the MBG scale to calculate euphoric effects, or they can be used to determine the potency of a given drug. However, Haertzen (1974) cautions against the exclusive use of the short forms because they are restricted and contain no validity items. Several specific sets of scales are described below.

The Empirical Drug Scales

The empirical drug scales consist of seven specific drug scales, including those for morphine (M), amphetamine (B), pentobarbital (P), lysergic acid diethylamide (L), pyrahexyl compound (Py), chlorpromazine (C), and alcohol (A), each reflecting changes in motivation, mood, sensation, perception, and along the "activity-sedation" continuum and the "euphoria-dysphoria" continuum. These scales were developed by comparing responses under each drug condition with the responses under placebo and control, and selecting those items which differentiated conditions at the 5% level. With respect to morphine, positive responses to the questions were most specific: "I have a pleasant feeling in my stomach," "I feel as if I would be more popular with people today," "I feel so good that I know other people can feel it," "My nose itches," "My speech is not as loud as usual" (Hill et al, 1963, p. 179). All drugs produce some elevation on each of the scales with these nonspecific drug effects in the direction of impaired functioning. The empirical scales appear to differentiate between placebo and all drug conditions but not between specific drug conditions. Hill et al (1963) note:

Judging from the results obtained to date with the ARC Inventory, it is quite apparent that considered individually very few of the subjective changes measured are unique for any of the drugs studied. On the other hand, it is quite clear that viewed as a spectrum of concurrent changes, subjective effects of drugs do exhibit a high degree of 'pattern specificity.' [p. 182]

Other ARCI Scales

Other groups of scales on the ARCI include the following: (a) the Group Variability scales, intended to isolate patterns of responses associated with morphine at a dose level of 20 mg, pentobarbital, chlorpromazine, LSD, amphetamine, pyrahexyl, or alcohol (Haertzen, 1966, 1974); (b) the Drug Correction scales, which, together with the Group Variability scales, help to differentiate different drug conditions (Haertzen, 1966, 1974); (c) the General Drug Predictor scale (Haertzen, 1974); (d) the General Drug Effect scale (Haertzen, 1965, 1974); (e) the Carelessness scale, devised to assess reliability in terms of response consistency; and the Opiate Withdrawal scale (Haertzen, Hill, and Belleville, 1963).

The Opiate Withdrawal Scale

The opiate withdrawal scale was developed by having former addicts estimate their feelings of withdrawal. A chi-square analysis was done on the responses of those subjects who were still experiencing withdrawal effects after the acute stage and those who were not. Those items on the ARCI which differentiated the two groups at the 0.05 level were combined in the long form of the opiate withdrawal scale (OPWL), and those differentiating at the 0.01 level were combined in the short form (OPW). The opiate withdrawal scale reflects the subject's reactivity, general discomfort, and feelings of physical distress. However, Haertzen and Meketon (1968) note that some proportion of the scale score is a reflection of general reaction tendencies independent of withdrawal, such as hostility and over-reactions to stress. There is also an alcohol withdrawal scale and a chronic opiate scale.

Conclusions

Haertzen, Hill, and Belleville (1963) comment that preliminary results with the ARCI suggest that morphine effects simulate the lack of concern and social disregard characteristic of the psychopathic individual. However, in general the ARCI is ". . . effective in differentiating various subjective effects of drugs and in discriminating some similarities and differences of naturally occurring and experimentally induced behavioral abnormalities" (Haertzen et al, 1963, p. 165).

THE HEROIN SCALE (HE) OF THE MINNESOTA MULTIPHASIC PERSONALITY INVENTORY

A number of modifications of the MMPI have been developed for restricted use in identifying specific target populations. Among these has been the development of a 57-item Heroin scale (He) by Cavior, Kurtzberg, and Lipton (1967). In developing the He scale, the responses to the 566 MMPI items of 63 incarcerated heroin addicts were compared with those of nonaddict prisoners. The heroin addicts had all used heroin daily for a minimum period of 1 year, had undergone detoxification, and had then returned to drug use. Fifty-seven items of the MMPI successfully discriminated the addict sample from the nonaddict inmates beyond the .001 level of significance, with the mean He score for the addict sample being 39.16 and for the nonaddict inmates 27.43 (Cavior et al, 1967). Further, Cavior et al (1967) found the He scores were not significantly correlated with length of time on heroin, the amount of heroin used, or with the age of onset of addiction. They therefore concluded that the response-differences evidenced by the two samples were not derivative of drug use itself. When an attempt was made to use the He scale with a cutoff score of 36 to identify a population of 160 addicts, Cavior et al (1967) were able to identify correctly 75% of the adult addicts and 67% of the adolescent addicts.

Sheppard, Ricca, Fracchia, Rosenberg, and Merlis (1972) attempted to cross-validate and extend the use of the He scale with a larger sample of male heroin addicts ($N = 274$) than that from which the original scale was derived. In addition, the authors investigated the ability of the He scale to discriminate between alcoholics and addicts relative to the addictive personality hypothesis. Results indicated that the sample of heroin addicts scored significantly higher than the nonaddict sample, thus supporting the earlier studies. Further, there were significant differences between the addict sample and two samples of alcoholic patients, with the heroin addicts scoring significantly higher on the He scale. Sheppard et al (1972) suggest that, in light of their data, there may not be a common personality "type" underlying addiction to both alcohol and narcotics. However, Sheppard et al (1972) found racial and ethnic differences in responses to the He scale and suggested that the items need additional refinement.

A study by Kranitz (1972) suggests, however, that the He scale needs further refinement not only relative to racial and ethnic differences. Three groups of subjects were compared on the He scale: heroin addicts, hospitalized alcoholics, and hospitalized nonalcoholics. While significant differences in scores were obtained in the expected direction, further investigation revealed that use of the suggested cutoff score of 36 (Cavior et al, 1967) incorrectly identified 59% of the heroin addict sample. The scale was much more powerful in classifying 80% of the alcoholics correctly as negatives, and in correctly classifying as valid negatives 96% of the nonalcoholics. Kranitz (1972) notes: "This failure in discriminating the target group (i.e., heroin addicts) reiterates the necessity for cross-validation of psychometric devices on independent groups from the original sample" (p. 717). Kranitz (1972) further comments that knowledge of base rates of heroin addiction in the population under study is essential because use of the He scale alone may represent a loss of efficiency in identification. He cautions:

. . . before making *either* clinical or research predictions based on psychometric instruments such as a Heroin Scale, we must be aware of the seemingly high rate of predictability that can be achieved by any instrument that is cross-validated on the same criterion group from which it was derived. [p. 719]

However, it is interesting to note that Sheppard et al (1972) offer a clinical picture of the heroin addict determined from a content analysis of the He scale. The addict is generally depressed, lacking meaningful goals and a sense of adequacy. Religious conflict is prevalent. "Family interactions can be characterized as marked with tension, irritability, resentment toward parents and siblings, and a general lack of support from family members" (Sheppard et al, 1972, p. 267). Peer-group membership is extremely important and the need to conform to peer pressure is strong. Addicts also appear to be strongly rebellious toward authority. In general, the picture of the heroin addict gleaned from the He scale appears to be fairly consistent with that which can be assessed from the literature.

Finally, in a cross-validation study of the He scale of the MMPI, Parr, Woodward, Rabinowitz, and Penk (1981) failed to differentiate heroin users ($N=336$) from polydrug abusers ($N=179$). Furthermore, white heroin users scored higher than black heroin users. These findings persisted even when potentially confounding covariates such as age, education, socioeconomic status and admission status were controlled for. The authors concluded that the scale showed promise for differentiating compulsive users of prescribed drugs generally, but not heroin users specifically, and that additional refinement was necessary.

THE HIMMELSBACH WITHDRAWAL SCALE

At the time Himmelsbach was conducting his studies of morphine addiction there was no adequate method of quantifying the severity of withdrawal from opiates. Certainly the existence of such a procedure would simplify comparisons between drugs of abuse potential and addiction liability and would also facilitate investigations of morphine addiction and treatment. The fairly straightforward scale based on the presence of specific objective symptoms of withdrawal is still in use over 40 years later in studies of antagonists and addicting drugs.

Kolb and Himmelsbach (1938) suggest that three examinations be made daily for the presence or absence of the following abstinence signs: yawning, lacrimation, rhinorrhea, perspiration, anorexia (40% decrease in caloric intake), dilated pupils, tremor, gooseflesh, restlessness, and emesis. In addition, blood pressure, weight, and temperature should be taken 1 to 3 times daily. The daily intensity of abstinence is then determined by scoring the increases in fever, hyperpnea, and blood pressure over addiction means. The average is taken for temperature and respiratory rate daily and weight loss is calculated from prewithdrawal levels. Himmelsbach (1938, 1941) assigned the following numerical values for the above symptoms: fever, 1 point for each $0.1°C$. increase; hyperpnea, 1 point for each increase in respiration per minute; systolic blood pressure, 1 point for each 2 mm increase; and weight, 1 point for each pound loss. Since the remaining symptoms cannot be accurately measured, they are scored only as being present. For example, 1 point is scored for the observation of each of the following signs: yawning, lacrimation, rhinorrhea, and perspiration; 3 points are scored for the presence of each of the following signs: anorexia, gooseflesh, dilated pupils, and tremors. Signs of restlessness are scored 5 points for their presence on any one day, while the presence of emesis receives 5 points for each time it is observed. The daily intensity of withdrawal is then calculated by summation of all points scored.

THE ADDICTION SEVERITY INDEX (ASI)

The Addiction Severity Index (ASI) was recently introduced to fill a need in the field of substance abuse for a normally valid system which could be used to assist in classifying the patient population. Noting the need for such an instrument to add focus to both research efforts and the effectiveness of treatment, McLellan, Luborsky, Woody, and O'Brien (1980) introduced the ASI "to fill the need for a reliable, valid, and standardized diagnostic instrument in the field of alcohol and drug abuse." (p. 26)

The Addiction Severity Index is based upon a view of addiction "as a unitary treatment problem manifested by a psychophysiological dependence upon a particular chemical agent" (p. 26). Acceptance of such a definition thus allows adequate description of the problem by means of "symptoms of amount, duration and frequency of chemical use." (p. 26). Its development was also aimed at meeting inadequacies of content or format and other problems in existing instruments.

The ASI itself considers addiction within the context provided by treatment problems related to substance abuse, both of a predisposing and a consequential nature. Its use results in a problem severity profile of the client, using six general areas relating to treatment problems: (a) chemical abuse, (b) medical, (c) psychological, (d) legal, (e) family/social, and (f) employment/support. *Severity* in any area is defined as "need for additional treatment." The use of the ASI involves the collection of (a) objective data in each of the six areas cited, as well as (b) the patient's judgment of severity of each problem area over the past 30 days. An unanchored scale from zero to nine is used to obtain severity estimates. McLellan et al (1980) report that the ASI may be administered by a trained technician in an average time of 25 to 30 minutes.

Validity and Reliability

Reported validity data for each scale is limited to correlations of scale scores with "other independent items having clear relationships to the particular problem area." While reported correlations are moderately high, the authors themselves note that their data "are only indicative of presumptive or face validity," and that they are pursuing a strategy of seeking measures of convergent validity. More data is presented with respect to reliability, which was initially found to be quite high, and a careful analysis resulted in the conclusion that the methodology used to analyze a patient's total condition by severity of his component problems was "reasonable."

Noting the early stage of development of the ASI, McLellan et al (1980) were quite encouraged by their preliminary findings as supporting its potential utility for the purpose for which it was developed. This purpose, analysis of "the total addiction profile into its component treatment problems," and the reliable and valid estimate of the severity of each of these problems, may indeed be met by the ASI, although the need for substantial additional test development is very clear.

REFERENCES

Abel, E. L. *Drugs and behavior: A primer in neuropsychopharmacology.* New York: Wiley, 1974.

Abeles, H., Plew, R., Landeutscher, I., and Rosenthal, H. M. Multiple-drug addiction in New York City in a selected population group. *Public Health Reports,* 1966, **81,** 685-690.

Abelson, H. I., Fishburne, P. M., and Cisin, I. *National survey on drug abuse: 1977.* Rockville, MD: National Institute on Drug Abuse, 1977.

Abrahams, J. L. Methadone maintenance patients' self-perceived factors responsible for successful rehabilitation. *International Journal of the Addictions,* 1979, **14,** 1075-1081.

Adler, P. T. and Lotecka, L. Drug use among high school students: Patterns and correlates. *International Journal of the Addictions,* 1973, **8,** 537-548.

Alexander, B. K. and Hadaway, P. F. Opiate addiction: The case for an adaptive orientation. *Psychological Bulletin,* 1982, **92,** 367-381.

Alksne, H., Lieberman, L., and Brill, L. A conceptual model of the life cycle of addiction. *International Journal of the Addictions,* 1967, **2,** 221-240.

American Institute of Public Opinion. Study Number 862. Cited in M. J. Hindelang, C. S. Dunn, L. P. Sutton and A. L. Aumick. *Sourcebook of criminal justice statistics, 1973.* Washington, D.C.: United States Department of Justice, 1973.

American Institute of Public Opinion. Special Drug Study, 1971. Cited in M. J. Hindelang, C. S. Dunn, L. P., Sutton and A. L. Aumick. *Sourcebook of criminal justice statistics, 1973.* Washington, D.C.: United States Department of Justice, 1973.

Angle, H. V. and Parwatikar, S. Methadone self-prescription by heroin addicts in an inpatient detoxification program. *Psychological Record,* 1973, **23,** 209-214.

Anglin, M. D., McGlothlin, W. H., and Speckart, G. The effect of parole on methadone patient behavior. *American Journal of Drug and Alcohol Abuse,* 1981, **8,** 153-170.

Anonymous. History of heroin. *Bulletin on Narcotics,* 1953, **5,** 3-16.

Archer, S. Historical perspective on the chemistry and development of naltrexone. *National Institute of Drug Abuse: Research Monograph Series,* 1981, **28,** 3-10.

Aronow, R., Paul, S. D., and Woolley, P. V. Childhood poisoning: An unfortunate consequence of methadone availability. *Journal of the American Medical Association,* 1972, **219,** 321-324.

Asher, H. Are methadone patients overprotected? *American Journal of Psychiatry,* 1973, **130,** 1041-1042.

Atkinson, C. A. and Crowley, T. J. A comparison of urine collection schedules with different predictability in a methadone clinic. In L. S. Harris (Ed.), *Problems of Drug Dependence*, 1981 (NIDA Research Monograph #41). Washington, D.C.: U.S. Government Printing Office, 1982. Pp. 460-465.

Ausubel, D. P. *Drug addiction: Physiological, psychological, and sociological aspects.* New York: Random House, 1958; 1964.

Ausubel, D. P. Causes and types of narcotic addiction: A psychosocial view. *Psychiatric Quarterly*, 1961, **35**, 523-531.

Axelrod, J. Cellular adaptation in the development of tolerance to drugs. In A. Wikler (Ed.), *The addictive states.* Baltimore: Williams and Wilkins, 1968. Pp. 247-264.

Babst, D. V., Chambers, C. D., and Warner, A. Patient characteristics associated with retention in a methadone maintenance program. *British Journal of Addiction*, 1971, **66**, 195-204.

Baden, M. M. Methadone related deaths in New York City. *International Journal of the Addictions*, 1970, **5**, 489-498.

Baden, M. M. *Pathology of the addictive states.* In R. W. Richter (Ed.), *Medical aspects of drug abuse.* Hagerstown, Md.: Harper and Row, 1975. Pp. 189-211.

Baer, D. J. and Corroda, J. Age of initial drug use and subsequent preference for other drugs. *Psychological Reports*, 1973, **32**, 936.

Baer, D. J. and Corrado, J. Heroin addict relationships with parents during childhood and early adolescent years. *Journal of Genetic Psychology*, 1974, **124**, 99-103.

Baganz, P. C. and Maddox, J. F. Employment status of narcotic addicts one year after hospital discharge. *Public Health Reports*, 1965, **80**, 615-621.

Bailey, W. C. Addicts on parole: Short term and long term prognosis. *International Journal of the Addictions*, 1975, **10**, 423-437.

Bale, R. N. Outcome research in therapeutic communities for drug abusers: A critical review 1963-1975. *International Journal of the Addictions*, 1979, **14**, 1053-1074.

Bale, R. N., Van Stone, W. W., Engelsing, T. M., and Zarcone, V. P., Jr. The validity of self-reported heroin use. *International Journal of the Addictions*, 1981, **16**, 1387-1398.

Ball, J. C. Two patterns of narcotic drug addiction in the United States. *Journal of Criminal Law, Criminology and Police Science*, 1965, **56**, 203-211.

Ball, J. C. Marijuana smoking and the onset of heroin use. In J. O. Cole and J. R. Wittenborn (Eds.), *Drug abuse: Social and psychopharmacologic aspects.* Springfield, Ill: Charles C. Thomas, 1966. Pp. 117-128.

Ball, J. C. and Bates, W. M. Nativity, parentage and mobility of opiate addicts. In *The epidemiology of opiate addiction in the United States.* Springfield, Ill.: Charles C. Thomas, 1970. Pp. 95-111.

Ball, J. C. and Chambers, C. D. (Eds.), *The epidemiology of opiate addiction in the United States*, Springfield, Ill.: Charles C. Thomas, 1970.

Ball, J. C., Chambers, C. D., and Ball, M. J. The association of marijuana smoking with opiate addiction. *Journal of Criminology and Police Science*, 1968, **59**, 171-182.

Ball, J. C., Thompson, W. O., and Allen, D. M. Readmission rates at Lexington Hospital for 43,215 narcotic drug addicts. *Public Health Reports*. 1970, **85**, 610-616.

Ball, J. C. and Urbatis, J. C. Absence of major medical complications among chronic opiate addicts. *British Journal of Addiction*, 1970, **65**, 109-112.

Barton, W. I. Drug histories and criminality of inmates of local jails in the United States (1978): Implications for treatment and rehabilitation of the drug abuser in a jail setting. *International Journal of the Addictions*, 1981, **17**, 417-444.

Bass, M. B., Friedman, H. J., and Lester, D. Antagonism of naloxone hyperalgesia by ethanol. *Life Sciences*, 1978, **22**, 1939-1946.

Bass, U. F., Brown, B. S., and Barry, S. Methadone maintenance and methadone detoxification: A comparison of retention rates and client characteristics. *International Journal of the Addictions*, 1973, **8**, 889-895.

Bass, U. F., III, and Woodward, J. A. *Skills training and employment for ex-addicts in Washington, D.C.: A report on TREAT* (Services Research Report). Rockville, MD: National Institute on Drug Abuse, 1978.

Bazell, R. J. Drug abuse: Methadone becomes the solution and the problem. *Science*, 1973, **179**, 772-775.

Beckett, A. H., and Casy, A. F. Synthetic analgesics: Stereochemical considerations. *Journal of Pharmacy and Pharmacology*. 1954, **6**, 986-999.

Beckett, H. D. and Lodge, K. J. Aspects of social relationships in heroin addicts admitted for treatment. *Bulletin on Narcotics*, 1971, **23**, 29-36.

Beggan, A. G. Malignant malaria associated with administration of heroin intravenously. *Transactions of the Royal Society of Tropical Medicine and Hygiene*, 1929, **23**, 147-155.

Beigel, A. and Bower, W. H. A classification of programs for drug abuse and drug addiction, *Journal of Drug Issues*, 1972, **2**, 65-72.

Bejerot, N. *Addiction: An artificially induced drive.* Springfield, Ill: Charles C. Thomas, 1972.

Bender, L. Drug addiction in adolescence. *Comprehensive Psychiatry*, 1963, **4**, 131-134.

Benvenuto, J. and Bourne, P. The Federal Polydrug Abuse Project: Initial report. *Journal of Psychedelic Drugs*, 1975, **7**, 115-120.

Berger, F. M. and Porterfield, J. Drug abuse and society. In J. Wittenborn (Ed.), *Drugs and youth.* Springfield, Ill.: Charles C. Thomas, 1969.

Berger, H. and Schwegler, J. J. Voluntary detoxification of patients on methadone maintenance. *International Journal of the Addictions.* 1973, **8**, 1043-1047.

Berger, P. A., Watson, S. J., and Akil, H. Beta-endorphin and schizophrenia. *Archives of General Psychiatry*, 1980, **37**, 635-640.

Berle, B. and Lowinson, J. Comparative study of three groups of patients at the Brown State Hospital Methadone Maintenance Program. In *Proceedings of the Third National Conference on Methadone Treatment.* Washington D.C.: U.S. Government Printing Office, 1970.

Berzins, J. I. and Ross, W. F. Locus of control among opiate addicts. *Journal of Consulting and Clinical Psychology.* 1973, **40**, 84-91.

Berzins, J. I., Ross, W. F., English, G. E., and Haley, J. V. Subgroups among opiate addicts—Typological investigation. *Journal of Abnormal Psychology*, 1974, **83**, 65-73.

Berzins, J. I., Ross, W. F., and Monroe, J. J. Crossvalidation of the Hill-Monroe acceptability for psychotherapy scale for addict males. *Journal of Clinical Psychology*, 1970, **26**, 199-201.

Berzins, J. I., Ross, W. F., and Monroe, J. J. A multivariate study of the personality of hospitalized narcotic addicts on the MMPI. *Journal of Clinical Psychology*, 1971, **27**, 174-181.

Bess, B., Janus, S., and Rifkin, A. Factors in successful narcotics renunciation. *American Journal of Psychiatry*, 1972, **128**, 861-865.

Bewley, T. H. and Ben-Arie, O. Morbidity and mortality from heroin dependence, II: Study of 100 consecutive patients. *British Medical Journal*, 1968 1, 727-730.

Bewley, T. H., Ben-Arie, O., and James, I. P. Morbidity and mortality from heroin dependence: I. Survey of heroin addicts known to the Home Office. *British Medical Journal*, 1968, 1, 725-732.

Biase, D. V. Who comes for drug rehabilitation: A comparison of two groups of adult addicts and abusers. In J. M. Singh, L. Miller and H. Lal (Eds.), *Drug addiction: Clinical and socio-legal aspects* (Vol. 2). Mount Kisco, New York: Futura, 1972. Pp. 133-136.

Bick, R. L. and Anhalt, J. E. Malaria transmission among narcotic addicts: A report of 10 cases and review of the literature. *California Medicine*, 1971, **115**, 56-58.

Biggam, A. G. Malignant malaria associated with the administration of heroin intravenously. *Transactions of the Royal Society of Tropical Medicine and Hygiene*, 1929, **23**, 147-155.

Blachly, P. H., Casey, D., Marcel, L. J., and Denney, D. D. A model for study of the treatment of the opiate abstinence syndrome. In E. Senay, V. Shorty and H. Alksne (Eds.), *Developments in the Field of Drug Abuse: Proceedings of the National Association for the Prevention of Addiction to Narcotics* (1974). Cambridge, MA: Schenkman, 1975. Pp. 327-335.

Blaine, J. D., Levine, G. L., Whysner, J. A., and Renault, P. F. Clinical use of LAAM. Paper presented at Conference on Recent Developments on Chemotherapy of Narcotic Addiction. Washington, D.C., November, 1977.

Bloch, H. A. and Geis, G. *Man, crime and society*. New York: Random House, 1965.

Blum, K., Hamilton, M. G., Hirst, M., and Wallace, J. C. Putative role of isoquinoline alkaloids in alcoholism: A link to opiates. *Alcoholism*, 1978, **2**, 113-120.

Blumberg, A. G. Covert drug abuse among voluntary hospitalized psychiatric patients. *Journal of the American Medical Association*, 1971, **217**, 1659-1661.

Blumberg, H. H., Cohen, S. D., Dronfield, B. F., Mordecai, E. A., Roberts, J. C. and Hawks, D. British opiate users: I. People approaching London treatment centres. *International Journal of the Addictions*, 1974(a), **9**, 1-23.

Blumberg, H., Cohen, S. D., Dronfield, B. E., Mordecai, E. A., Roberts, J. C., and Hawks, D. British opiate users: II. Differences between those given an opiate script and those not given one. *International Journal of the Addictions*, 1974(b), **9**, 205-220.

Blumberg, H. and Dayton, H. B. Narcotic antagonist studies with EN-1639A (*N*-cyclopropylnoroxymorphone hydrochloride). In *Fifth International Congress of Pharmacology*, Abstracts of volunteer papers, 1972, **23**.

Blumberg, H., Dayton, H. B. and Wolf, P. S. Analgesic and narcotic antagonist properties of noroxymorphone derivatives. *Toxicology and Applied Pharmacology*, *1967*, **10**, 406 (abstract).

Board of Directors, National Council on Crime and Delinquency. Drug addiction: A medical, not a law enforcement, problem. *Crime and Delinquency*, 1974, **20**, 4-9.

Bourne, P. G. The treatment of narcotics addiction in Georgia. *Journal of the Medical Association of Georgia*, 1972, **61**, 343-346.

Bourne, P. G. (Ed.) *Addiction*. New York: Academic Press, 1974.

Bourne, P. J. Issues in addiction. In P. J. Bourne (Ed.), *Addiction*. New York: Academic Press, 1974. Pp. 1-19.

Bowden, C. Determinants of initial use of opioids. *Comprehensive Psychiatry*, 1971, **12**, 136-140.

Bowden, C. L. and Langenauer, B. J. Success and failure in the NARA addiction program. *American Journal of Psychiatry*, 1972, **128**, 853-856.

Bowden, C. L. and Maddox, J. F. Methadone maintenance: Myth and reality. *American Journal of Psychiatry*, 1972, **129**, 435-439.

Bratter, T. E. Group therapy of affluent, alienated, adolescent drug abusers: A reality therapy and confrontation approach. *Psychotherapy: Theory, Research and Practice*, 1972, **9**, 308-313.

Bratter, T. E. Treating alienated, unmotivated, drug abusing adolescents. *American Journal of Psychotherapy*, 1973, **27**, 585-598.

Brecher, E. M. *Licit and illicit drugs*. Boston: Little, Brown, 1972.

Brehm, M. L. and Back, K. W. Self image and attitudes toward drugs. *Journal of Personality*, 1968, **36**, 299-314.

Brill, L. and Jaffe, J. H. The relevancy of some newer American treatment approaches for England. *British Journal of Addiction*, 1967, **62**, 375-386.

Brown, B. S., and Asherly, R. S. Aftercare in drug abuse programming. In R.I. Du-Pont, A. Goldstein, and J. O'Donnell (Eds.). *Handbook on drug abuse*. Washington, D.C. National Institute on Drug Abuse, 1979. Pp. 165-173.

Brown, B. S., DuPont, R. L., Bass, U. F., III, Brewster, G. W., Glendinning, S. T., Kozel, N. J., and Meyers, M. D. Impact of a large-scale narcotics treatment program: A six month experience. *International Journal of the Addictions*, *1973*, **8**, 49-57.

Brown, B. S., DuPont, R. L., Bass, U. F., III, Glendinning, S. T., Kozel, N. J., and Meyers, M. B. Impact of a multimodality treatment program for heroin addicts. *Comprehensive Psychiatry*, 1972, **13**, 391-397.

Brown, B. S., Guavey, S. K., Meyers, M. B., and Stark, S. D. In their own words, addicts' reasons for initiating and withdrawing from heroin. *International Journal of the Addictions*, 1971, **6**, 635-645.

Brown, B. S., Jackson, C. S., and Bass, U. F., III. Methadone and abstinent clients in group counseling sessions. *International Journal of the Addictions*, 1973, **8**, 309-316.

Brown, B. S., Jansen, D. R., and Bass, U. F., III. Staff attitudes and conflict regarding the use of methadone in the treatment of heroin addiction. *American Journal of Psychiatry*, 1974, **131**, 215-219.

Brown, B. S., Watters, J. K., and Iglehart, A. S. Methadone maintenance dosage levels and program retention. *American Journal of Drug and Alcohol Abuse*, 1983, **9**, 129-139.

Brown, G. F. and Silverman, L. P. The retail price of heroin: Estimation and applications. *Journal of the American Statistical Association*, 1974, **69**, 595-606.

Brown, R. R. Drug addiction in its relation to extroversion, ambiversion and introversion. *Journal of Applied Psychology*, 1935, **19**, 555-563.

Brown, R. R. The relation of body build to drug addiction. *Public Health Reports*, 1940, **55**, 1954-1963.

Brown, R. R. and Partington, J. E. The intelligence of the narcotic drug addict. *Journal of General Psychology* 1942(a), **26**, 175-179.

Brown, R. R. and Partington, J. E. A psychometric comparison of narcotic addicts with hospital attendants. *Journal of General Psychology*, 1942(b), **27**, 71-79.

Brown, T. *The enigma of drug addiction*. Springfield, Ill.: Charles C. Thomas, 1961.

Bruhn, P. and Maage, N. Intellectual and neuropsychological functions in young men with heavy and long-term patterns of drug abuse. *American Journal of Psychiatry*, 1975, **132**, 397-401.

Brust, J. C. M. and Richter, R. W. Quinine amblyopia related to heroin addiction. *Annals of Internal Medicine*, 1971, **74**, 84-86.

Buckman, J. Psychology of drug abuse. *Medical College of Virginia Quarterly*, 1971, **7**, 98-102.

Bucky, S. F. The relationship between past background and drug use. *Naval aerospace medical research report 1135*. Pensacola, Fla.: Naval Aerospace Medical Research Laboratory, 1971.

Bucky, S. F. The relationship between background and extent of heroin use. *American Journal of Psychiatry*, 1973, **130**, 709-710.

Burt and Associates, Inc. *Drug treatment in New York City and Washington, D.C. Follow-up Studies* (Services Research Monograph Series, DHEW Publication No. ADM 77-506). Washington, D.C.: National Institute on Drug Abuse, 1977.

Burt, M. R., Brown, B. S., and DuPont, R. L. Follow-up of former clients of a large mutimodality drug treatment program. *The International Journal of the Addictions*, 1980, **15**, 391-408.

Burton, J. F., Zawadzki, E. S., Weatherbell, H. R., and Moy, T. W. Mainliners and blue velvet. *Journal of Forensic Sciences*, 1965, **10**, 466-472.

Calicchia, J. P. Narcotic addiction and perceived locus of control. *Journal of Clinical Psychology*, 1974, **30**, 499-504.

Callahan, E. J., Price, K., and Dahlkoetter, J. Drug abuse. In R. J. Daitzman, (Ed.), *Clinical behavior therapy and behavior modification* (Vol. 1). New York: Garland STPM Press, 1980. Pp. 175-248.

Callahan, E. J., Rawson, R. A., McCleave, B., Arias, R., Glazer, M., and Liberman, R. P. The treatment of heroin addiction: Naltrexone alone and with behavior therapy. *International Journal of the Addictions*, 1980, **15**, 795-807.

Callner, D. A. Behavioral treatment approaches to drug abuse: A critical review of the research. *Psychological Bulletin*, 1975, **82**, 143-164.

Cambridge, M. A. Schenkman Publishing Co., pp. 321-326, 1975.

Campo, E. J., St. John, D., and Kauffman, C. C. Evaluation of the 21-day outpatient heroin detoxification. *International Journal of the Addictions*, 1977, **12**, 923-935.

Caplan, L. R., Hier, D. B., and Banks, G. Current concepts of cardiovascular disease-stroke: Stroke and drug abuse. *Stroke*, 1982, **13**, 869-872.

Caplovitz, D. *The working addict*. New York: City University of New York, 1976.

Casriel, D. H. and Bratter, T. E. Methadone maintenance treatment: A questionable procedure. *Journal of Drug Issues*, 1974, **4**, 359-375.

Cavior, N., Kurtzberg, R., and Lipton, D. S. The development and validation of a heroin addiction scale with the MMPI. *International Journal of the Addictions*, 1967, **2**, 129-127.

Challenor, Y. B., Richter, R. W., Bruun, B., and Pearson, J. Nontraumatic plexitis and heroin addiction. *Journal of the American Medical Association*, 1973, **225**, 958-961.

Chambers, C. D., Babst, D. V. and Warner, A. Characteristics predicting long-term retention in methadone maintenance program. In *Proceedings of the Third National Conference on Methadone Treatment*. Washington, D.C.: U.S. Government Printing Office, 1970.

Chambers, C. D. and Ball, J. C. Suicide among hospitalized opiate addicts. In J. C. Ball and C. D. Chambers (Eds.), *The epidemiology of opiate addiction in the United States*. Springfield, Ill.: Charles C. Thomas, 1970. Pp. 288-300.

Chambers, C. D., Hinesley, R. K., and Moldestad, M. Narcotic addiction in females: A race comparison. *International Journal of the Addictions*, 1970, **5**, 257-278.

Chambers, C. D. and Moffett, A. D. Negro opiate addiction. In J. C. Ball and C. D. Chambers (Eds.), *The epidemiology of opiate addiction in the United States*. Springfield, Ill.: Charles C. Thomas, 1970, Pp. 178-201.

Chambers, J. L. Need associations of narcotic addicts. *Journal of Clinical Psychology*, 1972, **28**, 469-474.

Chambers, J. L. and Lieberman, L. R. Differences between normal and clinical groups in judging, evaluating, and associating needs. *Journal of Clinical Psychology*, 1972, **21**, 145-149.

Chappel, J. W., Skolnick, V. B., and Senay, E. C. Techniques of withdrawal from methadone and their outcome over six months to two years. In Proceedings of the Fifth National Conference on Methadone Treatment. New York: National Association for the Prevention of Addiction to Narcotics, 1973. Pp. 482-489.

Cheek, F. E. and Mendelson, M. Developing behavior modification programs with emphasis on self-control. *Hospital and Community Psychiatry*, 1973, **24**, 410-416.

Chein, I., Gerard, D. L., Lee, R. S., and Rosenfeld, E. *The road to H: Narcotics, delinquency and social policy.* New York: Basic Books, 1964.

Chen, K. K. Pharmacology of methadone and related compounds. *Annals of the New York Academy of Sciences*, 1948, **51**, 33-97.

Cherkas, M. S. Synanon foundation—A radical approach to the problem of addiction. *American Journal of Psychiatry*, 1965, **121**, 1065-1068.

Cherubin, C. E. The medical sequelae of narcotic addiction. *Annals of Internal Medicine*, 1967, **67**, 23-33.

Cherubin, C. E. Liver disease in addicts. In R. W. Richter (Ed.), *Medical aspects, of drug abuse.* Hagerstown, Md.: Harper and Row, 1975, Pp. 212-219.

Christie, D. Drug use in the military. *New England Journal of Medicine*, 1972, **286**, 609.

Cimino, J. A., Doud, R. M., Andima, H. S., and West, S. A. Narcotic addiction in the United States: A nationwide survey. *Contemporary Drug Problems*, 1973, **2**, 401-415.

Clack, G. S. Drug use in New Orleans high schools. In J. M. Singh, L. Miller, and H. Lal (Eds.), *Drug addiction: Clinical and socio-legal aspects* (Vol. 2). Mt. Kisco, N.Y.: Futura, 1972. Pp. 169-178.

Cloward, R. A. and Ohlin, L. E. *Delinquency and opportunity: A theory of delinquent gangs.* Glencoe, Ill.: Free Press, 1960.

Cochin, J. Factors influencing tolerance to and dependence on narcotic analgesics. In S. Fisher and A. M. Freedman A. M. (Eds.), *Opiate addiction: Origins and treatment.* Washington, D.C.: Winston, 1974. Pp. 23-42.

Cochin, J. and Kornetsky, C. Development and loss of tolerance to morphine in the rat after single and multiple injections. *Journal of Pharmacology and Experimental Therapeutics*, 1964, **145**, 1-10.

Cochin, J. and Kornetsky, C. Factors in blood of morphine-tolerant animals that attenuate or enhance effects of morphine in nontolerant animals. In A. Wikler (Ed.), *The addictive states.* Baltimore: Williams and Wilkins, 1968. Pp. 268-279.

Cohen, A. K. and Short, J. F. Research in delinquent subcultures. *Journal of Social Issues.* 1958, **14**, 20-37.

Cohen, G. H., Garey, R. E., Evans, A., and Wilchinsky, M. Treatment of heroin addicts: Is the client-therapist relationship important? *International Journal of the Addictions*, 1980, **15**, 207-214.

Cohen, H. D., Graham, D., Fotopoulos, S. S., and Cook, M. R. A double-blind methodology for biofeedback research. *Psychophysiology*, 1977, **14**, 603-608.

Cohen, M. and Klein, D. F. Drug abuse in a young psychiatric population. *American Journal of Orthopsychiatry*, 1970, **40**, 448-455.

Cohen, M. and Klein, D. F. Age of onset of drug abuse in psychiatric inpatients. *Archives of General Psychiatry*, 1972, **26**, 266-269.

Cohen, S. Methadone maintenance: A decade later. *Journal of Drug Issues*, 1974, **4**, 327-331.

Coleman, S. B. Incomplete mourning and addict/family transactions: A theory for understanding heroin abuse. In D. S. Lettieri, M. Sayers, and H. W. Pearson, (Eds.), *Theories on Drug Abuse*. National institute on drug abuse (Research Monograph Series #30). Washington, D.C.: U.S. Government Printing Office, 1980. Pp. 83-89.

Coleman, S. B. and Davis, D. I. Family therapy and drug abuse: A national survey. *Family Process*, 1978, **17**, 21-29.

Coleman, S. B. and Stanton, M. D. The role of death in the addict family. *Journal of Marriage and Family Counseling*, 1978, **4**, 79-81.

Collier, H. O. J. A general theory of the genesis of drug dependence by induction of receptors. *Nature*, 1965, **205**, 181-182.

Collier, H. O. J. Tolerance, physical dependence and receptors. *Advances in Drug Research*. 1966, **3**, 171-188.

Collier, H. O. J. Humoral transmitters, supersensitivity, receptors and dependence. In H. Steinberg (Ed.), *Scientific basis of drug dependence*. London: Churchill, 1969. Pp. 49-66.

Collier, H. O. J. Drug dependence: A pharmacological analysis. *British Journal of Addiction*, 1972, **67**, 277-296.

Concool, B., Smith, H., and Stimmel, B. Mortality rates of persons entering methadone maintenance: A seven year study. *American Journal of Drug and Alcohol Abuse*, 1979, **6**, 345-353.

Coombs, R. H. Back on the streets: Therapeutic communities' impact upon drug users. *American Journal of Drug and Alcohol Abuse*, 1982, **8**, 185-201.

Coombs, R. H., Fry, L. J., and Lewis, P. T. (Eds.), *Socialization in drug abuse*. Cambridge, Mass.: Schenkman Publishing Co., 1976.

Cooper, J. R. Introduction. In J. R. Cooper, F. Altman, B. S. Brown, and D. Czechowicz. *Research on the treatment of narcotic addiction: State of the art.* Washington, D.C.: National Institute on Drug Abuse, 1983. Pp. xii-xvi.

Cooperstock, R. Sex differences in the use of mood-modifying drugs: An explanatory model. *Journal of Health and Social Behavior*, 1971, **12**, 238-244.

Corman, A. G., Johnson, B., Khantzian, E. J. and Long, J. Rehabilitation of narcotic addicts with methadone: The public health approach versus the individual perspective. *Contemporary Drug Problems*, 1973, **2**, 565-578.

Craig, R. J. Effectiveness of low-dose methadone maintenance for the treatment of inner city heroin addicts. *International Journal of the Addictions*, 1980, **15**, 701-710.

Craig, R. J. Personality characteristics of heroin addicts: Review of empirical research 1976-1979. *International Journal of the Addictions*, 1982, **17**, 227-248.

Craig, R. J., Rogalski, C., and Veltri, D. Predicting treatment dropouts from a drug abuse rehabilitation program. *International Journal of the Addictions*, 1982, **17**, 641-653.

Crawford, G. A., Washington, M. C., and Senay, E. C. Socio-familial characteristics of black male heroin addicts and their non-addicted friends. *Drug and Alcohol Dependence*, 1980, **6**, 383-390.

Crowley, T. The reinforcers for drug abuse: Why people take drugs. *Comprehensive Psychiatry*, 1972, **13**, 51-62.

Crowley, T. J., Chesluk, D., Dilts, S., and Hart, R. Drug and alcohol abuse among psychiatric admissions: A multidrug clinical toxicologic study. *Archives of General Psychiatry*, 1974, **30**, 13-20.

Crowther, B. Patterns of drug use among Mexican-Americans. *International Journal of the Addictions*, 1972, **7**, 637-647.

Crowther, B. The college opiate user. *International Journal of the Addictions*, 1974, **9**, 241-253.

Curtis, J., Richman, B. L. and Feinstein, M. Infective endocarditis in drug addicts. *Southern Medical Journal*, 1974, **67**, 4-9.

Cushman, P. Methadone maintenance in hard-core criminal addicts: Economic effects. *New York State Journal of Medicine*, 1971, **71**, 1768-1774.

Cushman, P. Methadone maintenance treatment of narcotic addiction. Analysis of police records of arrests before and during treatment. *New York State Journal of Medicine*, 1972, **72**, 1752-1755.

Cushman, P. Narcotic addiction and crime. *Rhode Island Medical Journal*, 1974(a), **57**, 197-204.

Cushman, P. Methadone maintenance treatment: An appraisal. *Journal of Drug Issues*, 1974(b), **4**, 376-380.

Cushman, P. and Dole, V. P. Detoxification of rehabilitated methadone-maintained patients. *Journal of the American Medical Association*, 1973 **226**, 747-752.

Dale, R. T. and Dale, F. R. The use of methadone in a representative group of heroin addicts. *International Journal of the Addictions*, 1973, **8**, 293-308.

De Fleur, L. B., Ball, J. C., and Snarr, R. W. The long-term social correlates of opiate addiction. *Social Problems*, 1969, **17**, 225-234.

De Leon, G. and Andrews, M. Therapeutic community dropouts, 5 years later: Preliminary findings on self-reported status. Paper presented at the Fourth National Drug Abuse Conference, San Francisco, May 5-9, 1977.

De Leon, G., Holland, S., and Rosenthal, M. S. Phoenix House. Criminal Activity of dropouts. *Journal of the American Medical Association*, 1972, **222**, 686-689.

De Leon, G., and Rosenthal, M. S. Therapeutic communities. In R. I. DuPont, A. Goldstein, and J. O'Donnell (Eds.). *Handbook on drug abuse*. Washington, D.C. National Institute on Drug Abuse, 1979. Pp. 39-47.

De Leon, G., Rosenthal, M., and Brodney, K. Therapeutic community for drug addicts, long-term measurement of emotional changes. *Psychological Reports*, 1971, **29**, 595-600.

De Leon, G., Skodol, A., and Rosenthal, M. S. Phoenix House. Changes in psychopathological signs of resident drug addicts. *Archives of General Psychiatry*, 1973, **28**, 131-135.

De Leon, G. and Wexler, H. K. Heroin addiction: Its relation to sexual behavior and sexual experience. *Journal of Abnormal Psychology*, 1973, **81**, 36-38.

Dembo, R. and Hendler, H. Typification of processing in a screening unit for drug abusers. *International Journal of the Addictions*, 1982, **17**, 1-18.

Densen-Gerber, J. and Drassner, D. Odyssey House: A structural model for the successful employment and re-entry of the ex-drug abuser. *Journal of Drug Issues*, 1974, **4**, 414-427.

Dewey, W. L., Fu, T. C., Ohlsson, A., Bowman, E., and Martin, B. R. Evidence for the release of endogenous opiates by morphine. In L. S. Harris (Ed.), *Problems of drug dependence, 1981* (NIDA Research Monograph #41). Washington, D. C.: U.S. Government Printing Office, 1982. Pp. 60-66.

Dogoloff, L. I. and Devine, C. M. International patterns of drug abuse and control. *Annals of the New York Academy of Science*, 1981, **362**, 16-21.

Dole, V. P. Methadone maintenance: Treatment for 25,000 heroin addicts. *Journal of the American Medical Association*, 1971, **215**, 1131-1134.

Dole, V. P., Foldes, F. F., Trig, H., Robinson, J. W., and Blatman, S. Methadone poisoning. *New York State Journal of Medicine*, 1971, **71**, 541-543.

Dole, V. P. and Joseph, H. The long-term outcome of patients treated with methadone maintenance. Paper presented at the New York Academy of Sciences Conference on Recent Developments in Chemotherapy of Narcotic Addiction, Washington, D.C., November 3-4, 1977.

Dole, V. P. and Nyswander, M. E. A medical treatment for diacetylmorphine (heroin) addiction. *Journal of the American Medical Association*, 1965, **193**, 646-650.

Dole, V. P. and Nyswander, M. E. Rehabilitation of heroin addicts after blockade with methadone. *New York State Journal of Medicine*, 1966, **66**, 2011-2017.

Dole, V. P. and Nyswander, M. E. Rehabilitation of the street addict. *Archives of Environmental Health*, 1967, **14**, 477-480.

Dole, V. P., Nyswander, M. E., and Kreek, M. J. Narcotic blockade. *Archives of Internal Medicine*, 1966, **118**, 304-309.

Dole, V. P., Nyswander, M. E., and Warner, A. Successful treatment of 750 criminal addicts. *Journal of the American Medical Association*, 1968, **206**, 2708-2711.

Dole, V. P., Robinson, J. W., Orraca, J., Towns, E., Searcy, P., and Caine, E. Methadone treatment of randomly selected criminal addicts. *New England Journal of Medicine*, 1969, **280**, 1372-1375.

Dole, V. P. and Warner, A. Evaluation of narcotics treatment programs. *American Journal of Public Health*, 1967, **57**, 2000-2008.

Dole, V. and Wolkstein, E. Vocational rehabilitation of patients in the Beth Israel methadone maintenance program. *Mount Sinai Journal of Medicine*, 1974, **41**, 267-271.

Drug Abuse Council. *Heroin maintenance: The issues*. Washington, D.C., 1973.

D'Orban, P. T. A follow-up study of female narcotic addicts: Variables related to outcome. *British Journal of Psychiatry*, 1974, **125**, 28-33.

Dudley, D. L., Rozell, D. K., Mules, J. E., and Hague, W. H. Heroin versus alcohol addiction—Quantifiable psychosocial similarities and differences. *Journal of Psychosomatic Research*, 1974, **18**, 327-335.

DuPont, R. L. Heroin addiction treatment and crime reduction. *American Journal of Psychiatry*, 1972, **128**, 856-860.

DuPont, R. L. and Greene, M. H. The dynamics of a heroin addiction epidemic. *Science*, 1973, **181**, 716-722.

DuPont, R. L. and Katon, R. N. Development of a heroin-addiction treatment program. *Journal of the American Medical Association*, 1971, **216**, 1320-1324.

Durkheim, E. *Suicide*. New York: Free Press, 1951.

Duvall, H. J., Locke, B. Z., and Brill, L. Follow-up study of narcotic drug addicts five years after hospitalization. *Public Health Reports*, 1963, **78**, 185-193.

Eddy, N. B., Halbach, H., and Braenden, O. H. Synthetic substances with morphine-like effect. Relationship between analgesic action and addiction liability, with a discussion of the chemical structure of addiction-producing substances. *Bulletin of the World Health Organization*, 1956, **14**, 353-402.

Eddy. N. B., Halbach, H., Isbell, H., and Seevers, M. Drug dependence: Its significance and characteristics. *Bulletin of the World Health Organization*, 1965, **32**, 721-733.

Einstein, S. and Garitano, W. Treating the drug abuser: Problems, factors and alternatives. *International Journal of the Addictions*, 1972, **7**, 321-331.

Einstein, S. and Jones, F. Group therapy with adolescent addicts: Use of a heterogenous group approach. In E. Harms (Ed.), *Drug addiction in youth*. New York: Pergamon, 1965. Pp. 132-147.

Eiseman, B., Lam, R. C., and Rush, B. Surgery on the narcotic addict. *Annals of Surgery*, 1964, **159**, 748-757.

Eisenman, A. J., Fraser, H. F., and Brooks, J. W. Urinary excretion and plasma levels of 17-hydroxycorticosteroids during a cycle of addiction to morphine. *Journal of Pharmacology and Experimental Therapeutics*, 1961, **132**, 226-231.

Eisenman, A. J., Fraser, H. F., Sloan, J., and Isbell, H. Urinary 17-ketosteroid excretion during a cycle of addiction to morphine. *Journal of Pharmacology and Experimental Therapeutics*, 1958, **124**, 305-311.

Eldred, C. A., Brown, B. S., and Mahabir, C. Heroin addict clients' description of their families of origin. *International Journal of the Addictions*, 1974, **9**, 315-320.

Eldred, C. A., Grier, V. V., and Berliner, N. Comprehensive treatment for heroin-addicted mothers. *Social Casework*, 1974, **55**, 470-477.

Eldred, C. A., and Washington, M. N. Female heroin addicts in a city treatment program: The forgotten minority. *Psychiatry*, 1975, **38**, 75-85.

Ellinwood, E., Smith, W., and Vaillant, G. Narcotic addiction in males and females: A comparison. *International Journal of the Addictions*, 1966, **1**, 33-46.

Emery, G. D., Steer, R. A., and Beck, A. T. Suicidal behavior among heroin addicts: A brief report. *Psychological Reports*, 1979, **44**, 237-238.

Emery, G. D., Steer, R. A., and Beck, A. T. Depression, hopelessness, and suicidal intent among heroin addicts. *International Journal of the Addictions*, 1981, **16**, 425-429.

English, G. E. and Tori, C. A. Psychological characteristics of drug abuse clients seen in a community mental health center. *Journal of Community Psychology*, 1973, **1**, 403-407.

Ervin, F. R. Effects of opioids on electrical activity of deep structures in the human brain. In A. Wikler (Ed.), *The addictive states*. Baltimore: Williams and Wilkins, 1968. Pp. 150-156.

Eveson, M. Drug addiction: A hypothesis for experimental test. *Canadian Journal of Corrections*, 1963, **5**, 110-113.

Falek, A. and Hollingsworth, F. Heroin and chromosome damage. *Archives of General Psychiatry*, 1980, **37**, 227-228.

Federn, E. A psycho-social view of "drug abuse" in adolescence. *Child Psychiatry and Human Development*, 1972, **3**, 10-20.

Feldman, H. Ideological supports to becoming and remaining a heroin addict. *Journal of Health and Social Behavior*, 1968, **9**, 131-139.

Felix, R. H. An appraisal of the personality types of the addict. *American Journal of Psychiatry*, 1944, **100**, 462-467.

Felton, C. P. Pulmonary infections in the addict. In R. W. Richter (Ed.), *Medical aspects of drug abuse*. Hagerstown, Md.: Harper and Row, 1975. Pp. 232-242.

Fielding, S., Wilker, J., Hynes, M., Szewczak, M., Novick, W. J., and Lal, H. A comparison of clonidine with morphine for antinociceptive and antiwithdrawal actions. *Journal of Pharmacology and Experimental Therapeutics*, 1978, **207**, 899-905.

Fields, F. R. J. and Fullerton, J. R. The influence of heroin addiction on neuropsychological functioning. *Journal of Consulting and Clinical Psychology*, 1975, **43**, 114.

Fink, M., Simeon, J., Itil, T. M., and Freedman, A. M. Clinical antidepressant activity of cyclazocine—A narcotic antagonist. *Clinical Pharmacology and Therapeutics*, 1970, **11**, 41-48.

Fink., M., Zaks, A., Resnick, R., and Freedman, A. M. Treatment of heroin dependence with opiate antagonists. In J. H. Masserman (Ed.), *Handbook of psychiatric therapies*. New York: Science House, 1966. Pp. 281-289.

Fink, M., Zaks, A., Sharoff, R., Mora, A., Bruner, A., Levit, S., and Freedman, A. M. Naloxone in heroin dependence. *Clinical Pharmacology and Therapeutics*, 1968, **9**, 568-577.

Finnegan, L. P. Narcotic dependence in pregnancy. *Journal of Psychedelic Drugs*, 1975, **7**, 299-311.

Finnegan, L. P. Women in treatment. In R. I. DuPont, A. Goldstein, and J. O'Donnell (Eds.). *Handbook on drug abuse*. Washington, D. C.: National Institute on Drug Abuse, 1979. Pp. 121-132.

Flaherty, J. E. *Army drug abuse programs: A future model*. Washington, D.C.: Drug Abuse Council, 1973.

Foldes, F. F., Lunn, J. N., Moore, J., and Brown, I. M. N-allylnoroxymorphone: A new potent narcotic antagonist. *American Journal of the Medical Sciences*, 1963, **245**, 23-30.

Fort, J.P. Heroin addiction among young men. *Psychiatry*, 1954, **17**, 251-259.

Fracchia, J., Sheppard, C., and Merlis, S. Some comments about the personality comparison of incarcerated and street heroin addicts. *Psychological Reports*, 1973(a), **33**, 413-414.

Fracchia, J., Sheppard, C., and Merlis, S. Early cigarette smoking and drug use: Some comments, data, and thoughts. *Psychological Reports*, 1974(b), **34**, 371-374.

Fraser, D. W. Methadone overdose. *Journal of the American Medical Association*, 1971, **217**, 1387-1389.

Fraser, H. F. and Isbell, H. Actions and addiction liabilities of alpha-acetylmethadols in man. *Journal of Pharmacology and Experimental Therapeutics*, 1952, **105**, 458-465.

Fraser, H. R. and Rosenberg, D. E. Comparative effects of (I) chronic administration of cyclazocine (ARC-II-C-3), (II) substitution of nalorphine for cyclazocine, and (III) chronic administration of morphine. Pilot crossover study. *International Journal of the Addictions*, 1966, **1**, 86-98.

Frederick, C. J. , Resnick, H. L. P., and Wittlin, B. J. Self-destructive aspects of hard-core addiction. *Archives of General Psychiatry*, 1973, **28**, 579-585.

Freedman, A. M., Fink, M., Sharoff, R., and Zaks, A. Cyclazocine and methadone in narcotic addiction. *Journal of the American Medical Association*, 1967, **202**, 191-194.

Freedman, A. M., Fink, M., Sharoff, R., and Zaks, A. Clinical studies of cyclazocine in the treatment of narcotic addiction. *American Journal of Psychiatry*, 1963, **124**, 1499-1504.

Freedman, R. R. and Czertko, C. T. A comparison of thrice weekly LAAM and daily methadone in employed heroin addicts. *Drug and Alcohol Dependence*, 1981, **8**, 215-222.

Friedmann, C. T., Dover, A. S., Roberto, R. R., and Kearns, O. A. A malaria epidemic among heroin users. *American Journal of Tropical Medicine and Hygiene*, 1973, **22**, 302-307.

Gardner, J. M. The adjustment of drug addicts as measured by the sentence completion test. *Journal of Projective Techniques and Personality Assessment*, 1967, **31**, 28-29.

Gardner, R. Deaths in United Kingdom opioid users 1965-69. *Lancet*, 1970(a), **2**, 650-653.

Gardner, R. Methadone misuse and death by overdosage. *British Journal of the Addictions*, 1970(b), **65**, 113-118.

Gearing, F. R. Evaluation of methadone maintenance treatment program. *International Journal of the Addictions*, 1970, **5**, 517-54

Gebhard, P. H. Situational factors affecting human sexual behavior. In F. A. Beach (Ed.), *Sex and Behavior*, New York: Wiley, 1965. Pp. 483-495.

Gendreau, P. and Gendreau, L. P. The "addiction-prone" personality: A study of Canadian heroin addicts. *Canadian Journal of Behavioral Science*, 1970, **2**, 18-25.

Gendreau, P. and Gendreau, L. P. Research design and narcotic addiction proneness. *Canadian Psychiatric Association Journal*, 1971, **16**, 265-267.

Gendreau, P. and Gendreau, L. P. A theoretical note on personality characteristics of heroin addicts. *Journal of Abnormal Psychology*, 1972, **82**, 139-140.

Gerard, D. L. and Kornetsky, C. Adolescent opiate addiction: A study of control and addict subjects. *Psychiatric Quarterly*, 1955, **10**, 457-486.

Gibbons, C. G., Brown, B. S., Greene, M. H., and DuPont, R. L. Initiation into heroin use. *International Journal of the Addictions*, 1981, **16**, 935-939.

Gilberstadt, H. and Duker, J. *A Handbook for clinical and actuarial MMPI interpretation.* Philadelphia: W. B. Saunders, 1965.

Gilbert, J. G. and Lombardi, D. N. Personality characteristics of young male narcotic addicts. *Journal of Consulting Psychology*, 1967, **31**, 536-538.

Ginzburg, H. Use of clonidine or lofexidine to detoxify from methadone maintenance or other opioid dependencies. In J. R. Cooper, F. Altman, B. S. Brown, and D. Czechowicz (Eds.) *Research on the treatment of narcotic addiction: State of the art.* Rockville, MD: National Institute on Drug Abuse, 1983. Pp. 174-211.

Glaser, F. B. Drug use in the military. *New England Journal of Medicine*, 1972, **286**, 609.

Glaser, F. B., Adler, F., Moffett, A. D., and Ball, J. C. The quality of treatment for drug abuse. *American Journal of Psychiatry*, 1974, **131**, 598-601.

Glaser, F. B. and Ball, J. C. Death due to withdrawal from narcotics. In J. C. Ball and C. D. Chambers (Eds.), *The epidemiology of opiate addiction in the United States.* Springfield, Ill.: Charles C. Thomas, 1970. Pp. 263-287.

Glass, L., Evans, H. E. and Rajegowda, B. K. Neonatal narcotics withdrawal. In R. W. Richter (Ed.), *Medical aspects of drug abuse.* Hagerstown, Md.: Harper and Row, 1975. Pp. 124-133.

Gold, M. S., Pottash, A. L. C., Extein, I., and Stroul, A. Clinical utility of clonidine in opiate withdrawal. In L. S. Harris (Ed.), *Problems of drug dependence.* Washington, D.C.: NIDA, 1980, Pp. 95-100.

Gold, M. S. Redmond, D. E., and Kleber, H. D. Clonidine blocks acute opiate withdrawal symptoms. *Lancet*, 1978, **1**, 599-601.

Goldberg, R. J., Greenwood, J. C., and Taintor, Z. Alpha conditioning as an adjunct treatment for drug dependence: Part I. *International Journal of the Addictions*, 1976, **11**, 1085-1089.

Goldenberg, I. I. *Employment and addiction: Perspective on existing business and treatment practices.* Arlington, Va.: National Technical Information Service, 1972.

Goldsmith, B. M., Capel, W. C., Waddell, K. J., and Stewart, G. T. Demographic and sociological implications of addiction in New Orleans: Implications for consideration of treatment modalities. In J. M. Singh, L. Miller, and H. Lal (Eds.), *Drug addiction: Clinical and sociological aspects* (Vol. 2). Mount Kisco, New York: Futura, 1972. Pp. 137-152.

Goldstein, A. Heroin addiction and the role of methadone in its treatment. *Archives of General Psychiatry*, 1972, **26**, 291-297.

Goldstein, A., Opioid Peptides (endorphins) in pituitary and brain. *Science*, 1976, **193**, 1081-1086.

Goldstein, A. and Goldstein, D. B. Enzyme expansion theory of drug tolerance and physical dependence. In A. Wikler (Ed.), *The addictive states*. Baltimore: Williams and Wilkins, 1968. Pp. 265-267.

Goldstein, A., Hanstein, R. W., and Horns, W. N. Control of methadone dosage by patients. *Journal of the American Medical Association*, 1975, **234**, 734-737.

Goldstein, A. and Judson, B. A. Three critical issues in the management of methadone programs. In P. Bourne (Ed.), *Addiction*. New York: Academic Press, 1974. Pp. 129-148.

Goldstein, A. and Sheehan, P. Tolerance to opioid narcotics: I. Tolerance to the "running fit" caused by levorphanol in the mouse. *Journal of Pharamcology and Experimental Therapeutics*. 1969, **169**, 175-184.

Golosow, N. and Childs, A. The soldier addict: A new battlefield casualty. *International Journal of the Addictions*, 1973, **8**, 1-12.

Goode, E. Multiple drug use among marijuana smokers. *Social Problems*, 1969, **17**, 48-63.

Goodkin, K. and Wilson, K. E. Amenability to counseling of opiate addicts on probation or parole. *International Journal of the Addictions*, 1982, **17**, 1047-1053.

Gordis, E. N. and Sereny, G. Effect of prior narcotic addiction on responses to treatment of alcoholism. *Alcoholism* (NY), 1980, **4**, 34-39.

Gossop, M., Strang, J., and Connell, P. H. The response of outpatient opiate addicts to the provision of a temporary increase in their prescribed drugs. *British Journal of Psychiatry*, 1982, **141**, 338-343.

Gottheil, E., Caddy, G. R., and Austin, D. L. Fallibility of urine drug screens in monitoring methadone programs. *Journal of the American Medical Association*, 1976, **236**, 1035-1038.

Graham, R. Relationship with business and industry. In The state of the art, vocational rehabilitation of the drug abuser: Counseling as the art. (Vol. 3). Washington, D.C.: Youth Projects, Inc., and DHEW Social and Rehabilitation Services, 1973. Pp. 49-53.

Grant, I., Adams, K. M., Carlin, A. S., Rennick, P. M., Judd, L. L., Schooff, K., and Reed, R. Organic impairment in polydrug users: Risk factors. *American Journal of Psychiatry*, 1978, **135**, 178-184.

Grant, I., Mohns, I., and Miller, M. A neuropsychological study of polydrug users. *Archives of General Psychiatry*, 1976(a), **33**, 973-978.

Grant, I. and Judd, L. Neuropsychological and EEG disturbances in polydrug users. *American Journal of Psychiatry*, 1976(b), **133**, 1039-1042.

Green, B. T. An examination of the relationship between crime and substance use in a drug/alcohol treatment population. *International Journal of the Addictions*, 1981, **16**, 627-645.

Green, J. and Jaffe, J. H. Alcohol and opiate dependence: A review. *Journal of Studies on Alcohol,* 1977, **38,** 1274-1293.

Greenstein, R. A., Evans, B. D., McLellan, A. T. and O'Brien, C. P. Predictions of favorable outcome following naltrexone treatment. In L. S. Harris (Ed.), *Problems of drug dependence, 1982* (NIDA Research Monograph #43). Washington, D.C.: U.S. Government Printing Office. Pp. 294-301.

Greenstein, R., O'Brien, C., Mintz, J., Woody, G.E., and Hanna, N. Clinical experience with naltrexone in a behavioral research study. In D. Julius and P. Renault (Eds.). *Narcotic antagonists: Naltrexone.* (Research Monograph Series) Washington, D.C.: National Institute on Drug Abuse, 1976.

Gritz, E. R., Shiffman, S. M., Jarvik, M. E., Haber, J., Dymond, A. M., Coger, R., Charuvastra, V., and Schlesinger, J. Physiological and psychological effects of methadone in man. *Archives of General Psychiatry,* 1975, **32,** 237-242.

Gould, R. E. Methadone reconsidered. *Drug Therapy,* 1971, **1,** 16-29.

Guzman, F., Braun, C., and Lim, R. K. S. Visceral pain and the pseudo affective response to introarterial injection of bradykinin and other analgesic agents. *Archives of International Pharmacodynamics,* 1962, **136,** 353-384.

Haddox, V. G. and Jacobson, M. D. Psychological adjustment—Mood and personality fluctuations of long-term methadone maintenance patients. *International Journal of the Addictions,* 1972, **7,** 619-627.

Haertzen, C. Subjective drug effects: A factorial representation of subjective drug effects on the Addiction Research Center Inventory. *Journal of Nervous and Mental Disease,* 1965, **140,** 280-289.

Haertzen, C. Development of scales based on patterns of drug effects using the Addiction Research Center Inventory (ARCI). *Psychological Reports,* 1966, **18,** 163-194.

Haertzen, C. An overview of Addiction Research Center Inventory Scales (ARCI): An appendix and manual of scales. Rockville, Md.: National Institute on Drug Abuse, 1974.

Haertzen, C., Hill, H., and Belleville, R. Development of the Addiction Research Center Inventory (ARCI): Selection of items that are sensitive to the effects of various drugs. *Psychopharmacologia* 1963, **4,** 155-166.

Haertzen, C. A. and Hooks, N. T. Changes in personality and subjective experience associated with the chronic administration and withdrawal of opiates. *Journal of Nervous and Mental Disease,* 1969, **148,** 606-614.

Haertzen, C. and Meketon, M. Opiate withdrawal as measured by the Addiction Research Center Inventory (ARCI). *Diseases of the Nervous System, 1968, 29,* 450-455.

Haertzen, C. and Panton, J. Development of a "psychopathic" scale for the Addiction Research Center Inventory (ARCI). *International Journal of the Addictions,* 1967, **2,** 115-127.

Hager, D. L., Vener, A. M., and Stewart, C. S. Patterns of adolescent drug use in middle America. *Journal of Counseling Psychiatry,* 1971, **18,** 292-297.

Halikas, J. A., Darvish, H. S., and Rimmer, J. D. The black addict: I. Methodology, chronology of addiction, and overview of the population. *American Journal of Alcohol and Drug Abuse*, 1976, **3**, 529-543.

Hampton, P. T. and Vogel, D. B. Personality characteristics of servicemen returned from Viet Nam identified as heroin abusers. *American Journal of Psychiatry*, 1973, **130**, 1031-1032.

Harford, R. J. and Kleber, H. D. Comparative validity of random-interval and fixed-interval urinalysis schedules. *Archives of General Psychiatry*, 1978, **35**, 356-359.

Harms, E. Two basic defaults in the present psychotherapy with drug addicts. *International Mental Health Research Newsletter*, 1972, **14**, 1-2.

Harrington, P., and Cox, T. J. A twenty-year follow-up of narcotic addicts in Tucson, Arizona. *American Journal of Drug and Alcohol Abuse*, 1979, **6**, 25-37.

Harris, W. D. M. and Andrei, J. Serologic tests for syphilis among narcotic addicts. *New York State Journal of Medicine*, 1967, **67**, 2967-2974.

Hartnoll, R. L., Mitcheson, M. C., Battersby, A., Brown, G., Ellis, M., Fleming, P., and Hedley, N. Evaluation of heroin maintenance in controlled trial. *Archives of General Psychiatry*, 1980, **37**, 877-884.

Havassy, B. E. and Hall, S. M. Urine monitoring of methadone maintenance clients: Does it prevent illicit drug use? In L. S. Harris (Ed.), *Problems of drug dependence, 1981* (NIDA Research Monograph #41). Washington, D.C.: U.S. Government Printing Office, 1982. Pp. 276-281.

Hawks, D. V., Mitcheson, M., Ogborne, A., and Edwards, G. Abuse of methylamphetamine. *British Medical Journal*, 1969, **2**, 715-721.

Hekimian, L. J. and Gershon, S. Characteristics of drug abusers admitted to a psychiatric hospital. *Journal of the American Medical Association*, 1968, **205**, 125-130.

Helms, D. J., Scura, W. C., and Fisher, C. C. Treatment of the addict in correctional institutions. In R. W. Richter (Ed.), *Medical aspects of drug abuse*. Hagerstown, Md.: Harper and Row, 1975. Pp. 360-366.

Helpern, M. Epidemic of fatal estivo-autumnal malaria. *American Journal of Surgery*, 1934, **26**, 111-123.

Helpern, M. and Rho, Y.-M. Deaths from narcotism in New York City. *New York State Journal of Medicine*, 1966, **66**, 2391-2408.

Helpern, M. and Rho, Y.-M. Deaths from narcotism in New York City: Incidence, circumstances, and post-mortem findings. *International Journal of the Addictions*, 1967, **2**, 53-84.

Hendler, H. I. and Stephens, R. C. The addict odyssey, from experimentation to addiction. *International Journal of the Addictions*, 1977, **12**, 25-42.

Henriques, E., Arsenian, J., Cutter, H., and Samaraweera, A. B. Personality characteristics and drug of choice. *International Journal of the Addictions*, 1972, **7**, 73-76.

Herz, A., Schulz, R., and Wuster, M. Development of selective tolerance to particular types of opiate receptors. In L. S. Harris (Ed.), *Problems of drug dependence,*

1981 (NIDA Research Monograph #41). Washington, D.C.: U.S. Government Printing Office, 1982. Pp. 215-222.

Hewetson, J. and Ollendorf, R. Preliminary survey of 100 London heroin and cocaine addicts. *British Journal of Addiction*, 1964, **60**, 109-114.

Hill, H. E. The social deviant and initial addiction to narcotics and alcohol, *Quarterly Journal of Studies on Alcohol*, 1962, **23**, 562-582.

Hill, H. E., Haertzen, C. A., and Davis, H. An MMPI factor analytic study of alcoholics, narcotic addicts and criminals. *Quarterly Journal of Studies on Alcohol*, 1962, **23**, 411-431.

Hill, H. E., Haertzen, C. A., and Glazer, R. Personality characteristics of narcotic addicts as indicated by the MMPI. *Journal of General Psychology*, 1960, **62**, 127-139.

Hill, H., Haerzen, C., Wolbach, A., and Miner, E. The Addiction Research Center Inventory: Standardization of scales which evaluate subjective effects of morphine, amphetamine, pentobarbital, alcohol, LSD-25, pyrahexyl, and chlorpromazine. *Psychopharmacologia*, 1963, **4**, 167-183.

Hill, H. E., Haertzen, C. A., and Yamahiro, R. S. The addict physician: A Minnesota Multiphasic Personality Inventory study of the interaction of personality characteristics and availability of narcotics. In A. Wikler (Ed.), *The addictive states*. Baltimore: Williams and Wilkins, 1968. Pp. 321-332.

Himmelsbach, C. The morphine abstinence syndrome, its nature and treatment. *Annals of Internal Medicine*, 1941, **15**, 829-839.

Himmelsbach, C. K. Clinical studies of drug addiction. Physical dependence, withdrawal and recovery. *Archives of Internal Medicine*, 1942, **69**, 766-772.

Himmelsbach, C. K. With reference to physical dependence. *Federation Proceedings*, 1943, **2**, 201-203.

Hirt, M. and Greenfield, H. Implosive therapy treatment of heroin addicts during methadone detoxification. *Journal of Consulting and Clinical Psychology*, 1979, **47**, 982-983.

Hoffman, M. Drug addiction and hypersexuality: Related modes of mastery. *Comprehensive Psychiatry*, 1964, **5**, 262-270.

Hofmann, F. G. *A handbook on drug and alcohol abuse*. New York: Oxford, 1975.

Hollonds, G. B., Oei, T. P., and Turecek, L. R. An evaluation of a behavior therapy programme as an intervention treatment for the fear of withdrawal with heroin-dependent persons. *Drug and Alcohol Dependence*, 1980, **5**, 153-160.

Holzman, R. S. and Bishko, F. Osteomyelitis in heroin addicts. *Annals of Internal Medicine*, 1971, **75**, 693-696.

Hough, G., Washton, A. M., and Resnick, R. B. Addressing the diversion of take-home methadone: LAAM as the sole treatment choice for patients seeking maintenance therapy. In L. S. Harris (Ed.), *Problems of drug dependence, 1982* (NIDA Research Monograph #43). Washington, D.C.: U.S. Government Printing Office. Pp. 302-309.

Householder, J., Hatcher, R., Burns, W., and Chasnoff, I. Infants born to narcotic-addicted mothers. *Psychological Bulletin*, 1982, **92**, 453-468.

Hubbard, R. L., Allison, M., Bray, R. M., Craddock, S. G., Rachal, J. V., and Ginzburg, H. M. An overview of client characteristics, treatment services, and during-treatment outcomes for outpatient methadone clinics in the Treatment Outcome Prospective Study (TOPS). In J. R. Cooper, F. Altman, B. S. Brown, And D. Czechowicz. *Research on the treatment of narcotic addiction: State of the art.* Washington, D.C. National Institute on Drug Abuse, 1983. Pp. 714-751.

Huberty, D. J. Civil commitment of the narcotic addict: Evaluation of a treatment model. *Crime and Delinquency,* 1972, **18**, 99-109.

Hughes, J., *Brain Research,* 1975, **88**, 295-308.

Hughes, P. H., Crawford, G. A., Barker, N. W., Schumann, S., and Jaffe, J. H. The social structure of a heroin coping community. *American Journal of Psychiatry,* 1971, **128**, 551-558.

Hunt, G. H. and Odoroff, M. E. Follow-up study of narcotic drug addicts after hospitalization. *Public Health Reports,* 1962, **77**, 41-54.

Hunt, L. G. *Recent spread of heroin addiction in the United States: Unanswered questions.* Washington, D.C.: Drug Abuse Council, 1974.

Hunt, W. A. and Bespalic, D. A. Relapse rates after treatment for heroin addiction. *Journal of Community Psychology,* 1974, **2**, 85-87.

Hunt, W. A. and General, W. R. Relapse rates after treatment for alcoholism. *Journal of Community Psychology,* 1973, **1**, 66-68.

Hutchings, D. E. Methadone and heroin during pregnancy: A review of behavioral effects in human and animal offspring. *Neurobehavioral Toxicology and Teratology,* 1982, **4**, 429-434.

Isbell, H. and Vogel, V. H. The addiction liability of methadone (amidone, dolophine, 10820) and its use in the treatment of the morphine abstinence syndrome. *American Journal of Psychiatry,* 1948, **105**, 909-914.

Isbell, H. and White, W. M. Clinical characteristics of addictions. *American Journal of Medicine,* 1953, **14**, 558-565.

Isbell, H., Wikler, A., Eisenman, S., Daingerfield, M., and Frank, K. Liability of addiction to 6-dimethylamino-4-4-diphenyl-3-heptanone (Methadone, "Amidone" or "10820") in man. *Archives of Internal Medicine,* 1948, **82**, 363-392.

Jackman, N. R., O'Toole, R., and Geis, G. The self-image of the prostitute. In E. Rubington and M. S. Weinberg (Eds.), *Deviance, the interactionist perspective,* Toronto: Macmillan, 1968.

Jaffe, J. H. Research on newer methods of treatment of drug dependent individuals in the United States of America. *Proceedings of the Fifth International Congress of the Collegium Internationale Neuropsychopharmacologicum,* 1966, **129**, 271-276.

Jaffe, J. H. Further experience with methadone in the treatment of narcotics users. *International Journal of the Addictions,* 1970(a), **5**, 375-389.

Jaffe, J.H. Treatment of drug abusers. In *Principles of psychopharmacology,* New York: Academic Press, 1970(b). Pp. 547-556.

Jaffe, J. H. Drug addiction and drug abuse. In L. S. Goodman and A. Gilman (Eds), *The pharmacological basis of therapeutics* (4th ed.). New York: Macmillan, 1970(c). Pp. 276-313.

Jaffe, J. H. Narcotic analgesics. In L. S. Goodman and A. Gilman (Eds.), *The pharmacological basis of therapeutics* (4th ed.). New York: Macmillan, 1970(d). Pp. 237-275.

Jaffe, J. The swinging pendulum: The treatment of drug users in America. In Dupont et al. (Eds.), *Handbook on drug abuse*, NIDA, 1979. Pp. 3-16.

Jaffe, J. H. and Brill, L. Cyclazocine, a long-acting narcotic antagonist: Its voluntary acceptance as a treatment modality by narcotics abusers. *International Journal of the Addictions*, 1966, **1**, 99-123.

Jaffe, J. H., Schuster, C. R., Smith, B. B., and Blachley, P. H. Comparison of acetylmethadol and methadone in the treatment of long-term heroin users. *Journal of the American Medical Association*, 1970, **211**, 1834-1836.

Jaffe, J. H. and Sharpless, S. K. Pharmacological denervation supersensitivity in the central nervous system: A theory of physical dependence. In A. Wikler (Ed.), *The addictive states*. Baltimore: Williams and Wilkins, 1968. Pp. 226-246.

Jaffe, J. H., Zaks, M. S., and Washington, E. N. Experience with the use of methadone in a multimodality program for the treatment of narcotics users. *International Journal of the Addictions*, 1969, **4**, 481-490.

Janssen, P. A. J. Development of new potent analgesics. In H. Steinberg (Ed.), *Scientific basis of drug dependence*. London: Churchill, 1969. Pp. 149-154.

Jasinski, D. R., Martin, W. R., and Haertzen, C. A. The human pharmacology and abuse potential of N-allylnoroxymorphone (Naloxone). *Journal of Pharmacology and Experimental Therapy*, 1967, **157**, 420-426.

Jasinski, D. R., Haertzen, C. A., Henningfield, J. E., Johnson, R. E., Makhzoumie, H. M., and Miyasato, K. Progress report of the NIDA Addiction Research Center. In L. S. Harris (Ed.), *Problems of drug dependence 1981* (NIDA Research Monograph #41). Washington, D.C.: U.S. Government Printing Office, 1982. Pp. 45-52.

Jasinski, D. R., Henningfield, J. E., Hickey, J. E., and Johnson, R. E. Progress report of the NIDA Addiction Research Center, Baltimore, MD, 1982. In L. S. Harris (Ed.), *Problems of drug dependence, 1982* (NIDA Research Monograph #43). Washington, D.C.: U.S. Government Printing Office, 1983. Pp. 92-98.

Jasinski, D. R., Perrnick, J. J., Clark, S. C., and Griffith, J. D. Therapeutic usefulness of propoxyphene napslate in narcotic addiction. *Archives of General Psychiatry*, 1977, **34**, 227-233.

Jessor, R., Graves, T. D., Hanson, R. C., and Jessor, S. L. *Society, personality, and deviant behavior: A study of a tri-ethnic community*. New York: Holt, Rinehart and Winston, 1968.

Joe, G. W. *Retention in treatment for drug users in the DARP: 1969-1971 admissions* (IBR Report No. 73). Fort Worth, Texas: Texas Christian University, Institute of Behavioral Research, May 1973.

Joe, G. W., Singh, B. K., Finklea, D., Hudiburg, R., and Sells, S. B. *Community factors, racial composition of treatment programs, and outcomes. National followup study of admissions to drug abuse treatments in the DARP during 1971-1973* (Services Research Monograph Series, DHEW Publication No. ADM 78-573). Washington, D.C.: National Institute on Drug Abuse, 1977.

Joe, V. C. Review of the internal-external control construct as a personality variable. *Psychological Reports*, 1971, **28**, 619-640.

Johns Hopkins School of Hygiene and Public Health. *An evaluation of treatment programs for drug abusers.* Baltimore, 1974.

Johnson, L. *Drugs and american youth.* Ann Arbor, Michigan: Institute for Social Research, 1973.

Jones, L. E. How 92% beat the dope habit. *Bulletin of the Los Angeles County Medical Association*, 1958, **19**, 37-40.

Judd, L. L., Janowsky, D. S. and Segal, D. S. Behavioral effects of methadone in schizophrenic patients. *American Journal of Psychiatry*, 1981, **138**, 243-245.

Judson, B. A., Carney, T. M., and Goldstein, A. Naltrexone treatment of heroin addiction: Efficacy and safety in a double-blind dosage comparison. *Drug and Alcohol Dependence*, 1981, **7**, 325-346.

Judson, B. A. and Goldstein, A. Symptom complaints of patients maintained on methadone, LAAM (Methadyl Acetate), and Naltrexone of different times in their addiction careers. *Drug and Alcohol Dependence*, 1982(a), **10**, 269-282.

Judson, B. A. and Goldstein, A. Prediction of long-term outcome for heroin addicts admitted to a methadone maintenance program. *Drug and Alcohol Dependence*, 1982(b), **10**, 383-391.

Judson, B. A. and Goldstein, A. Uses of naloxone in the diagnosis and treatment of heroin addiction. In J. R. Cooper, I. Altman, B. S. Brown, and D. Czechowitz (Eds.), *Research on the treatment of narcotic addiction: State of the art.* Washington, D.C., U.S. Government Printing Office, 1983. Pp. 1-9.

Kahn, E. J., Newman, L. L., and Polk, G. The course of the heroin withdrawal syndrome in newborn infants treated with phenobarbital or chlorpromazine. *Journal of Pediatrics*, 1969, **75**, 495-500.

Kahn, R. B., Schramm, N. T., and Joaquin, J. 21-day outpatient methadone detoxification: An evaluation. *International Journal of the Addictions*, 1976, **11**, 629-639.

Kandel, D. B., Treiman, D., Faust, R., and Single, E. Adolescent involvement in legal and illegal drug use: A multiple classification analysis. *Social Forces*, 1976, **55**, 438-458.

Kaplan, H. B. and Meyerowitz, J. H. Social and psychological correlates of drug abuse: A comparison of addict and non-addict populations from the perspective of self theory. *Social Science and Medicine*, 1970, **40**, 203-225.

Kaplan, K. Chronic liver disease in narcotics addicts. *American Journal of Digestive Diseases*, 1963, **8**, 402-410.

Kastenbaum, R. The dimensions of future time perspective: An experimental analysis. *Journal of General Psychology*, 1961, **65**, 203-218.

Katz, S. J., Long, J. M., and Churchman, D. A formative evaluation of a residential drug treatment center. *International Journal of the Addictions*, 1975, **10**, 643-657.

Katzker, E., Steer, R. A., and Schut, J. Differentiation of long-term methadone patients from their admission cohorts. *International Journal of the Addictions*, 1974, **14**, 281-287.

Kaufman, E. The relationship of alcoholism and alcohol abuse to the abuse of other drugs. *American Journal of Drug and Alcohol Abuse*, 1982, **9**, 1-17.

Kaul, B. and Davidow, B. Drug abuse patterns of patients on methadone treatment in New York City. *American Journal of Drug and Alcohol Abuse*, 1981, **8**, 17-25.

Kavaler-Menachem, F. Symposium for study of addiction, 1967. Cited by T. H. Bewley, O. Ben-Arie, and I. P. Jones. Morbidity and mortality from heroin dependence. I. Survey of heroin addicts known to home office. *British Medical Journal*, 1968, **1**, 725-732.

Kay, D. C., Pickworth, W. B., and Neider, G. L. Morphine-like insomnia from heroin in non-dependent human addicts. *British Journal of Clinical Pharmacology*, 1981, **11**, 159-169.

Kendall, S. R. and Gantner, L. M. Late presentation of drug withdrawal symptoms in newborns. *American Journal of Diseases of Children*, 1974, **127**, 58-61.

Khantzian, E. J., Mack, J. E., and Schatzberg, A. F. Heroin use as an attempt to cope: Clinical observations. *American Journal of Psychiatry*, 1974, **131**, 160-164.

Khantzian, E. J. Psychological (structural) vulnerabilities and the specific appeal of narcotics. *Annals of the New York Academy of Science*, 1982, **398**, 24-32.

Kilcoyne, M. M. Heroin-related nephrotic syndrome. In R. W. Richter (Ed.), *Medical aspects of drug abuse*. Hagerstown, Md.: Harper and Row, 1975. Pp. 243-250.

Kleber, H. Clinical experiences with narcotic antagonists. In S. Fisher and A. M. Freedman A. M. (Eds.), *Opiate addiction: Origins and treatment*. Washington, D.C.: Winston and Sons, 1973. Pp. 211-220.

Kleber, H. D. The interaction of a treatment program using opiates for mental illness and an addiction treatment program. In *Opioids in mental illness* (Vol. 398). New York: New York Academy of Sciences, 1982. Pp. 173-177.

Kleber, H. D. Concomitant use of methadone with other psychoactive drugs in the treatment of opiate addicts with other DSM-III diagnoses. In J. R. Cooper, F. Altman, B. S. Brown, and D. Czechowicz (Eds.), *Research on the treatment of narcotic addiction: State of the art*. Washington, D.C., U.S. Government Printing Office, 1983. Pp. 119-138.

Kleber, H., Kinsella, J. K., Riordan, C., Greaves, S., and Sweeney, D. The use of cyclazocine in treating narcotic addicts in a low-intervention setting. *Archives of General Psychiatry*, 1974, **30**, 37-42.

Kleber, H. and Klerman, G. L. Current issues in methadone treatment of heroin dependence. *Medical Care*, 1971, **9**, 379-382.

Kleinman, P. H. Onset of addiction: A first attempt at prediction. *International Journal of the Addictions*, 1978, **13**, 1217-1235.

Kliner, D. J. and Pickens, R. Indicated preference for drugs of abuse. *International Journal of the Addictions*, 1982, **17**, 543-547.

Koenigsberg, L. and Royster, E. *Jobs for drug abuse treatment program clients.* Washington, D.C.: National Institute on Drug Abuse, 1975.

Kolb, D., Gunderson, E. K. E., and Nail, R. L. Perceptions of drug abuse risks in relation to type of drug used and level of experience. *Journal of Clinical Psychology,* 1974, **30**, 380-389.

Kolb, D., Gunderson, E. K. E., and Nail, R. L. Pre-service drug abuse: Family and social history characteristics. *Journal of Community Psychology,* 1974, **2**, 278-282.

Kolb, L. Drug addiction in its relation to crime. *Mental Hygiene,* 1925, **9**, 74-89.

Kolb, L. and Himmelsbach, C. Clinical studies of drug addiction. III. A critical review of the withdrawal treatments with method of evaluating abstinence syndromes. *American Journal of Psychiatry,* 1938, **94**, 759-799.

Korin, H. Comparison of psychometric measures in psychiatric patients using heroin and other drugs. *Journal of Abnormal Psychology,* 1974, **83**, 208-212.

Kosten, T. R., Jalali, B., and Kleeber, H. D. Complementary marital roles of male heroin addicts: Evolution and intervention tactics. *American Journal of Drug and Alcohol Abuse,* 1983, **9**, 155-169.

Kosten, T. R., Rounsaville, B. J., and Kleber, H. D. Relationship of depression to psychosocial stressors in heroin addicts. *Journal of Nervous and Mental Disease,* 1983, **171**, 97-104.

Kozel, N. J., DuPont, R. L., and Brown, B. S. Narcotics and crime: A study of narcotic involvement in an offender population. *International Journal of the Addictions,* 1972, **7**, 443-450.

Kraft, T. Drug addiction and personality disorder. *British Journal of Addiction,* 1970, **64**, 403-408.

Kramer, J. C., Bass, K. A., and Berecochea, J. E. Civil commitment for addicts: The California program. *American Journal of Psychiatry,* 1968, **125**, 816-824.

Kranitz, L. A heroin addiction scale revisited. *International Journal of the Addictions,* 1972, **7**, 715-719.

Kreek, M. J. Medical safety and side effects of methadone in tolerant individuals. *Journal of the American Medical Association,* 1973, **223**, 665-668.

Kreek, M. J. Methadone maintenance treatment for chronic opiate addiction. In R. W. Richter (Ed.), *Medical aspects of drug abuse.* Hagerstown, Md.: Harper and Row, 1975. Pp. 167-185.

Kreek, M. J. Methadone in treatment: Physiological and pharmacological issues. In R. I. DuPont, A. Goldstein, and J. O'Donnell (Eds.). *Handbook on drug abuse.* Washington, D.C.: National Institute on Drug Abuse, 1979. Pp. 57-86.

Kreek, M. J. Metabolic interactions between opiates and alcohol. In *Research developments in drug and alcohol use.* New York. New York Academy of Sciences, 1981, **362**, 36-49.

Kreek, M. J. Health consequences associated with the use of methadone. In J. R. Cooper, F. Altman, B. S. Brown, and D. Czechowicz (Eds.). *Research on the treatment of narcotic addiction: State of the art.* Washington, D.C.: National Institute on Drug Abuse, 1983. Pp. 456-482.

Krueger, D. W. Stressful life events and the return to heroin use. *Journal of Human Stress*, 1981, **7**, 3-8.

Kuhar, M. J., Pert, C. B., and Snyder, S. H. Regional distribution of opiate receptor binding in monkey and human brain. *Nature*, 1973, **245**, 447-450.

Kurland, A. A., Henderson, J. M., Krantz, J. C., Jr., and Kerman, F. Naloxone and the narcotic abuser: A low-dose maintenance program. *International Journal of the Addictions*, 1973, **8**, 127-141.

Kurland, A. A., Krantz, J. C., Henderson, J. M., and Kerman, F. Naloxone and the narcotic abuser: A low dose maintenance program. *International Journal of the Addictions*, 1973, **8**, 127-142.

Kurland, A. A. and McCabe, L. Rapid detoxification of the narcotic addict with naloxone hydrochloride: A preliminary report. *Journal of Clinical Pharmacology*, 1976, **16**, 66-75.

Lahmeyer, H. W., and Steingold, R. G. Pentazocine and tripelennamine: A drug abuse epidemic? *International Journal of the Addictions*, 1980, **15**, 1219-1232.

Lambert, A., Benedict, S. R., Gregory, M. S., McGoldrick, T. A., Strauss, I., Wallace, G. B., and Williams, L. R. Report of the Mayor's Committee on drug addiction to the Honorable Richard C. Patterson, Commissioner of Correction, New York City. *American Journal of Psychiatry*, 1930, **87**, 433-538.

Langenauer, B. J. and Bowdwn, C. L. A follow-up study of narcotic addicts in the NARA program. *American Journal of Psychiatry*, 1971, **128**, 41-46.

Langrod, J., Brill, L., Lowinson, J. and Joseph, H. Methadone maintenance: From research to treatment. In L. Brill and L. Lieberman (Eds.), *Major modalities in the treatment of drug abuse*. New York: Behavioral Publications, 1972. Pp. 107-141.

Laskowitz, D. The adolescent drug addict: An Adlerian view. *Journal of Individual Psychology*, 1961, **17**, 68-79.

Leary, T. *Interpersonal diagnosis of personality*. New York: Appleton Century Crofts, 1957.

LeCompte, G. and Friedman, J. J. Chemotherapy in the treatment of heroin addiction: An alternative to methadone. *Journal of Drug Issues*. 1974, **4**, 332-341.

Lefcourt, H. M. Internal versus external control of reinforcement: A review. *Psychological Bulletin*, 1966, **65**, 206-220.

Lehmann, W. X. The use of I-alpha-acetyl-methadol (LAAM) as compared to methadone in the maintenance and detoxification of young heroin addicts. In J. D. Blaine and P. F. Renault (Eds.), *Rx: 3x/week LAAM, alternative to methadone* (NIDA Research Monograph Series No. 8). Washington, D.C.: U.S. Government Printing Office, 1976. Pp. 82-83.

Lennard, H. L., Epstein, L. J., and Rosenthal, M. S. The methadone illusion. *Science*, 1972, **176**, 881-884.

Lerner, A. M. and Oerther, F. J. Characteristics and sequelae of paregoric abuse. *Annals of Internal Medicine*, 1966, **65**, 1019-1030.

Lessin, B. and Siegel, L. Endocarditis in drug addicts. *Journal of the American Medical Association*, 1973, **224**, 1650.

Lettieri, D. J. Theories of drug use. In D. J. Lettieri (Ed.), *Drugs and suicide: When other coping strategies fail.* Beverly Hills, CA: Sage, 1978.

Levine, D. G., Levin, D. B., Sloan, I. H., and Chappel, J. N. Personality correlates of success in a methadone maintenance program. *American Journal of Psychiatry,* 1972, **129**, 456-460.

Levine, H. R. *Legal dimensions of drug abuse in the United States.* Springfield, Ill.: Charles C. Thomas, 1974.

Levine, R. R. *Pharmacology: Drug actions and reactions.* Boston: Little, Brown, 1973.

Levine, S. F. *Narcotics and drug abuse.* Cincinnati: W. H. Anderson, 1973.

Levy, B. S. Five years after: A follow-up of 50 narcotic addicts. *American Journal of Psychiatry,* 1972, **128**, 868-872.

Lewis, D., Hersch, R., Black, R., and Mayer, J. Use of narcotic antagonists (naltrexone) in an addiction treatment program. In D. Julius and P. Renault (Eds.), *Narcotic Antagonists: Naltrexone.* (Research Monograph Series). Washington, D.C. National Institute on Drug Abuse, 1976.

Lewis, S. A., Oswald, I., Evans, J. I., Akindele, M. O., and Tompsett, S. L. Heroin and human sleep. *Electroencephalography and Clinical Neurophysiology,* 1970, **28**, 374-381.

Lewis, V. A., Peterson, D. M., Geis, G., and Pollack, S. Ethical and social-psychological aspects of urinalysis to detect heroin use. *British Journal of Addiction,* 1972, **67**, 303-307.

Lidz, C. W., Lewis, S. H., Crane, L. E., and Gould, L. C. Heroin maintenance and heroin control. *International Journal of the Addictions,* 1975, **10**, 35-52.

Lieberman, J. J. The drug addict and the "cop out" father. *Adolescence,* 1974, **9**, 7-14.

Lifschitz, M. H., Wilson, G. S., Smith, E. D., and Desmond, M. M. Fetal and postnatal growth of children born to narcotic-dependent women. *Journal of Pediatrics,* 1983, **102**, 686-691.

Lincoln, L. Berryman, M., and Linn, M. W. Drug abuse: A comparison of attitudes. *Comprehensive Psychiatry,* 1973, **14**, 465-471.

Lindesmith, A. R. A sociological theory of drug addiction. *American Journal of Sociology,* 1938, **43**, 593-613.

Lindesmith, A. R. *Opiate addiction.* Bloomington, Indiana: Principia Press, 1947.

Lindesmith, A. R. *The addict and the law.* Bloomington: Indiana University Press, 1966.

Lindesmith, A. R. *The addict and the law.* New York: Vintage Books, 1967.

Lindesmith, A. R. *Addiction and opiates.* Chicago: Aldine Co., 1968.

Lindesmith, A. R. Patent medicine for the drug problem. *American Journal of Orthopsychiatry,* 1973, **43**, 512-514.

Lindesmith, A. R. and Gagnon, J. H. Anomie and drug addiction. In M. B. Clinard (Ed.), *Anomie and deviant behavior.* New York: Free Press of Glencoe, 1964. Pp. 158-188.

Ling, W., Blakis, M., Holmes, E. D., Klett, C. J., and Carter, W. E. Restabilization with methadone after methadyl acetate maintenance. *Archives of General Psychiatry,* 1980, **37**, 194-196.

Ling, W. and Blaine, J. D. The use of LAAM in treatment. In, R. I. Dupont, A. Goldstein and J. O'Donnell (Eds.), *Handbook of drug abuse.* Washington, D.C.: NIDA, 1979.

Ling, W., Chauvastra, V. C., Kaim, S. C., and Klett, C. J. Acetylmethadol and methadone as maintenance treatments for heroin addicts. A Veterans Administration Cooperative Study. *Archives of General Psychiatry,* 1976, **33**, 709-720.

Ling, W., Holmes, E. D., Post, G. R., and Litaker, M. B. A systematic psychiatric study of the heroin addicts. In National Association for the Prevention of Addiction to Narcotics, *Proceedings of the Fifth National Conference on Methadone Treatment.* New York: The Association, 1973. Pp. 429-432.

Lipscomb, W. R. Drug use in a black ghetto. *American Journal of Psychiatry,* 1971, **127**, 1166-1169.

Lipski, J., Stimmel, B., and Donoso, E. The effect of heroin and multiple drug abuse on the electrocardiogram. *American Heart Journal,* 1973, **86**, 663-668.

Litt, I. F., Cohen, M. I., Schonberg, S. K., and Spigland, I. Liver disease in the drug-using adolescent. *Journal of Pediatrics,* 1972, **81**, 238-242.

Loh, H. H., Shen, F. H. and Way, E. L. Inhibition of morphine tolerance and physical dependence development and main serotonin synthesis by cycloheximide. *Biochemical Pharmacology,* 1969, **18**, 2711-2721.

Lombardi, D. N., O'Brien, B. J., and Isele, F. W. Differential responses of addicts and nonaddicts on the MMPI. *Journal of Projective Techniques and Personality Assessment,* 1968, **32**, 479-482.

Lotti, V. J., Lomax, P., and George, G. J. Temperature responses in the rat following intracerebral microinjection of morphine. *Journal of Pharmacology and Experimental Therapeutics,* 1965, **150**, 135-139.

Louria, D. B., Hensle, T., and Rose, J. The major medical complications of heroin addiction. *Annals of Internal Medicine,* 1967, **67**, 1-22.

Lowinson, J. H., and Millman, R. B. Clinical aspects of methadone maintenance treatment. In R. I. DuPont, A. Goldstein, and J. O'Donnell (Eds.), *Handbook on drug abuse.* Washington, D.C.: National Institute on Drug Abuse, 1979. Pp. 49-56.

Lukoff, I. F., Quatrone, D. and Sardell, A. *Some aspects of the epidemiology of heroin use in a ghetto community: A preliminary report.* Washington, D.C.: National Institute of Law Enforcement and Criminal Justice, 1972.

MacGregor, I. S. and Lowenstein, A. Quinine blindness. *Lancet,* 1944, **2**, 566.

McCorkle, L., Elias, A., and Bixby, L. *The Highfields Story.* New York: Holt, Rinehart and Winston, 1958.

McDougall, W. A. A chemical theory of temperament applied to introversion and extroversion. *Journal of Abnormal and Social Psychology,* 1929, **24**, 293-309.

McCane, M. E., Stitzer, M. L., Bigelow, G. E., and Liebson, I. A. Initial opiate use and treatment outcome in methadone detoxification patients. In L. S. Harris (Ed.), *Problems of drug dependence, 1982* (NIDA Research monograph #43). Washington, D.C.: U.S. Government Printing Office. Pp. 280-286.

McGlothlin, W. H. California civil commitment: A decade later. *Journal of Drug Issues,* 1976, **6,** 368-379.

McGlothlin, W. H., and Anglin, M. D. *Long-term follow-up of clients of high and low-dose methadone programs.* Los Angeles, CA: University of California, Department of Psychology, 1981.

McGlothlin, W. H., Anglin, M. D., and Wilson, B. D. A follow-up of admission to the California Civil Addict Program. *American Journal of Drug and Alcohol Abuse,* 1977(a), **4,** 179-199.

McGlothlin, W. H., Anglin, M. D., and Wilson, B. D. *An Evaluation of the California Civil Addict Program* (National Institute on Drug Abuse, Services Research Monograph Series, DHEW Publication No. ADM 78-558). Washington, D.C.: U.S. Government Printing Office, 1977(b).

McKee, M. R. Addicts and rehabilitation. Whom to send where? *Psychological Reports,* 1972, **30,** 731-755.

McLellan, A. T., Luborsky, L., Woody, G. E., and O'Brien, C. P. An improved diagnostic evaluation instrument for substance abuse patients: The addiction severity index. *Journal of Nervous and Mental Disease,* 1980, **168,** 26-33.

McLellan, A. T., Luborsky, L., Woody, G. E., and O'Brien, C. P. Predicting response to alcohol and drug abuse treatments: Role of psychiatric severity. *Archives of General Psychiatry,* 1983, **40,** 620-628.

McLellan, A. T., O'Brien, C. P., Woody, G. E., Luborsky, L., and Druley, K. A. Is drug abuse treatment effective? In L. S. Harris (Ed.) *Problems of drug dependence, 1981* (NIDA Research Monograph #41). Washington, D.C.: U.S. Government Printing Office, 1982. Pp. 223-229.

McLellan, A. T., Woody, G. E., Evans, B. D., and O'Brien, C. P. Treatment of mixed abusers in methadone maintenance: Role of psychiatric factors. *Annals of the New York Academy of Science,* 1982, pp. 65-78.

McLellan, A. T., Woody, G. E., and O'Brien, C. P. Development of psychiatric illness in drug abusers: Possible role of drug preference. *New England Journal of Medicine,* 1979, **301,** 1310-1313.

McNamara, J. D. The history of United States anti-opium policy. *Federal Probation,* 1973, **37,** 15-21.

Macht, D. I. and Macht, M. B. Effect of cobra venom and opiates on mental efficiency tests. *American Journal of Physiology,* 1939, **126,** 574-575.

Maddux, J. F. and Bowden, C. L. Critique of success with methadone maintenance. *American Journal of Psychiatry.* 1972, **129,** 440-446.

Maddux, J. F., and Desmond, D. P. Residence relocation inhibits opioid dependence. *Archives of General Psychiatry,* 1982, **39,** 1313-1317.

Maddux, J. F. Desmond, D. P., and Esquivel, M. Outpatient methadone withdrawal for heroin dependence. *American Journal of Drug and Alcohol Abuse,* 1980, **7,** 323-333.

Madinaveitia, J. Search for addiction in a new analgesic. In H. Steinberg (Ed.), *Scientific basis of drug dependence*. London: Churchill, 1969. Pp. 155-165.

Mandell, W., Goldschmidt, P. G., and Grover, P. *Interdrug — An Evaluation of Treatment Programs for Drug Abusers*. Baltimore, Md.: Johns Hopkins University, School of Hygiene and Public Health, 1973.

Manning, F. J. and Ingraham, L. H. Drug "overdoses" among U.S. soldiers in Europe, 1978-1979. I. Demographics and toxicology. *International Journal of the Addictions*, 1983, **18**, 89-98.

Markoff, E. L. Synanon in drug addiction. In J. H. Masserman (Ed.), *Handbook of psychiatric therapies*, New York: Science House, 1966. Pp. 297-308.

Marks, P. A. and Seeman, W. *The actuarial description of abnormal personality*. Baltimore: Williams and Wilkins, 1963.

Martin, J. and Inglis, J. Pain tolerance and narcotic addiction. *British Journal of Social and Clinical Psychology*, 1965, **4**, 224-229.

Martin, W. R. Analgesic and antipyretic drugs. I. Strong analgesics. In W. S. Root and F. G. Hoffman (Eds.) *Physiological pharmacology* (Vol. 1). New York: Academic Press, 1963. Pp. 225-312.

Martin, W. R. Opioid antagonists, *Pharmacological Reviews*, 1967, **19**, 463-521.

Martin, W. R. The basis and possible utility of the use of opioid antagonists in the ambulatory treatment of the addict. In A. Wikler (Ed.), *The addictive states*. Baltimore: Williams and Wilkins, 1968(a). Pp. 367-377.

Martin, W. R. A homeostatic and redundancy theory of tolerance to and dependence on narcotic analgesics. In A. Wikler (Ed.), *The addictive states*. Baltimore: Williams and Wilkins, 1968(b). Pp. 206-225.

Martin, W. R. Drug dependence. In J. R. DiPalma (Ed.), *Drill's pharmacology in medicine*. New York: McGraw-Hill, 1971. Pp. 362-378.

Martin, W. R., Eades, C. G., Thompson, J. A., Huppler, R. E., and Gilbert, P. E. The effects of morphine and nalorphine-like drugs in the non-dependent and morphine-dependent chronic spinal dog. *Journal of Pharmocology and Experimental Therapeutics*, 1976, **197**, 517-532.

Martin, W. R. and Fraser, H. F. A comparative study of physiological and subjective effects of heroin and morphine administered intravenously in postaddicts. *Journal of Pharmacology and Experimental Therapeutics*, 1961, **133**, 388-399.

Martin, W. R., Gorodetzky, C. W., and McClare, T. K. An experimental study in the treatment of narcotic addicts with cyclazocine. *Clinical Pharmacology and Therapeutics*, 1966, **7**, 455-465.

Martin, W. R. and Jasinski, D. R. Physiological parameters of morphine abstinence, in man-tolerance, early abstinence, protracted abstinence. *Journal of Psychiatric Research*, 1969, **7**, 9-17.

Martin, W. R., Jasinski, D. R., Haertzen, C. A., Kay, D. C., Jones, B. E., Mansky, P. A., and Carpenter, R. W. Methadone: A re-evaluation. *Archives of General Psychiatry*, 1973, **28**, 286-295.

Martin, W. R., Jasinski, D. R., and Mansky, P. A. Naltrexone, an antagonist for the treatment of heroin dependence. *Archives of General Psychiatry*, 1973, **28**, 784-791.

Martin, W. R., Winkler, A., Eades, C. G., and Pescor, F. T. Tolerance to and physical dependence on morphine in rats. *Psychopharmacologia*, 1963, **4**, 247-260.

Martino, E. R. and Truss, C. V. Drug use and attitudes towards social and legal aspects of marijuana in a large metropolitan university. *Journal of Counseling Psychology*, 1973, **20**, 120-126.

Maurer, D. W. and Vogel, V. H. *Narcotics and narcotic addiction*. Springfield, Ill.: Charles C. Thomas, 1954; 1962; 1973.

Melchior, L., and Myers, R. D. Genetic differences in ethanol drinking of the rat following injection of 6-OHDA, 5, 6-DHT, or 5-7-DHT into the cerebral ventricles. *Pharmacology, Biochemistry and Behavior,* 1976, **5**, 63-72.

Mendelson, J. H. and Mello, N. K. Hormones and psychosexual development in young men following chronic heroin use. *Neurobehavioral Toxicology and Teratology*, 1982, **4**, 441-445.

Merton, R. K. *Social theory and social structure*. Glencoe, Ill.: Free Press, 1957.

Methadone Maintenance Evaluation Committee. Progress report of evaluation of methadone maintenance treatment program as of March 31, 1968. *Journal of the American Medical Association*, 1968, **206**, 2712-2714.

Miles, C. P. Conditions predisposing to suicide: A review. *Journal of Nervous and Mental Disease*, 1977, **164**, 231-246.

Miller, J. S. Addiction, a persistent cognition? *Contemporary Psychology*, 1969, **14**, 301-302.

Miller, J. S., Sensenig, J., and Reed, T. E. Risky and cautious values among narcotic addicts. *International Journal of the Addictions*, 1972, **7**, 1-7.

Miller, J. S., Sensenig, J., Stocker, R. B., and Campbell, R. Value patterns of drug addicts as a function of race and sex. *International Journal of the Addictions*, 1973, **8**, 589-598.

Minda, K. B. and Gorbach, S. L. Favorable experience with bacterial endocarditis in heroin addicts. *Annals of Internal Medicine*, 1973, **78**, 25-32.

Mirin, S. M., Meyer, R. E., and McNamee, H. B. Psychopathology, craving and mood during heroin acquisition: An experimental study. *International Journal of the Addictions*, 1976, **11**, 525-544.

Mirin, S. M., Meyer, R. E., Mendelson, J. H., and Ellingboe, J. Opiate use and sexual function. *American Journal of Psychiatry*, 1980, **137**, 909-915.

Mitcheson, M., Davidson, J., Hawks, D. V., Hitchens, L., and Malone, S. Sedative abuse by heroin addicts. *Lancet*, 1970, **1**, 606-607.

Mo, B. P. and Way, E. L. An assessment of inhalation as a mode of administration of heroin by addicts. *Journal of Pharmacology and Experimental Therapeutics*, 1966, **154**, 142-151.

Moffett, A. P., Soloway, I. H., and Glick, M. X. Post-treatment behavior of two populations of patients treated at a methadone outpatient facility. In J. M. Singh, L. Miller, and H. Lal (Eds.), *Drug addiction: Clinical and socio-legal aspects* (Vol. 2). Mount Kisco, New York: Futura, 1972. Pp. 133-136.

Monroe, J. J., Ross, W. F., and Berzins, J. I. The decline of the addict as "psychopath": Implications for community care. *International Journal of the Addictions*, 1967, **2**, 601-608.

Morell, J. A. The state of drug abuse program evaluation: A critical analysis. Paper presented at the 83rd annual meeting of the American Psychological Association, Chicago, Illinois, August, 1975.

Morell, J. Evaluating the outcome in correctional drug abuse treatment. In J. Platt, C. Labate, and R. Wicks (Eds.), *Evaluative research in correctional drug abuse.* Lexington, Mass.: D. C. Heath and Company, 1977.

Most, H. Falciparum malaria in drug addicts. *American Journal of Tropical Medicine,* 1940(a), **20,** 551-567.

Most, H. Falciparum malaria among drug addicts. Epidemiologic studies. *American Journal of Public Health,* 1940(b), **30,** 403-410.

Murphree, H. B. Narcotic analgesics. I. Opium alkaloids. In J. R. DiPalma (Ed.), *Drill's pharmacology in medicine.* New York: McGraw-Hill, 1971. Pp. 324-349.

Musto, D. F. *The American disease: Origins of narcotic control.* New Haven: Yale University Press, 1973.

Nash, G. *The impact of drug abuse treatment upon criminality: A look at 19 programs.* New Jersey. Montclair State College, 1973.

Nathan, P. E., and Lansky, D. Common methodological problems in research on the addictions. *Journal of Consulting and Clinical Psychology,* 1978, **46,** 713-726.

National Clearinghouse for Drug Abuse Information, Narcotic antagonists, Report Series 26, No. 1, 1973.

National Clearinghouse for Drug Abuse Information, Methadone: The drug and its therapeutic uses in the treatment of addiction, Report Series 31, No. 1, 1974.

National Institute on Drug Abuse. *CODAP quarterly reports.* Rockville, Md.: The Institute, 1976.

National Institute on Drug Abuse. *Developing an occupational drug abuse program: Considerations and approaches* (NIDA Research Monograph Series, Services Research Branch, Division of Resource Development, DHEW Publication No. ADM 79-692). Washington, D.C.: U.S. Government Printing Office, 1979.

National Institute on Drug Abuse. Treatment effectiveness. In *Treatment Research Notes.* September 1981, Pp. 4-7.

Nelson, J. E. Drug Abusers on the job. *Jom,* **23,** 403-408.

Newman, R. G. Detoxification treatment of narcotic addicts. In R. I. DuPont, A. Goldstein, and J. O'Donnell (Eds.), *Handbook on drug abuse.* Washington, D.C. National Institute on Drug Abuse, 1979. Pp. 21-29.

Newman, R. G., Bashkow, S., and Cates, M. Arrest histories before and after admission to a methadone maintenance treatment program. *Contemporary Drug Problems,* 1973, **2,** 417-430.

Newman, R. G., Cates, M., Tytun, A., and Werbell, B. Narcotic addiction in New York City: Trends from 1968 to mid-1973. *American Journal of Drug and Alcohol Abuse,* 1974, **1,** 53-66.

Ng, L. K. Y., Dauthitt, T. C., Thoa, N. B., and Herbert, C. A. Modification of morphine-withdrawal syndrome in rats following transauricular electrostimulation: An experimental paradigm for auricular electroacupuncture. *Biological Psychiatry,* 1975, **10,** 575-580.

Nichols, A. W., Salwent, M. B., and Torrens, P. R. Outpatient induction to methadone maintenance treatment for heroin addicts. *Archives of Internal Medicine*, 1971, **127**, 903-909.

Nightingale, S. Treatment for drug abusers in the United States. *Addictive Diseases*, 1977, **3**, 11-20.

Noble, P. and Barnes, G. G. Drug taking in adolescent girls: Factors associated with the progression to narcotic use. *British Medical Journal*, 1971 (June 12), 620-623.

Noble, P., Hart, T., and Nation, R. Correlates and outcome of illicit drug use by adolescent girls. *British Journal of Psychiatry*, 1972, **120**, 497-504.

Norman, B. Tetanus after hypodermic injection of morphine. *Lancet*, 1876, **1**, 873.

Nurco, D. N. Etiological aspects of drug abuse. In R. I. DuPont, A. Goldstein, and J. O'Donnell (Eds.), *Handbook on drug abuse*. Washington, D.C. National Institute on Drug Abuse, 1979. Pp. 315-324.

Nurco, D. N., Cisin, I. H., and Balter, M. B. Addict and careers II: The first ten years. *International Journal of the Addictions*, 1981, **16**, 1327-1356.

Nurco, D. N., Cisin, I. H., and Balter, M. B. Addict careers III: Trends across time. *International Journal of the Addictions*, 1981, **16**, 1357-1372.

Nurco, D. N. and Farrell, E. V. Narcotic abusers and poverty. *Criminology*, 1975, **13**, 389-399.

Nurco, D. N. and Lerner, M. Characteristics of drug abuses in a correctional system. *Journal of Drug Issues*, 1972, **2**, 49-56.

Nyswander, M. E. The methadone treatment of heroin addiction. *Hospital Practice*, 1967, **2**, 27-33.

Nyswander, M. E. Methadone therapy for heroin addiction: Where are we? Where are we going? *Drug Therapy*, 1971, **1**, 23-30.

Nyswander, M. E. and Dole, V. P. The present status of methadone blockade treatment. *American Journal of Psychiatry*, 1967, **123**, 1441-1442.

Obitz, F. W., Cooper, K. and Madeiros, D. C. General and specific perceived locus of control of heroin addicts. *Internatioanl Journal of the Addictions*, 1974, **9**, 757-760.

Obitz, F. W., Oziel, L. J. and Unmacht, J. J. General and specific perceived locus of control in delinquent drug users. *International Journal of the Addictions*, 1973, **8**, 723-727.

O'Brien, C. P., Greenstein, R., Evans, B., Woody, G. E. and Arndt, R. Opioid antagonists: Do they have a role in treatment programs? In L. S. Harris (Ed.), *Problems of drug dependence, 1982* (NIDA Research Monograph #43). Washington, D.C.: U.S. Government Printing Office, 1983. Pp. 71-78.

O'Brien, C. P., Greenstein, R., Mintz, J., and Woody, G. Clinical experience with naltrexone. *American Journal of Drug and Alcohol Abuse*, 1975, **2**, 365-377.

O'Brien, C. P., O'Brien, T. J., Mintz, J., and Brady, J. P. Conditioning of narcotic abstinence symptoms in human subjects. *Drug and Alcohol Dependence*, 1975, **1**, 115-123.

O'Brien, C. P., and Ng, L. K. Y. *Innovative treatments for drug addiction.* In R. I. DuPont, A. Goldstein, and J. O'Donnell (Eds.), *Handbook on drug abuse.* Washington, D.C. National Institute on Drug Abuse, 1979. Pp. 39-47.

O'Brien, C. P., Testa, T., O'Brien, T. J., Brady, J. P., and Wells, B. Conditioned narcotic withdrawal in humans. *Science*, 1977, **195**, 1000-1002.

O'Brien, J. S., Raynes, A. E., and Patch, V. D. Treatment of heroin addiction with aversion therapy, relaxation training and systematic desensitization. *Behavior Research and Therapy*, 1972, **10**, 77-80.

O'Donnell, J. A. *Narcotic addicts in Kentucky.* Washington, D.C.: United States Public Health Service Publication, No. 1881, 1969.

O'Donnell, J. A., Voss, H. L., Clayton, R. R., Slatin, G. T., and Room, R. G. *Young men and drugs: A nationwide survey* (NIDA Research Monograph 5). Washington, D.C.: U.S. Government Printing Office, 1976.

O'Donnell, J. A follow-up of narcotic addicts: Mortality, relapse, and abstinence. *American Journal of Orthopsychiatry*, 1964, **34**, 948-954.

Ogborne, A. C. Two types of heroin reactions. *British Journal of Addiction*, 1974, **69**, 237-242.

Ohler, R. L. Heroin use by veterans. *New England Journal of Medicine*, 1971, **285**, 692.

Oldendorf, W., Hyman, S., Braun, L., and Oldendorf, S. Blood-brain barrier: Penetration of morphine, codeine, heroin, and methadone after carotid injection. *Science*, 1972, **178**, 984-986.

Olds, J. Hypothalamic substrates of reward. *Physiological Reviews*, 1962, **42**, 554-604.

Olson, R. W. MMPI sex differences in narcotic addicts. *Journal of General Psychology*, 1964, **71**, 157-266.

O'Malley, J. E., Anderson, W. H., and Lazare, A. Failure of outpatient treatment of drug abuse: I. Heroin. *American Journal of Psychiatry*, 1972, **128**, 865-872.

Oppenheimer, E., and Stimson, G. V. Seven year follow-up of heroin addicts: Life histories summarized. *Drug and Alcohol Dependence*, 1982, **9**, 153-159.

Oswald, I., Evans, J. I., and Lewis, S. A. Addictive drugs cause suppression of paradoxical sleep with withdrawal rebound. In H. Steinberg (Ed.), *Scientific basis of drug dependence.* London: Churchill, 1969. Pp. 243-258.

Overall, J. E. MMPI personality patterns of alcoholics and narcotic addicts. *Quarterly Journal of Studies on Alcoholism*, 1973, **34**, 104-111.

Panton, J. H. and Behre, C. Characteristics associated with drug addiction in a state prison population. *Journal of Community Psychology*, 1973, **1**, 411-416.

Parr, W. C., Woodward, W. A., Robinowitz, R., and Penk, W. E. Cross validation of a heroin addiction (HE) scale in a treatment setting. *International Journal of the Addictions*, 1981, **16**, 549-553.

Paschke, W. R. The addiction cycle: A learning theory—Peer group model. *Corrective Psychiatry and Journal of Social Therapy*, 1970, **16**, 74-81.

Paton, W. D. M. The responses of, and release of acetylcholine by guinea-pig small intestine in response to coaxial electrical stimulation. *Abstracts of the Twentieth International Physiological Congress*, Brussels, 1956. Pp. 708-709.

Paton, W. D. The action of morphine and related substances on contraction and on acetylcholine output of coaxially stimulated guinea-pig ileum. *British Journal of Pharmacology*, 1957, **12**, 119-127.

Paton, W. D. A pharmacological approach to drug dependence and drug tolerance. In H. Steinberg (Ed.), *Scientific basis of drug dependence*. London: Churchill, 1969. Pp. 31-48.

Paton, W. D. Drug dependence: Pharmacological and physiological aspects. *Journal of the Royal College of Physicians* (London), 1970, **4**, 247-254.

Paton, W. D. and Zar, M. A. The origin of the acetylcholine released from guinea-pig intestine and longitudinal muscle strips. *Journal of Physiology*, 1968, **194**, 13-33.

Patterson, M. A. Effects of neuro-electric therapy (N.E.T.) in drug addiction: Interim report. *Bulletin on Narcotics*, 1976, **28**, 55-62.

Pearson, J. and Richter, R. W. Neuropathological effects of opiate addiction. In R. W. Richter (Ed.), *Medical aspects of drug abuse*. Hagerstown, Md.: Harper and Row, 1975. Pp. 308-319.

Pearson, J., Richter, R. W., Baden, M. M., et al: Transverse myelopathy as an illustration of the neurologic and neuropathologic features of heroin addiction. *Human Pathology*, 1972, **3**, 107-113.

Peck, M. L. and Klugman, D. J. Rehabilitation of drug dependent offenders: An alternative approach. *Federal Probation*, 1973, **37**, 18-23.

Penk, W. E., Robinowitz, R., Roberts, W. R., Dulan, M. P., and Atkins, H. MMPI differences of male Hispanic-American, black, and white heroin addicts. *Journal of Consulting and Clinical Psychology*, 1981, **49**, 488-490.

Penk, W. E., Robinowitz, R., Woodward, W. A., and Hess, J. L. MMPI factor scale differences among heroin addicts differing in race and admission status. *International Journal of the Addictions*, 1980, **15**, 329-337.

Perkins, M. E. Methadone maintenance: Expanding the concept of service. *American Journal of Psychiatry*, 1972, **129**, 461-462.

Perkins, M. E. and Bloch, H. I. Survey of a methadone maintenance treatment program. *American Journal of Psychiatry*, 1970, **126**, 1389-1396.

Perkins, M. E. and Bloch, H. I. A study of some failures in methadone treatment. *American Journal of Psychiatry*, 1971, **128**, 47-51.

Perkins, M. E. and Richman, A. Prevalence of participation in methadone programs. *American Journal of Psychiatry*, 1972, **129**, 447-450.

Pert, C. B. and Snyder, S. H. Opiate receptor: Demonstration in nervous tissue. *Science*, 1973, **179**, 1011-1014.

Pert, C. B. and Snyder, S. H. Properties of opiate-receptor binding in rat brain. *Proceedings of the National Academy of Sciences*, 1973, **70**, 2243-2247.

Pescor, M. J. Follow-up study of treated drug addicts. *Public Health Reports*. 1943, Supplement #170.

Phillipson, R. Methadone maintenance: Some uses, some limitations, some dangers. In J. M. Singh, L. Miller and H. Lal (Eds.), *Drug addiction: Clinical and sociolegal aspects* (Vol. 2). Mount Kisco, New York: Futura, 1972. Pp. 133-136.

Pin, E. J., Martin, J. M., and Walsh, J. F. A followup study of 300 ex-clients of a drug-free narcotic treatment program in New York City. *American Journal of Drug and Alcohol Abuse*, 1976, **3**, 397-407.

Platt, J. J. "Addiction-proneness" and personality in heroin addicts. *Journal of Abnormal Psychology*, 1975, **84**, 303-306.

Platt, J. J., Hoffman, A., and Ebert, K. Recent trends in the demography of heroin addiction among youthful offenders. *International Journal of the Addictions*, 1976, **11**, 221-236.

Platt, J. J. and Labate, C. Recidivism in youthful heroin offenders and characteristics of parole behavior and environment. *International Journal of the Addictions*, 1976(a), **11**, 651-657.

Platt, J. J. and Labate, C. Recidivism in youthful heroin offenders and pre-incarceration demographic characteristics. 1976 (b).

Platt, J. J., Labate, C., and Wicks, R. J. (Eds.) *Evaluative research in correctional drug abuse treatment*. Lexington, MA.: Lexington Books, 1977.

Platt, J. J., Metzger, D., and Perry, G. Evaluation of a heroin addiction treatment program within a correctional environment. In R. R. Ross and P. Gendreau (Eds.), *Effective correctional treatment*. Ontario: Butterworth, 1980. Pp. 421-435.

Platt, J. J., Morell, J., Flaherty, E., and Metzger, D. *Controlled study of methadone rehabilitation process: Final report*. National Institute on Drug Abuse, Grant No. R01-DA01929, July, 1982.

Platt, J. J., Scura, W. C., and Hannon, J. Problem-solving thinking of youthful incarcerated heroin addicts. *Journal of Community Psychology*, 1973, **1**, 278-281.

Platt, J. J., Scura, W. C., and Hoffman, A. Heroin addiction incidence among youthful offenders, 1968-1972. *Journal of Community Psychology*, 1973, **1**, 408-411.

Platt, J. J. and Spivack, G. Performance in important areas of life as a source of positive self-regard. *Proceedings, 81st Annual Convention, American Psychological Association*, 1973, **8**, 235-236.

Pomeranz, B., Cheng, R., and Law, P. Acupuncture reduces electrophysiological and behavioral responses to noxious stimuli: Pituitary is implicated. *Experimental Neurology*, 1977, **54**, 172-178.

Potter, H. P., Cohen, N., and Norris, R. F. Chronic hepatic dysfunction in heroin addicts. Possible relation to carrier state of viral hepatitis. *Journal of the American Medical Association*, 1960, **174**, 2049-2051.

Preble, E. and Casey, J. J. Taking care of business—The heroin user's life on the street. In R. H. Coombs, L. J. Fry and P. G. Lewis (Eds.), *Socialization in drug abuse*. Cambridge, Mass.: Schenkman Publishing Co., 1976.

Presnall, L. F. The employment and training of ex-drug users: A three-way interaction. In *Developments in the field of drug abuse: National drug abuse conference 1974*. Cambridge, Mass.: Schenkman Publishing Co., 1975.

Priestly, B. Drug addiction and the newborn. *Developmental Medicine and Child Neurology*, 1973, **15**, 200-201.

Primm, B. S. Dangerous new attacks on methadone maintenance. *Journal of Drug Issues*, 1974, Fall, 323-326.

Rado, S. The psychoanalysis of pharmacothymia (drug addiction). *Psychoanalytic Quarterly*, 1933, **2**, 1-23.

Rado, S. Fighting narcotic bondage and other forms of narcotic disorders. *Comprehensive Psychiatry*, 1963, **4**, 160-167.

Ramer, B. S. and Flohr, R. B. Rational planning for drug abuse services. In P. G. Bourne (Ed.), *Addiction*. New York: Academic Press, 1974.

Ramer, B. S., Zaslove, M. O., and Langan, J. Is methadone enough? The usage of ancillary treatment during methadone maintenance. *American Journal of Psychiatry*, 1971, **127**, 1040-1044.

Raubolt, R. R. and Bratter, T. E. Games addicts play: Implications for group treatment. *Corrective and Social Psychiatry*, 1974, **20**, 3-10.

Rawson, R. A., Mann, A. J., Tennant, F. S., and Clabough, D. Efficacy of psychotherapeutic counseling during 21-day ambulatory heroin detoxification. In L. S. Harris (Ed.), *Problems of drug dependence, 1982* (NIDA Research Monograph #43). Washington, D.C.: U.S. Government Printing Office. Pp. 310-314.

Ray, M. B. The cycle of abstinence and relapse among heroin addicts. *Social Problems*, 1961, **9**, 132-140.

Ray. O. S. *Drugs, society, and human behavior*. St. Louis: C. V. Mosby, 1972.

Razani, J., Chisholm, O., Glasser, M., and Kappeler, T. Self-regulated methadone detoxification of heroin addicts. *Archives of General Psychiatry*, 1975, **32**, 909-911.

Rector, M. G. Heroin maintenance: A rational approach. *Crime and Delinquency*, 1972, **18**, 241-242.

Reed, B. et al. *Women's drug research coordinating project* (summary report). Ann Arbor: Wayne County Department of Substance Abuse Services and the University of Michigan, 1977.

Reichle, C. W., Smith, G. M., Gravenstein, J. S., Macris, S. G., and Beecher, H. K. Comparative analgesic potency of heroin and morphine in post-operative patients. *Journal of Pharmacology and Experimental Therapeutics*, 1962, **136**, 43-46.

Remmer, H. Tolerance to barbiturates by increased breakdown. In H. Steinberg (Ed.), *Scientific basis of drug dependence*. London: Churchill, 1969. Pp. 111-128.

Renault, P. F. Methadone maintenance: The effect of knowledge of dosage. *International Journal of the Addictions*, 1973, **8**, 41-48.

Renault, P. Treatment of heroin-dependent persons with antagonists: Current status. In R. E. Willette and G. Barnett (Eds.), *Narcotic antagonists: Naltrexone pharmacology and sustained-release preparations* (NIDA Research Monograph Series #28). Washington, D.C.: U.S. Government Printing Office, 1981, pp. 11-22.

Resnick, R. Methadone detoxification from illicit opiates and methadone maintenance. In J. R. Cooper, F. Altman, B. S. Brown and D. Czechowicz (Eds.), *Research on the treatment of narcotic addiction: state of the art* (NIDA Treatment Research Monograph Series). Washington, D.C.: U.S. Government Printing Office, 1983. Pp. 160-167.

Resnick, R. B., Butler, P., and Waston, A. M. Patient self-regulation of methadone maintenance dose. In L. S. Harris (Ed.), *Problems of drug dependence, 1981* (NIDA Research Monograph #41). Washington, D.C.: U.S. Government Printing Office, 1982. Pp. 327-330.

Resnick, R. B., Fink, M., and Friedman, A. M. A cyclazocine typology in opiate dependence. *American Journal of Psychiatry,* 1970, **126,** 1256-1260.

Resnick, R. B., Kestenbaum, R. S., Gazanaga, P., Volanka, and Freedman, A. M. Experimental technique for rapid withdrawal from methadone maintenance: Results of pilot trials. In E. Senay, V. Shorty, and H. Alksne (Eds.), *Developments in the field of drug abuse.* Cambridge, Mass.: Schenkman, 1975.

Resnick, R. B., Kestenbaum, R. S., Washton, A., and Poole, D. Naloxone-precipitated withdrawal: A method for rapid induction onto naltrexone. *Clinical Pharmacology and Therapeutics,* 1977, **21,** 409-413.

Resnick, R. B., Schuyten-Resnick, E., and Washton, A. M. Treatment of opioid dependence with narcotic antagonists: A review and commentary. In R. I. DuPont, A. Goldstein, and J. O'Donnell (Eds.), *Handbook on drug abuse.* Washington, D.C. National Institute on Drug Abuse, 1979. Pp. 97-104.

Resnick, R. B. and Washton, A. M. Clinical outcome with naltrexone: Predictor variables and follow-up status in detoxified heroin addicts. *Annals of the New York Academy of Science,* 1978, **311,** 241-246.

Resnick, R., Washton, A., Stone-Washton, N., and Rawson, R. Psychotherapy and naltrexone in opioid dependence. In L. S. Harris (Ed.), *Problems of drug dependence, 1980* (NIDA Research Monograph #34). Washington, D.C.: U.S. Government Printing Office, 1981. Pp. 109-115.

Resnick, R. B., Washton, A. M., Garwood, J., and Perzel, J. LAAM instead of take home methadone. In L. S. Harris (Ed.), *Problems of drug dependence, 1981* (NIDA Research Monograph #41). Washington, D.C.: U.S. Government Printing Office, 1982. Pp. 473-475.

Richards, L. G. Demographic trends and drug abuse, 1980-1995. *National Institute of Drug Abuse: Research Monograph Series,* 1981, **35,** 1-98.

Richman, S. Return to productive community living: Reflections on the twenty year program experience of the New York State Vocational Rehabilitation Agency. In *Rehabilitating the Narcotic Addict,* Vocational Rehabilitation Agency, U.S. Department of Health, Education, and Welfare, 1966.

Richter, R. W. (Ed.) *Medical aspects of drug abuse.* Hagerstown, Md.: Harper and Row, 1975.

Richter, R. W., Baden, M. M., and Pearson, J. Clinical and neuropathological correlates of heroin addiction. *Annals of Internal Medicine,* 1970, **72,** 808 (abstract).

Richter, R. W. and Pearson, J. Heroin addiction related neurological disorders. In R. W. Richter (Ed.), *Medical aspects of drug abuse.* Hagerstown, Md.: Harper and Row, 1975, Pp. 320-337.

Richter, R. W., and Rosenberg, R. N. Transverse myelitis associated with heroin addiction. *Journal of the American Medical Association,* 1968, **206,** 1255-1257.

Riordan, C. E. and Kleber, H. D. Rapid opiate detoxification with clonidine and naloxone. *Lancet*, 1980, **1**, 1079-1080.

Ritland, D. and Butterfield, W. Extremity complications of drug abuse. *American Journal of Surgery*, 1973, **126**, 639-648.

Robbins, P. R. Heroin addicts' view of commonly abused drugs: A semantic differential approach. *Journal of Personality Assessment*, 1972, **36**, 366-370.

Robins, L. N. *Follow-up of vietnam drug users.* Special Action Office Monograph, Series A, No. 1, April 1973.

Robins, L. N. Estimating addiction rates and locating target populations: How to decomposition into stages helps. In J. D. Rittenhouse (Ed.), *Report of the task force on the epidemiology of heroin and other narcotics.* Merlo Park, CA: Stanford Research Institute, 1976.

Robins, L. N., Helzer, J. E., Hesselbrock, M., and Wish, E. D. Vietnam veterans three years after Vietnam: How our study changed our view of heroin. In L. Harris (Ed.), *Problems of drug dependence.* Richmond, VA: Committee on Problems of Drug Dependence, 1977.

Robins, L. N. Addict careers. In R. I. DuPont, A. Goldstein, and J. O'Donnell (Eds.), *Handbook on drug abuse.* Washington, D.C.: National Institute on Drug Abuse, 1979. Pp. 325-336.

Robins, L. N. and Murphy, G. E. Drug use in a normal population of young Negro men. *American Journal of Public Health*, 1967, **57**, 1580-1596.

Robins, L. N. and Wish, E. Childhood deviance as a developmental process: A study of 223 urban black men from birth to 18. In M. F. McMillan (Ed.), *Child therapy: Treatment and research*, Brunner-Mazel, 1977.

Rosenbaum, B. J. Heroin: Influence of method of use. *New England Journal of Medicine*, 1971, **285**, 299-300.

Rosenbaum, M. When drugs come into the picture, love flies out the window: Women's addicts' love relationships. *International Journal of the Addictions*, 1981, **16**, 859-877.

Rosenbaum, M., and Murphy, S. Getting the treatment: Recycling women addicts. *Journal of Psychoactive Drugs*, 1981, **13**, 1-13.

Rosenberg, C. M., Davidson, G. E., and Patch, V. D. Patterns of drop-outs from a methadone program for narcotic addicts. *International Journal of the Addictions*, 1972, **7**, 415-425.

Rosenthal, M. S. and Biase, D. V. Phoenix Houses: Therapeutic communities for drug addicts. *Hospital and Community Psychiatry*, 1969, **20**, 26-30.

Ross, D. H., Medina, M. A., and Cardenas, H. L. Morphine and ethanol: Selective depletion of regional brain calcium. *Science*, 1974, **186**, 63-65.

Rotter, J. B. Generalized expectancies for internal versus external control of reinforcement. *Psychological Monographs*, 1966, **80** (609), 1-28.

Rotter, J. B. *Social learning and clinical psychology.* Englewood Cliffs, N. J.: Prentice-Hall, 1954.

Rounsaville, B. J., Novelly, R. A., Kleber, H. D., and Jones, C. Neuropsychological impairment in opiate addicts: Risk factors. *Annals of the New York Academy of Science*, 1981, **362**, 79-90.

Rounsaville, B. J., Weisman, M. M., and Kleber, H. D. The significance of alcoholism in treated opiate addicts. *Journal of Nervous and Mental Disease*, 1982, **170**, 479-488.

Rozynko, V. V. and Stein, K. B. Social and psycholgical factors associated with length of stay in a drug treatment facility. *International Journal of the Addictions*, 1974, **9**, 873-878.

Rubington, E. Drug addiction as a deviant career. *International Journal of the Addictions*, 1967, **2**, 3-20.

Rubinstein, A., Sicklick, M., Grupta, A., Bernstein, L., Klein, N., Rubinstein, E., Spigland, I., Fruchter, L., Litman, N., Lee, H., and Hollander, M. Acquired immunodeficiency with reversed T4/T8 ratios in infants born to promiscuous and drug addicted mothers. *Journal of the American Medical Association*, 1983, **249**, 2350-2356.

Rush, A. J., Beck, A. T., Kovacs, M., and Hallon, S. Comparative efficacy of cognitive therapy and pharmacotherapy in the treatment of depressed out-patients. *Cognitive Therapy and Research*, 1977, **1**, 17-38.

Sabath, G. Some trends in the treatment and epidemiology of drug addiction: Psychotherapy and Synanon. *Psychotherapy: Theory, research and practice*, 1967, **4**, 92-97.

Sacks, L. L. Drug addiction, alcoholism, smoking, obesity treated by auricular staplepuncture. *American Journal of Acupuncture*, 1975, **3**, 147-150.

Sadove, M. S., Balagot, R. C., Hatano, S., and Jobgen, E. A. Study of a narcotic antagonist N-allyl-noroxymorphone. *Journal of the American Medical Association*, 1963, **183**, 666-668.

Sainsbury, M. J. Acupuncture in heroin withdrawal. *Medical Journal of Australia*, 1974, **2**, 102-105.

Salmon, R. W. and Salmon, R. J. The role of coercion in rehabilitation of drug abusers. *International Journal of the Addictions*, 1983, **18**, 9-21.

Santo, Y. Substance abuse by men and women: A comparison. Paper presented at the National Drug Abuse Conference, San Francisco, Calif., May, 1977.

Sapira, J. D. The narcotic addict as a medical patient. *American Journal of Medicine*, 1968, **45**, 555-588.

Sapira, J. D., Ball, J. C. and Cottrell, E. S. Addiction to methadone among patients at Lexington and Fort Worth. *Public Health Reports*, 1968, **83**, 691-694.

Sapira, J. D., Ball, J. C. and Penn, H. Causes of death among institutionalized narcotic addicts. In J. C. Ball and C. D. Chambers (Eds.), *The epidemiology of opiate addiction in the U.S.* Springfield, Ill.: Charles C. Thomas, 1970. Pp. 251-262.

Sarg, M. J. Heroin use in the Navy. *New England Journal of Medicine*, 1972, **286**, 111-112.

Savitt, R. A. Psychoanalytic studies on addiction. *Psychoanalytic Quarterly*, 1963, **32**, 43-57.

Schaumann, W. Influence of atropine and morphine on the liberation of acetylcholine from the guinea-pig's intestine. *Nature* (London), 1956, **178**, 1121-1122.

Schaumann, W. Inhibition by morphine of the release of acetylcholine from the intestine of the guinea pig. *British Journal of Pharmacological Chemotherapy*, 1957, **12**, 115-119.

Scher, J. M. The impact of the drug abuser on the work organization. In J. M. Scher (Ed.), *Drug abuse in industry*. Springfield, Ill.: Charles C. Thomas, 1973 (a), Pp. 5-16.

Scher, J. M. A chemical alternative to the narcotic antagonist thesis. *International Journal of the Addictions*, 1973 (b), **8**, 959-967.

Scherer, S. E., Ettinger, R. and Mudrick, N. Need for social approval and drug use. *Journal of Consulting and Clinical Psychology*, 1972, **38**, 118-121.

Schiff, S. A self-theory investigation of drug addiction in relation to age of onset. Unpublished doctoral dissertation, New York University, 1959.

Schulman, C. A. Alterations of the sleep cycle in heroin-addicted and suspect newborns. *Neuropaediatrie*, 1969, **1**, 89-100.

Schultz, R. and Goldstein, A. Morphine tolerance and supersensitivity to 5-hydroxytryptamine in the myenteric plexus of the guinea-pig. *Nature*, 1973, **244**, 168-170.

Scott, D. and Goldberg, H. L. The phenomenon of self-perpetuation in Synanontype drug treatment programs. *Hospital and Community Psychiatry*, 1973, **24**, 231-233.

Seevers, M.H. and Deneau, G. A. Physiological aspects of tolerance and physical dependence. In W. S. Root and F. G. Hoffman *Physiological pharmacology* (Vol. I). New York: Academic Press, 1963. Pp. 565-640.

Seevers, M. H. and Deneau, G. A. A critique of the "dual action" hypothesis of morphine's physical dependence. In A. Wikler (Ed.), *The addictive states*. Baltimore: Williams and Wilkins, 1969. Pp. 199-205.

Seevers, M. H. and Woods, L. A. Symposium on drug addiction. The phenomena of tolerance. *American Journal of Medicine*, 1953, **14**, 546-557.

Sells, S. B. (Ed.), *The effectiveness of drug abuse treatment: Evaluation of treatment* (Vol. I). Cambridge, Mass.: Ballinger Publishing Company, 1974.

Sells, S. B. Methadone maintenance in perspective. *Journal of Drug Issues,* 1977, **7**, 13-22.

Sells, S. B. Treatment effectiveness. In DuPont et al. (Eds.), *Handbook on drug abuse*, NIDA, 1979, pp. 105-117.

Sells, S. B., Chatham, L. R., and Joe, G. W. The relation of selected epidemiological factors to retention in methadone treatment. In *Proceedings of the Fourth National Conference on Methadone Treatment*. New York: NAPAN, 1972.

Sells, S. B., and Simpson, D. D. (Eds.), *The Effectiveness of Drug Abuse Treatment* (Vol. III). Cambridge, Mass.: Ballinger, 1976.

Senay, E. C. Methadone: Some myths and hypotheses. *Journal of Psychedelic Drugs*, 1971, **4**, 182-185.

Senay, E.C. Use of D-propoxyphene as a maintainer or detoxification agent for opiate addicts. In J. R. Cooper, F. Altman, B. S. Brown, and D. Czechowicz (Eds.), *Research on the treatment of narcotic addiction: State of the art*. Rockville, MD: National Institute on Drug Abuse, 1983. Pp. 225-235.

Senay, E. C., Dorus, W., Goldberg, F., and Thornton, W. Withdrawal from methadone maintenance: Rate of withdrawal and expectation. *Archives of General Psychiatry*, 1977, **34**, 361-367.

Senay, E. C., Dorus, W., Renault, P. F. and Morell, J. Three times a week LAAM equals seven times a week methadone. Paper read at the National Academy of Sciences, National Research Council, Committee on Problems of Drug Dependence, Washington, D.C., May 19-21, 1975.

Senay, E. C., Dorus, W., and Showalter, C. V. Short-term detoxification with methadone. *Annals of the New York Academy of Science*, 1981, **362**, 16-21.

Senay, E. C. and Renault, P. F. Treatment methods for heroin addicts: A review. *Journal of Psychedelic Drugs*, 1971, **3**, 47-54.

Senay, E., Shorty, V., and Alksene, H. (Eds.), *Developments in the field of drug abuse: National drug abuse conference 1974*. Cambridge, Mass.: Schenkman Publishing Co., 1975.

Shaffer, J. W., Kinlock, T. W., and Nurco, D. N. Factor structure of the MMPI-168 in male narcotic addicts. *Journal of Clinical Psychology*, 1982, **38**, 656-661.

Sharpless, S. and Jaffe, J. Withdrawal phenomena as manifestations of disuse supersensitivity. In H. Steinberg (Ed.), *Scientific basis of drug dependence*. London: Churchill, 1969. Pp. 67-76.

Sheppard, C., Fracchia, J., Ricca, E., and Merlis, S. Indications of psychopathology in male narcotic abusers, their effects and relation to treatment effectiveness. *Journal of Psychology*, 1972, **81**, 351-360.

Sheppard, C., Ricca, E., Fracchia, J., and Merlis, S. Indications of psychopathology in applicants to a county methadone maintenance program. *Psychological Reports*, 1973(a), **33**, 535-540.

Sheppard, C., Ricca, E., Fracchia, J. and Merlis, S. Personality characteristics of urban and suburban heroin abusers: More data and another reply to Sutker and Allain (1973). *Psychological Reports*, 1973(b), **33**, 999-1008.

Sheppard, C., Ricca, E., Fracchia, J., and Merlis, S. Psychological needs of suburban male heroin addicts. *Journal of Psychology*, 1974, **87**, 123-128.

Sheppard, C., Ricca, E., Fracchia, J., Rosenberg, N., and Merlis, S. Cross-validation of a heroin addiction scale from the Minnesota Multiphasic Personality Inventory. *Journal of Psychology*, 1972, **81**, 263-268.

Sideroff, S. I., and Jarvik, M. E. Conditioned responses to videotape showing heroin-related stimuli. *International Journal of the Addictions*, 1980, **15**, 529-536.

Siegel, H., Helpern, M. and Ehrenreich, T. The diagnosis of death from intravenous narcotism. *Journal of Forensic Science*, 1966, **11**, 1-16.

Siegel, S., Hinson, R. E., Krank, M. D., and McCully, J. Heroin "overdose" death: Contribution of drug associated environmental cues. *Science*, 1982, **216**, 436-437.

Silber, R. and Clerkin, E. P. Pulmonary edema in acute heroin poisoning. *American Journal of Medicine*, 1959, **27**, 187-192.

Simmons, L. R. S. and Gold, M. B. The myth of international control: American foreign policy and the heroin traffic. *International Journal of the Addictions*, 1973, **8**, 779-800.

Simon, E. J. In search of the opiate receptor. *American Journal of Medical Science*, 1973, **266**, 160-168.

Simon, E. J. Opiate receptors and opioid peptides: An overview. In *Opioids in Mental Illness*. New York: New York Academy of Sciences, 1982, **398**, 327-338.

Simpson, D. Treatment for drug abuse. *Archives of General Psychiatry*, 1981, **88**, 875-880.

Simpson, D. D., Joe, G. W., and Bracy, S. A. Six year follow-up of opioid addicts after admission to treatment. *Archives of General Psychiatry*, 1982, **39**, 1318-1323.

Simpson, D. D., Savage, L. J., Lloyd, M. R. and Sells, S. B. *Evaluation of drug abuse treatments based on the first year after DARP* (IBR Report No. 77-14). Fort Worth: Texas Christian University, Institute of Behavioral Research, 1977.

Simpson, D. D. and Sells, S. B. Patterns of multiple drug abuse: 1969-1971. *International Journal of the Addictions*, 1974, **9**, 301-314.

Simpson, D. D. and Sells, S. B. *Evaluation of drug abuse treatment effectiveness: Summary of the DARP follow-up research* (NIDA Treatment Research Report). Washington, D.C.: U.S. Government Printing Office, 1982.

Singh, B. K., Sells, S. B. and Demaree, R. G. *Measurement of Community Context Factors: National Followup Study of Admissions to Drug Abuse Treatments in the DARP during 1969-1972* (IBR Report 76-13). Fort Worth: Texas Christian University, Institute of Behavioral Research, 1976.

Sinnett, E. R., Arata, C. L., and Bates, R. A. Methods of administration of street drugs: Stereotypes, actuality, and perceived dangers. Unpublished manuscript, 1974.

Sinnett, E. R., Judd, B., Rissman, K., and Harvey, W. M. Temporal patterns of drug use by heroin addicts. *International Journal of the Addictions*, 1980, **15**, 1241-1248.

Sinnett, E. R., Wampler, K. S., and Harvey, W. M. Consistency of patterns of drug use. *Psychological Reports*, 1972, **31**, 143-152.

Small, C. B., Klein, R. S., Friedland, G. H., Moll, B., Emeson, E. E., and Spigland, I. Community acquired opportunistic infections and defective cellular immunity in heterosexual drug abusers and homosexual men. *American Journal of Medicine*, 1983, **74**, 433-441.

Smart, R. G. Comments on Sells' paper: " 'Reflections on the epidemiology of heroin and narcotic addiction from the perspective of treatment data.' " In *Epidemiology of heroin and other narcotics* (NIDA Research Monograph No. 16). Washington, D.C.: U.S. Government Printing Office, 1977.

Smith, D. E., Moser, C., Wesson, D. R., Apter, M., Buxton, M. E., Davison, J. V., Orgel, M., and Buffum, J. A clinical guide to the diagnosis and treatment of heroin-related sexual dysfunction. *Journal of Psychoactive Drugs*, 1982, **14**, 91-99.

Smith, G. M. and Beecher, H. K. Subjective effects of heroin and morphine in normal subjects. *Journal of Pharmacology and Experimental Therapeutics*, 1962, **136**, 47-52.

Smith, G. M., Semke, C. W., and Beecher, H. K. Objective evidence of mental effects of heroin, morphine and placebo in normal subjects. *Journal of Pharmacology and Experimental Therapeutics*, 1962, **136**, 53-58.

Smith, W. G., Ellinwood, E.H., and Vaillant, G. E. Narcotic addicts in the mid-1960's. *Public Health Reports*, 1966, **81**, 403-411.

Snarr, R. W., and Ball, S. C. Involvement in a drug subculture and abstinence following treatment among Puerto Rican narcotic addicts. *British Journal of Addiction*, 1974, **69**, 233-248.

Sorensen, J. L., Hargreaves, W. A., and Weinberg, J. A. Heroin addict responses to six weeks of detoxification with LAAM. *Drug and Alcohol Dependence*, 1982(a), **9**, 79-87.

Sorensen, J. L., Hargreaves, W. A., and Weinberg, J. A. Withdrawal from heroin in three or six weeks. Comparison of methadyl acetate and methadone. *Archives of General Psychiatry*, 1982(b), **39**, 167-171.

Soverow, G., Rosenberg, C. M. and Ferneau, E. Attitudes towards drug and alcohol addiction: Patients and staff. *British Journal of Addiction*, 1972, **67**, 195-198.

Spensley, J. The adjunctive use of tricyclics in a methadone program. *Journal of Psychedelic Drugs*, 1974, **6**, 421-423.

Stanton, M. D. The family and drug misuse: A bibliography. *American Journal of Drug and Alcohol Abuse*, 1978, **6**, 203-205.

Stanton, M. D. Family treatment of drug problems: A review. In R. L. Dupont, A. Goldstein and J. O'Donnell (Eds.), *Handbook on drug abuse*. Washington, D.C.: National Institute on Drug Abuse, 1979.

Stanton, M. D. A family theory of drug abuse. In D. J. Lettieri, M. Sayers and H. W. Pearson *Theomeson drug abuse: Selected contemporary perspectives* (NIDA Research Monograph #30). Washington, D.C.: U.S. Government Printing Office, 1980. Pp. 147-156.

Steer, R. A. Psychosocial correlates of retention in methadone maintenance. *International Journal of the Addictions*, 1980, **15**, 1003-1009.

Steer, R. A. Symptoms discriminating between heroin addicts seeking ambulatory detoxification or methadone maintenance. *Drug and Alcohol Dependence*, 1982, **9**, 335-338.

Steer, R. A., Herlick, L., and Diamond, H. Retention in ambulatory detoxification. *International Journal of Addiction*, 1981, **16**, 1505-1508.

Steer, R.A. and Schut, J. Moods of pregnant and non-pregnant heroin addicts. *International Journal of the Addictions*, 1980, **15**, 1279-1283.

Steigmann, F., Hyman, S., and Goldbloom, R. Infectious hepatitis (chomologous serum type) in drug addicts. *Gastroenterology*, 1950, **15**, 642-646.

Stein, L. Amphetamine and neural reward mechanism. In H. Steinberg, A. V. S. de Reuck and J. Knight (Eds.), *Ciba Foundation symposium on animal behavior and drug action*. London: Churchill, 1964. Pp. 91-118.

Stephens, R. C. and Cottrell, E. A follow-up study of 200 narcotic addicts committed for treatment under the Narcotics Rehabilitation Act (NARA). *British Journal of Addiction*, 1972, **67** 45-53.

Stephens, R. C. and Weppner, R. S. Legal and illegal use of methadone: One year later. *American Journal of Psychiatry*, 1973, **130**, 1391-1394.

Stern, R., Edwards, N. B., and Lerro, F. A. Methadone on demand as a heroin detoxification procedure. *International Journal of the Addictions*, 1974, **9**, 863-872.

Stimmel, B., Donoso, E., and Dach, S. Comparison of infectious endocarditis in drug addicts and nondrug users. *American Journal of Cardiology*, 1973, **32**, 924-929.

Stimmel, B., Goldberg, J., Rotkopf, E., and Cohen, M. Ability to remain abstinent after methadone detoxification: A six-year study. *Journal of the American Medical Association*, 1977, **237**, 1216-1220.

Stimmel, B., Hanbury, R., Sturiano, V., Korts, D., Jackson, G., and Cohen, M. Alcoholism as a risk factor in methadone maintenance. A randomized controlled trial. *American Journal of Medicine*, 1982, **73**, 631-636.

Stitzer, M. L., Bigelow, G. E., and Liebson, I. A. Comparison of three outpatient methadone detoxification procedures. In L. S. Harris (Ed.), *Problems of drug dependence, 1981* (NIDA Research Monograph #41). Washington, D.C.: U.S. Government Printing Office, 1982. Pp. 239-245.

Stitzer, M. L., Griffiths, R. R., McLellan, A. T., Grabowski, J., and Hawthorne, J. W. Diazepam use among methadone maintenance patients: Patterns and dosages. *Drug and Alcohol Dependence*, 1981, **8**, 189-199.

Stitzer, M., Bigelow, G. and Liebson, I. Contingent reinforcement of benzodiazepine-free urines from methadone maintenance patients. In L. S. Harris (Ed.), *Problems of drug dependence, 1981* (NIDA Research Monograph #41). Washington, D.C.: U.S. Government Printing Office, 1982. Pp. 282-287.

Stone-Washton, M. S., Resnick, R. B. and Washton, A. M. Naltrexone and psychotherapy. In L. S. Harris (Ed.), *Problems of drug dependence, 1981* (NIDA Research Monograph #41). Washington, D.C.: U.S. Government Printing Office, 1982. Pp. 505-507.

Strategy Council on Drug Abuse. *Federal strategy for drug abuse and drug traffic prevention 1973*. Washington, D.C.: U.S. Government Printing Office, 1973.

Suffet, F. and Brotman, R. Female drug use: Some observations. *International Journal of the Addictions*, 1976, **11**, 19-33.

Sutker, P. B. Personality differences and sociopathy in heroin addicts and non-addict prisoners. *Journal of Abnormal Psychology*, 1971, **78**, 247-251.

Sutker, P. B. Personality characteristics of heroin addicts: A response to Gendreau and Gendreau. *Journal of Abnormal Psychology*, 1974, **83**, 463-464.

Sutker, P. B. and Allain, A. N. Incarcerated and street heroin addicts: A personality comparison. *Psychological Reports*, 1973, **32**, 243-246.

Sutker, P. B., Allain, A. N., and Cohen, G. H. MMPI indices of personality change following short- and long-term hospitalization in heroin addicts. *Psychological Reports*, 1974, **34**, 495-500.

Sutker, P. B., Archer, R. P., and Allain, A. N. Volunteerism and self-reported psychopathology among opiate addicts. *Journal of Consulting and Clinical Psychology*, 1979, **88**, 59-67.

Sutker, P. B. and Moan, C. E. Personality characteristics of socially deviant women: Incarcerated heroin addicts, street addicts, and non-addict prisoners. In J. M.

Singh, L. Miller, and H. Lal (Eds.), *Drug addiction: Clinical and socio-legal aspects* (Vol. 2). Mount Kisco, New York: Futura, 1972. Pp. 107-114.

Sutker, P. B. and Moan, C. E. A psychosocial description of penitentiary inmates. *Archives of General Psychiatry*, 1973, **29**, 663-667.

Swiller, H. I., O'Brien, C. P., Forester, B. M. and Strange, R. E. Drug use patterns and demographic correlates among military psychiatric patients. In J. M. Singh, L. Miller, and H. Lal (Eds.), *Drug addiction: Clinical and socio-legal aspects*, (Vol. 2). Mount Kisco, New York: Futura, 1972. Pp. 133-136.

Switzer, A. *Drug abuse and drug treatment.* California Youth Authority, 1974.

Szapocznik, J. and Ladner, R. Factors related to successful retention in methadone maintenance: A review. *The International Journal of the Addictions*, 1977, **12**, 1067-1085.

Szara, S. and Bunney, W. E. Recent research on opiate addiction: Review of a national program. In *Opiate addiction: Origins and treatment.* Washington, D.C.: Winston, 1974. Pp. 43-57.

Taeusch, H. W., Carson, S., Wang, N. S. and Avery, M. E. The effects of heroin on lung maturation in fetal rabbits. *Pediatric Research*, 1972, **6**, 335 (abstract).

Tatum, A. L., Seevers, M. M. and Collins, K. H. Morphine addiction and its physiological interpretation based on experimental evidence. *Journal of Pharmacology and Experimental Therapeutics*, 1929, **36**, 447-475.

Taylor, P. L. and Albright, W. J., Jr. Non-drug criminal behavior and heroin use. *International Journal of the Addictions*, 1981, **16**, 683-696.

Taylor, W. J. R., Bowling, C. E. and Mason, H. M. Methadone iatrogenesis during narcotic substitution therapy. In J. M. Singh, L. Miller, and H. Lal (Eds.), *Drug addiction: Clinical and socio-legal aspects* (Vol. 2). Mount Kisco, New York: Futura, 1972. Pp. 133-136.

Taylor, W. J. R., Chambers, C. D., and Bowling, C. E. Addiction and the community (narcotic substitution therapy). *International Journal of Clinical Pharmacology, Therapy, and Toxicology*, 1972, **6**, 28-39.

Tenhouton, S. Sexual dynamics and strength of heroin addiction: A three factor model of an ideology. *Journal of Psychoactive Drugs*, 1982, **14**, 101-109.

Tennant, F. S. Treatment of heroin addicts with propoxyphene napsylate. In *Proceedings of the Committee on Problems of Drug Dependence of the National Academy of Sciences,* Chapel Hill, N.C.: Committee on Problems on Drug Dependence. 1973(a).

Tennant, F. S. Propoxyphene napsylate for heroin addiction. *Journal of the American Medical Association,* 1973(b), **226**, 1012.

Tennant, F. S. Propoxyphene napsylate treatment of heroin addicts. Paper presented at the 78th Annual Convention of the National Medical Association, New York, NY, 1973(c).

Tennant, F. S. Propoxyphene napsylate (Darvon-N) treatment of heroin addicts. *Journal of the National Medical Association*, 1974, **66**, 23-27.

Tennant, F. S. Outpatient heroin detoxification with acupuncture and staplepuncture. *Western Journal of Medicine*, 1976, **125**, 191-194.

Tennant, F. S. Influence of a cash fee on out-patient heroin detoxification. *International Journal of the Addictions*, 1980, **15**, 1249-1252.

Tennant, F. S., Jankowski, P., Shannon, J. A., and Bleich, R. Detoxification from methadone maintenance: Double-blind comparison of two methods. *Drug and Alcohol Dependence*, 1978, **3**, 85-92.

Tennant, F. S. and Rawson, R. A. Propoxyphene napsylate maintenance treatment for narcotic dependence: A non-methadone model. *Drug and Alcohol Dependence*, 1981, **8**, 79-83.

Tennant, F. S., Russell, B. A., Casas, S. K., and Bleich, R. N. Heroin detoxification: A comparison of propoxyphene and methadone. *Journal of the American Medical Association*, 1975, **232**, 1010-1022.

Tennant, F. S., Russell, B. A., Shannon, J. S., and Casas, S. D. Outpatient withdrawal from methadone maintenance with propoxyphene napsylate (Darvon-N). *Journal of Psychedelic Drugs*, 1975, **7**, 269-271.

Terenius, L. and Wahlström, A. *Acta Physiologica Scandanavica*, 1975, **94**, 74-81.

Tsau, K. and Jang, C. S. Studies on the site of analgesic action of morphine by intracerebral micro-injection. *Scienca Sinica*, 1964, **7**, 1099-1109.

Tseung, L. F., Loh, H. H., and Wei, T. E. Effects of clonidine on morphine withdrawal signs in the rat. *European Journal of Pharmacology*, 1975, **30**, 93-99.

Tyler, J. and Frith, G. H. Primary drug abuse among women: A natural study. *Drug and Alcohol Dependence*, 1981, **8**, 279-286.

Tyler, J. and Thompson, M. Patterns of drug abuse among women. *International Journal of the Addictions*, 1980, **15**, 309-321.

Tyler, J. and Sheridan, J. R. Patterns of primary drug abuse. *International Journal of the Addictions*, 1980, **15**, 1169-1178.

Uhde, T. W., Redmond, D. E., and Kleber, H. D. Psychosis in the opioid addicted patient: Assessment and treatment. *Journal of Clinical Psychiatry*, 1982, **43**, 240-247.

Ungerleider, J. T. The business of drugs. In J. M. Scher (Ed.), *Drug abuse in industry*. Springfield, Ill.: Charles C. Thomas, 1973. Pp. 45-48.

U.S. Department of Health, Education, and Welfare. Methadone—Listing as a new drug. *Federal Register*, 1972, **37** (242), 26790-26807.

U.S. Treasury Department, Bureau of Narcotics Register 5, Article 167, 1962(a).

U.S. Treasury Department, Bureau of Narcotics. Traffic in opium and other dangerous drugs for the year ended December 31, 1961. Washington, D.C.: U.S. Government Printing Office, 1962(b).

Vaillant, G. E. A twelve-year follow-up of New York narcotic addicts: I. The relation of treatment to outcome. *American Journal of Psychiatry*, 1966(a), **122**, 727-737.

Vaillant, G. E. A twelve-year follow-up of New York narcotic addicts: II. The natural history of a chronic disease. *New England Journal of Medicine*, 1966(b), **275**, 1282-1288.

Vaillant, G. E. A twelve-year follow-up of New York narcotic addicts: III. Some social and psychiatric characteristics. *Archives of General Psychiatry*, 1966(c), **15**, 599-609.

Vaillant, G. E. A twelve-year follow-up of New York narcotic addicts: IV. Some characteristics and determinants of abstinence. *American Journal of Psychiatry*, 1966(d), **123**, 573-585.

Vaillant, G. E. Parent-child disparity and drug-addiction. *Journal of Nervous and Mental Disease*, 1966(e), **142**, 534-539.

Vaillant, G. E. and Rasor, R. W. The role of compulsory supervision in the treatment of addiction. *Federal Probation*, 1966, **30**, 53-59.

Veatch, R. M., Adler, T. K., and Way, E. L. The importance of steric configuration in certain morphine-mimetic actions of synthetic analgesics. *Journal of Pharmacology and Experimental Therapeutics*, 1964, **145**, 11-19.

Verebey, K. The clinical pharmacology of naltrexone: Pharmacology and pharmacodynamics. In R. E. Willett and G. Barnett (Eds.), *Naltrexone: Pharmacochemistry and sustained release preparations* (NIDA Research Monograph #28). Washington, D.C.: U.S. Government Printing Office, 1980. Pp. 147-158.

Von Glahn, W. C. and Hall, J. W. The reaction produced in the pulmonary arteries by emboli of cotton fibers. *American journal of Pathology*, 1949, **25**, 575-595.

Wagers, P. K. and Smith, C. M. Responses in dental nerves of dogs to tooth simulation and the effects of systematically administered procaine, lidocaine and morphine. *Journal of Pharmacology and Experimental Therapeutics*, 1960, **130**, 89-105.

Waldorf, D. Life without heroin: Some social adjustments during long-term periods of voluntary abstention. *Social Problems*, 1970, **18**, 228-243.

Waldorf, D. *Careers in dope*. Englewood Cliffs, N.J.: Prentice-Hall, 1973.

Wallace, N. Future time perspective in schizophrenia. *Journal of Abnormal and Social Psychology*, 1956, **52**, 240-245.

Walsh, J. Methadone and heroin addiction: Rehabilitation without a "cure". *Science*, 1970, **168**, 685-686.

Wang, R. I. H., Kochar, C., Hasegawa, A. T., and Roh, B. L. Clinical comparison of propoxyphene napsylate and methadone in the treatment of opiate dependence. In L. S. Harris (Ed.), *Problems of drug dependence, 1981* (NIDA Research Monograph #41). Washington, D.C.: U.S. Government Printing Office, 1982, 253-260.

Ward, H. *Employment and addiction: Overview of issues*. Washington, D.C.: The Drug Abuse Council, Inc., 1973.

Washton, A. M., Resnick, R. B., and Rawson, R. A. Clonidine for outpatient opiate detoxification. *Lancet*, 1980, **1**, 1078-1079.

Washton, A. M., Resnick, R. B., and La Placa, R. Clonidine hydrochloride: A non-opiate treatment for opiate withdrawal. *Psychopharmacology Bulletin*, 1980, **2**, 50-52.

Washton, A. M. and Resnick. R. B. Recent advances in opiate detoxification: Clonidine and lofexidine. In L. S. Harris (Ed.), *Problems of drug dependence, 1982* (NIDA Research Monograph #43). Washington, D.C.: U.S. Government Printing Office, 1983. Pp. 44-50.

Washton, A. M. and Resnick, R. B. Outpatient opiate detoxification with clonidine. *Journal of Clinical Psychiatry,* 1982, **43,** 39-41.

Way, E. L. Distribution and metabolism of morphine and its surrogates. In A. Wikler (Ed.), *The addictive states.* Baltimore: Williams and Wilkins, 1968. Pp. 13-31.

Way, E. L. Some biochemical aspects of morphine tolerance and physical dependence. In S. Fisher, and A. M. Freedman (Eds.), *Opiate addiction: Origins and treatment.* Washington, D.C.: Winston, 1974. Pp. 99-120.

Way, E. L. and Adler, T. K. The pharmacologic implications of the fate of morphine and its surrogates. *Pharmacological Reviews,* 1960, **12,** 383-445.

Way, E. L. History of opiate use in the Orient and the United States. *Annals of the New York Academy of Science,* 1982, **398,** 12-23.

Weiss, W. U. and McFarland, A. W. Comparison of methadone clinic patients and methadone dropouts using the Leary interpersonal check list. *Proceedings of the 81st Annual Convention of the American Psychological Association,* 1973, **8,** 399-400.

Weissman, M. W., Slobetz, F., Prusoff, B., Mesritz, M., and Howard, P. Clinical depression among narcotic addicts maintained on methadone in the community. *American Journal of Psychiatry,* 1976, **133,** 1434-1438.

Wen, H. L. and Cheung, S. Y. C. Treatment of drug addiction by acupuncture and electrical stimulation. *Asian Journal of Medicine,* 1973, **9,** 138-141.

Wen, H. L. and Ho, W. K. Suppression of withdrawal symptoms by Dynorphin in heroin addicts. *European Journal of Pharmacology,* 1982, **82,** 183-186.

Weppner, R. S. Some characteristics of an ex-addict self-help therapeutic community and its members. *British Journal of Addiction,* 1973, **68,** 73-79.

Weppner, R. S., Stephens, R. C., and Conrad, H. T. Methadone: Some aspects of its legal and illegal use. *American Journal of Psychiatry,* 1972, **129,** 451-455.

Wesson, D. R. and Smith, D. E. Treatment of the polydrug abuser. In R. I. DuPont, A. Goldstein, and J. O'Donnell (Eds.), *Handbook on drug abuse.* Washington, D.C.: National Institute on Drug Abuse, 1979. Pp. 151-158.

White, W. B. and Barrett, S. Penile ulcer in heroin abuse: A case report. *Cutis,* 1982, **29,** 62-63, 69.

Wicks, R.J. *Correctional Psychology.* San Francisco: Canfield Press, 1974.

Weiland, W. F. and Chambers, C. D. Methadone maintenance: A comparison of two stabilization techniques. *International Journal of the Addictions,* 1970, **5,** 645-659.

Wikler, A. Studies on the action of morphine on the central nervous system of cats. *Journal of Pharmacology and Experimental Therapeutics.* 1944, **80,** 176-186.

Wikler, A. Recent progress in research on the neurophysiological basis of morphine addiction. *American Journal of Psychiatry,* 1948, **105,** 329-338.

Wikler, A. A psychodynamic study of a patient during self-regulated readdiction to morphine. *Psychiatric Quarterly,* 1952, **26,** 270-293.

Wikler, A. *Opiate addiction.* Springfield, Ill.: Charles C. Thomas, 1953.

Wikler, A. Conditioning factors in opiate addiction and relapse. In D. M. Wilner, and G. G. Kasselbaum (Eds.), *Narcotics.* New York: McGraw-Hill, 1965. Pp. 85-100.

Wikler, A. Present status of the concept of drug dependence. *Psychological Medicine*, 1971, **1**, 377-380.

Wikler, A. Dynamics of drug dependence. Implications of a conditioning theory for research and treatment. *Archives of General Psychiatry*, 1973, **28**, 611-616.

Wikler, A. Dynamics of drug dependence: Implications of a conditioning theory for research and treatment. In S. Fisher and A. M. Freedman *Opiate Addiction: Origins and Treatment*. New York: Wiley, 1973.

Wikler, A. and Carter, R. L. Effects of single doses of *N*-allylnormorphine on hindlimb reflexes of chronic spinal dogs during cycles of morphine addiction. *Journal of Pharmacology and Experimental Therapeutics*, 1953, **109**, 92-101.

Wikler, A., and Pescor, F. T. Classical conditioning of morphine abstinence phenomenon, reinforcement of opioid-drinking behavior and "relapse" in morphine-addicted rats. *Psychopharmacologia*, 1967, **10**, 255-284.

Wikler, A. and Rasor, W. Psychiatric aspects of drug addiction. *American Journal of Medicine*, 1953, **24**, 566-570.

Wilkins, L. H., Wintenitz, S. R., Oparil, S., Smith, L. R., and Dustin, H. P. Lofexidine and clonidine in moderate essential hypertension. *Clinical Pharmacology and Therapeutics*, 1981, **20**, 752-757.

Willett, E. A. Group therapy in a methadone treatment program: An evaluation of changes in interpersonal behavior. *International Journal of the Addictions*, 1973, **8**, 33-39.

Willis, J. H. The natural history of drug dependence: Some comparative observations on United Kingdom and United States subjects. In H. Steinberg (Ed.), *Scientific basis of drug dependence*. London: Churchill, 1969. Pp. 301-321.

Wilner, D. M. and Kassebaum, G. G. (Eds.) *Narcotics*. New York: McGraw-Hill, 1965.

Wilson, B. K., Elms, R. R. and Thomson, C. P. Outpatient versus hospital methadone detoxification: An experimental comparison. *International Journal of the Addictions*, 1975, **10**, 13-21.

Winick, C. Narcotics addiction and its treatment. *Law and Contemporary Problems*, 1957, **22**, 9-33.

Winick, C. The use of drugs by jazz musicians. *Social Problems*, 1959-60, 7, 240-253.

Winick, C. Physician narcotic addicts. *Social Problems*, 1961, 9, 174-186.

Winick, C. Maturing out of narcotic addiction. *Bulletin on Narcotics*, 1962, **14**, 1-7.

Winick, C. The 35 to 40 age drop-off. In *Proceedings of the White House Conference on Narcotic and Drug Abuse*. Washington, D.C.: U.S. Government Printing Office, 1962. Pp. 153-160.

Winick, C. Epidemiology of narcotics use. In D. M. Wilner and G. G. Kassebaum (Eds.), *Narcotics*. New York: McGraw-Hill, 1965. Pp. 3-18.

Wolkstein, E. and Richman, A. Treatment planning and clinical supervision. In *The state-of-the-art, vocational rehabilitation of the drug abuser* (Vol. 5). Washington, D.C.: Youth Projects, Inc., and DHEW Social and Rehabilitation Service, 1975.

Woody, G. E., McLellan, A. T., O'Brien, C.P., and Luborsky, L. Personality factors in methadone self-administration by heroin addicts. In T. Thompson, and C. E.

Johanson (Eds.), *Behavioral pharmacology of human drug dependence* (Research Monograph Series #37). Washington, D.C.: U.S. Government Printing Office, 1981. Pp. 63-74.

Woody, G. E., O'Brien, C.P., and Rickles, K. Depression and anxiety in heroin addicts: A placebo-controlled study of doxepin in combination with methadone. *American Journal of Psychiatry*, 1975, **132**, 447-450.

Wright, J. S. The rehabilitation of addicts. *Adolescence*, 1974, **9**, 437-442.

Yanagita, T., Katoh, S., Wakasa, Y. and Oinuma, N. Dependence potential of Buprenorphine studied in rhesus monkeys. In L. S. Harris (Ed.), *Problems of drug dependence, 1981* (NIDA Research Monograph #41). Washington, D.C.: U.S. Government Printing Office, 1982. Pp. 208-214.

Yorke, C. A critical review of some psychoanalytic literature on drug addiction. *British Journal of Medical Psychology*, 1970, **43**, 141-159.

Zahn, M. A. and Ball, J. C. Factors related to cure of opiate addiction among Puerto Rican addicts. *International Journal of the Addictions*, 1972, 237-245.

Zaks, A. Jones, T., Fink, M., and Freedman, A. M. Naloxone treatment opiate dependence. *Journal of the American Medical Association*, 1971, **215**, 2108-2110.

Zelson, C. Infant of the addicted mother. *New England Journal of Medicine*, 1973, **288**, 1393-1395.

Zelson, C., Lee, S. J., and Casalino, M. Neonatal narcotic addiction: Comparative effects of maternal intake of heroin and methadone. *New England Journal of Medicine*, 1973, **289**, 1216-1220.

Zimmering, P., Toolan, J., Safrin, R., and Wortis, S. B. Drug addiction in relation to problems of adolescence. *American Journal of Psychiatry*. 1952, **109**, 272-278.

Zimney, E. L. and Luke, J. L. Narcotic-related deaths in the District of Columbia: 1971-1979. *Journal of Forensic Science*, 1981, **26**, 462-469.

Zinberg, N. E. The search for rational approaches to heroin use. In P. G. Bourne *Addiction*. New York: Academic Press, 1974, 149-174.

Zuckerman, M., Kolin, E. A., Price, L., and Zoob, I. Development of a sensation-seeking scale. *Journal of Consulting Psychology*, 1964, **28**, 477-482.

Zuckerman, M., Neary, R., and Brustman, B. Dimensions of sensation-seeking. Paper presented at the annual meeting of the Eastern Psychological Association, Atlantic City, April, 1970.

Zuckerman, M., Sola, S., Masterson, J. W., and Angelone, J. V. MMPI patterns in drug abusers before and after treatment in therapeutic communities. *Journal of Consulting and Clinical Psychology*, 1975, **43**, 286-296.

Additional References

Cohen, G. Alkaloid products in the metabolism of alcohol and biogenic amines. *Biochemical Pharmacology*, 1976, **25**, 1123-1128.

Ho, A. K. S., Chen, R. C. A., and Kreek, M. J. Morphine withdrawal in the rat: An assessment by quantification of diarrhea and modification by ethanol. *Pharmacology*, 1979, **18**, 9-17.

Ho, A. K. S., Chen, R. C. A., and Morrison, M. J. Opiate-ethanol interaction studies. In K. Blum (Ed.) *Alcohol and opiates: Neurochemical and behavioral mechanisms.* New York: Academic Press, 1977, 189-202.

Ho, A. K. S., and Ho, C. C. Toxic interactions of ethanol with other central depressants: Antagonism by naloxone to narcosis and lethality. *Pharmacology, Biochemistry and Behavior,* 1979, **11**, 111-114.

Stimmel, B., Korts, D., Cohen, M., Jackson, G., Sturiano, V., and Hanbury, R. Opiate addiction and alcoholism: The feasibility of combined treatment approaches. In R. B. Millman, P. Cushman, and J. Lowinson (Eds.) *Research developments in drug and alcohol use.* New York: New York Academy of Sciences, 1981, 362, 50-56.

Author Index

Page numbers in *italics* refer to authors cited in reference sections at the end of Part One.

Subject Index